Rodney Bolt
with additional accounts by Kate Paice

KU-064-709

Holland

Cadogan Guides
West End House (3rd Floor), 11 Hills Place,
London W1R 1AG, UK
becky.kendall@morrispub.co.uk

The Globe Pequot Press
246 Goose Lane
PO Box 480, Guilford
Connecticut 06437–0480

Copyright © Rodney Bolt 2000
Chapter title pages taken from photographs
by Gerard van Vuuren and Kate Paice

Book and cover design by Animage
Cover photographs: front: Travel Library/Peter Terry
back: Travel Library/Stuart Black
Maps © Cadogan Guides, drawn by Map Creation Ltd

Editorial Director: Vicki Ingle
Series Editor: Linda McQueen

Editor: Linda McQueen
Proofreading: Susannah Wight
Indexing: Isobel McLean
Production: Book Production Services

A catalogue record for this book is available from the British Library
ISBN 1–86011–961–1

The author and publishers have made every effort to ensure the accuracy of the information in this book at the time of going to press. However, they cannot accept any responsibility for any loss, injury or inconvenience resulting from the use of information contained in this guide.

Printed and bound in Great Britain by Cambridge University Press.

For my parents, who have always been firm and unquestioning in their support.

About the Author

Rodney Bolt is seldom happier than when rattling along the canals of Amsterdam on his Miss Marple Dutch bicycle, or burrowing through papers in the Municipal Archive. Having lived in Greece, South Africa, Britain and Germany, he arrived in Amsterdam in 1991, and now nothing can convince him to leave. He has also written Cadogan Guides to Germany, Bavaria and Madeira, as well as other books and numerous articles on the Netherlands. In 1994 he won the German National Tourist Office's 'Travel Writer of the Year' award.

Acknowledgements

Heartfelt thanks to my editor Linda McQueen and to Vicki Ingle at Cadogan. Without their generosity of spirit, imagination in pursuit of the goal, flexibility, and sterling support, this book would not have been published in time. Special thanks to Linda for the late nights that were really my fault.

My particular gratitude goes to Kate Paice, who not only did a magnificent job researching and writing most of the chapter on the north, but buoyed up my spirits along the way.

Thanks too to Honkey Kaur for her help with fact-checking, to Vanessa Letts for adding so much practical information in the UK, to Susannah Wight for shouldering the task of proof-reading, and to Map Creation for the fine maps.

Please help us to keep this guide up to date

We have done our best to ensure that the information in this guide is correct at the time of going to press. But places and facilities are constantly changing, and standards and prices in hotels and restaurants fluctuate. We would be delighted to receive any comments concerning existing entries or omissions. Authors of the best letters will receive a copy of the Cadogan Guide of their choice.

Contents

Travel · 1–12

Practical A–Z · 13–32

History · 33–48

Introduction

*We had a pleasant time in Holland. They have reduced
work to a minimum there. They seem to be simple, polite
and dignified folk. Well set up men and girls and women
who laughed all the time.*

James Joyce, 1927

*The Dutch landscape has all the qualities that make
geometry so delightful. A tour in Holland is a tour through
the first books of Euclid.*

Aldous Huxley, 1925

If the word 'Holland' conjures up for you clogs, cheese, windmills and tulips, then think again. If it means prostitutes, drugs, and liberal sex laws, then you still have only a fraction of the picture. Should Rembrandt, Van Gogh and Mondrian also come to mind, that picture begins to become a little more complete. Add in prosperity, conviviality, efficiency, and an extraordinary laid-backness, and at last you're getting there.

Holland (or 'the Netherlands', to be more correct) is a small country. You can get almost anywhere in two to three hours. Yet for centuries it has packed a disproportionately big punch. The tidewater marks of those high historical moments are evident in abundance: medieval towns whose names were familiar to traders across the known world; museums packed with Old Masters and cities grand with the gables of the 17th-century Golden Age; sumptuous 19th-century architecture, and social institutions that seem to have adopted all that was good from 1960s counter-culture and honed it for efficient 21st-century use.

Most of Holland's delights are urban ones. Museums, fine buildings and the buzz of city life are more likely to lure you than any call of the wild. Nearly half of the country's population lives in the Randstad, an urban conurbation that includes Amsterdam, Rotterdam and The Hague. Yet even the largest cities have something of a grown-up village feel about them. The Dutch seem to have perfected the art of living comfortably in close proximity—perhaps helped by the fact that this is a remarkably prosperous society, and that everything seems to work properly. Trains run on time, strikes are almost unheard of, and you can go to sleep at night happy that no one in the country is starving.

But the Protestant work ethic is tempered by a serious devotion to leisure. A statutory 36-hour working week means that anyone who works a 40-hour week gets an extra day off every fortnight. Cafés and restaurants throughout the land hum with *gezelligheid*—that indefinable Dutch word that means something between cosiness and conviviality. And everyone seems remarkably relaxed. If locals are to be believed, this is especially true as you move farther south, to the predominantly Roman Catholic regions of Limburg and Noord-Brabant.

Nearly 24 per cent of Holland's land mass is below sea level, and it is flat, flat, flat. The few bumps and ridges that do exist seldom exceed a hundred metres high. The land is so flat that even the black and white cows make silhouettes along the skyline. Trees are laid out in neat rows, and canals criss-cross the pastures in straight lines. A fully laden cargo boat moves through the scene as if cutting a swathe through the grass.

This regularity can make the landscape monotonous, but it also gives it a minimalistic beauty, especially when softened by winter mists.

The countryside has an awesome geometry. In the spring, when the bulb fields around Haarlem and Leiden become solid squares of strong colour, it makes you think that Mondrian was a realist. But it's not all flat land and hard edges. The forests of the midlands, the wild islands in the north and the long, duney beaches of South Holland and Zeeland all provide ample refuge for wildlife—especially waterbirds—and offer comforting escape from the urban sprawl.

And of course there still are tulips for sale on street corners, shops full of round yellow cheeses, people who wear clogs in the garden, and windmills that whirr away working at their original purpose.

A Guide to the Guide

This guide begins its journey before you do, with **Travel** and **Practical A–Z** chapters packed with information to help you plan your trip; while **History** and **Art and Architecture** fill in the background to what you will see when you arrive.

Many visitors to Holland start with **Amsterdam**, and for many this is their only experience of the country. The city therefore has a chapter to itself, with practical information at the beginning and listings of hotels, restaurants, shopping, entertainment and gay life at the end of the chapter.

We have chosen not to divide this guide up simply by the official provinces of the Netherlands, the names of which will be unfamilar to most people. Overleaf is a map showing these provinces, and this guide covers them as follows:

The urban sprawl around Amsterdam on the western coast of the country is known as the **Randstad,** and stretches to cover *Zuid-Holland,* the very western edge of the province of *Utrecht* and the southwestern third of *Noord-Holland.*

The Midlands covers the rest of *Utrecht* including the city itself, the reclaimed province of *Flevoland,* and stretches east to cover points of major interest in *Gelderland* and southern *Overijssel.*

The North starts with the remaining northern and eastern part of *Noord-Holland,* taking you around the Meer, and then works its way through *Friesland, Groningen, Drenthe* and northern *Overijssel.*

The South covers *Zeeland* and the delta, *Noord-Brabant,* and finally the southerly province of *Limburg,* with its centre, Maastricht.

At the end of the guide, in **Language** you will find a selection of words and phrases to help you get around, a menu reader and a list of Dutch and Indonesian culinary treats for you to try. **Further Reading** suggests some more background to follow up, and a **Chronology** provides an easy reference to the country's history.

Holland: Provinces

25 km
15 miles

N

North

Sea

GRONINGEN

Leeuwarden
○ Groningen

FRIESLAND

DRENTHE

NOORD-HOLLAND

Zwolle

FLEVOLAND

OVERIJSSEL

AMSTERDAM

THE HAGUE

UTRECHT
○ Utrecht

GELDERLAND

ZUID-HOLLAND
Rotterdam

Nijmegen

NOORD-BRABANT

GERMANY

ZEELAND

LIMBURG

BELGIUM

Maastricht

Travel

By Air

The Netherlands' major international airport, **Amsterdam Airport Schiphol**, enjoys a reputation as one of the world's sleekest and most user-friendly airports, and has an impressive mall of duty-free shops. It serves direct flights from London, Manchester, New York, Los Angeles, Toronto, Vancouver and Sydney as well as many other airports around the UK and Americas. There are also smaller airports at **Rotterdam**, **Eindhoven** and **Maastricht**, which receive some international flights, mainly from continental Europe; VLM Flemish Airlines, for example, have a direct flight from London City Airport to Rotterdam for around £95 return (exclusive of airport taxes), and Air Exel fly from London Stansted to Maastricht. EasyJet have four flights daily from Luton Airport and one flight daily from Liverpool to Amsterdam from as little as £52 return.

Flights from London take about 45 minutes, from New York about 8 hours. Several carriers operate the London–Amsterdam route (*see* list below), so competition is strong. A browse through the travel ads in the British press (such as *Time Out* or the London *Evening Standard* will divulge any number of return flights priced below £100, even on scheduled airlines.

From **Ireland**, Aer Lingus has four flights daily from Dublin to Amsterdam, and daily flights from Cork; prices start at around IR£142 return. All other options involve travel via the UK and will cost more.

From **North America**, KLM, the Dutch national airline, operates in partnership with the American company Northwest Airlines. Together they offer a service that takes in most major US cities, including daily flights from New York, Baltimore, Los Angeles and Miami. KLM also flies daily to a number of Canadian cities, including Vancouver, Toronto and Montreal. Delta operates daily nonstop from New York, and Martinair, a Dutch airline, flies from many US cities and from Toronto. Prices direct from New York start at about $308 for special deals and go up to around $799 for more conventional fares. American travellers thinking of stopping over in London might find it cheaper to buy a ticket to Amsterdam in the UK.

transport from the airport

Schiphol airport is well served by road and rail connections—you can get almost anywhere in the country in an hour or two. Most people head first for Amsterdam (for connection details *see* p.74).

discount and student fares

UK

Europe Student Travel, 6 Campden Street, London W8, ✆ (020) 7727 7647, catering to non-students as well.

STA Travel, 6 Wright's Lane, London W8 6TA, or 85 Shaftesbury Avenue, London W1V 7AD, ✆ (020) 7361 6161/6262; Bristol, ✆ (0117) 929 4399; Leeds, ✆ (0113) 244 9212; Manchester, ✆ (0161) 834 0668; Oxford, ✆ (01865) 792800; Cambridge, ✆ (01223) 366966 and many other branches in the UK.

Airline Numbers

Schiphol Airport (info) (0900) 0141

Air Exel   UK   (020) 8750 9002

Aer Lingus   UK   (020) 8899 4747
Dublin   (01) 886 8888
Amsterdam   (020) 520 5288

American Airlines
USA   (800) 433 7300
Amsterdam   (06) 022 7844

British Airways UK   (0345) 222 111
Amsterdam   (020) 346 9559

British Airways City Flyer
(London Gatwick to Rotterdam)
UK   (0345) 222 111

British Midland UK   (0345) 554 554
Amsterdam   (06) 601 2301

Canadian Airlines
(Toronto)   Canada   (800) 665 1177
UK   (020) 7745 5000
Rotterdam   (0800) 022 8270

Delta   USA   (800) 241 4141
Amsterdam   (06) 504 0606

easyJet   UK   (0870) 6000 000
Amsterdam   (023) 568 4880
www.easyjet.com

KLM   UK   (0990) 750 900
USA   (800) 3 747 747
Amsterdam   (020) 474 7747
www.klm.com
(direct flights to Amsterdam from New York, LA,
Vancouver, Toronto, Belfast, Bristol, Birmingham,
Cardiff, London Heathrow, Southampton)

KLM uk   UK   (0990) 074 074
Amsterdam   (020) 474 7747
(flights to Amsterdam from Aberdeen, Edinburgh,
Glasgow, Leeds and Newcastle)

KLM Cityhopper UK   (020) 8750 9002
(flights from London Heathrow to Rotterdam,
Eindhoven and Amsterdam)

Martinair   USA   (800) 627 8462
Amsterdam   (020) 601 1767

TWA   USA   (800) 892 4141
Holland   (023) 548 3777
UK   (0845) 733 3333

VLM   UK   (020) 7476 6677
(flights from London City Airport to Rotterdam)

Trailfinders, 194 Kensington High St, London W8 7RG, ℗ (020) 7938 3939 (for non-students as well).

Travel Cuts, 295a Regent St, London W1R 7YA, ℗ (020) 7255 1944.

USIT Campus Travel, 52 Grosvenor Gardens, SW1W OAG, or 174 Kensington High Street, London W8 7RG, ℗ (020) 7730 3402 with branches at most UK universities, including Bristol, ℗ (0117) 929 2494; Manchester, ℗ (0161) 833 2046; Edinburgh, ℗ (0131) 668 3303; Birmingham, ℗ (0121) 414 1848; Oxford, ℗ (01865) 242 067; Cambridge, ℗ (01223) 324283, or see their website at *www.usitcampus.co.uk.*

Ireland

Budget Travel, 134 Lower Baggot St, Dublin 2, ℗ (01) 661 1866.

United Travel, Stillorgan Bowl, Stillorgan, County Dublin, ℗ (01) 288 4346/7.

USIT, Aston Quay, Dublin 2, ℗ (01) 679 8833; Cork, ℗ (021) 270 900; Belfast, ℗ (01232) 324 073; Galway, ℗ (091) 565 177; Limerick (061) 415 064; Waterford, (051) 72601. **Ireland**'s biggest student travel agents.

USA and Canada

It's worth sifting through the small ads in newspaper travel pages (e.g. the *New York Times, Chicago Tribune, Toronto Globe & Mail*) before contacting travel clubs and agencies, some of whom may require an annual membership fee.

Airhitch, 2472 Broadway Suite 200, New York, NY 10025, ✆ (212) 864 2000.

Council Travel, 205 E 42nd St, New York, NY 10017, ✆ (800) 743 1823.

Last Minute Travel Club, 132 Brookline Avenue, Boston, MA 02215, ✆ (800) 527 8646.

STA Travel, 10 Downing St, New York, NY 10014, ✆ (212) 627 3111 or (800) 777 0112; 51 Grant Avenue, San Francisco, CA 94108, ✆ (415) 391 8407.

Travel Cuts, 49 Front St East, Toronto, ON M5E 1B3, ✆ (416) 365 0545.

Internet

Some of the tastiest bargains of all are posted on the **Internet**. Check out *www.lastminute.com* or *www.travelocity.com*

By Train

A direct **Eurostar** service from London Waterloo to Amsterdam through the Channel Tunnel is scheduled to go into operation one day. Until it does, you have to catch the train through the tunnel and make a simple platform change at Brussels. It is possible to book a through-ticket, which costs £75–105 return if you stay for a minimum of three nights, one of which must be a Saturday, otherwise up to £270 for a standard return. There are frequent special offers that can bring the price down even further. The journey time is 2hrs 40mins to Brussels, involving a wait between trains of approximately 25–30 minutes, and 3hr journey on from Brussels to Amsterdam Centraal Station (new high-speed rail links in Holland should speed up the journey considerably by 2003). Note that you absolutely must check in 20mins before the train departure time from Waterloo or you will not be allowed to board. For information and bookings call ✆ (0990) 186 186.

If you are travelling from Scotland or the north of England, especially Edinburgh, Glasgow, Newcastle, Manchester, York or Birmingham, ask Eurostar when you book about special subsidized national train fares to London.

Stena Line, ✆ (08705) 70 70 70, *www.stenaline.co.uk*, offers combined rail and ferry tickets from London to Amsterdam, departing from Liverpool Street via Harwich and the Hook of Holland. The total journey time is about 7 hours, and standard fares start at about £79 return, although there are often promotional fares like the 3-day Apex return which can bring the price down to a mere £49.

There's a talking **timetable** for Amsterdam on ✆ (0891) 888 731. Centraal Station's European enquiries number is ✆ (0900) 9296.

By Bus

This is the cheapest way to go, but it can also be the nastiest. Overnight journeys, in particular, seem maliciously planned so that you're woken at a border crossing every few hours. **National Express/Eurolines** (✆ (0990) 80 80 80/✆ (01582) 404 511) offer two options from London Victoria daily. On the morning departure you cross the Channel by Hovercraft; the overnight trip involves the ferry and takes 2hrs longer. The current return price for either choice is £44 (or £31 single), under-26/over-60 £39 (or £28 single).

By Car

To bring your car into the Netherlands you'll need a valid insurance document (such as the EU 'green card'), current registration and road safety test certificates, an international identification disc and an EU or international driving licence. The shortest **ferry crossing** (6½hrs by day or 8hrs by night) is Harwich–Hook of Holland (Stena Line, ℰ (0990) 707 070)—though, depending on where you're setting off from, you might find other lines more convenient: P&O North Sea Ferries (Hull–Rotterdam, ℰ (01482) 377177, 13½hrs) or Scandinavian Seaways (Newcastle–IJmuiden–Amsterdam, ℰ (01255) 240 240).

You can also take your car through the Channel Tunnel with **Eurotunnel**, ℰ (0990) 35 35 35. You enter the tunnel at Folkestone (take Junction 11a off the M20), and exit south of Calais on the French A16. You do not have to book ahead to use the tunnel, but it will be faster if you have.

Entry Formalities

passports and visas

EU nationals and citizens of Australia, Canada, New Zealand and the USA need only a valid passport to visit the Netherlands if their stay is for less than three months. If you intend to stay for longer than three months you should get your passport stamped on entry, and will need a **resident's permit**.

Dutch Embassies and Consulates Abroad

Australia, 120 Empire Circuit, Yarralumla, Canberra ACT 2600, ℰ (02) 6273 3111.
Canada, 350 Albert St, Ottowa, Ontario K1R 1A4, ℰ (613) 237 5030.
New Zealand, Investment House, Tenth Floor, Ballance St, Wellington, ℰ (04) 471 6390.
UK, 38 Hyde Park Gate, London SW7 5DP, ℰ (020) 7590 3200.
US, 4200 Linnean Ave NW, Washington DC, 20008, ℰ (202) 244 5300.

customs

People travelling within the European Union are no longer allowed to buy **duty free**, but if you are coming from outside the EU and are over 17, you can enter the Netherlands with 200 cigarettes (or 50 cigars or 250g/8.82oz of tobacco), 1 litre of spirits (or 2 litres of fortified wine) and 2 litres of non-sparkling wine, 50g/1.76oz of perfume and ƒ300 worth of gifts. If you've bought goods tax-paid within the EU then there are no restrictions, within reasonable limits. You should leave any meat, fruit, plants, flowers, radio transmitters and offensive weapons at home. If you bring in your **dog or cat** it must be accompanied by a certificate stating that it's been inoculated against rabies.

The exporting of **flower bulbs** is permitted to the UK, but you need an inoculation certificate for the USA. It's best to have bulbs posted home to avoid border hassles. Most reputable dealers will do this, and all the necessary paperwork, for you.

Tour Operators and Special-interest Holidays

It can work out cheaper to get to Holland with a package tour, especially if you will be spending much of your time in Amsterdam. Tour operators can also arrange specialist holidays, cycling tour and trips that include Belgium and Luxembourg as well as the Netherlands. Try these suggestions below.

in the UK

Amsterdam Travel Service, Bridge House, 55–59 High Road, Broxbourne, Hertfordshire EN10 7DT, ✆ (01992) 456 056, *www.amsterdamtravel.co.uk.* Offers a comprehensive range of holidays in Holland, from accommodation only (1–5-star hotels), to excursions to Rotterdam, Haarlem, Delft and Utrecht, 8-day cycling holidays, dinner cruises, 'cheese and markets' escorted tours and Amsterdam by Night and Day. Can also tailor-make holidays.

Bridge Travel Service, Bridge House, 55–59 High Rd, Broxbourne, Herts EN10 7DT, ✆ (01992) 456 654. Self-drive holidays throughout Holland, staying in 3–4-star hotels, and including a two-hour Amsterdam by Candlelight cruise.

Cresta Holidays, Tabley Court, Victoria Street, Altrincham, Cheshire WA14 1EZ, ✆ (0161) 927 7000, *www.crestaholidays.co.uk.* City breaks in Amsterdam, The Hague and Delft staying in 2–4-star hotels, also a wide range of themed excursions: windmills and Edam, bulbfields and canal cruises.

Crystal Holidays, Crystal House, The Courtyard, Arlington Road, Surbiton, Surrey KT6 6BW, ✆ (020) 8390 9900. City breaks and tailor-made excursions throughout Holland.

DFDS Seaways, Scandinavia House, Parkeston, Harwich, Essex CO12 4QG, ✆ (08705) 333 111, *www.dfdsseaways.co.uk.* Two-night cruise breaks visiting the bulb fields of Holland from £54; also cruise-and-city breaks in Amsterdam, Haarlem staying in 2–4-star accommodation.

Eurobreak, 10–18 Putney Hill, London SW15 6AX, ✆ (020) 8780 7700. Short breaks/weekend breaks in Amsterdam.

Gran Dorado Holiday Villages, 17 Rodney Road, Cheltenham, Glos GL50 1HX, ✆ (01242) 255 000, *www.grandorado.com.* Holiday villages including tropical paradise pools, clubs, restaurants and sports facilities in Port Zélande, Amsterdam Beach and Loohorst, with discount entrance to the 170 acres of roller coasters, rides and attractions in De Efteling theme park.

Kirker Holidays, 3 New Concordia Wharf, Mill St, London SE1 2BB, ✆ (020) 7231 3333. Tailor-made weekend breaks in Amsterdam.

Osprey Holidays, Broughton Market, Edinburgh, Scotland EH3 6NU, ✆ (0131) 557 1555. More weekend breaks in Amsterdam.

Stena Line Holidays, Charter House, Park St, Ashford, Kent TN24 8EX, ✆ (01233) 647022/✆ (08705) 747474. City breaks in Amsterdam, The Hague and Rotterdam and excursions to Utrecht, Arnhem, Zandvoort, Maastricht and The Golden Circle. Can also arrange self-catering accommodation in the Gran Dorado holiday villages (see above) and visits to De Efteling theme park and the 80 acres of tulips and hyacinths at Keukenhof bulb park.

Thomson Breakaway, Centenary House, 3 Water Lane, Richmond, Surrey TW9 1TJ, ✆ (020) 8210 4210. City breaks and package tours in Amsterdam.

Time Off, 1 Elmfield Park, Bromley, Kent BR1 1LU, ✆ (0990) 846 3633. City breaks in Amsterdam.

Travelscene, Travelscene House, 11–15 St Annes Road, Harrow, Middlesex HA1 1LQ, ✆ (020) 8427 8800, *www.travelscene.co.uk*. City breaks and driving holidays in Amsterdam, Rotterdam, The Hague, Delft, Arnhem and the bulb fields of Noorwijk.

in the USA

Abercrombie & Kent, 1520 Kensington Road, Oakbrook, IL 60523, ✆ (800) 323 7308 / (630) 954 2944, *www.abercrombiekent.com*. Six-day tulip cruises on the Princesse Royale through Holland, stopping off at the Keukenhof Gardens, and continuing on south through Belgium, stopping off in Bruges, Ghent, Antwerp and Willemstad.

Above & Beyond Tours, 230 N. Via las Palmas, Palm Springs, CA 92262, ✆ (800) 397 2681, *www.abovebeyondtours.com*. Escorted tours to the Queens' Day floating gay pride parade in Amsterdam, as well as tailor-made tours.

BA Holidays, ✆ (800) 359 8722. Package tours to Amsterdam.

First Cultural Tours, 225 West 34th, New York, NY 10122, ✆ (212) 563 1202; *istny@aol.com*. Organizes weekly barge trips from Amsterdam to Brussels, with two nights' 4-star hotels at either end.

Grand Travel, 6900 Wisconsin Avenue, Suite 706m Chevy Chase, Maryland, MC 20815, ✆ (800) 247 7651; *www.grandtrvl.com*. Fully escorted summer tours specially designed for grandparents travelling with grandchildren: highlights include Amsterdam, Utrecht, Delft, The Hague, the windmills of Kinderdijk, Gouda and a canal trip on to Bruges, Ghent and Brussels.

Hibiscus Tours, 885 3rd Ave, 29th floor, New York, NY 10022, ✆ (800) 653 0802, ✆ (212) 759 9087, *www.hibiscustours.com*. Garden, art and Jewish Heritage escorted tours for small groups of 15 or under, also weekend breaks.

Hilliard and Olander, 608 2nd Ave S, Suite 181, Minneapolis, ✆ (800) 229 8407. Package and driving tours all over Holland, de luxe accommodation.

Holland Approach, 550 Mountain Ave, Gillette, New Jersey 07922, ✆ (800) 225 1699, *www.globaltravelsolution.com*. Two 9-day escorted tours (April– Sept) through Holland, Belgium and Luxembourg: transportation by motor coach, staying in 3-star hotels.

Holland Bicycling Tours, PO Box 6068, Huntington Beach, CA 92615, ✆ (800) 852 3258, *faygrassi@earthlink.net.* Escorted bicycling tours in Northern and Southern Holland, visiting museums and bulb fields, staying in 3-star hotels, excellent food.

KLM/Northwest World Vacations, ✆ (800) 800 1504. City breaks in Amsterdam.

Mayflower Tours, PO Box 490, 1225 Warren Avenue, Downers Grove, Illinois 60515, ✆ (800) 323 7604. Nine-day horticultural tours in spring through the Netherlands and Benelux countries and visiting the Amsterdam flower auction and the bulb fields of Keukenhof.

Maupintours, 1421 Research Park Drive, Suite 300, Laurence, Kansas 66049, ✆ (800) 255 4266. Organizes two 2-week tours in April: 'Holland in Bloom' and 'Gardens and Treasures of Holland and Belgium'.

Saga International, ✆ (800) 952 9560. City breaks in Amsterdam.

Getting Around

*A telephone call to the national travel information service ✆ (0900) 9292 will put you in touch with someone who can give you **information** in English on all forms of public transport (including trains) nationwide.*

*See the **Language** chapter, pp.369–72, for some basic travelling vocabulary.*

By Train

Travelling around the Netherlands by rail is cheap and easy. You don't have to book, as services are extremely frequent and efficient, and you can hop off a train to explore towns en route to your destination without paying extra. Holland is a small country, and nowhere is more than about three hours' journey time from Amsterdam, which is the hub of most national travel. Fares are calculated by distance in a very fair and systematic way, so there shouldn't be any surprises. The table below should give you a rough idea of average fares:

Return fare Amsterdam to:			
Alkmaar	ƒ19.50	Kampen	ƒ55.00
Amersfoort	ƒ23.00	Leiden	ƒ22.00
Deventer	ƒ45.00	Leeuwarden	ƒ73.50
Gouda	ƒ29.25	Maastricht	ƒ51.00
Groningen	ƒ74.50	Rotterdam	ƒ39.25
Haarlem	ƒ10.75	Zwolle	ƒ48.00
The Hague	ƒ29.25		

Return fare Rotterdam to:	
Dordrecht	ƒ11.00
Middelburg	ƒ56.00

Tickets and Passes

Domestic as well as international rail tickets, passes and tabletables can all be purchased in advance (though slightly more expensively) from **Holland Rail**, Chase House, Gilbert Street, Ropley, Hants SO24 OBY, ✆ (01962) 773646, *www.hollandrail.com.* A free brochure called *Exploring Holland By Train* is available from Holland Rail or Netherlands Tourist Board offices, and the NTB *www.holland.com/uk* also includes full details of international train travel timetables.

If you're planning on hopscotching your way through Holland, the **Euro Domino** pass (available to non-EU as well as EU visitors) is brilliant value: *f* 130, *f* 200 and *f* 350 will buy three, five or ten days' unlimited train travel within a one-month period. There are special rates for under-26s and senior citizens, and tickets can be upgraded to a **Euro Domino Plus** pass to include travel by train, bus and metro as well. You can purchase both kinds of tickets in advance (they'll cost a little more than in Holland, but will get you 50% off ferries and 25% off train fares to Harwich). Holland Rail also has a special **Holland Rail Pass** giving three or five days' unlimited travel within the month for £38 or £57 (with a friend/partner travelling at half-price).

The information desk at most stations will give you details of all the various tickets and passes offered by the network—as well as a condensed version of the national rail timetable costing *f* 2. The most popular is the **Day Pass** (*f* 71.50), entitling the holder to 24 hours' unlimited travel throughout the country (for another *f* 8 it can be upgraded to include tram, bus and metro as well). Available in July and August, the **Summer Tour Rover** entitles you and a friend to a two-for-the-price-of-one 72 hours' unlimited travel within a 10-day period. Don't forget as well to find out about the **Rail Idee**, a special package deal combining train tickets with discounted admission to top sights, attractions and museums all over Holland.

Senior citizens in the UK should also consider buying a **Rail Europe Senior Card** which gives holders 30% reductions on all international travel (details available from UK stations).

Many rail stations in Holland also include a bike depot, and will hire out **bikes** at specially reduced rates for rail passengers (these can even be reserved in advance via Holland Rail). In smaller stations that are poorly served by other forms of public transport, you'll find **Trein Taxis**. Available at 160 of Holland's 350 railway stations, these communal taxis will take you to any address in the town or village for a flat fare of *f* 7/£3 (tickets available from the ticket office or ticket machine in the station hall).

Journey Times

Amsterdam–Zuiderzee Museum: 1hr 4mins.
Amsterdam–Zandvoort: 32mins.
Amsterdam–Het Loo Palace: 1hr.
Hoek van Holland–Delft: 46mins.
Hoek van Holland–Eindhoven: 1hr 55mins.
Rotterdam–Maastricht: 2hrs 18mins.

By City Public Transport

Public transport in the Netherlands is safe and relatively inexpensive. Most larger cities have tram as well as bus networks (and in Arnhem you'll still find electric trolley buses). Rotterdam and Amsterdam have small metro systems.

tickets and travel information

Although you can buy single tickets on boarding trams and buses, it's much cheaper and easier to buy a **strip ticket** (*strippenkaart*, *f* 11.75). This is valid on the Amsterdam and Rotterdam metros, and on all buses and trams throughout the Netherlands. The *strippenkaart* is divided into 2, 3, 8 or 15 units. Each time you make a journey allow 1 unit for 'boarding', then one more for each zone you travel through: a journey in one zone needs 2 units, through two zones 3 units, and so on. Fold the card over at the appropriate unit and slip it into the slot of the stamping machine (on board buses and trams and at the entrance to metro stations). Your card is then stamped with the zone and time and is valid for an hour, even if you swap lines. *Strippenkaarten* are valid for a minimum of 12 months. You can buy them from stations, newsagents, supermarkets, and the GVB (Amsterdam Muncipal Transport Authority, Stationsplein 15, opposite Centraal Station, Amsterdam). Available in summer only, the slightly more expensive *zomerzwerfkaart* (*f* 16) gives open access to all bus routes for 24 hours.

Uniformed and plain-clothes inspectors will spot-fine you *f* 60 if they catch you travelling without a valid ticket. Playing the confused foreigner will get you nowhere.

By Bicycle

Bicycles are the quintessential Dutch mode of transport. Everyone uses them, from hip young things to grannies and cabinet ministers. The land is flat, of course, and it's easy to get about. Cities generally have safe, separate cycle paths, and there are marked routes all over the countryside (ask local tourist offices or the ANWB motoring organization for maps and booklets). You can weave around as blithely as you like, secure in the knowledge that Dutch law holds that in an accident between a motorist and a cyclist, the cyclist is always right, whatever the circumstances (and even if you're riding without a light in the middle of the night in the wrong direction up a one-way street). This makes drivers very careful.

Most main railway stations will have a bicycle storage depot with **bikes for hire**, and you'll find hire shops in nearly every town. Bike renting is cheap (seldom more than *f* 10 a day). You'll need to take your passport, and a deposit. This ranges from *f* 50 to *f* 200, but you can usually get around it by leaving an imprint of your credit card. If you're around for a while, you might consider buying one second-hand—*f* 150 should get you a reasonable machine from a local market. It's possible to take bicycles on trains, though you need to pay extra and buy a ticket first, and you may not travel during the morning and evening rush hours.

Bicycle theft is endemic, especially in Amsterdam. Never leave your bike unlocked. The best way to secure it is with a solid metal U-shaped lock (thieves go armed with clippers that cut through chains in seconds). Lock the front wheel and the frame to a railing or high post. It's a good idea, when you're hiring a bike, to check your liabilities under the rental firm's terms of insurance.

The tourist board publishes a free booklet, *Cycling in Holland*, detailing some of the country's choicest cycle routes; 1:100,000 cyling track maps for every province in Holland are available from all Netherlands Tourist Board VVV tourist offices for *f* 12.

By Car

An EU or international **driving licence** is valid. Speed limits are 50kph (31mph) in built-up areas, 80kph (50mph) on the open road, and 100kph (75mph) on motorways. Drive on the right, and give way to traffic approaching from the right, except where you have clear right of way. Be wary of sightseeing pedestrians, give way to cyclists and remember that trams give way to no one. Finding **parking** can be a nightmare, especially in Amsterdam.

The national **emergency car-repair** service is ANWB Wegenwacht (✆ (0900) 0888; open 24 hours daily). ANWB shops in larger cities are useful sources of maps and route planners.

Below is a list of words you may come across on road signs.

alle richtingen	all directions
bromfietsen	mopeds
bushalte	bus stop
doorgaand verkeer	through trafic
drempels	speed humps
fietsen	bicycles
file	traffic jam
file vrij	free of traffic jams
the above two phrases flash on electronic signs above motorway, when there are alternative routes to somewhere	
filevorming	get in lane
geen	no
gestemd	forbidden, obstructed
gevaar	danger
m.u.v.	except for
as in 'm.u.v. (brom)fietsen' below a no-entry sign	
parkeerbeheer	parking authority
parkeeren	parking
tussen	between (parking periods)
uit	exit

Most major **car hire** companies have offices at Schiphol airport and in the larger cities. You'll need your driving licence, passport and a credit card (to pay a deposit).

Avis ✆ (020) 655 6050 or ✆ (020) 430 9609
Budget ✆ (0800) 0537 or ✆ (070) 384 4385
Cars for Less ✆ (020) 7287 2625—up to 80% off local rates in Holland
Europcar ✆ (020) 683 2123 or ✆ (020) 316 4190
Hertz ✆ (0800) 23 54 37 89 or ✆ (020) 504 0554

Prices are comparable with the UK and Ireland, but North Americans will find them a little steeper than they are used to.

Practical A–Z

Addresses

The Dutch write the house number after the street name, and follow it by Roman numerals indicating the storey: Bloemstraat 56 II would be an apartment two floors above street level at No.56 Bloemstraat. An apartment at street level is shown by the letters 'hs' (*huis*, house). Postcodes are written before the name of the city. (Postcode directories are available in post offices.)

Addresses in Amsterdam are discussed in the **Amsterdam** chapter, *see* p.79.

Children

Parents don't have to go to extraordinary expense or exercise great feats of imagination to give children a good time in Holland. Cycle lanes make bicycling about quite safe, a boat or pedalo on a canal can while away hours, even a ride on a clanging tram can be an event. If trams prove to be a hit, try one of the antique trolleys that go to the **Amsterdamse Bos**, a woody parkland outside Amsterdam where the children can ride horses, eat pancakes, swim and run about and shout to their hearts' content.

Some museums have special facilities for children. In Amsterdam, the **New Metropolis Center of Science and Technology**, Prins Hendrikkade, at the entrance to the IJ tunnel, is a paradise for young computer enthusiasts. All the high-tech displays have explanations in English and most of them invite fiddling fingers. At the other end of the scale is the Kindermuseum (Children's Museum) at the **Tropenmuseum** (Tropical Museum), Linnaeusstraat 2, © (020) 568 8300 (*open Wed for tours at 1.45 and 3.30, Sat and Sun at noon, 1.45, 3.30; special events some Saturdays; adm children ƒ7.50 adults ƒ2.50; children's programme lasts 1½hrs, adults join children after 1 hour; children between 6 and 12 years old only; reservation recommended*). The staff, who have all had experience of a third-world country, create a village-like environment where children can spend time learning first-hand about aspects of another culture—such as drumming, ricemaking or dancing.

Of the theme parks out of town, by far the most exciting is **De Efteling**, Europalaan 1, Kaatsheuvel, Noord Brabant, 110km from Amsterdam, © (0416) 288 111 (*see* pp.355–6). This is a surreal fantasy-land with an enormous Enchanted Forest, flying carpets, mysterious boat journeys, a Sleeping Beauty whose breasts heave, and all the usual (and some very unusual) rides. If you visit The Hague then the **Madurodam Mini-town** is a welcome diversion (*see* p.198). Over Christmas there's a popular circus at the **Carré Theatre** in Amsterdam (*see* pp.132–3).

Climate and Packing

The songs, and all the clichés, about tulips and the **spring** are right: it's a heady time to be in Holland, especially Amsterdam. Café owners tentatively put out a few tables and chairs to catch the new sun, there are flowers everywhere and everyone seems to be in a good mood. In **summer** the atmosphere becomes almost feverish. Tourists crowd the streets and bars, the air gets heavy and humid and mosquitoes breed abundantly on the canals. But it's a great time for countryside cycle jaunts. Gable-spotters enjoy **autumn** and early **winter**, as long lines of houses reappear from behind the summer foliage. Brick, cobblestone and leaves mingle in a subtle spectrum of browns. **January** and **February** can be punishing. As you teeter along the slippery pavements, you're assassinated by the icy blasts of wind that howl down the narrow streets and lash around corners. But as the door bangs behind you in a warm café, you'll discover the true meaning of the Dutch word '*gezelligheid*' (*see* p.23). The one thing common to all seasons is rain—sudden showers more than the monotonous drenching sort. It's a good idea to pack an umbrella at any time of the year. The temperature can drop rather suddenly, even in summer, so a few warm clothes are a wise precaution.

The Dutch are not ostentatious dressers. The dress code seems to be that if it feels good, it looks good.

English-language books are readily available, though expensive, so it's better to buy your holiday reading before you go.

Consulates and Embassies

Australia	Carnegielaan 4, 2517 KH, The Hague, ✆ (070) 310 8200.
Britain	Koningslaan 44, 1075 AE, Amsterdam, ✆ (020) 676 4343.
Canada	Sophialaan 7, 2514 JP, The Hague, ✆ (070) 311 1600.
Ireland	Dr Kuyperstraat 9, 2514 BA, The Hague, ✆ (070) 363 0993.
New Zealand	Carnegielaan 10, 2517 KH, The Hague, ✆ (070) 346 9324.
USA	Lange Voorhout 102, 2514 EJ, The Hague, ✆ (070) 310 9209.

Crime and Drugs

Police ✆ 112

Holland is comfortably safe. Even in larger cities you need have little fear of serious street crime at any time of day or night (though women walking alone would be well advised to avoid red-light districts after midnight).

Contrary to received opinion, soft drugs are not legal in Holland, though an official blind eye is turned to the possession of under 28g (1oz) of cannabis. The tolerance goes as far as allowing some coffeeshops to sell cannabis over the counter; here people smoke marijuana on the premises. But this is not true of all coffeeshops and cafés, and anyone found in possession of hard drugs, such as heroin or cocaine, can expect swift prosecution.

Bicycle theft, theft from cars and pickpocketing are something of a problem. You'll often see quite abusive signs on car windows informing all who might be tempted that there is nothing at all inside to steal. The Dutch sometimes spend more on a lock than on their bicycle ('And I'd just bought a new lock!' is a common wail after a bike has been stolen). A favourite trick of pickpockets is to sidle up close and offer to sell you something illicit. In your annoyed efforts to get rid of them (or keenness to see what they've got) you don't notice that your wallet is being gently removed. Sensible vigilance is the only way to avoid these petty crimes: don't leave valuables in your car, always lock your bike securely (*see* p.11) and don't carry a wallet in your back pocket or leave it on top of a shop counter when paying. Keep traveller's cheques and stubs separate and don't carry large amounts of money in one pocket.

The Dutch police generally keep a low profile and are a relaxed and sympathetic lot.

Disabled Travellers

Cobbled streets and tiny houses with narrow doorways and steep stairs can pose problems for those with limited mobility. Older trams have high steps, and are not accessible at all, though newer models are more wheelchair-friendly. In Amsterdam, however, there is a special taxi service for wheelchair-users (✆ (020) 613 4134) and the metro is accessible. The Netherlands Railways publishes timetables in Braille and a leaflet on *Rail Travel for the Disabled*, available at larger stations, or through their London office (✆ (01962) 773646, ✉ 773625, *www.hollandrail.com*).

The Dutch government takes an enlightened and constructive view of the problems faced by disabled people. They have, for example, introduced banknotes with raised shapes in the corner that indicate their value to the visually impaired. You'll find that nearly all museums, cinemas and churches have wheelchair access and many have facilities for the visually impaired and hard of hearing. Local tourist offices or the London branch of the **Netherlands Board of Tourism** (PO Box 523, London SW1E 6NYT, ✆ (020) 7828 7900) will have lists of accommodation, restaurants, museums and tourist attractions with facilities for the disabled. For information on specialized holidays contact:

RADAR, 12 City Forum, 250 City Rd, London EC1V 8AF, ✆ (020) 7250 3222, minicom ✆ (020) 7637 5315.

Holiday Care Services, 2nd Floor, Imperial Building, Victoria Road, Horley, Surrey RH6 9HW, ✆ (01293) 774535.

Disability Action Group, 2 Annedale Ave, Belfast BT7 3JH, ✆ (01232) 91011.

SATH (Society for the Advancement of Travel for the Handicapped), 347 Fifth Avenue, New York, NY 10016, ✆ (212) 447 7284.

Mobility Internation USA, PO Box 3551, Eugene, OR 97403, ✆ (503) 343 1284.

Mobility International Nederland, Heidestein 7, 3971 ND Driebergen, ✆ (0343) 521 795, ✉ (0343) 516 776. Will give advice on accommodation.

Wheelchair Hire in Amsterdam, Beumer de Jong, Haarlemmerstraat 49–53, 1058 JP Amsterdam, ✆ (020) 615 7188. Wheelchair hire from ƒ40/week; book in advance, especially in the summer.

Stichting Recreatie Gehandicapten, Boedapeststraat 25, Hoofddorp, Postbus 4140, 2003 EC Haarlem, ✆ (023) 536 8409. Organizes holidays and excursions in Holland for disabled people.

Electricity

The voltage in the Netherlands is 220 AC, which is compatible with the UK, but you'll need a transformer for American electrical equipment. Wall sockets take rather flimsy two-pronged plugs.

Police, ambulance, fire brigade, ☎ 112. The operators speak English.

For medical emergencies, see 'Health' below. Lost or stolen credit cards can be reported on the following numbers: American Express, stolen cheques ☎ (0800) 022 0100, stolen cards ☎ (020) 504 8000/504 8666 after 6pm; Diners Club ☎ (020) 557 3407; Mastercard/Access ☎ (0800) 022 5821; Visa ☎ (020) 660 0611.

Entertainment

Film

The Dutch are avid movie-goers. Most cafés and some restaurants and takeaways have a list of the week's films pinned up on the wall. Home-grown products haven't, however, made much of an impact on the international scene—though director **Paul Verhoeven** is known for *Robocop* and *Total Recall*, a Dutch film, *Antonia*, picked up the 1996 Oscar for Best Foreign Film, and the British director **Peter Greenaway** operates largely with Dutch funding.

Cinema prices range from ƒ10 to ƒ15 and there are often discounts on week nights. In the rare cases where an English film has been dubbed over you'll see '*Nederlands Gesproken*' on the publicity. The internationally important **Rotterdam Film Festival** is held in January/February. Information is available from any Dutch tourist office.

Theatre

Like England, the Netherlands experienced a 17th-century **Golden Age** of the theatre. Playwrights of that era, such as Vondel, Hooft and Bredero, are still performed in Holland. The 18th and 19th centuries saw the growth of extravagant stage spectacles. (On the nights they went to the theatre, wealthy families would send their maids and cooks on ahead to swell the ranks of the extras.) By the end of the 19th century, theatre had ossified from a popular into an élitist form. The '**Tomato Action**' of 1968 put an end to that. A disgruntled new generation of actors began throwing tomatoes at their older colleagues during performances and sparked off a theatrical revolution. In the decade that followed, Amsterdam theatres like the **Mickery** and the **Shaffy** earned a worldwide reputation for high quality avant-garde work. Government cuts and changing tastes have curtailed the mud-wading and body-painting, but there is still a strong tradition of excellent, highly visual theatre (look out for work by Orkater theatre company and spectacular outdoor romps by the Dogtroep). There is no national theatre company; the chief mainstream company is the rather stolid Toneelgroep Amsterdam, resident at the Westergasfabriek in Amsterdam.

Dance

Until recently, Dutch dance was sagging sadly, propped up by a rather univivacious Nationale Ballet in Amsterdam and the practically moribund Scapio Ballet in Rotterdam. Only The Hague's **Nederlands Dans Theater** had the verve and energy to prevent complete artistic prolapse. But at the moment the Netherlands is rising towards the crest of a new wave of dance, inspired perhaps by the big stage at Amsterdam's **Muziektheater**, an influx of foreign dancers and traditional rhythms from the former colonies. The **Nationale Ballet** has imported Canadian Wayne Eagling to be its Artistic Director, has expanded its repertoire, and is benefiting from the visits of touring companies who, at the Muziektheater, now have a suitable Amsterdam venue. The **Scapio** is dusting off the cobwebs and under new artistic direction has appointed Ed Wubbe as their daring new choreographer; the Nederlands Dans Theater keeps up a salvo of fine ballet and modern dance. Look out also for work by **Djazzex** (jazz dance) and **Dansgroep Krisztina de Chatel** (vivid, fairly theatrical style).

Classical Music

After a lull during the 1980s, when government cuts guillotined five of the Netherlands' thirteen major orchestras and public interest began to wane, Dutch music seems to be undergoing a renaissance. Baroque and period instrument orchestras are reaching particularly high standards (try to catch the **Amsterdam Baroque Orchestra** or the **Orchestra of the 18th Century** when they are not on tour). The **Nederlandse Opera** (also based in Amsterdam) repeatedly comes up with sharp, adventurous productions, often of 20th-century works, and the contemporary music scene is very lively (look out for pieces by **Louis Andriessen** and performances by the refreshingly unorthodox **Ricciotti Ensemble**). The famed **Royal Concertgebouw Orchestra** first established its reputation before the Second World War under the baton of Willem Mengelberg. He built up a close working relationship with Mahler and Richard Strauss and devoted 50 years to establishing his orchestra as one of the greatest in the world, only to be sacked after the war for pro-German sympathies. In the 1960s the orchestra was propelled to even greater heights by Bernard Haitink. It too has been through a dry patch, but conductor Riccardo Chailly is giving it new life.

Tickets

Tickets for opera, ballet and concerts will seem cheap if you're used to London or New York prices, but they sell out quickly. You can try for returns half an hour before a performance, but there are no last-minute discounts and systems of selling return tickets can be disorganized. Churches are favourite venues for concerts and recitals.

Rock Music

Chart-busters and rock and pop stadium-packers like Madonna and Prince used to give Amsterdam a miss and head for the larger venues such as the **Rotterdam Ahoy**. But in 1996 Amsterdam gained a state-of-the-art sports and entertainment stadium. The **Amsterdam ArenA** looks like a giant spaceship, hovering on the southeast outskirts of the city. It opened with concerts by Tina Turner and Michael Jackson, and has been packing in the audiences ever since. Keep an eye out also for Dutch stars who have made it internationally—such as Mathilde Santing, Eton Crop and the not so gently ageing Golden Earring—who have a loyalty to the old country and come back for a gig every year or two. Young British bands are often the best bet if you're looking for good rock. Many of these head for Paradiso or De Melkweg in Amsterdam. The Netherlands' large Indonesian and Surinamese populations swell many a bar with pulsating ethnic rhythms—the Latin and South American music scene is especially lively. Summer is the time for lively music festivals (*see* individual festival listings under Amsterdam, pp.80–82, Rotterdam, p.208, and The Hague, p.192).

Jazz

The mellow tones of jazz seem to suit the atmosphere of Dutch 'brown cafés', and many will have a live band on a Saturday night or Sunday afternoon. But the excellent **North Sea Jazz Festival** in The Hague (*see* p.192) is the jazz gig of the year. Surinamese and other South American immigrants crowd out a number of vibrant drinking and dancing venues—the music is great, and often live. Bars and cafés with live music often don't charge entrance, but have more expensive drinks.

Clubs

Dutch clubbers don't suffer the fashion neuroses of their London or New York counterparts. You can dress up, down, wild or straight: there's seldom any need to shock or impress some cool doorman before you're let in. The mood is carefree and unpretentious—late-night clubbing seems just an extension of early evening café life. Club nights on the beach at **Zandvoort** are the current focus of the summer dance scene.

Festivals and Events

Details of smaller local festivals and market days are given in the relevant chapters.

Feb: Carnival (sometimes in March). The annual last-minute bash before the rigours of Lent is most lively in the Catholic south, with Maastricht, Den Bosch and Bergen-op-Zoom putting on the best shows. Events go on for three or four days up to Shrove Tuesday, and usually involve at least one fancy-dress parade, and a lot of drunken fun.

Mar/ April: The best time to drive through the bulb fields or visit flower-filled gardens is in late March and early April.

National Museum Weekend is usually held on the third weekend in April. All museums are free—and crammed to capacity. A date to avoid unless you are particularly hard up.

Queen's Day, the Dutch monarch's official birthday, is held on 30 April, and celebrated across the country with street parties and a 'Free Market', which means that anyone can sell just about anything anywhere. Amsterdam used to be the best place to be, but during the late 1990s mayor Patijn introduced more strictures on the fun with each passing year, and current gossip has it that Utrecht is now more lively, especially on the night of 29 April, when things get going around midnight and don't stop.

The **World Press Photo Exhibition** is a show of the winning and finalists' pictures from the world's top annual photo-journalism competition. The award ceremony and opening exhibition are always held in Amsterdam in mid-April/early May.

May: **Dodenherdenking** (Remembrance Day) on 4 May is a sober, low-key occasion during which people lay flowers at monuments and places of significance (such as points from which Jews were deported). There is a genuine, nationwide two-minute silence at 8pm.

The next day, **Bevrijdingsdag** (Liberation Day) is usually celebrated in much the same manner as Queen's Day, though these days it is generally declared a public holiday only once every five years.

On **Nationale Molendag** (National Windmill Day, usually the second Saturday in May) about 600 of the country's 1,000 or so windmills are in full sail and open to the public. The same day is also declared **National Bicycle Day**, which doesn't mean much except that everyone cycles out to see the windmills.

Jazz in Duketown, a four-day festival in Den Bosch around Whitsun, doesn't quite rival the North Sea Jazz Festival (*see* below), but it can be more fun. Standards are high, it's less crowded, more relaxed, and the beer flows.

June: The **Holland Festival** is the country's leading arts event and attracts world names in music, opera, dance and theatre. Emphasis has been mainly on music, but in recent years focus has changed to performance of a more avant-garde nature.

In the second half of June, The Hague's substantial Indonesian community get together for the **Pasar Malam Besar**, a bonanza of music and dance, traditional puppet shows and cookery demonstrations, all centred on a large and colourful market on the Malieveld.

July: The famous **North Sea Jazz Festival** is held for three days in mid-July in The Hague, attracting top-drawer performers from around the world.

Not to be outdone, Rotterdam responds with a **Summer Carnival** on the last Saturday in the month. This is carnival very much in the Caribbean mode.

Aug: Culture vultures can dip their beaks in a variety of fare during the two-day-long **Uitmarkt** in Amsterdam at the end of August. The country's leading dance and theatre troupes, orchestras, and opera companies—and just about everybody else in the arts too—give a flavour of their programme for the forthcoming season, at (mostly free and open-air) venues all over Amsterdam.

Sept: On **Monumentendag** (Monument Day, second Saturday) historical buildings all over the country that are not usually open to the public throw open their doors. Queues can be long, but you get a fascinating glimpse of interiors that are usually hidden from view.

Prinsjesdag (third Tuesday) is the official opening of the Dutch parliament. Queen Beatrix whisks through The Hague in a golden coach to make a speech in the Ridderzaal.

The **Bloemencorso** (Flower Parade) is a parade of floats smothered in flowers from the Aalsmeer (site of the Netherlands' main flower auction houses) to Amsterdam, on the first Saturday of the month.

Nov: In mid-month **Sinterklaas** (St Nicholas) arrives, usually by steamboat and with an uncanny ability to appear in many places at once, all over the country. He then rides his dappled horse through town. He is accompanied by his servant Zwarte Piet (Black Pete), who to most outsiders appears a grotesque racist caricature (he's invariably a blacked-up white person with thick red lips and a fuzzy wig). Even liberal-minded Dutch people go into angry denial mode if you point this out.

Dec: The high point of the Sinterklaas festivities, which continue throughout November and early December, is **Sinterklaasavond** (a.k.a. Pakjesavond) on 6 December, very much an at-home affair at which families swap small gifts, often accompanied by mildly insulting doggerel about the recipients' various foibles.

Oudejaarsavond (31 December) is celebrated with gusto. Vast numbers of *oliebollen* (literally 'oil-balls', and that's what they are—deep-fried lumps of dough) are consumed, and fire crackers are let off everywhere, with apparent complete disregard for safety. You need nerves (and sometimes limbs and other organs) of steel to survive.

Erasmus, the great 16th-century Dutch humanist and man of letters, was pleased to note that his fellow countrymen were not given to much wild or ferocious behaviour, treachery or deceit, indeed were 'not prone to any serious vices except, that is, a little given to pleasure, especially to feasting'. Two centuries later the national ability to tuck in and drink up was still impressive enough to shock the British—themselves no mean feasters. In 1703 the seven or so deacons of the Arnhem guild of surgeons dispatched, at one sitting, 14lb of beef, 8lb of veal, six fowl, stuffed cabbages, apples, pears, bread, pretzels, assorted nuts, 20 bottles of red wine, 12 bottles of white wine and some jugs of coffee. Today, eating is still a supreme Dutch enthusiasm.

Paradoxically, **native Dutch cuisine** is not all that inspiring. The Dutch culinary clichés are *hutspot* ('hotchpotch'), a well-boiled stew that was much appreciated by starving citizens after the siege of Leiden and still requires a similar state of ravenousness before it can really be enjoyed; and *erwtensoep*, a porridgy pea soup which comes (vegetarians beware) with bits of sausage floating in it and a side dish of bread and raw bacon. The quality of *erwtensoep* is judged by testing whether or not your spoon will stand up on its own in the middle of the bowl. These are the staples of many a 'tourist menu', but (like the English) the Dutch have recently begun to explore more exciting avenues in their local cuisine—with game and fish especially. Other palatable traditional foods include *pannekoeken* (pancakes) which come with sweet or savoury fillings and *haring* (herring) eaten raw by tossing your head back and dropping a whole fillet down your throat, holding it by the tail. (If you can stomach it, this is a marvellous cure for a hangover.) *Belegde broodjes* are crusty rolls filled with a delicious variety of fillings—travellers' tales of sliced beef layered on buttered bread predated anecdotes about Lord Sandwich's invention by about a century. Waffles, dripping with syrup or smothered with fruit and cream, are sold on the streets. Cones of *frites* (potato chips), usually with a large dollop of mayonnaise, are ubiquitous. They're normally cooked with good-quality potatoes in clean oil.

In the absence of a stimulating local tradition, Dutch chefs have looked further afield. **French cuisine** first came into fashion during the Napoleonic occupation, and remains the cornerstone of many of the best kitchens. Nowadays most menus are tantalizingly eclectic, showing influences from Japan, Indonesia, Surinam and Turkey. Don't be surprised to find peanut sauce, saffron pasta and oysters on the same menu. The Dutch were enjoying '**fusion cuisine**' years before trendy London and New York chefs could distinguish lemongrass from lime leaves.

Specialist **ethnic restaurants** abound. Reasonable Indian and Italian food is to be had all over town, though the increasingly popular Thai and Japanese restaurants make a more exciting alternative. It's the culinary heritage of Holland's imperial past, however, that makes for the best ethnic binge. Treat yourself to an **Indonesian *rijsttafel***—a personal banquet of rice or noodles with a myriad spicy side dishes. (*See* **Language**, pp.373–4, for a selection of Dutch and Indonesian food terms.)

Vegetarians will have a difficult time in the Netherlands. The Dutch are great carnivores. Fish doesn't seem to count as meat, so if you enquire about vegetarian dishes you're often offered *kabeljauw* (cod). However, in the 1970s the tastes of the hippies spawned a few vegetarian restaurants and more have opened recently. Chefs in better kitchens are beginning to be more imaginative with their vegetarian options, and most restaurants will have at least one vegetarian meal on the menu.

Restaurants and Eating Out

Ingredients are usually market-fresh and microwave cookers are pleasingly thin on the ground. Food is cooked to order in most restaurants, so expect an unhurried meal. The Dutch **eat early** in the evening—between 7 and 9pm—and many kitchens are closed by 10 or 11pm. You may well find Dutch restaurants, bars and cafés **smoky**—the non-smoking revolution has not hit Holland by any means, and no amount of huffing and menu-flapping will even be understood let alone complied with. As in France, cafés and even some restaurants allow dogs in with their owners.

Budget eating is easy, and needn't be boring. Many restaurants offer a three-course 'Tourist Menu' for under ƒ30, but you're generally better off looking out for signs advertising a *dagschotel* (dish of the day). You usually end up with an oversized white plate with some well-prepared meat and a constellation of pickles and salads. Many cafés serve food—menus change daily and often offer the best value of all.

Takeaway foodstalls punctuate markets and shopping streets all over the country. As well as *frites*, *haring* and waffles you can sample all sorts of foreign delights: Turkish kebabs, Israeli falafel, Japanese sushi and spicy nibbles from Surinam and Indonesia. Under signs flashing '**Automatiek**' you can select a deep-fried croquette from a row of tiny windows displaying this and similar wares: drop in your ƒ1.50, pull a lever and collect your reward. 'Snack' was originally a Dutch word. Snack bars are the Dutch equivalent of street food. At worst they sell pre-prepared mushy croquettes, but at best they are tiny family-run establishments that hover in the middle ground between restaurant and takeaway.

Note that many smaller restaurants **don't accept credit cards**, and there's an air of reluctance about those that do. Even some of the larger establishments don't like plastic—so it's always a good idea to check in advance. Most good restaurants fill up pretty quickly, so it's wise to **reserve** a table by telephone.

The restaurants in the guide are all graded according to the approximate price of a three-course meal, without wine.

Restaurant price ranges (for a 3-course meal)

expensive	over ƒ80 (though seldom more than ƒ175)
moderate	ƒ55–ƒ80
cheap	under ƒ55

The bill will include tax and a 15% service charge—though if you feel you've been well looked after you can leave extra. It's usual to leave small change (or round up larger bills to the nearest ƒ5). It's worth checking out expensive restaurants, even if they seem above your budget, as many offer special three- or four-course meals for between ƒ45 and ƒ75.

Cafés and Coffeeshops

The term 'café' covers a wide range of establishments. At one end of the spectrum are the poky bars, where you go to knock back a few beers (with the odd *jenever* chaser); you might also be able to buy bread rolls, *tostis* (pale toasted sandwiches) or *bitterballen* (balls of meat purée, coated in breadcrumbs and deep-fried). At the other end you'll find enormous, airy **grand cafés** and places that offer such sumptuous fare that they're really indistinguishable from small restaurants. These often call themselves ***eetcafés*** (literally 'eating cafés') or even ***petit restaurant cafés***.

Most Dutch drink beer. Ordering *een Pils* at the bar will get you a small glass of lager topped with a finger or two of froth. Or you might prefer a *jenever* (Dutch gin—oilier and weaker than its British counterpart, with a whiff of juniper berries). In this case ask for a *borrel*. You can have either *oud* (old—more mellow) or *jong* (young—sharper). *Jenever* may also be flavoured: *citroenjenever* (lemon) or *besenjenever* (blackberry) are popular. Ask for a *kamelenrug* (camel's back) and your glass will be filled to the rim. Traditionally, you knock back all of your *jenever* with a single gulp. Should you require both beer and gin simultaneously, request a *kopstoot* (literally: 'knock on the head'). On freezing winter days a quick visit to a ***proeflokaal*** will warm your blood. These were once free tasting houses attached to spirit-merchants and taphouses. These days you have to pay, but the procedure is much the same: walk in, drink up, walk out.

Coffeeshops serve tea, coffee and wonderful cakes and pastries. Sometimes they serve snacks and fuller meals, but never alcohol. Tea is seldom served with milk, unless you specifically ask for it. Coffee will come black or with strange processed *koffiemelk*, unless you order *koffieverkeerd* (literally 'coffee wrong'), in which case you'll get a delicious 50:50 mixture with fresh milk. Since the 1970s some coffeeshops (the so-called **smoking coffeeshops**) have openly sold marijuana. These are easily distinguishable at first glance/sniff. They are painted psychedelic colours, often have leaf designs on the windows and emit loud music and fazed customers.

Gezelligheid

Dictionaries translate the Dutch word *gezellig* as 'convivial' or 'cosy'. A 1970s historian defined it, in the idiom of his time, as 'partly a sort of cosiness and partly a living togetherness'. *Gezelligheid* is the stuff of the Dutch temperament, and Amsterdammers pride themselves that their town bulges with it.

A café with nicotine-stained walls and scuffed leather chairs is *gezellig*; when you move into a new apartment you hang a few pictures, buy in some pot plants, adjust the lighting and make the flat *gezellig*; the mood in a neighbourhood bar on a cold winter's afternoon is *gezellig*; the behaviour of British lager louts in the bars of Leidseplein is definitely not. Sometimes *gezelligheid* seems subconscious. During the street riots of the 1960s the police were equipped, not with aggressive-looking anti-riot gear but with large round wicker shields. It must have been almost impossible to hurl a missile at a policeman who was sheltering behind something resembling a dog basket. In its extreme forms *gezelligheid* becomes oppressive—the lace window screens, shelves of knick-knacks and safe respectability of a stolid *burgher* sitting room. At worst *gezelligheid* inhabits a trim, embroidered world somewhere between kitsch and twee. A nice, *gezellig* family hotel in a small seaside town would probably be the *last* place you'd choose to spend your summer holiday.

The up-side of *gezelligheid* is to be felt in the warm conviviality that suffuses Dutch cafés, and even markets and town squares. Living in cramped houses in a small-scale city has honed Amsterdammers' social behaviour to a fine edge. They seem to have discovered that the best way of getting on when your neighbours are at such close quarters is by developing a frank, easy-going tolerance—a subtle decorum. Rules are clear, universally understood and sometimes broken if the occasion demands. In 17th-century Calvinist Amsterdam, Roman Catholics were allowed to worship freely, provided that their churches were discreetly hidden behind domestic house-fronts. Today Amsterdam authorities turn a blind eye to the sale and smoking of marijuana (technically still illegal) in certain cafés. Centuries of reasonableness have produced a culture that, perhaps more than any other in Europe, deserves the epithet 'civilized', and at its core are the virtues of *gezelligheid*.

Health and Insurance

Ambulance, ℗ 112

It is always advisable to take out travel insurance before any trip abroad—and to do so as soon as you buy your tickets. Specially tailored travel insurance packages cover medical expenses, lost luggage and theft, and also offer compensation for cancellation and delayed departure. The cost of travel insurance is steadily rising, but is still insignificant when compared with the potential costs of a serious emergency, or even the value of your tickets should you have to cancel your trip. Consult your insurance broker or travel agent. In the event of needing to make a claim, be sure to check the small print of your policy to see what documentation (police report, medical forms, invoices, etc.) is required by the insurance company.

That said, EU nations are entitled to receive free or reduced-charge medical treatment in the Netherlands: British visitors will need a form E111 (fill in application form SA30, available from DSS branches or post offices). Theoretically you should organize this two weeks before you leave, though you can usually do it over the counter in one visit. The E111 does not insure personal belongings.

Maps

Falk publish a variety of city and country maps (available in larger bookshops and VVV tourist offices throughout Holland). Offices of the **ANWB** motoring organization are also a good source of motoring maps and cycle routes.

In the UK, try **Stanford's** (12–14 Long Acre, London WC2 9LP, ℗ (020) 7836 1321; **Waterstone's Piccadilly**, 203–6 Piccadilly, London W1V 9LE, ℗ (020) 7851 2400; **The Travel Bookshop**, 13 Blenheim Crescent, London W11 2EE, ℗ (020) 7229 5260; or **The National Map Centre**, 22 Caxton St, London SW1H OQU, ℗ (020) 7222 2466.

In the USA, try the **Traveler's Bookstore**, 22 West 52nd St, New York NY 10019, ✆ (212) 664 0995; branches of the **Complete Traveler** in New York (199 Madison Ave, New York, NY 10016, ✆ (212) 685 9007) and San Francisco (3207 Filmore St, CA 92123, ✆ (415) 923 1511); and **Rand MacNally** in New York (150 East 52nd St, New York, NY 10022, ✆ (212) 758 7488) and San Francisco (550 Jackson St, CA 94105, ✆ (415) 981 7520).

Media

Don't be surprised if you find yourself chatting over a coffee with a local about the previous night's BBC TV soap opera. Amsterdam gets BBC1 and 2, Radio 4 (198kHz LW) and the World Service (6045 kHz AM). Even on Dutch television British and American shows tend to be subtitled rather than dubbed. Most homes and hotels are connected to cable. You can get about 20 stations (including CNN) and can decide what to watch by flicking through to **Infokanaal**—two alternating screens with simultaneous broadcasts of what's on offer on all channels. Non-Dutch speakers might like to tune in to Netherlands Radio 3 (96.8 mHz) for pop or Radio 4 (98.9 mHz) for classical music.

International **newspapers** are available all over the Netherlands, usually on the day of publication. If you want to pigeonhole the person opposite you on the tram by the newspaper he's reading, here's a short list. *De Telegraaf* is right-wing, sensationalist press. It was the only paper allowed to publish during the Nazi occupation. The *NRC Handelsblad* is the favourite of intellectuals. *Het Parool* started life as a Resistance news-sheet in Amsterdam during the war. *Trouw* also went underground, and *De Volkskrant* was banned. These three now form the nucleus of the left-wing press. *Het Financieel Dagblad* gives business news, and has an English summary. The *Algemene Dagblad* is middle-of-the-road, and one of the few papers to be based in Rotterdam.

Money

For lost credit cards, see 'Emergencies'.

The unit of Dutch **currency** is the guilder, which is abbreviated as *f*, f, fl (for the old Dutch term florin) or NLG (in business and banking contexts). On price tags, 'guilders' is often written as /−. A guilder is divided into 100 cents (shortened to 'c'). There are around *f*2.5 to the pound sterling, and about *f*1.66 to the US dollar. The notes are said to be the prettiest in Europe, and come in *f*10, *f*25, *f*50, *f*100, *f*250, *f*500 and *f*1000 denominations (though you seldom see notes above *f*100, and may have trouble finding shops that accept larger denominations). There are six types of coin: a *stuiver* (5c, copper); the *dubbeltje* (10c), *kwartje* (25c), *f*1 and *rijksdaalder* (*f*2.50)—all silver-coloured; and the *f*5 (gold-coloured). All prices are rounded up to multiples of five. Once you've got used to counting in 25s and 2.5s, it's pretty straightforward.

Credit cards are not as widely accepted as you might expect—the Dutch generally prefer cash in shops, restaurants and even hotels. It's always a good policy to double-check. The small commission that banks charge businesses on credit card payments seems to sit uncomfortably with the Dutch sense of financial prudence. A number of shops will charge you extra if you pay by credit card. Eurocheques and traveller's cheques are a better idea. If you have appropriate identification, many establishments will accept them direct. Nowadays hole-in-the-wall cash dispensers are the most convenient way of getting money. Check before you leave that your bank card is programmed for overseas withdrawals, and that your bank doesn't make any outrageous charges for the service. You can usually withdraw up to *f*300 a day.

Banks are open 9–4/5 Mon–Fri (some stay open until 7 on Thursdays).

Head offices of the main Dutch banks in Amsterdam

> ABNAMRO, Vijzelgracht 32, © (020) 629 9111.
> ING, Bijlmerplein 888, © (020) 563 9111.
> Rabobank, Wilhelminaplantsoen 124, © (020) 495 0950.
> VSB Bank, Singel 548, © (020) 624 9340.

Some foreign bank head offices

> Barclays Bank, World Trade Center, Stravinskylaan 3051, © (020) 301 2364.
> Citibank NA, Hoogoorddreef 541B, © (020) 651 4211.

The **Postbank** (at post offices) and **GWK** (Grens Wissel Kantoor—official *bureaux de change*) are the best places to change your money. ***Bureaux de change*** often offer the same rates as banks, but take more commission; however, the GWK exchanges at Amsterdam's Centraal Station and Schiphol (both open 24 hours daily) are a better bet than the deals offered by hotel receptions, and even many banks.

If you exchange traveller's cheques at a company branch, you don't have to pay commission at all. In Amsterdam, you'll find offices of American Express at Amsteldijk 166, Damrak 66 (with 24-hour cash dispenser for cardholders and automatic traveller's cheque refund service) and Van Baerlestraat 39; and Thomas Cook at Dam 23–25, Damrak 1–5 (open Mon–Sat 8–8 and Sun 9–8), and Leidseplein 31a.

Museum Admissions and Discount Cards

> *In the text of this book, you will see 'adm' after the opening hours if there is an admission charge, and 'adm exp' if the charge is more than f 15.*

Museums in the Netherlands are seldom free, but for *f*55 (*f*25 for under-24s and *f*45 for over-55s) you can buy an **Annual Museum Card** (*Museumjaarkaart*/**MJK**) which gets you into most museums in Holland for nothing, or at a substantial discount. Buy one at the museum ticket office, and ask for the booklet listing the 300–400 museums the discount applies to.

If you're under 26 the **CJP** (***Cultureel Jongeren Passport***) entitles you to discount at museums, theatres and cultural events. It's available from tourist offices, many theatres, and some libraries and other cultural institutions for *f* 20.

You will need a photograph for all these discount cards, and proof of age for the CJP.

Post Offices

The Dutch postal service logo is a white **ptt post** on a red background. Post offices are generally open Mon–Fri 8.30–5. Larger branches may also open Sat 9–12 noon. Here you can buy stamps, and send letters, express letters and telegrams (make sure you're in the right queue—sometimes counters are labelled for certain functions only). Stamps (*postzegels*) can also be bought from tobacconists. At the time of writing it costs ƒ1 to send a postcard to the UK, ƒ1 to send an airmail letter to the UK or a postcard to the USA and ƒ1.30 to send an airmail letter to the USA (prices for letters under 20g). The slot for overseas mail on post boxes is marked 'Overige'. A poste restante service is available. Letters should be addressed to: Poste Restante, Hoofdpostkantoor PTT, Singel 250, 1016 AB Amsterdam. You'll need a passport to claim your mail.

Public Holidays

New Year's Day, Good Friday, Easter Sunday and Monday, Queen's Day (30 April), Ascension Day, Whit Sunday and Monday, Christmas Day and Boxing Day. On public holidays most things close, and towns can be very quiet indeed.

Shopping

Weekday opening hours are generally 9–6. On Saturdays shops close around 5pm, and some do not open on Monday mornings either. Some shops in larger city centres now open from noon to 6pm on Sundays. Many of the smaller shops can be quite idiosyncratic about when they open, but all will have a little black and yellow timetable of opening hours posted on an outside window. Most neighbourhoods have one or two shops that open around 5pm and stay open until between 11pm and 1am. Here you can buy, at a suitably inflated price, emergency bottles of wine, groceries and gooey cakes for late-night munchies. Some of the more upmarket establishments sell gourmet meals and chocolates to bring tears to your eyes. Look out for signs reading 'Avondverkoop' or 'Nightshop'.

Dutch sales tax (BTW—17.5% on most goods) is included in the marked price, though many stores offer tax-free shopping to non-EU tourists. They'll help with the paperwork.

Sport

The most popular national sport is **football**. The Dutch team have not had many resounding international successes, but the local teams such as Amsterdam Ajax, PC Eindhoven, and Feyenoord (Rotterdam) have a vociferous and enthusiastic following. Important matches will almost certainly turn your neighbourhood brown café into a silent room of tense men fixated on a flickering TV. Hockey (field hockey), on the other hand, is a sport in which both the men's and the women's national teams have been world champions, and ice hockey is proving increasingly popular. But the one sporting event certain to grip the whole land is the **Elfstedentocht** ('eleven-city marathon') which takes place on the canals and waterways between 11 towns in Friesland. It is only rarely that the freeze is good enough, but if the weather is really cold you'll hear talk of nothing else for weeks but whether or not the **Elfstedentocht** is going to happen. If you hear that it's on, then it's certainly worth a trip north.

The Netherlands is also home to more esoteric sports. Every year, from May to October, squads of eager '**horizontal mountain-climbers**' don shorts and sneakers and slop knee deep through sucking quagmires of black mud off the Frisian coast. This they do for two to four hours at a time, before returning home. Another odd national pastime is **pole-sitting**. Every year, around the beginning of August, men sit on poles in the North Sea (at Noorderwijkerhout just north of The Hague) until they fall off. The last one to do so is the winner. *Korfball* is an indigenous hybrid of netball and volleyball played between teams comprising equal numbers of men and women. It's a rule-bound battle of the sexes where players have to toss a ball around at great speed and try to shoot it into a hoop 11½ feet (3.5m) off the ground.

Telephones, E-mail and the Internet

Dutch telephone boxes are green, with a white ptt telecom logo. Payphones take 25c, ƒ1, ƒ2.50 and coins. Increasingly, cardphones are taking the place of payphones. Many accept credit cards, and all operate with phonecards, which you can buy at post offices, railway stations and newsagents. Instructions in phone boxes are clear, but don't be confused by the local ringing tone, a long continuous sound rather like the British 'engaged' signal. A busy line in Holland is indicated by rapid tones. Another confusing surprise is the dalek voice you get when phoning popular numbers such as airports or taxis. You're told: '*Er zijn nog drie (three)/twee (two)/een (one) wachtenden voor u*'—an indication of how many people are patiently waiting ahead of you in an electronic queue.

Numbers preceded by 0800 are free; those beginning 0900 are charged at a special rate, usually between 50c and ƒ1 a minute (for these calls a recorded voice will tell you how much you are having to fork out).

Directory Enquiries: ✆ (0900) 8008

International Operator (also for collect calls): ✆ (0800) 0410

International Directory Enquiries: ✆ (0900) 8418

International direct dialling codes:

From Holland to USA: ✆ (00 1)—area code without the first 0
From USA to Holland: ✆ (011 31)—area code without the first 0
From Holland to UK: ✆ (00 44)—area code without 0
From UK to Holland: ✆ (00 31)—area code without 0

International calls are cheaper between 8pm and 8am, but calls to other European countries don't count as international.

Most cities now have an abundance of Internet cafés and, uniquely, Amsterdam has Internet booths on street corners. These look just like telephone booths, but are marked with an @. A normal telephone card gives you access to the Net and e-mail facilities.

Time

The Netherlands is 2 hours ahead of Greenwich Mean Time in the spring and summer, and 1 hour ahead in winter and autumn. It is 6 hours ahead of Eastern Standard Time and 9 hours ahead of Pacific Standard Time.

Tipping, Etiquette and Service

Restaurant and bar bills in Holland are inclusive of tax and service, so a tip isn't really necessary. It's customary, though, to round the amount up to the nearest guilder (or ƒ5 for a big bill). If the service has been exceptional, it's quite acceptable to add a little more. Don't leave money on the bar counter after buying your drink; the Dutch will either think it a little vulgar, or take it for a tip. Taxi drivers expect 10%—especially if they've helped with luggage.

Queuing at supermarket delicatessens, some banks and public institutions is controlled by an electronic ticketing system. You tear off a ticket as you enter and wait for your number to flash up on a screen. At cash machines and bank and post office counters, the rest of the queue keeps a polite metre or so's distance from the person transacting business. Sometimes there's a boundary line painted on the floor. Step over this mark (visible or otherwise) and the atmosphere turns icy.

English is spoken almost as a second mother tongue through most of the Netherlands. Some Hollanders seem to resent this, but many (especially those working in restaurants, bars and shops) seem insulted if you ask 'Do you speak English?' One way round this is to open with a cheery *Dag!* ('*darhg*'—good day) and then speak English. '*Dag*'— called out with a friendly upward lilt in the voice—is used at all times of day or night, on entering and leaving shops, and when speaking to barmen, policemen, cabbies and tram drivers.

When you meet a Dutch person for the first time, it's polite to shake hands and say your name clearly.

If you are used to slick New York service, or even to the slightly less brisk British style, then you are in for a sad surprise when you visit Holland. Bring a bottle of Valium to help keep calm and a pack of cards to while away the time, or you will find your holiday intensely frustrating. It is not unknown for customers to sit for twenty minutes to half an hour in a café before there is even a whiff of a waiter, though when they do come they are so full of shiny-eyed friendliness that it is difficult to be angry. Expect to wait at least half an hour to forty minutes for your dinner to arrive once you have ordered it. The knowledge that everything is being prepared fresh rather than subjected to the microwave is scant consolation to a rumbling stomach.

The maxim that the customer is always right does not hold true in the Netherlands. If you dare to complain, it will be pointed out to you in no uncertain terms that it is in fact you who is at fault. Inform the receptionist that something has been stolen from your room, and rather than an offer of sympathy you will be told off for not putting it in the hotel safe—and will probably have to pay for the phone call to the police. Dare to order a meal 15 minutes before the advertised closing time of the kitchen (usually astonishingly early anyway) and you'll have a strip torn off you for eating so late. Even situations where it seems self-evident that you are in the right—such as a complaint about the lack of a shower curtain—can lead to a brush-up with the management that leaves you feeling you are to blame.

Paradoxically, service is cheery, relaxed and friendly. Just be prepared to wait...and don't complain.

Toilets

Apart from those at railway stations and the odd foul-smelling urinoir, there are few public toilets in the Netherlands. The best option is to duck into a café. This is perfectly acceptable practice, though bars in some of the busier tourist areas discourage it. The better hotel foyers provide classier options, but this takes a certain amount of poise, as you have to stroll through the lobby as if you're a resident, all the time darting your eyes about for the relevant sign—not easy if you're caught in a last-minute dash. Station loos—and sometimes those in larger cafés—are guarded by fierce women, who require you to drop at least 25c into a saucer before passing.

Tourist Information

There is a nationwide tourist office at Schiphol airport, Holland Tourist Information (HTi, Schiphol Plaza, Mon–Sun 7am–10pm). You can get information on the Internet at the official website: *www.holland.com*. The Netherlands Board of Tourism (NBT) offices abroad can give you details of hotels and events:

UK   PO Box 523, London SW1E 6LB, information line ✆ (0906) 871 7777 (charged at premium rate), (recorded info) ✆ (0891) 717 777, *www.holland.com/uk*.

USA   355 Lexington Av, 19th Floor, New York, NY 10017, ✆ (212) 370 7360, or toll free (1 888) GO HOLLAND, *www.goholland.com*, *info@goholland.com*.

Canada   25 Adelaide Street E., Suite 710, Toronto, Ontario, M5C 1Y2, ✆ (1 888) GO HOLLAND, or, for French speakers, (1 888) PAYS BAS, *www.goholland.com*, *info@goholland.com*.

VVVs

Most towns and villages in Holland have a local tourist office or **VVV** (look out for the eye-catching blue triangle sign containing the letters VVV in white) which will be able to advise you on accommodation, opening times and local sights etc. They should also have a wide range of motoring, cycling and tourist maps for sale. You can write directly to a VVV from abroad by addressing your letter to VVV followed by the name of the town you are visiting.

Where to Stay

All sorts of old houses—poky, grand and resonantly historical, beside canals and in the middle of forests—have been given new life as hotels in the Netherlands. Many of these are privately owned and have been lovingly turned into little havens of *gezelligheid* or storehouses of antiques. These are the best places of all to stay—but most have built up a dedicated clientele and require booking some time in advance. Rooms in the same house will vary enormously in size and en suite bathrooms tend to have showers only. If you hear of a particularly desirable room, try to book it specifically by number.

Reservations

Reservations can be made direct to the hotel or, once you're in the country, through local tourist offices or VVV (phone the Netherlands Tourist Board on © (070) 419 5544 for their details). VVVs charge around *f* 5 booking fee and a *f* 10 room deposit which is later deducted from your bill. The Netherlands Board of Tourism in your home country can give you a list of hotels, but can't make bookings. If you need to book in advance the **Netherlands Reservation Centre** (NRC) offers a broad choice from budget to 5-star on © 0031 (0)70 419 55 44, *www.hotelres.nl, info@hotelres.nl.*

Because accommodation is at such a premium, you'll find that most hotels will ask for a deposit or the security of a credit card number.

Accommodation Categories

Standards of cleanliness and service are high and, unless you're scraping along at the very bottom of the price range, you're unlikely to find yourself sharing your room with local fauna, thumping faulty electrical equipment or speculating about the origins of the hairs on the sheets. Facilities can be quite spartan, however, and a lot of the smaller hotels offer rooms of the bed/bedside table/wardrobe-only variety. Yet even these are usually tastefully done up and almost invariably impeccably clean.

Hotels are graded by the Benelux star system (one to five stars), though this isn't a particularly useful guide as it is based on an inventory of facilities and tells you nothing about location, service or ambience. Facilities vary in direct relation to price—you get what you pay for. Around the top end of the 'moderate' range (*f* 220–*f* 280) you should be assured of a TV and telephone in your room. Beyond that lies the world of mini-bars, en suite jacuzzis and telephones in the loo.

The hotels in the 'expensive' range tend to be business hotels. Here you're paying for facilities like fax machines and meeting rooms. Such places are briskly efficient, but are often soulless and used to expense-account customers. You can be just as comfortable, and probably far happier, in a more idiosyncratic hotel from the top of the 'moderate' range. Price ranges given in this guide are as follows:

Hotel price ranges used in this guide	
luxury	*f* 450 and over
expensive	*f* 280–*f* 450
moderate	*f* 180–*f* 280
inexpensive	*f* 100–180
cheap	under *f* 100

These prices are for a double room with bath or shower en suite in season, and include services and taxes and (unless otherwise stated) Dutch breakfast. For prices of single rooms deduct 15–20 per cent.

Self-catering

Amsterdam Apartments, Kromme Waal, 1011 BV, ✆ (020) 626 5930, ✉ 626 9544. Privately owned flats around town—usually flats let by Amsterdammers away on holiday—*from f700 per week*.

GIS Apartments, Keizersgracht 33, 1015 CD; ✆ (020) 625 0071, ✉ 638 0475. From simple to luxurious. *From f2,000 per month, minimum 3 months*.

Global Home Network, Suite 205, 110-D Elden Street, Herndon, Virginia, USA; ✆ +1 703 318 7081, ✉ + 1 703 318 7086 have a number of canalside apartments on their books, for short- and medium-term lease. *Prices on application*.

Centre Parcs, Head Office, Rufford Newark Nottinghamshire NG22 9DP UK, ✆ (01623) 872 997, ✉ 872 399. Chalet accommodation amidst covered tropical swimming paradises, with golf and tennis facilities.

Hikers' Cabins: For the rugged at heart only, a network of wooden cabins with beds, cooking, washing and toilet facilities throughout Holland. Cost per night for a maximum of four people is f55: bring your own sleeping bags and kitchen utensils. Brochures with more information available from Stichting Trekkershutten Nederland Ruigeweg 49, 1752 HC Sint Maartensbrug, ✉ (0224) 563 318.

Bed & Breakfast

Bed & Breakfast Holland, T. de Bockstraat 3, 1058 TV Amsterdam, ✆ (020) 615 7527, ✉ 669 1573.

Bed & Breakfast in Holland & Amsterdam Information, Kraneweg 86a, 9718 JW Groningen, ✆ (050) 313 2424, *www.holidaylink.com*, *b&b@holidaylink.com*.

Camping and Caravanning

Holland Tulip Parcs, M. Meustraat 112, 4818 LW Breda, ✉ (076) 520 7305, *www.hollandtulipparcs.nl*. Network of 25 campsites across Holland, some with facilities including restaurants and swimming pools.

RCN, Recreatiecentra Nederland Campings Bungalows, Postbus 38, 3970 AA Driebergen, ✆ (343) 513 547. Group of ten campsites on beauty spots across Holland, many with water and sports centres.

History

Until quite recently—1831 to pinpoint a date—the borders of what we now know as the Netherlands were as fluid as its ever-shifting shoreline. And it is 'the Netherlands' we're talking about. Holland does not exist. 'North Holland' and 'South Holland' are both provinces of the country that the Dutch themselves call 'Nederland'. It's only foreigners who insist on applying the name Holland to the whole land. Just how this all came about needs a little untangling.

Watery Beginnings

As long ago as 150,000 BC there were nut-nibblers and hewers of flint tools near Utrecht. The Ice Age did for them. Next came hungry hunters and nomads, most of whom were flooded out by the fickle North Sea. It wasn't until about 6000 BC that farmers began to settle on what high muddy banks they could find, and it was only around 750 BC that they began to build their own mounds to protect farmsteads from the floods.

By the time written records began, in 57 BC, most of the territory was occupied by **Germanic tribes**, whom the Roman writer Tacitus dismissed as 'proud, touchy and warlike'. It was around this time that the Romans pushed their way in, conquering all but the Frisians in the very north of the land. But the North Sea again intervened, turning most of the west of the country to bog (Pliny was miserable near Leiden in AD 50). Disheartened, and with their empire crumbling behind them anyway, the Romans eventually withdrew. The end of Roman rule in the area is generally set at AD 406, when the Romans surrendered their forts along the Rhine.

Tribal Gatherings

Gradually, the remaining Germanic folk formed themselves into larger groups—the Saxons in the east, the Franks to the south of the great rivers (the Rhine and the Maas), and the plucky Frisians on their mounds in the north. At the beginning of the 6th century the Frankish **King Clovis I** converted to Christianity in the heat of a battle. That would appear to have been a good move, because not only was he victorious, but the Franks went on to establish a far-reaching empire—this was eventually to develop into the Holy Roman Empire, with the coronation of **Charlemagne** in AD 800.

Officially, the Netherlands was part of the **Holy Roman Empire** until 1648, but in reality power was held (after a brief and violent Viking interlude) by a number of local overlords, who were constantly at each other's throats. During the Middle Ages the most powerful rulers to emerge were the **Counts of Holland**, the **Bishops of Utrecht**, and the **Dukes of Gelderland** and of **Brabant**. No one ever really managed overall domination over the rebellious Frisians, who fought among themselves for most of the 14th and 15th centuries.

A Measure of Independence

By 1350, most of the future regions of the Netherlands had established themselves as **independent states**. Wars between local nobles continued to rage, with two main factions forming—the 'Hoeksen' (Hooks) and the 'Kabeljauwsen' (Cods), who fought for succession in the counties of Holland, Zeeland and Hainault. At the same time a power struggle developed between increasingly wealthy cities and the landed aristocracy.

As early as the 11th century, once the Vikings had stopped raiding and the weather had improved, the occupants of the Low Countries had begun to get the hang of reclaiming marshland and building **dykes** against the incursions of the sea. Soon they formed **water boards** (to regulate water levels in low-lying parts of the countryside) and constructed inland waterways. Trade along these routes flourished, and wealthy towns began to grow up. Some of these towns joined the powerful Baltic trade organisation, the **Hanseatic League**.

Town councils were well organized, and enjoyed considerable freedom. Town charters were granted to these wealthy merchant strongholds, guaranteeing their privileges in return for financial support for the local lord's war. One of the first towns to gain such a charter was **'s Hertogenbosch** (Den Bosch) in 1185. Similar privileges were granted to **Haarlem** by Count William II of Holland in 1245 and, after a struggle involving the Lord of the Amstel, the Count of Holland and the Bishop of Utrecht (*see* p.69), **Amsterdam** emerged as a powerful force, gaining its charter in 1300.

Part of Burgundy

Meanwhile, machinations in the upper realms of European royal courts were beginning to have an effect back down on the ground. In 1363 the King of France had given the Duchy of Burgundy to his son **Philip the Bold** (1342–1404). Philip married **Margaret of Flanders**, and subsequent clever unions and fortuitous inheritances meant that Burgundian influence spread ever northwards. By the middle of the 15th century, Philip's grandson **Philip the Good** (1396–1467) managed to unite a large chunk of what we now known as the Netherlands, together with Flanders and Luxembourg, under **Burgundian rule**. The Frisians, of course, held out, as did their neighbours in Groningen and Gelderland.

Burgundian expansion continued under **Charles the Rash** (1433–77), and links with the Hapsburgs were made when his daughter Mary married Emperor Maximilian I of Austria. Their son **Philip the Fair** (1478–1506) married Joanna of Castile and Aragon, thus adding her lands to the empire. Their heir **Charles** (1500–58) inherited the Austrian States from his grandfather Maximilian, and canoodled his way into being declared Holy Roman Emperor.

A Country Forms

By the time Philip the Fair died in 1506, the counties and duchies around the county of Holland were already being termed 'the Netherlands'. By the mid-16th century, Friesland, Groningen and Gelderland had finally been subsumed into Burgundy, and this northwestern corner of the empire became known as the '**Seventeen United Netherlands**'. Charles appointed his aunt Margaret, dowager Duchess of Savoy, to the post of 'royal governor' over the area. But the increasingly powerful cities were opposed to this Burgundian centralization. As early as 1464 various regional assemblies had convened in Bruges to decide whether Philip the Good should be financed to go on a crusade. This convention, called the '**States-General**', became a permanent and increasingly important feature of regional government.

Growing Prosperity

The blossoming of trade in the Netherlands was principally due to grain, herring and beer. Enormous quantities of grain were needed to feed the growing population in western Europe (bread was still the staple diet). The Netherlands was able to tap rich Baltic and central European supplies through its traditional trading connections. Dordrecht, on the river Rhine, and Amsterdam played a leading role in this activity.

Other towns near Amsterdam, such as Hoorn and Enkhuizen, also prospered. Leiden and Haarlem became busy centres of cloth manufacture. Gouda, Delft and Amersfoort were just three of many **brewing towns**—and as most people drank beer rather than the poisonous local water, merchants began to get rich. Then in 1384 one Willem Beukels hit upon a way of **preserving herring** more efficiently—by gutting them before salting. This meant that ships could stay out at sea even longer and travel further afield. At about the same time, as if obeying some cosmic plan, the herring moved their spawning ground from the Baltic to the North Sea, and the industry prospered. It needed salt (from Portugal) and wood for the barrels (from Germany and Scandinavia).

Amsterdam merchants had no qualms, as they moved further into the Baltic, about breaking in on the Hanseatic League's trade and developing new routes. Soon the city's ships were also carrying furs, iron ore, cloth, and wine. Wily merchants began building warehouses all over the city to store goods until the best price could be fetched. Amsterdam became a thriving commercial centre and a nexus for European trade. It fought a bitter trade war with the Hanseatic towns, but by the mid-15th century was indomitable. By 1500 the region around Amsterdam (most of the county of Holland) had taken the lead in the economy. This had a crucial effect on politics in the centuries to come.

Reformation and Revolt

At the beginning of the 16th century Europe was firmly in the grip of the Roman Catholic Church. But on 31 October 1517 a hitherto obscure Augustinian monk called **Martin Luther** calmly walked up to the chapel of Wittenberg Castle and nailed his '95 Theses' to the door. The 'Theses' condemned superstition in the Church and the practice of indulgences. Luther's act marked the beginning of the Reformation—theologians everywhere became braver and more audible in their criticism. In Rotterdam **Erasmus** propounded an idealized man as the pinnacle of creation, rather than the miserable sinner after the Fall. In Geneva **Calvin** appealed to the Age of Reason with his impeccably logical 'Institutes': the State should be separated from the Church, and be in the hands of morally upright citizens. The Catholic Church responded swiftly and thousands were tried for heresy.

Trade routes also served as channels for new ideas. The revolutionary theology caught on quickly in the Netherlands and there were heresy trials, but the Dutch were traditionally tolerant and didn't always carry out sentences they were obliged to impose. In fact Calvin's austere doctrines, and the notion of civic power, rather appealed to a number of wealthy merchant families.

By this time the Netherlands was ruled, as a consequence of marriages made in the stratosphere of the royal courts of Europe, by **Philip II of Spain** (later husband of Mary Tudor). Philip was head of the mighty Austro-Spanish Catholic house of Hapsburg which dominated much of Europe, owned most of South America and even laid claim to the English crown. Unlike his reassuringly named predecessors (Philip the Good, Charles the Bold and Philip the Fair), Philip II was a cruel and fanatical despot. He also took ages to reach decisions, so his subjects spent most of their lives in a terrified limbo. Action was dangerous, no orders came from above and political situations had the habit of deteriorating around the protagonists. This was particularly aggravating in territories as far-flung as the Netherlands. Even Dutch Catholics, outraged by the Inquisition and this distant monarch's cruel repression, became antagonistic. Opposition to Philip began to grow along nationalist as well as religious lines. Philip took a quiet step back, leaving his half-sister, **Margaret of Parma**, to deal with any unpleasantness—though in effect power was wielded by a scheming civil servant Antoine Perrenot, later **Cardinal Granvelle**.

Meanwhile, several leading local nobles had been declared the king's lieutenants—or '*stadhouders*'—in the main provinces. Among these was one **William of Orange**, lord-lieutenant of Holland, Zeeland, West Frisia and Utrecht. Granvelle tried to exclude the *stadhouders* from discussions in the Council of State, but in 1562 dissatisfied court nobles united under William of Orange and demanded Granvelle's dismissal. They were tacitly backed by Margaret of Palma, who was no friend of the scheming upstart, and in 1564 Granvelle left the Netherlands 'to visit his family', and never returned. Margaret was persuaded to sign the '**Moderation**', which implied some measure of religious tolerance. Protestants from around Europe began to see the Netherlands as the only safe haven outside Germany and Switzerland. Protestant services were permitted outside city walls; during the summer of 1566, hundreds of people left city churches to listen to these open-air 'hedge-sermons'. Meanwhile, a crop failure the previous winter had caused a famine. Southern Flanders, especially, was in the grip of a depression caused by the decline of the cloth trade with England. All this gave an even sharper edge to the religious rancour being stirred up in the polders outside the cities. In August 1566, this erupted in a frenzy of destruction. Puritan iconoclasts smashed church windows and battered or burnt all popish treasures, graven images and artworks.

Persecution and War

Philip II was livid. He sent an army of 10,000 men under the **Duke of Alva**—the 'Iron Duke'—to punish the heretics. Most of the Protestant leaders, sensing what was coming, hastily left the country. When the Duke arrived in Amsterdam, 170 merchants' houses lay empty. A reign of terror began. So many people were executed by the Duke's **Council of Blood** that the city was nicknamed 'Murderdam'.

In 1568, the date taken as the beginning of the **Eighty Years' War** with Spain, the exiled William of Orange attempted a campaign against Alva. (William's previous discretion about his Protestant sympathies had earned him the name 'William the Silent'.) Terrified local Protestants gave him little support and the invasion was a failure. William didn't have enough money to pay his soldiers and had to creep away from them in the night. He wandered around France gathering another army, and by 1572 was meeting with a little more success, capturing Brill, Vlissingen (Flushing) and Veere. He was assisted by the **Sea-beggars**, a rough and ready bunch of quasi-pirates, who proved an embarrassment to their sober general by pillaging churches, massacring clergy, dressing up in desecrated vestments and getting drunk (but they were later to form the basis of the Dutch navy).

Most towns (except Amsterdam) now rallied to William's aid. In the town of Dordrecht he was elected overall '*stadhouder*' by the United Provinces, which meant that, technically, he was lord-lieutenant of the King he was rebelling against. As the fighting wore on, this allegiance became a fiction, but initially the intention really was to maintain fealty while demanding that the Netherlands keep control over its own internal policies. In a battle song of the time beginning 'William of Nassau, I am of Dutch blood', William sings, 'I have always honoured the King of Spain.' Curiously, though in the 20th century this song became the Dutch national anthem, the line was not changed, which must make the Netherlands the only country in the world that sings the praises of another land in its national song.

Vengefully, Alva sent troops to punish towns that supported William. But the rebels relieved Alva's **sieges of Alkmaar** (on 8 October 1573) and **Leiden** (3 October 1574)—events still celebrated today. Soon William controlled all the towns around Amsterdam. Meanwhile, the populace was turning against Alva—less as a result of his vicious persecutions than because of the 10th penny tax he had imposed (which diverted 10 per cent of all citizens' income into the Duke's personal coffers). The profligate Alva slipped away one night in 1573, just a few hours before he was due to face a meeting of angry creditors.

In the winter of 1575–6 William laid siege to **Amsterdam**. The town officials were so worried about infiltrators that they banned skating on the canals and even stood guard at important gates themselves. Cattle from the fields were brought within the city walls and stabled in the deserted merchants' houses. Priceless silver was melted down and minted into coins in an attempt to keep business ticking over. The ever-prudent Amsterdam city fathers had only been supporting Philip II because Spain seemed the stronger side. After a long siege, it became clear that William was going to win the war so, in 1578, the city judiciously swapped allegiance and made peace with William. This signalled the virtual end of Spanish dominion over the Netherlands (though they were to retain sovereignty for another 70 years).

The *Stadhouders*

Each province of the United Provinces was headed by a *stadhouder* (the title that had traditionally been used for the king's lieutenant in the area). In theory, provinces could choose separate *stadhouders*, but in practice all opted for members of the House of Orange, and gradually this became centred on just one member of the family. Successive generations continued to elect heirs to the House of Orange, so the title became all but hereditary. William's son, Maurits, was styled 'Prince', and soon the family was considered grand enough for a match with an English princess—William II married Mary Stuart, daughter of Charles I, an arrangement that did not please the various city regents, as England was a trade rival.

The *stadhouder* was commander-in-chief of the country's armed forces, and this also brought him into conflict with the regents. Peace was better for business than war, and after the final defeat of the Spanish in 1648 the State of Holland wanted to cut back on military spending. William II of Orange wanted to keep his armies. The traditional unease between Amsterdam and the House of Orange bristled into tension. On 23 June 1650 the *stadhouder* visited Amsterdam and demanded an official reception. The regents refused, and condescendingly invited him for dinner instead. 'If we are to wine and dine together,' sniffed a piqued William, 'then we would have to be better friends than we are at present.'

He left the next day, gathered troops and sent them to take Amsterdam by surprise. Civil war was narrowly averted. The invading army had got lost in a fog and were spotted by a postman on his way over from Hamburg. The city was warned, and William was forced to negotiate. When he died of the pox some months later, it was decided not to appoint another *stadhouder* for the while.

In 1654, as part of the peace negotiations that ended the first Anglo-Dutch War (1652–4), the State of Holland succeeded in passing a law, known as the Act of Seclusion, stating that no member of the House of Orange should ever become *stadhouder* again. This was supported by Cromwell, who feared that the House of Orange might lend support to the deposed English royals. But when the Stuarts returned to the English throne in 1660 they reinforced the position of the Oranges, and when the Act of Seclusion was revoked in 1672 William III was made *stadhouder* of all the provinces (except Friesland), with strengthened powers. His marriage to another Mary Stuart, daughter of James II, was his stepping stone to becoming King of England in 1689, and paved the way to the Grand Alliance, uniting England, the Republic, Spain and parts of Germany against France.

In 1579 the southern, Catholic and largely French-speaking provinces signed the **Union of Arras** and declared their allegiance to Spain. This gave Spain a base for attacks on the north (most notably the punishing **Siege of Antwerp** in 1584–5). Seven northern provinces responded with the **Union of Utrecht**, a Protestant military federation with The Hague as the centre of power. The provinces—Holland, Zeeland, Utrecht, Groningen, Gelderland, Friesland and Overijssel—agreed to remain 'in perpetual alliance', united 'as if they were one'. The Union upheld the 'freedom of religious belief'. Each state would decide on religious matters separately, and persecution would end.

In response, Philip II outlawed William, who subsequently advised the States General to elect a new king. By the Act of Abjuration on 22 July 1581, the States General withdrew allegiance from Philip and appointed his brother the **Duke of Anjou** as their monarch. The notion still existed that a state needed a sovereign, though in effect power lay in the hands of William of Orange. But William was assassinated on 10 July 1584. The States General placed the administrative power of the Union in the lap of the Council of State. William's 17-year-old son Prince Maurits was made a member of the Council, and one of his nephews, John of Nassau was elected *stadhouder*. On the death of Anjou a year later, sovereignty was offered to the King of France, who declined, and to Elizabeth of England, who sent along the Earl of Leicester as governor general. Leicester was not popular, and left after two years.

Meanwhile, Philip II was not sitting still. In autumn 1588 he sent along an '**invincible Armada**' to crush the rebellion once and for all—and to teach the English a lesson along the way. And that, as every English schoolchild knows, was a big mistake.

Realizing A Republic

In 1585 **Prince Maurits** was elected *stadhouder* of Holland, largely as the result of the machinations of a senior civil servant **John van Oldenbarneveldt** (1547–1619). It was beginning to dawn on the states that the position of *stadhouder* was really an embodiment of their own power, and that they didn't need to offer allegiance to an external sovereign after all. It was around this time that people began to refer to the northern provinces of the Netherlands as the **Republic of the Seven United Dutch Provinces**. By 1596 both France and England were prepared to acknowledge the United Provinces as an independent power, and to support them against Spain. This was known as the **Triple Alliance**.

With his characteristic knack of avoiding sticky situations, Philip gave the Netherlands to his daughter Isabella as a wedding present in 1598. Van Oldenbarneveldt persuaded her to conclude a truce in 1609. She agreed to acknowledge the sovereignty of the Republic for the duration of the truce. Meanwhile, antagonism grew up between Van Oldenbarneveldt and Maurits (who was all for continuing the war)—a conflict which eventually resulted in Van Oldenbarneveldt's execution, and in Maurits assuming the *stadhoudership* of the provinces of Groningen and Drenthe, in addition to that of Holland. By the end of the Twelve Years' Truce in 1621, Maurits was the leading power in the land. When he died in 1625, he was succeeded by his half-brother Frederick Henry. The *stadhoudership* was on its way to becoming hereditary.

Peace at Last

The war with Spain, which had dragged on since the Union of Utrecht in 1579, was exhausting the coffers of both sides. By the 1640s everyone had had enough. In 1646 delegates of the States General arrived in the German town of Münster to begin talks with Spain, France and the German Emperor. It took two years to argue out a peace plan, but by the 1648 **Treaty of Münster**, the sovereignty of the United Netherlands was finally recognized, marking the end of the Eighty Years' War.

The seven united provinces had the right to vote in the States General. Drenthe had some degree of sovereignty, but the southern states of Brabant, Vlaanderen (Flanders) and Limburg, who had sided with the Spanish, were seen as spoils of war and were not granted independent assemblies or representation in the States-General.

Rather sneakily, the northern Dutch negotiators at the Treaty of Münster had ensured that the Scheldt (the river serving Antwerp, which had been blockaded during the war) was to remain closed. This ensured that the port of Amsterdam had no rival, and it became the hub of international trade—a position that did not appeal to the English. In 1651 England passed the **Navigation Act**, heavily protecting English trade. Two **Anglo-Dutch wars** ensued, the first (1652–4) ending in defeat for the Republic, but the second culminating in one of the Netherlands' most celebrated victories, that of **Admiral Michiel de Ruyter**, who sailed up the Medway and trounced the English fleet in 1667.

The Golden Age (17th Century)

A map worked into the floor of Amsterdam's 17th-century Stadhuis (town hall) places the city at the centre of the universe—and for much of the century that must have seemed true. Goods flowed into the port from around the world, paused for a while in one of the hundreds of brimming warehouses and, as soon as prices went up, were packed off to distant and lucrative markets. Guilds flourished as the abundance of raw materials attracted craftsmen from around Europe, and even the lowliest workers earned nearly twice as much as their English counterparts. The Amsterdam Bourse (Exchange) thronged with merchants from countries as far away as India and Turkey. They conducted a resounding trade in property and shares, and merchandise of all sorts. Isaac le Maire had the idea of trading *in blanco*—dealing on paper with goods he didn't yet own—and the first futures market was begun. In 1609 the city council founded the **Amsterdam Wisselbank** (Bank of Exchange) in the cellar of the town hall. It drew up bank drafts to replace coins (which could be clipped, melted down or stolen), gave quick mortgages and lent at a good rate of interest (an encouraging 3½–4 per cent; England dragged behind at 6 per cent). Amsterdam notes of exchange were accepted throughout the world.

The **arts and intellectual life** flourished. Not only were Rembrandt, Vermeer and Frans Hals kept busy, but lesser painters churned out an estimated 20 million pieces of work during the first part of the century. Even the poorest houses had paintings. Books suppressed elsewhere rolled off Amsterdam's uncensored presses—and if you hung about the right cafés you could bump into Spinoza or Descartes.

The economy was solidly based on the Baltic grain trade (it filled four-fifths of Amsterdam's warehouses), but the spirit of the Golden Age shines clearest in the romance, daring and glamour of the **trade with the East**. Initially the Dutch hadn't bothered to send ships further than Lisbon, relying on intrepid Portuguese sailors for booty from the Spice Islands. In 1580, however, Philip II conquered Portugal and closed its ports to his arch-enemy. It was clear that the Dutch would have to send their own ships to the East. Jews fleeing the Inquisition brought inside information about trade routes, and in 1595 Jan Huyghens published *Itinerario*, a book which told temptingly of the precariousness of Portuguese government in the colonies. Later that year Cornelis Houtman set off with four ships and 200 men on a voyage of discovery. Only 99 men limped back in battered ships on 23 August 1597, and investors just managed to break even, but the port of Amsterdam buzzed with excitement.

When a second voyage realized a profit of 400 per cent, merchants exploded into action. In 1597 the romantically named 'Compagnie van Verre' (Far Away Company) began direct trade with the East Indies. Everybody wanted to get in on the act. So many new companies were formed that they looked likely to put each other out of business before they'd really started. On 20 March 1602 they all united to form the **Verenigde Oostindische Compagnie (VOC—United East India Company)**. The whole country seemed greedily caught up in the spirit of adventure: domestic servants and seamstresses were among the thousands of early shareholders. The company had the monopoly of Dutch trade from the Cape of Good Hope to Cape Horn, and at the peak of its influence it had over 150 merchant vessels protected by 40 fighting ships and its own army of 10,000 soldiers. It sailed all over the East Indies and also to India, Ceylon, China, the South Pacific Islands and South Africa. For nearly two centuries it was the most powerful trade organization in the world. The VOC could establish colonies, sign treaties and declare war and it became the cutting edge of Dutch colonialism. A contemporary English traveller remarked that it was 'a commonwealth within a commonwealth'.

In 1624 the **West India Company** was formed. It was a copycat venture, smaller and much less prosperous than the VOC, and had the trade monopoly over the seas between Africa and the Americas. It teetered along largely on the profits of the slave trade, but exhausted its coffers waging colonial wars against the Portuguese and Spanish. The company's main claim to fame was that it administered the American colony of New Amsterdam—later captured by the British and renamed New York.

The trading companies' economic clout gave Amsterdam tremendous sway over the rest of the Netherlands. Eight of the Chamber of Seventeen, the powerful governing body of the VOC, had to be Amsterdam citizens, and managers were appointed by the *burgemeester*. The city itself was ruled by the **Heren (Lords) XLVIII**, a council of four *burgemeesters*, a sheriff, seven jurists and 36 advisers. These 'Regents' often came into conflict with national government.

The Decline

In the first half of the 17th century Germany was battling through the Thirty Years War, the Roundheads and Cavaliers were roughing each other up in England, and France had been left rather limp by the war with Spain. Around 1650 the dust began to settle, and the pugnacious neighbours turned their attention to the prosperous little country in their midst. The conflicts of the late 17th and 18th centuries drained the United Provinces' coffers and gave the warfaring House of Orange a useful step-up back to power.

Squabbles over herring and punitive anti-Dutch import laws led to wars with England in 1652–4 and 1664–7. Rather unwillingly, the Provinces found themselves fighting France in the **War of the Spanish Succession** (1701–14). There was another war in 1780 when England discovered the Dutch had secretly been trading with rebel American colonies. London and Hamburg began to take over as mercantile centres, while Amsterdam's old trade routes were threatened. England's increasing sea power began to erode the East Indies trade, and in 1791, after years of false accounting, the VOC went into liquidation. The river Schelde was reopened as a trade route, putting Antwerp back on the map as an important port. Trade became a less important part of the economy, and while Amsterdam focused its attention on banking, the early industrial revolution passed the country by.

As the money business boomed, the Amsterdam oligarchy became increasingly corrupt and complacent. Children of influential families would be given public posts as christening presents, and they would draw the salary while a menial did the work. The city fathers happily pocketed a large portion of the taxes they collected. The rich got ostentatious, and the poor got angry and subversive. On 24 June 1748 an Amsterdam merchant noticed a 'shameless slut' in the buttermarket who turned her back on a guard and 'several times raised her skirt, smacking her bare buttocks saying, "That's for you."' The guard shot her ('in her bare fundament') and she later died. This was all that was needed to spark off some well-organized street violence. Armed with lists of tax collectors' addresses, a mob stormed the grand canals, sacking houses and destroying anything of value. The **Tax Farmers' Riot** was swiftly suppressed, but the civil guard had to beat drums below the scaffold to drown out the slogans shouted by the ringleaders as they went to the gallows.

Vociferous, fantastically dressed bands of volunteers, heady with Rousseau's ideas, began to roam the countryside spreading the gospel of democracy. They had the support of some sympathetic patricians, such as Hendrik Hooft (affectionately known as 'Father Hooft'). Soon these **Patriots** had taken over the governments of many smaller towns, and on 27 April 1787 they staged a coup in Amsterdam. The Prince of Orange had had enough. With the armies of his brother-in-law, the King of Prussia, he sent the Patriots packing. Many fled to France, where they were just in time for the Revolution. In 1795 a French Republican army, with the support of exiled Patriots, crossed the frozen Rhine and advanced on Amsterdam. There was, by this time, strong pro-French feeling in the Netherlands. The invading armies were seen as liberators, and the Regents were bloodlessly deposed in what became known as the **Velvet Revolution**. A 'Freedom Tree' was erected on the Dam and Amsterdammers danced around it celebrating the newly declared **Batavian Republic** (the Batavians were the ancient tribe of the Netherlands). But the *liberté*, *égalité* and *fraternité* were not to last for long.

In 1806 Napoleon created his younger brother, **Louis Bonaparte**, King of the Netherlands. Louis converted Amsterdam's prized Stadhuis into a palace and demolished the ancient public weighhouse on the Dam because it spoiled his view. The outraged city was not consoled by the fact that it was now the new capital.

A Kingdom Again

On his first day in the new job Louis announced to his ministers, in heavily accented Dutch, '*Ik ben uw Konijn*' ('I am your rabbit') rather than '*Ik ben uw Koning*' ('I am your king'). But though he had started off on the wrong foot, Louis soon endeared himself to the people by visiting the stricken during smallpox epidemics, actively supporting the arts and sciences and rather foolishly standing up to his older brother. (He allowed Dutch smugglers to break Napoleon's blockade of British ports.) Napoleon hadn't expected his young sibling to be such an upstart, so in 1810 he deposed him and incorporated the Netherlands into the French Empire. But **Waterloo** was just around the corner. Even before that battle, in 1813 (after Napoleon's retreat from Moscow) the French garrison withdrew from Amsterdam and the Netherlands was proclaimed a constitutional monarchy under the House of Orange. The 1814 **Congress of Vienna** united all the Netherlands provinces (north and south) for the first time, under **King William I** (1772–1843), son of *stadhouder* William V (who had died in 1806), as a constitutional monarch. But the proud new kingdom lasted only until 1831, when the predominantly Catholic and anti-Orangist southern provinces rebelled and formed a new independent kingdom called **Belgium**, unrecognised by the north until eight years later, when the disputed southern province of Limburg was finally ceded to the north.

From Gloom to Boom

After months of bickering with The Hague, Amsterdam had become the capital of 'the Netherlands', and home to the Netherlands Bank. But the new nation was in something of a decline. The city's coffers were empty. Napoleon's blockade of English ports and the British occupation of Dutch colonies during the Napoleonic wars had strangled trade, the money market had slipped across the channel to London, and Dutch entrepreneurs had disdained the inventions of the Industrial Revolution. The trading companies' dainty sailboats were soon to be eclipsed by heavy steamships, too bulky to negotiate the Zuider Zee. In 1824 the North Holland Canal (between Amsterdam and Den Helder) was given a festive opening, but the bravado was misplaced. The numerous bends and locks compelled such creeping progress that it was hardly worth the merchants' while. From now on it was **Rotterdam**, rather than Amsterdam, that was destined to become the country's premier port.

As the disconsolate country limped through the early decades of the 19th century, a few valiant paladins of the new industries set their minds to revitalizing her. The king set up the **Nederlandse Handelsmaatschappij** (Netherlands Trading Company) to perk up the drooping trade in tropical products. In 1825 Paul van Vlissingen started running regular steamship services to London and Hamburg and built an engineering works on Oostenburg island in east Amsterdam. Peppy doctor and philanthropist Samuel Sarphati founded a commercial college, several banks, a construction company, the Amstel Hotel (still one of the best in the country) and an efficient and profitable refuse disposal service (Amsterdam's stinking waste was shipped out in sealed barges, composted and sold to farmers). He founded the **Vereniging voor Volksvlijt** (Industrial Society) to knock new life into flagging manufacturers and to inject new technology into factories. His sparkling glass Palace of Industry rose up dramatically on Frederiksplein in Amsterdam and was home to countless displays, exhibitions and concerts until it burnt down in 1929.

Towards the end of the century the Netherlands began to thrive once more. New industries—even a motor car factory—flourished. The opening of the Suez Canal in 1869 meant easier access to the Orient, and in 1876 the North Sea Canal was cut through the dunes to give Amsterdam proper access to bigger ships. The Netherlands became the main supplier to a newly unified Germany, and manufacturing and ship-building industries revived. The discovery of diamonds in South Africa led to a boom in the diamond-cutting trade, with workers becoming deliriously rich overnight. In 1839 the first railway in the Netherlands ran from Amsterdam to Haarlem; fifty years later there were nearly 200 trains running to destinations all over Europe, and grand new railway stations were springing up in cities along the way. During the 1880s the first trams and bicycles made their appearance. The arts blossomed: national institutions such as the Rijksmuseum and Concertgebouw have their origins in the last two decades of the century. By 1883 the Netherlands had regained enough of her former grace for Amsterdam to host the **World Exhibition**.

The 19th century also saw an increase in **parliamentary democracy** in the Netherlands. The 1848 revolts in the rest of Europe made King William II nervous. In 1848 the king set up a reform committee under the liberal Rudolph Thorbecke and changes were hurried through after a mob stormed around the Dam in Amsterdam in 1849, with the alarming proclamation that 'All men are brothers.' As the franchise was extended, support grew for the socialist movement. A Socialist Party was founded in the 1880s, without much success, but the Social-Democratic Workers' Party (SDAP) founded in 1894 was the forerunner of today's Partij van de Arbeid (PvdA—Labour Party).

Amsterdam entered the 20th century on the crest of a boom. The Netherlands remained neutral in the First World War. The Dutch happily traded in arms with both sides, and emerged comparatively unscathed—though the rest of the country's trade had taken a blow and food shortages in 1917 had provoked riots in Amsterdam. The population had been growing fast—from 3 million in 1846 to 6 million in 1913.

In 1920 two converted De Havillands, carrying two passengers apiece, began to fly regularly to London. The world's first air travel booking office opened at Schiphol in the following year. In 1928 Amsterdam hosted the Olympic Games, but the 1929 Wall Street Crash slid the country into an economic depression. The 1930s also saw the growth of a small but vociferous Dutch Nazi Party (NSB)—though the fascist movement didn't gather anywhere near the support it did in Germany.

The Second World War

The Netherlands hoped to remain neutral in the Second World War, as they had in the first. But on 10 May 1940 the Germans attacked Dutch airports and military barracks. Queen Wilhelmina and the Dutch government lost little time in skipping across the Channel to the relative safety of England. They left Supreme Commander Winkelman to deal with the advancing Germans. He held out for five days, during which Rotterdam was mercilessly bombed from the air. On 15 May the German army occupied the Netherlands and Hitler declared the cool Austrian Nazi Arthur Seyss-Inquart *Rijkscommissaris* (State Commissioner). Members of the NSB who had collaborated with the invaders were catapulted to positions of high office.

At first life carried on much the same as before, with the Dutch exercising their indefatigable capacity to turn a blind eye to anything that threatened to ruffle the smooth flow of daily business. However, when Seyss-Inquart's early softly-softly attempt to *nazificeren* ('nazify') Holland met with stolid Dutch inertia, he became more brutal. Young Dutchmen were sent off to work in Germany, soldiers who had been captured during the invasion and then released were re-arrested as prisoners-of-war. Jews, especially, were the butt of systematic oppressive decrees. The wearing of yellow stars was compulsory and Jews were banned from driving or from using trams. They had to hand in their bicycles, be indoors by 8 o'clock (not even out in their own gardens), were allowed to shop only in Jewish shops between 3 and 5 o'clock in the afternoon, and couldn't visit theatres, cinemas or sports grounds. Soon they were forbidden to visit Christians, had to go to separate schools and were fenced off in ghettos. On 22 February 1941 German trucks rumbled into the Jodenhoek (Jewish Quarter) in Amsterdam and the first round-up of Jews began. In the years that followed nearly all of Amsterdam's Jews (10 per cent of the city's population) were transported, along with gypsies and homosexuals, to concentration camps in Germany. Hardly any survived.

The February *razzia* (raid on Jews) sparked off a spontaneous Amsterdam-wide strike that was viciously put down. Right through the occupation heroic Resistance fighters sabotaged German munitions and supplies stores, attempted to assassinate Nazi leaders, spawned batches of false documents and reeled off secret newspapers to keep the public properly informed. Nazi retaliation was diabolical. If they couldn't dig out the ring-leaders, whole groups of innocent people would be shot in reprisal for any Resistance activity. Opposition also went on in quieter, but no less courageous ways. Many non-Jews wore yellow stars in sympathy and thousands gave shelter to *onderduikers* ('divers')—members of the Resistance, or Jews (like the Frank family), who went into hiding around the city. On Prince Bernhard's birthday, thousands imitated his habit of wearing a white carnation, much to the confusion of the Nazis who didn't know quite what to legislate against. Queen Wilhelmina re-established herself in the good opinion of many Amsterdammers by broadcasting cheering messages to her people from the security of a BBC studio.

By the winter of 1944—'Hunger Winter'—the fabric of life had all but collapsed. Everybody was starving (especially those sharing ration books with *onderduikers*), as the Germans had restricted the flow of food in retaliation for a Dutch railwaymen's strike. Walking was the only means of transport and rubbish bins and sewers overflowed. Fuel was impossible to come by, so people stole any wood they could lay their hands on. Sleepers were torn from the tram tracks, parks thinned out mysteriously overnight and any empty houses were stripped of furniture, beams and floorboards.

On 5 May 1945 the Netherlands was liberated. On 7 May jubilant crowds crammed the streets of Amsterdam to greet the Canadian liberation force. In a final lash of malice, German soldiers opened fire on the crowd, killing 22 people.

Post-war Blues

The Netherlands was devastated by the war. Its transport system was paralyzed, industrial production had slumped by 30 per cent and the Germans had broken dykes, flooding much of the countryside. Despite chronic shortages of almost everything, the Dutch bounced back with a lively resilience, enthusiastic for a quick recovery. They even managed city-wide street parties in 1948 to celebrate Queen Juliana's coronation and Dutch victories in the Olympic Games. The granting of independence to former colonies knocked the edge off the tropical trade, but the Netherlands soon got down to the more mundane business of keeping the hungry new Ruhr industries fed. From the outset, the country participated in the economic recovery that swept continental Europe in the 1950s. After the widening of the North Sea Canal and construction of the new Amsterdam-Rhine Canal in 1952, regeneration was meteoric. Garden-city suburbs sprang up to house the swelling population.

Unity and Prosperity

The Netherlands, together with Belgium and Luxembourg, formed the **Benelux Customs Union** in 1948, and the **Benelux Economic Union** in 1958—organizations that played an important role in the establishment of NATO and of the **European Economic Community**.

The 1960s saw increasing prosperity, and the foundation of the Dutch welfare state. Old patterns began to emerge. The solid Calvinist burgers were still very much in control, but the traditional tolerance of minorities and deviants soon made space, not for the naked dancing Anabaptists of yore, but for a new phenomenon of dreamy hippies and tatty youth. In the 1960s Amsterdam became a mecca of the blossoming youth culture. Troupes of long-haired, denim-clad, gently stoned young people hung out and slept around Centraal Station, the National Monument on the Dam and in Vondelpark. In 1969 John Lennon and Yoko Ono staged their week-long 'Bed-in' for world peace in the Hilton Hotel. An old church near Leidseplein was converted into the Paradiso—a place where you could puff away on marijuana without fear of arrest, and have your ears blasted by the latest music. Homosexuals began to join the party, and soon Amsterdam was known as the gay capital of Europe.

The 1980s and 1990s have seen an era of extraordinary wealth and economic stability for the Netherlands—even during the rollercoaster rides other European economies were taking at the end of the 1980s boom years. Based on open and easy industrial relations and good Protestant moderation, the 'polder model' economy, as it has come to be known (after Dutch '*polders*'—reclaimed land) has been the envy of many an EU finance minister. At one point, the Netherlands was almost the only country that met all the criteria for entry into the single currency without having to resort to imaginative accounting.

The 21st century began early in the Netherlands. The first non-military **Internet** connection point in Europe was in Amsterdam, set up in 1988 at the Centre for Mathematics and Computer Science (CWI). And the city remains one of the six biggest Internet nodes in the world, transmitting over 100 million bytes per second. By the late 1990s, Amsterdam already had public Internet booths alongside telephone boxes on street corners. With a long history of formal and informal unions and alliances behind it, the Netherlands seems unruffled about entering a new millennium as part of a united Europe.

Art and Architecture

Dutch Painting

Sacheverell Sitwell wrote that painting is as endemic among the Dutch as poetry is among the English. During the 17th-century Golden Age (a high-water mark for painting, as well as an economic boom) an estimated 20 million paintings were executed. Even the humblest homes had the odd oil tacked up on the wall. A 17th-century English traveller observed that 'many times blacksmiths, cobblers, etc. will have some picture or other by their forge or in their stall. Such is the general notion, inclination and delight that these country natives have to painting.' These days there is still a feeling that art matters, is part of everyday life, and that even the zaniest of new painters belongs to a long continuum of artists working in Holland.

Before the Golden Age

It is important to draw a distinction between Dutch and Flemish art. In 1579 the Netherlands polarized into a Flemish, predominantly Roman Catholic south, and an alliance of seven Dutch, Protestant northern provinces. Eugène Fromentin, the 19th-century art critic, observed that 'Holland had never possessed many national painters. While she was blended with Flanders, it was Flanders that took upon herself to think, invent and paint for her.' Early Flemish art resounds with familiar names like Breughel, Bosch and van Eyck, while Holland musters Cornelis Ketel, a portrait painter who grew bored with his craft and, as a ruse to liven up his technique, started painting with his toes, with no noticeable loss in quality. However, in the 17th century migrations of prominent painters to the Protestant north, a blossoming national confidence and snowballing economic prosperity stimulated a new Dutch School. This exclusively Dutch painting was influenced by Flemish artists, but also by Italians and a small heritage of local painters less disgruntled with their lot than Cornelis Ketel.

In his *Book of Famous Men*, the 15th-century humanist Barolemmo Fayio lists only two Flemish artists: Jan van Eyck and Rogier van der Weyden—painters we still consider pivots of the period. Both had a strong influence on later Dutch painting. **Jan van Eyck** (1385–1441) and his shadowy brother, Hubert (some say they collaborated, some say that Hubert never existed) are credited with the discovery of oil paint. In reality, they merely perfected a technique that northern European painters had been using for some time. Oil paints, which can be applied in layers, give a rich, deep tone which was much favoured by artists who were fascinated by appearances—the glowing colours of objects as they were touched by light. Italian artists, on the other hand, tended to be more concerned with structure, bodies and movement: they worked in tempera (egg-based paint) which rendered sharper, brighter colours—but soon latched on to the practical and artistic merits of oils.

Early Netherlandish art was mainly devotional. Static groups of bodies crowded pictures crammed with detail and heavily symbolic bric-a-brac. **Rogier van der Weyden** (1399–1464) swept the canvas clean. He focused tightly on a few figures and injected a passionate, authentic emotional intensity into his work. This was extremely rare in religious art of the time, and had a powerful impact on later Dutch painters.

Albert Ouwater (active 1450–80) was the man who took these ideas north. He settled in Haarlem around the time that a book by the Florentine Leon Battista Alberti was being passed around painters' studios. Alberti argued that historia (narrative) was crucial to good art. Dutch painting became less static; small dramas and conflicts began to emerge from the canvas. **Geertgen tot Sint Jans** (*c.* 1460–95) was much influenced by Ouwater. He painted bright, beautiful pictures, still laden with symbolic references but with a much freer arrangement of figures. The figures themselves, however, were still rigid, with little real eloquence of human movement. **Lucas van Leyden** (1489–1553), a child prodigy who was already engraving in his native Leiden at the age of nine, burst on to the scene with sparkling, dynamic, densely peopled paintings that revolutionized Dutch art. As these various strands combine we can see, in the work of painters like Van Leyden and **Jan Mostaert** (1475–1555), the first signs of a separate Dutch school of painting.

In 1604 Karel van Mander, a painter and theorist working in Haarlem, published *Het Schilderboek*—a collection of biographies and a theoretical handbook for artists. It was the first full-scale work of art theory to delineate Dutch and Flemish traditions. Van Mander exalted Haarlem as the cradle of Dutch art. The school of painters working there was developing its own style of Italian Mannerism. The Mannerists believed their work shouldn't slavishly imitate Nature, but improve upon it with imagination and Art. Paintings (even those with innocent titles like John the Baptist Preaching) swarm with lumpy nude musclemen and elongated female figures. They sport about in exotic settings in which piled-up fragments of Roman art, stylized plants and fabulous beasts abound.

The first Dutch painter to travel to Renaissance Italy (it later became de rigueur for any artist who wanted to be taken seriously) was **Jan van Scorel** (1495–1562). He passed through Germany and Venice on a pilgrimage to Jerusalem. On his way back he visited Rome, and was given the job of curator of the massive papal art collection by Hadrian VI, the only Dutch pope in history. This experience changed his painting style completely, and he returned to Haarlem (as Van Mander puts it) as 'the lantern-bearer and road-paver of the Arts in the Netherlands'. Others would claim that honour for Lucas van Leyden, but Van Mander thought that Van Leyden was a show-off—and, besides, he didn't come from Haarlem. Van Scorel's pupil **Martin van Heemskerck** (1498–1574) also travelled to Italy and was one of the main propagators of Mannerist ideas in Holland.

Mannerism made Dutch painting far more lively and flexible, but painters began to tire of its ornament. A move to greater realism and narrative clarity—more Nature, less Art—can be seen in the works of **Hendrik Goltzius** (1558–1616), another member of Van Mander's Haarlem mafia.

By the 1620s another school of painters had sprouted in Utrecht. Artists such as **Hendrick Terbrugghen** (*c.* 1588–1629) and **Gerrit van Honthorst** (*c.* 1590–1624) were ardent followers of the Italian painter Caravaggio, whose chiaroscuro technique (strong contrasts of light and shadow) influenced successive waves of Dutch painters all the way through to Rembrandt and Vermeer. Terbrugghen was the first Dutch Caravaggist to return to Holland (after a ten-year stay in Italy), but he was self-effacing and a bit of a misfit—he wasn't even elected to office in the Utrecht guild. The flattering and flamboyant Van Honthorst, on the other hand, ran up impressive lists of patrons wherever he went and became the best known of the Dutch Caravaggists. His beautiful nocturnal scenes—candlelight and shadow playing over huddles of faces—earned him the nickname 'Gherardo delle Notti'.

The Golden Age

France has shown a great deal of inventive genius, but little real faculty
for painting. Holland has not imagined anything, but it has painted
miraculously well.

Eugène Fromentin, art critic, writing in 1875

In 1565 mobs stormed through the Netherlands breaking church windows and destroying religious paintings and statues. In their enthusiasm to eliminate idolatry, these iconoclasts wiped out much of the country's artistic heritage. There seemed little call to replace it. The austere Calvinists who took control of the northern provinces after 1579 whitewashed the insides of churches and had no time for papish decoration. Italy and its art went out of fashion. The rising merchant classes seemed suspicious of unprofitable aristocratic foibles like patronage of the arts. Artists were in a dilemma: what were they to paint, and who would pay them for it? Eugène Fromentin comes right to the point.

The problem was this: given a bourgeois people, practical, not inclined to
dreams, very busy withal, by no means mystic, of anti-Latin tendency,
with broken traditions, a worship without images, parsimonious habits—
to find an art to please [them]...there remained nothing for such a people
to propose to themselves but a very simple and daring thing...to paint its
own portrait.

And so the Dutch set about painting 'the portrait of Holland, its external image, faithful, exact, complete, life-like, without any adornment'. In the Golden Age that followed, you find few flamboyant devotional paintings or pompous, heroic battle scenes. Instead, you are given portraits of merchants, town squares, street scenes, glimpses of daily life, breakfast tables, brothels, taverns, the countryside, or moments in history. No other nation has managed a more intimate and beautifully executed chronicle of its life and times.

Genre Painting

Early English critics called the pictures of scenes from everyday life 'drolleries'—nowadays we refer to them as genre paintings. By the mid-17th century, genre was one of the most popular art forms in Holland, and the cheapest to buy. These were straightforward, unembellished paintings of taverns, brothels and family life, but they often contained a covert moral message. Sometimes the signal was crude—wildly copulating dogs in a doorway behind a flirting couple refer to the saying 'As with the woman, so with her dog.' Sometimes complex allegorical references and obscure symbols were knitted into the apparently simple pictures. Unravelling these was, for an educated 17th-century viewer, half the fun of genre paintings.

There are examples of genre work in the paintings of the Caravaggists Hendrick Terbrugghen and Gerrit van Honthorst, and in the work of some Mannerists, but it was the writing and painting of **Willem Buytewech** (1591–1624) in Haarlem, and the short visit to the town of Flemish painter **Adriaen Brouwer** (1605–38), that really established the style in Holland. Brouwer was a disorderly bohemian and a popular painter. Both Rubens and Rembrandt went to great lengths to add his work to their collections, though Haarlem society took some time to recover from his high spirits. He was strongly influenced by his compatriots Breughel and Bosch, and would sit about in pothouses knocking off cruelly realistic sketches of the clientele. The grotesque portrayal of peasants appealed to his Haarlem pupil **Adriaen van Ostade** (1610–85), and became a feature of one strain of Dutch genre painting. (As Van Ostade grew older and richer, however, his work became calm, cosy and far more respectable.)

Another style of genre grew up in Leiden around the painter **Gerard Dou** (1613–75). His meticulous, highly finished, almost slick work was widely imitated and gave rise to the school of Leiden *fijnschilders* ('fine painters'). The paintings, often of genteel middle-class interiors, have subtle chiaroscuro lighting effects and some very abstruse symbolic references. Leiden seemed to enjoy especially difficult allusions, maybe because it was a university town. Dou's pupils **Gabriel Metsu** (1629–67) and **Frans van Mieris** (1635–81) excelled in elegant genre work.

In far-away Deventer **Gerard ter Borch** (1619–81) was developing his own style— highly attentive to detail and with an especially fine touch in painting fabrics. In Delft **Jan Vermeer** (1632–75) was painting the hushed, softly lit interiors that have earned him the reputation (with Rembrandt and Frans Hals) of being one of the three great painters of the age. Vermeer produced 11 children, and only three times that many paintings in his life. In the midst of his tumultuous household, he would lock himself away and work painstakingly on tranquil portraits of Dutch homes without a single child in sight. The reticent, and poor, painter would even hide from influential art dealers when they came to call.

The best recorder of riotous domestic uproar was tavern-keeper **Jan Steen** (1625–79). He paints the lewd, sozzled and wanton inhabitants of his sitting rooms, taverns and brothels with such verve and good humour that it's difficult to judge just what his moral attitude really is. The paintings of **Pieter de Hooch** (1629–after 1688) and **Nicholaes Maes** (1629–93), on the other hand, are closer to the subdued interiors of Vermeer. De Hooch is especially known for his sensitive portrayals of mothers and children. His paintings of the dark interiors of burgher homes with, somewhere in the picture, a door opening on to the bright outdoors, set a pattern for many other genre painters.

Historical and Biblical Painting

The 16th-century Mannerists had used Biblical and historical subjects as a pretext for fanciful flights of imagination, an excuse to adorn paintings with naked bodies and elaborate ornamentation. As we have seen, there was no place for this in respectable 17th-century merchants' sitting rooms, and the austere Calvinists proscribed art in churches. Most artists were launched into an open market of more acceptable styles—portraits, landscapes and genre scenes—but a few soldiered on in the grand old style. Many of these painters were simply out of touch with the spirit of the new age, but others came up with an innovative, more realistic style of historical painting.

The Dutch Caravaggists (*see* above) were prime movers in the new direction. Their bold realism appealed to painters in this Age of Reason. The new style of historical painting leant on experience, rather than invention, and had a much clearer narrative. Unlike the Mannerists, who had indulged themselves in flashy virtuoso performances without any deference to period, 17th-century painters painted scenes from the Bible or from history (especially banquet scenes or intimate group studies of Christ with the apostles), attempting to portray clothing, buildings and utensils with some sort of historical accuracy. (They were, however, usually quite spectacularly off the mark.)

The Amsterdam painter **Pieter Lastman** (1583–1633) was the spearhead of the new generation of history painters. It was to study as his pupil that **Rembrandt van Rijn** (1606–69, *see* p.111) went to Amsterdam in 1624. Rembrandt clearly wanted to be part of the modern movement of realism. Kenneth Clark calls him 'the great poet of that need for truth and that appeal to experience which had begun with the Reformation'. His quest was for naturalness and authenticity. He used his neighbours in the Jewish Quarter for Biblical paintings, and infused his pictures with a powerful psychological realism. By the 1640s he was undoubtedly the best history painter in Holland, but it was a lonely mission, as the style remained unpopular during his lifetime. Only one of his pupils, the last, **Aert de Gelder** (1645–27) concentrated exclusively on history painting. He worked in a lighter, more sentimental style than Rembrandt would ever have allowed himself to fall into.

Portraiture

Portraiture is the most conservative of all the categories of visual art. Painters commissioned to record the wealthy, pompous and important for posterity usually opt for well-tried, acceptable forms. The Golden Age brought some exciting innovators—especially with double and group portraits—but the changes were subtle and the style soon hardened once more into an emptier, more formalized genre.

Anthonie Mor (1519–74), who Italianized his name to Antonio Moro, spent some time in the court of Emperor Charles V, and introduced the fashionable classical style of Italian portraiture to the Netherlands. It was taken up by **Michiel Miereveld** (1567–1641). He had a comfortable job in the court of Frederick Henry in The Hague, churned out competent, formal pictures and became the leading portraitist of the early Dutch Republic.

It was **Frans Hals** (1585–1666) who brought verve to portrait-painting. His acute psychological perception, comic wickedness and lightness of touch give his portraits an unprecedented vibrancy. For the first time the sitters seem unconstricted, even friendly. Though his work became very dark towards the end of his life, his early group portraits are exuberantly stage-managed and really capture the high spirits and optimism of Holland's new-found freedom.

Rembrandt's portraits are more introspective, with subtle nuances of light and mood, but portraiture was, for him, primarily a source of income. The earlier 'jugs on a shelf' approach to sitters had been corrected by Hals, but it was Rembrandt who gave canvasses real vitality, particularly in larger works. His dynamic arrangement of the guardsmen in the *Night Watch* (1642; *see* pp.111–12) revolutionized group portraiture. Although he brings his full artistic weight to the task, he reserves any radical experimentation for pictures of himself and his family. In these you find a sensitivity and flair quite beyond the formal traditions of the art.

Govert Flinck (1615–60) and **Ferdinand Bol** (1616–80), both students of Rembrandt, are admired as portraitists. Bol followed Rembrandt so slavishly that even art historians can't always tell them apart. Flinck had the awkward honour of being commissioned to paint for Amsterdam's new town hall after his teacher's sketches had been rejected. He died before completing his drawings, and Rembrandt was one of the painters employed to finish the job.

Frans Hals and Rembrandt gave portraiture a fresh burst of life, but by the middle of the century other artists were cementing their innovations into a new repertory of poses and gestures. Dutch society was becoming grander and more pompous, and the artists it commissioned to paint its picture—like **Bartholomeus van der Helst** (1613–70)—thought Hals' and Rembrandt's work too plain. Once again the portraits lost spontaneity and energy and, though often stylish, became formalized and rhetorical.

Landscape, Still Life and Specialist Paintings

In his *Natural History*, Pliny marvels at the exactness with which some ancient painters could imitate Nature: birds would crash into a wall on which Zeuxis or Apelles had painted a still life. Early Netherlandish painters were impressed by this idea and paid loving attention to background rocks, trees and landscapes—so much so that Sir Henry Wotton, a 17th-century English Ambassador to the Low Countries, could marvel at their 'Artificiall Miracles'. (Michelangelo, however, is reputed to have scoffed at the mundaneness and literalness of this Netherlandish style, saying it was fit only for young or very old women, monks, nuns and certain tone-deaf members of the aristocracy.) Although no painters actually took an easel out of doors until the 19th century, this interest in realism did mean that landscape established a sturdy niche for itself in Dutch art during the Golden Age.

The 16th-century Mannerists used natural scenery, laced with fantastical creatures, as an exotic backdrop to biblical and classical scenes. The well-travelled **Gillis van Coninxloo** (1544–1607) painted very much in the Mannerist style, but is generally regarded as the first Dutch landscapist. Mannerist pictures were usually painted from a high viewpoint. It was **Esaias van de Velde** (1591–1632) who, quite literally, brought things down to earth. He painted dry, rather matter-of-fact country scenes from a low, more naturalistic, viewpoint—a style adopted by practitioners of what became known as the **tonal phase** of Dutch landscape painting.

Paintings of the tonal phase, which lasted until the 1640s, are delicate, almost monochromatic and are animated by the atmosphere they create. The 17th-century poet and critic Constantijn Huygens praised the school for its ability to evoke 'the warmth of the sun and the movement caused by a cool breeze'.

The first tonal painter was van de Velde's pupil **Jan van Goyen** (1596–1656). Although he began painting in the bolder colours of his master, he was soon producing translucent worlds of hazy greens, browns and greys. **Salomon van Ruysdael** (1600–70) painted refined, spacious landscapes and is generally considered the second major tonal painter. **Hercules Seghers** (b.1590) painted some inspired and original scenes of waterfalls, desolate valleys and stormy mountains. Although he worked at the same time as the tonal painters, his unique style evoked the power of a much grander Nature. He had a reputation for being drunk and depressed, and disappeared in 1633. Nowadays the whereabouts of only 15 of his works are known, though there are records of another 30.

Rembrandt was a great admirer of Seghers, and owned eight of his paintings. His small oeuvre of landscapes strongly reflects Seghers' influence. From the 1650s a new generation of landscape painters started producing rugged, grandiose works with more solid forms and stronger contrasts of light and colour than the rather pale pictures of the tonal phase artists. Leaders of this new **classical phase** were **Jacob van Ruisdael** (1628–82; Salomon's nephew, though they spelled their names differently) and **Albert Cuyp** (1620–91). Ruisdael is acknowledged as the greatest Dutch landscapist and is especially admired for his stormy skies. Cuyp combined clarity and a firm classical structure with (especially in his late work) Italianate lighting that suffuses his pictures with a soft glow. Ruisdael's pupil **Meindert Hobbema** (1638–1709) produced paintings very much derivative of his master's work before marrying the burgemeester's kitchen maid and becoming a wine gauger in the Amsterdam customs house, abandoning painting almost entirely.

Cuyp, like many other Dutch landscapists, fell under the spell of Italy. Many Hollanders were drawn south by the warmth and shimmering light. Right from the beginning of the century Italianate landscapes existed alongside the more typically Dutch pictures. (The term, however, refers more to the subject matter than to the influence of Italian art.) The escapist, rather nostalgic paintings by artists like **Jan Both** (c. 1618–52) and **Nicolaes Berchem** (1620–83) were very popular with the Dutch public. The landscapes are imaginary (some of these painters didn't even visit Italy) and are populated by the beautiful shepherdesses and antique ruins also found in the pastoral literature of the time.

By the 19th century the style was beginning to lose favour. The English painter John Constable, in a lecture in 1836, berated Both and Berchem as specious painters whose reputation was propped up by dealers demanding high prices. When, reeling from the vehemence of the attack, an avid collector remarked that he had better sell his Berchems, Constable replied: 'No sir, that will only continue the mischief, *burn them*.'

The English term **'still life'** comes from the Dutch '*stilleven*', the word that began to be used around the 1650s to describe a theme in Dutch painting that was very typical of the 17th-century taste for the domestic and realistic. The stylistic development of still life painting parallels that of landscapes. Early works are 'tonal'—suspended against a plain background, suffused by a transparent, dull light. The objects painted are simple everyday things. The *ontbijtje* (breakfast piece) with bread, cheese and pewter mug is a favourite subject. Later *Vanitas* still lifes, reminding us of the ephemerality of life and earthly pleasures, became popular. Fruit is seen at its *toppunt*, the point of ripeness just before it goes bad, and darker symbols like skulls and snuffed out candles make an appearance. As the Golden Age society prospered, the simple *ontbijtjes* were replaced by *pronkstilleven* (*pronk* means ostentation). The style of these luxurious pieces is similar to that of the classical phase of landscape painters. Colours are brighter and each object seems sharply picked out, as if by spotlight. Gold, silver, china, expensive seafood and exotic fruit replace the simpler fare of earlier work.

Paintings of flowers were a specialized branch of still life. Real blooms were often cripplingly expensive, and short-lived. The 17th-century Dutch preferred pictures of flowers in their houses. The paintings were often complete fantasies—exotic blooms from all over the world, that flowered at different times of the year, would all be arranged in one vase. They were painted with an exacting and extravagant realism. Samuel Pepys enthuses in his diary over a 'little flower pott' done by **Simon Verelst** (1644–1721), marvelling that it was 'the finest thing that ever I saw in my life—the drops of Dew hanging on the leaves, so as I was forced again and again to put my finger to it to feel whether my eyes were deceived or no'. (Verelst was asking £70 for the painting. The notoriously mean Pepys 'had the vanity' to offer £20, which wasn't accepted.) **Ambrosius Bosschaert the Elder** (1573–1621) and his three sons were the most prolific flower painters of the period. By the time he died, Bosschaert could command 1,000 guilders a painting.

Sea, Buildings and Animals

Despite Holland's reliance on the sea, **marine painting** doesn't occupy an important position in its art. Early painters like **Jan Porcellis** (1584–1632) seem primarily concerned with atmosphere of the sea and sky, while later artists like **Willem van de Velde the Younger** (1633–1707) begin to reflect the nation's pride in the ships themselves. Of the **architectural paintings**, **Pieter Saenredam**'s (1597–1695) exquisitely executed church interiors are the most pleasing—and so accurate that they are still used as blueprints for restoration work. The most interesting **animal painter** is **Paulus Potter** (1625–54), whose bulls and cows have an intense reality that is almost nightmarish.

The 18th and 19th Centuries

After decades of entrepreneurial adventure, Amsterdam settled back to enjoy its wealth, and seemed to lose the drive that had propelled it through the Golden Age. Society began to look to France as a model of graceful living, and associations for the promotion of French ideas and culture sprang up.

With the deaths of Frans Hals (1666), Rembrandt (1669) and Vermeer (1675), the Golden Age of Dutch painting also came to an end. The achievements of the 17th century were so great that they seemed to haunt 18th-century painters, who didn't dare do anything new. Paintings became over-refined and uniform in their imitation of French styles and reworking of old ideas. Much 17th-century painting had reflected the stern ethics of Calvinism, but the 18th century began to shed the moral sobriety that had been the dominant humour of the previous age. The freshest painting of the period comes from the few artists who reflected this change in mood and worked playfully with the established Dutch styles. The most impressive of these lighter-hearted painters was **Cornelis Troost** (1697–1750), whose delicately composed satires have earned him the title of the 'Dutch Hogarth'.

Much work was to be had painting the ceilings of grand mansions and decorating the interiors of new public buildings. **Gerard de Lairesse** (1640–1711) was the market leader in this field. His somewhat over-enthusiastic admirers dubbed him the 'Dutch Raphael'. His successor, **Jacob de Wit** (1695–1754), excelled as a trompe l'œil artist and a decorator of churches. Protestant churches were still bare, but Catholicism was tolerated provided that (a 1730 decree cautioned) care was taken 'that the meeting places of the Catholics do not have the appearance of churches or public buildings, nor should they strike the public eye'. There were no such restrictions, however, on interiors, and De Wit made his fortune on commissions from wealthy parishes.

During the 19th century, painting became more documentary—any allegorical meaning or high moral purpose disappeared entirely. Romantic painters such as **Jozef Israëls** (1824–1911) and **A. H. Bakker Korff** (1824–82) did imbue their work with emotion, but it was of the sober, cosy Dutch variety rather than anything explosive or passionate. Landscapists ploughed on in a neoclassical or grand Romantic manner, though in the world of **A. G. Bilders** (1838–65) you can see the beginnings of a simpler naturalism. In place of the distant, artificially constructed views found in previous paintings, the landscape is seen from close to. This radical change, which gave paintings the sort of perspectives seen in photographs, characterized much work later in the century. (This is particularly evident in the city scenes of the Amsterdam Impressionist **G. H. Breitner** (1857–1923). The landscapes and seascapes of **Johann Barthold Jongkind** (1819–91), drawn from the 17th-century tonal tradition, influenced later French Impressionists and Dutch artists of the Hague School.

The Hague School was active between 1870 and 1890, an Art for Art's Sake movement made up of an enthusiastic group of Impressionistic painters. They became famous for their grey skies, and paintings of the long flat beaches and rainswept polders around The Hague. Subject matter was less important than personal feelings and style. **Anton**

Mauve's (1838–88) gently coloured landscapes are the best known. **Hendrik Mesdag** (1831–1915) was a skilled seascapist, and painted the impressive *Panorama* in The Hague (*see* p.197). The brothers **Maris-Jacob** (1837–99), **Matthijs** (1839–1917) and **Willem** (1844–1910)—contributed landscapes and nature studies to the movement.

Undoubtedly the greatest painter of the century was the man that a director of the Stedelijk Museum called 'the lowliest, most human', **Vincent Van Gogh** (1853–90). During his short, troubled painting career, Van Gogh produced work quite unlike any other Dutch artist; his work also takes its own quite individual course in the stream of postimpressionist painting in general (*see* pp.116–20).

Jan Toorop (1858–1928) trailed along with the stylistic changes of the century—from Pointillism to Expressionism. His best work, like that of his contemporary **Johan Thorn Prikker** (1868–1932), was in a delicate, almost fairytale Symbolist style that begins to point towards Art Nouveau.

The 20th Century

The individualism of the late 19th century undermined the supportive strength of the great painting traditions of the past. Twentieth-century Dutch artists were left not only with the question that had dogged their 17th-century forebears (what to paint), but also by a new problem: *how* to paint. There was no longer a framework of assumptions within which they could make their decisions. Twentieth-century art fragments into splinter groups trying to find their way through the dilemma.

The artists of *De Stijl* ('Style', or 'The Way') came up with a new set of assumptions, a theory they believed would take the place of the old traditions. This theory was propounded in a series of polemical articles in the periodical from which they got their name (published from June 1917 to January 1932). They claimed that they were getting rid of all the inaccuracies, obscurity and casual accidents of individualism, and had discovered the essence of art—a Platonic ideal that the world could understand. The best known visual expression of this great universal principle is the straight black lines and blocks of primary colours in the work of **Piet Mondriaan** (1872–1944). (He dropped the second 'a' in his name in order to appear more French—a pretension that most Dutch museums ignore.) Mondriaan gives us a one-man lesson in the development of abstract art. Even in early, recognizable landscapes you can see the germs of his fascination with horizontal and vertical lines. Gradually the figurative images dissolve and you're left with the dashes and criss-cross lines of what is aptly known as his 'plus-minus' period. Then the lines get straighter and bolder, and the colours resolve into bright, flat reds, yellows and blues. Mondriaan claimed he was aiming for the 'lucid tidiness' that the new age demanded. In this he is, paradoxically, very much part of a Dutch tradition of stillness and quiet, careful composition. As Kenneth Clark suggests: Mondriaan is Vermeer without the light.

The prime motivator of *De Stijl*, and editor of the periodical, was **Theo van Doesburg** (1883–1931). His paintings were more dynamic than Mondriaan's, and caused the final rift between the two artists. The work of a third member of the group, **Bart van der Leck** (1876–1958), is instantly recognizable—coloured triangles scattered on a white canvas. Van Doesburg was the real energy behind the movement. When he died, the magazine ceased publication and formal contacts between members dissolved. Though *De Stijl* lasted only 15 years, its impact was felt all over the world, not only in painting, but also in architecture, interior design, typography and even literature and music. The images are still plagiarized by trendy designers for company logos, coffee mugs and T-shirts.

Most of the major art movements of the early 20th century seemed to pass Holland by. There were, however, two Dutch schools of Expressionists active before the Second World War. The **Bergen School** centred on the recalcitrant work of **Charley Toorop** (1891–1955; daughter of the 19th-century painter Jan Toorop). **De Ploeg** ('The Plough') was led by **Jan Wiegers** (1893–1959) and influenced by Van Gogh and the German Expressionists. They painted angular and explosively coloured pictures, often of the countryside around Groningen.

The hard, nightmarish quality of the Dutch **Magic Realists** is reminiscent of Salvador Dali's Surrealism, but their scenes are not as hallucinatory. **Pyke Koch** (b. 1901) paints alluring, pithy works with awe-inspiring prowess. He is shamefully little known outside Holland. **Carel Willink** (1900–83) and **Raoul Hynckes** (b.1893) are two other prominent Magic Realist painters, if not quite as inspired.

The most exciting movement to emerge after the war was **COBRA** (made up of artists from **CO**penhagen, **BR**ussels and **A**msterdam). These painters were inspired by primitive art and children's paintings to develop a *volwassen kinderstijl* (grown-up child style). Their keywords were vitality and spontaneity. **Karel Appel** (b. 1921) remarked 'I just mess about' and 'I paint like a barbarian in a barbarous age.' The gaudy, vibrant and topsy-turvy paintings of COBRA appear to represent a purposeful effort to wipe out any vestige of classical tradition.

During the 1960s minimalistic monochrome canvasses and white reliefs made an appearance. Work by **Jan Schoonhoven** (b. 1914) was influenced by the German **Zero/Nul** movement, which was trying to create a new beginning for art by reducing individual influence to nothing. **Ad Dekkers** (1938–74) and **Edgar Fernhout** (1912–74; Charley Toorop's son) produced similar work, but were more in the abstract geometrical tradition of Mondriaan.

The technological revolution has had its impact on Dutch art. **Peter Struycken** (b. 1939) began very much in the vein of Dekkers, but since 1968 has been using a computer to generate the colour and patterns of his work. **Jan Dibbets** (b. 1941) uses montages of photographs geometrically arranged on clean white canvases, in a way that seems to link him to Mondriaan and Saenredam (the 17th-century painter of church interiors). Nowadays, the club scene and the computer revolution is spawning exciting multimedia art. Colourful pieces by **Dadara**, rather in the manner of Keith Haring, are proving commercially very popular, and finding their way on to T-shirts and mouse pads. Among contemporary artists, keep an eye open for witty sculptures by **Servaas**, innovative painting by **Aldert Mantje** and **Ger van Elk**, **Gijs Bakker**'s poised mixed-media pieces, **Arjan Lancel**'s inspired installations and sculpture, and beautifully shaped ceramics by **Wouter Dam**.

The delights of Dutch architecture are generally small-scale, domestic ones. Wealthy merchants over the centuries have built some grand mansions, but they're not gargantuan. Though you're unlikely to be bowled over by the sheer magnificence of some glittering edifice, you're sure to be stopped in your tracks, suddenly captivated by an ornamented gable, a witty façade decoration or a neat, perfectly poised little house.

In the Beginning...

The first houses made of wood, but soon people began building in brick, which was more resistant to the fires that could sweep through crowded cities. At first this only applied to the lower walls; the gables (which formed the outer walls of attics and were often shaped to give interesting definition to steep triangular roofs) were still wooden.

The shapes of early brick gables, called **spout gables**, are a direct reflection of their wooden ancestry. Wooden constructions were built with each successive storey sticking out a little further than the previous one, so that rainwater would drip on to the street and not seep back into the body of the building. Early **brick gables** leant over for the same reason, which is another contributing factor to the many tilting façades you see in Dutch streets. Most of the pre-17th-century buildings still standing around the country belonged to the city fortifications, built in stone after the 15th century to deflect the impact of newly invented gunpowder.

New Ideas

Towards the end of the 16th century, architectural pattern books from Italy made an appearance in Holland. The Dutch architects who pored over translations of these books were inspired both by the classical system of proportion, and by the ornamental designs. In the buildings these architects subsequently produced, the simple spout gable gave way to the more decorative **step gable**, and red-brick façades were lavishly decorated with plaster scrolls, escutcheons, vases and masks. The ornamentation reached a high point in the playful work of the Amsterdam architect **Hendrick de Keyser** (1565–1621). It took until the end of the 17th century for people to stop building in the Renaissance style, but the adventurous were already experimenting with a purer form of classicism in the 1620s. This new wave reacted against lavish ornament, and was far more intrigued by the strict lines and proportions of classical design. Fruit, flowers, animals and human figures do join the line-up of gable adornments, but not in such profusion. The larger houses begin to resemble temple-fronts, with garlands and festoons under windows. Smaller buildings sport **neck gables**. Simpler and more suitably classicist than the cascading step gables, neck gables are often topped off with a purely classical fronton and are a compromise between a vision of architecture that imitates the buildings of Greek and Roman antiquity, and the practicalities of building for a rainy climate. (The tall 'necks' mask steep roofs, something a conventionally classical straight cornice could not do. It was only in the 19th century that reliably leak-proof flat roofs could be built, and straight cornices became more widespread.) Notable architects of the period are **Jacob van Campen** (1595–1657), who built the city hall on the Dam in Amsterdam (*see* p.86) and **Philips Vingboons** (1607–78) and his brother **Justus** (1620–98), famed for their domestic architecture.

Decoration and Decline

Towards the end of the 17th century austerity set in, and architects began to emphasize simplicity and harmony. **Adriaan Dortsman** (1625–82) is the master of the school of 'Restrained Dutch Classicism'. Windows were made larger and façades became simpler and more rhythmical in design. In the 18th century, as the economy picked up, many merchant families gave their homes a facelift during which brick façades were plastered over or replaced by sandstone. But more money to spend also meant more decoration. The century is marked by a fascination with things French. Gables became draped with acanthus leaves (Louis XIV), encrusted with asymmetrical fripperies (Louis XV) or strung with modest garlands (Louis XVI). Sometimes buildings were crowned with excessively ornate balustrades—a nifty way of hiding a steep roof with what appeared to be a classical straight cornice. The 18th century also saw the advent of the standardized, **pre-fabricated gable**—a sort of architectural mix-and-match.

Public Pomp

The Netherlands suffered an economic slump for most of the 1800s. Little building went on until money began to dribble back into the coffers in the last decades of the century. The driving force behind 19th-century Dutch architectural innovation was

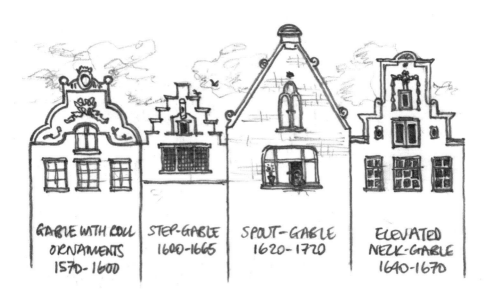

GABLE WITH SCROLL ORNAMENTS 1570–1600 | STEP-GABLE 1600–1665 | SPOUT-GABLE 1620–1720 | ELEVATED NECK-GABLE 1640–1670

P. J. H. Cuypers (1827–1921), the designer of the Centraal Station and Rijksmuseum in Amsterdam (*see* pp.82–4 and 110). He based his work on indigenous brick and wood architecture, but was easily lured towards neo-Gothic extravagance. His belief that the entire building, from basic structure to the smallest detail of decoration, should be governed by a single coherent principle became the basis for modern Dutch architecture. Two other styles dominated 19th-century building: the upstarts of the **Architectura et Amicitia** society went in for idiosyncratic fantasies that outdid even Cuypers' ornamentation, while the more conservative members of the **Maatschappij ter Bevordering der Bouwkunst** (Society of Architects) favoured an eclectic approach, resulting in a mixture of diluted styles. Most of the interesting 19th-century buildings in the Netherlands today come from the boom period of the latter part of the century, and reflect this divergence of taste.

Modern Times

H. P. Berlage (1856–1934), the designer of the Beurs (Stock Exchange, *see* p.84), is known as the father of modern Dutch architecture. Like Cuypers, he used traditional Dutch materials. He relished displaying a building's structure with graceful brickwork, but was never tempted into frivolous ornamentation. The most exciting 20th-century school of Dutch architecture arose as a reaction to Berlage's homespun, rational buildings. Younger architects, many of them in the employ of Amsterdam's housing department, began experimenting with decorative folds and turrets of brickwork shaped around a more solid inner skeleton of concrete. These modern, quirky brick fantasies of the **Amsterdam School** (active from around 1912 to 1924, *see* pp.134–6)

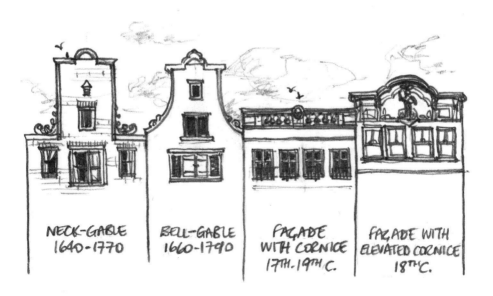

NECK-GABLE 1640-1770   BELL-GABLE 1660-1790   FACADE WITH CORNICE 17TH-19TH C.   FACADE WITH ELEVATED CORNICE 18TH C.

have, until recently, been neglected, but an exhibition of photographs and architects' drawings at the Stedelijk Museum in the 1980s shot them back into fashion.

But the work of the Amsterdam School stands beside the mainstream Dutch architecture, and prime examples are confined to the capital. A second modern movement, which emerged as an extension of rather than a reaction to Berlage's work, was to prove more influential. Under the influence of *De Stijl* (*see* p.59), Bauhaus in Germany, Frank Lloyd Wright in the USA and Le Corbusier in France, a new style of building emerged— all sharp edges, concrete, steel and glass. Like Berlage, the architects of what became known in the Netherlands as **Nieuwe Zakelijkheid** (New Functionalism), believed that they should use their materials to emphasize, not disguise, the basic structure of their buildings. Nieuwe Zakelijkheid dominated the middle decades of the century. Though it produced some neat and attractive buildings, and some fine domestic architecture by **Gerrit Rietveld**, it must also take the blame for the thinking behind high-rise 1960s horrors.

The Netherlands has suffered more than its fair share of architectural atrocities in recent years—tacky façades of insensitively used modern materials and buildings hugely out of scale. Notable exceptions are work by architects such as **A. Alberts**, who offers quirky exceptions to the norm with his gas-company headquarters building in Groningen, and the ING Bank headquarters on the outskirts of Amsterdam. This extraordinary brick building has hardly a right angle in sight, mineral water fountains instead of air-conditioning, a system that warms the building by recycling the heat generated by computers, and installations of mirrors and stone that play light tricks at the solstices.

The country's most impressive contemporary architecture is to be seen in Rotterdam, which embarked on a brave and adventurous programme of rebuilding after being flattened during the Second World War (*see* pp.204ff). Elsewhere, the economic boom of the past two decades has resulted in competitive construction of showpiece office blocks. Dutch architects are encouraged to take chances, and business parks sprouting around Amsterdam and The Hague especially sparkle with glittering towers that show bravura and flair. Foreign architects invited to work on projects in the Netherlands have also made their mark in recent years: **Alessandro Mendini**'s zany and colourful Groningen Museum in Groningen, fellow Italian **Renzo Piano**'s New Metropolis Science & Technology Centre in Amsterdam, and Japanese architect **Kisho Kurokawa**'s new wing to the Van Gogh Museum, to name but a few.

attiek (stress the second syllable—'teak'), not the same as English 'attic', but the line of ornaments above a cornice (*q.v.*) that hides the roof from the street.

bel-étage (rhymes with massage), the floor above the souterrain (*q.v.*), reached by a short flight of steps, but functionally the ground floor.

cartouche elaborate sandstone ornamentation often seen around small oval windows or hoist beams (*q.v.*).

claw-piece the ornamentation that fills in the right-angled step made by the side of a neck-gable and the wall below.

console a supporting bracket (rather like a shelf bracket), often ornamented and supporting a cornice (*q.v.*).

cornice a moulded projection which crowns a façade and runs the width of the building. It may be simple and flat, or ornamented.

festoon ornament in the form of a garland—usually with fruit or flower motifs.

fronton triangular (though sometimes rounded) piece that crowns a façade. It runs the width of the gable only (not the whole building, like a cornice). In some classical designs the fronton is very large, often supported by pillars and running almost the full width of the building—this is called a **tympan**.

gable the Dutch word *gevel* refers to the whole façade, but technically this is just the part of the wall that covers the triangular end of the roof.

gable stone stone tablet, with a picture or symbol carved on it, embedded in the façade. In the 17th century it acted as a house number.

hoist beam beam sticking out from the top of a façade. It has a hook on the end through which a block and tackle can be hung to hoist goods to the upper floors.

œil-de-bœuf ('bull's eye'), small oval windows, often with an elaborate sandstone framing, seen in the tops of façades.

pilaster flattened pillar that projects slightly from a façade. May be decorative or have a structural function.

pothouse an extension of the kitchen with a separate entrance slightly below street level. (Originally used to store pots, later as workshops for craftsmen.)

souterrain the part of the house below street level. Because of Amsterdam's high ground-water level, the souterrain is not as low as a conventional cellar, and is usually reached by a door under the stoop (*q.v.*).

stoop   the steps leading up to the front door of a building (which is usually a little above street level). In most houses the steps rise across the façade, rather than extending frontally from the door down to the street. The landing is sometimes big enough for a few chairs, and there is occasionally a small bench built into the railings.

volute   scroll-like whorls which form part of claw-pieces (*q.v.*), or fill in the 'shoulder' of a gable.

Amsterdam

Amsterdam is a practised but subtle temptress. Her gentle charms begin to work the moment you arrive, as they have for generations of travellers before you. You'll find yourself drawn along to nooks of curious architecture, and enticed into far more tantalizing cafés than could possibly be good for your health. You'll be lured down alleyways to glimpse the rough underside of town, then whisked back to the trim respectability of leafy canals. You'll be invited to admire wondrous treasures, and have secrets revealed to you that no other city would dare. Daily, you'll be launched into a farrago of sleek business people, droves of tourists, scruffs, bohemians and persons of decidedly ill repute. Yet everyone seems to get on remarkably well together, and the chance encounters with people here will be one of the lasting pleasures of your visit.

Amsterdam has an edge and verve that will keep you on your toes. As Henry James wrote after a visit to the Netherlands in the 1870s, it will 'at least give one's regular habits of thought the stimulus of a little confusion'. Three strands of life continually interweave: reminders of the wealthy Golden Age trading city dominated by a few Calvinist families, the sleazy port, and the radical hippie mecca of the 1960s grown comfortably liberal.

Over the past decade Amsterdam has notched up a high status in the business world, and seems anxious to become a little more respectable. Politics are becoming more conservative, police are clearing out junkies and dealers from the more squalid areas of the red-light district, and restaurants and galleries are appearing in their wake. But Amsterdam will never lose its alternative tang. It has a long tradition of liberal tolerance and is, after all, a port, with a port's hard edge. For centuries its heretics, whores and disruptive politicians have tugged, nudged and needled other Amsterdammers away from any tendency to complacency. Today you will still find a relaxed and tolerant city. Same-sex couples kiss in the street, whiffs of marijuana waft from psychedelic coffeeshops, clinics and crisis centres exist to help addicts with more severe drug habits.

Amsterdam offers all the advantages of a great metropolis, with few of the drawbacks. You can admire some of the greatest art in the world, listen to top-notch orchestras, and enjoy the summits of gourmet cuisine. Yet Amsterdammers are down-to-earth people, and in their compact city are more often to be seen cycling and walking than whizzing about in cars. The town's greatest attractions are still its simplest pleasures: strolls along the canals, time spent in front of a painting that takes your breath away and long conversations in quiet cafés where centuries of tobacco smoke have turned the walls quite brown.

See inside back cover for an overview map of Amsterdam.

Amsterdam's first inhabitants were probably fishermen and farmers who built a dam near where the River Amstel petered out into the tidal flats of the IJ. Little is known about this early period, until the 12th century, when a local bigwig, **Gijsbrecht**, built himself a castle at the spot where the River Amstel was dammed (on the site of the present day Dam Square). He called himself the first Lord of Amstel and laid claim to the countryside emerging from the water around him. The **Lords of Amstel** were answerable to the **Bishops of Utrecht**, and rather resented it. In the late 13th century Gijsbrecht IV felt he was powerful enough to rebel, but he didn't reckon on his neighbour, **Floris V**, the **Count of Holland**, joining in the fray. Floris had wooed popular support in 1275 by granting special **toll privileges** to the people who lived beside 'the Aemstelle Dam'. Floris defeated Gijsbrecht, but later Gijsbrecht crept up on Floris and murdered him. The Bishop of Utrecht took advantage of the confusion and confiscated Gijsbrecht's land. In 1300 he granted the town of 'Aemstelledamme' its **first charter**. When he died in 1317 he ceded Amsterdam and the surrounding countryside to his nephew, William III, the new Count of Holland. The people of Amsterdam took full advantage of their toll privileges and of William's wide influence and settled down to serious trading and money-making. In 1323 the Count of Holland granted Amsterdam the sole right to import beer from Hamburg—at that time northern Europe's largest brewing town and a prominent member of the powerful alliance of Baltic trading ports, the **Hanseatic League**. That, together with the growing grain trade, laid the foundation for Amsterdam's future prosperity.

During medieval times the town remained small—a cosy cluster of wooden houses stretching along the banks of the Amstel. In 1300 Amsterdam had one church (the Oude Kerk) and two streets—the present day Warmoesstraat and Nieuwendijk. The town was razed by **great fires** in 1421 and 1452. Wooden buildings were forbidden after the second blaze, and only two remain today (*see* pp.91 and 93). By the 15th century the boundaries extended as far as Oudezijds Voorburgwal, Nieuwezijds Voorburgwal and Spui. There was a new church as well as a clump of monasteries, chapels and inns built to cope with pilgrims flocking to the scene of the **Amsterdam Miracle**. In 1345 a dying man had vomited up the host after his last communion. It was thrown on a fire but didn't burn. Later it developed healing powers, and would transport itself overnight between churches. A chapel of its own seemed to make it stay in one place and, though this burnt down, the host survived. It became an object of worship, and is still honoured today in the **Stille Omgang** (Silent Procession, *see* pp81 and 84). One of those healed by the magic wafer was **Maximilian I**, Emperor of Austria (later Holy Roman Emperor). Amsterdam had further earned his gratitude by supporting his faction, the Kabeljauwen (Codfish), against the conservative Hoeken (Hooks) in the struggle for domination of the Low Countries. In 1489 he upped Amsterdam's prestige by granting the city the right to use his royal insignia in its coat of arms. Trade flourished, and by 1500 Amsterdam bustled with 9,000 inhabitants contained within its first city wall (following the line of the present day Gelderskade, Kloveniersburgwal and Singel canals).

During the **Reformation** (*see* **History**, pp.36–8), Amsterdam held out longer than most cities against the Protestant forces of **William of Orange**, but judiciously swapped sides when it was clear that he was winning. On 26 May 1578, as the city made peace with William, all the Catholic officials and most of the clergy were bundled into a boat, escorted to the outskirts of the city, and cast off to find their way to more hospitable climes. A Protestant city government was set up by members of the leading Calvinist families. With characteristic Amsterdam grace, the events of 26 May were tactfully referred to as the '**Alteration**'.

Having weathered seige and iconoclasts during the Reformation, the city became even more prosperous. By the time of the **Union of Utrecht** in 1579 (*see* **History**, p.40), Amsterdam was by far the most economically powerful city in the Dutch federation. The siege of Antwerp had not only wiped out a major trade rival, but had despatched droves of refugees who made straight for the haven in the north. Amsterdam's tolerance paid off. The newcomers brought skills, like diamond-cutting, that fired the city's crafts and industries into a new life. Though the war with Spain had closed off normal trade routes, local merchants had kept rich by supplying both sides in the conflict. Through much of its history Amsterdam seemed to operate on the principle that 'if we didn't supply the enemy, we couldn't afford to fight them'. Arms dealers would support entire wars all over Europe, and brokers of marine insurance (introduced in the late 15th century) had no qualms about insuring both sides in a battle. Amsterdammers excelled at making money. At the end of the 16th century they were on the brink of the most resplendent era of their history.

The **Dutch Golden Age** in the 17th century (*see* **History**, p.41) was centred primarily on Amsterdam, which was home to both the Dutch East India Company (VOC) and the West India Company. People flooded into the city and by 1650 the population had shot past the 200,000 mark. As early as 1613, far-sighted town planners had begun an extension of three new **canals** around the perimeter of the city. Initially the Herengracht (Gentlemen's Canal), Keizersgracht (Emperor's Canal) and Prinsengracht (Princes' Canal) went only as far as the present day Leidsegracht, but further construction in 1662 gave Amsterdam its familiar half-moon shape. Malodorous industries and the poor were banished to the fields beyond, to the area now known as the **Jordaan** (*see* pp.107–8). The wealthiest merchants built themselves mansions along the new canals and the city built a Stadhuis that was proclaimed the eighth wonder of the world.

Power in the city itself was grasped by a handful of patrician families. The Catholic clique ousted during the Alteration was replaced by a Protestant oligarchy that became known as the **Magnificat**. Family names like Hooft, Pauw, Bicker, van Beuningen and Six can still raise an Amsterdammer's eyebrow. Wives and daughters sat on the boards of charities and almshouses (housed in confiscated monasteries) and sons would serve in the civil guard on their way up to becoming *burgemeesters* or magistrates.

But as the glory days of the Dutch Golden Age slumped into the **depression years** of the early 1800s, Amsterdam's fortunes sank too. The sagging city almost collapsed under the burden of a population that doubled in the latter part of the 19th century. Living conditions were horrific. Whole families were crammed into dark cellars. Areas like the Jordaan and De Pijp became squalid, overcrowded slums, ravaged by **cholera**. (There were 2,273 victims of the 1848–9 epidemic alone.) Amsterdam had fallen far from the glory days of the Golden Age. In 1838, with deft symbolism, the piles under the Stock Exchange gave way and the building collapsed.

Amsterdam figures such as **Paul van Vlissingen** and **Samuel Sarphati** (*see* **History**, pp.44–5) were in the forefront of the country's revival at the end of the century, and though Amsterdam did suffer in the early **1930s Depression**—when gangs of unemployed were set to work creating the Amsterdamse Bos (Amsterdam Forest) outside the city—the city approached the **Second World War** with renewed prosperity.

The city was ravaged by Nazi occupation (*see* **History** pp.46–7), but made a quick recovery during the 1950s, and by the 1960s was entering one of its all-time halcyon periods, when it was a prime focus of the Youth Revolution that swept Europe. At the centre of the Amsterdam counter-culture was a group of flamboyant jesters, the **Provos** (from '*provocatie*'—'provocation'). Philosophy student Roel van Duyn, and magician and one-time window cleaner Robert Jasper Grootveld, with a motley gang of accomplices staged 'happenings' on the Dam and around the statue of the Lieverdje ('Little Darling') on the Spui. The Provos were against capitalism, traffic and tobacco, and for free bicycles and free sex. The demonstrations were light-hearted, theatrical and endearing. Whenever the police were needled into retaliation, onlookers in the elegant cafés around the square branded them bullies. However, when Crown Princess Beatrix married a German, Claus von Amsberg, in the Westerkerk in March 1966, the mood soured. The royal family was, to the Provos, the distillation of the Establishment. Not only the Provos were angry. There was a traditional coolness between Amsterdam and the House of Orange, and ratepayers resented having to foot the bill for the celebrations. The older generation—still raw from the Occupation—was appalled that their princess could marry a German. Demonstrators lined the route of the wedding procession waving banners demanding 'Republic' and 'Give me my bike back' (the Nazis had confiscated bicycles during the war). Smoke bombs were thrown and, though the day passed without serious incident, discontent bubbled on right through the spring. One hot June day a minor industrial dispute over construction workers' holiday pay erupted into violence. During a scuffle with the police in the Jordaan, one worker, Jan Weggelar, died of a heart attack. Rumour spread that the police had killed him, and a full-scale riot spread right across the city, sucking in Provos, Nozems (youth gangs) and anyone who enjoyed a good fight. Shops were looted, cars burned and parking meters ripped out of the ground. By nightfall the *burgemeester* was about to call in the army, but Chief Commissioner van der Molen of the Amsterdam Police took the matter in hand. He donned full dress uniform, called for his sword and strode out bravely into the midst of a bemused crowd. At midnight he met union leaders and, though he didn't entirely defuse the situation, the disruption fizzled out two days later after the mob had stormed the Port van Cleve Restaurant and the offices of the right-wing newspaper, *De Telegraaf.*

Later that year, violence broke out again over proposals to build a huge bank on Frederiksplein. Amsterdammers felt that big money was destroying the heart of the city by denuding it of anything but banks and offices. But despite concerted opposition, the city regents voted in favour of the bank by 30 to 14.

Meanwhile, the crowds camping out, especially those around the new National Monument (a war memorial), had begun to test the patience of upright, patriotic citizens. In 1967 off-duty Marines had descended on unsuspecting hippies outside the Centraal Station and cut off their hair. The mess left by the impromptu campsites was an affront to the obsessively neat Amsterdammers and a by-law passed in the summer of 1969 banned sleeping around national monuments. Initially it wasn't enforced—though the police would occasionally hose everyone down. In 1970, after violent clashes with the police had failed to oust the Dam dropouts, the Marines once again decided on unofficial unilateral action. Bands of strapping lads singing barrack-room songs belted arm-in-arm down the Damrak, and frightened the hippies away forever. Good burghers looked on from the surrounding balconies and cheered. Though the next morning the establishment press felt compelled to condemn, ever so lightly, the Marines' behaviour. Amsterdam's youth culture survived the attack, but was more formally accommodated in hostels and Sleep-Ins.

The Provos had broken up in 1967 'in order to avoid bloodshed', but Roel van Duyn went on to establish the **Kabouters** ('helpful gnomes')—a whimsical party of idealists with occasional flashes of common sense—they wanted more trees, fewer banks and polluting industries, a ban on traffic in central Amsterdam, and free white bikes for all. In the 1970 municipal elections they polled 11 per cent of the vote and won five seats on the city council. As the decade wore on, they lost their appeal and were finally disbanded in 1981.

Though the Provos were no more, and the Kabouters were on the wane, the late 1970s and early 1980s saw some spectacular battles. The council's plan to build a **Metro**—largely to serve the outer suburbs—met with outrage. It was expensive, and meant pulling down more houses in the inner city. Many people refused to move and on 25 March 1975—'**Blue Monday**'—there were violent demonstrations when officials tried to clear the first houses for demolition. Police fired tear gas through the windows and drove armoured cars into the doors. The ferocity of the opposition increased until 1978, when the council agreed to build new homes and renovate areas of the inner city. Skirmishes went on right up until the opening of the Metro in 1980.

In 1980 13 per cent of the city's population was on the housing list. Squatting had become a popular solution to the chronic shortages. Properties that had been vacated for the Metro, factories left empty when companies moved outside the city and houses bought by speculative investors (and then left to rot and fall down so that the land could be developed more profitably) were occupied by the paint-pot and hammer-wielding homeless. A lot of work went into the renovation of squatter homes, and the building of accompanying studios and cafés. The network became highly organized, and, with 10,000 members by 1982, was a force to be reckoned with. Police attempts to evict squatters were heavy-handed (they used tanks on a squat in the Vondelstraat) and not always successful. Battles would rage for days, and at one point the *burgemeester* had to declare a state of emergency. By 1984 the last of the big squats had fallen. On others a compromise had been reached—the council bought up the property, renovated it and let it back cheaply to the inhabitants. Squatting, and evictions, still go on, but in a calmer atmosphere.

Ed van Thijn, Amsterdam's (socialist) *burgemeester* for most of the 1980s and the early 1990s, was tough on squatters when he first came to office, but then initiated a strong programme of *stadsvernieuwing* (urban renewal) to help ease the severe housing crisis and to transform the city's image. Every few decades, the city fathers get it into their heads that Amsterdam is backward and old-fashioned and needs to be promoted as a modern metropolis. This usually leads to big new buildings in the centre of town. In the 1890s the Centraal Station, a temple to the new railways, blocked off Amsterdam's view of its harbour forever; in the 1920s the enormous Nederlandse Handels-maatschappij (Chamber of Commerce) building pushed aside rows of historic gabled houses near Rembrandtplein; during the 1960s concrete and glass monstrosities appeared all over town, the most controversial being the Nederlandse Bank on Frederiksplein. The 1970s and early 1980s saw the arrival, amidst violent protest, of the Metro and the 'Stopera', a combined city hall and opera house on Waterlooplein (*see* p.96). In the 1990s Burgemeester Van Thijn began to emphasize Amsterdam's role as a tourist, banking and congress metropolis. (It is now Europe's fourth tourist city after London, Paris and Rome, and in the world's top ten as a congress venue.) Vast new development went on in the area around Centraal Station, a glittering casino complex was built alongside Leidseplein, and business parks bristling with skyscrapers appeared—though this time on the outskirts of town.

Van Thijn's successor, **Schelto Patijn**, assumed office in 1994. Amsterdam's mayors are not elected by the citizenry, but appointed (ostensibly by the Queen). Yet they wield extraordinary civic power. Unlike Van Thijn, Patijn is not a born-and-bred Amsterdammer. What makes matters worse is that he hails from The Hague, Amsterdam's arch-rival. It did not help his image at all when the news leaked out that he didn't even intend to live in Amsterdam—though this decision was hastily revoked. At first, mutterings in Amsterdam cafés had it that this outsider did not understand the city at all, and is trying to change it into The Hague (which has a reputation for staid prissiness). His efforts at giving Amsterdam a more upmarket, businesslike image resulted in such moves as the towing away some of the old houseboats on the canals (seen as illegal and messy), and an attempt at closing down a number of café terraces (which was thwarted by rousing local opposition).

Yet the city's notorious drugs problem does seem more under control. Heroin dealers have been cleared out of the tourist areas around Zeedijk and Nieuwmarkt and now hole out in the south of the city. The *stadswacht* (modern-day equivalents of the Civil

Guards in the Old Masters' portraits) wander about, unarmed, in smart uniforms with red trimmings, keeping an eye on public behaviour and making sure that buskers don't sing too loudly. Tourist figures over the past few years have risen steadily. Amsterdam is enjoying a quiet, rather comfortable moment in its history, but its age-old tolerance of mischief remains the finest antidote to complacency. Amsterdam's flourishing gay community, the bustling red-light district, the newest wave of immigrants (from Turkey and Surinam), the Kabouters' heritage of environmental awareness and the Amsterdammers' nose for disruptive politics keep the cafés alive and the old port rough beneath its smooth veneer.

Orientation

For an overview map of Amsterdam, see inside back cover.

Amsterdam is small. If you were single-minded about it, it would take only 40 minutes to traverse its spider's web of canals all the way from Centraal Station to the Rijksmuseum on the other side of town. But you would need to know where you were going. The cobweb shape is confusing and disorientating. Arm yourself with a good map (those published by Falk are recommended). Along the way you'll be constantly surprised by the changes in pace and atmosphere of the *kwartiers* you passed through, some no bigger than a courtyard and a few gabled houses, yet every one of them has a distinctive, quite particular character of its own. Visit the **'Negen Straatjes'** (*see* pp.105–6) for quirky shopping, the Jordaan (*see* pp.107–8) for quiet charm; wander along the **Grachtengordel** ('Canal Belt' *see* pp.100ff) for elegance and grandeur, or sink into the tat surrounding the **Damrak** and **red-light district** (*see* pp.84 and 87).

Amsterdam is a sedate city. Pedestrians and cyclists set the pace, and you'll find most places you want to visit within comfortable walking distance. If your legs are tired, or you're in a hurry, yellow trams will whisk you to almost anywhere you want to go. A car is a liability. Parking is expensive (when it's possible), and driving in the narrow streets, which throng with bicycles and jaywalking tourists, is a nightmare. Public transport on the other hand is efficient, safe and cheap, and to be recommended.

Getting There from the Airport

Taxis into Amsterdam will cost you at least *f*60, and hardly seem worth it given the ease, frequency and price of public transport. Trains leave for Centraal Station every 15 minutes (until 1am, then hourly until 5am). The journey takes about 20 minutes and tickets cost *f*6.50.

Alternatively, you can swan into town on the plush KLM Hotel Bus. The service is available to anyone, even if you sneaked over on a bucket flight and intend sleeping in the Vondelpark. Buses leave at 15min intervals from 6.30am to 9.15pm and tickets cost *f*17.50. Route A stops include the Pulitzer, Krasnapolsky, Jolly Carlton and Okura (i.e. mainly central Amsterdam). Route B focuses more on southern Amsterdam, stopping at such hotels as the Hilton, Beethoven and Apollo.

Maps, information and tickets are available from the **GVB** (Amsterdam Municipal Transport Authority), Stationsplein 15, opposite Centraal Station (open Mon–Fri 7am–7pm, Sat and Sun 8am–7pm, ✆ (0900) 92 92). In the summer there's often a mobile branch on Leidseplein.

Once you've grasped the quirky logic behind it, the ticketing system used on public transport seems quite sensible. Although you can buy single tickets on boarding, it's cheaper and easier to buy a **strip ticket** (*strippenkaart*, ƒ11.75). Most tourist sights are within the central zone, but there are maps at all stations and stops, should you be in any doubt.

If you intend to use a lot of public transport, the most economical ticket will be a **day ticket** (*dagkaart*). This allows unlimited travel in Amsterdam and costs ƒ12 for 1 day, ƒ15 for 2 days, ƒ19 for 3 days, ƒ23 for 4 days, and ƒ27 for 5 days. You can buy *dagkaarten* from drivers or the GVB. Weekly, monthly or annual season tickets (*abonnement*) are also available from the GVB, starting from ƒ17.75.

Bus and tram drivers can also sell you an **hourly ticket** (*uurnetkaart*, pronounced 'oornetkart') for ƒ4.50 which allows you to travel anywhere in Amsterdam within an hour of its validation.

by tram

Trams run from 6am Mon–Fri and 7.30am Sun. Last trams are around midnight. On most trams you can get on or off through any one of the three doors (which open after you press the adjacent metal button). Some lines have conductors, who sit at the back. On these trams you can only alight through the rear door. Tram stops have yellow boards showing the numbers of the trams they serve and listing further destinations along the route. Of special benefit to visitors is the **Circle Tram**, running from Centraal Station to all the major sights and back.

by bus

Buses work on the same system as trams, though you must board at the front door. You're much less likely to use them, unless you need a **night bus**. A black square with the bus number printed on it is shown on the board of night bus stops. By some inscrutable logic the night buses decrease in frequency at about the time the bars close (2am). After this time there is only one bus an hour on some routes, and none at all until 4am on others. So your alternatives are a late night out, a very late night out, or walking home. You can, of course, always get a taxi.

by metro

The metro is used mainly by commuters from the eastern and southeastern suburbs. There are only two lines, both terminating at Centraal Station. Running times and ticketing are the same as for trams.

Theoretically, you can hail an Amsterdam cab in the street, but you're unlikely to have any luck at all. Best bet is to pick one up at a rank, or telephone the 24-hour central control, ✆ 677 7777 or ✆ (0900) 0724. The main **ranks** are at Centraal Station, Rembrandtplein and Leidseplein. Cafés, restaurants or night-clubs will usually phone a cab for you, and one will arrive within minutes. When you set off, the meter should be blank, except for the minimum charge. Even short journeys are expensive, with a flat rate of *f*5.80 for starters, then *f*2.85 a kilometre (*f*4.50 a mile) and increasing after midnight.

by bicycle

Cycling is the perfect means of transport in Amsterdam. It's convenient and gets you about at just the right speed to enjoy the city to the full. It's also a very Dutch way to travel. There are 700,000 people living in Amsterdam, and 550,000 bicycles. The city has an excellent network of cycle lanes, and bicycles are cheap to hire, though it can be more economical to pick up a second-hand one. This you can do from markets or cycle shops for around *f*150.

For bike hire try Rent-A-Bike (Pieter Jacobsdwarsstraat 11, ✆ 625 5029) or Macbike (Mr. Visserplein 2, ✆ 620 0985) and Take-A-Bike (Stationsplein 6, near Centraal Station, ✆ 624 8391), which are a little cheaper.

by water

If you have the time for the leisurely journeys, canal trips can give you an eye-opening perspective on the city. The moment you step on a boat you seem to cross a mysterious boundary. People on shore carry on with their lives—nicking bicycles, arguing, making love—apparently oblivious of you sailing past only a few feet away. The **Canal Bus** takes you on a gentle dawdle along some fine stretches of canal between the Rijksmuseum and Centraal Station, stopping at Leidseplein, Leidsestraat/Keizersgracht and the Anne Frank Huis. Buses leave at 45min intervals between 10am and 6pm. A day ticket costs *f*22. The new **All Amsterdam Transport Pass** is a day pass that for *f*27.50 includes all public transport as well as unlimited use of the canal bus.

Water Taxis can be great fun if you're in a party mood—the company will even lay on a guide, food and drink for appropriate extra charges. If you're lucky you can hail an empty water taxi as it putters past (they can stop anywhere along the canalside). You can also order them from the **Water Taxi Centrale** (Stationsplein 8, ✆ 530 1090; open daily 9am–1am; major credit cards accepted). Fares are metered—an 8-seater boat works out at around *f*125 for the first half an hour irrespective of the number of passengers, and *f*75 for every subsequent half-hour.

If you're feeling energetic you can hire a **Canal Bike** (a pedalboat that seats two or four people; costs *f*25 per hour for two people and *f*40 for four; deposit *f*50; no credit cards). Explore the canals for a while, then drop it off at any one of the hire company's four moorings—at Leidseplein (between the Marriott and American Hotels), at the Rijksmuseum, at the Anne Frank Huis, and on the Keizersgracht near Leidsestraat. Remember to keep to the right, and keep an ear open for warning hoots emitted by the long canal boats as they approach sharp corners or narrow tunnels. **Canal Motor Boats** (on Kloveniersburgwal, ✆ 422 7007) offer electric boats for hire at *f*65 for the first hour, and a declining rate for subsequent hours.

by car

If you do find yourself lumbered with a car in Amsterdam, you can find covered **car parks** (indicated by a white P on blue background) at De Bijenkorf (on Beursplein), Byzantium (Stadhouderskade, opposite Leidseplein), Europarking (Marnixstraat 250), RAI (on the Europa Boulevard) and under the Muziektheater (Waterlooplein). Charges are around *f*5 an hour. Parking beside the road works out at about *f*4 an hour, and street parking works by the 'pay-and-display' method. You put your money into a machine (often cunningly concealed behind a tree halfway down the street), estimate your time of return, then leave the ticket it prints out on your dashboard. If you park illegally your car will be towed away before you've had a chance to buy an ice-cream. It will cost you at least *f*400 to get it back from the pound (Dani, 1 Goedkoopstraat 7, ✆ 553 0333), and they won't take credit cards. If you overstay your time in a parking bay, your car will be clamped. A yellow sticker on the windscreen tells you where to pay the fine (which will be at least *f*126). Some meters are free after 7pm and on Sundays, but in the city centre you have to pay up to 11pm, Sunday inclusive. It's always best to check before abandoning your car to the clampers.

If you are in Amsterdam with a car for any length of time, it is a good idea to buy a **parking card**. This costs *f*30 (9am–7pm), *f*33 (9am–11pm), or *f*7 (7pm–11pm), and is available from the Dienst Stadstoezicht (Weesperstraat 105a, Beukenplein 50, Ceintuurbaan 159, Kinkerstraat 17, ✆ 553 0333). A **park-and-ride system** (known to the Dutch as a Transferium) operates from the Amsterdam Arena, in Amsterdam southeast. Amsterdam city council hopes to open more park-and-ride lots around the outskirts of town.

The most convenient 24-hour petrol stations are at Marnixstraat 250 and Sarphatistraat 225.

If you'd like to **hire a car**, you'll find the international companies well represented: Avis (Nassaukade 380, ✆ 683 6061); Budget (Overtoom 333, ✆ 612 6066) and Hertz (Overtoom 85, ✆ 612 2441). Local companies provide a good service, sometimes at less than half the price. Try Diks (Van Ostadestraat 278–80, ✆ 662 3366); Drive Yourself (Cruquiuskade 5, ✆ 627 4001) or Kuperus (Middenweg 175, ✆ 693 8790).

guided tours

On the jetties around Centraal Station you'll find a cluster of boat companies offering canal tours, candlelight cruises and dinner cruises. Prices and standards are almost uniform, but **Lovers Rondvaarten** (Prins Hendrikkade 25–27, ✆ 530 1090) has the best reputation.

The **Amsterdam Tourist Board** (*see* below) not only takes bookings for canal cruises, but constantly comes up with new ideas for touring the city—its staff can suggest all sorts of walking and cycling routes in and about Amsterdam. **Yellowbike** (NZ Kolk 29, ✆ 620 6940) also offers guided cycle tours around the city and surrounding waterlands. **Audiotourist** (Oude Spiegelstraat 9, ✆ 421 5580) will rent you a personal stereo plus guided tour on cassette for *f*15 (plus deposit). There are three different walks that last two to three hours each.

More rewarding than the commercially organized tours are the informal walk-abouts with old Amsterdam residents offered by **Mee in Mokum** (✆ 625 1390; open Mon–Fri 1–4 pm). The guides aren't professional, but give a homely, resident's touch that you're unlikely to find elsewhere. The tours are usually done in Dutch, but since the groups are small (about eight people), it's often possible to arrange an English alternative. **Archivisie** (✆ 625 8908) offers specialist architectural tours.

Amsterdam ✆ (020–)   ***Tourist Information***

The **Amsterdam Tourist Board** has English-speaking staff who can help with information about tourist sights, events and transport. They can change money and (for a *f*3.50 fee) arrange hotel and theatre bookings. They sell a range of maps and brochures and can suggest tours and walks. The main Amsterdam branch is opposite Centraal Station at Stationsplein 10. There is another, less busy branch at Leidseplein 1, a small branch in Centraal Station and one in the south of town on the corner of Stadionplein and Van Tuyll van Serooskerkenweg. All these branches are open Mon–Sat 9–5. During the high season some offices may extend their hours, and open on Sunday. There is a central information telephone number: ✆ (0900) 400 4040, but it costs *f*1 a minute and you are usually kept for ages in an electronic queue (paying for every second of the wait), often to be told at the end of it all that the office is too busy anyway and that you should phone back later.

Information about public transport is given by the **GVB** (Amsterdam Municipal Transport Authority), Stationsplein 15 (open Mon–Fri 7–7, Sat and Sun 8–7).

The **AUB Uitburo** (Leidseplein 26, ✆ 621 1211; open Mon–Sat 10–6) gives information and sells advance tickets (booking fee *f*2) for the city's theatres and concert halls and for many other cultural events. It also distributes leaflets and listings magazines. Entertainment info is also at the end of a phone line: Uitlijn, ✆ (0900) 0191.

The information desk at Schiphol Airport can give you a free English copy of the *Visitors' Yellow Pages*, a slim book of useful telephone numbers. You can also pick it up at police stations or from the Amsterdam Tourist Board.

You can visit the city **website** on *www.amsterdam.nl*. For business-orientated information visit the website of the Amsterdam Promotion Foundation at *www.amsterdampromotion.nl.*

Amsterdam ✆ (020–)

Practical A–Z

addresses

Houses on the main canals are numbered from west to east, even numbers on the outer circumference. Amsterdammers seem to have run out of imagination when naming their streets. If they think they've hit on a good name they'll use it again and again, so you get not only Eerste/1e (1st) Helmersstraat but also Tweede/2e (2nd) Helmersstraat and Derde/3e (3rd) Helmersstraat. Transverse streets get the epithet 'dwars', and also appear in multiples, so Tweede Egelantiersdwarsstraat will be the second street off Egelantiersstraat. The Oudezijd (old side of the city, east of Damrak) and the Nieuwezijd (new side, west of Damrak) are abbreviated in addresses to OZ and NZ—Oudezijds Voorburgwal, for example, is usually written OZ Voorburgwal.

babysitters

If you've had enough of the little darlings, you can get hold of vetted and reliable babysitters from **Oppascentrale Kriterion** (✆ 624 5848; open 24 hours). Prices start at about *f*7 an hour and you're expected to provide drinks, food for long sessions and the cost of transport home after midnight. Over weekends there is a minimum charge of *f*20.

discounts

The **Amsterdam Culture and Leisure Pass** entitles you to all sorts of discounts on museums and restaurants. It costs *f*39.50—though it can pay for itself within a few days. It's available from the Amsterdam Tourist Board.

emergencies

The national emergency number is ✆ **112**.

Main police stations are at Elandsgracht 117 and Warmoesstraat 44. Report any theft immediately, and get a written statement for your insurance claim. The **Amsterdam Tourist Assistance Service** (ATAS, NZ Voorburgwal 114/8, ✆ 625 3246) is on hand to offer victim support, should you have been shaken up by your experience, or feel at a loss as to what to do.

If you are a victim of rape or sexual abuse contact **De Eerste Lijn** (The First Line) on ✆ 613 0245 (24 hours). You'll find main **police stations** at Elandsgracht 117 and Warmoesstraat 44. It's a good idea, for insurance purposes, to report lost or stolen property to the police as soon as possible. There are **lost property offices** at Centraal Station, GVB Head Office, Prins Hendrikkade 108–14 (open Mon–Fri 9–4, for items lost on public transport), and at Waterlooplein 11 (open Mon–Fri 11–3.30, for items lost in parks and on the streets). It's best to allow a day or two for your property to filter through the system before trying to reclaim it.

The most useful place to ring if you are ill or need a dentist is the **Central Medical Service** on ✆ (0900) 503 2042. This 24-hour service will refer you to a duty practitioner. The most central **hospital** with an outpatients department is Onze Lieve Vrouwe Gasthuis, Eerste Oosterparkstraat 179, ✆ 599 9111. **Chemists** (*drogisterij*) sell non-prescription drugs and toiletries. If you need a prescription made up you should go to an *apotheek*. The Central Medical Service can also advise you on this. If you've crushed your contact lenses or dropped your specs in a canal, try **York Optiek**, Heiligeweg 8; ✆ 623 3295 (open Mon–Fri 9.30–6, Sat 9.30–5, appointment advisable, major credit cards accepted). If your dentures take a crunch try **Accident**, Amstelveenseweg 51, ✆ 664 4380 (open 24 hours). There's a free and confidential VD clinic at Groenburgwal 44, ✆ 555 5822 (open Mon–Fri 8–10.30 and 1–3, but arrive before 10.30am for first consultation; appointment not necessary). The **Polikliniek Oosterpark**, Oosterpark 59, ✆ 693 2151 (open Mon–Fri 9–5) offers contraception, abortion and morning after pills, but its services are not free.

post

The main **post office** is at Singel 250 (open Mon–Fri 9–6, Sat 10–1.30; late opening Thurs until 8; ✆ 556 3311) and, as well as the usual facilities, has phones, photocopiers, a gift shop and a philately counter. Parcels can be sent only through this office, or the **sorting office** (Oosterdokskade 3, near Centraal Station; open Mon–Fri 8.30–9, Sat 9–12 noon; ✆ 622 8272).

religious services

Roman Catholic services in English are held at an old clandestine church: St John and St Ursula (Begijnhof 30, ✆ 622 1918; Sun 12.15 pm). There's a Latin High Mass at De Papegaai (St Peter and Paul, Nieuwezijds Voorburgwal 293; also entrance on Kalverstraat, Sun 11.15am).

Protestant services in English are held in the serene English Reform/Scottish Presbyterian Church (Begijnhof 48, ✆ 624 9665; Sun 10.30am) and at the Anglican Church (Groenburgwal 42, ✆ 624 8877; Sun 10.30am and 7.30pm).

Times of **Jewish** services vary. You can contact the Liberal Community at Jacob Soetendorpstraat 8 (✆ 642 3562) and the Orthodox Community at PO Box 7967, Van der Boechorstraat 26, 1008 ad (✆ 646 0046).

Festivals

Perhaps because of Amsterdam's Puritan heritage, you'll find little civic or royal pomp. Instead, the city lets its hair down at a number of fairs, arts festivals and street parties—the best celebration of all being Koninginnedag on 30 April. *See* also **Practical A–Z**, pp.19–20 for nationwide festivals, but here in Amsterdam here are some dates to aim for.

February: Commemoration of the February Strike—a solemn gathering on 25th at the Dokwerker statue on J. D. Meijerplein (*see* p.99).

March: The Stille Omgang (Silent Procession) takes place at night on the Sunday closest to the 15th. Roman Catholics from all over the world walk in silence along the Heiligeweg and up to Sint Nicolaaskerk to celebrate Amsterdam's 'Miracle' (*see* pp.69 and 84).

The Meervaart Theatre hosts a Blues Festival and there's a boat show featuring the latest pleasure craft at the RAI Congress Centre (on Europaplein).

April: 30 April is Koninginnedag (Queen's Day—a national holiday to celebrate the Queen's birthday). Amsterdam declares a 'free market'. Anyone can sell anything anywhere and all bar and restaurant takings are tax-free. The whole city turns into a cross between the Notting Hill Carnival and a fleamarket. Holland converges on the town to eat, drink, dance and be exceptionally merry, but with the usual charming Dutch relaxed tolerance. Up to three million people throng the streets (Amsterdam's population is only 700,000), yet you hardly *see* a policeman, there are no barricades, no rules and no problems—seldom upwards of ten arrests over the whole day, and those are usually for pickpocketing. The best time to join in is after midnight on the 29th, when everyone is setting up stalls and people are as fresh and excited as children on Christmas Eve.

An internationally respected World Press Photo Exhibition displays the pick of newspaper and magazine photography from the preceding year. (In the Nieuwe Kerk from mid-April to mid-May.) Watch out also for GRAP Day at De Melkweg (*see* p.165), when Amsterdam's best new bands blast away well into the night.

June: The Holland Festival runs for the whole month of June. This is Amsterdam's answer to the Edinburgh Festival, with an impressive constellation of international performers booked into opera, dance and theatre venues around the city. The festival forms part of the Amsterdam Arts Adventure, which keeps everyone from opera-lovers to movie-buffs entertained well into the summer.

On the 2nd Sun 5,000 people go for a jog around the canals in the Grachtenloop (*see* p.137).

Around the beginning of the month (or at the end of May) the RAI Congress Centre plays host to Kunst RAI, an international contemporary art fair. Later in the month, the World Roots Festival—nine days of music, dance and theatre from non-Western cultures—takes place at De Melkweg.

July: If the Holland Festival sounds too staid for your tastes, try the July Summer Festival—a bonanza of the avant-garde that goes on all over town (sometimes in the strangest places).

August: For most of the month of August the Martin Luther King Park, beside the Amstel on the southern outskirts of town, is the scene of De Parade, a 'theatre funfair'. Various theatre groups and performers arrange bright show booths, some of them dating back to the first half of the century, in a vast circle, and offer everything from cabaret to performance art. The Masters (and Mistresses) of Ceremonies present the players on stages outside the booths, then everyone troops in for the show. There's lots to eat and drink too.

The Uitmarkt (Entertainment Market) takes place in the last week of August. Groups from all over the Netherlands offer tantalizing snippets of what the coming cultural season has to offer. It's free, and takes place in theatres, in the open air—in fact anywhere a company can find a suitable space.

More open-air music is played during the three-day-long Grachtenfestival (Canal Festival)—this time from boats opposite the Pulitzer Hotel (Prinsengracht 315–31; also in the last week of August).

September: Bloemen Corso (Flower Parade) is a parade of floats from Aalsmeer ('the flower capital') to Amsterdam on the first Saturday of the month. Check with the Amsterdam Tourist Board (*see* p.78) for details of the route and arrival times. Vijzelstraat and the Dam are the best places to watch from.

The Jordaan Festival is the liveliest of a series of neighbourhood street parties. All over the Jordaan, the residents come out into the streets to booze, barbecue and try their luck in the often unabashedly dire local talent contests.

November: In mid-November St Nicholas (Sinterklaas/Santa Claus) arrives by steamboat at Centraal Station (supposedly from his home in Spain). He parades through the city on a white horse with his slave Black Pete (an oddly persistent tradition in modern, racially aware Amsterdam) and is given the keys of the city by the *burgemeester* on the Dam. Relax with a coffee on Rembrandtsplein and watch the early part of the procession in relative comfort.

Central Amsterdam (West)

Stationsplein

The **Centraal Station**, built between 1884 and 1889 atop thousands of wooden piles on an artificial island, is such an elaborate and sustained exercise in 19th-century ornament that it can almost be forgiven for screening off Amsterdam's view of the old harbour. The architect P. J. H. Cuypers (also responsible for the Rijksmuseum) succumbed to every temptation to gild bits of his red-brick extravaganza, so that it sparkles in the sunlight like a Walt Disney palace. Its twin towers are adorned not only by a clock, but also by a wind-rose, a delightfully superfluous instrument that rotates languidly showing the frequency of winds blowing from the various leading points of the compass. The roof bristles with stone and iron spikes and the central section sports classically inspired reliefs showing allegories of sailing, trade and industry. There's a large section over the entrance depicting the peoples of the world paying homage to the maiden Amsterdam.

The building seems very much in the tradition of the triumphal arch or elaborate city gate and is indeed a grand place to arrive in Amsterdam. The city is laid out like a semi-

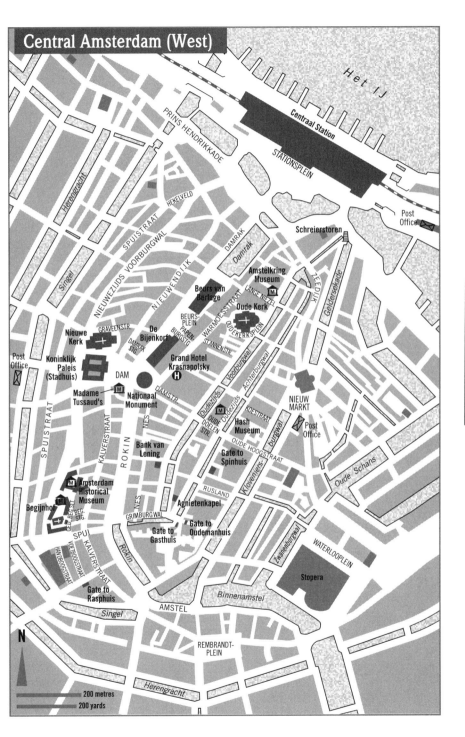

Central Amsterdam (West)

Het IJ

Centraal Station

STATIONSPLEIN

PRINS HENDRIKKADE

Post Office

Schreierstoren

HEKELVELD

SPUISTRAAT

Singel

Herengracht

NIEUWEZIJDS VOORBURGWAL

NIEUWENDIJK

DAMRAK

Damrak

Amstelkring Museum

Beurs van Berlage

LANGE NIEZEL

ZEEDIJK

Oude Kerk

BEURS-PLEIN

WARMOESSTRAAT

GRAVEENSTR.

Nieuwe Kerk

De Bijenkorf

PAPEN. BURGSTG.

DAMRAK STG.

STANNENSTR.

OUDEKERKSPLEIN

OUDE KERKSTEEG

Geldersekade

Post Office

Koninklijk Paleis (Stadhuis)

DAM

Grand Hotel Krasnapolsky

Voorburgwal

Achterburgwal

Madame Tussaud's

Nationaal Monument

DAMSTR.

Oudezijds

Oudezijds

NIEUW MARKT

SPUISTRAAT

KALVERSTRAAT

NES

ROKIN

Bank van Lening

OUDE DOELEN STR.

Hash Museum

ROESTRAAT

Post Office

Gate to Spinhuis

OUDE HOOGSTRAAT

Kloveniers burgwal

Oude Schans

Amsterdam Historical Museum

NES

RUSLAND

Begijnhof

GRIMBURGWAL

Agnietenkapel

BEG. STG.

Gate to Oudemanhuis

Gate to Gasthuis

SPUI

Zwanenburgwal

WATERLOOPLEIN

VOORBOOMSTRAAT

HANDBOOGSTRAAT

KALVERSTRAAT

Rokin

Stopera

Gate to Rasphuis

Singel

AMSTEL

Binnenamstel

REMBRANDT-PLEIN

N

Herengracht

200 metres
200 yards

circular spider's web with the Centraal Station in the middle. As you step out of the main entrance you get the full impression, across the shapeless open space of **Stationsplein**, of the spires, gables and cupolas of Amsterdam's delicate skyline. To the left across the square is **Sint Nicolaaskerk** (St Nicholas Church; *open April–Oct, Mon–Fri 11–4, Sat 2–4*), a sprucely restored 19th-century neo-Renaissance building with a murky interior. A small ship set above the door at the back is the only remainder that it was a seamen's church. Every March during the Stille Omgang (Silent Procession), Roman Catholics walk silently through the streets to the Sint Nicolaaskerk to commemorate Amsterdam's miracle (*see* p.69). Paintings in the left-hand transept depict the story.

Along the Damrak

From Stationsplein leads the **Damrak**, once a busy port built along the Amstel, but these days a street lined with the fast food joints, rip-off bureaux de change, tacky restaurants and tackier hotels that usually cluster around tourist inlets. The only remaining patch of water is a tiny dock filled with the glass-covered boats that bus you around on hour-long canal trips (for details, *see* p.76).

The original settlement of Amsterdam grew up in the early 13th century along Kerkstraat (Church Street, later renamed Warmoesstraat) on the left (east) side of the river. Towards the end of the last century the village expanded along Windmolenstraat (Windmill Street) on the right (west) bank. The Church Side and the Windmill Side soon became known as Oude Zijd (Old Side) and Nieuwe Zijd (New Side) and the corresponding sides of Damrak are still called that today.

Halfway up Damrak, on the left-hand side, you come to the **Beurs van Berlage** (*museum open Tues–Sun 10–4; basic adm, includes visit to tower*).The first Beurs (Exchange) was built by the prolific 17th-century architect Hendrick de Keyser in 1608. The city council thought it necessary to confine all the outdoor wheeling and dealing that took place along Damrak and around the Oude Kerk to one (warmer and drier) venue. The result was deafening. As international trade expanded, such exotica as Turks, Indians and Hungarians joined the locals packed around the pillars and arcades of the small hall on the Rokin, bargaining madly for silks, shares, tobacco and tulips—or anything the boats brought in. De Keyser's Beurs held out for two hundred years. The building that replaced it (on the site of the present De Bijenkorf department store) was universally unpopular and in 1874 the city held a competition for a new design. When it was revealed that the winner had cribbed the façade from a French town hall, H. P. Berlage (who had come third) smartened up his original plans and landed the prize. Many revisions later (he was still at the drawing board while the builders were at work), he came up with a building that has become an Amsterdam landmark and earned him the reputation of being the father of modern Dutch architecture. The Beurs van Berlage (completed in 1903) is all clean lines and functional shapes. Berlage allows himself some gently patterned brickwork, but there's not one extraneous twirly bit nor a glimmer of 19th-century Gothic fantasy. The pillars and arcades inside are an echo of the original Beurs.

These days part of the Beurs is used for concerts, while the rest is a museum (comprising a modest display on the history and design of the building) and exhibition hall. A visit to the museum gives you access to the clock tower and a view over the oldest part of town. In the smaller of two concert halls you sit and listen to the music in an enormous glass box which has solved the problem of abysmal acoustics without defacing the original interior. You can get a glimpse inside without buying a concert or a museum ticket by popping into the café at the south end.

The café opens out on to **Beursplein**. To the right the traffic on Damrak hurtles past. The dainty neoclassical **Effectenbeurs** (Commodities Exchange) on the left is the place where the real trading now happens. Across the square, a row of silently chewing, blank faces stare out at you from behind a sheet of plate glass. These are exhausted shoppers propped up along a snackbar in the back window of De Bijenkorf, though they look as if they're for sale.

The Dam

Riots, garrottings, camping hippies—the Dam has seen it all. Reputedly the site of the original dam across the Amstel, it hit its zenith as city centre in the 17th century. Pragmatic Amsterdam merchants wouldn't stand for any decorative open space at the heart of the city and the Dam bustled with a fishmarket, a public weighing house, a communal crane and a dock that allowed ships to sail right up into the middle of town to offload. Popular tunes rang out from the Stadhuis carillon and, above all the racket, the town crier's horn would from time to time blast out (once for good news, twice for bad). When you needed to go home, you could ring a bell to summon a taxi. After a brief wait for the drivers to throw dice to decide who should take you, you'd set off at reckless speed in a slide carriage (wheels presented a problem on the hump-backed bridges), accompanied by packs of sprinting boys throwing water and greased rags under the runners to make the carriage go faster, or straw to make it stop. You'd have to drop out coins at intervals to ensure your rapid progress, and a few more at the humpy bridges to the stalwart lads who hung around to give a much-needed extra push.

Traffic on the Dam these days is just as frantic, but the square has lost all its verve. It's still the city centre and the carillon still peals out pop tunes, but the Dam is soulless, fumid and dull. The eastern end is dominated by the towering, phallic **Nationaal Monument**, erected in 1956 as a memorial to the people killed in the Second World War. In the 1960s it became a sort of hippie totem pole and hundreds of people would sleep around it in the summer. Police attempts to put a stop to this (such as washing it down with firehoses) led to protest riots, but in 1970 a marauding group of off-duty marines chased away the campers forever (*see* p.72).

At its southern end the Dam leads into **Kalverstraat**, a pedestrianized shopping street where shoulder-to-shoulder consumers push in and out of Euro-high-street stores, scrabble about in the sales baskets and devour pungent fast food. While on the north-western corner stands the **Nieuwe Kerk** (*open daily 11–5*). The construction of the Nieuwe Kerk actually began nearly 600 years ago. It's a soaring Gothic heap without a steeple. (In the 17th century, Oude Kerk parishioners, who had always been jealous of the flash rival church, were delighted when the city council stopped construction of the tower because it was going to be higher than the town hall.) Until 1890 all the city's clocks were set weekly by the church's sundial. Like most of Amsterdam's large churches, the Nieuwe Kerk is now used mainly for exhibitions and concerts. Even if you can't catch a recital on the sumptuous Great Organ, the instrument itself, fluttering with angels and cherubs and surrounded by soft-painted shutters, is worth a visit. Admiral de Ruyter, the Dutch naval hero, is buried in the choir. (His invasion of the River Medway in England caused Sir William Batten, Surveyor of the British Navy, to explode to Samuel Pepys: 'I think the devil shits Dutchmen.') There's a memorial to the poet Vondel near the west door. Before you leave, have a look also at the richly carved pulpit and ornate copper choir screen.

Next door to the Nieuwe Kerk, taking up the entire western end of the square is the **Koninklijk Paleis** (Royal Palace; *opening times vary, in summer generally daily 11am–5.30pm, sometimes closed for state functions; information on © (020) 620 4060*). The Koninklijk Paleis was the **Stadhuis** (City Hall) until Louis Bonaparte decided he wanted to live there in 1808. It's been a royal palace ever since, though Queen Beatrix prefers the leafier groves of Huis ten Bosch in The Hague and never spends the night here. The area in front of the Stadhuis was a favourite spot for theatrical public executions. On the right, above the entrance arches, you can still see the blocks where the scaffold slotted into the wall. The ornate street lamps along the front were commissioned by King Willem Frederik in 1840. They were the city's first gas lamps, but were so expensive to run that the council secretly turned them off whenever the king was out of town.

When the Stadhuis was built in the mid-17th century, only St Peter's, the Escorial and Venice's Palazzo Ducale rivalled it in grandeur. The poet Constantijn Huygens dubbed it 'the eighth wonder of the world', and a passing Englishman wrote of 'a most neat and splendid pile of a building'. But Sir William Temple, the British Ambassador to the Netherlands, harrumphed that it was '*una gran piccola cosa*' ('a big little thing'—he was quoting someone else's remark about the Louvre). The architect, Jacob van Campen (designer of the ill-fated Nieuwe Kerk tower), had produced a grandiose celebration of Amsterdam's mercantile supremacy and civic might—a classicist heap of windows, pilasters and relief carving. On the front pediment, collected water deities worship an allegorical Maid of Amsterdam; at the back of the building the trading nations of the world grovel to her. Peace stands high under the dumpy dome (a cornucopia overflowing at her feet) holding not only an olive branch, but also Mercury's staff (a symbol of commerce). Atlas buckles under a copper globe so heavy that it needs iron rods to prop it up. Despite all this confident symbolism, there's no grand entrance (the eight little arches along the front look more like tradesmen's gates or the way into the stables) and nowadays you are more likely to agree with Sir William Temple than Constantijn Huygens: the rather grimy palace in a busy city centre has as much architectural impact as a main post office or magistrates' court.

However, if you're passing during the rather restricted opening hours, don't miss the chance of popping inside to be dazzled by the **Burgerzaal** (Citizens' Hall). It's a vast space encrusted with marble carving that glints in the light pouring in from all sides. Rows of chandeliers drip from the distant ceiling, and brass inlaid maps on the floor show the heavenly and terrestrial worlds (with Amsterdam very much at the centre of things and the enthroned Maid of Amsterdam proudly surveying it all). The few chairs around the edges, even a grand piano for the inevitable recital, look like doll's house furniture. Scattered throughout the building are delicate and often witty marble reliefs (Icarus takes a tumble outside the Bankrupts' Court, caryatids look bored with holding up the cross-beams). Most of them are by Artus Quellinus, the noted Golden Age sculptor who also carved the pediments outside. The city fathers, however, blundered when it came to commissioning the wall paintings: they sent Rembrandt packing after he had presented his preliminary sketches.

The Empire furniture dispersed around the building was left behind by Louis Bonaparte. When he took over the Stadhuis he carpeted the marble floors, boarded up the galleries, turned the virtually empty upper storey into living accommodation and also had the weighing house on the Dam demolished because it spoiled his view. When the bored and wayward Queen Hortense granted a royal pension to a foundling abandoned at the palace door, he forestalled an inundation of hapless infants by surrounding the entrance with cobblestones and appointing guards to prevent anyone from stepping on them. His wooden-partitioned upstairs apartments lasted well into this century and were such a fire risk that whenever Queen Wilhelmina used the palace everyone was instructed not to smoke and to sleep with the doors open. A fireman in gym shoes would creep about at night to catch offenders.

The Red Light District

Amsterdam's much-hyped red-light district (known to locals as 'De Walletjes'—the little walls) lies east of the Damrak, and you can reach it from the Dam along Warmoesstraat or Damstraat. **Warmoesstraat** is Amsterdam's oldest street. Originally a cluster of wattle and daub cottages, it was by the 16th century a row of prosperous merchants' houses and powerful banks. The Duke of Alva lived here in 1574 during his reign of terror (the rest of the street was understandably empty at the time) and left without paying his rent. Vondel (the 'Dutch Shakespeare') had a small hosiery business at the Dam end before he became a famous poet; and Sir Thomas Nugent, a seasoned 17th-century traveller, recommended it as the only street where you'd find English inns and so avoid being cheated by wily Dutchmen. In 1766 Mozart senior held court in the tavern of De Goude Leeuw and sold tickets for his son's recitals at $f2$ apiece; and a century later Karl Marx pondered and scribbled away in the inn next door. These days Warmoesstraat is the first layer of the red-light district, and a strange mixture of past respectability and the seediness which lies beyond. It's a grubby, dishevelled street, but no one seems to take it seriously enough for it to be sordid.

In the alleys off Warmoesstraat women sit, barely clad and deeply bored, perched on bar stools in the windows. Catch someone's eye and immediately there's a bright smile and a sparkle which disappears the moment you look away. If business is bad, or if you walk with eyes downcast, you'll hear the windows being rapped noisily. In the mornings the little alleys, some narrower than a doorway, are inhabited only by the desperate (on both sides of the glass) and the area has a feeling of secrecy and expectancy, rather like an empty theatre. Off-duty prostitutes join friends to go out shopping, or wander off in groups to the clinic for a check-up. In the afternoons it all seems too blatant and seedy, but later a wild festivity sets in as the lanes fill with the merry, the lecherous and the plain curious. Phalanxes of Japanese businessmen troop about aching to take photographs, drunken schoolboys gawp and try to pluck up courage, tight clutches of Dutch families from the provinces ooh and aah and snicker at all the wickedness.

In the heart of it all is Amsterdam's oldest building, the **Oude Kerk** (Old Church; *open summer Mon–Sat 11–5, Sun 1–5; adm*). Only the tower of the Oude Kerk actually dates from 1300. The original basilica disappeared behind an increasingly haphazard outgrowth of side chapels, transepts and clerestories. Most of what you see today is lofty early 16th-century Renaissance, but even that has a crust of warden's offices, choir rooms and houses, built over a period of three centuries. The interior has survived frequent bouts of heavy-handed restoration, an engulfing coat of Prussian blue paint in the 18th century and violent attacks by iconoclasts. In August 1566, roused by the sight of fragments of statuary from smashed-up churches in Antwerp, Protestant mobs stormed the church, breaking windows and destroying all graven images. A local girl, Lange Weyn, threw her shoe at a picture of the Virgin Mary in the excitement, and was later drowned in a barrel on the Dam for the outrage.

After what is discreetly called the 'Alteration' of 1578, when the Protestants finally took control of the city, the new Calvinist city fathers stripped the church of its dedication to St Nicholas (patron saint of sailors and so, aptly, of Amsterdam) and the popular title of Oude Kerk became official. They also set about turning it into a more sombre place of worship. It had become a hearty communal gathering place. Dossers and travellers slept in the corners, pedlars set up stalls in the aisles, merchants clinched deals on the square outside and dog-owners crowded the entrance. (Only certain classes of Amsterdam society were allowed big dogs, and if your mutt couldn't squeeze through the special iron hoop at the church door, its days were numbered.) These days the church plays host to travelling exhibitions and the occasional concert. Inside you can see the **tomb of Rembrandt's wife**, Saskia van Uylenburgh (near the Weitkoperskapel on the north side); some beautifully restored and remade stained glass (especially the windows depicting the Annunciation in the Mariakapel); and the secret door (once covered by plaster, 5m above the ground in St Sebastiaanskapel) to the **IJzeren Kapel** (Iron Chapel), a hiding place for important city documents until 1892.

Oudezijds Voorburgwal

Oudezijds Voorburgwal was the canal immediately inside (voor, 'in front of') the first city wall. Today it's a brash, brazen strip of porn shops, video booths and peep-shows, though some stylish gables and façades poke out above the lurid layer at street-level.

Look out for: the diving dolphins opposite the Amstelkring; a mask- and bust-encrusted house by Hendrick de Keyser opposite the Oude Kerk; Africans and Indians relaxing on tobacco bales on the neck-gable at No.187; and an elegant neoclassical building by one of the three great 17th-century domestic architects, Philips Vingboons, at No.316.

At No.40 you'll find one of Amsterdam's most charming small museums, the **Amstelkring Museum** (*open Mon–Sat 10–5, Sun 1–5; adm*). Also known as Ons Lieve Heer op Solder (Our Lord in the Attic), the Amstelkring was a '*schuilkerk*'—a clandestine church. During the 17th and 18th centuries Roman Catholic services were illegal, but ever-tolerant Amsterdam turned a blind eye to what was going on behind domestic façades. The attic of the little spout-gabled house joins up with two others in the houses behind and was consecrated as a church in 1663. Inside the museum you can wander about an 18th-century reception room, into a classic 17th-century Dutch '*sael*' (living-room) with symmetrical black and white marble flooring and a monumentally grand walnut fireplace, up through bedrooms with quaint box-shaped cupboard-beds, higher and higher to a small wooden staircase. Turn the corner at the top of the stairs and suddenly you're in what seems an enormous church with two galleries, light streaming in, an abundance of carving and painting and a voluptuous organ that must have been audible throughout the neighbourhood. The church is filled with treasures and mementoes of oppressed Catholicism (you can get an explanatory pamphlet downstairs). Try to get there early in the day, when you can appreciate the dream-like atmosphere in relative solitude.

Halfway down Oudezijds Voorburgwal the sleaze shops suddenly come to an end and you find yourself in a leafy nook of old Amsterdam. At No.300 is the Municipal Pawn Broker—the **Bank van Lening**, euphemized as 'Ome Jan' (Uncle John's). For the past three hundred years it has been a more sympathetic alternative to professional moneylenders—interest is fixed at a rate that corresponds to your ability to pay. Vondel, bankrupted by his playboy son, spent his septuagenarian years here as a clerk, going to work each day through a gateway that had one of his own poems inscribed in the arch. (It's still there, advising the rich to hurry past, as they have no business inside.)

On the opposite side of the canal is the **Agnietenkapel** (*open Mon–Fri 9–5, though phone © (020) 525 3341 first to check; adm*), a 15th-century convent church that houses a specialized and not particularly captivating collection of prints, photographs and ephemera centring on academic life.

Oudezijds Achterburgwal

Oudezijds Achterburgwal was the canal just outside (*achter*, 'behind') the first city boundary. Most of the buildings in this area are now part of the University of Amsterdam, but they were once (in the words of a 17th-century visitor) a collection of 'almshouses which look like princes' houses, hospitals for fools and houses where beggars, frequenters of taphouses, women who feign great bellies and men who pretend they have been taken by Turks' were confined and set to hard work.

These institutions, a product of prosperous and Calvinistic Amsterdam, were considered far-sighted and revolutionary by the rest of Europe. The gateway on the corner, copied from a Michelangelo design, led to the **Gasthuis** (hospital). A little further down you come to another elaborate arch, the entrance to the **Oudemanhuis**, an old men's almshouse. These days glass doors slide back as you approach and you find yourself in a dim arcade of second-hand bookstalls with medieval-looking proprietors. A shaft of light halfway along comes from a door that leads to the elegant almshouse courtyard. It's a private court belonging to the university, but nobody will stop you if you want to have a look.

The **Spinhuis** (on Spinhuissteeg) was a place where 'incorrigible and lewd women' were made to spin cloth for the poor. A rather alarming relief above the door shows women whipped with a cat-o'-nine-tails. Underneath is the not entirely convincing inscription:

> *Schrik niet, ik wreek geen quaat maar dwing tot goet.*
> *Straf is mijn hand, maar Lieflijk mijn gemoed.*
>
> *Cry not, for I exact no vengeance for wrong, but force you to be good.*
> *My hand is stern, but my heart is kind.*

The altruism of successive custodians seems to have been directed more towards passing gentlemen. For a small fee they were given access to the wicked inmates.

Modern attractions on Oudezijds Achternurgwal include the **Hash and Marijuana Museum**, at No.148 (*open daily 11am–10pm; adm*), devoted to a history of hemp and dope, and the **Tattoo Museum** at No.130 (*open Tues–Sun noon–6; adm*), which is not as tacky and sensationalist as one might expect, but a genuinely well-researched survey of the history of tattooing and body art in a variety of cultures.

Around the Nieuwmarkt

The Nieuwmarkt (New Market) is an open, brick-paved square that connects some of the more sinister alleys of the red-light district. Furtive men pop out of side streets, blink uncertainly in the bright light, then slip away. The police have cleared out the junkies and dealers who used to hang about the square, and it's been given a facelift. Now that the underworld is banished, Nieuwmarkt is moving upmarket. The once barren square is beginning to fill up with terraces and regain some of its old liveliness. On Sundays in the summer months there's a bustling antiques market and on feast days you can sometimes find a fairground or one of the old Dutch travelling dance halls.

A ring of modern street lamps, like giant mauve praying mantises, seem about to devour the solid medieval **St Antoniespoort** which huddles, flanked by dumpy towers, in the middle of the square. St Antoniespoort began life in 1488 as one of the main gates in the city wall. It was a popular spot for public executions. If you have a look on the south side you can see the rectangular holes (now bricked up) where the support beams of the scaffold slipped in. In one of the octagonal towers was a *galgekamertje* (little gallows room). From here the hapless prisoner got a foretaste of what was to happen to him: a small window looked out on the hangings, brandings and chopping off of bits going on a few feet below. In 1617 the gate was converted into a public weighing house. As all wholesale goods had to be weighed for taxes, 'De Waag' was the centre of trading activity. Liveried porters carried produce to and fro. Fierce armed guards were posted everywhere to keep an eye on the filling coffers and to arrest defaulters. (The sewer below the square was a highway for smugglers and bandits.) In 1691 St Antoniespoort housed the dissecting room of the Guild of Surgeons (cadavers being so conveniently at hand). You can just make out their inscription above the door in the south tower. On the other side bricklayers decorated the door to their guild room with elaborate wreaths of trowels. Today De Waag houses a trendy café.

Leading off the top end of Nieuwmarkt are Zeedijk and Geldersekade. In the 14th century **Zeedijk** marked the city limits. Modern Amsterdammers associate it with the *rode knipoog en witte kick* (the 'red wink' of prostitution and 'white kick' of heroin). A massive clean-up campaign by the council and police has got rid of the drug dealers and turned most of Zeedijk into a respectable street of restaurants and galleries.

The timber house at No.1 is one of the oldest buildings in the city and one of the two remaining wooden buildings in central Amsterdam. It was built in 1550 as a seamen's hostel. The innkeeper allowed sailors who'd drunk or gambled away their wages to leave pet monkeys in payment. The hostel became infested with apes and fleas and became known as 'In 't Aepjen': you could always spot the poor scratching seamen who'd slept 'in the monkeys'. The Dutch still say of someone who is in difficulty that they have *in de aap gelogeerd* (literally, 'stayed in the monkey'). **In 't Aepjen** is now a café. The drinking-houses on the right-hand side of **Geldersekade** were notorious. A 17th-century British ambassador to the Netherlands was horrified: 'There are tolerated in the city of Amsterdam, amongst other abuses, at least 50 musick-houses where lewd persons of both sexes meet to practise their villainies.' His moral outrage didn't preclude him from having a detailed knowledge of the prices and opening times of the 'Long Seller', a public meeting house where 'rogues and whores make their filthy bargains'. The red-light district has moved fractionally eastward (*see* p.86), and Geldersekade is now the backbone of Amsterdam's small Chinatown.

At the northern end of Geldersekade is the **Schreierstoren** (built 1480), a dwarfish brick tower with a pixie-hat roof. It's one of the few remnants of Amsterdam's first city wall. Romantics maintain the tower gets its name because sailors' wives would gather on the battlements to see the men off the sea. Well might they weep and wave. Voyages could take up to four years and, on average, two-thirds of the men who set off never returned. More pedantic linguists point out that '*schreier*' comes from the old Dutch word for 'astride' or 'angle' and that the tower straddles two canals. The romantics win: a stone tablet on the wall depicts the wailing wives. Henry Hudson also has a plaque, as it was from here, in 1609, that he went off to discover a new route to the East Indies and found Manhattan instead, giving his name to the Hudson River. The Schreierstoren was originally a solid defence tower; the top storey, windows and doors were all added later. Nowadays it houses a café.

Amsterdam Historical Museum

Kalverstraat 92; open Mon–Fri 10–5, Sat and Sun 11–5; adm.

Situated in the old Burgerweeshuis, a home founded in 1520 for orphans from the top ranks of Amsterdam society, the Amsterdam Historical Museum offers a compact and accessible introduction to the city's history. In the quiet loggia and courtyard of what was the boys' section, now the terrace of In de Oude Goliath café, the boys' wooden lockers are still visible in the wall. Through the next arch is the girls' courtyard, a sober red brick court with sensible Ionic pilasters. The girls had their own gate, on the right side of the courtyard. The thrifty governors transferred it stone by stone from a building that was being demolished nearby and had a mason carefully alter the date stone from 1571 to 1634. Boys and girls were effectively kept separate by an open sewer that ran between their respective dormitories. The sewer has been covered and the resulting passageway converted into a promenade gallery for civic guard portraits which are too big to hang anywhere else, but they don't make particularly riveting viewing.

Inside the museum proper, the exhibition is arranged chronologically from Amsterdam's foundation right up to the 20th century and, armed with a file of English explanations of all the exhibits (free from the ticket desk), you can skim round quickly or stop to pick up details about periods that interest you. A map on the ground floor lights up in sections showing different phases of Amsterdam's growth. There's a sudden expansion in the Golden Age and an even bigger one in the late 20th century, after which all the lights go out with an alarming thud. You can get a bird's eye view of early Amsterdam from a medieval painting (quite a feat of imagination for an artist who had never been higher than the top of the Oude Kerk tower); see a collection of the surprisingly basic navigational instruments that guided the Dutch East Indiamen all over the world; and push buttons that make period music come out from behind models and paintings. There's a whole room of paintings, banners and relics connected with Amsterdam's 'miracle' (*see* pp.69 and 84). Up a spiral staircase at the top of the building you can listen to recordings of the city's various carillons and even have a go at playing the one taken from the medieval Munttoren (*see* opposite)—though if you get too carried away an attendant clambers up to glower at you. The museum also stages excellent temporary exhibitions on specialist aspects of Amsterdam's history.

The Begijnhof

Tucked behind the Amsterdam Historical Museum, the Begijnhof has the atmosphere of a quiet village square. You can hardly believe, in the leafy calm walled in by its neat gables, that the busiest parts of the city are only a few metres away. The Béguines were an order of lay nuns, founded in the 15th century, who, through self-effacement and powerful family connections, remained undisturbed by the religious upheavals of the following centuries. Sister Antonia, the last of the order, died in the house at No.26 in 1971. The small mound near the gate (covered by flowers in the spring) is the grave of another Béguine, Sister Cornelia Arens. When she died in 1654 she was buried, at her own request, in the gutter. Most of the houses were rebuilt in the 17th and 18th centuries, but at No.34 you can see the last remaining original façade, one of only two medieval wooden houses left in Amsterdam. Next door is an old clandestine church which still holds weekly mass. The church across the pathway was the original Begijnkerk, consecrated in 1419 and the only medieval church in the city with the tower in its original state. After a period of disuse during the Reformation, it was offered to Protestant dissenters fleeing England in 1607 and became known as the **English Church**. A plaque on the tower and stained glass in the chancel commemorate the fact that this group formed the core of the Pilgrim Fathers who sailed for America in 1620.

Some of Amsterdam's most enduringly popular cafés lie just outside the Begijnhof, around the Spui. At the southern end of this attractive square, the diminutive statue of **Het Lieverdje** ('The Little Darling', an impish Amsterdam rascal) was the focal point of provocative 'happenings' in the 1960s (*see* p.71). Down Voetboogstraat is the outrageous gate of the old **Rasphuis**, the male equivalent of the Spinhuis, where men had to saw wood into a fine powder used for dye. Carved figures are tied down by real chains. A castigating Amsterdam raises her hand high, but someone has pinched her flail. The Calvinist custodians of the Rasphuis thought up a most ingenious method of compelling the inmates to good soul-saving work. A 17th-century British consul in Amsterdam was much impressed: 'They are beaten with a bull's pissel [penis] and if yet they rebel and won't work, are set in a tub, where if they do not pump, the water will swell over their heads.'

Central Amsterdam (East)

The Flower Market and Rembrandtplein

After all the fuss that's made about it in the brochures, Amsterdam's **floating flower market** can be a bit of a disappointment. It's not very long, not all that cheap, you can't tell from the street that it's floating, and it's full of confused tourists clutching maps and asking each other: 'Is this it?' But the buckets of cut flowers and rows of potted plants are pretty to look at, and on hot days the mingling scents of the flowers fill the whole passage. If you're a keen gardener there's a tempting variety of seeds and bulbs that can be posted home (but *see* p.6).

At the eastern end of the market you come to **Muntplein** and the **Munttoren** (Mint Tower), a solitary clock tower with a polygonal base, that is yet another steeple by Hendrick de Keyser—a verticomaniac responsible for nearly every spike on Amsterdam's skyline. The base dates from 1490 and was part of Regulierspoort, one of the gates in the old city wall. The structure gets its name because the guard house was briefly used as a mint in 1672–3, when the French were occupying much of the rest of the Netherlands and the Amsterdam merchants couldn't get at their usual source of Rijksdollars and ductatoons.

Halfway along Reguliersbreestraat—the road that conects Muntplein and Rembrandtplein—you'll find the **Tuschinski Cinema**. Abraham Tuschinski, a Jewish refugee from Poland, saw his first film in 1910 and immediately wanted to own a cinema. He got a friend to write to Pathé in French, requesting the machinery and

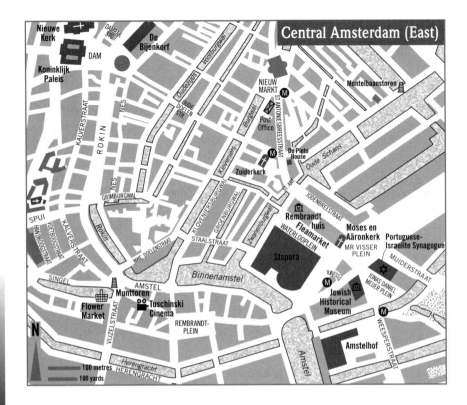

rights to show films. His first 'bioscope' opened in 1911 in a disused seamen's church with a converted outside lavatory as the box office. But Tuschinski wanted a cinema where his 'guests' could lose themselves in another world. In 1921 he was wealthy enough to achieve his dream. You walk through a soaring Art Deco façade with flag-poles, camp statuary and curly iron lamps into an interior that lurches between heady luxury and high kitsch. It's a stylistic cocktail of five different colours of marble, Persian carpets, thousands of electric lights, wall decorations, stained glass and exotic *objets d'art.* You can go on a guided tour (*Sun and Mon during July and Aug, 10.30am; adm*), or come back later and see a film. Ask for a balcony ticket in the main cinema. It doesn't matter what's showing; the interval will be reward enough. On the first Sunday of each month during the winter, there's a special morning screening of a silent movie, with musical accompaniment and sound effects from the original Wurlitzer organ.

The concrete and glass **Cineac** (opposite the Tuschinski) seems from another century. It's hard to believe it was built only 13 years later. The architect, J. Duiker, was a movie fanatic. The auditorium opened directly on to the street and the projectionist could be seen from outside through the glass wall on the first floor. Rebuilding in the 1960s and 1980s all but destroyed the original concept. In the late 1990s Cineac got yet another facelift, this time emerging as a restaurant in the Planet Hollywood chain owned, appro-priately, by a group of movie stars.

Reguliersbreestraat opens on to **Rembrandtplein**, which was a butter market until the mid-19th century when a group of worthy burghers plonked a statue (Amsterdam's first) in the middle and grew some grass around it. Cafés sprang up. Variety artists from the halls along the Amstel would meet their agents at the posh Café Kroon, then retreat across the square to the darker recesses of the Hotel Schiller where they felt more at home among the artists, writers and other friends of proprietor Frits Schiller (whose paintings still decorate the walls). Nowadays the square is a favourite after-work stopover and a magnet to tourists, who come for the relaxed Amsterdam conviviality. You can lie about on the grass (among masses of tulips if it's spring) or sit and drink at one of the pavement cafés. Traffic is banished from most of the square but buskers keep the noise level high. When the sun sets, things get even livelier. The cafés change gear as the night staff come on duty. Music systems are turned on full, jazz from one corner, Dutch sing-along from another. Congas of drunken Dutchmen snake out of pubs and around bemused policemen. Spanish schoolgirls move about in wide-eyed groups. At one bar the three barmen break out at intervals into a well-rehearsed dance routine. Whether you're carousing with the revellers, or just sitting and watching it all, it's a cheerful place to stop for a drink.

Waterlooplein

Waterlooplein was originally the manmade island of Vlooyenburg, so named because the Amstel flooded it with monotonous regularity. (*Vlooyen* means 'flow', and also 'fleas', which seems rather more appropriate these days as Waterlooplein is the site of a fleamarket.) Vlooyenburg was built on a sandbank in the Amstel in 1593, and soon became a popular neighbourhood for Sephardic Jews arriving from Spain and Portugal. In the mid-17th century they were joined by the Ashkenazim (from eastern and central Europe), and Vlooyenburg became the heart of the Jewish quarter. Despite its sogginess, it was at first quite well-to-do. Prosperous Sephardim lived along the water's edge but, with the great influx of poorer Ashkenazim, buildings were constantly subdivided and more and more people were crammed into less and less space. The economic decline of the 18th and 19th centuries made conditions even worse. A contemporary traveller complained that everywhere there were 'horrible piles of excrement and offal, the walls around drenched with urine'. Later in the 19th century, however, the economy boomed and conditions improved. In 1882 the council reclaimed more land, and filled up two canals to create a large market square to replace the squalid, crowded network of alleys. In 1886 the clusters of market traders who had overrun the side streets were moved to the newly created Waterlooplein. There was much grizzling because it was so open and windy (an objection you're sure to sympathize with if the weather is bad) but soon the market had the reputation of being the busiest and most cheerful in Amsterdam.

The district was devastated during the Nazi occupation. Convoys of trucks would rumble into the market and cart away hundreds of people at a time. Of the 130,000 Jews living in Amsterdam in 1938 (10 per cent of the total population), 100,000 did not survive the war. The empty houses they left behind were stripped of anything burnable during the freezing winters. For a long time the old Jewish quarter lay empty and derelict, as if the buildings themselves were in a state of shock.

When the city council announced plans (in 1979) to build a combined city hall and opera house on the site, there was public outrage. The city hall was ugly, the opera house seemed unnecessary, and the few people still living in the neighbourhood would have to be evicted. The building was nicknamed the **Stopera**—from *stadhuis* (city hall) and opera. 'Stop the Stopera' campaigns were held all over Amsterdam but, as always, the council won.

The new **Muziektheater** (the opera house) opened in 1986, followed two years later by the Stadhuis. The city hall is indeed bland and ugly, but most Amsterdammers grudgingly admit to the beauty of the Muziektheater. Its glass walls, sweeping stairways, soft pink colour scheme and marble coliseum-like shell look their best in the early evening. As the light fades, the whole building seems to glow. The artists themselves are delighted with the state-of-the-art equipment and huge dressing rooms. There are even colour-coded stairways backstage (yellow for opera, pink for ballet and blue for technicians). But there were some massive architectural blunders backstage as well—the ballet rehearsal rooms have ceilings so low that dancers couldn't practise lifts, the orchestra didn't have a rehearsal room at all and the scenery lifts were at the opposite end of the building from the loading entrances. Both the Netherlands Ballet and Opera are resident, and the programme is varied, with many international visitors (*see* p.163, 'Entertainment and Nightlife').

In a passageway connecting the Stadhuis and Muziektheater three water columns show the tides at IJmuiden and Vlissingen (below knee-level) and the sobering sight of the level reached during the 1953 Zeeland flood (way above your head). You can walk down a flight of stairs, below sea level, and touch the bronze knob (its position calculated in the 17th century) which represents the zero point from which heights in much of Europe are calculated.

Around the Stopera stretches Amsterdam's famous **fleamarket**. There's a wonderful lack of logic in its layout and a pervasive air of bargain-hunting and money-making. Antiquarian booksellers rub shoulders with purveyors of used porn. Lines of Peruvians, Balinese and Indonesians sell bright national clothing and jewellery. There are heaps of mildewy second-hand overcoats and racks of precision-selected designer classics, tables of used kitchenware and haphazard conglomerations of expensive antiques. The rows of oddities and exotica are punctuated by more down-to-earth stalls selling bicycle parts, underwear or cleaning equipment. A fringe of derelicts gathers around the edge of the market, returning day after day with little spreads of unwanted (and sometimes unidentifiable) bric-a-brac. In one corner a muttering clump of old men surreptitiously flash watches and bits of gold at each other. A relentless stream of collectors, tourists, Amsterdammers looking for bargains and the openly curious flows up and down between the stalls.

Around Waterlooplein

The eastern corner of the fleamarket is dominated by the **Mozes en Aäron Kerk**. In 1649 it was a clandestine Roman Catholic church, named after the gable stones (one depicting Moses and the other Aaron) on the two house-fronts that hid it. The present rather heavy-looking neoclassical church (with wooden towers painted to look like sandstone) was built in the 19th century, but you can still see the original gable stones round the back. The church was famous for its choir and even the local Jews would come in for the music on Christmas night. The Jewish philosopher Spinoza lived in the house next door to the original church; the Sephardic community excommunicated him for his secular beliefs, but regretted their haste when he went on to become one of the most lauded intellectuals of his time.

Diagonally across from the church is the **Oudezijds Huiszittenhuis** (the rather Dickensian-sounding 'Old Side Home for the Domiciled Poor', built in 1654). The Alms Board Wardens would enter through a grand public staircase on the other side of the building. Paupers would huddle for hours in the courtyard waiting for handouts of bread, cheese and peat. The peat was stored next door in the Arsenaal (built 1610), and the road down the side of this warehouse is still called Turfsteeg (Peat Alley).

Off the northern end of the market, on Jodenbreestraat, is the **Rembrandthuis** (*open Mon–Sat 10–5, Sun and holidays 1–5; adm*). Rembrandt lived at Jodenbreestraat 4–6 for nearly twenty years (*see* p.111) and his old house is now a museum. It has been carefully restored to its original state, using old plans and descriptions to ensure authenticity. In the adjoining modern wing you can see the pick of Rembrandt's etchings, including a series of tiny self-portraits of the painter pulling funny faces. Rembrandt used himself as a model more than any other 17th-century painter. He even slips into crowd scenes on some of his larger canvases. There's a slide-show on Rembrandt's life, in English, in the basement (hourly on the hour until 3pm).

Following St Antoniesbreestraat north from the Rembrandthuis, you come to the skull-and-crossbones adorned churchyard gate of the **Zuiderkerk** (*open Mon–Fri 12.30–4.30, Thurs 6–9; tower open June–Sept Wed–Sat 2pm–4pm, adm*), built between 1603 and 1614, which was the first Protestant church to be built after the Reformation, and is a triumph of Amsterdam's great steeple designer, Hendrick de Keyser. The soaring spire with its decorative Ionic columns and its clusters of slightly oriental pinnacles was much admired by Christopher Wren, and inspired the designs of his City of London churches. During the harsh winter of 1944–5 more people died in the neighbourhood than the authorities were able to bury, and the church had to be used as a temporary mortuary. Today it's a deeply uninteresting information centre for urban development.

Northeast of the church, on Oude Schans, is the **Montelbaanstoren**, a defence tower built in 1512 when the wharves were still outside the city walls. In 1606 (when the tower was no longer used for defence) the builder Hendrick de Keyser added a wonderfully gratuitous spire. This was an activity he apparently enjoyed: he's responsible for much of Amsterdam's spiky skyline. Five years after it was built, the Montelbaanstoren began to tilt over. Unlike their more flamboyant counterparts in Pisa, the good burghers of Amsterdam would have none of it: they attached ropes to the top and pulled it straight again. Rembrandt loved to draw it, and it's still a favourite subject for visiting artists. VOC sailors left from the Montelbaanstoren to join the large seafaring East Indiamen which were too bulky to navigate as far as Amsterdam and were moored far to the north. These days it houses the city water authority.

The Synagogues

Amsterdammers nickname their city 'Mokum', from the Yiddish '*Mokum aleph*', 'the best city of all', and they'll often leave you with a cheery '*de mazzel*'—'good luck'. As early as the 16th century, Amsterdam's religious tolerance was attracting Jews fleeing persecution in other European countries. This tolerance stemmed less from the milk of Christian kindness than from sound commercial reasoning. The Sephardic Jews brought good inside information on Portuguese colonies and trade routes. The Ashkenazim had skills that fuelled the Golden Age boom. The city's trade guilds, however, refused to admit Jews and so Jews could only find work in fields that did not present direct competition to locals. Many were physicians or apothecaries, or worked in high-risk finance and in the new trades associated with the cotton or diamond industries. But they could retain their religion and didn't have to live in ghettos or wear distinguishing badges. Amsterdam soon became known as the 'Jerusalem of the West'.

To the east of Waterlooplein, a complex of four old Ashkenazi synagogues now houses the **Jewish Historical Museum** (*open daily 11–5 except Yom Kippur; adm*).The Ashkenazim, fleeing pogroms in Poland and massacres in Germany, arrived in Amsterdam in the mid-17th century. They soon outnumbered the Sephardim (who had begun arriving half a century earlier) by ten to one, but were pitifully poorer. They really had to struggle to build themselves a synagogue. Just as they were about to begin, their attention was diverted by Sabbatai Zvi, a false Messiah who claimed he would lead them back to the Holy Land. They waited for four years before giving up on him and building the Grote Sjoel (Grand Synagogue) in 1671. As the congregation expanded, more temples were built on adjacent plots. The Obbene Sjoel (Upstairs Synagogue, 1686) was followed by the Dritt Sjoel (Third Synagogue, 1700). The Neie Sjoel (New Synagogue, 1752) opened with great ceremony. Tickets were sold at an outrageous ƒ10 (though crowds of poor were let in for free). Ashkenazi Congregation records revel in the pomp of the occasion and bristle with anti-Sephardic rivalry: 'An orchestra pit has been placed next to the bima (raised central platform), where the musicians took their places with their music. Below that there was an uncircumcised musician playing a contrabass and for the rest only Jews who played for free and even one Portuguese Jew.' The complex was gutted during the Second World War and remained empty until the 1980s, when the temples were restored and reopened as the historical museum.

The museum's displays do not dwell on gruesome images of the Holocaust and tales of woe, but are a combination of works of art, memorabilia and artefacts aimed at explaining Jewish life. Naturally it is moving to see one of the yellow stars Jews had to wear during the war, but the museum also diffuses a positive energy from the delicately embroidered prayer shawls, photographs of Bar Mitzvahs and overwhelmingly extravagant silverware also on show. The 'Jewish identity' displays in the New Synagogue explain aspects of tradition, Zionism and the reaction to persecution. Most of the Great Synagogue is given over to expositions of the religion itself—the rituals, festivals and rites of passage. You can see the original Mikveh (ritual bath) unearthed during the renovations, a rather cute circumcision set and some stylish modern temple silverware. In the galleries of the Great Synagogue paintings and old documents illustrate the history of Jews in Amsterdam. The connecting walkways house temporary exhibitions and work by Jewish artists (Jaap Kaas's fierce, funny bronze monkeys are worth looking for). The museum also has a library and media centre, a kosher café and a good bookshop.

Across the way from the museum is the **Portuguese-Israelite Synagogue** (*open April–Oct, Sun–Fri 10–4; Nov–March Mon–Thurs 10–4, Fri 10–3, Sun 10–12; adm*). There was little love lost between the Sephardim and Ashkenazim. Even today old Sephardic Jews can remember being warned off '*vrotte Tedesco*' (filthy Germans) with: '*Je kan nog beter met een Goya trouwen dan met een Tedesco.*' ('Rather marry a gentile than an Ashkenazi.') The Sephardim were a smaller but more powerful community with a class of wealthy professionals, and were happily welcomed into Dutch society. Their Portuguese-Israelite Synagogue (or 'Snoge' after the Spanish *esnoga*) was built between 1671 and 1675 as a showpiece. It was more than twice the size of the Ashkenazi temple completed the year before on the site next door. Only in Amsterdam could Jews make such an open display of their place of worship. There was no established building style for synagogues, and the architect, Elias Bouman (who had also designed the Ashkenazi building), claimed he was creating an imitation of Solomon's temple following descriptions in the Old Testament. However, the building he produced, with its mahogany pews and brass chandeliers, bears a remarkable resemblance to the larger Christian churches of the period. It's an imposing brick block that dwarfs the buildings around it. The Hebrew letters of the name 'Aboab' are worked into the text above the door (which translates as 'And I—in Thy great love—shall enter Thy House') in acknowledgement of Rabbi Isaac Aboab de Fonseca's efforts to get the synagogue built.

Beside the synagogue is a peaceful square, the **Jonas Daniël Meijerplein**. Jonas Daniël Meijer (1780–1834) whizzed through his school years and was a Doctor of Law by the time he was 16. He was the first Jew admitted to the Bar and one of the first to fight for and get full Dutch citizenship. As a favourite of the potty but enlightened Louis Bonaparte and under William I, Meijer did a lot to improve the legal position of the Jews. In the middle of the square, standing stalwartly, his sleeves rolled up and chin cocked defiantly—ready for a fight—is Mari Andriessen's bronze statue **De Dokwerker** (The Dockworker, 1952). Every year on 25 February people lay flowers at its feet to commemorate the resistance to Nazi occupation. This is the anniversary of the general strike which swept through a shocked Amsterdam in a matter of hours as an expression of solidarity with the Jews after the first Nazi round-ups. During his brief spell as a theology student in Amsterdam, Van Gogh could be seen 'with his books clamped under his arm, holding snowdrops in his left hand in front of his chest, his head stooped forward slightly', making his way across this square to the third floor of the house at No.13, where he studied classics with Mendes da Costa for *f*1.50 a lesson. (The original house has been demolished.)

The Canals

Amsterdam's population increased tenfold between 1550 and 1650. In the early 17th century the far-sighted city fathers were already planning to push the city boundaries outwards with three grand concentric canals. The Prinsengracht (Princes' Canal), Keizersgracht (Emperor's Canal) and Herengracht (Gentlemen's Canal, rather than Kings', a nice move by bourgeois Amsterdam) were intended for rentiers and rich merchants who wanted to live away from the smells and noise of the harbour. The shops and industries there were banished to poorer parts of town. The city hall parcelled out the land in 30ft, rather than the usual 20ft lots (though wily speculators would buy up two adjacent plots and split them into three and the really opulent merchants would combine two into a single house). Space was at a premium in Amsterdam and you were taxed on the width of your house, so height often became an expression of wealth and the boastful decoration was applied to the inside, or to the gables. Even the rear façades got special attention. ('Our Lord finished off a canary's behind as neatly as its front,' remarked one contemporary architect.) Narrow houses mean winding stairways, uncongenial to four-poster beds and heavy carved dressers, hence most Amsterdam buildings have a hoist beam poking out from the gable so you can winch your furniture up the outside. Many lean dangerously over the street, not necessarily because they're about to subside into the city's soggy soil, but because this shows off the gables to passing pedestrians and makes the building more imposing. It also stops rising furniture from crashing into the wall. Angles became so alarming that a bye-law was introduced in 1565 to put a stop to the more adventurous tilts.

The Herengracht

Fashion has claimed each canal, at one time or another, as Amsterdam's best address, but it was the Herengracht that was really built to impress. It's more grand than pretty, a little ravaged by centuries of ostentation. Subsequent occupiers have (until recently) thought nothing of pulling down old buildings to make way for bigger and better displays of wealth, but the survivors have an endearing panache. Some extraordinary gables poke up out of the trees that line the canal. Monumental sandstone frontages seem to push aside the traditional dainty gabled brick façades. Cornices curled with acanthus leaves, strung with garlands and surmounted by urns lord it over the modest step-gables, though the odd defiant bell or neck-gable might reply with an extravagant claw-piece.

At No.120 you can see one of the few smaller 17th-century houses to have kept its façade free of later additions and amendments. Farther along, at Nos.170–2 is the Bartolotti House, built in 1617 by Hendrick de Keyser (who designed most of Amsterdam's spiky towers) for West India Company director Van den Heuvel. (It was

The Canals

paid for by Van den Heuvel's mother-in-law who stipulated the house be called after her late husband.) Its enormous neck-gable is all but invisible under the encrustation of pilasters, pinnacles and decorative reliefs. These days part of it houses the **Nederlands Theater Instituut** (*open Tues–Fri 11–5, Sat and Sun 1–5; adm*) which always has good exhibitions, usually of the sort where you push buttons or pull levers and make things happen. If there are three of you, you can raise a storm with the wind, thunder and lightning machines on the ground floor.

The white sandstone house next door (known as the White House), built in 1668, was the first by the later famous 17th-century domestic architect, Philips Vingboons. The dignified row of four houses (Nos.364–70) farther down the canal, with clean lines, stately neck-gables and quiet decoration are also by Vingboons.

At No.366 is the **Bijbels Museum** (Bible Museum; *open Mon–Sat 10–5, Sun 1–5; adm; partially closed for renovation until late 2000*) worth a visit only if you are interested in models of Solomon's temple and the history of the Dutch Bible over the past millennium—though the interior does preserve ceiling paintings by the 18th-century design supremo Jacob de Wit.

No.380–2 is an outrageous confection—a late 19th-century imitation of a French Renaissance château scrunched down to city mansion size. Just up the canal is a pretty little 17th-century house with a simple festooned neck-gable (No.394), and across the way, No.401 manages to lean in three different directions at once.

The bit of the canal between Vijzelstraat and Leidsestraat is known as the **Golden Bend**, perhaps more for the wealth of the inhabitants than the refinement of the architecture. There are two clusters of more gorgeous and more graceful dwellings further up the canal that better deserve the epithet, though the elegant Louis XIV building with curved balustrades at No.475 does have the reputation of being Amsterdam's most beautiful house.

Amsterdam *burgemeesters* have been officially resident at No.502 since 1927, and next door (Nos.504–10) is a little stretch of wildly decorative claw-pieces. Tigers, dolphins and seagods curl about the gables and for once upstage the grander buildings.

At No.605, you'll come to the **Willet-Holthuysen Museum** (*open Mon–Fri 10–5, Sat and Sun 11–5; adm*), a 17th-century canal house. For two centuries it was occupied by a succession of Amsterdam glitterati. The last, Sandrina Holthuysen, had spent most of her life married to Abraham Willet, an avid collector of paintings, art books, glass, ceramics and silver. When she died in 1895, alone, riddled with cancer and surrounded by cats, she left the house and contents to Amsterdam as a museum. The city then filled it with pickings from a number of similar bequests. Most of the rooms are now reconstructed as 18th-century period pieces, with the different collections scattered about the house, mainly in rather stiff salons and boudoirs; there's also a crisp formal garden. Everything seems in its Sunday best—including the surreal headless mannequins that stand strategically about, sporting 18th-century costume. It's a good place to get an insider's view of one of the more stately canal houses.

The Keizersgracht

Less ostentatious than the Herengracht, the Keizersgracht nevertheless offers some architectural gems. At No.319 you can see the first house (built in 1639) in which architect Philips Vingboons combined classic elements (the Doric pilasters) with the traditional Dutch style. Nearby is the imposing classicist **Felix Meritis building** (No.324 on the left-hand side; *open daily 5pm–midnight*). It was built in 1778 to house an arts and scientific society founded in the spirit of Voltaire and Rousseau. With an observatory, library, laboratories and a small concert hall, the Felix Meritis Foundation became the cultural centre of the Dutch Enlightenment. When Napoleon made his triumphal entry to Amsterdam, he was punted up the canal and ushered with pride into the building. He got no further than the foyer, spat on the floor, said the place stank of tobacco smoke, and strutted back to the boat. Towards the end of the 19th century the society went into terminal decline. The building was later used as the Communist Party headquarters, but won back its cultural prominence in the 1970s when it housed the Shaffy Theatre, in the forefront of the European avant-garde. The theatre lost some of its significance and impact during the 1980s, but the Felix Meritis Society has been revived. As an arts complex and the home of Amsterdam's Summer University, the building is once again playing host to artists and intellectuals from around the world.

A wander farther along the canal reveals more architectural delights. The startlingly large windows of No.440 (built 1897) originally lit a clothing design studio and factory. It must have been the world's most gracious sweatshop. The bank at No.452 was once a private residence. Designed by Outshoorn in 1860, it is one of the last of a series of grand canal houses, influenced by French and Italian architecture, that were built by the three great domestic architects—Vingboons, van Campen and Outshoorn—over a period of 200 years. At No.546 nothing of the façade, except the windows, has changed since it was built in 1760. The bell-gable is a good example of the playful cake-icing Louis XV decoration. The ornately decorated building that cuts the corner with Leidsestraat is German-inspired—the Dutch were more into solid right angles at corners. A frieze of fat naked babies, lurking in shrubberies and grumpily pushing carts and canoes, runs around the wall. The bust commemorates the 17th-century poet Pieter Cornelisz. Hooft. The pompous building on the opposite corner was built on the site of Van Gogh's uncle's art shop for an insurance company in the late 19th century, but is now the refined **Metz** department store. Inside, you can mount stairs, passing racks of tasteful kitchenware and mounds of Liberty prints. As you climb, the atmosphere becomes increasingly rarefied and the floors emptier and emptier. By the time you're nearing the top, there's hardly anything for sale at all. The few pieces of designer furniture scattered about look more like museum pieces than anything you could put in the dining-room. At the top is a café designed by Gerrit Rietveld. Gazing through its glass cupola, you have a rare opportunity to view Amsterdam's spider's web from on high. Back down on ground level, try to get to the **Van Loon Museum** at Keizersgracht 672 (*open Fri–Mon 11–5; adm*). The house still belongs to the Van Loon family (who live in a small apartment next door) and offers the best example of all of Amsterdam patrician home life.

The patch where the Keizersgracht crosses Nieuwe Spiegelstraat is renowned for its antiques shops and art galleries. Known as the **Spiegelkwartier**, this is one of the two quarters in Amsterdam dedicated to one particular business (the only other one being the red-light district). Here you'll find top-quality antiques galore—shops crammed with elaborate clocks, solemn rows of carved wooden dressers and ornate gilded furniture. Enormous chandeliers hang at eye-level, and gold, silver and colourful gems shine at you from all sides. Tucked amongst all this grandeur, you can still find idiosyncratic little shops, obviously the domain of a single collector. Aalderink (Spiegelgracht 15) has a sparse but expertly selected range of oriental pieces and Africana. Thom and Lenny Nelis (Keizersgracht 541) sell curious and unmentionable medical antiques. Anneke Schat (Spiegelgracht 20a) makes delicate, sculpted jewellery inspired by spiders' webs and butterflies and much favoured by Dutch glitterati and the royal family. If your souvenir budget runs to multiple noughts you could pop into Elisabeth den Bieman de Haas for a little Chagall litho or bright modern oil from COBRA, the post-war expressionist movement (*see* p.60). Roel Houwink (Nieuwe Spiegelstraat 57) has one of those shops you could potter about in for ages—everything from musical boxes to escutcheons nicked from under the nose of a Prince of Orange. Kramers (Nieuwe Spiegelstraat 64) has tangles of old jewellery and trinkets, barrels of clay pipe bowls and a roomful of Delft tiles ranging from the 15th to 20th centuries and costing anything from the price of a sandwich to double your air fare.

The Prinsengracht

The Prinsengracht is the site of one of the most enduring symbols of Amsterdam—the spire of the Westerkerk. The **Westerkerk** (West Church) was consecrated in 1631. Its sober Protestant interior is brightened by large painted organ shutters showing a dancing King David and a voluptuous Queen of Sheba laden with gifts for Solomon. Rembrandt was buried here, but no one knows where the body is. There's a flutter of academic excitement every time old bones are found, but it's most likely that he was crunched up during the digging of an underground car park. A memorial plaque has been put up near his son Titus's grave. The church tower, known as the Westertoren, built by (you guessed it) Hendrick de Keyser, is Amsterdam's highest (85m) and contains its heaviest bell (7500kg). The Westertoren has something of the significance to Amsterdammers that St Paul's has to Londoners. Sentimental songs are addressed to it, and you can only be a true Jordaaner (*see* below) if you were born in its shadow. In the 1940s a fervent engineer climbed out on to the top of the tower during a violent storm and, with the help of a theodolite, worked out that it swayed all of 3cm. During the summer months you can climb up rather more sedately for a rare view of Amsterdam from high up (*open April–Sept, Mon–Sat 10–4; adm*). At the top is the gaudily painted imperial crown of Maximilian of Austria. Amsterdam's merchants gained considerable international clout when, out of gratitude for support given to the Austro-Burgundian princes, he granted them the right to use the crown in the city coat of arms.

If you walk around the outside of the church you can see the house where Descartes lived when he was in Amsterdam (Westermarkt 6); the pink marble triangles of the Homomonument which commemorates gays killed in the concentration camps; and a sad little statue of Anne Frank, who wrote her diary just around the corner.

The **Anne Frank Huis** is at Prinsengracht 263 (*open Sept–May Mon–Sat 9–5, Sun 10–5; June–Aug Mon–Sat 9–7, Sun 10–7; adm*). Anne Frank, the second daughter of German-Jewish immigrants living in Amsterdam, got her diary for her 13th birthday on 12 June 1942. Three weeks later her family were '*onderduikers*' ('divers')—in hiding from the Nazi occupying forces. They lived for two years in a small suite of rooms at the back of Anne's father's herb and spice business on the Prinsengracht. The windows had always been painted over to protect the herbs previously stored there, the entrance was hidden behind a hinged bookcase and, apart from four trusted office workers who supplied them with food, nobody knew they were there. Later they were joined by a dentist Fritz Pfeffer (whom Anne calls 'Dussel') and the Van Pelses ('Van Daans') and their son Peter. For two years they were cooped up in what became known as the Annexe, and Anne wrote in her diaries about life with the petulant and demanding Mrs Van Daan and her hen-pecked spouse, of the tiresomely childish Dussel, and of moments of joy and desperation within her own family. No one knows who betrayed them, but in August 1944 German police barged into the offices, walked straight up to the bookcase and demanded entry. All the hideaways, except Anne's father, died in concentration camps in Germany. The office cleaner found the diary in which Anne had written with astonishing lucidity about life in the 'Annexe' and about growing up. When it was given to her father, he found that she'd already began to edit it for publication. It appeared in 1947 with the title The Annexe, the one Anne herself had chosen. Now it's printed in over 50 languages and an estimated thirteen million copies have been sold. Well over half a million people visit the Anne Frank Huis annually. The house has been restored to its pre-war condition, giving moving impression of what life was like for the families who hid there. In new premises next door you'll find an exhibition on Jews in Amsterdam and racial oppression.

Towards the eastern end of the Prinsengracht, south of Rembrandtplein, you'll find **Amstelveld**, a secluded square with a white wooden church and small Monday flower market, tucked away from the surrounding bustle. The recently restored 17th-century **Amstelkerk** has a popular left-wing preacher and is the one of the few churches in central Amsterdam that packs in a congregation. It isn't continuously open to the public, but sometimes stages chamber recitals. In front of the church, crossing the Prinsengracht, runs the Reguliersgracht, held by many to be the prettiest canal in town with its quiet gables and humpback bridges.

De Negen Straatjes

Crisscrossing the main canals, De Negen Straatjes ('The Nine Alleys') offer the most intriguing shopping in Amsterdam. **Huidenstraat** has trendy second-hand clothes stores and shops crammed with lamps and light fittings—from original Art Nouveau to bright and bulbous 1960s products. Pompadour at No.5 sells impossibly tempting hand-made chocolates. Across the Keizersgracht bridge in **Runstraat** is the Witte Tanden Winkel (White Teeth Shop) for nothing but the tooth—psychedelic and electric tooth-brushes, pastes galore, curious aids and sound clinical advice. Just the place to expiate your sins after Pompadour. All along the way, furniture from antiques shops tumbles out into the streets, though they're not always as cheap as the image suggests. **Wolvenstraat** has more second-hand clothes shops (one with Queen Mother hats) and a button shop (some in such shapes and sizes that their function is barely recognizable). **Berenstraat** is home to some of the younger, trendier art galleries. One, Animation Art: 'Name that Toon' sells storyboards and cels (the acetate originals from which cartoons are made) of everyone from Betty Boop to Winnie-the-Pooh. Hartenstraat has more fashion shops and another eccentric collector's outlet—this time vintage electronic equipment. The jolly naked illustrations of Eddie Varekamp that have found their way on to T-shirts and coffee mugs are on sale from his studio shop (No.30). Reestraat has a *poppendokter* (doll's doctor). Puppets hang from the ceiling, dolls of all sorts crowd the window and a disconcerting catalogue of dolls' faces hangs on the wall. Next door is a candle shop. Coloured, scented, sculpted, altar candles and erotic candles hang from the ceiling, are stacked on shelves or poked into odd candlesticks and elaborate cande-labra—and they're not at silly prices.

Leidseplein and Around

On the outer edge of the 'Canal Belt', Leidseplein is Amsterdam's tourist vortex, with more than the usual complement of British boys in Union Jack shorts learning the strength of Dutch lager. Fire-eaters and itinerant musicians busk while your pockets are picked, though at night the atmosphere improves a little as the square becomes the festive hub of late-night transport. As a 17th-century traveller cautioned, 'Here be sure to furnish yourself with money.' The neon alleys leading off the square are lined with expensive and nasty restaurants and nightclubs with names like 'Cash'. Leidsestraat, the northern exit, is clogged with pedestrians and bicycles travelling on no particular side until, bells clanging, a yellow tram hurtles down the central rails scattering all. Mainly airline offices, 24-hour bureaux de change and shops selling clogs and Taiwan Delft, Leidsestraat is happily avoided.

On the southern end of the square, is the **Stadsschouwburg** (Municipal Theatre; *open nightly; backstage tours in summer daily at noon; adm; duration 1hr*). State theatres in Amsterdam were usually out in the sticks, and kept burning down. The first one on this site was built in 1774 (when Leidseplein was on the edge of town) and, after suffering the usual fate, was replaced by the present building in the late 19th century. The new building was designed by Jan Springer, the bohemian kingpin of Architectura et Amicitia, a wickedly unrestrained artists' society. Budget cuts put a stop to his more florid decorations, yet still the public disapproved of the result. Springer went into a sulk and virtually abandoned his career. The building has a small stage and the new Muziektheater on Waterlooplein has rather stolen its thunder, but it continues to host local and international productions.

Next door, the jutting balconies and odd protruding windows of the **American Hotel** are a Dutch interpretation of an original Art Nouveau design. The architect, W. Kromhout, is considered a forerunner of the fanciful Amsterdam School (*see* pp.134–6). The writers and artists who once frequented the Café Américain (*open daily 10am–midnight*) have fled the tourist armies of the Leidseplein, but it's still worth a visit for the glass Japanese parasol lampshades and patterned windows that filter the hard Amsterdam light into a soft and playful kaleidoscope.

The Jordaan

The inviting side streets, alleys and intimate canals of the Jordaan are lined with cosy cafés, curious shops and good restaurants, all luring you to ferret about in your own way. Jordaan comes from the French '*jardin*', but during the housing crisis in the 19th century this 'garden' on the outskirts of the city disappeared under rows of working-class housing. The houses were small, dark and close together and all the smellier industries (such as tanning) were banished to the Jordaan from the posher areas of town. Naming the streets after flowers didn't cheer things up much. Conditions were appalling, but the Jordaaners developed a pride and a culture akin to London's cockneys.

The true Jordaaner is born in the small patch bound by Prinsengracht, Brouwersgracht, Lijnbaansgracht and Looiersgracht, in the shadow of the Westertoren (*see* inside back cover map). The church tower is the symbol of the Jordaan. Jordaaners have their own accent and are renowned for a wry sense of humour and for being adept pigeon-fanciers. Everyone over the age of forty is known as '*ome*' or '*tante*'—uncle or aunt. (Until a decade or so ago, you could still be woken by Ome Hein, a professional 'waker-up', as he made his early morning rounds with a pet goat.) They're a rebellious lot. There have been a number of historical riots, including one in 1886 when police tried to put a stop to the gory-sounding pastime of 'eel-jerking'; and another when the council threatened to reduce the dole in 1934. Recently, traditional Jordaan life has been given a new edge by an influx of artists and music students. You're quite likely to be accompanied on your walk by strains of Mozart and will probably encounter odd art objects suspended over the street.

Lovers of curiosa and antiques should head for the area around **Looiersgracht**. At No.38 is the Rommelmarkt (literally 'rubbish market'), an indoor fleamarket that seems almost subterranean. Entering through a small street door, you seem to walk forever down a long, dim corridor lined with piles of old toys, tea caddies, zippo lighters, 1960s records and magazines. The further you penetrate, the more precious things become. You might even pick up some antique Japanese lacquerware or an Art Deco vase.

At the end of the canal you come to the **De Looier Indoor Antiques Market**, a collectors' and dealers' market pitched halfway between Rommelmarket junk and Spiegelkwartier splendour. Stallholders have a lively commercial spirit—they even have their own newspaper and weekly bridge drives. There are regular specialist fairs in this honeycomb of little stands selling furniture, glass, old lace and even older Delftware.

Marking the northeastern corner of the Jordaan is the **Noordermarkt**. The square is quiet, and usually empty, but if you come back early on a Monday morning you'll find a crush of trendies, students and down-and-outs at Amsterdam's cheapest clothes market. The Noorderkerk was Hendrick de Keyser's last church and, as befits an old man, is solemn and austere with only the teeniest of spires.

The northern boundary of the Jordaan is formed by the **Brouwersgracht** (Brewers' Canal). This is quintessential Amsterdam; the canal's neat, gabled houses, humped bridges and shady towpaths feature in almost every brochure intended to lure you to the city. Yet the crowds that tramp up and down the grand canals seem to pass it by. There are no neon lights or noisy cafés. It's a quiet, residential canal for the hopelessly romantic. Most of the houses are converted warehouses. In the 17th century this canal, right at the harbour's edge, seethed with traders and reeked of fish and beer. Stockfish warehouses and no fewer than 24 breweries crowded its banks. Amsterdam had to import fresh water from the surrounding countryside to feed its industries and populace. Most of the long flat boats carrying this water entered the city along the Brouwersgracht, so breweries sprang up along the canal that afforded them the pick of the incoming supplies. Just off Brouwersgracht, the small square of the Herenmarkt is dominated by **Westindisch Huis** (West India House). The dumpy red-brick exterior dates from the 19th century, when it was rebuilt as a Lutheran orphanage. Nowadays it's an adult education college, but you can usually nip in for a glimpse of the 17th-century courtyard—the only remnant of the building's romantic past as headquarters of the West India Company. In the courtyard there's a memorial to Peter Stuyvesant, the notoriously grouchy peg-legged Governor of Nieuw Amsterdam—the Company's chief American trading post. In 1664 he surrendered the settlement to the British, who renamed it New York.

From the eastern end of the canal you can see the enormous copper dome of the old Lutherse Kerk (Lutheran Chuch). The church (also known as the **Ronde Lutherse Kerk**—Round Lutheran Church) was built in 1668 by Adriaan Dortsman, a leading light of the appropriately named Restrained Dutch Classicists. A careless plumber caused a fire which burnt it down in 1822; it was rebuilt the following year and was used as a church until the early 1930s, when dwindling congregations resulted in its closure. After some years of disuse, the church was converted into a conference hall for the hotel across the road, but in 1993 it burned down again. The gutted building cost ƒ4 million to restore and opened for business again in 1995. The round brick walls look impenetrable (conference delegates reach it through an underground tunnel).

The Museum Area

Museumplein

Amsterdam's (if not the nation's) greatest cultural institutions border Museumplein—the Rijksmuseum and Concertgebouw at either end, the Van Gogh and Stedelijk Museums up one side. Until recently Museumplein was bisected by a busy road nicknamed 'Europe's's shortest motorway', and was windswept, deserted and nasty. But

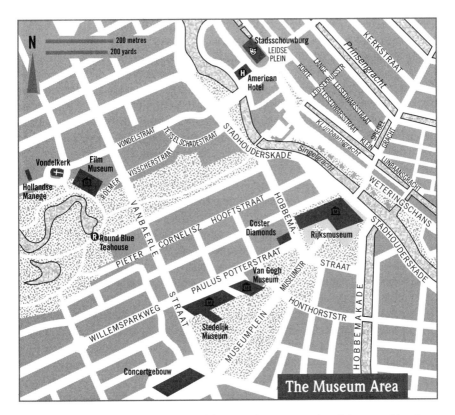

The Museum Area

dramatic re-landscaping in the late 1990s created a green and stylish spot with a long pool, a café and underground garages that suck up all the cars and coaches.

As you wander through the square, stop briefly to look at the Vrouwen van Ravensbrück memorial, a series of vertical steel slabs erected to commemorate the 92,000 women who died in concentration camps during the Second World War. The text translates as 'For those women who until the bitter end refused to accept fascism.' The flickering light and thumping sound emanating from the sculpture are intended as a beacon to call people to the monument and to continue the fight.

The Rijksmuseum

Open daily 10–5; adm exp, with free floor-plan. If there's a long queue at the ticket office, nip around the back to the entrance to the new South Wing, where there is usually hardly anyone waiting at all. There is an excellent guided tour to the museum on CD-ROM, obtainable on the shop level for f7.50. You can walk around at your own pace, punching in codes to learn more about individual paintings and, if you wish, tapping ever deeper into more detailed background information. The CD comes with a printed sugges-tion of 15 paintings to see if you're in a hurry.

The Rijksmuseum (National Museum, pronounced 'reyks-museum') was completed in 1885 to house the national collection of paintings and sculpture. The collection has evolved from a hoard of 200 paintings confiscated from the exiled Prince William V in 1798. First they had been gathered in the Huis ten Bosch palace in The Hague, and later were brought to the Trip brothers' 17th-century mansion in Amsterdam. By the 1860s it was clear that the Trippenhuis was going to be too small for the growing collection. The quest for a new temple for the nation's art sparked off a conflagration of chauvinism, in-fighting and intrigue that would have impressed the Borgias. When the winners of an anonymous competition for a new museum design turned out to be German, the plan was rejected as 'non-Dutch'. Once a suitable Dutch architect was found in P. J. H. Cuypers (of Centraal Station fame) a new scandal emerged. The architect, project co-ordinator, government advisor and decorator were all Roman Catholics. Protestant Holland scented nepotism and popery. The building Cuypers produced was thought altogether too extravagant, too churchy and too foreign to house the treasures of Dutch culture. What made it worse was that Cuypers, having had a more sober Romanesque plan accepted, managed, while building was in progress, to slip in more fantastical bits of a previously rejected Gothic plan. Good patriotic Calvinists found this mish-mash of foreign styles deplorable. One critic railed: 'For two million guilders we now have the most sorry spectacle of a building that anyone could have thought to call a museum.' In response to the gilding and plethora of sculptures, portraits and tiling depicting Dutch artists that adorns the outside walls, another critic compared the museum to 'a garishly decorated house of a rich parvenu'. Even the king pleaded a prior engagement on the day of the opening ceremony.

Ironically, Cuypers thought his red-brick and wood building with its clean, simple lines to be quintessentially Dutch, and today one would be inclined to agree with him. Like the Centraal Station on the other side of town, the Rijksmuseum was designed as a grand entrance to the city. (When it was built there were only fields beyond it.) A walkway through the middle of the building has bright bathroom acoustics that attract anything from opera-singing accordionists to steel bands. Though not as magical as the Centraal Station, 'De Rijks' is one of Amsterdam's most conspicuous landmarks, and has become a cultural icon. When it reopened after the Second World War the waiting queue of pallid, underfed Amsterdammers in slightly shabby formal dress stretched all the way down Stadhouderskade.

In the years following the completion of the Rijksmuseum in 1885 so many people left their complete collections to the museum that it had, almost immediately, to embark on a programme of expansion. Not all the additions have been happy ones. In 1906 a committee of artists and architects spent months fiddling about in a life-sized model of a hall intended to show off Rembrandt's *Night Watch*. They finally decided that light from the left, tempered by carefully placed curtains, would be ideal. It wasn't. The room was a disaster, ended up being used for minor exhibitions and earned the monicker 'De Puist' (the pimple).

All of Cuypers' ornate interior decorations have been removed and today the museum is a maze of whitewashed rooms. Prince William V's modest collection has become:

5,000 paintings, 30,000 sculptures and works of applied art, 17,000 historical objects, 3,000 works of Asiatic art and a million prints and drawings.

On the first floor, an archway leads to the **Gallery of Honour**. If your time is really tight, this is the one place to visit. It gives a good introduction to Golden Age painting, and houses the Rembrandt for which the museum is famous. At the far end, taking up the full wall, is Rembrandt's *Night Watch*.

Rembrandt

Rembrandt Harmensz. van Rijn (1606–69) was the son of a Leiden miller. When the poet Constantijn Huygens, who was also something of an art critic, visited Leiden in 1628, he went into raptures over Rembrandt's paintings (though he reprimanded the then unknown youth for his puniness and lack of manly exercise). A few years later Rembrandt upped sticks for the big city. He had made his mark in Leiden, and as the *burgemeester* wryly remarked: 'His portraits and other pictures pleased the citizens of Amsterdam, who paid him well for them.' And indeed they did. Wealthy burghers, trades guilds and companies of the civic guard all spent handsome sums to be painted by the fashionable young artist. His unromanticized portraits hit just the right note in rationalistic, post-Reformation Holland. Even his biblical and historical paintings have a truth and psychological rigour, especially in the faces, that seem to suggest direct experience of the world he's depicting. In 1634, already a rich and celebrated painter, he married heiress Saskia van Uylenburgh and five years later felt confident about paying a swingeing ƒ13,000 for a house in the Jewish quarter (*see* p.97). (This was where he had always wanted to live—he found Hebrew culture fascinating and preferred Jewish models for his religious painting.)

Saskia died in 1642, having just changed her will to leave everything to their infant son Titus, with the estate to be held in usufruct by Rembrandt for as long as he didn't remarry. The painter got round this by having a clandestine affair with Titus' nurse, Geertghe Dircx. Then, in 1649, he fell in love with a younger servant, Hendrickje Stoffels. Geertghe sued successfully for breach of contract. This came at a bad time. Rembrandt was receiving fewer commissions now— perhaps because of gossip about his domestic affairs, perhaps because he was becoming increasingly uncompromising in his work, or maybe he was just going out of fashion. He'd also spent far too much on paintings and the house. In 1656 he was declared bankrupt. The property that had been his home for some 20 years was sold, and he moved out to live on the Rozengracht with Hendrickje and Titus. They were going to try to revive his flagging fortune by working as his agents, but Hendrickje died within two years, followed by Titus in 1669, only months after he had married. Rembrandt was so hard up that he had to sell Saskia's tomb to pay for Hendrickje's funeral. When he himself died, he was buried in an unmarked grave in the Westerkerk.

The *Night Watch* was commissioned in 1642 by the militiamen of the Kloveniersdoelen (the Arquebusiers' Guildhall) to hang in their banqueting room alongside five other portraits of companies of the civic guard. It's officially called *The Company of Captain Frans Banning Cocq and Lieutenant Willem van Ruytenburch* and got its present title in the 19th century because ageing layers of varnish made it murky. For years it's had the reputation of being the work that signalled Rembrandt's decline. This is ill-deserved—he still had some of his most important commissions ahead of him. It is true though, that the 17th-century public didn't like it very much, and when it was moved to the Town Hall in 1715 the city fathers thought nothing of lopping a bit off the left-hand side so that it would fit on the wall: two of Captain Cocq's militiamen disappeared forever.

Today, together with *The Syndics*, it's considered the prize of the Rijksmuseum's collection. It was usual to paint group portraits in fairly static compositions, giving each member equal prominence. Rembrandt, however, paints the company in a flurry of movement, as if about to set off on a march. Rich clothes and a wonderful collection of plumed and pointed hats all add to the sense of grandeur and motion (this is all pure invention—the guards' uniforms were in reality rather dull, and they never marched). A little girl in a luminous gold dress, possibly the company mascot, looks bewildered by all the activity. (The rather surreal touch of a dead chicken tied to her waist is an allusion to the militia's coat of arms.) The captain and his lieutenant, in fine clothes, dominate the scene. The rest of the company look far less important—which is possibly why the painting was initially unpopular: they had after all each paid their ƒ100, and deserved the same billing.

When the controllers of the Drapers' Guild (the 'Staalmeesters', or 'Syndics') commissioned Rembrandt to paint their portrait in 1662, they were determined not to make a similar mistake, and stipulated a more traditional composition. Rembrandt obeyed, yet still managed to create a work that brims with life. The Syndics look up from their table, and the viewer has the odd sensation of having just walked into the room and disturbed them at work. It's one of the finest group portraits ever painted—Kenneth Clark goes as far as acclaiming it 'one of the summits of European painting'—and seems to be the image picture librarians most reach for to evoke old Holland.

As you wander through the Gallery of Honour, keep an eye open for three more of Rembrandt's paintings: *The Jewish Bride* (1667), a glowing, tender portrait of a couple, no longer all that youthful, but very much in love; a rather depressed, world-weary *Self-portrait as the Apostle Paul* (1661); and *St Peter's Denial* (1660), showing a very troubled, down-to-earth apostle. Other paintings in the Gallery of Honour may change from time to time, but you can probably see **Nicholas Maes**' delicately detailed *Old Woman at Prayer* and work by one of Rembrandt's better-known pupils—**Ferdinand Bol**. Massive *penschilderijen* ('pen paintings', rather like etchings) of naval battle scenes by Willem van de Velde I are also on show.

The other halls on the left wing of the first floor take you off on a chronological journey through Dutch painting. In Rooms 201–6 you'll find works from the Middle Ages and the Renaissance (which reached the Netherlands a century later than Italy).

You'll probably want to save your energy for the Golden Age, but as you pass through the early rooms have a look at **Geertgen tot Sint Jans**' brightly detailed *Holy Kinship* (1485), crammed with emblems and symbolic references and his *Adoration of the Magi* (1490), set against an intricate backdrop of ruined landscapes, processions and misty forests. *The Seven Works of Charity* (1504), instructive panels by the **Master of Alkmaar**, have survived attacks by iconoclasts and creeping damp, and still preach their catalogue of worthy acts. **Lucas van Leyden**'s *Adoration of the Golden Calf* (1530) is suitably riotous and a good example of the way Dutch Renaissance painters introduced realistic landscape settings for mythological scenes. The youth trying hard not to break the egg on the tavern floor in Pieter Aertsen's *Egg Dance* (1557) prefigures the scenes of everyday life that were to be such a feature of the Golden Age. The **Dutch Mannerists**, who worked in Haarlem between 1580 and the 1620s, get a good showing; Cornelis Cornelisz.'s enormous *Fall of Man* (1592) teems with animals mythical and domestic. In Karel van Mander's *The Magnanimity of Scipio* (1600), the 3rd-century BC Roman hero nobly refuses the offer of a beautiful captive for his slave and returns her to her betrothed.

Rooms 207–36 are filled with paintings from the 17th century, the '**Golden Age**' not only of Dutch art but of the Netherlands' political and economic might. Intense realism and the naturalistic rendering of domestic and everyday life are the hallmarks of the Golden Age. There are precise, calm interiors, minutely detailed still lifes, wild taverns and salacious brothel scenes. Homely Dutch mothers and their *onnozele schaapjes* (innocent lambs) take the place of the Madonna and Child, and you'll see businessmen and civic guards rather than generals and fantastical battle scenes. As you walk around the collection you'll see more of Rembrandt and his pupils, but there are a number of other artists particularly worth searching out.

Frans Hals' happy and rather cheeky-looking *Wedding Portrait of Isaac Abrahamsz. Massa and Beatrix van der Laen* (1622), and the florid *Merry Drinker* (1628–30)—seemingly dashed off with swift brushstrokes and scratches in the wet paint—testify to his greatness as a portrait-painter. **Pieter Saenredam**'s church interiors are so still, and he pays such close attention to architectural shapes, that they seem almost abstract, Pieter de Hooch—especially in *Woman and Child in a Pantry* (1658) and *Women beside a Linen Chest* (1663)—is a master of quiet family scenes. Light from the busy outside world streams in through a door or window in the background, while in the spotless rooms with their symmetrical black and white floor tiles all is order and calm—though the impish children seem just on the verge of disrupting it.

A somewhat sadder *schaapje* can be seen in **Gabriel Metsu**'s touching, yet unsentimental *Sick Child*. **Jan Steen** gives quite another idea of family life. He used his experiences as a tavern-keeper to create scenes of such jolly domestic upheaval—as in *The Merry Family* (1670)—that the Dutch still use the expression 'a Jan Steen household' for any chaotic but cheerful home. You'll also find still lifes which, at the beginning of the century, are sober arrangements of herring, bread and cheese, but later overflow with ornate tableware, full-blown flowers and juicy fruit at its *toppunt* (literally: top-point)—the last moment of perfection before decay. **Abraham van Beyeren**'s 1665 painting shows fat peaches, seafood, leaking melons and a toppled silver candlestick in meticulous detail. Look out also for **Gerard ter Borch**'s exquisite fabrics—poor little *Helena van der Schalke* (1648) is weighed down by her fine silk dress and in *Gallant Conversation* the young woman's silver gown shimmers. (The conversation wasn't really that gallant—the man holding up his hand in gentle admonition was originally offering her a coin. A pious owner painted it out.)

Skim as fast as you like through the rest of the collection, but don't miss the Vermeers (Room 221a). Only 30 works by **Johannes Vermeer** (1632–75) exist; the Rijksmuseum has four of them. He had a passion for light and his paintings seem translucent. Light from a window reflects off a white wall, a jug, or softly glowing fabric. The tranquil *Kitchen Maid* (1658) and *Woman Reading a Letter* (1662–3) are totally without stylistic artifice, yet come close to perfection. In quiet, everyday scenes, Vermeer captures a sense of eternity.

If you walk through the rooms in numerical order you'll end up back in the Gallery of Honour. From here you can totter downstairs for a coffee. Before you do, have a look in Room 248, tucked away behind the film hall. Here you'll find the small Italian Collection with some chubby pink Rubens, Carlo Crivelli's elegant tempera *Mary Magdalene* (1485–90) and Piero di Cosimo's warts-and-all portraits of a Florentine architect and his cauliflower-eared father (1485).

It's probably a better idea to come back another day to see the rest of the museum, but if time is short refresh yourself as best you can in the museum café and head back up the stairs, this time to the right wing of the building, devoted to sculpture and applied art.

The museum's collection of **sculpture and applied art** includes ceramics, china, glass, furniture, costumes, lace, tapestries, jewellery and silver from the Middle Ages to the 20th century, and can be utterly overwhelming. On a first visit the best idea is to give yourself a gentle overview. In the rooms leading off the entrance hall (Rooms 238–42), you'll find some of the best pieces in the collection. Ten 15th-century bronze figures, poised in graceful attitudes of mourning, have been filched from the tomb of Isabella de Bourbon in Antwerp. There's a tiny portable altar, carved in gold and encrusted with enamel, that some lucky nun used for her private devotion in the Abbey de Chocques in France in the 16th century. Look out also for Adriaen van Wesel's busy and energetic oak carving of *The Meeting of the Three Magi* (1475–7). A little further on, in Room 245, you can see Late Gothic German carvings of *Christ and the Last Supper*, still with some original polychrome and gilding.

If you have a taste for camp, head straight for Room 251a and Wenzel Jamnitzer's extraordinary *Table Ornament*, made for the city of Nuremberg in 1549. Mother Earth stands, one hip cocked, in a rockery of flowers, lizards and shrimps (all silver casts of real specimens) and supports on her head an enormous birdbath of cherubs rampant, scrolls, snakes and more flowers. All this is surmounted by yet another posy of enamelled silver foliage. Its ornate gilded wood and leather carrying case is displayed alongside.

The collection of **Delftware** (Rooms 255–7) has some prize polychrome as well as more traditional blue and white pieces. The people of Delft first started making cheaper imitations of the Chinese porcelain brought back by the Dutch East India Company in the 17th century. (Things have turned a full circle: now souvenir shops sell imitation Delftware made in Taiwan.) Among the usual plates and cups you can see a functioning Delftware violin and towering tulip pagodas with space for forty stems (which, in the 17th century, would have cost a fortune to fill).

Back downstairs (in Room 164) you can see two exquisite early 18th-century **doll's houses**—collectors' pieces assembled by the lady of the house, rather than toys. The museum is full of choice life-size furniture too, but it's rather coldly presented and, unless you have a specialist interest, the canal-house museums earlier in this chapter will probably appeal to you more—though do keep an eye open for the rich **Gobelin tapestries** (Room 165) and an ornate oak table-leaf veneered with tortoiseshell and inlaid with a mass of birds, monkeys, fruit and putti worked in copper, brass and mother-of-pearl. If you appreciate good porcelain, the **Meissen collection** (Rooms 170–71) is one of the best in the world. An alchemist in the German town of Meissen, near Dresden, discovered the secret of Chinese porcelain manufacture while trying to make gold for the king, and the pieces subsequently produced in the area have been collectors' items for centuries.

The **South Wing** houses a small but carefully selected **costume and textile collection** (in Room 15, near the door to the walkway) and **18th- and 19th-century art**, including bright, ethereal pastels by the Swiss artist Jean-Etienne Liotard (1702–89)—mostly of aristocrats and socialites. The best 19th-century work is by painters of two movements from the second half of the century. The three Maris brothers were leading artists of the **Hague School** (nicknamed the 'grey' school after its heavy, cloudy skies). Jacob painted beaches and townscapes, Matthijs portrayed romantic fairy-tale scenes and Willem seemed preoccupied with ducks. Anton Mauve's pearly grey *Morning Ride along a Beach* (1876) is characteristic of the movement. The **Amsterdam Impressionists** are well represented by George Breitner, who liked to paint Amsterdam in the rain, and Isaac Israëls, whose brighter pictures are closer to the work of the French Impressionists.

Downstairs in the South Wing, you'll find the **Asiatic Art Collection**. Three hundred years of Dutch trade connections have resulted in a glittering stash of treasures from the East. You can see lacquerwork, ceramics and textiles from Japan, Javanese sculptures, and religious works from China and India. A small, bronze dancing Lord Shiva (the Hindu god of creation) from the 12th century and an elegantly relaxed Chinese Buddhist saint, the Bodhisattva Avalokitesharva, from the same period, make the trip across to the South Wing worthwhile.

In the **Rijksprentenkabinet** (Print Room) exhibition hall, on the ground floor near the museum café, you can see temporary exhibitions from a vast collection of prints, drawings and watercolours by the likes of Rembrandt, Dürer, Goya and Canaletto. To see works from the collection not on view, you need written permission (from the Director, Jan Luykenstraat 1a).

On the ground floor of the left wing of the main building, you'll find the **Dutch History Collection**. The history collection comprises paintings, documents and memorabilia dating from the Middle Ages to the Second World War. There's an understandable emphasis on ships and sea battles, but the presentation is not very exciting. If you have the time, pop in for a look at some of the more amusing curiosities—like a deceptively gorgeous copper crown with glass jewels sent as a trade bribe to an African king by the 17th-century Duke of York (via the Dutch naval hero Admiral de Ruyter), or the grand but diminutive jackets worn by the toddler Prince William V.

The Van Gogh Museum

The Rijksmuseum Vincent Van Gogh (National Vincent Van Gogh Museum; *open daily 10–6; adm f12.50*) has really cornered the Van Gogh market with 200 paintings, 500 drawings, a collection of works by Van Gogh's contemporaries, the letters from Vincent to his brother Theo, Vincent's collections of Japanese woodcuts and 19th-century engravings, a press archive dating from 1899—and publishing copyright for the lot. The museum was completed in 1973 and is based on an initial drawing by the influential Dutch architect, Gerrit Rietveld (*see* p.64), who died before working the plan through. Brave efforts by later architects to realize his rather sketchy ideas produced a hard-edged and unsympathetic building. But in 1999, a new wing by renowned Japanese architect Kisho Kurokawa gave the museum the sort of proud architectural profile it deserves.

Works from the permanent collection are displayed in the old part of the museum; the Kurokawa wing is used for temporary exhibitions and houses the darkened Print Room, where you can find Van Gogh's drawings and studies, and trace some of his influences—sketches by friends, pictures he copied and his collection of Japanese prints and magazine engravings. The selection on display changes frequently, but you can usually follow his development through some rather conventional Dutch landscapes, with all the expected perspectives, and studies of gnarled hands and heavily jowled peasant faces to the wild movement of *Women Dancing* (1885). Millet's *Labours of the Field* and woodcuts by Hiroshige and Kesai Yeisen clearly had an influence on some of Van Gogh's better known oils. The museum has an exceptionally good library, where you can view photographs of Vincent's letters to Theo. Training courses, and all sorts of activities to help working artists, are held regularly. (Details are available from the museum.)

Vincent van Gogh was born in 1853 in the tiny village of Zundert, near the Belgian border. We have an image of him as a wild, schizophrenic bohemian; a simpleton, out of touch with the world and reliant on his younger brother's handouts. This isn't the full truth. He came from an old Dutch family of clerics, naval officers and gallery owners. Though he was constantly at odds with his relations, and indeed offended almost everyone he met, he was in many ways part of the Establishment. He spoke three languages fluently, had a wide knowledge of European art and had the business acumen and connections needed to organize two exhibitions of friends' work in Paris. He signed himself 'Vincent' because he thought his surname, difficult for foreigners to pronouce, would be bad salesmanship. (You say it with two guttural 'g's—'fun HGoHG'). Even the money he got from his art-dealer brother he excused as a business arrangement—an advance on the money Theo would one day make selling his work. Yet all his life he was desperately lonely, dogged by a sense of failure and frustrated by how few people appreciated his art. Towards the end he was beset by bouts of madness which left him exhausted and depressed. He was acutely sensitive to his surroundings. The colours, people, light or weather in one environment would become loathsome to him and the need to move would become consuming. Suddenly he'd up sticks and go—to the sun, to the city, to the country. These moves would often be reflected in a change in his work, so it's interesting to approach the paintings with some knowledge of what was going on in Van Gogh's life at the time.

Vincent's first job, at the age of 16, was as an assistant with the art dealer Goupil & Cie in The Hague. In 1873 he went to work at the London branch and was impressed by Constable, Turner and especially the Pre-Raphaelite John Everett Millais. An unhappy love affair made him grumpy at work. He began to be rude to customers about their taste, was shuttled between London and Paris and finally, despite family connections (his uncle was a partner in the firm), dismissed. Still obsessed by his English rose, he returned to Britain as a teacher, but was soundly rebuffed. She married someone else and he went back to Holland to work in a bookshop. He still didn't know what he wanted to do with his life.

But in May 1877 it all suddenly seemed clear: following in his father's footsteps, he set off for Amsterdam to study theology. Greek and Latin proved an uphill struggle and he was entirely defeated by algebra; after less than a year he went to a crammer for evangelists in Brussels, where mathematical aptitude was not a prerequisite. But he couldn't preach either. Yet again the family pulled strings. The Brussels Evangelist Committee reluctantly sent him to prove his worth among the coalminers of the Borinage—a wasteland in south Belgium. After seven months he was dismissed for over-zealous involvement with the poor.

He stayed on in a hovel for another year, almost starving to death, and began to draw. He was 26 and had found his direction. His younger brother, Theo, rescued him and started to pay him the monthly allowance that was to be Vincent's only income for the rest of his life.

Van Gogh was largely self-taught, though he spent a brief period studying perspective and anatomy in Brussels in 1880. The following year he fell in love with his widowed cousin, Kee Vos. He walked to Amsterdam from his parents' home in south Holland, stormed into her father's house on the Keizersgracht and held his hand over a candle yelling, 'Let me see her for as long as I can hold my hand in the flame.' But Kee had fled. Van Gogh left without seeing her and with a hole burned into his flesh. The incident caused a family row; he was thrown out of home and went to The Hague. Here he met members of the Hague School of painting, a movement characterized by muddy colours and gloomy skies. He was given lessons by one of its leading members, Anton Mauve (a cousin by marriage), and was also much influenced by Jozef Israëls' earthy studies of peasants. He was especially friendly with a young painter called George Breitner, who later became known as one of the best Amsterdam Impressionists. They discovered a mutual interest in Zola and together drew the street life in the seedier parts of town. An uncle who had commissioned 12 views of the city was horrified by Vincent's unconventional approach and refused to pay up. The relationship with Mauve grew tense when Van Gogh began to reject the older painter's advice, and family relations soured on a wider scale when it became known that he was living with the prostitute Sien Hoornik 'in order to reform her'.

In September 1883 Van Gogh suddenly left The Hague for the countryside of Drenthe in the north of Holland. He had begun to paint in oils, but still with a muddy Dutch palette. The good people of Drenthe thought him a dangerous lunatic and a tramp, and refused to pose for him—so this became a period of landscapes with small figures in the distance. After a few months, loneliness drove him to a reconciliation with his parents and he went back south to live with them in Nuenen. Weavers and peasants in the surrounding Brabant farmland were his dominant motif. The period culminated in the dim glow and gravy browns of *The Potato Eaters* (1885). Van Gogh loved this 'real peasant picture'—he felt you could smell the bacon, smoke and potato steam, and that the rough hands that dipped into the dish were the same hands that had dug the earth.

In *The Old Church Tower at Nuenen*, the tower stands crooked and solitary in a flat, empty churchyard. A few crows flutter against the overcast sky. Van Gogh painted it in May 1885, a few months after his father had been buried there, and just before it was demolished and all the wood—including the graveyard crosses—sold to peasants. His father had been an unpopular preacher in a declining sect. *Open Bible, Extinguished Candle and Book* (1885) has been seen as Vincent's homage to their difficult relationship. Next to the huge Bible and snuffed candle (a convention for death) is a French novel—something his father would not have allowed in the house.

Margot Begemann, a neighbour, took poison after her family refused permission for her to marry Vincent. She survived, but Vincent got the blame and the village turned against him. He went to Antwerp, studied Rubens, covered his walls with Japanese prints and enrolled in the academy—which he left a few months later without ever learning of the academy's decision to demote him to the beginners' class. He then went to Paris. The first Theo (who was working there for Goupil & Cie) heard of the move was a note brought by a messenger asking him to meet Vincent in the Louvre. Vincent moved into Theo's tiny apartment, but was such a chaotic and irritating flatmate that Theo had to find somewhere bigger, with a separate studio space for his brother. The first few canvases in Paris (such as *View over Paris*, 1886) still use the Dutch browns and greys. But when Theo introduced him to a few Impressionist friends, the shock of their fresh, bright canvases changed Vincent for life. At first the colour creeps in gradually (*Woman Sitting in the Café du Tambourin*, 1887) but soon he is copying the flat colours of the Japanese prints and painting some of the familiar bright self-portraits. He began to long for harder light and a less hectic milieu than Paris could offer. Writing to his sister Wil about *Self-portrait at the Easel* (1888), he draws her attention to his sad expression. He's had enough of Paris and wants the sun. He gives himself pinkish-grey skin against a greyish-white wall, his tightly drawn features contrast with a bristly, unkempt, bright red beard. On the palette he holds are all the colours of the painting except this fiery orange of the beard.

On 20 February 1888 Vincent escaped to the Mediterranean warmth of Arles in the south of France. Here in the famous 'Yellow House', which he shared for a while with Gauguin, his best known works were painted. It is hard to believe that the raucous yellows and bright reds and blues of *Harvest at La Crau* were painted only three years after *The Potato Eaters*. Look closely at one of the versions of *Sunflowers*. Between the greens and yellows are bright streaks of ice blues, mauves and reds—colours you never notice in the reproductions. Portraits of the postman, Roulin, and his wife are drenched in sun and colour. Even the *Night Café* has a bright, steamy heat. The solitary *Sower at Arles* works under an enormous yellow orb in a green and pink sky. The most ordinary things around him evoke intense response. *Vincent's Bedroom at Arles* is filled with a brilliant light but the smooth paintwork, the mauves and blues of the walls have a calming effect. (The green splodge under the chair is the result of a botched repair job after the painting was damaged in transit to Theo.)

Van Gogh was very excited by Gauguin's arrival on 20 October 1888 and went to great pains to furnish his room comfortably. The money to do this, of course, came from Theo. *Gauguin's Chair* shows a piece Vincent bought for his friend (elaborate in comparison with his own). On the seat are novels intended to indicate Gauguin's spirituality and modernism. A candle burns as well as the gas light, to suggest Gauguin's fiery nature. Together they visited nearby towns such as Les Saintes-Maries-de-la-Mer, where Vincent painted *Boats on the Beach*. The small red, green and blue boats had reminded him of flowers. He paints them with the flat colours and definite lines of a Japanese print, while the sea eddies and swirls with a shimmering complexity of colouring.

Gauguin's stay was not a happy one. The two artists had tempestuous arguments. After a particularly violent dispute on Christmas Eve, Vincent threatened Gauguin with a razor, then slashed off his own right ear and presented it to a prostitute who had complimented it. Gauguin left for Paris. Another nervous crisis followed Van Gogh's recuperation, and he was voluntarily admitted to the asylum of St-Paul-de-Mausole at Saint-Rémy. Paintings from this period—usually of fields around the asylum, the hospital garden or of individual trees and flowers—are in softer hues. In February 1890 Vincent painted *Branches of an Almond Tree in Blossom* for Theo's newly born son—blossom-laden branches stand out against an eggshell-blue background.

By May he felt well enough to leave the asylum, though he could only bear Paris for three days. He travelled to Auvers-sur-Oise where an eccentric art-lover, Dr Gachet, promised to keep an eye on him. But Vincent became more and more overwrought: his colours became harder, brush strokes more violent. In *Crows in the Wheatfields* (July 1890) it seems difficult for the birds to fly into the thick, dark sky. A path curves and goes nowhere. One of his last paintings, *Roots and Tree Trunks*, has even more disorientating perspectives and thick layers of paint in unexpected colours. The painter seems completely self-engrossed, and the viewer is quite alienated.

On 27 July Vincent went into the fields and shot himself, but he bungled even this. He staggered back to the inn where he was staying and died on 29 July, in Theo's arms. After a short illness, Theo himself died six months later, at the age of 32. The brothers are buried side by side in the churchyard at Auvers-sur-Oise.

Dedication, or desperation, drove Theo's widow—Johanna van Gogh-Bonger—to promote the works stacked all over her apartment. The art world began to take notice. In 1891 there was an exhibition in Brussels, followed by numerous others all over the Netherlands and in Paris. Paintings started to fetch high prices and national museums added Van Goghs to their collections. After Johanna's death in 1925 her son, Vincent's namesake, took over the collection and in 1931 put it on permanent exhibition in the Stedelijk Museum in Amsterdam. To prevent the break-up of the collection after his death, the Van Gogh Foundation was formed in 1960 and set about building the present museum. With three members of the Van Gogh family on the board of the foundation, there's a feeling that it's still very much a family concern—and Vincent, once the black sheep, is again part of the Establishment.

The Stedelijk Museum of Modern Art

The Stedelijk Museum ('Municipal Museum'; *open daily 11–5; adm*) is a solid 19th-century red brick building with fussy plaster decorations and spiky gables. A row of rather haughty architects stares down at you from niches on the first floor. The widened entrance and glass box extension at the back were part of a drive in the 1950s to make art more accessible: the guiding principle was that a museum loses its sense of mystery when works can also be viewed from the street. A good idea—if the blinds didn't have to be drawn every afternoon against the damaging sunlight.

Don't be deceived by appearances. It's a bright, lively museum of modern art. You'll find not only conventional paintings, but all sorts of applied art (designer chairs, feather hats and gaudy teapots) and work by less established artists. As you queue for your ticket, the person in front may just as likely be a professor of art history as some painter's proud mother.

The museum owes its existence to two benefactors. Sophia Augusta de Bruyn, the eccentric dowager of Jonkheer (Lord) Lopez Suasso, spent as little as she could on clothes (scandalizing Amsterdam society by wearing the same dress more than once). Instead she amassed as many jewels, trinkets, curios (and especially clocks) as she could. When she died, she left everything to the City of Amsterdam. There was so much that the council felt obliged to build a museum to display it all. At the same time the wealthy Vereeniging tot het Vormen van eene Openbare Verzameling van Heedendaagsche Kunst (Society for the Formation of a Public Collection of Contemporary Art) or VvHK, was looking for a home.

The city council and the 'society with the long name' (as it was understandably nicknamed) got together and the museum opened in 1895. It wasn't until the early 1970s that the last of Sophia Augusta's bric-a-brac was dispersed to specialist museums and the Stedelijk became devoted exclusively to modern art.

Successive directors have left their imprint on the collection, but it was the imagination, energy and skill of Willem Sandberg—'part poet, part artist, part designer, part administrator, part magician'—that between 1945 and 1963 established the Stedelijk as one of the world's leading modern art museums. He built up an important collection and held a series of notable, usually controversial, exhibitions. In 1949 there were fisticuffs in the foyer at the opening of the first COBRA exhibition. (COBRA was a group of artists from Copenhagen, Brussels and Amsterdam whose colourful, childlike painting was the first to provoke the response that 'a three-year-old could do better'.) Though that's not happened again, daring new acquisitions still spark off public uproars.

Space is limited, so only a small portion of the collection is shown at any one time. Outside the summer months (May–September) you may even find that much of the museum is taken over by a special exhibition, though present museum policy is to show the core of the permanent collection on a more stable, long-term basis. A plan of what is currently on view is available from the information desk (to the left of the entrance).

You'll find whatever is being exhibited of the **permanent collection** up the wide marble staircase, on the top floor. In 1972 the large **Van Gogh** collection, which had been kept at the Stedelijk, moved next door to its own museum. Because Van Gogh is considered so important to modern art, a few paintings were left behind. *La Berceuse* (The Cradle) was inspired by a story Gauguin told Van Gogh about fishermen who pinned prints of their patron saint—Stella Maris (Maria, Star of the Sea)—to the cabin wall. Van Gogh felt that a portrait of Madame Roulin (a postman's wife), holding a cord for a rocking cradle, would be ideal for such a print. He imagined the seamen 'would feel the old sense of being rocked come over them and remember their own lullabies'. It's a pity that the painting isn't hung the way Van Gogh suggested—as a triptych with sunflower paintings on either side. Don't miss the paintings by **George Breitner**, Van Gogh's contemporary and drinking partner. In *De Dam*, a view of Dam square, he captures that special Amsterdam light in a way that makes the exact time of year, even the time of day, immediately recognizable. Keep an eye open also for his highly patterned, exotic *Woman in a Red Kimono* (in reality a hat shop assistant).

The museum has a good collection of modern art classics. You'll probably find Manet's picture of a barmaid (staring at you saucily from under a crystal chandelier), a study for his famous *Bar at the Folies-Bergère*. There are some gentle Cézanne landscapes and a whole range of **Picassos**—from bright early collages to nudes from his Blue Period. One wall is sure to be filled by **Matisse**'s vast paper cut-out *The Parakeet and the Mermaid*, done towards the end of his life when his eyesight was too poor for painting, and painstakingly restored in 1996. You'll find at least one of **Kandinsky**'s vivid Improvisations—paintings where he used colour to represent the sounds of various musical instruments—and some rather good **Chagall**s.

The 1960s are well represented by **Warhol** screen-prints, **Roy Lichtenstein**'s comic strip blow-ups and **Bruce Nauman**'s neon light installations, and the museum comes right up to date with works by some of the best living European and American artists.

The high point is the museum's collection of the Russian artist **Kazimir Malevich** and the Dutch movement, *De Stijl*. Side by side, these two collections show how abstract art began and we see the gradual disappearance of any reference to outside reality. The visionary director of the museum, Willem Sandberg, was responsible for tracking down the Malevich collection, unearthing a treasury of works that had been forgotten in a cellar in Germany for three decades. Malevich had left the entire contents of an exhibition for safe-keeping with a friend in Beieren, but was subsequently never allowed to leave Russia. He died in 1935, so there the cache remained (under a pile of rubble after the war) until Sandberg swooped down and bought it in the late 1950s. The museum has a complete range of his work, from early Impressionist pieces, through a Cubist period to the completely abstract—solid shapes of colour (oblongs, squares, triangles) on a white background. Malevich composes these shapes at such angles that the paintings seem full of movement.

At around the same time (1917) **De Stijl** artists were coming up with very similar work. The best known is that of **Piet Mondriaan** (he dropped the last 'a' to appear French, but the Dutch prefer the original). His *Compositions* of vertical and horizontal black lines with blocks of primary colours, so shocking at the time, now appear on everything from oven gloves to shampoo bottles. When Theo van Doesburg (co-founder of De Stijl) after ten years of rectilinear painting produced a Contra-composition, in which he daringly tilted his lines through 45°, Piet left the movement in a huff. They were never reconciled, though Mondriaan later took up the challenge by tilting his canvas through 45° and keeping the lines vertical.

In the Print Room, halfway down the main staircase, you could find anything from a Toulouse-Lautrec poster to Mapplethorpe's startling close-up photographs of male nudes. Keep an eye open for the innovative work of Dutch photographer Cas Oorthuys, and Roland Topor's blackly comic cartoons. Work not on display can be viewed by appointment in the study-room.

Most of the ground floor is given over to travelling exhibitions and applied art. The small door to the left of the ticket office leads to rooms of odd-shaped furniture, gaudy ceramics and lumpy mats. There's a video art room under the stairs, and the glass box extension at the back of the building occasionally displays work (often dire) by contemporary Amsterdam artists. Two installations on the ground floor shouldn't be missed. The *Appelbar* (through a door to the right of the information desk), adorned with murals of colourful birds, fish and children, is the work of the COBRA artist Karel Appel. It was used as a café until the opening of the present restaurant in 1956. The commission was offered to Appel as a palliative after a débâcle at the Town Hall in 1951: a mural in the canteen, commissioned by the Building Department, had to be boarded over when the Catering Department insisted that it would put people off their food. Edward Kienholz's *Beanery* is a near-life-sized version of a poky Los Angeles bar. You can wander about in the dim light, examining the bric-a-brac. Rusty music scratches away in the juke-box. There's a murmur of conversation. A couple sit at the bar. Someone has passed out in the corner. A waitress clears the remnants of a disgusting meal. But all the faces of the figures are clock-faces, and as you're the only thing that moves it is a surreal and rather disorientating experience. Luckily, the real bar (bright and airy) is just across the corridor. (Unlike the *Appelbar*, the *Beanery* is not a permanent installation, so sometimes disappears into storage or off on tour.)

The Concertgebouw

The Concertgebouw at the southern end of the square was designed by A. L. van Gendt (one of the collaborators on the Centraal Station design) and completed in 1888. It is solid Dutch neo-Renaissance; no frivolity here—indeed, the few urns and obelisks he included in the design either never went up for lack of funds, or have fallen off through lack of funds. The twin staircase towers are intended to harmonize with Cuypers' Rijksmuseum across the way (more out of toadyism than artistic integrity—Cuypers headed the committee that chose the design). Busts of Beethoven, Bach and Sweelinck (Holland's one claim to musical fame) grace the façade. The gilded lyre on top is a 1960s replacement of the original (which fell off). The entrance is no longer through the front, but through a shiny glass extension built in 1988 as part of a complete renovation of the building, which had been subsiding dangerously. The portico, classical shapes and colouring of the extension mean that it does fit in reasonably well and it certainly meets the general manager's stipulation that if there was to be a new front door, he didn't want to have to hang an 'Entrance around the Corner' notice on the old one.

In the 1870s Amsterdam, a city with metropolitan aspirations, found itself without a concert hall and with Brahms's admonition ringing in its ears: '*Ihr seid liebe Leute aber schlechte Musikanten*' (You are lovely people but awful musicians). The government maintained that art was not its business, so it was a committee of private citizens that raised the money, bought some cheap land outside the city limits next to an evil-smelling candle factory and commissioned Van Gendt (more for his figures than his design). Van Gendt prided himself on being a salesman rather than an artist and was completely unmusical. It is ironic that he should have produced a concert hall with possibly the best acoustics in the world. The area soon became very fashionable. The candle factory was replaced by ostentatious mansions and every Thursday the streets would be crammed with the carriages of season-ticket holders.

Under the baton of conductors like Mengelberg (who was sacked for his Nazi sympathies in 1945 after 50 years' service) and Haitink, the resident Royal Concertgebouw Orchestra has become world-famous. If you're passing on a Wednesday, pop in for a free '**lunchconcert**' (*12.30pm, through it's a good idea to be there by 12*). These are usually recitals given in the Kleine Zaal (Small Hall—a chamber music room upstairs), but if you're lucky you might catch the RCO itself in open rehearsal in the Grote Zaal (Big Hall—the main auditorium).

Walk down the left-hand side of the building following Jan Willem Brouwersstraat and turning left into Johannes Verhulststraat.

At the turn of the century there was a garden behind the Concertgebouw. On summer afternoons it would rustle with silk as Amsterdam's élite gathered for outdoor concerts. Those (literally) outside the charmed circle would have to crush around the railings. In 1922 the garden was sold to developers to raise money for a pension fund for the orchestra, and disappeared behind a housing development. If you walk a short way up J. Verhulststraat and look back you'll get the only view now available of the little gilded mermaid blowing her trumpet on top of the Kleine Zaal.

Beyond Museumplein

Almost next door to the Rijksmuseum, on the corner of Hobbemastraat, is **Coster Diamonds** (*open daily 9–5; adm free*). Jews fleeing persecution in Antwerp set up the diamond-polishing industry in Amsterdam in the 16th century. Roaring trade with South Africa established it in the 19th century. (Diamond-cutters would light their cigars with a *f*10 note, more than the average weekly wage.) The city is still a focus for diamond-dealing and processing. What this means in practical terms is that you can buy the gems for half the price you'd pay in London or New York. All over the city factories invite you in to see the craftsmen at work in order to lure you into their salerooms.

Coster Diamonds is one of the biggest. The 'Koh-I-Noor' (Mountain of Light), one of the prize gems in the British crown jewels, was cut here, and there's a glassy replica in the exhibition hall. Smart, uniformed hostesses conduct you on a short tour through the cutting and polishing works (done with whizzing discs coated with diamond dust and olive oil) and then propel you past a room temptingly labelled 'Self-Service' (it turns out to be a café) into the jewellery shop. It's an interesting ten minutes, though if you want to buy it might be worth shopping around.

A block or two away from Museumplein is **Pieter Cornelisz. Hooftstraat**, Amsterdam's most chic shopping street, named after a 17th-century poet. It's one of the few streets in the city where you can confidently window-shop without fear of stepping in dog turds. There are a few exotic delis, certificated Delft porcelain at Focke & Meltzer (No.65) and some elegant, but dull, cafés. Mostly it's clothes: shops for the hip toddler or the fashion-anxious adolescent. If you're past voting age then things range from well-cut classics to the outré (well, almost). All the favourite names (Armani, Gucci, Hamnett) can be found. Some (like MaxMara and Stephane Kelian) have their own shops. P. C. Hooftstraat and Van Baerlestraat, which crosses it further up, are also home to some of the better Dutch designers—Edgar Vos, Rob Kroner and Sissy Boy.

Around the Vondelpark

During the so-called 'Second Golden Age' at the end of the 19th century, when the butter market was turned into Rembrandtplein and the neighbourhood around the museums was being developed as an upmarket residental area, some local burghers got together to create the Vondelpark to commemorate the poet Joost van Vondel.

Joost van Vondel

Joost van Vondel (1582–1674; pronounced in the way an old English army officer might say 'fondle') is proclaimed the Dutch answer to Shakespeare. He excelled in ornate poems in celebration of public events, clocking up over a thousand lines for the opening of the Town Hall alone. The lack of action in his dramas is notorious: he went in for static pictorial representations accompanied by long flowery descriptions of anything exciting. His play *Gijsbrecht van Amstel* is a Dutch literary classic. It's said that one of the scenes inspired Rembrandt's *Night Watch*. By all accounts the Master would have had quite enough time to paint it during the performance. From humble beginnings in his father's busy hosiery shop on the edge of the red-light district, Vondel built up a considerable reputation and small fortune. The former counted for little in mercantile Amsterdam when his son squandered the latter. At the age of 70 he had to go back to work in the city pawnbrokers. He was sacked after 10 years' service for writing poetry in office hours and finally, in his eighties, was granted a state pension. He died at 92 of hypothermia, and suggested his own epitaph:

> *Hier ligt Vondel zonder Rouw,*
> *Hij is gestorven van de kou.*
>
> *Here lies Vondel, without regret [or unmourned],*
> *He was killed by the cold.*

It's a large park by Amsterdam standards and J. D. Kocher's informal English land-scaping gives it calm, graceful lines and wide perspectives. Curved tree-lined avenues, irregularly shaped lakes and ponds, little furrow-like paths through shrubberies, hidden gardens and wide stretches of lawn attract Amsterdammers from all over the city—especially at weekends. A lone accordionist sits on a bench and plays for the ducks. Refugee guitarists from South America play heartrending tunes, homesick for a stronger sunlight. Jugglers meet to learn, practise and show off. There's a party atmosphere whenever the sun shines, and in the summer the festivities go on well into the night with concerts, theatre performances and an open-air cinema. On holidays (especially Queen's Day) enjoyment reaches carnival pitch.

There are dainty bridges, a few sculptural surprises and some odd architecture to catch your eye. As you enter the park, you can see, across the pond, one of the more attractive examples of Nieuwe Zakelijkheid (Functionalist) architecture: H. J. Baanders' **'t Ronde Blauwe Theehuis** (Round Blue Teahouse), a cross between a pagoda and a flying saucer that seems to hover over the water. Across the way Vondel himself, in badly fitting laurels, looks gouty, prosperous and entirely oblivious of the Muses playing about his ankles. His ornate pedestal was made in 1867 by P. J. H. Cuypers (architect of the Centraal Station and Rijksmuseum).

The pavilion near the main entrance to the park was designed in 1881 by P. J. and W. Hamer, and is now the **Netherlands Film Museum** (no exhibition—cinema shows from the archive only, details published in listings magazines). The first director, Jan de Vaal, was a voracious but secretive collector. He hoarded his treasures and seemed wary of the outside world. The result was that not many people bothered about the film museum until the dynamic duo—director Hoos Blotkamp and film buff Eric de Kuyper—took over in the late 1980s and discovered an archive of world significance. Funding was secured, the building was revamped, the long process of cataloguing begun (unearthing such gems as hand-coloured silent movies) and the occasional screenings were boosted to three times a day. There are all sorts of special events and films are shown in the original language. On summer Saturdays there are free screenings on the terrace (around 10pm), when you can buy a beer and have a giggle at Charlie Chaplin or Abbott and Costello. The main hall is worth a peek: its interior is from Amsterdam's first cinema, the Cinema Parisien built in 1910. The Parisien had declined ungracefully into a porn pit when the daughter of the original owner heard, in 1987, that it was about to be gutted by the hotel next door. Armed with coffee flask and screwdriver she went to rescue the interior (still intact after a 1930s redecoration) and, aided by the Monuments Trust, the old atmosphere was bottled and transferred to the Film Museum. The **library** (*open Tues–Fri 10–5, Sat 11–5; adm free*), with a good selection of magazines and reference works and a stash of posters and publicity material, is in the building alongside the pavilion.

The grand 19th-century Gothic of the **Vondelkerk** (Heilige Hartkerk) fills a tiny oval in Vondelstraat, which runs parallel to the park. The architect P. J. H. Cuypers was highly respected for his churches, and this is acknowledged as one of his best. Unfortunately it's been converted to offices, so the interior is lost. The houses at Nos.73–9 Vondelstraat were also designed by Cuypers. The tiled tableaux on the wall show the architect, the mason and the jealous critic. The motto translates as: 'Jan conceives it, Piet realizes it, Claes tears it apart. Oh, who cares?'

Further up Vondelstraat, at No.140, through the arch and up a long passage lies one of Amsterdam's best kept secrets. As you walk up towards the black door at the end of the passage, you'll notice a clue—the earth and cumin-musty smell of horses. Open the door and immediately you are in the vast, light and eerily silent **Hollandse Manege** (*open daily, usually from 10am—midnight*). The architect, A. L. van Gendt (who also designed the Concertgebouw), was influenced by the Spanish Riding School in Vienna. The beautifully plastered interior, with horses' heads worked into the classical design and elegant, open iron roofing, comes as a complete surprise. The one marked 'Tribune' leads to a balcony overlooking the arena. Sawdust muffles all sound and the occasional sharp command from the instructor is all that breaks the thick silence. The door marked 'Foyer' takes you to a café that runs the width of the building. It has the relaxed grandeur of a palace stables. You can see the horses in the arena through glass doors all up one side of the café—and the drinks are the cheapest in town.

The Port of Amsterdam

The Western Islands

The Western Islands, in the old Western Docks beyond Central Station, are man-made. They're close together, criss-crossed by canals and connected by little wooden bridges. There's an eerie sense of isolation, even though they are nowadays very much part of the mainland. In the 17th century Amsterdam burst beyond the boundaries that had contained it for generations. More and more land was created by draining off water into new canals. The area of the city increased by nearly 40 per cent. The poet Vondel wrote some histrionic verse in praise of the achievement (as was very much his wont), using the sort of hyperbole usually reserved for military victories. Travellers marvelled at the size and number of the warehouses. Buildings shot up all over the new islands, and were immediately filled with tobacco, salt, tin, wine, draperies, spices, copper, furs, gold—almost any commodity that could realize a profit.

On **Bickerseiland** (Bicker's Island, named after the original developer), modern concrete apartment blocks with bright red and blue window frames line one side of the narrow walkway. The other side is a jumble of houseboats. Rafts, tugs, canal boats, barges—anything that floats (and some things that almost don't) have been commandeered to solve Amsterdam's chronic housing problem. In the 1950s, when the canal transport industry went into an almost terminal decline, skippers were only too pleased to offload their craft on the oddballs who wanted to live on the water. By the 1970s there were around 800 legally licensed moorings and countless illegal ones. The council

The Port of Amsterdam

outlawed all newcomers and granted an amnesty to over a thousand of the unlicensed boats that were already occupied. Recently, moves have begun again to get rid of them.

Their occupants were allowed (like those on the legal boats) to connect up to the water and electricity supplies. Arrangements for the latter are alarmingly Heath Robinson. Wonky home-made poles hold up yards of black flex as it snakes along the canalside and between the boats. Wet washing flutters from these improvised clothes lines. Originally houseboats were the domain of the weird and rebellious, but now lawyers and stock-brokers sun themselves on deck and talk for hours about waterproofing techniques. One boat even houses a community of nuns. Streetnames like 'Sailmaker's Street' and 'Blockmaker's Street' are all that's left of the shipbuilding yards for which Bickerseiland was renowned. (It was also famous for its dogs. There were so many that the local church had to employ two dog-chasers to keep the aisles free during services.) Most of the island is taken up by soulless 1970s housing estates. At Zeilmakerstraat 15, in one of the few buildings to escape post-war redevelopment, you'll find the **Amsterdams Beeldhouwers Kollektief** (Amsterdam Sculptors' Collective; *open Thurs–Sun 1–5*). The sixty members (some of the city's best young sculptors among them) keep the gallery well supplied. Exhibitions change frequently. Most work is on sale, and not all of it is of a size to preclude taking it home in your overnight bag.

Realeneiland is named after Jacob Real, the original owner. Ahead of you as you cross the bridge on to the island is a neat little row of 17th-century houses. Jacob Real's own, rather modest house (now a restaurant) is at the end. He was a fervent Catholic. The gold-painted coin on the gable stone commemorates the treasures he saved from the icon-oclasts by smuggling them out of a monastery in the nick of time. Real's surname (also the name of a coin) afforded an appropriate pun, and the house became known as **'De Gouden Reael'**. There's a tang of tar and varnish in the air. The diligent occupants of the rather stately row of boats on the dockside seem perpetually involved in maintenance.

Hidden in the middle of the Western Islands, **Prinseneiland** is the best of all. Its little lanes are a mish-mash of architectural styles. Tumbledown warehouses crumble quietly next to smart, sharp-edged new apartments. Tall, carefully restored façades grace the canal. The island is perfumed by freshly sawn timber from the working boatyard. There's seldom any traffic. All you hear is the sound of sawing, workmen calling to each other and (to jolt you back down to earth) pop music from their ghetto-blasters. The bridge at the eastern end of Galgenstraat used to afford a fine prospect of the city's Golgotha ('Galg' means 'gallows'). The curious were not always afforded a view of the whole process. Offenders were often executed in the city centre. The heads, sometimes with the heart stuffed into the mouth, were posted on the city wall and only the discarded bits ended up on the grassy mound near the Galgenbrug.

Around Haarlemmerplein

On the busy square of Haarlemmerplein, some way west of Central Station, stands the massive **Willemspoort** (a.k.a. Haarlemmerpoort), a neoclassical gatehouse built for the entrance of King William II in 1840. The masons botched the rather special *trompe-*

l'œil effect that has to be achieved to keep the perspectives right: the central columns appear to taper rather suddenly at the top. It's never been a popular structure. At a town council meeting at the turn of the century it was saved from demolition by only four votes. If you walk through the gate you'll see four small rectangles set into the second pillar on the left. They mark the position of the old *stokmaat*, the measure by which horses were judged large enough for military service. It was used right up to the First World War.

Over the past few years the streets leading to the square, **Haarlemmerdijk** and **Haarlemmerstraat**, have developed into one of the quirkiest and most varied shopping quarters in town. New Age stores, junk shops, galleries, zany boutiques and ethnic gift shops all contribute to the appeal. Among the more curious attractions is Beune's confectioners at No.156. If you take them your photograph, they'll reproduce it in icing on the cake of your choice. The result is a white slab with a sombre sepia image, rather like a Portuguese tombstone. There's a chess and go shop (No.147) and a shop selling wildly coloured hand-woven Tibetan tiger rugs. A church by the 19th-century grandfather of modern Dutch architecture, P. J. H. Cuypers, has (like so many of his others) been converted into offices. Towards the end of the street you'll have to concentrate hard not to miss De Groene Lanteerne which, at 128cm wide, claims to be the world's narrowest restaurant.

Going East

Skirting the top edge of inner Amsterdam, going east from Central Station you come to the **Scheepvaarthuis** (Shipping House), built in 1916 (on the site of the place where the first Dutch fleet set sail for the East Indies) as the offices for six big shipping companies. After serving as the headquarters of the municipal transport authority during the 1980s and most of the 1990s it was closed for renovation, and will probably reopen as a hotel. It was the first building designed by the team of architects (Van der Meij, Kramer and De Klerk) who became known as the Amsterdam School, a sort of fantastical Dutch Art Nouveau movement (*see* pp.134–6). Nothing escapes decoration. The building comes to a prow-like point crowned by a statue of Neptune. He waves his trident while his wife Salicia takes the wheel. Four female figures represent the points of the compass. The walls are encrusted with unflattering reliefs of sea heroes. Doors, stairs, window frames and any wall space left are patterned with appropriate images—wave forms, sea horses, dolphins, anchors, seals and ship's wheels. The roof line is a cheval-de-frise of moulded lead. It's as if you're viewing the building in a distorting mirror: there's hardly a smooth surface in sight. The maritime motifs continue inside with filigreed metalwork ornamentation, beautiful stained-glass skylights and windows and much of the original furniture (also designed by the architects). Doorknobs, lamps, wall-panels, floor patterns all reflect the theme. No detail is missed.

Farther along Prins Hendrikkade you come to the eye-catching **New Metropolis Science & Technology Centre** (*open Tues–Sun 10–6, Sat open until 9pm; adm f24, after 4pm f14, under 17s f16*), featuring all sorts of interactive equipment in a giant ship-shaped museum designed by Italian architect Renzo Piano. Just across the water is the sturdy **Nederlands Scheepvaart Museum** (Maritime Museum), built as an admiralty warehouse in 1655 (*open Tues–Sun 10–5; adm f14.50*). It's a wonder the building's still upright: workers were bribed with *drinkgelt* (drinking money) and finished it in an amazing nine months and fourteen days. The new warehouse had a system of cisterns and sprinklers to put out fires and an army of rat-catching cats with their own office and keeper. The museum's main attraction—a full size replica of the *Amsterdam*, one of the VOC's ships—is moored outside (though occasionally it pays visits to other ports). You can swan about the captain's cabin, have a look at his tiny loo then descend into the ship's murky maw where up to 200 sailors would live for months at a stretch. From the upper deck you can look across to the VOC warehouses on the end of Prins Hendrikkade. Back in the museum you can see a cutaway of an 1840s outrigger and the ostentatiously gilded (and rather uncomfortable) Royal Barge used for state occasions and for paddling visiting dignitaries around the canals. You can also climb up to the Second World War room to peer out at Amsterdam through a periscope. The rest of the museum comprises room after room of maps, navigational equipment from previous eras, and models and pictures of ships. Everything is informatively labelled in Dutch and English, giving you a good introduction to the history of Dutch seafaring. The 'Time Voyage' multimedia show takes you a step further, portraying—with smoke machines, movies, slide shows and special effects—how unjolly it was to be a tar in the 17th century. The museum shop is well-provisioned with books on ships, and is a treasure chest of maritime flotsam and jetsam. In an unmarked room in the cellar a man sells model kits of awesome complexity (*Thurs–Sat only*).

Across the bridge to the right is the **Kromhout Museum** (*open Mon-Fri 10–4; adm f3.50*), one of Amsterdam's oldest shipbuilding yards, and one of the few to survive the 19th-century decline in the trade. It had a new lease of life in the 20th century when it produced the diesel engine used by most Dutch inland craft. In the 1960s it moved to larger premises and the old yard became a museum. Some boat building and restoration still goes on, but rows of diesel engines form the bulk of the exhibits. It's very much a place for the enthusiast.

Further Afield

The Plantagebuurt

The elegant, wide streets of the **Plantage** ('Plantation') district east of Waterlooplein were once a bushy parkland where Amsterdammers would lounge about on feast days, or go on long evening walks. At the end of the 19th century this was flattened by rows of showy neoclassical houses with outrageous colonial embellishments (pineapple pinnacles, exotic festoons, negro figurines propping up the beam ends). Many of the wealthier Jews moved into the grand new houses and by the 1920s it was the suburb of the Jewish élite. In 1897 the **Hollandse Schouwburg** (Holland Theatre) at Plantage Middenlaan 24, after a false start as an operetta theatre, became the home of the Nederlandsche Toneelvereeniging (Dutch Drama Society)—the company that propelled Dutch theatre into the 20th century. Because of the large number of Jews in both the audience and the theatre group itself, the occupying forces during the Second World War renamed it the Joodsche Schouwburg (Jewish Theatre). In 1942 it was designated an assembly point for Jews waiting to be deported. People were kept in the darkened building for days and then herded on to trains bound for Westerbork and then on to the death camps at Auschwitz and Sobibor. Understandably, after the war no one much wanted to use the Hollandse Schouwburg as a theatre again; in the 1960s it was declared a memorial to the deported Jews who never returned. Today only a secluded memorial garden lies behind the façade. Every year on 4 May (Remembrance Day) the city keeps a two-minute silence at 8pm to commemorate those who died in the war.

Nearby is the **Desmet Cinema**. During the war, German Jewish refugees staged theatre and cabaret here. The shows were so good that even the Nazi officer in charge of deportation would slip in to watch. Across the way is the **Wertheimpark**, the last remaining patch of the old Plantage gardens. At the entrance, two sphinxes with lanterns on their heads glower from the top of disproportionately large gateposts. Most of the park seems taken up by a fountain in memory of A. C. Wertheim (1832–97), a philanthropic banker who lived out his motto: 'Be a Jew in the synagogue and a human being in society', by being available in his office for an hour every morning to anyone, Jew or gentile, who needed to appeal to his charity. In one corner of the park, built over an urn of ashes brought back from Auschwitz, is a monument to Jews who perished in the concentration camps. Smashed mirrors lie flat on the ground: a symbol that the Earth can no longer reflect Heaven without distortion.

Just a little nearer to town, the **Hortus Botanicus** (*Botanical Gardens; open 1 April–1 Oct, 9–5 on weekdays and 11–5 other days; from 1 Oct to 1 April it closes at 4pm; adm f7.50*), was originally an apothecaries' herb garden in a marshy corner of the Plantage. It was later inundated by tropical plants pillaged by the Dutch East India Company, and has ended up with one of the biggest botanical collections in the world. A coffee shrub cultivated at the Hortus was presented to Louis XIV in 1714. Its seeds

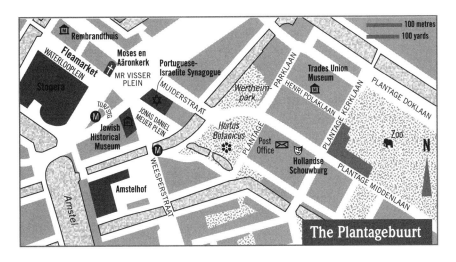

were used to initiate the cultivation of coffee in South America. A century later the gardens narrowly survived Louis Bonaparte's attempt to turn them into a zoo. The animals arrived before any cages had been built and the orangery became a volatile dormitory for wolves, lions, monkeys and porcupines. Tranquillity was restored when, after the king's untimely departure from the Netherlands, a relieved directorate put the animals up for auction. During the first half of this century, the gardens' biggest attraction was the massive Victoria Amazonica water lily. People would queue for hours on the one night of the year when it flowered, and—so the stories go—could stand, three at a time, on the broad lily pads. The sturdy plant survived this abuse, but not the demolition of its greenhouse in the 1960s. For decades there was no Victoria Amazonica at the Hortus, but in the 1990s a new greenhouse was built, and the giant lily once more has pride of place. The Hortus is a tranquil spot, a pocket-sized patch of green that's not really part of the tourist circuit. It won't take you long to nip in and see the ancient varieties of tulip, visit the world's oldest pot plant, warily observe the cabinet of flesh-eating plants, enjoy the tropical climes of the glass-domed palm house or the balmy air in the new three-climate hothouse. Then you can cool off with a fruit juice in the Orangery.

Along the Amstel

On the Amstel river just south of its crossing with Prinsengracht is a lively classical building with a cornice of jesters and grinning clowns. This is the **Royal Carré theatre**, built as a circus for Oscar Carré in 1887. Until 1875, Amsterdam had held an annual fair in September. It was a three-week beanfeast that engulfed the entire city with balls, celebrity performances, sideshows and circuses. One of these was Carré's, which King Willem III had granted the honorary title of 'Royal Dutch'—the equivalent of an official 'By Appointment' stamp. But the revels had grown a little too unleashed for the tastes of the Protestant patricians, and the city council declared that the 'Kermis' of 1875 was to be the last. Despite rioting in the streets (which destroyed much of the original mauve 17th-century

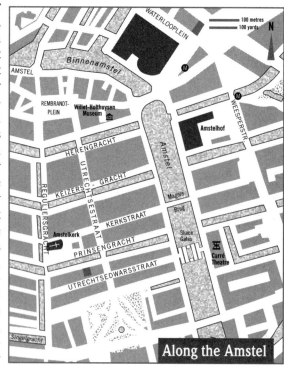

glass in canal-house windows), their edict was carried out and Amsterdam lost its annual wassail. But Carré decided he was going to stay. He built a 'temporary' wooden circus tent beside the Amstel and, when the council wasn't looking, erected a stone façade. Outraged city fathers declared that he should take it down, but Carré fought on tenaciously throughout the 1880s, and eventually got his way. The striking building you see today was built within months as the circus's permanent home. Now it hosts mainly musicals, but the best time to see its circular plush interior is when it reverts to being a circus over the Christmas holiday.

A little way up the river you can see the **Magere Brug** ('Skinny Bridge'). It was built in the 17th century for two spoilt young maidens who were too lazy to walk the long way round from their house in Kerkstraat to their stables across the river. A public outcry prevented its being replaced by a steel bridge in 1929, but the old structure was rotting and today's delicate white wooden swing bridge is a replica.

De Pijp

The area just south of the Singelgracht, east of Museumplein, is known as De Pijp (The Pipe) for the long thin passages that run between the 19th-century tenement houses. Once a slum, it's now a lively neighbourhood populated by artists and immigrant communities. The main north–south street is Ferdinand Bolstraat, but the streets seem to get brighter, busier and nosier as you get closer to the **Albert Cuyp Market**, where it all explodes into a cacophony of national musics, a kaleidoscope of colour and a press

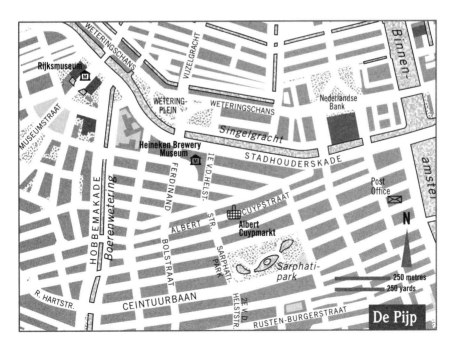

of eager shoppers that stretches for over a kilometre. Eating seems to be an important reason to be here. Between the piles of silk, gaudy modern clothes and cheap shoes, boxes of dried herbs and teas, people slip raw herrings down their throats, guzzle home-made chocolates, queue for freshly cooked waffles, taste farm cheese and stock up on fish, fruit and vegetables for even greater feasting at home. Behind the stalls there's yet another layer of life—tacky clothing shops, ethnic stores and cheap Indian and Surinamese restaurants. An old hippie busker sings exactly the same repertoire, on the same corner, every day.

The **Heineken Brewery Museum** (*guided tours only: Mon–Fri 9.30 and 11am,1pm and 2.30pm Saturdays in July and Aug also noon and 2pm; allow 2 hours; adm f3, which goes to charity*) on the corner of Ferdinand Bolstraat and Stadhouderskade is the birthplace of Heineken beer. The brewery, established here in 1867, stopped production on this site only a few years ago when Amsterdam began to drink more than the brewery could produce. Now smart guides lead you through the stables (old dray horses *in situ*) and past huge copper vats. You learn how beer is made and how the Heineken family made its fortune. The real purpose of the visit for many people, however, seems to be the free beer at the end of the tour.

Amsterdam School Architecture and the New South

The Nieuw Zuid (New South) was created by the architect H. P. Berlage (1856–1934), the father of modern Dutch architecture (*see* p.63), after a new law had revolutionized Amsterdam housing conditions. In 1915–17 he drew up a plan of wide avenues and narrow side streets that reflected the 17th-century canals. He died before he could implement it, and his work was taken on with even greater enthusiasm by Michel de Klerk and Pieter Kramer, architects of what became known as the Amsterdam School. De Klerk was a working-class wunderkind headhunted from primary school to begin work with the city's leading architectural firm at the age of 14. He and Kramer set out to design buildings that were, in his words, 'sensationally shocking'. They were successful. When the Nieuw Zuid was finished nobody wanted to live there. The area eventually became a ghetto for Jews fleeing persecution in Germany. (The Frank family lived on Merwedeplein before going into hiding.) In the past few years there's been a revival of interest in the Amsterdam School. Houses, bridges and even public lavatories are being declared national monuments.

In reacting against their sober, rational Dutch predecessors, the Amsterdam School produced an idiosyncratic cross between Old Dutch and Art Nouveau, which has led to some quirky and amusing, but also rather beautiful building. You can see why they're sometimes called the 'Gaudís of the North'. Their whimsical brick buildings are instantly recognizable by the curves and bulges of their façades. The buildings are constructed around a reinforced concrete frame, so the bricks can do what they like. The pleats and folds earned the movement's work the nickname *schortjesarchitectuur* (apron architecture). Decorative, polychromatic, almost sculptural brickwork is used

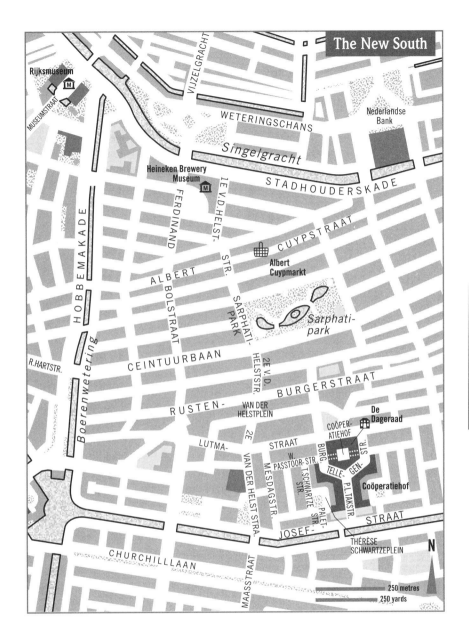

lavishly. Odd parabolic and trapeziform windows and angulated carved doors contrast startlingly with the general symmetry of the buildings. Stone and brick sculptures are integrated into the building's design, especially at corners and on bridges. In the Nieuw Zuid these are usually the gnome-like mythical figures by Hildo Krop (1884–1970).

Features of the Amsterdam School

Shape: Their whimsical brick buildings are instantly recognizable by the curves and bulges of their façades. Entire blocks were seen as one building—waves of roofs and balconies give a delightful sense of horizontal movement. Soaring chimneys and stairways accentuate the vertical lines.

Bricks: Decorative, polychromatic, almost sculptural brickwork is used lavishly. Like Berlage, the new builders used 'honest' Dutch materials of wood and brick, but the buildings are constructed around a reinforced concrete frame, so the bricks can do what they like. The pleats and folds earned the movement's work the nickname *schortjesarchitectuur* (apron architecture). Straight edges are often softened by a frill of vertically placed roofing tiles.

Windows and Doors: Odd parabolic and trapeziform windows and angulated carved doors contrast startlingly with the general symmetry of the buildings.

Sculptures: Stone and brick sculptures are integrated into the building's design, especially at corners and on bridges. In the Nieuw Zuid these are usually the gnome-like mythical figures by Hildo Krop (1884–1970). Krop was the municipal sculptor for many years and his chunky work is all over Amsterdam. Recently it was revealed that for much of that time he was working for the Soviet KGB, and it's even been suggested that he was involved in the recruitment of Anthony Blunt and other famous British spies.

Details: House numbers, letterboxes and hoists are all designed to fit into the larger scheme. Egyptian and oriental influences are evident in the metalwork.

You can see prime examples of Amsterdam School in the area around **Burgemeester Tellegenstraat**, a patch of streets and squares designed entirely by Kramer and De Klerk. In 1918 the housing association **De Dageraad** (Daybreak) gave the young men free rein to design the neighbourhood. Strikingly curved staircase towers, wavy rooftops, jutting sharp-edged windows and fancy coloured brickwork are the results of this freedom from restriction. The buildings are wonderful to look at, but residents complain their furniture doesn't fit in the odd-shaped rooms. The two crescents of Burgemeester Tellegenstraat are completely symmetrical. Look at the lettering in the doorways. You'll occasionally even find corresponding lettering on one side reflected in mirror image on the other.

Amsterdam ✆ (020–)

Sports and Activities

spectator sports

The Amsterdam **football** team, Ajax, is one of the best and most popular in the country. Important matches have even been known to cause the city council to adjourn sessions. Ajax won European Cups three times in the 1970s, and managed again in 1995. If you want to see the team for yourself, head for their flashy new home, the Amsterdam ArenA, ☏ 311 1333, next to the Bijlmer metro station in Amsterdam South East. A good **ice hockey** team (S IJ S Amsterdam 89) plays at the Jaap Edenhal rink, Radioweg 64, ☏ 694 9652, from Oct to Feb. The local **basketball** team, Canadians Amsterdam, is one of the best in the country. They play at the Apollohal, Stadionweg, ☏ 671 3910. Fans of **American football** might be lucky enough to catch an Amsterdam Admirals, ☏ 465 0550, home game at the Amsterdam ArenA or at the old Olympic Stadium.

do-it-yourself

The 1980s health mania hit Amsterdam as soundly as it did other major cities in the Western world, and has persisted into the 1990s. You can find a number of well-equipped **gyms and fitness centres** around town. Two of the best are: Splash, Looiersgracht 26–30, ☏ 624 8404 (*open daily 7am–midnight; weights, machines, sauna, steam, massage and aerobics; f35 per day/f65 per week/f135 per month all inclusive*) and Garden Gym, Jodenbreestraat 158, ☏ 626 8772 (*open Mon, Wed, Fri 9–11, Tues and Thurs 12–11, Sat 11–6.30 and Sun 10–5 mainly, though not exclusively, for women; weights, dance, sauna, solarium, massage, self-defence; day pass f15, with sauna/shower f22.50, sauna only f17.50*). Sauna Deco, Herengracht 115, ☏ 623 8215 (*open Mon–Sat 11–11, Sun 12–6 adm f17.50 before 2pm, or f25 per day*) is an exhilarating experience. You sweat away those extra inches in a stylish Art Deco interior rescued from a famous 1920s Parisian department store.

Swimming pools in Amsterdam are clean, well-maintained and supervised. They often have small bars or coffeeshops at the water's edge so you can top up the calories after an energetic swim. Opening times are complicated, with periods set aside for club and naked swimming, so it's a good idea to phone first. The Marnixbad, Marnixplein 9, ☏ 625 4843 (*adm f4.50*) has waterslides and a whirlpool. The Mirandabad, De Mirandalaan 9, ☏ 642 8080 (*adm f7*) has tropical temperatures, a pebble beach and a wave machine. There's an outdoor pool for good weather and a slide and whirlpool. The Zuiderbad, Hobbemastraat 26, ☏ 679 2217 (*adm f4.5*) is just a plain, rectangular pool of water for swimming quietly up and down in. It was built at the beginning of the century and still has most of its original features, including some beautiful tile work and a neat perimeter of wooden changing cubicles opening on to the edge of the pool.

Walking and **cycling** are the two great national pastimes, and the attractive canals and well-laid out cycle paths make both a joy. If you want to be more serious about things, or would like an uninhibited jog, head for the Vondelpark or the Amsterdamse Bos. The Amsterdam Tourist Board can offer suggestions for cycling or walking tours (*see* p.76 for bicycle hire). They will also be able to give you information on the **Grachtenloop** ('canal run'), Amsterdam's equivalent of the London Marathon. One Sunday early in June thousands of people come together to spend the best part of the day jogging set distances up and down the main canals.

In the winter walking gives way to **skating**. If you're lucky you may be in Amsterdam in a year when the canals freeze over, and everyone whizzes around the city on skates. (Be careful, though, the ice can be thin and sometimes doesn't freeze under bridges.) If you don't have your own skates, head for Jaap Edenhal, Radioweg 64, ℘ 694 9652, a large indoor rink where you can hire skates for ƒ9 (you'll need your passport or a ƒ100 deposit).

If bats, rackets and balls are your forte, you'll find **squash** and **indoor tennis** courts at the Frans Otten Stadion, Stadionstraat 10, ℘ 662 8767 (*open Mon–Fri 9–11, Sat 9–8, Sun 9–10; tennis ƒ37.50 per hour/ƒ50 after 5pm, squash ƒ30/ƒ37.50 per hour; racket hire ƒ5*). There are 36 tennis courts, most of them outdoor, at the Amstelpark, Koenenkade 8, ℘ 644 5436 (*open daily 8am–11pm; indoor courts ƒ35 per hour, outdoor courts ƒ30; racket hire ƒ5*). Squash City, Ketelmakerstraat 6, ℘ 626 7883 (*open Mon–Fri 8.30–midnight, Sat and Sun 8.30–10; ƒ17.50 for 45 minutes after 5pm Mon–Fri and on Sun, ƒ13.50 before 5pm and on Sat; racket hire ƒ5*) also has a weights room and sauna for players to use. For **table tennis** enthusiasts, there's the Table Tennis Centre Amsterdam, Keizersgracht 209, ℘ 624 5780 (*open Sun 1–7.30pm, Mon 2–6pm, Tues–Sat 2pm–1am; ƒ12.50 per table per hour*).

As gentler form of relaxation, you might try a little **billiards**, **snooker** or the pocketless Dutch variation called *biljart* (countless volunteers willing to explain the rules and offer advice around every table). You'll find all three played at the Biljartcentrum Bavaria, Van Ostadestraat 97, ℘ 676 4059 (*open daily 11am–1am; snooker ƒ10 per hour until 2pm, then ƒ15*). The Snookercentrum de Keizer, Keizersgracht 256, ℘ 623 1586 (*open Mon–Thurs and Sun noon–1am, Sat noon–2am; ƒ8.50 per hour before 7pm, then ƒ12 for pool and ƒ15 for snooker*) is in a 17th-century canal house. The tables are in private rooms and you can phone down to the bar for drinks.

Shopping

> *What is there that's not found here*
> *Of corn; French or Spanish wine*
> *Any Indies goods that are sought*
> *In Amsterdam may all be bought*
> *Here's no famine—the land is fat.*

Constantijn Huygens, 17th-century Dutch poet

Amsterdam's prosperity in the Golden Age turned it into an exotic emporium mundi. The little shops below the decorative *uithangborden* (painted signs) were crammed with Nuremberg ceramics, Lyons silk, Spanish wines, mysterious Egyptian potions and an abundance of local pastries, cheeses, linen and boots. When Marie de Médicis made her grandiose entry into Amsterdam in 1638, the first thing she did when she had a moment's spare time (amidst the lavish ceremonies celebrating her arrival) was to swoop down on the

Amsterdam shops where, apparently, she haggled with the adept confidence of someone reared in a marketplace.

Amsterdam's markets, boutiques and eccentric speciality shops are still one of the city's greatest allures. The range of goods and oddity of the shops can keep you browsing for hours. The only barriers against your absolute financial ruin are the inconvenient opening hours. Calvinism wins over tourism—despite the recent relaxation of laws governing shop hours, you'll find very few places at all open on a Sunday. Amsterdammers enjoy their weekends, and the fun tends to overflow into Monday: many shops also stay closed on Monday mornings, if not for the whole day. However, most stay open late on Thursday nights. (Thursday, the night before the weekenders descend on the city, has a wild feeling of local festivity that dissipates under the influx of outsiders.)

after-hours shopping

Amsterdam night shops include **Baltus**, Vijzelstraat 127, **Big Bananas**, Leidsestraat 76, with big price tags and rude assistants, and **Heuft's First Class Nightshop**, Rijnstraat 62, for late-night oysters and champagne. In addition to these, the **Albert Heijn Supermarket** on Koningsplein is open 10–10 Mon–Sat and noon–6 on Sunday. It is a conventional supermarket with normal prices. Some larger stores in the city centre (such as **Hema** and **De Bijenkorf**) are now also open on Sunday afternoons.

To locate a late-night pharmacy contact an information service on ℗ 694 8709.

antiques

The Rokin (the street running from the Dam to Muntplein) was once the traditional stretch for antique dealers. Now there are only a few crusty die-hards here—the sort of shop where you have to comb your hair and ring a bell before they let you in. These days the most stylish, outlandish and enticingly chaotic treasure-troves are to be found in the Spiegelkwartier (*see* p.104) and around the Looiersgracht.

bicycles

Macbike, Mr Visserplein 2. Second-hand bikes. Parts, repairs and sympathy when your machine falls to bits or the front wheel gets caught in the tram lines.

't Mannetje, Frans Halsstraat 35. Tandems, three-wheelers and other curious designs, as well as repairs.

books

Good antiquarian bookshops pop up all over the city, but especially around the university at the southern end of the red-light district. New books in English are usually quite expensive in Amsterdam.

American Book Center, Kalverstraat 185. After W.H. Smith's, the best stock in town of English fiction and non-fiction, magazines and children's books.

Architectura & Natura, Leliegracht 44. Just what it says, with an impressive collection of books on Amsterdam.

Atheneum, Spui 14–16. Stamping ground of the city's intelligentsia. Good selection of magazines and English non-fiction.

The Book Exchange, Kloveniersburgwal 58. Essential in this town of outrageous prices.

La Carte, Utrechtsestraat 110–12. Maps, streetplans and guide books.

The English Bookshop, Lauriergracht 71. Carefully selected range, with some second-hand.

Intertaal, Van Baerlestraat 76. Everything you need to learn Dutch or to teach English.

Lankamp & Brinkman, Spiegelgracht 19. Children's books in English.

Lambiek, Kerkstraat 78. Cheery comic shop. Collectors' pieces and a cartoonists' gallery.

Robert Premsela, Van Baerlestraat 78. Art books a cut above the museum shops.

De Slegte, Kalverstraat 48–52. Discount and antiquarian megastore.

Waterstones, Kalverstraat 152. Large well-stocked branch of the British chain.

cameras and photography

Foto Amsterdam, Rokin 22. Official dealer for all the big names.

Superfoto, Leidsestraat 80, and around town. Colour film ready in an hour. Two days for slides.

Ruad Foto, Jan Toroopstraat 47. Cameras, computers and camcorders to hire.

clothes

Dutch designers don't cause many tremors in world fashion, but you will find tasteful, well-cut clothes in fine fabrics at much lower prices than in other capitals. The second-hand clothes shops attract stall-grubbers from around the globe. **P. C. Hooftstraat** and **Van Baerlestraat** are the corridors of high fashion— here you'll find international labels as well as Dutch designers.

Cora Kemperman, Leidsestraat 72. Slightly off-the-wall yet supremely stylish.

Edgar Vos, P. C. Hooftstraat 134. Nifty suits for the high-powered businesswoman.

Fever, Prinsengracht 192. Hot little numbers for hot little people.

Sissy Boy, Van Baerlestraat 15. Middle-of-the-road elegance at fast-lane prices.

Rob & Rik, Runstraat 30. Leatherwear from functional to fetish.

Tothem, Nieuwezijds Voorburgwal 149. Swimsuits and sexy underwear for men.

La Culotte, P. C. Hooftstraat 111. Pricey, sensuous silk lingerie.

Clubwear House, Herengracht 265. Clubwear for the brave and the beautiful.

For children's clothes there's **Bam Bam**, Magna Plaza, Nieuwezijds Voorburgwal 182, where there's treasure-trove for trendy toddlers, and **Oilily**, P. C. Hooftstraat 133, for tiny tots whose mums and dads have big pockets.

Clusters of second-hand shops rub elbow patches with each other in the zigzag of lanes from Huidenstraat to Hartenstraat. You could also try **Hans en Grietje**,

Overtoom 255, for ethnic and colonial bits and bobs, and **Petticoat**, Lindengracht 99, for Fifties retro, hats, shawls and cufflinks, and zooty under-wear.

If you're into something tasteful or demure, head for P.C. Hooftstraat again. Alternatively try **Shoebaloo**, Koningsplein 7–9, with glitz, ruffs and teetering heels for the oddly shod (unisex); **Big Shoe**, Leliegracht 12, for big feet (either gender), or **Candy Corson**, St Luciensteeg 19, for stylish leather bags and belts.

department stores

De Bijenkorf, Dam 1. 'The Beehive'—aptly named. Bustling shop with a wide range of good quality merchandise, and no pretensions to being Harrods.

Hema, Kalvertoren, Kalverstraat (and all around town). The Dutch Woolworth's or five-and-dime—but all in good taste. An excellent one-stop shop to stock up on essentials.

Metz & Co., Keizersgracht 455. Liberty prints, stylish kitchenware and design-museum furniture. Superb view of Amsterdam from the glass-walled café on the top floor.

Delftware, clogs and gifts

Rinascimento Gallerie d'Arte, Prinsengracht 170. Old and new Delftware (the real thing, not souvenir shop tat). Watch the designs being painted on by hand.

De Klompenboer, Nieuwezijds Voorburgwal 20. Clogs and other wooden goodies carved on the premises. Also pewter and lace.

diamonds

Where you buy depends on your personal taste, but do shop around and stick to established dealers. You can watch diamonds being cut in a number of shops, including **Coster Diamonds**, Paulus Potterstraat 2–6, Rokin Diamonds, Rokin 12, and **Van Moppes**, Albert Cuypstraat 2–6.

dry cleaning, laundry and repair

Clean Center, Ferdinand Bolstraat 7–9. Open Mon–Fri 8am–9 pm, Sat 8–5.

Cleaning Shop Express, Huidenstraat 24a. Dry cleaning, laundering, repairs.

food

Look out for two kinds of **bakery**. A *warme bakker* sells breads and biscuits and a *banketbakker* sells pastries and all the wonderful creamy things that the doctor forbids. Many also sell hand-made chocolates. Try **Runneboom**, 1e van der Helststraat 49, for delicious ryebread, Greek village loaves, healthy wholemeals and crispy white rolls, **Hendrikse**, Overtoom 472, with tarts and cream cakes fit for Queen Beatrix, and closer to the centre of town, **C. O. Hotkamp**, Vijzelgracht 15.

In the better **cheese** shops you'll be given a sliver to taste before buying. Choose from mild *jong* (young), or the more tangy *belegen* (matured) or *extra belegen*. **Arxhoek**, Damstraat 19, has a large selection, especially of farm cheeses. **Pasteuning Deliwijn**, Willemsparkweg 11, is a traditional Italian deli with a good selection of wines. **A Taste of Ireland**, Herengracht 228, sells British provisions for the homesick; and the chain **Natuurwinkel**, Weteringschans 133, and all around town, provides everything from organic vegetables and wine to vitamins and tofu-burgers.

Albert Hein is the most popular chain of supermarket. You'll find branches on Waterlooplein, Koningsplein and Vijzelstraat. The largest—the one behind the Royal Palace—is also open on Sundays.

For tea and coffee, go to **Keizer**, Prinsengracht 180, with wondrous aromas and odd utensils in an early 19th-century setting; or **Geels & Co**, Warmoesstraat 67, the city's oldest tea and coffee specialist, in the middle of the red-light district.

De Bierkoning, Paleisstraat 125, a cosy shop behind the palace, sells glasses of all shapes and around 750 brands of bottled beer. **Hart's Wijnhandel**, Vijzelgracht 3, has a wide range of wines and spirits.

markets

Albert Cuyp Markt, Albert Cuypstraat, *Mon–Sat 9–4.30*. Foodstuffs, clothes and hardware (*see* p.133).

Bloemenmarkt (Flower Market), Singel, between Muntplein and Koningsplein, *Mon–Sat 9–6*. Amsterdam's floating flower market (*see* p.93).

Boerenmarkt, Noordermarkt, *Sat 10–3*. Organic produce, ethnic crafts.

Lapjesmarkt, Westerstraat, *Mon 7.30–1*. Bargain clothes and spectacular fabrics.

Lindengracht, *Sat 9–4*. Small general market, but the best.

De Looier Indoor Antiques Market, Elandsgracht; *Mon–Thurs 11–5, Sat 9–5*. Mid-price antiques market. There's also a *rommelmarkt* (junk market) just around the corner.

Nieuwmarkt, *May–Sept, Sun 10–5*. Good quality antiques in the shadow of a medieval city gate and weighing house.

Noordermarkt, *Mon 7.30–1.30*. Pile upon pile of junk. Get there early for a treasure hunt.

Oudemanhuis Book Market, Oudemanhuispoort, *Mon–Sat 10–4*. A dim alley smelling of musty binding and yellowing paper.

Stamp Market, near Nova Hotel, Nieuwezijds Voorburgwal 276; *Wed, Sat 11–4*. Grizzled collectors swap stamps, currency, medals and esoteric jokes.

Waterlooplein; *Mon–Sat 10–4*. Amsterdam's famous fleamarket.

specialist shops

Amsterdam abounds in idiosyncratic speciality shops: old family businesses, outlets for some personal obsession or the fantasies of quixotic visionaries. Here are but a few:

De Beestenwinkel (The Animal Shop), Staalstraat 11. Stuffed bunnies, tiger puppets and teddy bears to put your pyjamas in.

Brillenwinkel, Gasthuismolensteeg 7. Classic spectacle frames, from Mahatma Gandhi to Dame Edna.

Condomerie Het Gulden Vlies, Warmoesstraat 141. Condom as consumer item.

Joe's Vliegerwinkel, Nieuwe Hoogstraat 19. Kites weird and wonderful.

Hangmatten Maranón, Singel 488–90. Bright and breezy hammocks from around the world.

P. G. C. Hajenius, Rokin 92–6. Tobacconist with famed house-brand cigars.

The Head Shop, Kloveniersburgwal 39. Accessories for dope devotees.

Kitsch Kitchen, 1e Bloemdwarsstraat 21. Gaudy plastic goodies, brightly patterned enamel bowls and curious kitchen implements.

Knopenwinkel, Wolvenstraat 14. Buttons of all shapes and periods.

Kramer, Reestraat 20. Candles and candlesticks—ethnic to high altar.

Klamboe Imports, Prinsengracht 232. Mosquito nets—the best way to ward off the pests.

Olivaria, Hazenstraat 2a. An entire shop devoted to olive oil; there's even a tasting bar.

Poppendokter, Reestraat 20. Dolls and parts of dolls.

Vlieger, Amstel 34. Pencils, pigments and piles of inspiring paper.

Waterwinkel, Roelof Hartstraat 10. Over 100 types of mineral water from around the world, and mud from the Dead Sea.

De Witte Tanden Winkel, Runstraat 5. Champagne-flavoured toothpaste and tooth-brushes, toothbrushes, toothbrushes.

Amsterdam ✆ (020–)   ***Where to Stay***

It's a summer Friday afternoon. The Amsterdam Tourist Board information office opposite Centraal Station is brimming with hopeful weekenders looking for accommodation. But by 4 o'clock Amsterdam is full. Frustrated visitors are being despatched to surrounding towns like Leiden or Haarlem—pretty towns, and commuting is swift and cheap, yet this is always going to be second-best.

The truth is, to relish Amsterdam you need to stay right in the centre, preferably on a canal, and to do that you should book a hotel room well in advance—two to three weeks at least, more in the summer or over holiday weekends. There is, of course, always the chance of catching a cancellation, and some hotels do keep back a room or two until the last minute; if you cannot book in advance, try calling the hotel direct just before noon—the witching hour between check-out and check-in—and try your luck.

As Amsterdam is such a compact city, hotels in this list are graded by price rather than area. Nearly all of them are within easy walking distance of the main tourist sites, and have been chosen because of their pleasant atmosphere, location or historical significance. An asterisk ★ indicates hotels that are especially recommended.

Hotels:

1 American Hotel
2 Amstel Hotel Intercontinental
3 Blakes
4 Hotel de l'Europe
5 Le Grand Amsterdam
6 Grand Hotel Krasnapolsky
7 Hotel Pulitzer
8 Amsterdam Hilton
9 Hilton International Schiphol
10 Seven One Seven
11 Hotel Ambassade
12 Golden Tulip Doelen
13 Dikker and Thijs Fenice
14 Jan Luyken
15 Schiller Karena
16 Acca International
17 Hotel Acro
18 Hotel Agora
19 Hotel Amsterdam Prinsengracht
20 Hotel Belga
21 Het Canal House
22 La Casaldó
23 Hotel de Filosoof
24 Hotel Orlando
25 Owl Hotel
26 Hotel Seven Bridges
27 Quentin Hotel
28 Hotel Toren
29 Hotel Washington
30 Hotel Wiechmann
31 Hotel de Admiraal
32 Hotel Adolesce
33 Hans Brinker
34 Hotel Brouwer
35 Hotel Engeland
36 Hotel de Harmonie
37 Hotel Hoksbergen
38 Hotel Impala
39 Hotel Prinsenhof
40 Hotel de Westertoren

Hostels:

h1 Vondelpark
h2 Stadsdoelen
h3 Arena
h4 Eben Haezer Christian Youth Hostel
h5 The Flying Pig Park

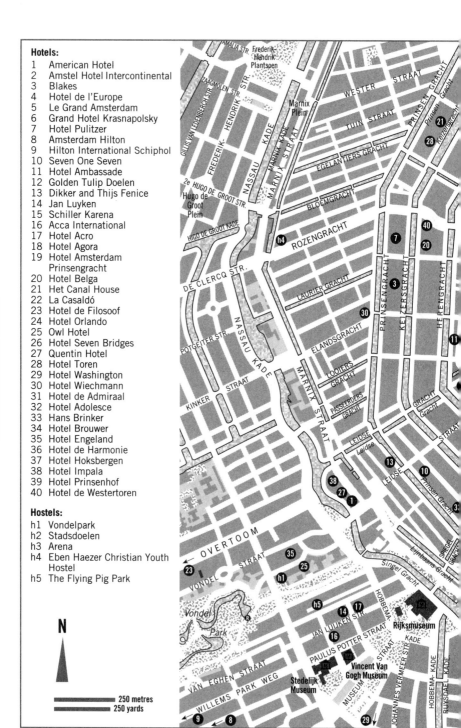

N

250 metres
250 yards

Amsterdam Hotels

American Hotel, Leidsekade 97, 1017 PN, ✆ 556 3000, 🖃 625 3236 (*luxury*). An
① Art Deco extravaganza overlooking the thronging Leidseplein. The café downstairs was once the meeting place for Amsterdam's literati.

★Amstel Hotel Intercontinental, Professor Tulpplein 1, 1018 GX, ✆ 622 6060,
② 🖃 622 5808 (*luxury*). A gracious and sedate hotel on the banks of the Amstel. If you're stuck for transport you can use the hotel's motor yacht or limousine.

Blakes, Keizersgracht 384, 1016 GB, ✆ 530 2010, 🖃 530 2030 (*luxury*). Style diva
③ Anouska Hempel brings her touch to a grand canal house. Bedrooms range from voluptuous to Buddhist minimalist. Guests are rich and famous. Well, rich anyway.

★Hotel de l'Europe, Nieuwe Doelenstraat 2–8, 1012 CP, ✆ 531 1777, 🖃 531 1778
④ (*luxury*). An elegant 19th-century hotel in the grand old style. Knocks spots off the Doelen down the road.

The Grand Amsterdam, Oudezijds Voorburgwal 197, 1001 EX Amsterdam, ✆ 555
⑤ 3111, 🖃 555 3222 (*luxury*). Built as an inn in 1578, then used as Admiralty Headquarters, and finally served as Amsterdam's city hall (from 1808 to 1988). Many fine 1920s interior fittings remain (including the Wedding Room in which Queen Beatrix plighted her troth), but some people are put off by the proximity of the red-light district.

Grand Hotel Krasnapolsky, Dam 9, 1012 JS, ✆ 554 9111, 🖃 626 1570 (*luxury*).
⑥ Right in the centre of town. Very grand from the outside, and inside a mix of period charm and all mod cons.

★Hotel Pulitzer, Prinsengracht 315–31, 1016 GZ, ✆ 523 5235, 🖃 627 6753 (*luxury*).
⑦ Twenty-four canal houses linked up to form a warren of oak-beamed rooms. There's a peaceful garden and a magnificent 18th-century restaurant.

Amsterdam Hilton, Apollolaan 138–140, 1077 BG, ✆ 710 6005, 🖃 710 6000
⑧ (*luxury*). Modern building in the south of the city, not in the centre.

Hilton International Schiphol, Herbergierstraat, 1118 ZK, ✆ 710 4000, 🖃 710 4080
⑨ (*luxury*). Part of Schiphol complex around the airport. Shuttle bus from airport.

Seven One Seven, Prinsengracht 717, 1017 JW, ✆ 427 0717, 🖃 423 0717 (*luxury;*
⑩ *special weekend rates*). Superb, antique-filled suites on one of the smartest canals in town. The owners have aimed at creating a relaxed, homey atmosphere—albeit an extremely chic and well-appointed home.

Hotel Ambassade, Herengracht 335–353, 1016 AZ, ✆ 626 2333, 🖃 624 5321
⑪ (*expensive*). Eight converted houses, dotted about with antiques and with a magnificent breakfast-room overlooking the canal.

Golden Tulip Doelen Hotel, Nieuwe Doelenstraat 24, 1012 CP, ✆ 554 0600, 🖃 622
⑫ 1084 (*expensive*). One of Amsterdam's oldest hotels, though fading in grandeur. Rembrandt painted the *Night Watch* here in 1642.

★Dikker & Thijs Fenice Hotel, Prinsengracht 444, 1017 KE, ✆ 626 7721, 🖃 625
⑬ 8986 (*expensive*). Plum in the middle of it all, in a hectically lively area of town. Modern furnishings in a 100-year-old shell.

Jan Luyken Hotel, Jan Luykenstraat 58, 1071 CS, ✆ 573 0730, 📠 676 3841 (*expensive*). Smart, efficient business hotel in quiet area near the Concertgebouw.
(14)

★**Schiller Karena Hotel**, Rembrandtplein 26–36, 1017 CV, ✆ 554 0700, 📠 626 6381 (*expensive*). Decorated with the paintings of its 19th-century owner, the downstairs café was once the meeting place of actors and artists. The hotel itself is smart, comfortable and overlooks a lively square.
(15)

Acca International, Van de Veldestraat 3a, 1071 CW, ✆ 662 5262, 📠 679 9361 (*moderate*). Modern, functional hotel near the main museums.
(16)

Hotel Acro, Jan Luykenstraat 44, 1071 CR, ✆ 662 0526, 📠 675 0811 (*moderate*). Sparkling, simple, if a little soulless. Set in the quiet museum district.
(17)

Hotel Agora, Singel 462, 1017 AW, ✆ 627 2200, 📠 627 2202 (*moderate*). The owner is interested in fine furniture—and it shows. Rooms overlooking the canal or back garden are the best.
(18)

Hotel Amsterdam Prinsengracht, Prinsengracht 1015, 1017 KN, ✆ 623 7779, 📠 623 8926 (*moderate*). Friendly staff, all mod cons and canal views, though the décor is a little bland.
(19)

Hotel Belga, Hartenstraat 8, 1016 CB, ✆ 624 9080, 📠 623 6862 (*moderate*). Unpretentious, family-run hotel in a quaint shopping alley.
(20)

★**Het Canal House**, Keizersgracht 148, 1015 CX, ✆ 622 5182, 📠 624 1317 (*expensive–moderate*). Stunning converted canal houses, filled to the brim with the owner's carefully chosen antiques. A breakfast-room with a piano and drippingly beautiful crystal chandelier. The hotel has the feel of a tastefully (if grandly) decorated private home, and it has a lift (quite a rarity in these historic houses).
(21)

★**La Casaldó**, Amsteldijk 862, 1079 LN, ✆ 642 3680, 📠 644 7409 (*moderate*). Romantic houseboat with a waterside terrace and just four rooms, all individually decorated. It's on the outskirts of town, so a car or bicycle is a good idea.
(22)

★**Hotel De Filosoof**, Anna Vondelstraat 6, 1054 GZ, ✆ 683 3013, 📠 685 3750 (*moderate*). Each room is named after a well-known thinker, and decorated accordingly. The hotel can arrange consultations with one of Holland's practising philosophers, many of whom frequent the bar.
(23)

Hotel Orlando, Prinsengracht 1099, 1017 JH, ✆ 638 6915, 📠 625 2123 (*moderate*). Canalside house with just five rooms, individually decorated in a modern style. Book well in advance.
(24)

Owl Hotel, Roemer Visscherstraat 1–3, 1054 EV, ✆ 618 9486, 📠 618 9491 (*moderate*). Smart family hotel with garden. In the museum neighbourhood.
(25)

★**Quentin Hotel**, Leidsekade 89, 1017 PN, ✆ 626 2187, 📠 622 0121 (*moderate*). Popular with musicians playing at De Melkweg around the corner. Posters of past (now famous) residents adorn the walls. Spotless, tastefully decorated and good views over the canal.
(27)

★**Hotel Seven Bridges**, Reguliersgracht 31, 1017 LK, ✆ 623 1329, no fax (*expensive–moderate*). The most charming of the small hotels. Beautifully decorated rooms—and breakfast served in bed.
(26)

Hotel Toren, Keizersgracht 164, 1015 CZ, ✆ 622 6033, ✉ 626 9705 (*moderate*).
(28) Seventeenth-century canal house with high moulded ceilings, and antiques scattered among the modern furniture.

Hotel Washington, Frans van Mierisstraat 10, 1071 RS, ✆ 679 6754, ✉ 673 4435
(29) (*moderate*). Large 19th-century house on a peaceful avenue near the Concertgebouw. Room furnishings are simple but tasteful, and there's a small back garden. A friendly, homey atmosphere much appreciated by visiting concert musicians.

★Hotel Wiechmann, Prinsengracht 328–30, 1016 HX, ✆ 626 3321, ✉ 626 8962
(30) (*moderate*). Carefully converted canal houses with an air of old world charm, and a noble breakfast-room.

Hotel De Admiraal, Herengracht 563, 1017 CD, ✆ 626 2150, ✉ 623 4625 (*inexpensive*). Friendly owner, views over two canals, and a good breakfast.
(31)

Hotel Adolesce, Nieuwe Keizersgracht 26, 1018 DS, ✆ 626 3959, ✉ 627 4249 (*inexpensive*). Cheerful, simple hotel with a sunny breakfast-room. A good one if
(32) you have children, as it is one of the few establishments that genuinely welcomes them.

Hans Brinker, Kerkstraat 136, 1017 GR, ✆ 622 0687, ✉ 638 2060 (*inexpensive*).
(33) Prides itself on its no-frills good value and central situation.

Hotel Brouwer, Singel 83, ✆ 624 6358, ✉ 520 6264 (*inexpensive*). A gem. Canal
(34) house with rooms tastefully done up with lovely old furniture. Most have a good view.

Hotel Engeland, Roemer Vischerstraat 30, 1054 EZ, ✆ 689 2323, ✉ 685 3148 (*inexpensive*). The English representative in a quaint row of 19th-century houses
(35) built to show seven different national architectural styles.

Hotel de Harmonie, Prinsengracht 816, 1017 JL, ✆ 625 0174, ✉ 622 8021 (*inexpensive*). Bright, jolly, family-run hotel.
(36)

Hotel Hoksbergen, Singel 301, ✆ 626 6043. ✉ 638 3479 (*inexpensive*). No-
(37) nonsense knotty pine, some canal views, clean rooms and friendly management.

Hotel Impala, Leidsekade 77, 1017 PM, ✆ 623 4706, ✉ 638 9274 (*inexpensive*).
(38) Clean, laid-back hotel with young crowd.

Hotel Prinsenhof, Prinsengracht 810, 1017 JL, ✆ 623 1772, ✉ 638 3368 (*inexpensive*). Quiet, thoughtfully decorated hotel with friendly management.
(39)

Hotel de Westertoren, Raadhuisstraat 35b, 1016 DC, ✆/✉ 624 4639 (*inexpensive*).
(40) Well-kept, if a little noisy.

bed and breakfast

Despite their easy assimilation of things British, Amsterdammers do not seem much taken by B&B. When you do find private accommodation, it probably won't be all that much cheaper than (or very different from) a room in a small hotel.

Bed and Breakfast Holland, Theophile de Bockstraat 3, 1058 TV, ✆ 615 7527, ✉ 669 1573, has a number of B&Bs on its books. *Prices range from ƒ95 for a minimum 2-night stay and there is a ƒ20 booking fee per reservation. Advance bookings only.*

h1 The two official International Youth Hostel Federation hostels are **Vondelpark**,
h2 Zandpad 5, 1054 GA, ✆ 589 8999, ✉ 589 8955; and **Stadsdoelen**, Kloveniersburgwal 97, 1011 KB, ✆ 624 6832, ✉ 639 1035. *Members ƒ28 per person (incl. breakfast); non-members ƒ33; sheet hire ƒ6.25.*

h3 There are also **Arena**, 's Gravesandestraat 51, 1092 AA, ✆ 694 7444, ✉ 663 2649, an erstwhile seedy hippy Sleep-Inn, now considerably smartened up and attracting a friendly crowd of backpackers, *double room ƒ135, dormitories*
h4 *from ƒ27.50, bedding ƒ5*; **★Eben Haezer Christian Youth Hostel**, Bloemstraat 179, 1016 LA, ✆ 624 4717, ✉ 627 6137, a spotless, not oppressively religious and the best value of the lot. *ƒ27.50, including breakfast and*
h5 *bed linen, no membership required, lockers available*; and **The Flying Pig Park**, Vossiusstraat 46, 1071 AJ, ✆ 400 4187, ✉ 470 5159, friendly crowd, clean dorms, free lockers and a cosy café beside the Vondelpark, *dorm beds from ƒ26.50 per person, double room ƒ120.*

Amsterdam ✆ (020–)   ***Eating Out***

The following list is a very personal selection from the hundreds of good restaurants Amsterdam has to offer. An exploratory wander around the Jordaan, through the alleys that criss-cross the canals (from Reestraat to Huidenstraat), or along Utrechtsestraat will reveal even more. Restaurants are listed in three areas. '**Central**' refers to the semi-circle bounded by the three main canals. The **Jordaan** is the area in the west of the city, just beyond the canals. Restaurants in the north, south and east will be found under '**Further Afield**'.

Amsterdam is very much a cash city. Many smaller restaurants don't accept **credit cards**, and there's an air of reluctance about those that do. Even some of the larger establishments don't like plastic—so it's always a good idea to check in advance. Feasting Amsterdammers and hungry tourists fill up most good restaurants pretty quickly, so it's wise to reserve a table by telephone.

Really good, inexpensive foreign food can be found in foreign-national snack bars. Try **Bird** (Thai; Zeedijk 77), **Kismet** (Turkish; Albert Cuypstraat 64), **Maoz** (Israeli falafel; Reguliersbreestraat 45), **Riaz** (Surinam; Bilderdijkstraat 193).

Central

Excelsior, Hotel l'Europe, Nieuwe Doelenstraat 2–8, ✆ 531 1705 (*expensive*). Grand without being pompous. Waiters in tails bring you *haute cuisine* classics or the very best in new Dutch cooking, and there's a superb view over the Amstel. Dress: jacket and tie.

Koriander, Amstel 212, ✆ 627 7879 (*expensive*). The view is even more sublime than from the Excelsior, but the menu and décor more down-to-earth. The *gezellig* atmosphere and no-nonsense (yet imaginative) fare are a great attraction to artistes from the nearby Opera House. *Open till midnight; closed Sun/Mon.*

Sichuan Food, Reguliersdwarsstraat 35, ✆ 626 9327 (*expensive*). Proud possessor of the first Michelin star awarded to a Chinese restaurant in the Netherlands. There are aperitifs made from flowers, sautéed oysters with tangy sauces, lobsters and fish cooked in ways that local western restaurants are beginning to imitate.

De Silveren Spiegel, Kattengat 4–6, ✆ 624 6589 (*expensive*). The building, all Delft tiles and cosy corners, dates from 1614. The visionary chef comes up with such dishes as guinea fowl with rose petal sauce, and uses prime local ingredients, such as lamb from the North Sea island of Texel (where the creatures frolic freely and eat wild herbs). Service is personal and friendly.

't Swarte Schaep, Korte Leidsedwarsstraat 24, ✆ 622 3021 (*expensive*). Up a steep staircase in a 300-year-old building you'll find oak beams, antiques, superb wines, an eclectic cuisine and passing members of the Dutch royal family.

De Utrechtsedwarstafel, Utrechtsedwarsstraat 107, ✆ 625 4189 (*expensive*). Igor works single-handedly in the kitchen, Hans is front-of-house. Igor is a culinary whizz, and Hans an expert on wines. There's no menu, just a grid offering three, four or five courses, at a simple, medium or gourmet level. Wine is included in the price. You pick your level, tell them if there is anything you prefer not to eat, and wait to be surprised. Igor comes out to tell you about the meal; Hans chats about the wine, tailor-making choices as you go along. It's like going to dinner at a friend's, who just happens to be a heavenly cook and have an enviable cellar. *Closed Sun/Mon.*

D'Vijff Vlieghen (The Five Flies), Spuistraat 294–302, ✆ 624 8369 (*expensive*). An intriguing conglomeration of antique-filled rooms in a wonky 17th-century inn. It gets its unfortunate name from the original owner, Jan Vijff Vlieghen. In the 1950s and 1960s it was frequented by the likes of Orson Welles, Benjamin Britten, Jean Cocteau and Walt Disney. These days the restaurant rests on its laurels, and doesn't give good value for money.

Van Harte, Hartenstraat 24, ✆ 625 8500 (*moderate*). Modest, yet an excellent kitchen. Berries and wild mushrooms in the sauces, tender meats and charming service.

Vasso, Rozenboomsteeg 12–14, ✆ 626 0158 (*moderate*). Fresh pasta and fine Italian food in a restaurant that has the lively atmosphere of the kitchens of a faded palazzo.

1ᵉ Klas, Platform 2B, Centraal Station, ✆ 625 0131 (*moderate*). Well-prepared (though not wildly adventurous) Dutch fare in the beautifully restored First Class restaurant.

De Compagnon, Guldehandsteeg 17, ✆ 620 4225 (*moderate*). Down an alley in the red-light district, and through a green door, you'll find a series of tiny rooms, perched on top of each other, filled with antique bric-a-brac, and with views across the little harbour on the Damrak. It is an unexpected find, romantic and intimate—but sadly one of those restaurants where the atmosphere outdoes the cuisine, which is run-of-the-mill Franco-Dutch.

Hemelse Modder, Oude Waal 9, ✆ 624 3203 (*moderate*). Haunt of writers. Before you get to the divine chocolate mousse that gives the restaurant its name ('Heavenly Mud'), try some of the fish or vegetarian dishes. *Closed Mon.*

Kort, Amstelveld 2, ✆ 626 1199 (*moderate*). Freshly prepared food with simple sauces. Somewhere for the health-conscious gourmet. Quiet terrace on the water's edge, and a coolly rational Wiener Werkstätte interior.

Krua Thai, Spuistraat 90a, ✆ 620 0623 (*moderate*). After much audible campery in the kitchen, spectacular dishes issue forth. The hot-and-spicy beef salad is unbeatable, and the stuffed chicken wings divine.

Maison Descartes, Vijzelgracht 2, ✆ 622 4936 (*moderate*). In the depths of the French cultural institute, surrounded by the Delft tiles of a 17th-century Dutch kitchen, you can enjoy regional French cuisine. Menus change nightly.

Memories of India, Reguliersdwarstraat 88, ✆ 623 5710 (*moderate*). Top-class Indian cuisine in curious sub-continental post-modern surrounds. Sit between copper palm trees and stubs of marble column and enjoy fried pomfret, chicken with cinnamon and cardamom sauce, or searing curries. Run by the same family who own the renowned Khan's restaurant in London.

Pier 10, De Ruyterkade Steiger 10 (behind Centraal Station), ✆ 624 8276 (*moderate*). A little wooden hut, once a shipping line office, right on the end of a pier in the IJ. Watch the boats chug past as you devour scrumptious Dutch/French food.

Saturnino, Reguliersdwarsstraat 5h, ✆ 639 0102 (*moderate*). Trendy Italian restaurant on the city's main gay street. You can pop in for a pasta, or linger for a full meal. The atmopshere is glitzy, but the food has a wholesome home-made touch.

Sluizer Visrestaurant, Utrechsestraat 45; and **Sluizer**, Utrechtsestraat 41–3, ✆ 622 6376 (*moderate*). Two adjacent trendy restaurants, evocative of the thirties with marble-topped tables and fringed lamps. Both are usually packed, and the fish restaurant especially has a good reputation. Both open till midnight.

Tujuh Maret, Utrechtsestraat 73, ✆ 427 9865 (*moderate*). All too often an Indonesian rijsttafel turns out to be a series of bowls of barely distinguishable spicy gunge, served with piles of rice. But here you can treat yourself to a flavoursome feast. The soto ayam (chicken broth) has a fine bouillon base, and the different chicken and meat dishes are just that: different. You can enjoy beef in a mild sauce of soya and nutmeg, or a zippier version cooked with red peppers and tamarind; chicken as a tangy curry, or with a gentle coconut sauce.

Turquoise, Wolvenstraat 22–24, ✆ 624 2026 (*moderate*). A bizarre combination of wood-panelled Art Nouveau décor and Turkish cuisine. Under Tiffany lamps, beside cherubs rampant, you can tuck into a feast made up of different starters or try such main courses as chicken breast with cheese and garlic. Warm, homey service.

Le zinc...et les dames, Prinsengracht 999, ✆ 622 9044 (*moderate*). A converted 17th-century warehouse, adorned with portraits of women. The clientele may all seem under 25 and on their first date, but the French cuisine is robust and tasty, with dishes from various regions and wines-by-the-glass to match. *Closed Mon.*

Zuid Zeeland, Herengracht 413, ✆ 624 3154 (*moderate*). Specializes in fish dishes from Belgium and the south of Holland, but also meat dishes with a French and Japanese influence. *Closed Sat, Sun.*

Anda Nugraha, Waterlooplein 339, ✆ 626 6046 (*cheap*). Tasty home-cooked Indonesian food. *Rijsttafel f45 for two people.*

Axum, Utrechtsedwarsstraat 85–87, ✆ 622 8389 (*cheap*). Authentic Ethiopian cuisine—which means a giant communal pancake and a few sizzling pots of stews and curries. Toss on some salad and yoghurt sauce, add a spoon of stew, and roll up mouth-sized bites with your fingers. Appropriately ethnic décor and utterly charming service.

Balthazar's Keuken, Elandsgracht 108,✆ 420 2114 (*cheap*). Every Wednesday Alain Parry and his cousin Karin have breakfast together, and decide the week's menu. The kitchen takes up a third of the room, and diners crowd around a few small wooden tables, three nights a week. You take pot luck, though there's a fish-or-flesh choice for the main course. Starters are usually meze-style and might include cockles with ginger and parsley or a red-pepper salad with anise pepperoni. For a main course you may have buttery pink salmon in a crackly coat of nori, scattered with crisp-fried green asparagus, served with sepia risotto and a perky anchovy sauce. *Open Wed–Fri.*

Bird, Zeedijk 77, ✆ 420 6289 (*cheap*). Tiny Thai snack bar with a kitchen one end, a trendy crowd squashed around a few tables, and tantalizing Thai cuisine.

De Blauwe Hollander, Leidsekruisstraat 28, ✆ 623 3014 (*cheap*). Cheap and cheerful, if rather heavy, Dutch cooking.

Casa di David, Singel 426, ✆ 624 5093 (*cheap*). Wooden beams and canalside charm give this pizzeria a special edge. The food is good too: pasta made on the premises, an excellent array of antipasti, and fragrant, crusty pizzas cooked in a wood-burning oven.

Centra, Lange Niezel 29, ✆ 622 3050 (*cheap*). Busy, garish, cafeteria-like atmosphere, and the best Spanish food in town.

Et Alors, Nes 35, ✆ 421 6056 (*cheap*). Run by two sisters in the heart of the alternative theatre district. Suzanna serves at table, while Sandra slaves single-handedly in the kitchen. Dedicated Francophiles, they have decorated their small restaurant with a comfortable clutter of old furniture picked up on treks through France. It's all for sale, even the plates you eat off. The cuisine, of course, is French—unpretentious fare, with a cared-for, home-cooked touch. Try tasty home-made sausages with rocket salad, or monkfish with an aïoli and vegetable sauce.

Goodies, Huidenstraat 9, ✆ 625 6122 (*cheap*). Arty hangout that sells good sandwiches and salads by day, and pasta by night.

Haesje Claes, Spuistraat 273–5, ✆ 624 9998 (*cheap*). Touristy, but unhurried. Folksy Old Dutch interior, solid tasty Dutch food, lots of salad and vegetables.

Keuken van 1870, Spuistraat 4, ✆ 624 8965 (*cheap*). Began as a soup kitchen in 1870. Punks, pensioners and passing backpackers come in for enormous, tastily cooked meals for under ƒ17. *Kitchen closes 8pm weekdays, 9pm Sat–Sun.*

Pancake Bakery, Prinsengracht 191, ✆ 625 1333 (*cheap*). The best pancakes in town.

La Place, Rokin 162, ✆ 620 2364 (*cheap*). Serve yourself at various counters—a great salad bar, fresh pastas and grilled meats cooked while you wait. Most of the ingredients are organic, you sit in one of a honeycomb of rooms in an atmospheric 17th-century building.

Rose's Cantina, Reguliersdwarsstraat 38, ✆ 625 9797 (*cheap*). Crowds of Bright Young Things, tasty Tex-Mex food and lethal margaritas.

Song Kwae, Kloveniersburgwal 14, ✆ 624 2568 (*cheap*). The place to go for Thai food when you've been unable to squeeze into Bird (*see* above). Lots more space, and good food too.

Surinam Express, Halvemaansteeg 18, ✆ 622 7405 (*cheap*). Tiny sandwich shop off Rembrandtplein with seeringly authentic Surinamese food—spicy vegetable and tangy curry fillings. But you can order fuller meals too, and eat at a counter along the wall.

d'Theeboom, Singel 210, ✆ 623 8420 (*cheap*). Georges Thubert scorns rip-off prices and culinary pretension. He runs his restaurant, in a converted canalside warehouse, in classic French style, and offers excellent value and fine cooking.

Upstairs Pannekoekhuis, Grimburgwal 2, ✆ 626 5603 (*cheap*). Teeny pancake parlour suspended above a bustling lane.

Woeste Walmen, Singel 46, ✆ 638 0765 (*cheap*). Run by squatters, who have decorated a large canal-house parlour with quirky flair and who come up with food that they have enjoyed cooking. The menu changes daily, and there is usually one meat and one non-meat option for the main course. *Open Sat and Sun only.*

The Jordaan

Christophe, Leliegracht 46, ✆ 625 0807 (*expensive*). The atmosphere can be a little frigid, but Algerian-born Jean-Christophe Royer comes up with superb French cuisine enlivened by zesty north-African flavours, which makes up for all.

De Luwte, Leliegracht 26, ✆ 625 8548 (*moderate*). Candlelight, wooden tables and chairs, subtle *trompe l'œil* scenes on the walls, and windows looking on to a small canal make for a romantic evening. Delicious meals with fresh (often organically grown) ingredients and tangles of salad complete the picture.

Speciaal, Nieuwe Leliestraat 142, ✆ 624 9706 (*moderate*). Many say the best Indonesian restaurant in town.

Stoop, 1ᵉ Anjeliersdwarsstraat 4, ✆ 639 2480 (*moderate*). Small, busy restaurant with an open kitchen and an all-embracing cuisine. Try home-made beef pastrami salad with ginger-and-yoghurt dressing, or Peking duck with a chutney of aubergines and dried figs.

Ristorante Toscanini, Lindengracht 75, ✆ 623 2813 (*moderate*). Cavernous, rowdy and very Italian. A gastric and sensual delight, but service is exceeding slow. Bring a pack of cards. *Closed Tues.*

Caramba, Lindengracht 342, ✆ 627 1188 (*cheap*). Lively South American restaurant where an arty crowd consumes tortilla and gets poleaxed by vicious margaritas.

De Eettuin, 2e Tuindwarsstraat 10, ✆ 623 7706 (*cheap*). Forests of greenery, generous Dutch portions and a modest salad bar.

Moeders Pot (Mother's Cooking), Vinkenstraat 119, ✆ 623 7643 (*cheap*). Meat and ten veg cuisine. A one-person affair run by a huge hairy man who must have 'mother' tattooed somewhere under his white T-shirt.

Further Afield

Beddington's, Roelof Hartstraat 6–8, ✆ 676 5201 (*expensive*). Austere décor, but sumptuous meals by a chef who combines culinary experience from Derbyshire, the Far East and the summits of French haute cuisine. *Closed Mon.*

Ciel Bleu, Okura Hotel, Ferdinand Bolstraat 333, ✆ 678 7111 (*expensive*). God's-eye view of Amsterdam from the 23rd floor of one of the city's lone tower blocks. The cuisine is appropriately *haut*. *Dress: jacket and tie.*

Vis aan de Schelde, Scheldeplein 4, ✆ 675 1583 (*expensive*). Minimalist décor, no muzak, subdued conversation, and above all a gentle hand in the kitchen. Fish comes perfectly cooked: tuna with just a tinge of pink, meltingly soft monkfish. The chef's imagination roams free without running rampant. For a starter try marinated salmon with asparagus steeped in vanilla and orange. Classics are there too, such as an excellent bouillabaisse, or you can be more adventurous, with dishes such as tuna in a red wine and flageolet bean sauce.

Yamazato, Hotel Okura, Ferdinand Bolstraat 333, ✆ 678 7111 (*expensive*). Supreme Japanese cuisine, from the appropriately named 'Emperor's Menu' to the smallest sushi, all exquisitely presented on lacquered platters and in hand-made bowls, brought to you by waitresses in kimonos..

Yoichi, Weteringschans 128, ✆ 622 6829 (*expensive*). Amsterdam's oldest Japanese restaurant, and still up there with the best. Traditional décor, traditional food, traditional high prices.

Basak, Frans Halsstraat 89, ✆ 664 9534 (*moderate*). Unassuming Turkish restaurant lit by multicoloured glass lanterns, and serving tasty casseroles as well as the usual grills. Everything comes with heaps of fresh salad.

La Brasa, Haarlemmerdijk 16, ✆ 625 4438 (*moderate*). One of the more intimate of the Argentinian grills. Very much a place for carnivores: hairy cowhide seats and juicy beef on a wood grill.

De Gouden Reael, Zandhoek 14, ✆ 623 3883 (*moderate*). A 17th-century house on a quayside in the Western Islands. Renowned for its French provincial cuisine—a different area every three months.

Griet Manshande, Keerpunt 10, ✆ 622 8194 (*moderate*). Hidden in a corner of a modern housing estate on the Bickerseiland. Choose your meal from the daily selection in the vitrine—anything from classic coq au vin to roast skate with beurre noir. There's a relaxed, neighbourhood atmosphere, the service is friendly and the cooking subtle and skilled.

De Groene Lanteerne, Haarlemmerstraat 43, ✆ 624 1952 (*moderate*). The narrowest restaurant in the world—in places just a doorway wide, run by a couple who are becoming renowned for their hearty French fare.

Bodega Keyzer, Van Baerlestraat 96, ✆ 671 1441 (*moderate*). Writers and musicians have been coming here for nearly a century to eat smoked eel and fresh sole. (The Concertgebouw is right next door.) *Closed Sun; open till midnight.*

Kilimanjaro, Rapenburgerplein 6, ✆ 622 3485 (*moderate*). A tabletop tour of Africa. Begin with a delicious fish soup from Guinea, then crocodile from Senegal, or a spicy Tanzanian red snapper curry. Wash it all down with Castle lager from South Africa, home-made ginger beer or a hibiscus and baobab cocktail.

De Knijp, Van Baerlestraat 134, ✆ 671 4248 (*moderate*). Near to the Concertgebouw. Fresh oysters are a speciality. *Open till midnight.*

The Movies, Haarlemmerdijk 159, ✆ 626 7069 (*moderate*). Crowded restaurant attached to an old Art Deco cinema offers 'Cuisine Sauvage'—challenging concoctions such as red bass with kumquats.

De Ondeugd, Ferdinand Bolstraat 15, ✆ 672 0651 (*moderate*). Just minutes' barrow-trundle from the Albert Cuyp market. The fish and vegetables are alarmingly fresh. Try the goose liver on apple compôte, Thai soup or grilled swordfish with tomato *beurre blanc*. Main dishes come with frites and mayonnaise—but here the mayo is homemade and the chips hand-hewn and delicious.

Sparks, Willemsparkweg 87, ✆ 676 0700 (*moderate*). Friendly neighbourhood brasserie, with a small garden courtyard and understated décor. Amster-dammers in the know come here to savour Sander van Ommeren's inspired Mediterranean-influenced cooking. Start with marinated octopus with rocket and artichoke crème, then try a brochette of lamb with sea lavender, bulgur pilaf and thyme-lavender gravy, and round off with a refreshing blood-orange sorbet.

De Witte Uyl, Frans Halsstraat 26, ✆ 670 0458 (*moderate*). Big tables, comfortable chairs, a carefully chosen wine list, and a menu of imaginative medium-sized dishes. Just the place to come with a group of friends, order a few bottles, and share the food. *f80.*

Witteveen, Ceintuurbaan 256–58, ✆ 662 4368 (*moderate*). Peter Greenaway meets Zeffirelli. Vast red, black and gilt interior; dressed-up waiters, and tables smothered with white linen. Folk from the neighbourhood, looking a little stiff and uncomfortable in their Sunday best, tuck in the napkins and sit down to some of the best traditional Dutch cooking in town.

Zabar's, Van Baerlestraat 49, ✆ 679 8888 (*expensive–moderate*). It doesn't look much from the outside—a tatty jalousie and plants squashed up against the window. But inside you'll find a cheery crowd of Amsterdammers enjoying flavourful food from all over the Mediterranean region, from Moroccan lamb casserole to crunchy Greek halva. And it's just a few minutes' walk to the Concertgebouw.

Arena, 's Gravesandestraat 51, ✆ 694 7444 (*cheap*). Backpackers and assorted budget travellers chomp their way through stews and other tummy-filling fare in café-like surrounds. The occasional cloud of hashish smoke wafts by.

Kong Kha, Rijnstraat 87, ✆ 661 2578 (*cheap*). Small, bustling restaurant and take-away, where you'll find authentic Thai home-cooking. A bit out of the way, but well worth a short ride on the number 4 tram. The *tod man plaa* (fishcakes) are delicious, and the *tom kha kai* (chicken and coconut soup) is sweet and soothing to the palate, a perfect contrast to some of the more fiery main dishes.

Riaz, Bilderdijkstraat 193, ✆ 683 6453 (*cheap*). Great Surinamese curries, which you can order with rice or roti—a pancake in which you roll up your food then eat with your fingers.

De Vrolijke Abrikoos (The Jolly Apricot), Weteringschans 76, ✆ 624 4672 (*cheap*). Pastel shades, pine tables and bio-dynamic ingredients combined with subtlety and flair. Try giant roast mushroom with a creamy sauce, delicate oriental soups, or bass with a robust tomato sauce. In good weather you can sit at tables in the back garden. *Closed Tues.*

Waroeng Asje, Jan Pieter Heijestraat 180, ✆ 616 6589 (*cheap*). Surinamese/Indonesian takeaway with a few tables for eating-in, near the Vondel park. The *soto soep* (spicy meat-and-veg soup with a bowl of rice alongside, *f7*) is a meal in itself.

vegetarian

Bolhoed, Prinsengracht 60, ✆ 626 1803 (*cheap*). Exotic Thai statues, quirky lamps and candelabra, bright colours (but soft lighting) make a far remove from clichéd knotty pine. The cuisine has a Mexican touch, and is imaginative and tasty. There are vegan dishes available, fish too, and the daily special three-course menu (*f30*) is excellent value.

Golden Temple, Utrechtsestraat 126, ✆ 626 8560 (*cheap*). Simple décor, but tasty food with strong Indian flavours. Vegan options.

De Waaghals, Frans Halsstraat 29, ✆ 679 9609 (*cheap*). Vegetarian cuisine with organic ingredients and international influences. Try the Tunisian bean casserole, or coconut and aubergine soup—though flavours are sometimes subtle to the point of blandness.

Zest, Prinsenstraat 10, ✆ 428 2455 (*moderate*). Trendy restaurant in fusion mode, but offering good vegetarian choices. Try Thai risotto with sugarsnap beans and mushrooms.

Restaurants that put special effort and imagination into the vegetarian options on the menu are: **Hemelse Modder** (Central); **Woeste Walmen** (Central); **De Luwte** (Jordaan); **De Vrolijke Abrikoos** (Further Afield); **Griet Manshande** (Further Afield).

late night

Of the restaurants listed above, a few keep their kitchens open until midnight: **Bodega Keyser** (Further Afield), **De Knijp** (Further Afield), **Koriander** (Central), **Sluizer** (Central), and **Saturnino** (Central). The downstairs **Diner** at the Holland Casino is open until 2am and serves good food. You don't have to buy a casino ticket to get in. **Bojo** (Lange Leidsedwarsstraat 51) is an Indonesian restaurant open until 2am during the week and until 5.30am on Fri and Sat. **Maoz** (Reguliersbreestraat, near Tuschinski Cinema) serves scrumptious falafel and salads on the street all through the night. **Gary's Late-Nite Bagel Shop** (Reguliersdwarsstraat 53) sells genuine New York bagels, cheesecake and muffins until the wee hours.

Amsterdam ✆ (020–)   ***Cafés and Coffeeshops***

Cafés are at the centre of an Amsterdammer's social life. Wooden floors and furniture, and walls stained by years of cigarette smoke, have inspired the name **'brown café'**. Here you can have a drink or just a coffee, nibble snacks or plough through hefty Dutch meals. But most of all you sit and talk, or while away the time leafing through the day's papers or glossy magazines. There's seldom any grating background music—though in friendly neighbourhood bars the clientele may burst into song. Whether it's in a tiny café supported by a handful of locals, or a stylish new bar with an arty crowd, you'll find that Amsterdammers create an atmosphere where they can relax and feel both *uit* and *thuis* ('out' and 'at home').

The term 'café' covers a wide range of establishments. At one end of the spectrum are the poky **bars**, where you go to knock back a few beers (with the odd jenever chaser); you might also be able to buy snacks. At the other end you'll find enormous, airy grand cafés and *eetcafés* (see p.23). Some rather startling newcomers made an appearance during the 1980s: the designer bars are the complete antithesis of the brown café—hard metal furniture, bright light and colours and loud music—but are now very much part of the Amsterdam scene.

Café-crawling is the best way to discover Amsterdam: between museum visits, on rainy afternoons, on long, hot summer evenings. There are nearly 1,500 cafés to visit, and you're sure to rootle out a few favourites for yourself—but here is a list of a few special ones to help you on your way. Most cafés close at 1 or 2am over weekends. They begin opening their doors around 11am, though some don't get it together until 3 or 4pm.

An asterisk (*) indicates cafés particularly recommended for their food. The letters after the address give you some indication of where the café is: C— the central area bounded by the main canals; J—the Jordaan and northwestern Amsterdam; S—south and southeast of the centre.

cafés

*Aas van Bokalen, Keizersgracht 335 (C). Arty brown café.

In't Aepjen, Zeedijk 1 (C). A *'rariteitencafé'*, crammed with antiques.

*Américain, American Hotel, Leidseplein (C). Splendid Art Deco grand café.

*Eetcafé Van Beeren, Koningsstraat 54, ✆ 622 2329. Quiet neighbourhood café with an imaginative chef.

*Belhamel, Brouwersgracht 60 (J). Art Nouveau décor on a pretty canal.

De Blaffende Vis, Westerstraat 118 (J). Cheery Jordaan café.

Cul de Sac, Oudezijds Voorburgwal 99 (C). Tucked away down a side alley—one of the few really good bars in the red-light district.

Dantzig, Zwanenburgwal 15 (C). Attractive corner of the ugly new Stadhuis. A grand café that frequently fills with wedding parties.

De Druif, Rapenburg 83 (near Maritime Museum) (C). Dates from 1631.

Dulac, Haarlemmerstraat 118 (J). Fantasy grand café, inspired by the French fairytale illustrator Edmund Dulac.

*De Duvel, 1ᵉ van der Helststraat 59–61. Busy café with a large terrace near the Albert Cuyp market.

Eik en Linde, Plantage Middenlaan 22 (near Zoo) (C). Local brown café with mixed, arty crowd.

Eland, Prinsengracht 296 (C). Traditional brown café.

*Engelbewaarder, Kloveniersburgwal 59 (C). Writers gulp down pasta and scribble away on wooden tables. Heated discussions about art and life echo from the corners.

*1ᵉ Klas (First Class), Platform 2B, Centraal Station. Lose yourself in the great age of rail travel.

De Gijs, Lindengracht 249 (J). Tiny two-tier bar with an edge of Jordaan eccentricity.

Gollem, Raamsteeg 4 (C). Home of a hundred (or more) beers.

*De Groene Olifant (The Green Elephant), Sarphatistraat 510 (S). Huge windows flood this cosy bar with light. The folk are friendly and the food delicious.

Het Hok, Lange Leidsedwarsstraat 134 (C). A refuge from the hordes on Leidseplein. Filled with quiet people playing chess.

Hollandse Manege Café, Vondelstraat 140 (S). Overlooks an exquisite 19th-century riding school arena.

Hoppe, Spui 18–20 (C). Dates from 1670. These days it's an after-work watering hole.

*Huyschkamer, Utrechtsestraat 137 (C). Trendy café in a former male brothel.

De IJsbreker, Weesperzijde 23 (S). Attached to Amsterdam's leading venue for serious contemporary music, with appropriate background sounds. Tranquil riverside terrace.

*De Jaren, Nieuwe Doelenstraat 20 (C). Light and airy grand café. Home of the arts and media set.

Karpershoek, Martelaarsgracht 2 (C). Claims to be Amsterdam's oldest café (this is challenged by Café Chris).

De Kat in de Wijngaert, Lindengracht 160 (J). Quiet and friendly Jordaan café.

Koophandel, Bloemgracht 49 (J). Converted warehouse that only begins to fill up around midnight, then throbs till dawn.

*Kort, Amstelveld 2 (C). Modern café with a quiet canalside terrace.

*De Kroon Royal Café, Rembrandtplein 17 (C). Historic meeting place of variety artistes and their agents, with a view over Rembrandtplein.

Luxembourg, Spui 22–24 (C). Grand café that attracts well-heeled office workers.

*Het Molenpad, Prinsengracht 653 (C). A brown café that sometimes crams a live jazz band into one corner. A smoky, dreamy place to while away a Sunday afternoon.

Nol, Westerstraat 109 (J). Outrageously kitsch Jordaan bar. Locals, gangsters and astonished visitors get swept into uproarious sing-songs.

L'Opera, Rembrandtplein 19 (C). Sedate Art Deco café on a bustling square.

Papeneiland, Prinsengracht 2 (C). Built in 1642, with a secret passage to the house across the canal.

De Prins, Prinsengracht 124 (C). Pretty canalside pub popular with students.

*Van Puffelen, Prinsengracht 377 (C). Sawdust on the floor, and cherubs on the ceiling. A good restaurant at the back, a terrace on a barge on the canal in front, and a very smart clientele.

Rooie Nelis, Laurierstraat 101 (J). A Jordaan institution. Bursting with Jordaaners and visitors all having a good time.

*Rosereijn, Haarlemmerdijk 52 (J). Cosy brown café with a good selection of magazines and cheap, tasty food.

*Schiller, Rembrandtplein 26 (C). Cosy Art Deco bar tucked away from the rumpus of Rembrandtplein. Excellent cuisine.

't Smalle, Egelantiersgracht 12 (J). An 18th-century *proeflokaal* converted into brown café. Gets packed most evenings.

De Tuin, 2e Tuindwarsstraat 13 (J). Dim light, board games and a twinge of eccentricity. All the ingredients of a classic brown café.

Twee Prinsen, Prinsenstraat 27 (C). Heated terrace and a friendly, alternative Jordaan crowd who profess great rivalry with the 'yuppies' at the Vergulde Gaper on the opposite corner.

Twee Zwaantjes, Prinsengracht 114 (C). Electric organ music, accordions and big ladies with big voices from the Jordaan will make any visit unforgettable.

*Vertigo, Vondelpark 3 (S). Wonderful terrace on Vondelpark for good weather, cosy cellar under the Film Museum for bad.

*De Waag, in the old Waag (Weighing House) on Nieuwemarkt (C). Vast café, decorated with medieval austerity and lit entirely by candles.

Welling, J. W. Brouwerstraat 32 (C). Traditional brown café convenient for the Concertgebouw.

De Wetering, Weteringstraat 37 (C). A real log fire in winter and an ancient television that is used only for crucial football matches.

Wildschut, Roelof Hartplein 1–3 (S). Art Deco interior and noisy, smoky but none the less popular terrace.

designer bars

Esprit, Spui 10 (C). Plate-glass and aluminium showcase for the trendy.

Krull, Corner of 1e van der Helstraat and 1e Jan Steenstraat (S). Friendly café near the Albert Cuyp market.

*Morlang, Keizersgracht 451 (C). Brittle trendier-than-thou atmosphere, but good food.

*Het Land van Walem, Keizersgracht 449 (C). Friendlier than the Morlang next door, with a bigger terrace and a garden at the back.

Schuim, Spuistraat 189 (C). Shop-window café that fills up with students during the day, and at night artsy types who admire their friends' paintings on the walls.

Seymour Likely Lounge, Nieuwezijds Voorburgwal 250 (C). Real creation of a fictitious artist, and one of the trendiest spots in town.

Proeflokaalen (see p.23)

De Admiraal, Herengracht 319 (C). Enormous, with comfy chairs—stretches the definition somewhat.

De Drie Fleschjes, Gravenstraat 18 (C). More traditional *proeflokaal*. Some nearby offices have their own marked barrels.

Het Proeflokaal, Pijlsteeg 31 (C). Delightfully cramped and crooked old *proeflokaal* with a range of flavoured jenevers and sticky liqueurs.

coffeeshops

Backstage Boutique, Utrechtsedwarsstraat 65–7 (C). The zaniest coffeeshop in town.

Granny, 1e van der Helstraat 45 (S). Near Albert Cuyp market. Some of the best *appelgebak* in town.

Greenwoods, Singel 103 (C). Real English afternoon tea for the homesick. The owner is most frequently seen up to her elbows in flour making the next batch of scones or sponge cake.

Pompadour, Huidenstraat 12 (C). Refined hand-made chocolates in a splendid setting.

Puccini, Staalstraat 17 (C). Irresistible cakes and outrageous chocolates near the Waterlooplein fleamarket.

Reibach, Brouwersgracht 139 (J). German specialities, such as wickedly alcoholic fruit from the Rumtopf jar, and a view over a beautiful canal.

smoking coffeeshops

The Bulldog, Leidseplein 13–17/Oudezijds Voorburgwal 90 (C). Oldest and most commercial.

Rusland, Rusland 16 (C). Privately owned, intimate and relaxedly scruffy.

Pink Poffertje, moored at southern end of Oude Schans (C). Cosy boat that even sells marijuana beer.

Prix d'Ami, Haringpakkersteeg 5 (C). Deeply respectable-looking branch of a chain of coffeeshops.

Amsterdam ✆ (020–)   ***Entertainment and Nightlife***

Amsterdam's nightlife centres on cafés. They offer everything from a quiet evening over the backgammon board to jolly sing-songs in just about any language you choose. There are even some cafés where you can dance, though a handful of good nightclubs serve those who really like to bounce and sweat. The more genteel spectator entertainments are quite accessible to foreigners. Films are usually shown in their original language, with Dutch subtitles; there's a strong tradition of highly visual theatre, and many performances in English; the new Muziektheater provides a venue for touring opera and dance companies and Amsterdam has high international status in the various music worlds. Up-and-coming British rock bands test the water here before facing jaded audiences at home; there are some good jazz festivals, and recent immigration has upped the quality of salsa and Latin American music. The acoustically superb Concertgebouw attracts leading classical artists and conductors, and there's a very healthy contemporary music scene.

listings information

The various listings magazines will guide you through the maze. The tourist office publish a monthly *What's On In Amsterdam* (ƒ4, available at Amsterdam Tourist Board and around town). The free monthly **Uitkrant** (from Amsterdam Tourist Board, AUB (*see* p.78), libraries, museums and theatres) is more comprehensive and although it's in Dutch, fairly easy to follow. An even better bet (though also in Dutch) is the *PS Weekend* supplement to *Het Parool. Shark/Queer Fish* (ƒ2.50 from larger newsagents) is a twice-monthly guide to trendy Amsterdam, focusing mainly on clubs and with a strong gay slant. *Oor* (available from newsagents) is the Dutch equivalent of NME, the British rock music newspaper. Both the Amsterdam Tourist Board and the AUB booking office can reserve tickets. The AUB also has an up-to-the-minute 'What's On' noticeboard (good for pop music) and a few rainforests' worth of leaflets. If you're on line, access *www.aub.nl* for up-to-the-minute information on shows and exhibitions, and a bookings service too; or call Uitlijn on ✆ (0900) 0191.

You'll find most of the multi-screened commercial cinemas in the area around Leidseplein, where they offer pretty standard fare. The six-screen Tuschinski must be a hot contender for the most beautiful cinema in the world and is worth a visit no matter what's showing.

Desmet, Plantage Middenlaan 4, ✆ 627 3434. Ornate Art Deco cinema used by a Jewish cabaret company in the early years of the Second World War. These days known for its imaginative mini-festivals and weekend gay screenings.

Netherlands Film Museum, Vondelpark 3, ✆ 589 1400. Frequent changes of programme, usually with something from the museum's unique and extensive archive—such as tinted silent movies (*see* p.125).

Kriterion, Roeterstraat 170, ✆ 623 1708. Cult American movies and erotic French late-nights.

The Movies, Haarlemmerdijk 161, ✆ 638 6016. Some of the programming verges on the mainstream, but the 1920s interior is a delight and there's a vibrant café/restaurant.

Rialto, Ceintuurbaan 338, ✆ 675 3994. Good on retrospectives, science fiction, animation and children's films.

De Uitkijk, Prinsengracht 452, ✆ 623 7460. Amsterdam's oldest cinema (dating from 1913) squashed into an even older canal house. It features a white grand piano that has long since tinkled its last notes, but is too big to be removed.

See also **De Melkweg,** 'Multimedia Centres' below.

Two local English-speaking companies compete with foreign touring productions for the Amsterdam audience. The In Theatre presents small-scale productions, usually upstairs in a converted prop room at the Stadsschouwburg, and Boom Chicago offers improvised comedy in their own supper theatre next door. The Nes (off Damstraat) and the banks of the Amstel are traditionally Amsterdam's theatreland, but these days no old warehouse, factory or stable is safe from troupes of eager actors.

If you want to go to the theatre, the best thing to do is check the listings magazines for touring companies—but here's a short list of venues where you're most likely to find good work in English.

't Fijnhout Theater, Jacob van Lennepkade 334, ✆ 685 3755. A popular theatre with English-language touring companies.

Koninklijk Theater Carré, Amstel 115–25, ✆ 622 5225. Built for a circus—a function it still performs over the Christmas period when Dutch children regard a visit as de rigueur. It's the home of most big Amsterdam musicals, but more off-the-wall performances slip into gaps in the programme.

Felix Meritis, Felix Meritis Building, Keizersgracht 324, ✆ 626 2321. A descendant of the Shaffy, which was at the forefront of the avant-garde during the 1970s and

1980s, and housed in a building with a rich cultural past, the Felix Meritis is still a place to catch exciting new work.

De Stadsschouwburg, Leidseplein 26, ✆ 624 2311. Amsterdam's municipal theatre. The programme includes not only a wide range of national productions but also visiting international companies. There's a good theatre bookshop near the main entrance.

See also **De Melkweg**, 'Multimedia Centres' below.

dance

Bellevue, Leidsekade 90, ✆ 624 7248. Often host to modern dance touring companies.

Frascati, Nes 63, ✆ 626 6866. A venue for more established modern dance.

Muziektheater (Stopera), Waterlooplein 22, ✆ 625 5455. If you want to see something in this new opera house, ballet may be the best choice as the acoustics are a little iffy (*see* below).

classical music

AGA Zaal and Yakult Zaal, Damrak 213, ✆ 627 0466. Home to the Netherlands Chamber Orchestra and the Netherlands Philharmonic respectively. Beautifully converted concert halls in the old Beurs van Berlage (*see* pp.84–5).

Concertgebouw, Concertgebouwplein 2–6, ✆ 671 8345. The Grote Zaal (Large Hall) has perfect acoustics and is used for orchestral concerts and occasionally for visiting pop stars and jazz bands. Nervous students from the Sweelinck Conservatorium across the road make their professional débuts in the Kleine Zaal (Small Hall). There are free lunchtime concerts on Wednesdays (*see* p.123).

De IJsbreker, Weesperzijde 23, ✆ 693 9093. A deservedly famous centre for contemporary music. It brings out its own news-sheet and offers a stimulating programme of local and international composers and improvisers.

Muziektheater (Stopera), Waterlooplein 22, ✆ 625 5455. Home to the national ballet and opera companies, but subject of one of the biggest architectural and property development controversies of the century, and of angry complaints by musicians and audience alike about the bad acoustics (*see* p.96). It does, however, have an attractive, cosy auditorium—rare for a modern theatre.

De Rode Hoed, Keizersgracht 102, ✆ 638 5606. Varied programmes in a converted church.

Scan the listings magazines to find out about church concerts at the Oude Kerk, the Nieuwe Kerk, the Engelse Kerk and the Waalse Kerk.

rock and pop music

Akhnaton, Nieuwezijds Kolk 25, ✆ 624 3396. Recording studios, rehearsal facilities and a forum for much of the liveliest new music, hip-hop, Latin and other ethnic bands.

Amsterdam ArenA, Arenaboulevard 1, ✆ 311 1333. Sports stadium that is the venue for visiting megastars.

Arena, 's Gravesandestraat 51, ✆ 694 7444. The old hippy Sleep Inn has undergone a transformation into one of the trendiest music and dance venues in town.

Cruise Inn, Zeeburgerdijk 272, ✆ 692 7188. Flotsam and jetsam from the 1950s shake, rattle and roll in an old wooden clubhouse.

Korsakoff, Lijnbaansgracht 161, ✆ 625 7854. A venue for headbanging post-punks, which nods towards heavy metal and gothic teeny-boppers.

Paradiso, Weteringschans 6–8, ✆ 626 4521. An Amsterdam institution. A gloomy looking church that has been converted into a bright and buzzing venue for good music—anything from big rock names to jazz, African, Latin and even contemporary classical.

Prices range from free entrance to around ƒ20 and starting times are usually between 9 and 11pm.

See also **De Melkweg**, 'Multimedia Centres', and 'Nightclubs' below.

jazz, Latin and folk

Jazzcafé Alto, Korte Leidsedwarsstraat 115, ✆ 626 3249. Live jazz every night in a cosy brown café tucked away in a brash touristy street.

De Badcuyp, 1ᵉ Sweelinckstraat 10, ✆ 675 9669. Neighbourhood café-cum-arts centre in a converted bathhouse, and a lively venue for jazz and salsa.

Bimhuis, Oudeschans 73, ✆ 623 1361. The city's major jazz venue plays host to visiting artistes and the cream of the locals, and has free sessions on Mondays and Wednesdays.

Brasil Music Bar, Lange Leidsedwarsstraat 70, ✆ 626 1500. Live Samba and a gyrating throng of Latin expatriates.

Casablanca, Zeedijk 26, ✆ 625 5685. Café hosting mainstream and standards bands, with the occasional jam session.

Jazz Cruise, tour starts at Rijksmuseum, Saturdays, April to Nov; 8pm and 10pm, ✆ 623 9886. An hour and a half of jazz on a canal boat, with beer, wine and cheese thrown in.

Maloe Melo, Lijnbaansgracht 163, ✆ 420 4592. Enduring, if somewhat poky, blues café.

Meander, Voetboogstraat 3, ✆ 625 8430. Lively café where, on alternate nights, students and their kind swing to salsa, bop to funk and chill out to jazz.

Mulligan's, Amstel 100, ✆ 622 1330. Rousing Irish sing-a-longs.

Odeon Jazz Kelder, Singel 460, ✆ 624 9711. Trad jazz in an intimate atmosphere.

Rembrandt Bar, Rembrandtplein 3, ✆ 623 0688. Plays Dutch folk music. But for a real knees-up and noisy accordion rather visit Café Nol or De Twee Zwaantjes (*see* 'Cafés', p.159).

Rum Runners, Prinsengracht 277, ✆ 627 4079. Glitzy Caribbean bar/restaurant with live Latin bands on Sunday afternoons and early evening.

Soeterijn, Linnaeusstraat 2, ✆ 568 8500. The city's top venue for music from Africa, Indonesia, Eastern Europe and the Middle East.

The commercial discos (chart music, plastic palm trees, expensive drinks and posses of drunken men) cluster around Leidseplein. What follows is a list of places for those with rather different tastes. Most venues close at 4am (5am over weekends). You should tip the doorman as you leave (about *f*5), and avoid using cabs cruising outside. Legal cabs will be found at a nearby rank—or the club may phone for one for you.

Dansen bij Jansen, Handboogstraat 11, ✆ 620 1779. A bit like a Students' Union bop. You usually need to prove membership of a college or university to get in. Frequent theme and fancy-dress nights.

Escape, Rembrandtsplein 11, ✆ 622 1111. A cavern of a place that has shed its commercial image to become a hyper-trendy club, complete with shops and even a hairdresser.

Mazzo, Rozengracht 114, ✆ 626 7500. Comfortable club with a good atmosphere and an excellent range of music, often live with local bands.

Odeon, Singel 460, ✆ 624 9711. Multi-roomed venue in a converted canal house, but often overpopulated by adolescent tourists.

Scandals Lounge, Reguliersdwarsstraat 13, ✆ 422 6220. Glitzy hip and garage.

Sinners in Heaven, Wagenstraat 3, ✆ 620 1375. Weird 'n' wonderful décor; world-famous-in-Holland clientele.

Soul Kitchen, Amstelstraat 32, ✆ 620 2333. The sort of music that thirty-somethings can understand and dance to, in a friendly refreshingly untrendy atmosphere. No under 25s allowed.

Trance Buddha, Oudezijds Voorburgwal 216, ✆ 422 8233. Young New Age crowd with appropriate soundtrack.

West Pacific, Haarlemmerweg 8, ✆ 488 7778. Fun, hip dance-café that is part of an arts complex in an old gasworks.

See also **De Melkweg** below.

multimedia centres

De Brakke Ground, Nes 45, ✆ 626 6866. Attractive venue for Flemish art and performance. Dance programmes are especially worth catching.

De Meervaart Centrum, Meer en Vaart 1, ✆ 610 7498. A modern arts centre that stages a good variety of film, theatre, dance and music (both classical and jazz).

De Melkweg, Lijnbaansgracht 234a, ✆ 624 1777. Converted from an old dairy in the 1960s, De Melkweg (Milky Way) has managed to slough off its old hippie image, and emerge as a vibrant centre for the arts. The theatre has an extraordinarily imaginative programme and plays host to companies from around the world (performances are often in English). There is a small cinema that shows a range of films from mainstream to cult; and a concert hall that stages excellent African and South American bands, and acts as a try-out venue for a lot of up-and-coming rock groups. At weekends, when the bands have finished, an alternative disco takes over. The coffeeshop was one of the first where the sale of marijuana was tolerated by the authorities. If you're going to use the centre a lot, it's a good idea to take out membership (ƒ15, valid three months) which gives you considerable discount on admission prices.

Amsterdam RAI, Europaplein 12, ✆ 549 1212. A business congress centre which frequently houses large concerts and touring musicals. It is also the venue for KunstRAI, an annual fair of contemporary art.

Westergasfabriek, Haarlemmerweg 8–10, ✆ 681 3068. Amsterdam's most recently opened arts centre is in a converted gasworks. It's home to the Toneelgroep Amsterdam and is the European base for the Cirque du Soleil. Visiting shows are usually in an experimental vein. Every night after 11pm the chairs in the café are moved aside and the customers bop until late.

Amsterdam ✆ (020–)   **Gay Amsterdam**

In the heady social upheaval of the 1960s and 70s, when pixie-hatted members of the Gnome Party held protest meetings on the Dam and troupes of hippies camped out in the Vondelpark, Amsterdam's lesbians and gays joined in the frolic. Homosexuality had been decriminalized in 1811, but the gay community wanted a city free of the petty prejudices and subtle discrimination they ran up against in day-to-day life. In many ways they succeeded. Today Amsterdam is known as the Gay Capital of Europe. Gay bars and cafés, though often in clusters, aren't in ghettos. Nobody bats an eyelid if two men kiss or hold hands in public. The city was quick off the mark in coping constructively with HIV, the council housing department gives gay couples the same status as married heterosexuals, and in 1987 the world's first memorial to persecuted lesbians and gays, the Homomonument, was unveiled (the three triangles of pink granite between the Westerkerk and the Keizersgracht are the focal point of many a party, protest or commemoration service).

There are gay bars, clubs, hotels, bookshops and restaurants all over town. You'll find most of the heavier leather bars lurking up the north end of **Warmoesstraat**, ribbons of coffeeshops, restaurants and bars along **Kerkstraat** and **Reguliersdwarsstraat**, a jolly throb of clubs and pubs along the **Amstel** off Rembrandtplein, and scores of local neighbourhood cafés. Despite accusations that the Amsterdam gay scene is stagnating, gay tourists flock to the city. Over weekends, the hunk at the end of the bar is more likely to be a computer programmer from South London than a local lad. Many Amsterdammers respond to this invasion by staying at home, venturing out on Thursdays and Sundays when the occupying forces are thinner on the ground. The atmosphere, though, is friendly and welcoming. Most gay venues distribute free **maps of gay Amsterdam**, leaflets and free magazines (such as *Rainbow*) giving you an idea of what's on about town; but as people are so open and chatty, word of mouth is often the best way to find out what the evening might have in store.

Here is an idiosyncratic selection of places to go; some are well known but others are quirky, local establishments, out of the tourist maelstrom.

cafés, coffeeshops and restaurants

Backstage Boutique (a.k.a. 'The Twins'), Utrechtsedwarsstraat 75; *open Mon–Sat 10am–6pm*. Not exclusively gay, but with an atmosphere of stratospheric camp that shouldn't be missed.

Café Secret, Kerkstraat 346; *open Sun–Thurs 9pm–3am, Fri–Sat 9pm–4am*. Cosy café that sometimes has live entertainment.

COC, Rozenstraat 14; coffeeshop *open Wed–Sat 1–5pm*. Spartan but amiable haven in Amsterdam's lesbian and gay 'culture centre'.

Downtown, Reguliersdwarsstraat 31; *open daily 10–8*. A friendly day-time coffeeshop, popular with tourists and locals, in one of Amsterdam's gay streets. It serves food and has a sprawl of pavement tables on sunny days.

Getto, Warmoesstraat 51; restaurant/café *open Wed–Sat noon to 1am, Sun noon–midnight; closed Mon and Tues*. A young, friendly crowd and good food make this one of the most popular recent additions to the gay scene.

Le Monde, Rembrandtplein 6; *open daily 8am–midnight*. Tiny, cheery snack café with a terrace on Rembrandtplein.

La Strada, Nieuwezijds Voorburgwal 93; *open daily noon–1am*. Brown café with good food and friendly staff, popular with local lesbians.

Reibach, Brouwersgracht 139; *open daily 10–8, but closes 6pm Oct–Mar*. Trendy café with a Germanic edge, great cakes and a pleasant, small terrace on one of Amsterdam's most tranquil canals.

bars

Amstel Taveerne, Amstel 54; *open daily 3pm–1am, to 2pm at weekends*. Beer mugs and bric-a-brac hang everywhere. Dutch reproductions on the walls. Dutch originals around the bar. A provincial pub in the middle of the city with sing-alongs and good cheer (all Dutch).

April, Reguliersdwarsstraat 37; *open daily 2pm–1am*. More than double its previous size (and more attractively designed) after a 1996 renovation. Popular with young Amsterdammers during the week. Over the weekend tourists swell numbers until the bar bursts into a street party.

Argos, Warmoesstraat 95; *open Mon–Thurs 9pm–3am, to 4pm at weekends*. Amsterdam's oldest leather bar sweats with bikers' jackets, cowboy chaps and denim. As you wander into the dimmer recesses, what the gay guides coyly term 'action' becomes quite lively.

Havana, Reguliersdwarsstraat 17; *open daily 4pm–1am, to 2am at weekends*. Comfortable café/bar with an exhausting constellation of beautiful people. There's a small dance floor upstairs, so you can pop up for an early bop.

Casa Maria, Warmoesstraat 60; *open Sun–Thurs noon–1am, Fri–Sat noon–2am.* In the heart of the red-light district. A jukebox full of uproarious kitsch, a gregarious Spanish owner, and a picture window that offers the best people-watching possibilities in town.

Montmartre, Halvemaansteeg 17; *open daily 4pm–1am, to 2am on Fri and Sat.* Dancing barmen, original 1920s décor, loud music and a tight squeeze.

Le Shako, 's Gravenlandseveer 2; *open daily 9pm–2am, to 3am at weekends.* A miniscule bar that attracts students, writers, academics and a good load of local scruffs. Cheap beer on Tuesdays and free snacks on Thursdays.

clubs

COC, Rozenstraat 14. Amsterdam's Gay Centre runs a disco on Friday nights (*10pm–2am*) which attracts a local crowd and ingénues from the provinces.

C'ring (or Cockring), Warmoesstraat 96; *open daily 11pm–4am, to 5am on Fri and Sat.* Steamy, sweaty, swarming venue for emergency sex.

Exit, Reguliersdwarsstraat 42. April's busy disco-sister.

De Trut, Bilderdijkstraat 165; *open Sun 11pm–4am.* A trendy, but relaxed and pose-free club with a wide range of music, a (mainly) young crowd and a mix of lesbians and gay men. The Trut is in the cellar of what was once one of Amsterdam's biggest squats. The entrance is unmarked, but if you turn up between 11 and midnight, you'll see where to go. Often the club gets so full you have to wait for someone to leave before you're allowed in.

accommodation

Hotels are forbidden by law to discriminate against gay couples, but here's a selection of specifically gay places to stay. The prices are for a double room with shower in season, with breakfast included. (Addresses are given with the Amsterdam postcode.)

Amsterdam House Hotel, 's Gravelandseveer 3, 1011 KM, ✆ 624 6607, ✉ 624 1346 (*inexpensive*). Friendly canalside hotel just minutes from gay hotspots.

International Travel Club/ITC, Prinsengracht 1051, 1017 JE, ✆ 623 0230 (*inexpensive*). Quiet hotel overlooking one of Amsterdam's finest canals, popular with an older crowd.

Jordaan Canal House, Egelantiersgracht 23, 1015 RC, ✆ 620 1545, ✉ 638 5056 (*moderate–inexpensive*). Beautifully situated, exclusively gay 17th-century canal house.

Hotel New York, Herengracht 13, 1015 BA, ✆ 624 3066 (*moderate*). Swish hotel with all mod cons, hiding behind three 17th-century canal houses at a tranquil end of Amsterdam's grandest canal.

GIS Apartments, Keizersgracht 33, 1015 CD Amsterdam, ✆ 625 0071, offers furnished apartments *from f150–250 per night.*

Many of Amsterdam's best 'straight' hotels are sympathetic places to stay, and many are gay-owned. See especially the Quentin Hotel (which has a large lesbian clientele), Seven Bridges Hotel and Hotel Engeland under 'Where to Stay'.

lesbian Amsterdam

Lesbians are not as well catered for as gay men in Amsterdam, but there's a lively, friendly scene in places such as:

Sarah's Grannies, Kerkstraat 176; *Mon–Sat 9am–6pm.* Offers good Dutch meals in a relaxed atmosphere. Not exclusively gay, but popular with local women.

Café Saarein, Elandsstraat 119; *open Mon 8pm–1am, Tues–Thurs and Sun 3pm–1am, Fri and Sat 3pm–2am.* A cosy local café, currently the citadel of Amsterdam's lesbian life.

Café Vive-la-Vie, Amstelstraat 5; *open daily noon–1am, to 2am at weekends.* Sociable crowd in a vaguely Art Deco bar with music that increases in volume as the night wears on.

COC (see under 'clubs' above) holds a house-oriented women-only disco on *Saturdays from 8pm–2am.*

You II, Amstel 178, *open Thurs to Saturday 11pm to 5am; Sunday 4pm to 1am.* More of a disco than Vive-la-Vie, and less heavily house than COC. Much-needed hip, yet pretty, relaxed lesbian meeting place.

other attractions

If the sun's shining, the place to be is **Zandvoort**, on Amsterdam's gay beach. Zandvoort is not the forgotten patch in the dunes that such places usually are, although it's a bit of a trek to reach it. There are two gay bars (Eldorado and Sans Tout) on the beach. Both are open from 8am until midnight. You can get there by train from Centraal Station (about 30mins, frequent trains right through the day). Once you get to the beach, walk south along the promenade and then on past the 'Naakt Strand' (nudist beach) for about 5km.

There's a **gay cinema** every Saturday and Sunday at Desmet, Plantage Middenlaan 4a, ✆ 627 3434. It shows a selection of popular and independent films and attracts a local crowd.

You can spend hours browsing around **gay bookshops** like Intermale, Spuistraat 251—mostly for men—or Boekhandel Vrolijk, Paleisstraat 135, which has a wide selection of literature, biographies and non-fiction of interest to lesbians and gay men. The American Discount Bookshop, Kalverstraat 185, has a good gay section.

Mandate, Prinsengracht 715 (*open Mon–Fri 11am–10pm; Sat noon–6pm, Sun 2–6pm; daily membership f18, six visits f63*) is a well-equipped **gay gym** with a busy coffee bar; and the notorious Amsterdam saunas are Thermos Day, Raamstraat 35 (*open Mon–Fri noon–11pm, Sat and Sun noon–10pm; adm f30*) and Thermos Night, Kerkstraat 60 (*open daily 11pm–8am; adm f30*).

COC is Amsterdam's lesbian and gay social centre (Rozenstraat 14, ℂ office 626 3087/information ℂ 623 4079; *open Mon–Thurs 9–5; for disco and coffeeshop hours*, see 'Clubs' and 'Lesbian Amsterdam' above).

Gay and Lesbian Switchboard (ℂ 623 6565; *open 10am–10pm*) gives information and advice in English.

The Randstad

Amsterdam, The Hague and Rotterdam—and their surrounding towns—have moved so close together over the centuries that they now almost form a single giant metropolis. The Dutch even give this conurbation a name: the Randstad—which translates literally as 'Edge City', or 'Border City'. (The towns form a rough line along the coast and rivers that marked the traditional boundaries of the State of Holland, *see* pp.34–5).

Yet there are patches of green in-between each urban sprawl—patches of red, yellow and mauve too, if you happen to be travelling in early spring, when the bulb fields are in bloom. And the cities preserve their particular styles and atmospheres so determinedly that they could be on far sides of the country. The Hague, graceful and sedate, is the age-old rival of rough, quirky Amsterdam. Rotterdam, an architecturally edgy phoenix that pushed its way out of the ashes left by the Second World War, is perhaps the one place in the Netherlands that actually feels like a city, rather than a grown-up village. Haarlem and Leiden recline and revel with university-town abandon, and Delft quietly preserves its historical air.

Getting Around the Randstad
by train

Travelling **by train** is by far the most sensible way to get about the Randstad, as trains are fast and frequent. One line connects Amsterdam, Leiden, The Hague and Rotterdam; another bypasses Leiden and goes to Haarlem instead, before joining up the other cities. If you buy a ticket to (for example) Rotterdam, you are permitted to get off along the way, on the day the ticket is valid. (Though just to be safe, you should mention this when buying the ticket, and they will print 'via Leiden' or 'via Den Haag' on it.)

From Amsterdam Centraal Station to:

Haarlem: Trains leave every 10 minutes, and the trip takes 15mins.

Keukenhof Gardens: Centraal Station will usually have details of special discount offers on a combined rail/bus ticket to the Keukenhof. Alternatively, there's a bus connection from both Leiden and Haarlem stations to the Keukenhof in the season (details from local tourist offices).

Leiden: There's a train every 15–20mins. Journey time is half an hour.

The Hague: Trains take 50 minutes. There are about four an hour. The Hague has two railway stations: Den Haag HS (Hollands Spoor) and Den Haag CS (Centraal Station). There are frequent tram and rail links between the two, but the CS is the more convenient. **Delft** and **Scheveningen** are part of The Hague's urban transport network; tram journeys take 20 and 15mins respectively. There are also train connections between The Hague CS and Delft.

Rotterdam: There are 4–5 trains an hour, and the journey takes an hour.

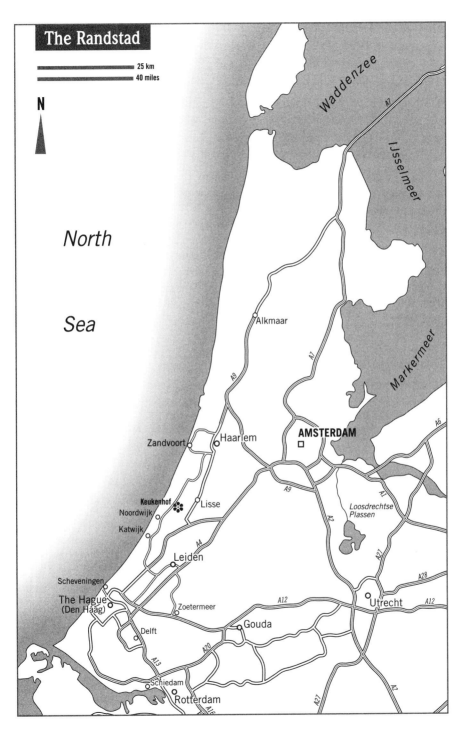

All the cities are linked by motorways, though traffic jams are common in the rush hours.

Haarlem: Just a few minutes up the A9 or A5 from Amsterdam.

Leiden: It's 40km (25 miles) along the A4 between Amsterdam and Leiden, and then another 10km (6 miles) to The Hague.

The Hague: 48km (30 miles) along the A4 southwest of Amsterdam.

Rotterdam: 45 miles (72km) south of Amsterdam along the A4 and A13, and 18 miles (28km) from The Hague (southeast along the A13).

Haarlem

Just 15 minutes by train from Amsterdam, Haarlem has a cosy, provincial atmosphere quite different from the capital—but it's by no means dull. You'll find hordes of friendly cafés, the much-painted St Bavo's church, tiny *hofjes* tucked behind over-the-top public architecture, Holland's oldest and most intriguing museum and an important collection of paintings by Frans Hals. Haarlem acts as an overflow for students who have accommodation problems in Amsterdam and Leiden, and this gives the town a youthful, carefree air.

Getting Around

Most of the tourist sights are within easy walking distance, but your *strippenkaart* (*see* p.10) will be valid on bus trips.

Tourist Information

The VVV tourist office is outside the railway station, open Mon–Sat 9–6; ℗ (0900) 616 1600, and can supply you with maps and public transport information.

Around the Grote Markt

Most people arriving in Haarlem head straight for the **Grote Markt** (Market Square) and the imposing Gothic **Grote of St Bavokerk** (Great or St Bavo's Church; *open Mon–Sat 10–4; Sept–March 10–3.30; adm*). The view across the square hasn't changed much over the centuries, and on a quiet morning you feel you could be looking at one of Gerrit Berckheyde's 17th-century paintings of the church. The interior is bright and painted white. A gleefully ostentatious Baroque organ upstages even the soaring Gothic arches. It was built by the Amsterdammer Christian Muller in 1738, and is said to be one of the biggest in the world. Clusters of musical putti and graceful maidens cling to the pipes. Handel, Mozart and Albert Schweitzer have all had a go on the ivory and tortoiseshell keyboard. Before you leave, have a look at the fading tapestry designs painted on the columns at the side of the church and fluid lines of a marble relief by The Hague sculptor Xavery: Poetry and Music paying homage to the town patroness. In the centre column of the Brewers' Chapel (near the south transept) two little lines mark the heights of past Haarlem residents: Giant Cajanus (2.6m/8ft 8ins) and Paap (94cm/37ins).

Outside the church is a statue of **Laurens Coster**. Local legend has it that while he was carving his lover's name in a tree trunk, a letter fell into the sand. He was inspired by the imprint to invent printing. Though Haarlem is proud of him today, his contemporaries took him for a sorcerer and drove him out of town. He went to live in Germany—which might explain why the rest of the world believes that printing began with Gutenberg.

The oldest part of the **Stadhuis** across the square is a 14th-century hunting lodge built for the Count of Holland. It's been altered and expanded over the years, and the present complex incorporates a medieval monastery. During office hours you can have a look at the old heavy-beamed **Gravenzaal** (Count's Hall). On the south side of the square is the relentlessly ornamented **Vleeshal** (the former Meat Market, built in 1602). Sacheverell Sitwell remarked that we should 'regard it less as a building, than as Dutch cabinet work on a most capricious scale'. The cellar houses a small **Archeological Museum** (*open Wed–Sun 1–5; adm free*) displaying local finds from prehistory onwards.

Just off Grote Markt, above a clock shop once owned by the Ten Boom family is the **Corrie Ten Boom House** (Barteljorisstraat 19; *open Nov–March Tues–Sat 11–3; April–Oct Tues–Sat 10–3.30; adm by donation*). The Ten Boom family offered refuge to Jews in the Second World War in a cupboard-like hideaway, which the Gestapo never found—even though they once spent nearly a week living in the house, hoping to starve out any *onderduikers* (literally 'under-divers' *see pp.46–7*). Most of the Ten Boom family were active in the Resistance and perished in concentration camps, but Corrie returned, and told the story in a book, *The Hiding Place*.

Hofjes

Haarlem is renowned for its *hofjes*—secluded almshouse courtyards dating from the 15th century. Wander down a passageway, peer through a half-open door on the street and you'll find them—hidden formal gardens, surrounded by dainty gables and white-painted front doors. Most are still lived in, but if you're discreet you can have a quick look around. The best ones are in the western part of the city around Barrevoetestraat and Tuchthuisstraat.

Frans Hals Museum

Groot Heiligland 62; open Mon–Sat 11–5, Sun 12–5; adm.

Haarlem's star attraction is housed in one of the town's grander *hofjes*, a 17th-century Old Men's Home. The museum isn't devoted entirely to Hals—there's a batch of other Golden Age painters, a wide range of furniture and applied art and an extensive modern collection. The corridors are pervaded by a steady ticking of clocks, and the displays give you some sharp surprises. In a dim 17th-century period room, you'll see an enormous drawing by the 1930s Magic Realist, Pyke Koch. Bright contemporary pieces hang alongside Old Masters or in rooms displaying antique silver. All this gives the museum a quirky liveliness. Don't miss the exquisitely crafted 18th-century doll's house or the Restoration Workshop. (You stand behind a glass wall and watch painters work painstakingly on the tiny patch of an Old Master that will occupy them for months.)

The most intriguing of Frans Hals' works in the museum are the portraits of the *Regents* and *Regentesses of the Old Men's Home*, painted in 1664 when Hals was in his eighties. The story that he was a bitter occupant of the almshouse is not true, but he certainly seems to be taking some sort of revenge with his brush. The Regentesses, in particular, are a sour and terrifying lot. Their expressions range from rosy stupidity to pure evil, and the white faces are thrown into stark relief by the sombre surround. You can see why Van Gogh said that Hals had at least 27 shades of black.

Teylers Museum

Spaarne 16; open Tues–Sat 10–5, Sun 12–5, winter until 4; adm.

The Netherlands' oldest purpose-built museum first opened its doors in 1784. It's the best sort of small museum—one based on the taste of an erudite, eccentric private collector, in this case the 18th-century merchant Pieter Teyler van der Hulst. A succession of astute directors have, in making new acquisitions, skilfully developed the diverse themes of Teyler's original collection. You'll find a fascinating hoard of old scientific instruments and machines, fossils, paintings and drawings (including some by Michelangelo and Rembrandt). Much of the collection is housed in beautiful wooden display cases in the original 18th-century museum building. The superb drawing collection is in a modern wing, that has been added with taste and discretion.

Provinciehuis Noord-Holland

Guided tours by arrangement, contact the VVV.

Slightly out of the centre of town, the Provinciehuis Noord-Holland (North Holland Provincial Government Building) is certainly worth the 20–30-minute walk. It was built as a home and private art gallery by an eccentric Amsterdam banker in 1796, and during its chequered history has been a palace to Louis Bonaparte and a museum. It's a sumptuous neoclassical building with exquisite stucco work, gorgeously moulded ceilings and patterned parquet flooring, whose rooms abound with marble statues and period furniture.

Haarlem ✆ (023–)   **Where to Stay**

Most visitors to Haarlem stay either in Amsterdam or in Zandvoort on the coast (*see* p.219), as the local hotel selection is not exciting.

Golden Tulip Lion d'Or, Kruisweg 34, 2011 LC, ✆ 532 1750, ✉ 532 9543 (*moderate*). Solid 19th-century building near the city centre, with comfortable rooms.

Carillon, Grote Markt 27, ✆ 531 0591, ✉ 531 4909 (*inexpensive*). Old-fashioned hotel with friendly staff, in the shadow of St Bavo's.

Haarlem ✆ (023–)   **Eating Out**

The street behind St Bavo's, at the far end of the market, is a good place to look for restaurants and cafés—though you really need go no further than the wood panelling and hanging lampshades of the beautifully restored **Stations Restaurant** (on Platform 2). For a treat there is also **De Componist**, Korte Veerstraat 1, ✆ 532 8853 (*expensive*), a stylish restaurant that is rapidly gaining the reputation of being one of the best in the country. Up-and-coming star chef Michel Lambermon turns out such tasty Franco-Dutch fare as marinated salmon with tomato bouillon and samphire. **Café Brinkmann**, Grote Markt 9–13, ✆ 532 3111 (*moderate*) is an elegant Art Deco establishment overlooking St Bavo's.

In the cheaper range, De Karmeliet, Spekstraat 6, ✆ 531 4426 (*inexpensive*) provides a cheery stopover for a simple snack or sandwich, and **In den Uiver**, Rivier Fischmarkt 13, ✆ 532 5399 (*inexpensive*) is a cosy *proeflokaal* for an invigorating Dutch *jenever.*

Keukenhof

Open late March–late May, daily 8–7.30; adm exp.

In spring, the fields between Haarlem and Leiden glow with the colours of millions of tulips and other bulbs, and attract nearly that number of tourists. Coachloads pour out of Amsterdam, to return traumatized by the sight of great cutting machines churning through the bulbfields scrunching up the flowers. (Most plants are grown for the bulb rather than the bloom, and a swift blade to the stalk makes the bulb subdivide.) The Amsterdam Tourist Board (*see* p.78) and various agencies around town can help with organized tours, but it's a far better idea to go on your own by train or car. The town to head for is **Lisse**, and the garden to see is the **Keukenhof**.

The Keukenhof (literally 'Kitchen Garden') was, in the 15th century, the herb and vegetable patch of the Countess Jacoba van Beieren. Whatever she grew there enabled her to get through four husbands (including a Duke of Gloucester and a Dauphin of France) before her own death at the age of 35. In 1949 a group of Dutch bulb-growers took over the land as a shop window for the bulb industry. It turned out to have a much wider appeal. Today there are some 30ha (74 acres) of nearly 7 million plants and a further 5000sq m (54,000sq ft) of flowers under glass. The best time to go is from mid to late April, when tulips, daffodils, narcissi and hyacinths are all flowering at once.

Tulip Mania

Tulips—homely, suburban and pure—have become a national cliché. Yet behind these apparently innocent blooms lurks a past of envy, greed and intemperance almost unparalleled in Dutch history.

Tulips were first spotted in Adrianople, Turkey, by Dutch diplomats at the Ottoman court. In the early 17th century the flowers made a spring début in some of French and Dutch society's best gardens. Soon, Johan van Hooghelande, a Leiden botanist, had found out how to vary the colour and shape of the blooms. Connoisseurs queued up, money pouches bulging, for the latest varieties and by the 1620s the tulip was *the* flower of fashionable aristocracy. This alchemical combination of scientific research, visual allure and the chance of profit—three great Dutch enthusiasms—incited the Great Tulip Mania. At first, the bulbs were seen as exotic rarities. The Calvinist Church even regarded them as dangerous—perhaps because the flamed petals reminded them of the ribbons, ruffs and other vanities that ministers railed against from the pulpits. The bulbs were swapped and grown by a handful of aristocratic connoisseurs who, as was their wont, imposed a strict hierarchy on the tulip world. The noblest were the roses (red and pink on white), then came the violets (lilac and purples on white) and finally *bizarden* (red or violet on yellow). Humble plain colours barely merited an estate. It was the irregular, flamed and striped varieties, like the red and white Semper Augustus and the Viceroy, that mattered. (The democratically minded Dutch, however, preferred to call their nobler varieties 'Admiral' or 'General' followed by the name of the grower.)

Gradually *hoi polloi* began to edge in on the scene. Tulips were easily reproducible for a wider market. Delftware, an imitation of expensive Chinese porcelain, was already decorating more modest homes. The Flemish carpet industry had its foundations in copying Turkish rugs. Tulips copied themselves, so by the mid-1630s weavers, blacksmiths and bakers were able to buy the bulbs at village fairs. The fashion spread and a tulip fever gripped the nation. Prices took off, then went into orbit. An Admiral de Maan that sold for *f*15 in 1634 went for *f*175 three years later. At the height of the boom an *f*800 Scipio changed hands after a few weeks for *f*2,200. People went to any lengths for a prized bulb. One farmer met the *f*2,500 demanded for a single Viceroy by payment in kind: two *last* of wheat, four of rye, four fat oxen, eight pigs, a dozen sheep, two oxheads of wine, four tons of butter, 1,000 pounds of cheese, a bed, a suit of fine clothes and a silver beaker.

The rocketing prices were fuelled not only by demand, but by the growth of a futures market. In 1634 one bright dealer had the idea of buying in the winter for future delivery, and then selling to a new buyer before he actually possessed the stock. Soon deals were being done on negotiable pieces of paper, with the time of delivery as an expiry date. A quick turnover meant a quick paper profit. Dealers were selling bulbs they didn't yet possess, for amounts they couldn't possibly raise. As the delivery date drew closer, the danger that you would actually have to pay up increased, but so did the possibility of making an intoxicating profit as prices rose by the hour. At the bottom of the pile, and in danger of ending up with a heap of worthless bulbs if the market collapsed, were the growers. (The actual tulips would be the last thing on the mind of a merchant facing bankruptcy and trying to settle his paper debts.)

And collapse it did. By 1636 this *windhandel* (literally 'trading in the wind') was beginning to worry the city magistrates and outrage the Church. Whether it was the rumour of intervention that caused the panic, or the panic that caused the intervention, is unclear. But on 2 or 3 February 1637 a warning whisper shot round Haarlem and dealers went all-out to sell. Prices plummeted, the bubble burst and the magistrates had to intervene with special legislation to rescue the innocent growers from the debris of bankrupts. It wasn't until the spring of 1638 that the market found a normal level, but the passion for tulips was there to stay. As the scandal subsided they quietly assumed their place alongside clogs, cheese and blue and white china as part of the nation's iconography.

Eating Out

The cafés around the Keukenhof are crowded and unexciting. Pack yourself a picnic.

Leiden

The plan of a Dutch town is: a bridge a canal: under an arch into a street: pointed stepped houses; 1620: on brand new garages: a great red brick tower, then a vast church, shut up... Some frescoes on white-washed walls... Flights of cyclists. Immense profusion of highly civilised shops—flower shops, shoes, bicycles, books, everything the more solidly placed wealthy but not frivolous citizen can eat or wear or use: all shining spick & span.

Virginia Woolf, *Diary: May 8, 1935*

Leiden fits the plan perfectly, and even throws in a couple of windmills for good measure. This was Rembrandt's birthplace and home to the Pilgrim Fathers, the site of the most famous battle in Dutch history and of the first tulips grown in Holland. Yet despite its wealthy air and historical resonance, Leiden is no stuffy museum piece. The local university, founded in 1581, is one of the most prestigious in the country and student life gives the town spirit and verve. 'A new harvest of sanskrit!' exclaims the sign on a bookshop window; the 'frescoes on whitewashed walls' are texts by the world's greatest poets; glimpses through canal-house windows reveal the chaos of communal student kitchens; doors of ancient Student Corps' headquarters fly open and tipsy young men tumble out into the night air. Inside, the sounds of carousing continue. In surrounding cafés people are locked in earnest conversation.

Just a few minutes' journey from Amsterdam, Leiden is a popular day-trip destination. But if you spend a night there, when most of the visitors have gone, you're more likely to appreciate the university-town atmosphere. Just visiting the museums could easily consume a day of your time. The Molenmuseum Valk gives a fascinating insight into the innards of a windmill, the collection of Japanese artefacts at the Rijksmuseum voor Volkenkunde is so impressive that people make pilgrimages from Japan to view it, and the Egyptian antiquities at the Rijksmuseum van Oudenheden are of world renown.

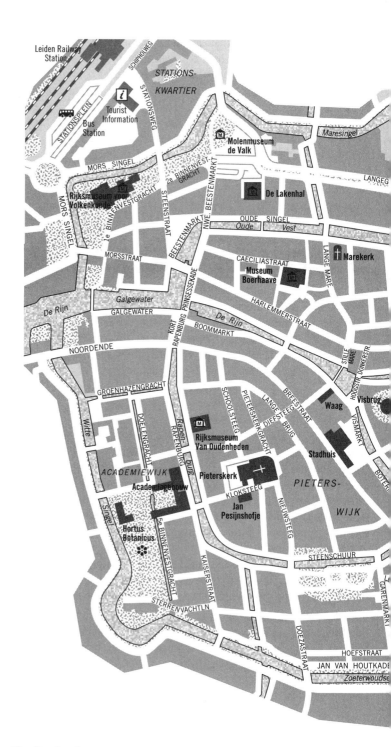

200 metres
200 yards

N

NGEGRACHT

OOSTDWARS-
GRACHT

VEST

Oude

Vest

Oude Heren-

gracht

Biekerspark

MAREDORP

PELIKAANSTRAAT

Haven-
plein

HAVEN

De Haven

VAN DER WERFSTRAAT

HARLEMMERSTRAAT

OUDE RIJN

KAASMARKT

ZUIDSINGEL

Amker-
park

Singel

Zijl

Burcht

MIDDELWEG

HOOIGRACHT

GROENE

MIDDELSTEGRACHT

UITERSTEGRACHT

VESTESTRAAT

PANCRASWIJK

HERENGRACHT

LANGESTRAAT

ORANJEGRACHT

OOSTERKERKSTRAAT

STEEG

Katoen-
park

Nieuwe

Rijn

NIEUWE RIJN

'DAAL

LEVENDAAL

GEREGRACHT

GORTESTRAAT

LEVENDAAL

AAT

KADE

Singel

History

Locals ('Leijenaars') like to claim that the Leiden grew from the Roman settlement of Lugdunum, but it's safer to pinpoint the town's origin at the appearance of De Burcht (The Stronghold, *see* below) around AD 1000. Around 1050 the powerful Counts of Holland moved into town, so ensuring Leiden's prosperity for centuries. At the beginning of the Eighty Years' War, the Spanish besieged Leiden (1573–4). The starving town was eventually relieved by William the Silent, who broke down the dykes and, to the Spaniards' utter surprise, came sailing across the fields with the Dutch navy. The Spanish made off with such haste that they left their dinner—an enormous pot of stew—still simmering on the fire. It was found by a city marksman (romantics say a wandering orphan). He carried it back to the hungry Leijenaars who were already laying into the white bread and herring that the navy had brought. Every year, on 3 October, the town celebrates the anniversary of its relief with festive public consumption of bread, herring and *hutspot* ('hotch-potch'). As a reward for their endurance William offered the people of Leiden either eternal relief from taxation, or Holland's first university. With characteristic far-sightedness they chose the latter.

Leiden went on to become a prosperous wool-trading town, but towards the end of the 18th century the trade (and the city) went into decline as the industrial revolution passed Holland by and British towns cornered the wool market. It was the university that helped the town keep its head above water—and it still does. Although Leiden's suburban sprawl now links up with the industries and larger cities of the Randstad, it is the university and its associated research institutes that drive Leiden's economy.

Getting Around

All the main tourist sites are within easy walking distance of the centre and the railway station. They are all very well signposted, and there are helpful maps dotted all over the city centre (look for the **i** sign). *Strippenkarten* (*see* p.10) are valid on public transport here too, though Leiden's buses tend to skirt the historic core of the city and are of limited use to tourists. For **information** on public transport, telephone the national information line on ✆ (0900) 9292.

Bicycle rental: Behind the station, ✆ (071) 512 0068; ƒ8 per day. You'll need to leave ƒ100 deposit and have proof of identification.

Taxi: ✆ (071) 521 2144 or 512 3300.

Boat trips: Rederij Sleutelstad (dep. Beestenmarkt, ✆ (071) 513 4938) offer trips through the city's canals (mid-April–mid-Sept); Schuitje Vaart (dep. Stille Mare, ✆ (071) 512 0394) does the same, but in smaller boats (May–Sept).

Tourist Information

The VVV tourist office is right near the railway station at Stationsplein 210, ✆ (0900) 222 2333, ✆ (071) 512 5318; open Mon–Fri 9–5.30, Sat 9–4; *www.tref.nl/3355/sport/vvv.htm*. Here you can pick up a map and advice on routes of walks around the town.

Leiden erupts in a city-wide party on **3 October** (as it has done for over 400 years) to celebrate the relief of its siege in 1574. Traditional white bread, herring and *hutspot* (*see* above) are served, and celebrations in restaurants and cafés spill out into the street.

The Centre

Rijksmuseum voor Volkenkunde

National Museum of Ethnology, Steenstraat 1; open Tues–Fri 10–5, Sat and Sun 12–5; adm. Until 2001 the museum will be undergoing extensive renovation, and only a small part of the collection will be on view at any one time. Adm will be only f3.50 during the renovation period.

You have barely stepped off the train when you come across one of Leiden's weighty museums. In a converted 19th-century hospital beside what was once part of the city moat, you'll find Javanese puppets, Bornean ear-jewellery made from the beaks of hornbills, a Greenlander's Sunday best, and other riches from around the world.

But the real attraction is the **Siebold Collection** of Japanese art and artefacts. In 1825, Philipp von Siebold went to Japan as a doctor, under the auspices of the Dutch government. He had instructions to collect as much information as he could about what was then a relatively unknown culture. Siebold came back laden with 6,000 objects, ranging from fans to enormous 17th-century statues of Buddha. This stash forms the core of what has become one of the most noted representations of traditional Japanese culture in the world. There are rooms set out ready for a tea ceremony, cabinets of beautiful lacquerware, suits of Samurai armour and ceremonial swords. The display of prints boasts work by Utagawa Hiroshige (1797–1858), including the well-known *Sudden Shower over the Bridge of Atake*. Keep an eye open for the 17th-century clocks. At that time the Japanese divided the daylight hours into six equal periods, named after animals in the Chinese astrological chart. The length of these periods varied according to season. The mechanisms of these first clocks were copied from western models, but a clockmaker had to visit every month to adjust them to follow seasonal fluctuations.

Molenmuseum de Valk

2e Binnenvestgracht 1a, open Tues–Sat 10–5, Sun 1–5; adm.

A restored 18th-century grain mill, 'De Valk' offers a rare inside view of how windmills work. You can potter about the lower storeys, where the last miller lived until the turn of this century. Then leave the cosily furnished rooms to clamber past millstones and flour chutes to the grinding cogs, seven storeys high. On the way you can step out on to the reefing stage (the platform that runs around the middle of the windmill) for a view over the city.

De Lakenhal

Oude Singel 32, open Tues–Fri 10–5, Sat and Sun 12–5; adm.

'The Cloth Hall' was built in 1640 as the administrative centre of Leiden's prosperous cloth industry. In 1874 it was converted into a municipal museum. Much of the original interior wall panelling and stucco work is intact, and there are good collections of silver and furniture. But the star attractions are the paintings. Look out especially for Lucas van Leyden's fine and delicately coloured triptych, *The Last Judgement* (1572); works by the young Rembrandt and his studio-mate Jan Levens; Gerard Dou's tiny, intense oils (which established a Leiden style); and the lecherous abandon of Jan Steen's *Amorous Couple* (1660). There's a painting depicting the brave Burgemeester van der Werff who, at the height of the siege, offered his own body as food to the faltering citizens. They refused but were fired by his courage to hold out even longer. (In the painting they look well-fed and a little embarrassed by the offer.)

Museum Boerhaave

Lange St Agnietenstraat 10, open Tues–Sat 10–5, Sun 12–5; adm.

The idea of a museum of scientific and surgical instruments might not have you immediately reaching for your wallet, but this one is worth every cent of the entry fee. First off, on the ground floor, is a reconstruction of a wooden Anatomy Theatre—a mini-colosseum with steep rakes of spectators' seats surrounding a central operating table. It was in theatres like this that Rembrandt's *Anatomy Lesson of Professor Tulp*, and countless other paintings of the genre, were set. Next, you wander through five centuries' worth of medical instruments and scientific paraphernalia. There's a 17th-century painting depicting God as a doctor (complete with a urine specimen jar), and the world's first herbarium—a book of pressed herbs, all still intact, put together by one Leohart Rauwolf in 1560. Next comes a range of beautifully crafted early microscopes, one of the first ever pendulum clocks, and astronomy globes and instruments galore. Look out for the 19th-century Zander equipment, such as the 'Apparatus for Massaging the Chest and Back'—an eccentric contraption made of cast iron, with all sorts of cogs, belts and rubber hammers. You can also see a prototype heart-lung machine, and one of the first commercially produced electron microscopes. Along the way there are models of machines to play with, and everything is given clear labelling in English.

Hofjes

Beside the Boerhaave museum is a green door with 'Zion' elaborately scripted on the jamb. Through it you'll find a pretty garden courtyard surrounded by dainty houses. This is the **Groot Sionshof**, a court of almshouses built for elderly married couples in 1668. There are many such *hofjes* around Leiden, hidden behind unassuming doors. On your wanderings, pop in for a glimpse of the rather grand 18th-century **Coninckshofje** (Oude Veste 15); **St Stevenshof** (Haarlemmerstraat 48–50), founded in 1487; and the **Groeneveldstichting** (Oude Veste 41), built for the widows of clergy in 1882. All are still private residences, but provided you respect that you are usually welcome to look around quietly. Though if you see a sign reading '*Verboden Toegang Art. 461*', bear in mind that means 'Trespassers will be Prosecuted'.

Around the Stadhuis

Leiden's **Stadhuis** (City Hall) was built in 1597, though the unattractive brick pile you see today dates back to the 1930s, rebuilt after the old Stadhuis had been razed. All that was left was the front façade (which you can still see, in Breestraat). At one corner of the City Hall stands a sturdy 17th-century **Waag** (Weighing House), once the focus of an enormous market place: many of the street names in the area still end with '*markt*', from Kaasmarkt (cheese) to Aalmarkt (eels) and Beestenmarkt (cattle), giving you an idea of just how large the market was. A walk through the elegant classicist buildings that once accommodated the fish market brings you to **De Burcht** (The Stronghold). The dumpy fortress was built around AD 1000 on a mound between two branches of the Rhine to protect a small settlement of fishermen and farmers from marauding Vikings, fractious local lords and the fickle water levels. You can still march around its sturdy battlements and look out over the whole city.

The University District

Rijksmuseum Van Oudenheden

> *National Museum of Antiquities, Rapenburg 28; open Tues–Sat 10–5, Sun 12– 5; adm.*

The country's leading archaeological museum houses the entire 1st century AD *Temple of Taffeh* donated in 1960 by the Egyptian government to the Dutch in gratitude for their contribution to UNESCO excavations in Abyssinia. The squat stone building is in the museum foyer (it was a condition of the gift that no one should pay to see it) and overhead lighting simulates the passage of the sun (a second stipulation). The museum has a thrillingly gruesome collection of mummies (including one of a crocodile), and good stores of Greek and Roman antiquities. Star exhibits are the *Tomb Statues of Maya and Merit*. Maya was Director of the Treasury to Tutankhamun; his wife was a priestess. Although the statues arrived in Holland in 1832, their provenance was obscure, and it was only in 1986 that the tomb was rediscovered (a CD-ROM tells the story). The top floor of the museum is devoted to choice finds from local excavations, giving a clear and very manageable picture of civilization in Holland from prehistoric to medieval times.

The University

Founded in 1581, the University of Leiden now spreads throughout the city, rather in the manner of Oxbridge colleges. But the focus of university life is the **Academiegebouw**, Rapenburg 73, one of the oldest parts of the unversity. Once a nunnery, it has for centuries been used as an exam hall. Inside, up a spiral wooden stair-case, you'll find the 'Sweat Box'—the room where anxious candidates sat before exams and later awaited their results. The room is now hermetically sealed to protect the generations of signatures they left behind them on the walls. There is also a small **Academic History Museum** (*open Wed, Thurs, Fri 1–5; adm free*) with displays of mortar boards, gowns and students' bric-a-brac down the ages.

Hortus Botanicus

Open April–Sept Mon–Sat 9–5, Sun 10–5; Oct–Mar Mon–Fri 9–5, Sun 10–5; adm.

The part of the university most worth visiting is its Botanical Garden. Planted in 1594, it is one of the oldest botanical gardens in Europe. A 17th-century traveller described the Hortus as 'ravishing in rare curiosities', and it is here that the botanist Clusius planted the first tulip bulbs in Holland. They had come from Turkey via an embassy garden in Switzerland, where Clusius had spotted them. Unfortunately, the professor never saw his plants bloom: they were stolen one night before spring came. Today, Clusius' garden has once again been laid out in its original form. Later, when you have inhaled the perfume of scores of roses, visited the 350-year-old laburnum, and grown tired of the elegantly laid-out shrubberies, you can push your way through hothouses of sticky exotica, past signs warning you to 'Beware of the Butterflies' to the massive Victoria Amazonia lily, reputed to be able to support the weight of three men on its pads, and which flowers but one night a year.

Pieterskerk and Pilgrims

The 15th-century **Pieterskerk** (*open daily 1.30–4*) is in the heart of the student quarter. The surrounding cafés are favourite places to meet and relax, and on a fine summer's day there appear to be more live bodies stretched out in the former cemetery than dead ones. The church was originally called St Pieters, but was stripped of its saintly title, and any other papist ornamentation, during the Reformation. By far the most interesting thing to see in the plain, cavernous church is a mummified body. It was found, dried out by the draught, in a secret room under the pulpit and now lies in the church with its ankles neatly crossed and its head on a pillow. No one knows how it got there, or even how old it is. Some suspect murder, or a priest's secret lover; members of the older generation mutter darkly about Nazis and the Occupation.

Pieterskerk's other attractions include the tomb of Jan Steen, the 17th-century Dutch painter. Rembrandt's parents are also buried at Pieterskerk, though their graves are unmarked. Very little remains in Leiden to remind you of the painter's early years in the town. (A plaque on the side of a 1960s block of flats in Weddesteeg, halfway between the railway station and the university, marks the spot where he was born.)

In the church, you can also see a chart tracing ex-President George Bush's family tree, showing his descent from the Pilgrim Fathers. From 1609 to 1620 a group of Puritans, finding the religious atmosphere in Holland more congenial than in England, settled in Leiden with their preacher, John Robinson. **Jan Pesijnshofje** (Pieterskerkhof 21), a late 17th-century almshouse near the church, now marks the site where Robinson lived and preached. The congregation felt the need for an even freer climate, so in 1620 they headed back to Plymouth, boarded the *Mayflower* and set sail for the New World. Robinson didn't go with them; he died in 1625 and is buried in the Pieterskerk.

Naturalis

Darwinweg 2, ✆ (071) 568 7600; open Tues–Sun noon–6pm, adm.

Naturalis is the National Museum of Natural History, situated just behind Leiden station. The entrance building was originally put up in the 17th century as a *pesthuis* (hospital for sufferers from the plague). Nowadays a covered walkway transports you past a couple of life-size rhinos to a modern high-rise that's been hollowed out and filled with tiers of dinosaur skeletons, minerals, stuffed animals, preserved fish and thousands of plants and neatly ranged insects. No mangy bears and faded parrots here: everything is in top-top better-than-real-life condition, and interestingly presented. There are intriguing displays on environment and the planet, and a wealth of multimedia facilities—though it's a new museum and as yet much of the labelling and all of the multimedia is in Dutch only.

Shopping

Haarlemmerstraat is the main shopping drag, with branches of all the Dutch high street stores. But you'll find well-stocked bookshops, junk shops and quirkier boutiques around the top end of Nieuwe Rijn and in the alleys around the Pieterskerk.

Leiden ✆ (071–)   ### *Where to Stay*

Golden Tulip Leiden, Schipholweg 3, 2316 XB, ✆ 522 1121, ✉ 522 6675 (*expensive*). Smart business persons' hotel just a bleeper's pip from the railway station.

Mayflower, Beestenmarkt 2, 2312 CC, ✆ 514 2641, ✉ 512 8516 (*moderate–inexpensive, price includes breakfast*). Overlooking the newly renovated Beestenmarkt square, though with a slightly eerie, furniture-warehouse atmosphere.

Nieuw Minerva, Boommarkt 23, 2312 EA, ✆ 512 6358, ✉ 514 2674 (*inexpensive; includes breakfast*). Long having worn the mantle of Leiden's best bet for lower budgets, it is now tired—especially when it comes to furnishings and service. But it does have an attractive canalside location.

De Doelen, Rapenburg 2, 2311 EV, ✆ 512 0527, ✉ 512 8453 (*inexpensive; includes breakfast*). Converted from a grand canal house. The rooms are tastefully furnished and the public areas still bear traces of sumptuous décor. Good value.

The Rose, Beestenmarkt 14, 2312 CC, ✆ 514 6630, ✉ 521 7096 (*inexpensive; includes breakfast*). Small hotel above a café, overlooking the

Beestenmarkt and a canal. Friendly owners, though the rooms are spartan, and could be cold in winter.

Pension In de Goede Hoek, Diefsteeg 19a, 2311 TS, ℰ 512 1031 (*cheap*). Cosy little pension in the heart of student land.

Youth Hostel, Lange Scheistraat 9, 2312 CR, ℰ 512 8457, ⊜ 512 8763 (*f23.50 for dormitory room, f5 sheet hire*).

Leiden ℰ (071–)   ***Eating Out***

The best place for cafés and restaurants is around **Pieterskerkhof** and **Hooglandskerk**.

Fabers, Kloksteeg 13, ℰ 512 4012 (*expensive*). Cool service, *haute cuisine* and a good price to quality ratio.

Malle Jan, Nieuwsteeg 11, ℰ 512 3888 (*moderate*). Lively brasserie offering good, substantial Franco-Dutch favourites, with lots of salad and potatoes.

Het Panacee, Rapenburg 97, ℰ 566 1494 (*moderate*). Realm of the deans and professors. Amidst gapers (yawning carved heads that once signalled apothecaries' shops) and stained glass, you can tuck into such dishes as venison with forest mushrooms and honey-truffle sauce.

Scarlatti, Stille Mare 4, ℰ 512 2114 (*moderate*). Friendly café atmosphere, candlelight and excellent cooking. Try *machi badam malai*, a Malaysian starter made from marinated fish cooked in yoghurt and almonds.

De Brandery, Middelweg 7, ℰ 513 3728 (*moderate*). Multi-tiered restaurant made with galleries rescued from an old church, but with a curious Wild West bordello atmosphere. Good hearty cooking.

Koetshuis, Burgsteeg 13, ℰ 512 1688 (*moderate*). A converted 17th-century carriage house at the foot of the Burcht. Serves good light lunches and fairly standard fare in the evenings.

Mangerie de Koekop, Lange Mare 60, ℰ 514 1937 (*moderate*). Fresh décor, Lloyd's loom chairs and tasty vegetarian options on the menu.

Lunchroom Snijders, Botermarkt 15, ℰ 512 2583 (*inexpensive*). Behind a richly carved 19th-century shop front, through a tempting patisserie, is a room with a gently fading 1930s atmosphere. Good for a quick sandwich or gooey cake.

Annie's Verjaardag Brasserie, Oude Rijn 1a, ℰ 512 5737 (*inexpensive*). A dripping cellar full of students and a waterside terrace. Snacks, soups and sandwiches during the day, and more substantial fare in the evenings.

De Waterlijn, Prinsessekade, ℰ 512 1279 (*inexpensive*). Floating, angular, modern glass-walled café with a view up the canal to a windmill. Apple pie and light meals.

Student cafés are the best places to meet up with people, and to find out about the current club scene. **Barrerra** (cnr Kloksteeg and Rapenburg) is a good place to start, night and day, and **Leidseplein** (cnr Diefsteeg and Pieterskerkgracht) also has a friendly crowd. The current music and dance hotspot is **LVC**, next to the post office on Breestraat.

The Hague

A 17th-century travel guide describes The Hague as 'the fairest village in the world, both for the pompous buildings, and for the largeness thereof'. Two centuries later Matthew Arnold wrote: 'I never saw a city where the well-to-do classes seem to have given the whole place so much of their own air of wealth, finished cleanliness and comfort; but I never saw one, either, in which my heart would so have sunk at the thought of living.' And early this century, Aldous Huxley observed that The Hague 'tries to be elegant and only succeeds in being respectable and middle class'. Little has changed. People still call The Hague 'the largest village in Europe' and the many ex-colonials who have retired here have generated another nickname: 'the widow of Indonesia'.

The wide boulevards and graceful architecture *do* speak of quiet, established wealth, and Amsterdammers, in particular, complain that The Hague is a stuffy domain of diplomats, civil servants and businessmen. (Though Amsterdam is the capital of the Netherlands, The Hague is the centre of government and the chosen seat of the present queen.) It may not be the place you would go to bop until dawn or throng singing through the streets, but the spotless architecture, acres of greenery and inimitable museums give it an atmosphere of tranquil refinement which is rather alluring. The Hague offers the bonus of the seaside resort of Scheveningen, on its northwestern perimeter, and the town of Delft to the south. Most of the main sites in the city are centrally situated, though if you really want to appreciate all The Hague has to offer, you'll need more than a day.

History

Around the year 1230, Floris IV, Count of Holland, built himself a country cottage beside a pond in the North Sea dunes. His son William II, who was elected King of the Romans and Emperor of Germany in 1247, thinking that a grander hunting lodge better befitted his status, began to put up a small palace on the site. The settlement that grew up around it was known as 's-Gravenhage (the Count's Hedge), and this is still The Hague's official name. Over the centuries, successive counts added to the original buildings and put up new palaces. They progressed from being mere counts to becoming *stadhouders* and eventually kings of Holland (*see* **History** pp.34–9). The Hague became their official seat and, after 1578, the meeting place of the States General, the predecessor of the present-day Dutch parliament. Yet the counts and their successors contrived to keep The Hague detached from the strife of day-to-day politics. Great battles were fought at Leiden, Breda and Utrecht. Assemblies were held and treaties signed at Brussels and Bruges. Amsterdam swept to glory and heady riches on the back of the Dutch East India Company during the Golden Age. The Hague remained serenely apart from the fray, and was officially classed as a 'village' well into the 19th century. But all the time it was gaining importance as an administrative and judicial centre. In 1511 the highest court of Holland was established here, and by the 17th century The Hague had become such a vortex of intrigue among foreign diplomats that it was called 'the whispering gallery of Europe'.

In 1899 the Permanent Court of Arbitration (later to become the International Court of Justice) was established in The Hague, giving this long tradition a mark of respectability. But in the meantime, the 'village' had suffered a sharp blow to its pride. During the French occupation (1806–13), King Louis Napoleon had lingered in The Hague just a few months, before deciding to move his

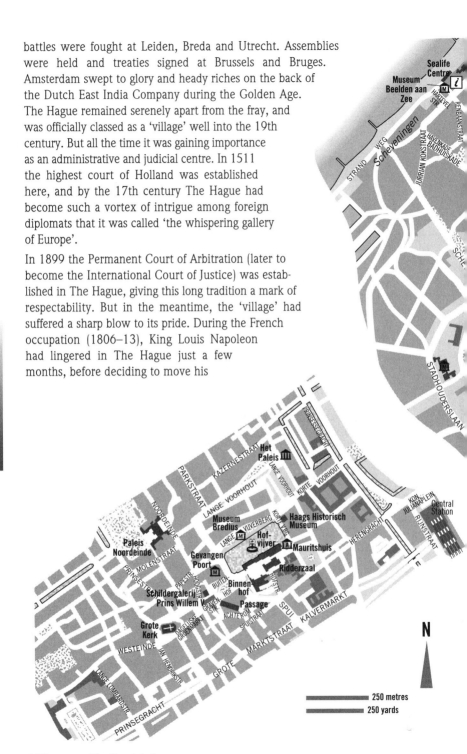

750 metres
800 yards

N

urhaus
rist Office

ZWOLSE
STRAAT

Nieuwe
Scheveningse
Bosjes

Westbroek
Park

HARINGKADE

Madurodam

Hubertuspark

NGSEWEG

Scheveningse

Bosjes

Huis ten Bosch

/Omniversum/
nte Museum

Haagse-

Bos

CARNEG
PLEIN Museum Mesdag

Vredespaleis

LAAN VAN MEERDERVOORT

ZEESTRAAT

Panorama
Mesdag

Tourist
Office

Centraal
Station

See Inset Map

STATIONSWEG

Station HS

The Hague (Den Haag)

capital to Amsterdam. After the French had withdrawn from the Netherlands, Amsterdam retained this status—although the new Dutch king, William I, moved the seat of parliament back to The Hague. Rivalry between the two cities remains intense. As recently as 1953 there was a massive attempt to have The Hague reclassified as the Dutch capital, and the public wrangling was finally resolved only after an appeal to original documents signed by King William I. But each city still regards the other as in some way second-best.

Getting Around

You can use your *strippenkaart* (*see* p.10) on buses and trams in The Hague, or buy a *dagkaart* (day card) from the VVV tourist office. The national information number for public transport is ✆ (0900) 9292. Most of the tourist sites are within very easy walking distance of each other, though you will probably prefer to hop on to Tram 8 for the Panorama Mesdag and the Museon. Tram 9 takes you via Madurodam to Scheveningen, and Tram 1 will trundle you through the Scheveningense Bosjes to the sea.

Bicycle hire: Beside Station Hollands Spoor, ✆ (070) 389 0830.

Taxi: ✆ (070) 390 7722 or ✆ 364 2828.

Tourist Information

The VVV tourist office (open Mon–Sat 9–5.30, in July and Aug also Sun 10–5, ✆ (0900) 340 3505) is on Koning Julianaplein, just outside Centraal Station. Staff can supply you with maps and information about tours and public transport.

Festivals

The Hague lets its hair down with some lively summer festivals. In June there's a 10-day long Indonesian market, the **Pasar Malam Besar**; the **International Kite Festival** at Scheveningen; and a two-day **international horse show** on the Lange Voorhout, a large green square in the middle of town. The **North Sea Jazz Festival**, held annually in The Hague in mid-July, is one of the world's most important jazz festivals.

City Centre

Binnenhof

Guided tours of the Binnenhof and Houses of Parliament Mon–Sat 10–4; adm; ✆ (070) 364 6144 to book in advance. All tours start at the Ridderzaal, but after that itinerary varies according to which house is in session. Try to get on a tour that visits the old, rather than the new chambers.

The count's courtyard, the **Binnenhof**, remains the centre of town, though now it's an amalgam of architectural styles. On the third Tuesday in September, Queen Beatrix sweeps into the courtyard in a gold carriage to open parliament. The ceremony takes place under the high oak vaulting and delicate turrets of the **Ridderzaal** (the 'Hall of Knights') in the centre of the Binnenhof. The Ridderzaal, the oldest building in the complex, was built to host the early Counts of Holland's hunting parties. Later it served as a court. High up in the rafters of the barrel-vaulted roof are small carved heads. The judges encouraged miscreants and witnesses to tell the truth by warning them that these 'eaves-droppers' listened to all they said and passed it on up to God. By far the best view of the Binnenhof is from the outside—across the **Hofvijver** (Court Pond), a glassy expanse of water with a softly spraying fountain.

The First Chamber of the States General (the equivalent of the British House of Lords or the US Senate) still meets within the Binnenhof complex, in a grand Baroque ball room. The Second Chamber (the effective governing body of the Netherlands) now meets in a modern building around the corner from the Ridderzaal. Completed in 1993, the new chambers are decorated in a way intended to portray the Dutch landscape. This is done with disarming honesty: one wall represents sheets of pouring rain, and the ceiling of the plenary hall is painted to symbolize a low blue-grey sky. A glance at the staff list reveals another, rather charming aspect of life in the Netherlands: the government employs 75 people to clean the house, and only 50 to guard it.

Mauritshuis

Open Tues–Sat 10–5, Sun 11–5; adm.

Next to the parliament buildings, on a corner of the Hofvijver, the Mauritshuis, a grand 17th-century mansion built for a favoured general, is now home to the Royal Collection of paintings once owned by *stadhouders* William IV and William V. High points of three centuries of Dutch and Flemish art cover the walls, stacked one above the other (a fashionable way of displaying pictures in the 18th century); there's hardly an inch of wood-panelling or flock wallpaper to be seen between the gilt frames. It's a heady experience. You can see Rembrandt's first Amsterdam commission, *The Anatomy Lesson of Professor Tulp* (1632)—the corpse, like the painter, had just arrived in Amsterdam from Leiden; and the erudite surgeon was renowned for his advice that patients drink 50 cups of tea a day. There are three of Vermeer's rather minimal œuvre, Frans Hals's manic *Laughing Boy*, Paulus Potter's nightmarish, meticulously finished *Young Bull* (complete with frogs and flies) and works by Rubens and Holbein. There are also nine paintings by the 17th-century innkeeper Jan Steen. His postcard-sized cheekily lascivious *Girl Eating Oysters* alone would make a visit to the museum worthwhile.

Schildergalerij Prins Willem V

Prince William V Gallery, Buitenhof 35, open Tues–Sun 11–4; adm.

In 1773 Prince William V had an art gallery built in his palace, and condescended to allow the general public in for a look on three days a week. This gives the *Schildergalerij* some justification in its claim to be the oldest museum in the Netherlands, though the palm really goes to the Teylers Museum in Haarlem, which was purpose-built in 1784. Today, the better part of the royal collection is housed across the pond in the Mauritshuis. But although the larger museum has creamed off the masterpieces, the *Schildergalerij* has the edge when it comes to atmosphere. There are seldom many people in the long gallery, with its high Louis XVI stucco ceilings and walls plastered with paintings. At times it feels almost as if the prince himself had invited you up to see his collection.

Museum Gevangenpoort

Prison Gate Museum; open Tues–Fri 11–5, Sat and Sun 12–5; guided tours only, on the hour; adm.

Once the gate to the Binnenhof, this solid, step-gabled building served as a prison from 1420 to 1828, though warders seldom managed to outwit The Hague's maidservants, who were notorious for their ability to spring incarcerated lovers and brothers. Nowadays it houses a gory collection of torture instruments, from thumbscrews and whipping benches to a branding iron bearing The Hague's coat of arms. Give it a shudder as you pass by. A tour is of interest only to the morbidly curious.

Museum Bredius

Lange Vijverberg 14, open Tues–Sun 12–5; adm.

Erstwhile director of the Mauritshuis Museum and renowned art scholar Abraham Bredius (1855–1946) managed over the years to build up an impressive private collection of 17th-century Dutch art. He also established a reputation for being stubborn and cantankerous, and had some very public set-tos with his superiors at the museum. He invariably came out on top. Wrapped in furs, Bredius would spend days in chilly archives researching his beloved 17th-century paintings—it is his research that showed a number of works previously attributed to Rembrandt to be by the Master's pupils. The collection that he accumulated for himself is notable not so much for its big names (though there are enough of these) as for the way it reveals the astonishing high quality that existed across the spectrum of Dutch art in the Golden Age.

The Bredius Museum is filled with extraordinarily good paintings by artists most people would not have heard of. Look out for Godfried Schalken's delicately rendered *Lady Playing a Lute*, Willem Drost's poised *Portrait of a Lady* and Aert van der Neer's wintry *Scene on the Ice outside the Town Walls.* You'll also see work by better-known artists: a *Bust of Christ* by Rembrandt; a floral still-life by Simon Verelst (such as the one that sent Samuel Pepys into rhapsodies, *see* p.57) and some exceptional paintings by Jan Steen—including one that until recently was cut in half. It was Bredius who, in the 1920s, realized that the two halves belonged together, but it wasn't until 1996 that the painting was restored to its original state. Bredius donated some 46 paintings to the Rijksmuseum in Amsterdam, loaned another 25 to the Mauritshuis and, when he retired and went to live in Monaco, gave his entire collection to the municipality of The Hague, so that it would remain in the Netherlands. Today the paintings are hung in the intimate domestic setting of an 18th-century patrician mansion, just across the pond from the Mauritshuis.

Haags Historisch Museum

The Hague Historical Museum, Korte Vijverberg 7; open Tues–Fri 11–5, Sat and Sun 12–5; adm.

Completing the circuit of museums around the Hofvijver, the Historisch Museum is housed in the former barracks of the civil guard, built in 1636. Tucked in between countless paintings of views of The Hague and Scheveningen and memorabilia of municipal history are some interesting old doll's houses. The most intriguing is the one that belonged to one Lita Tholen-de Ranitz in 1910. It comes equipped with such state-of-the-art conveniences as running water, central heating, a telephone and even a vacuum cleaner.

Beyond the Binnenhof

The Counts of Holland were incorrigible palace-builders. On Noordeinde you can see the classicist pile of the **Paleis Noordeinde** (restored to the appearance it had in 1640). Paleis Noordeinde is where Queen Beatrix, very much a workaday monarch, clocks in to do her share of the country's administration, and it is not open to the public.

Queen B.

Queen Beatrix of the Netherlands arrives to open an art exhibition. There are only about four police officers in evidence. None of the guests has been screened. There is no ripple of curtsies as she walks up the aisle to her seat. The Dutch do not have to bow before their sovereign…and no one has even thought of taking a pot shot at a Dutch monarch since an assassin hiding behind a pillar did for the first William of Orange in 1584. Queen Beatrix's departure doesn't stop the traffic. A blue limousine, accompanied by just two outriders, glides her away; only to reduce speed to a gentle cruise when it gets stuck behind a bus around the corner. This is a down-to-earth, democratically minded monarchy. Yet it commands a loyalty so fierce that the British royals must glance across the Channel with envy. In Holland you can joke about anything. You can even be quite rude about the Dutch. But make a disparaging remark about 'our Queen', and the room plummets into icy silence.

Queen Beatrix's hands-on approach to running her country has a lot to do with this. Hard work, in a Protestant country, is always a strong plus. Beatrix does her fair share of ribbon-cutting, smiling and waving, but most of her time is spent in an office in The Hague, involving herself directly with government (so much so that a recent headline raised eyebrows with *'Beatrix Bemoeial?'*—'Busybody Beatrix?'). For decades every Dutch government has been run by a coalition. After an election the process of choosing a Prime Minister and cabinet involves much discussion. The Queen is at the heart of it all, a mover and shaker rather than simply the wielder of a rubber stamp.

Yet the Dutch royal family could be Dallas to the Brits' Dynasty. Juliana, the Queen Mother, was embroiled in a Rasputin-like relationship with a faith healer after one of her daughters was born blind. The young princess grew up to marry a penniless Cuban refugee, later divorced him and sold the contents of her house (everything from potpourri holders to priceless works of art) to finance a move to the USA. Another daughter married a Roman Catholic, renounced her Protestant religion and gave up all the trappings of royal life and any claim to the throne. The present Crown Prince cavorted, clad in orange bermuda shorts, with a victorious Dutch hockey team at the Atlanta Olympics. Such behaviour may cause muttering and murmurs, but the public remains relatively unobtrusive and unconcerned. The most passionate reaction in the past few decades was saved for when Beatrix married a German: people pelted them with tomatoes at their wedding in Amsterdam. But Prince Claus's charm, fluent Dutch and air of gentle vulnerability has defused even that.

No-nonsense Hollanders appreciate the common touch, and their royal family has it in large measures. Before she married, Beatrix studied social work, and did a stint with the Salvation Army, which at the time had its headquarters in Amsterdam's red-light district. The entire royal family arrived in Amsterdam in a bus for the service to celebrate Beatrix and Claus's silver wedding anniversary. A few years ago, on Queen's Day (the Queen's official birthday, when people party on the streets all day and there is a free-for-all fleamarket) Beatrix decided on the spur of the moment to visit Amsterdam. She wandered about the streets of the Jordaan with a few family and friends. It was a while before somebody recognized her. Then a young man in the crowd yelled out: '*Meid, geef me een kus*' (roughly translated: 'Oi, gi's a kiss, old girl').

Beaming, the Queen took hold of his shoulders and obliged.

In the centre of town, on **Lange Voorhout**—a vast tree-filled square, part of which was a medieval tournament field—you can see the neat, modest 18th-century **Het Paleis** (Lange Voorhout 74; *open Tues–Sun 11–5; adm*). Het Paleis, once the winter home of Queen Emma (Beatrix's great-grandmother) now hosts temporary art exhibitions. Behind Het Paleis, on Prinsessegracht, is the **Museum van het Boek** (Museum of the Book, Prinsessegracht 30; *open Tues–Fri 11–5, Sat and Sun 12–5; adm*). In the rich mahogany cases of an 18th-century library you can see such treasures as fragments of a 6th-century bible, a copy of *Le Roman de la Rose* (1370) and the 17th-century *Blaeu Atlas*, one of the earliest and most beautiful ever atlases of the world.

Just south of Paleis Noordeinde is the imposing, rather gloomy **Grote Kerk** (Great Church, ✆ (070) 365 8665; *open by request*). It dates back to 1539, though most of the structure you see today was built a century later, after a fire had destroyed the earlier church. Next door is the elaborately decorated **Oude Stadhuis** (Old City Hall), built in the 17th century, and now a restaurant.

North of the Centre

Vredespaleis

Peace Palace, Carnegieplein 2; open May–Oct Mon–Fri 10–5; Nov–April Mon–Fri 10–4; tours 10, 11, 2 and 3; adm.

The 1899 Hague Peace Conference established the Permanent Court of Arbitration—a court with global jurisdiction, still widely respected and considered neutral—but gave it a rather dingy home. In 1903 the American millionaire Andrew Carnegie donated $1.5 million to build a more appropriate palace for the court. Countries from all over the world contributed ironwork, stained glass, statuary and furniture to create a quirky hotchpotch of a building, which you can visit by guided tour only.

Panorama Mesdag and Museum Mesdag

Hendrik Willem Mesdag (1831–1915) was a leading member of the Hague School of painters (*see* pp.58–9). He considered his *Panorama*—painted in the 1880s during a craze for such entertainments—to be his most important work, because it gave 'such an awesome impression of nature'. At the **Panorama Mesdag** (Zeestraat 65; *open daily 10–5; adm*) you walk about under a canvas canopy and look out on all sides, across real sand dunes littered with clogs and empty gin bottles, at a huge, circular view of Scheveningen. The painting is done with such realism that contemporaries accused Mesdag of having projected new-fangled photographs on to the canvas and traced them. Though it was an artistic success, the *Panorama* was a commercial failure, helping drag the Belgian company that funded it into bankruptcy. Eventually it was bought by the artist himself, and is now jointly owned by 33 of his descendants. A few minutes' walk away is the **Museum H. W. Mesdag** (Laan van Meerdervoort 7f; *open Tues–Sun 12–5, adm*), where you can see the artist's own collection of Hague School paintings, as well as works of the related French Barbizon School and a reconstruction of Mesdag's living quarters and studio.

The Gemeente Museum Complex

The superb **Gemeente Museum** (Municipal Museum, Stadhouderslaan 41; *open Tues–Sun 11–5; adm*) was designed in 1935 by the influential architect H. P. Berlage. The spacious tiled interior looks, at first glance, like a bank—or a very upmarket public lavatory. It houses a beautiful collection of glass and silverware, some important 19th-century paintings, superbly reconstructed period rooms and one of the best modern art collections in the country. You'll find lots of familiar names from the first half of the century—Monet, Picasso, Egon Schiele—as well as the pick of modern Dutch artists like Jan Toorop, Pyke Koch and the painters of the COBRA movement, Karel Appel and Constant (*see* p.60). There are a number of early works by Mondriaan—realistic landscapes and bright impressionistic studies—that hint only slightly at the abstract style for which he later became famous (*see* p.59).

The collection of contemporary work gives you the rare impression of a healthy budget being intelligently spent. Don't leave without visiting the **music department**, which displays instruments ranging from exquisitely crafted harpsichords and viols to an Indonesian gamelan.

Adjoining the Gemeente Museum is the **Museon** (Stadhouderslaan 41; *open Tues–Fri 10–5, Sat and Sun 12–5; adm*), which offers a romp through the world of popular science. Computers, CD-i players and imaginative displays bring to life everything from the Big Bang to contemporary electronics. A passageway leads on to a 1990s version of a panorama, the **Omniversum** (President Kennedylaan 5; *programmes on the hour Tues–Sun 11–5; adm exp; call ✆ (070) 354 7479 or contact VVV for programme details*). Lasers and films (such as *Speed* and *The Future of Time*) are projected on to a dome-shaped screen, sounds explode all about you and special 'sub-woofers' produce bass notes so deep you can only feel them.

On the Edge

A few minutes' ride east of the centre (on Bus 4 or 43), in the thickets of the Haagse Bos, you can peer through the trees at the present Royal residence—the dinky, domed **Huis ten Bosch** ('House in the Woods', built 1654), though it isn't open to the public. Just north of the city centre is the **Scheveningse Bosjes**, an urban forest so rambling that you can quite easily get lost in it. If you make your way across the wilds you'll come to the miniature town of **Madurodam** (*open daily March–Aug 9–8; Sept–Mar 9–5; adm exp*). You can see models of landmarks from all over the Netherlands, little residential canals, football grounds, an airport, railways and a harbour—all on a scale of 1:25. By far the most enjoyable sight, however, is from up on the coffee terrace where you can watch the visitors tramp, Gulliver-like, up and down the paths.

Scheveningen

At its northwestern end, The Hague merges with the fishing port and seaside resort of **Scheveningen**. (Don't worry if you can't pronounce it—only the locals can. During the Second World War Dutch Resistance fighters made suspected German infiltrators say it as a test of their true nationality.) The long, white stretch of sand, lapped by the grey-brown waters of the North Sea, somehow seems in its element on blustery days when tiny figures, buttoned up and bent over, battle against the wind. The pink bodies that stretch out in deckchairs on sunny days look curiously out of place.

Badly bombed during the war and hastily rebuilt, Scheveningen is a tacky resort, thronged mainly by German visitors. But you will find the **Kurhaus**, a gracious *grande dame* of a hotel, built in 1885 and now a national monument. The kings and queens of Europe have stayed here; Dietrich, Piaf, Chevalier and even the Rolling Stones have played in the concert hall. A little further along the promenade in the only other old building of note in Scheveningen, a pavilion built for King William I in 1826, is **Museum Beelden am See** (Sculptures by the Sea, Harteveltsraat 1; *open Tues–Sun 11–5; adm*). Set in a tranquil hollow in the dunes, it is devoted to sculptures of the human form. Have a look at Igor Mitoraj's mysterious, veiled marble reliefs, then don a sou'wester off the rack and step out on to the terraces to see Arthur Spronken's idiosyncratic portrayal of the Dutch royal family. Nearby the **Sealife Centre** (Strandweg 13; *open daily 10–6, July and August 10–8; adm exp*) is home to creatures of the deep, from shrimps to stingrays. Presentation is imaginative (at one point you walk through an underwater glass tunnel, with sharks swimming above your head), and the centre is a great hit with children.

If you feel like escaping the crowds, **Kijkduin**, a few kilometres up the promenade, is a quieter spot where you can sit undisturbed on the windy dunes and look out over the grey North Sea.

Shopping

The **Passage** (off Gravenstraat, near the Buitenhof) is a grand neoclassical shopping arcade lined with *chocolateries*, boutiques and specialist shops—including one that sells only teddy bears. There's a branch of the stylish department store, Maison de Bonneterie, near the Oude Stadhuis on Groen Markt. Nearby Hoogstraat and the alleys leading off it are the location of classy clothes shops and antiques stores. There is a traditional **market** around the Grote Kerk on Wednesday afternoons, and an **antiques and book market** on Lange Voorhout on Thurs and Sun in the summer.

The Hague/Scheveningen ☎ (070–)   ### Where to Stay

Hotel Des Indes Inter-Continental, Lange Voorhout 54–56, 2514 EG, ☎ 361 2345, 🖷 361 2350 (*luxury*). Once a splendid patrician mansion, converted into a hotel in the 19th century, the Des Indes has been home to the likes of Mata Hari and Cecil Rhodes. The circular lobby is redolent of the grand old days, a great place for afternoon tea—but the furnishings in some of the rooms show signs of wear that you would not expect in a hotel of this class.

Steinberger Kurhaus Hotel, Gevers Deynootplein 30, 2586 CK Scheveningen, ☎ 416 2636 (*expensive: f380 land side, f430 sea side*). A battle rages inside the stately old seaside hotel between what is left of the original fittings and insensitive (if not downright kitsch) modern décor. Alas the latter usually wins, but the rooms are comfortable, and the staff pleasant.

Carlton Ambassador Hotel, Sophialaan 2, 2514 JP, ☎ 363 0363, 🖷 360 0535 (*luxury*). Quietly plush, ever so tasteful hotel in the embassy district. Rooms are done up in Dutch and English repro antique style.

Parkhotel Den Haag, Molenstraat 53, 2513 BJ, ☎ 362 4371, 🖷 361 4525 (*luxury–expensive; price includes breakfast*). Back-to-back with the Paleis Noordeinde, decorated in soothing pastel shades and with a small enclosed garden.

Paleis Hotel, Molenstraat 26, 2513 BL, ☎ 362 4621, 🖷 361 4533 (*moderate*). In a quiet alley near the Binnenhof, and convenient for sights and shops. Rooms are on the small side, and rather functionally decorated.

Hotel Petit, Groot Hertoginnelaan 42, 2517 EH, ✆ 346 5500, 🖷 346 3257 (*moderate–inexpensive*). In a smart suburb near the Vredespaleis. Bright, airy rooms and personable owners.

Hotel City, Renbaanstraat 1–3, 2586 EW, Scheveningen, ✆ 355 7966, 🖷 354 0503 (*inexpensive*). Scrupulously clean and well-run family hotel just a few minutes' walk from the beach.

Albion, Gevers Deynootweg 118–20, 2586 BP, Scheveningen, ✆ 355 7987, 🖷 355 5970 (*inexpensive*). Good, solid Dutch hospitality in a converted 1930s house a block away from the sea.

Aristo, Stationsweg 164–66, 2515 BS, ✆ 389 0847 (*cheap*). Simply furnished but clean hotel just a short totter from Station Hollands Spoor.

Youth Hostel: Gevers Denooytweg 2, ✆ 354 7003 (*f45 for dorm bed*).

The Hague/Scheveningen ✆ *(070–)*   ***Eating Out***

The side streets and canals to the east of Lange Voorhout are well-stocked café and restaurant hunting grounds. The Hague is renowned for the quality of its Indonesian restaurants.

Le Restaurant, Hotel Des Indes, Lange Voorhout 54–56, ✆ 361 2345 (*expensive*). A small restaurant opening on to the sumptuous circular lobby of the hotel. Service is impeccable and the cuisine a skilful combination of the best of Dutch and French traditions, with a touch of Indonesian exoticism. Try the guinea fowl with a secret Des Indes sauce (there are vanilla and cardamom in there somewhere).

Da Roberto, Noordeinde 196, ✆ 346 4977 (*expensive*). Top-class Italian restaurant, under the personal eye of owner-chef Roberto de Luca. He uses trad ingredients in imaginative ways: lasagne with pigeon and spinach, or polenta with snails. There's an excellent list of Italian wines.

Greve, Torenstraat 138, ✆ 360 3919 (*moderate*). Long trestle tables, boards of steaming home-made bread, and friendly service. Go for the chicken soup, thick with vegetables, and then one of the daily specials.

Bogor, Van Swietenstraat 2, ✆ 346 1628 (*moderate*). Excellent Indonesian cooking in an elegant *Jugendstil* house.

The Raffles, Noordeinde 196, ✆ 345 8587 (*moderate*). An Indonesian restaurant that dares to be a little different, with a cook who doesn't feel bound to produce the usual Indonesian fare, but experiments within the tradition.

Le Haricot Vert, Molenstraat 9a, ✆ 365 2278 (*moderate*). Intimate, candlelit restaurant in a 17th-century house that once accommodated palace flunkies. French-inspired cuisine with a robust Dutch hand.

Tampat Senang, Laan van Meerdervoort 6, ✆ 363 6787 (*moderate*). Elaborate décor, fine Indonesian food and, from time to time, a live gamelan orchestra.

Bengel, Hooikade 2, ✆ 364 2898 (*moderate*). Cherubs, chandeliers and push drapes everywhere. A relaxed, arty crowd tuck in to such dishes as lamb with grapes, garlic and thyme.

De Dageraad, Hooikade 4, ✆ 364 5666 (*cheap*). Plain pine décor, but inspired vegetarian cuisine. There's a wide selection of cheese fondues (including cider and Calvados, and beer, mustard and garlic) as well as special seasonal and regional set menus with such adventurous combinations as goat's cheese with dates and orange sauce.

Schlemmer, Lange Houtstraat, ✆ 360 9000 (*cheap*). A 19th-century officers' mess, still sporting grand fireplaces, Schlemmer has both café and restaurant sections. The atmosphere in both is informal and friendly. Dawdle over a coffee, or enjoy duck bouillion, or omelette with mascarpone and grilled aubergine.

Broeders, Buitenhof 19, ✆ 356 2900 (*cheap*). Buzzing, trendy Grand Café in the city centre. The pastas and salads make a good quick lunch.

De Posthoorn, Lange Voorhout 39a, ✆ 346 2338 (*cheap*). Serves light snacks and sandwiches and has a pleasant terrace overlooking the tree-lined marketplace.

Achterommetje, Achterom 71, ✆ 364 5876 (*cheap*). Friendly place in an alley behind the Passage shopping arcade in the city centre. They play jazz, sell good, healthy, home-cooked food and delicious cakes.

't Syndicaat, Nieuwe Molstraat 10, ✆ 360 0053 (*open 5pm–8pm Mon, Wed and Fri only; cheap*). Vegetarian eating-house in a small alternative arts complex. Menus vary according to what's in the market.

The Hague/Scheveningen ✆ *(070–)*　　　***Entertainment and Nightlife***

The Hague has a rich cultural life. The city orchestra, **Het Residentie Orkest**, is almost as good as the Royal Concertgebouw. Its home is the **Dr Anton Philipszaal**, Spuiplein 150, ✆ 360 9810, which offers a varying programme of classical music from top-quality Dutch and international orchestras.

The national modern dance company, the renowned **Nederlands Danstheater**, can be found performing next door, at the **Lucent Danstheater**, Spui 152, ✆ 360 4930, and you'll find drama (sometimes in English) at the **Koninklijke Schouwburg**, Korte Voorhout 3, ✆ 346 9450.

The Hague's most famous cultural event, the **North Sea Jazz Festival**, is held annually over a weekend in mid-July at the city's Congres Centrum (information from the VVV, *see* above).

There's a vibrant live music scene centered on **Paard**, Prinsengracht 12, ✆ 360 1618, Syndicaat, Nieuwe Molstraat 10, ✆ 360 0053, and **Backstage**, Lange Houtstraat 9, ✆ 364 8464, all of which have dance floors and party nights.

Boko Bar, Nieuwe Schoolstraat 1, ✆ 362 1614 is a friendly place to begin an exploration of The Hague's relatively small **gay** scene.

Delft has as many bridges as there are days in the year and a like number of canals and streets with boats passing up and down.

William Crowne, on visiting Delft with the
Duke of Arundel in December 1636

Though overrun by tourists in season, of all the towns on the Randstad Delft manages to preserve its ambience of age. You might not be able to count as many bridges and canals as did the rather excitable Will Crowne, but get up early before the crowds descend and you might suddenly glimpse an alley, a skyline, a stretch of façades that could come right out of the *View of Delft* by the city's most famous son, the painter Johannes Vermeer (*c.* 1632–75).

Established early in the 11th century, Delft soon became a prosperous weaving and brewing town. By the end of the 16th century it held such control over the surrounding land traffic and waterways, and was so well fortified, that William the Silent (*see* p.38) chose it as his HQ during the Dutch revolt against Spain. He was assassinated here in 1584, and so resides in Delft for ever more, in a tomb that has become the Dutch royal family mausoleum.

In 1645, an exploding arsenal destroyed much of the medieval town, but a massive rebuilding programme soon restored its former glory. It was around this time that De Porceleyne Fles started making and exporting the blue and white earthenware that was to make the town famous.

Tourist Information

VVV, Markt 85, ✆ (015) 212 6100; open April–Oct Mon–Fri 9–6, Sat 9–5, Sun 10–3; Nov–March Mon–Fri 9–5.30, Sat 9–5, closed Sun.

Getting Around

Most sights are within **walking** distance, ranged around the Markt. To reach the Markt from Delft station, cross the Westsingelgracht and Oude Delft canals and turn left at Koornmarkt.

There are **tram** connections to The Hague, and your *strippenkaart* (*see* p.10) is valid on public transport.

The Markt

Facing each other proudly across the market square are the Stadhuis and the Nieuwe Kerk. In between come rows of cafés, restaurants, souvenir shops selling tacky ersatz Delftware, and—on Thursdays—a busy general market. Of the medieval **Stadhuis** only the 13th-century tower remains. The surrounding solid grey stone building, with its scarlet shutters and fussy cornice, was put up in 1618 by leading Renaissance architect Hendrick de Keyser (*see* p.61), after a fire had destroyed the original city hall. The late-Gothic **Nieuwe Kerk** (*open April–Oct Mon–Sat 9–6; Nov–March Mon–Fri 11–4;*

adm free) took more than a century to build, between 1383 and 1510. Even then the stonemasons could not down chisels, because the church was badly damaged by the fire that swept Delft in 1536 and by the arsenal explosion a hundred years later. It wasn't until 1872 that the flamboyant architect P. J. H. Cuypers (*see* pp.63 and 82–4) shot the tower up to its present 109 metres. Inside the church is the sumptuous black marble and alabaster tomb of William of Orange, together with a carving of the prince and, nearby, his small dog, which pined to death after William was assassinated. A stone slab in the floor marks the entrance to the royal mausoleum, where all but a few Dutch monarchs have been buried ever since.

Oude Delft

A walk along the Oude Delft canal, lined with elegant patrician mansions, provides a charming impression of the old city. At one end the tower of the **Oude Kerk** (*open Mon–Sat 9–6; adm free*) seems to tilt in four directions simultaneously—with a two-metre tilt to the east and one metre to the north. The tower houses a 9,000kg carillon that, understandably, is rung only on special occasions. The church was begun in the 13th century, though much of its austere interior dates from 200 years later. Inside you'll find the graves of Vermeer, and famous Dutch admirals Martin Tromp and Piet Hein.

Across the way from the church, off a quiet courtyard, is the **Prinsenhof Museum** (*open Tues–Sat 10–5, Sun 1–5; adm*). The former cloister houses the Delft historical museum—stocked with pottery, silver, tapestries and royal portraits—but is more famous as the spot where William of Orange was assassinated by Catholic fanatic Balthasar Geraerts. You can still see the bullet holes the murderer left behind in the wall of the stairwell. Across the courtyard is the **Nusantara Museum** (*open Tues–Sat 10–5, Sun 1–5; adm*), which has a colourful and fascinating collection of costumes and artefacts from the Dutch East Indies—much of it booty brought back during the 17th century by members of the Dutch East India Company. Further up the canal, just beyond the Prinsenhof, is the **Museum Lambert van Meerten** (*open Tues–Sat 10–5, Sun 1–5; adm*), which offers a fine opportunity to view a canal house from inside. As well as finely furnished rooms, you'll find a vast collection of Delft tiles and ceramics from around the world.

Further Afield

South of the Markt, along the Koornmarkt, is the **Koninklijke Leger- an Wapenmuseum** (Royal Army and Weapon Museum; *open Mon–Fri 10–5, Sat and Sun noon–5pm; adm*) which has swords, guns and other implements of warfare and traces the history of Dutch battles up to the 20th century. But if it's porcelain rather than pistols you're after, then head farther south to **De Porceleyn Fles** (Rotterdamseweg 196, © *(015) 256 0234, Mon–Sat 9–5; adm*), the famous **Delftware** factory, where you can see the blue and white ceramics being hand-painted, and buy the real thing rather than the repro tack sold in most souvenir shops.

Delft Museum Hotel, Oude Delft 189, 2611 HD, ✆ 214 0930, ✉ 214 0935 (*moderate*). Eleven beautifully restored canalside houses, converted into a comfortable hotel. Antiques and contemporary art in the lounge areas, with quietly tasteful more modern furniture in the rooms.

De Plantaan, Doelenplein 10, 2611 BP, ✆ 212 6046, ✉ 215 7327 (*inexpensive*). Pleasantly run hotel with somewhat wacky design—some rooms sporting eccentric *trompe l'œil*. There's a good restaurant downstairs too.

Les Compagnons, Markt 61–65, ✆ 214 0102 (*cheap*). Clean, simple family-run pension in the heart of town. If there's no room at the inn, and you can afford the price hike, ask the same family about their three- and four-star hotels nearby, but make sure you specify this branch if you want the cheap one.

Explore the side streets between Koornmarkt, Oude Delft and Phoenixstraat for the cosiest cafés and best eats.

Le Vieux Jean, Heilige Geestkerkhof 3, ✆ 213 0433 (*moderate*). Long-time family-run favourite (soon to celebrate its 25th anniversary). Son Robert-Jan Polman is giving new vim and verve to his parents' traditionally good cooking by slipping the odd bit of curry in with the langoustines, or adding figs to the duck with red wine sauce.

De Prinsenkelder, Schoolstraat 11, ✆ 212 1860 (*moderate*). Rich Franco-Dutch cuisine in the cellar of the Prinsenhof cloisters.

Kleyweg's Stads-Koffiehuis, Oude Delft 133, ✆ 212 4625 (*cheap*). Good coffee, crispy pancakes, a relaxed neighbourhood-café atmosphere, and a view on to the prettiest canal in town.

Rotterdam

For over 25 years Rotterdam, on the delta of the river Maas, has topped the list of the world's largest ports. Unlike anywhere else in the Netherlands, Rotterdam has the skyline, pace and aggressive edge of a big city. Locals dub it 'Manhattan-on-the-Maas'.

Old Rotterdam was all but flattened by bombs early in the Second World War. The imagination and sense of adventure that the authorities brought to rebuilding their city has resulted in some bravura feats of modern architecture. As you step out of Rotterdam Centraal Station, you are confronted by the tallest office block in the Netherlands—a shard of black glass 150m high, belonging to an insurance company. The shapes, angles and colours of the buildings beyond it grow increasingly weird. But Rotterdammers take to this innovation with gusto, even giving some of the odder buildings nicknames. 'Rotterdam,' they say, 'will never be finished.' But there is another side to the city. Recently, the few patches of historic dockland that survived the bombing have been restored and injected with new life, largely in the form of cafés and restaurants. These romantic little harbours, coupled with some excellent museums, make Rotterdam worth at least a day or two of your time.

History

Towards the end of the 13th century, three people settled beside the river Rotte (part of the Maas delta) and built a dyke to reclaim some of the boggy land that stretched out around them. They paid a rent to Count Floris V of 12 chickens a year. Soon a mildly prosperous settlement grew up, relying on fishing, farming and trade with passing ships to trickle gold into the coffers. By 1328 Rotterdam had its own sheriff, and in 1340 the town was granted a charter by Count William IV. Rotterdam became the port serving the textile towns of Delft and Leiden and trade flourished—even through an English embargo. Canny Rotterdammers named a dockside tavern 'Calais', so that visiting captains could stop off for a drink and quite honestly record that they had been to Calais.

At the end of the 16th century, after suffering catastrophic floods and the privations of the Eighty Years' War, Rotterdam was quick to recover—European trade was shifting its focus from the Baltic to the North Sea. In 1585, when the Duke of Parma seized Antwerp, refugee merchants fleeing to Rotterdam brought secrets of the new spice routes and trade burgeoned as never before. But during the 17th-century Golden Age, Amsterdam (the seat of the Dutch East India Company) took over as the larger and more prosperous port, and Rotterdam went into decline. An 18th-century British trade embargo (Holland had become embroiled in the war between Britain and France) made the situation even worse. The 1800 ships that visited Rotterdam annually had, by 1799, dropped to just 140. The city fathers' Luddite attitude towards steamships and the railways didn't help the local economy either.

But improving trade relations with Britain, and the growth of the Ruhr industrial area (to which Rotterdam is connected by inland waterways), gave the port a much-needed boost in the late 19th century. Expansion and excavation of the port gave access to even the largest ocean-going ships and laid the foundations for the massive harbour of today. Rotterdam became an important passenger port, especially for emigrants to the Americas. Between 1880 and 1940 around a million people passed through Rotterdam on the way to the USA, many of them Jews fleeing persecution in Eastern Europe. As an important international harbour, Rotterdam was a prime target for German bombers, and was razed to the ground on 14 May 1940. During the Nazi occupation Allied bombers had a go at the harbour facilities, and occasionally hit the town by mistake. But within a few years of the war the port was back to its normal capacity, and was one of the first in Europe to respond to the new demands of containerization. Today it stretches on for some 25 miles (40km) and has one of the most advanced technological support systems in the world.

Getting Around

If the weather is good, and you take time to stop off in cafés along the way, it is perfectly possible, even pleasant, to **walk** from Blaak in the east, through old

Rotterdam

Centraal Station

S. GRAVENDIJKWAL

Nederlandse
Architectuurinstituut

ROCHUSSENSTRAAT

WITTEMAWEG

NIEUWE BINNENWEG

Delfshaven

Coolhaven

S. GRAVENDIJKWAL

ROCHUSSENSTRAAT

Coolhaven

Oude Kerk

Coolhaven

De Dubbelde
Palmboom

PIETER DE HOOCHWEG

Coolhaven

BUYTEWECHSTRAAT

VOORHAVEN

VOORHAVEN

WILLEM

Delfshaven

HOFFSTRAAT

Euromast

Parkhaven

Pa

SCHIEHAVEN

St. Jobshaven

Parkhaven

Schiehaven

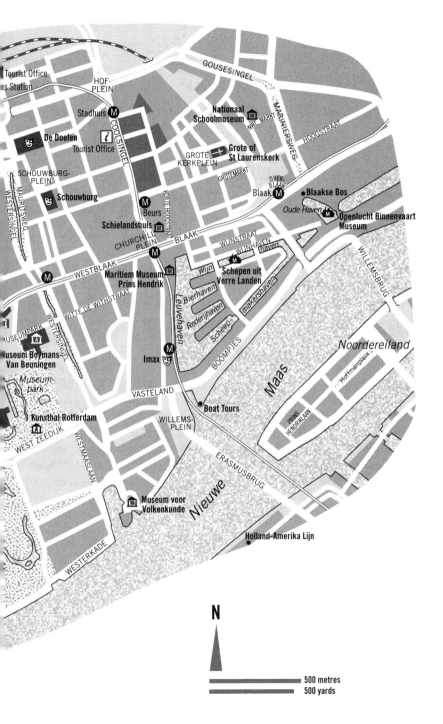

Tourist Office
us Station

HOF-
PLEIN

GOUSESINGEL

Stadhuis

Nationaal Schoolmuseum

NWE. MARKT

MARIANERSWEG

HOOGSTRAAT

COOLSINGEL

De Doelen

Tourist Office

GROTE
KERKPLEIN

Grote of St Laurenskerk

SCHOUWBURG-
PLEIN

GROTEMART

OVER-
BLAAK

Schouwburg

MAURITSWEG

WESTERSINGEL

Beurs

KORTE HOOGSTRAAT

Blaak

Blaakse Bos

Oude Haven

Openlucht Binnenvaart Museum

Schielandshuis

CHURCHILL
PLEIN

BLAAK

WIJNSTRAAT

WINHAVEN

Inaven

WESTBLAAK

Maritiem Museum Prins Hendrik

Wijn

Schepen uit Verre Landen

WITTE DE WITHSTRAAT

Leuvehaven

Bierhaven

makershaven

WESTERSINGEL

Rederijhaven

USEUMPARK

Scheep-

BOOMPJES

Noordereiland

useum Boymans Van Beuningen

Imax

Hoffmanplein

*Museum-
park*

VASTELAND

Maas

PRINS
HENDRIKLAAN

Kunsthal Rotterdam

Boat Tours

WILLEMS-
PLEIN

WEST ZEEDIJK

WESTMAASLAAN

ERASMUSBRUG

Museum voor Volkenkunde

Nieuwe

Holland-Amerika Lijn

WESTERKADE

N

500 metres
500 yards

docklands and along the Maas to the Euromast. After that it's a dull ten-minute walk to Delfshaven.

If you don't feel like legging it, the most convenient form of public transport is the **metro**. There are four lines running roughly east to west, and two going south from Centraal Station. Lines going in a similar direction stop at the same stations for most of their length, only fanning out in the distant suburbs—so the metro is easy to negotiate. There's also an efficient network of **trams** and **buses**. *Strippenkaarten* (*see* p.10) are valid, and you can get **information** from the national information line on ✆ (0900) 9292.

Should you want a close-up view of the world's largest port, you can go on a **harbour tour**. Spido Havenrondvaarten (situated at Leuvehoofd on the Leuvehaven, ✆ (010) 275 9988) offers a variety of boat tours starting from ƒ16.50.

Bicycle hire: Rijwiel Shop, Stationsplein 1, ✆ (010) 412 6220.

Taxis: ✆ (010) 462 6060.

Tourist Information

The main branch of the VVV tourist office is at Coolsingel 57, ✆ (010) 402 3200; open Mon–Thurs 9.30–6, Fri 9.30–7, Sat 9.30–5, Sun 10–4. Not only can staff supply maps and the usual information, but they can suggest walking routes for people interested in modern architecture.

Festivals

The **Rotterdam Film Festival**, held in late January and early February, screens the pick of the latest art movies as well as commercial hits. In August, the **Heineken Jazz Festival** fills cafés (and sometimes streets) with eager fans of popular jazz and improvised music. There is also a two-month-long **Summer Festival** in July and August, which involves a wide variety of outdoor events and street entertainment.

The Museum Quarter

Museum Boymans-Van Beuningen

Museumpark 18–20; open Tues–Sat 10–5, Sun 11–5; adm.

Amsterdam and The Hague both cornered royal art collections for the foundation of their showpiece museums. Not only did Rotterdam lack the advantages of royal patronage, it had to contend with a series of philistine city councillors, who turned down offers of at least two magnificent private collections. Yet today the Boymans-Van Beuningen Museum can stand shoulder to shoulder with the Rijksmuseum and the Mauritshuis as one of the finest collections of art and design in the country.

It was Frans Jacob Otto Boijmans who, in 1841, finally persuaded the council to accept his collection, provided they could find suitable accommodation for it. The eccentric hotchpotch of paintings, drawings and porcelain, which Boijmans had previously been unable to sell at auction or unload on the Utrecht city council, was housed in the Schielandshuis (*see* below), and much of it was lost when the building burnt down in 1864. But the museum's second major benefactor, the industrialist Daniel George van Beuningen (1877–1955), donated a treasury of masterpieces, including *Child in a Landscape*, the only **Titian** in any Dutch collection. Successive museum directors championed modern art and design. In 1903 the museum acquired *Lane of Poplars near Nuenen*, the first **Van Gogh** ever to appear in a public collection. More recently, director Wim Beeren has established the museum's reputation in the art world by commissioning work from the likes of Joseph Beuys, Andy Warhol, Bruce Nauman and Claes Oldenburg.

Today, the 'Boymans' is housed in a building designed in 1935 and extended in the 1970s. Navigating through the warrens of rooms, arranged around two courtyards, can be utterly bewildering, but it is a pleasure getting lost. A **floorplan** (available free at the ticket office) is essential.

Downstairs, in the west wing, you'll find **decorative art and design**, ranging from a 16th-century Nautilus cup that belonged to the Czar of Russia (an iridescent shell covered with silver-gilt and rubies) to an Olivetti calculator. There is an especially good collection of 20th-century chairs, and also glass and ceramics. The **Print Room** in the east wing reveals just part of a rich store that includes work by Dürer, Bellini and Rembrandt. The two floors of the southern extension are devoted to **modern art**. Here highlights include Degas' *Little Dancer, fourteen years old*, a delightful sculpture in bronze, muslin and satin; work by Pyke Koch and other Dutch Magic Realists (*see* p.60); and a world-class collection of Dali, Magritte and other surrealists, much of it from the collection of English eccentric (and alleged illegitimate son of Edward VII), Edward James.

But the cream of the museum's collection is on the first floor of the west wing. Here you'll find a wealth of canvases by the likes of **Rubens, Frans Hals** and **Rembrandt** (including a touching portrait of his son Titus). Famous images, such as **Breughel**'s *Tower of Babel* and **Hieronymus Bosch**'s *The Vagabond*, hang alongside lesser-known but nonetheless exquisite pieces like **Bartholomeus van der Helst**'s intimate, 17th-century *Portrait of Abraham del Court and Maria de Keerssegieter*, in which Maria wears a breathtakingly beautiful silver satin dress. The Boymans is renowned for the quality of its temporary exhibitions, and has a large museum shop, well stocked with art books and designer knick-knacks.

Around the Museumpark

Adjoining the Boymans-Van Beuningen Museum, the Museumpark is really no more than a vast, rather barren city square. At the southern end are the blank slabs of the **Kunsthal Rotterdam** (Weestzeedijk 341; *open Tues–Sat 10–5, Sun 11–5; adm*), a giant exhibition space built in 1992. Here you are sure to catch some travelling block-buster—anything from African sculpture to classic cars. Beside a pond at the northern end of the square is the **Nederlands Architectuurinstituut** (Netherlands Architecture Institute, Museumpark 25; *open Tues–Sat 10–5, Sun 11–5; adm*), designed by local architect Jo Coenen in 1993. A glass box, apparently suspended from scaffolding and with an arcaded offshoot that lights up in different colours at night, this is a zany home for the nation's architectural archive. There is no permanent display, but the institute holds temporary exhibitions on architectural themes.

Het Schielandshuis

Korte Hoogstraat 31; open Tues–Sat 10–5, Sun 11–5; adm.

Built between 1662 and 1665 as government offices for the surrounding province of Schieland, the pristine white Schielandshuis is a beautiful example of the poise and proportion of Restrained Dutch Classicism. Though the building burnt down in 1864 (by which time it was already in use as a museum), the façade survived, and the rest was carefully restored. Today it houses a Historical Museum, most noted for the *Atlas van Stolk*. In 1835, the timber merchant Abraham van Stolk began to compile an 'historical atlas' of prints that depicted events in Dutch history and which portrayed his own life and times. The tens of thousands of prints he collected came into the possession of the Rotterdam municipality in 1967. Only a tiny fragment of the *Atlas* goes on show at any one time, on the ground floor, usually in the form of an exhibition arranged around a specific theme. Also on the ground floor is a series of exceptional Baroque- and Rococo-style rooms, taken from mansions around Rotterdam and reassembled in the Schielandshuis. Upstairs you'll find displays on the history of Rotterdam (including some intriguing old children's toys) and a small collection of costumes, featuring not only little sequinned numbers from the 1920s, but hippie and flower-child garments too.

The Eastern Docklands

Blaak

Emerging from the space-age metro station at Blaak, you are confronted with two of Rotterdam's most photographed modern buildings, an apartment block nicknamed 'the Pencil' (for reasons that are quite evident), and the **Blaakse Bos** (Blaak Forest). The 'forest' comprises a thicket of cube-shaped apartments, up-ended on one corner and perched on tall stalks. Designed by Piet Blom in 1984, these curious homes are all occupied except one, which you can visit: the **Kijk-Kubus** (Show-Cube, Overblaak 70; *open March–Dec daily 11–5; Jan–Feb Fri–Sun 11–5; adm*). It is surprisingly ordinary inside. Sticking up incongruously in these modern surrounds is the Gothic tower of the **Grote of St Laurenskerk**, Grote Kerkplein 3 (*open Tues–Sat 10–4, but closed Thurs in winter and sometimes closed for conferences; adm free*). Built between 1449 and 1525, the church is a lonely survivor of Second World War bombs, and contains three organs by the Danish Marcussen company—the oldest dating back to 1540. There's a coffee corner at the back of the nave, where you can sit, sip a hot drink, and possibly be deafened by a blast from the main organ, which is one of the biggest in Europe.

Across the busy marketplace behind the church you'll find the **Nationaal Schoolmuseum** (Nieuwemarkt 1a; *open Tues–Sat 10–5, Sun 1–5; adm, children under 16 free*), a series of classrooms down the ages, starting in the 12th century, all reconstructed using authentic furniture. By 1910 school slates have given way to exercise books and by 1960 communal tables have replaced long wooden desks, and there is a TV set in the corner. In a 1930s classroom, a message chalked up on the blackboard invites you to sit down and try your hand at using a dip-pen.

Oude Haven

Stretching out on the other side of the Blaakse Bos is the Oude Haven (Old Harbour), the first of a series of docks that were the predecessors of today's busy port. Nowadays the Oude Haven is filled with boats of the **Openlucht Binnenvaart Museum** (*open access; adm free*), workaday vessels that have plied the inland waterways over the centuries. The old warehouses that surrounded the docks have gone, but as you wander from Oude Haven to Scheepmakershaven ('Shipbuilders' Harbour') and Wijnhaven ('Wine Harbour') these colourful, much-used old boats stand in startling contrast against a backdrop of angular modern architecture. There is even a whiff of tar and diesel in the air. At Wijnhaven you'll find the floating museum of **Schepen uit Verre Landen** (Ships from Far Countries, Wijnhaven 20a; *open Tues–Fri 10–4, Sat and Sun 12–5; adm*). Inside is a fascinating collection of craft, from painted sampans to tiny reed rafts from the Andes, and a fishing boat on which 16 Vietnamese refugees were found floating on the ocean in 1981.

Maritiem Museum Prins Hendrik

Leuvenhaven 1; open Tues–Sat 10–5, Sun 11–5; adm.

Models and paintings of ships abound in the Maritime Museum. Unless your interest is passionate, you could skim through the first two floors stopping off only at the **Schatkamer** (Treasury), where the choicest examples are kept. After that, displays become more varied and interesting, with lots of hands-on exhibits for children. In a reconstructed warehouse office you can open drawers and sniff the aromas of a variety of cargoes—from cinnamon to bananas and peanuts. You can peer out at Rotterdam through a submarine periscope (accompanied by appropriate sound effects), and push buttons to guess at the speed of the wind that a machine blows in your face. Grown-ups might prefer the old sea charts and navigation instruments—Lucas Waghenaar's *Spieghel der Zeevaert* (1584), the first printed maritime atlas, is on show—and there's an informative display on the history of the port of Rotterdam. But by far the most riveting part of the museum is moored in the harbour outside: the 19th-century warship *Buffel*. The ship has been perfectly restored, from the rows of enamel basins in the crew's washroom to the polished mahogany and leather of the captain's cabin. You can see the shining, pumping engines and drop in on the ship's jail, situated in the bow just behind the battering ram.

The Western Docklands

Along the Maas

The Boompjes ('little trees') was once a tree-lined promenade along the river Maas. Today it is a wall of high-rise blocks skirted by speeding traffic and dotted with nervous-looking pedestrians. But it does offer a fine view of the bridges over the river—the bright red **Willemsbrug** (built in the 1980s), and the spectacular white **Erasmusbrug**, a 410m-long suspension bridge hanging from a single 139m-high pylon. Nicknamed 'the swan' by those who like it, and 'washing-up brush' by those who don't, it opened in 1996—only to close again a few weeks later because the cables flapped alarmingly in the first strong wind. Across the water you can see the twin towers of the former head-quarters of the **Holland-Amerika Lijn**, the company that ferried so many people across the Atlantic to a new life in the USA. (Nowadays the building is a hotel.)

A little further down the river, around Veerhaven, old Rotterdam reasserts itself. The quays are lined with turn-of-the-century buildings, there are flourishes of greenery, and smart yachts moored in the docks. In a 100-year-old building beside the harbour, the **Museum voor Volkenkunde** (Ethnological Museum, Willemskade 25; *open Tues–Sat 10–5, Sun 11–5; adm*) offers three floors of changing exhibitions on the cultures of distant lands. Nearby, through a small park, is Rotterdam's post-office tower, the **Euromast** (Parkhaven 20; *open April–Sept daily 10–7; Oct–March 10–5; July and Aug until 10.30pm; adm exp*). A lift takes you up 92m to the viewing platform, then—amidst much roaring and dry-ice smoke—the **Space Adventure** capsule will shoot you up to the top of the tower, 185m above the ground, for a view that extends to the North Sea.

Delfshaven

The most appealing of all Rotterdam's historic harbours is Delfshaven, which got through the Second World War relatively unscathed. Delfshaven was once a separate town, made rich by *genever* distilleries and as the main port serving the textile factories and potteries at Delft. The narrow harbour (it's more like a canal) runs past an old wind-mill, once used to grind grain for the distilleries, and is edged with dainty gabled buildings, mostly dating from the 17th century. Nowadays they house art galleries, antiques shops and a string of cafés and restaurants, giving Delfshaven a sedate, leisurely air that makes it seem quite detached from the rest of Rotterdam.

In **De Dubbelde Palmboom** (Voorhaven 12; *open Tues–Fri 10–5, Sat and Sun 11–5; adm*), a converted 19th-century warehouse, you can see exhibits on working life in the area—from an Iron Age farmstead to a reconstruction of the interior of a worker's cottage built early this century. A few minutes' walk further up the harbour is the **Oude Kerk** (*open Sat 2–5; adm free*), the church where, on the 21 July 1620, the Pilgrim Fathers spent their last night on Dutch soil, praying for safe conduct and sleeping on the pews. Next morning they embarked on the *Speedwell* for Plymouth, where they changed ships for the *Mayflower*.

The centre of Rotterdam is on the way to becoming one huge shopping mall. It was one of the first inner-city areas in Europe to be pedestrianized. Plans are already being implemented to link up existing shops with brand new buildings to create a 'shopping environment', canopied by glass and full of eager Euro-shoppers. If this is how you enjoy spending your money, head for **Beurs metro station**. If you prefer a more individual approach, try **Nieuwe Binnenstraat**, where you'll find magic mushrooms, music, designer furniture, and a branch of the Witte Tandenwinkel (more varieties of toothbrush than you could imagine). There are some adventurous **art galleries** on Witte de Withstraat, and antiques shops in Delfshaven. Every Tuesday and Saturday you'll find a good **antiques and fleamarket** on Grotemarkt and Hoogstraat, near the Blaak metro station.

Rotterdam ✆ (010–)   *Where to Stay*

Bilderberg Parkhotel, Westersingel 70, 3015 LB, ✆ 436 3611, ✉ 436 4212 (*expensive*). A gracious turn-of-the-century mansion with a giant metallic annexe, just around the corner from the Boymans-Van Beuningen Museum. Staff are super-friendly and the rooms are modern and comfortable. From ƒ305.

Hotel Central, Kruiskade 12, 3012 EH, ✆ 414 0744, ✉ 412 5325 (*inexpensive*). Just what it says. In the heart of the shopping district, and with a faded air of the 1970s.

Hotel New York, Koninginnenhoofd 1, 3072 AD, ✆ 439 0500, ✉ 484 2701 (*moderate–inexpensive: from ƒ160 to ƒ275 with river view*). Trendy, stylish hotel in the converted headquarters of the Holland-Amerika Lijn. Rooms are furnished in a hip modern style and have great views across the harbour.

Hotel Van Walsum, Mathenesserlaan 199–201, 3014 HC, ✆ 436 3275, ✉ 436 4410 (*inexpensive; price incl. breakfast*). A gem: one of those family-run hotels managed by people who take a pride in what they're doing. In a 19th-century building just a short walk from the Museumpark, and offering excellent value for money. (Check out the restored 1890s loo on the 3rd floor.)

Alexander Hotel, Pieter de Hoochweg 115a/b, 3024 BG, ✆ 476 5277, ✉ 425 4201 (*inexpensive*). Simple hotel with friendly management and a restaurant downstairs. Near Delfshaven.

Hotel Baan, Rochussenstraat 345, 3023 DH, ✆ 477 0555, ✉ 476 9450 (*cheap*). A comfortable family-run hotel on the waterside near Delfshaven.

Youth Hostel, Rochussenstraat 107–9, 3015 EH, ✆ 436 5763, ✉ 436 5569 (*from ƒ32.25 p.p. for a bed in a dorm including breakfast*).

Rotterdam ✆ (010–)   *Eating Out*

Parkheuvel, Heuvellaan 21, ✆ 436 0766 (*expensive*). Modern restaurant with a view over the Maas, a classic ambience and a reputation almost unrivalled by any in the land. Imagine scallops with acorn bread and truffles; langoustines and sole with sun-dried tomatoes and grilled artichoke. Or don't even attempt to imagine, just try it.

De Engel, Eendrachtsweg 19, ✆ 413 8256 (*expensive*). Owned and operated by a chef whose favourite movie is *The Cook, the Thief, his Wife and her Lover.* Sumptuous décor in a patrician mansion, and a menu that depends on what's fresh and special in the market that day. Delicious dishes that rely more on good ingredients and subtle combinations of flavour than on fancy sauces.

Parkzicht, Kievitslaan 25, ✆ 436 8888 (*moderate*). A pavilion in the middle of a park beside the Maas. On one side is a bar and brasserie where you can have light meals, or just a drink. On the other is a pricier candlelit restaurant where pigeon cooked with goose liver is more the order of the day.

Eten, Nieuwe Binnenweg 153, ✆ 436 4474 (*moderate*). An interior design that manages to be both hyper-modern and cosy, painted in deep blues, greens and browns, with a sweeping, curved leather bench and a plethora of fish sculptures. Fish dishes are indeed a speciality. Start with excellent seafood tapas, then try brill steamed with asparagus and thinly layered with duck liver.

De Tijd Geest, Oost Wijnstraat 14, ✆ 233 1311 (*moderate*). Popular lunchtime spot overlooking the Oude Haven (though it's open for dinner too). Formal décor under the high ceilings of a 19th-century building—with the occasional startling flash of fake cheetah-skin upholstery. Join Rotterdam business folk for such dishes as duck breast with lavender honey and shiitake mushrooms.

Eethuisje de Parel, Voorhaven 54b, ✆ 476 5558 (*moderate*). A tiny restaurant beside the harbour at Delfshaven. Oddball décor—as if Dali had been let loose in an aquarium, though the food is less bizarre. Try the smoked pork chops with mushrooms, or duck with forest berries.

Henkes, Voorhaven 17, ✆ 425 5596 (*moderate*). An enormous *grand café*, with an interior that 100 years ago belonged to a Brussels insurance office. Tasty fare with a traditional Dutch touch, such as brown bean soup with smoked eel, or halibut with leeks and home-ground mustard.

Loos, Westplein 1, ✆ 411 7723 (*moderate*). Big, noisy, perennially popular brasserie. A lively, slightly artsy Rotterdam crowd tuck in to such delights as sea bass wrapped in Chinese greens and served with stir-fried veg and hazelnut sauce.

Wester Paviljoen, Nieuwe Binnenweg 136, ✆ 436 2322 (*cheap*). 'Brown café' writ large, with a young friendly crowd. Dishes such as lasagne or rabbit casserole are uneventful, but good value for money.

Cambrinus, Blaak 4, ✆ 414 6702 (*cheap*). In the shade of the Blaakse Bos. You can sit inside on plush, comfy chairs in winter or join the crowds on the large, waterside terrace in good weather. There are tasty *hapjes* (snacks to accompany your drink) and fuller meals, such as squid stir-fried with chickpeas, green beans and bamboo shoots.

The **Rotterdam Philharmonic Orchestra**, as well as any visiting artiste of note in the classical music world, plays at **De Doelen** concert hall, Schouwburgplein 50, ✆ 217 1717. Rotterdam also boasts one of the best modern dance troupes in the country, Scapino Ballet, which performs at the **Rotterdamse Schouwburg**, Schouwburgplein 25, ✆ 411 8110. Visiting rock stars head for **Ahoy Rotterdam**, Zuiderparkweg 20–30, ✆ 481 2144.

There is a flourishing live music scene centred mainly on **Café Dada**, Westewagenstraat 58, Popular, Westkruiskade 26, and **Rotown**, Nieuwe Binnenweg 19. **Nighttown**, Westkruiskade 26, is the city's trendiest club, and also often features live music, and **Heksenkethel** (underground, entrance opposite Centraal Station) is popular for its retro Seventies vibes. The new, multi-level **Hollywood Music Hall**, Delftestraat 14 and the tropical **Baja Beach Club**, K. Doormanstraat 10–12 are hottest on the disco scene.

Around Rotterdam

Schiedam: Five Windmills

The town of Schiedam, now practically a suburb of Rotterdam (*you can get there on Tram 1 or 4*) gives you some impression of what Rotterdam must have been like before Second World War bombers and post-war architects set to work on it. Avoid the Hoogstraat, full of shoppers and glitzy high-street façades, and wander instead down **Lange Haven** (Long Harbour), a canal-like harbour lined with gabled houses, and with beautiful old boats moored along the walls.

Founded in 1250, Schiedam survived as a port and fishing village until the 18th century, when in order to be more competitive with Rotterdam and Delfshaven it began to specialize in distilling *jenever* and other liqueurs. Today you can visit the **Nederlands Gedistilleerd Museum** (Netherlands Distillery Museum; *open Tues–Sat 11–5, Sun 12.30–5; adm*), which is centred on De Gekroonde Brandersketel, a traditional working distillery where the kettles are still heated by coal fires. After seeing how it's done, you can climb upstairs past various displays on *jenever* and distilling (*summarized English explanations on walls, but detailed text available from ticket office*), to a *proeflokaal* (tasting room) where you get a free sip or two of the house brand *jenever* and a few other liqueurs.

Almost next door is the **Nationaal Coöperatie Museum** (*open Thurs 1.30–5pm and 7–9pm, Fri 1.30–5pm, Sat 11–5; adm free*), a restored 1920s Co-op shop, complete with live little old lady behind the counter and jars of sweets. Nearby on Hoogstraat, the **Stedelijk Museum** (Municipal Museum; *Tues–Sat 11–5, Sun 12.30–5; adm free*) has a fine collection of COBRA paintings (*see* p.60) and contemporary art. Just off the Hoogstraat, the **Grote of Sint Janskerk** (Great or St John's Church; *open Fri and Sat 10–4; adm free*), built in the early 16th century, has an elegantly simple Gothic interior, reminiscent of the poised paintings of church interiors by artists such as Saenredam.

Schiedam is also known for its five 18th-century **windmills**, claimed to be the tallest old-style windmills in the world. Ranged along Nieuwe Haven and Noordvest, each about 30m high, they make an impressive sight. A couple still grind meal: one, De Noordmolen (Noordvest 38; ✆ *(010) 473 1141*) is a restaurant, and one, De Nieuwe Palmboom (Noordvest 34; *open Tues–Sat 11–5, Sun 12.30–5; adm*) is open to the public.

Kinderdijk: Nineteen Windmills

If Windy Miller really was a childhood obsession, just beyond the southeastern edge of Rotterdam, set in a meadow near a tributary of the Lek, are the 19 windmills of **Kinderdijk** (*bus 154 from Rotterdam suburban station Lombardijen, or from Utrecht Centraal Station*). The name (which means child's dyke) comes from a cutesy legend about a baby who was washed up here in a cradle after great floods in 1421, with a cat sitting on its tummy to keep it from tipping out. The windmills were once crucial in draining the area (and they are still used in emergencies), pumping water into nearby *boezems*—a word which causes as much mirth among visiting Dutch children as it is likely to with English-speaking ones, but which also means a reservoir for excess polder water. Every Saturday afternoon in July and August the windmills are set in motion, and from April to September one of them is always open to visitors (*Mon–Sat 9.30–5.30*).

Dordrecht

Just 15km southeast of Rotterdam on the A16, Dordrecht stands on one of the busiest river junctions in Europe. Here the Oude Maas, the Noord and the Merwede—all very much working rivers—meet and feed into the port of Rotterdam. Ships and barges float past on their way to the Europoort, but nowadays most of Dordrecht's own harbours are filled with pleasure craft. The town managed to avoid damage by the bombs that rained down on Rotterdam during the Second World War, and its 800 or so historical buildings have also escaped over-zealous restoration. It preserves its haphazard medieval street plan and rough edges, and so has far more of the atmosphere of a port than many of the pristine historical harbour towns farther north.

Founded nearly a thousand years ago on the banks of the river Thuredrith (which no longer exists), Dordrecht soon became a prosperous trading town, receiving its city charter in 1220. The 1421 flood that destroyed much of the surrounding countryside (and washed the baby up at Kinderdijk, *see* above) left Dordrecht, which was protected by its city walls, unscathed—an island in an inland sea. Over the centuries this sea subsided a little to become the Biesbosch waterlands (*see* below). A marker of the city's importance is that it was chosen as the venue for the Eerste Vrije Statenvergadering, the first meeting of the Free Assembly of the Seven Provinces. This gathering, at which William of Orange was elected *stadhouder*, is often seen as the beginning of the United Republic of the Netherlands. Later Dordrecht was the venue for a number of milestone church synods, the most notable of which (in 1618–19) ordered a new translation of the bible. This *Statenbijbel* was to become the foundation of modern Dutch.

Trains leave from Rotterdam for Dordrecht six times an hour. The journey takes 15 minutes and costs ƒ11 return.

There is no adequate public transport to the Biesbosch from Dordrecht, though bus 5 gets you to within 45mins' walk of the visitors centre. You can also take a *trein-taxi* (*see* p.9) from Dordrecht Station.

VVV, Stationsweg 1, ✆ (078) 613 2800, Mon–Sat 9.30–5.

The Old Harbours

Dordrecht's old harbour area, on the northeastern edge of town beside the Oude Maas, is a romantic place for a wander, day or night. 'When the sun set and reflected off the water and in the windows, and threw a strong golden glow over everything, it was like a painting by Cuyp,' wrote an entranced Vincent van Gogh after an evening walk. Most of the harbours were laid out in the 17th century, when trade was booming. Now, graceful old sailing boats and inland waterways barges, as well as smart new yachts, are moored along the jetties. The old warehouses, and some merchants' houses with very grand façades, have been converted into apartments and galleries. Keep an eye open for the former fish market on the Kornhaven, resplendent with carved sea monsters, and now used as a beer terrace.

Near the entrance to the Nieuwe Haven is the **Grote Kerk** with its tilting tower— some two metres off the perpendicular (*closed for renovation at time of writing*). Building began on the church in the 12th century, though a fire destroyed all but the tower in 1457, so most of today's building is 15th-century Gothic. Inside, you will find richly carved 16th-century choir benches, 15th-century murals, and an exuberant rococo pulpit. Across the harbour, you'll find the **Museum Mr Simon van Gijn** (Nieuwe Haven 29; *open Tues–Sun 11–5; adm*), an 18th-century patrician mansion that was occupied by banker and art collector Simon van Gijn from 1864 to 1922. He left his home and collection to the city—there are superb period rooms (including an 18th-century kitchen), vast stashes of silver, and an excellent collection of antique toys and doll's houses. At the far end of the harbours, you come to the **Groothoofdspoort**, a city gate originally built between 1440 and 1450—though what you see today is a Renaissance cladding built around the medieval structure. Through the gate, you come to the exact confluence of the Oude Maas, the Noord and Merwede rivers.

Around Town

A walk from the Grote Kerk past the large neoclassical **Stadhuis** takes you to **Het Hof** ('the court'), originally an Augustinian monastery, built in the 13th century but rebuilt in the Renaissance style after a 1512 fire. Here, in the **Statenzaal** (*open Tues–Sat 1–5; adm free*), the first meeting of the Free Assembly of the Seven Provinces was held (*see* above).

Beyond Het Hof, you come to Museumstraat, where at No.56 you can see the **Arend Maartenszhof**, an almshouse for war widows founded around 1600. Push the doorbell button to the right of the entrance, and the 1707 Regents' Office lights up, allowing you to peer in through the window. Further along Museumstraat you come to the **Dordrechts Museum** (Museumstraat 40; *open Tues–Sun 11–5; adm*), which has a magnificent collection of Dutch art, including work by Dordrecht-born landscape artist Albert Cuyp (*see* p.56), good Hague School work by Mauve and Mesdag, as well as more modern work by Constant and Karel Appel. There is no permanent exhibition, rather the museum offers various themed shows of work from its depots.

Outside Dordrecht

About 5km east of the city centre, the **Biesbosch** is one of the largest national parks in the Netherlands, and one of the few remaining unspoiled freshwater tidal zones in Europe. It's a sprawling wetlands area of marshland, meadows and reedlands, interspersed by rivers and creeks. Birds abound, as well as other animal life, such as beavers (which were introduced in the 1980s to control the spread of willows). Some of the rivers are navigable, and you can hire canoes or join a boat trip at the **Biesbosch Visitor Centre** (Baanhoekweg 53, ✆ (078) 630 5353; *open Tues–Sun 9–5; April–Oct also Mon 12–5 ; booking advisable*).

Shopping

Dordrecht is known for its **antiques shops**, many of them situated along Voorstraat (where, in 1877, Vincent Van Gogh worked for a few months in a book shop). As you work your way up the street towards the Groothoofd area, so prices drop and shops have a more rough-and-tumble junkshop appearance.

Dordrecht ✆ (078–) **Where to Stay and Eating Out**

Hotel Bellevue, Boomstraat 37, 3311 TC, ✆ 613 7900, ✉ 613 7921, *bellevue@dordt.nl* (*moderate*). Once a sailor's inn beside the Groothoofdspoort, the Bellevue has been going for 300 years. Nowadays it has something of a 19th-century seaside hotel air. The rooms have inoffensive modern décor, though a few are quite small. Some look out over the river. There's a good breakfast buffet, and the downstairs restaurant is popular with locals.

Dordrecht, Achterhakkers 72, 3311 JA, ✆ 613 6011, ✉ 613 7470 (*moderate*). Grand old patrician mansion beside one of the old harbours. The rooms are comfy and well-appointed, some way beyond expectations for the price range (witness Jacuzzi and four-poster bed).

De Kop van 't Land, Zeedijk 32, 3329 LC, ✆ 616 6397 (*inexpensive–cheap*). Bewitching little hotel cum restaurant (just three rooms) on the edge of the Biesbosch. Not much to look at, but laid-back and rather romantic. The owner-chef comes up with inspired dishes with a home-cooking touch.

De Stroper, Wijnbrug 1, ✆ 613 0094 (*moderate–inexpensive*). White-painted wood, fishing nets and the odd plastic marlin give this fish restaurant a curious

Cape Cod quality. The service is warm and friendly, and the food good. You can opt for a cheap brasserie menu, with standards like salmon pasta or baked trout, or embark on such adventures as sea bass with mango and red onion sauce, served with wild rice patties.

For a quick coffee and a nibble, try **Café Mignon** at the Dordrechts Museum, facing out into a beautiful courtyard shaded by an enormous tree.

The Coast

Canal water can be pretty poisonous, so if the weather is hot inhabitants of the Randstad head for the coast.

Getting There and Around

Trains to Zandvoort from Haarlem run every 15 minutes, and the trip takes 15 minutes.

Bus connections (No.90 to Den Haag) Haarlem/Katwijk/Noordwijk/Leiden.

Tourist Information

Zandvoort; Schoolplein 1, © (023) 571 7947; open Tues–Fri 10–12.30 and 1.30–4.30, Sat 10–3.30.

Katwijk; Vuurbaakplein 11, © (071) 407 5444, ✆ (071) 407 6342; open Jan–April Mon–Fri 9–5, Sat 9–1; April–July Mon–Sat 9–6; July–Sept Mon–Sat 9–6, Sun 11–1; Sept–Jan Mon–Fri 9–5, Sat 9–1.

Although **Zandvoort** is just beyond Haarlem (another 15 minutes on the train) it has achieved the honorary status of being 'Amsterdam's beach'. It's a crowded and commercial resort, though if you wander farther up the coast you'll find a nudists' beach, a gay beach and lots of quieter spots among the dunes. On hot summer's nights Zandvoort is the scene of trendy Ibiza-style beach-party clubbing.

Following the N206 south, you pass through bulb fields (making slabs of bright colour in early spring) to the dune reserve of **Noordwijkerhout** (free access). Marked paths wind through stubby forests and scrubby coastal grassland to the windswept North Sea coast. It's a great place for walking and cycling, and outside weekends can even achieve a measure of romantic loneliness.

The resort of **Noordwijk** on the other hand is a tacky little town that cowers behind a ghastly row of high-rise hotels. **Katwijk**, a little farther on, is a mild improvement; then, after a wild and open area of rolling dunes and marshy lakes, you reach the resort of **Scheveningen** (*see* above, p.198). Located between Katwijk and Noordwijk is the sprawling European Space Research and Technology Centre, the nerve centre of the European Space Agency. Attached to it is a **Space Expo** (Bus 32 from Leiden or 90 from Haarlem or The Hague; *open Tues–Sun 10–5; adm*), which has exhibitions on the history of space travel and what life is like for astronauts (including a cut-away space suit and a suction loo). Eerie music and blue light permeate the large hall, giving it the atmosphere of a James Bond set, but presentation is a little dull and there are surprisingly few interactive exhibits (*though at the time of going to press the Space Expo was due for a revamp*).

Noordwijk ℗ (071–)   **Where to Stay**

Hotel Edelman, Koningin Astrid Boulevard 48, 2202 BE, ℗ 361 3124, ✉ 361 0773 (*moderate–inexpensive*). Old-fashioned hotel just outside Noordwijk that gives you some idea of how attractive the resort must have been before crass development spoiled it. Many rooms have wooden balconies with a sea view, and, if asked nicely, Mr Edelman will do his John Cleese impersonation.

Noordwijk ℗ (071–)   **Eating Out**

This is not gourmet territory. The coastal towns have rows of barely distinguishable beachfront cafés and pancake houses, and there's a passable pizzeria at the northern entrance to the Noordwijkerhout reserve. One exception is **Latour**, Konigin Astridboulevard 5, Noordwijk, ℗ 365 1239 (*lunch moderate, dinner expensive*). A piano tinkles in the background as you savour such delights as *coquilles St Jacques*, smoked salmon and sweetbreads, in classically stylish surrounds, and with a view of the sea to boot.

The Midlands

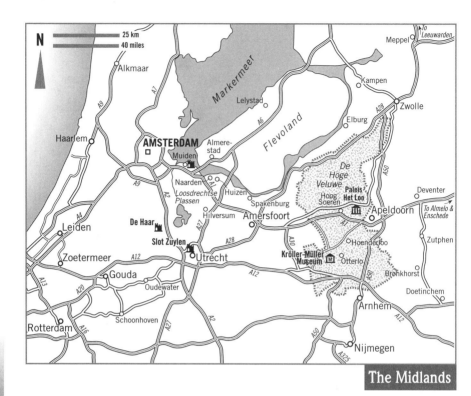

The Midlands

East of the Randstad conurbation, the bristling business parks and brown brick suburbs give way to primly laid-out farmland, which relaxes into the forests, wild dunes and meadows of the Hoge Veluwe National Park—justly nicknamed the 'Green Heart' of the Netherlands. Ranged around this verdant patch, a variety of small towns lures you back to urban delights: grand architecture at Gouda and Utrecht, echoes of past glories at Hanseatic towns like Zutphen and Zwolle. Replica sailing ships, scales for weighing witches, live apes, and the country's smallest village are all yours for the visiting.

Getting Around the Midlands

By car: A comprehensive network of motorways connects all the major towns. The A1 is the main artery east out of Amsterdam, through the middle of the Hoge Veluwe and off into Germany; the A2 takes you south via Utrecht; and the A28 is the most useful for the northern towns. But unless you're intending to stop at lots of smaller villages, the train is a more convenient way of getting around.

By train: Outside Amsterdam, Amersfoort and Utrecht are the main junctions. Direct lines run north from Amersfoort to Zwolle, and east to Apeldoorn and Deventer. Trains via Utrecht go to Gouda, and Arnhem. There is also a direct Zwolle–Deventer–Zutphen–Arnhem connection.

The stretch to the east of Amsterdam, around the dull broadcasting town of **Hilversum**, is officially known as 't Gooi, but more popularly as '*Het Gooise Matras*' (The Gooi Mattress)—an arch reference to the happy romping of the media types who populate the area (in both senses of the word).

Getting There from Amsterdam

Muiden: Bus 136 from Amstel Station (50mins), or a local train from Centraal Station to Weesp, then bus 153 (45mins).

Naarden: Bus 136 from Amstel Station (55mins); train from Centraal Station to Naarden Bussum then take bus 136 (twice every hour) to Naarden Vesting.

Tourist Information

Naarden: VVV, Adriaan Dortsmanplein 1b, ✆ (035) 694 2836; open May–Sept Mon–Fri 9.15–5, Sat–Sun 10–4; Oct–April Mon–Fri 10.30–2, Sat 10–2.

Festivals and When to Go

These days the *St Matthew Passion* alternates with the *St John Passion*, and is performed in the Naarden Grote Kerk on the Thurs, Fri and Sat of the Easter weekend (*St Matthew* in 2000). Tickets range from ƒ50 to ƒ100 and sell out long in advance. Information from De Nederlands Bach Vereniging, ✆ (030) 251 3413.

Muiden and Muidenslot

First stop out along the A1, at the mouth of the river Vecht, is the village of **Muiden**— hardly more than a cluster of dinky gabled houses along the waterfront. But on the village outskirts is the **Muiderslot** (*guided tours only, every half-hour, duration one hour; open April–Oct, Mon–Fri 10–5, last tour at 4, Sat and Sun 1–4, last tour at 3; Nov–May Sat and Sun only; adm*), a stumpy castle that stands firmly fixed in the national psyche for two reasons. It was here in 1296 (a date almost as familiar to Dutch schoolchildren as 1066 is to British) that Count Floris of Holland was imprisoned and murdered. Over three centuries later, the castle was the focus of the Muiderkring (Muiden Circle), the country's most famous ever literary circle, centring on the poet P. C. Hooft.

Tesselschade

One rough night, towards the end of the 16th century, a small trading ship ran aground on one of the treacherous sandbanks around the island of Texel off the coast of North Holland. The young Dutch merchant and man of letters, Roemer Visscher, was one of the few survivors. That very night his wife (snug in their house on the Engelsekaai in Amsterdam) gave birth to a daughter. Although she was christened Maria, her father felt compelled to mark the coincidence and celebrate his survival by burdening her with the sobriquet 'Tesselschade' (literally Tessel/Texel-damage, but with gentler connotations of mischief).

Despite her nickname (and an accident involving a spark from a blacksmith's anvil) Tesselschade went on to become the one-eyed doyenne of Amsterdam salon culture. Her father made sure that Maria and her sister Anne got a sound classical education (a younger daughter, Geertruid, seemed content with embroidery) and that they picked up all the subsidiary skills required to sparkle in erudite society. By the time she was a young woman the handsome (if slightly imperfect) Tesselschade could supply fluent translations of the most complex Latin, Greek or Italian texts, was an accomplished poetess, would entertain delightfully on harpsichord, lute and viol and had a singing voice of high repute. When some of the older Chambers of Rhetoric (medieval literary societies) joined forces in 1630, it was Tesselschade who won the competition to write a poem celebrating the union.

In the first two decades of the 17th century, the house on the Engelsekaai became Amsterdam's foremost literary and philosophical salon. When their father died, the daughters were snapped up by the poet Pieter Cornelisz. Hooft to join his famous literary circle at Muiden Castle, where they held court until their respective marriages. The list of Tesselschade's suitors had read like a *Who's Who* of Dutch letters—men like Vondel, Bredero, Constantijn Huygens and P. C. Hooft plied her with eulogistic verses. But she finally married a sea captain from Alkmaar. Anne fulfilled her merchant family's social ambitions by marrying a minor nobleman. Tesselschade returned to Amsterdam as a widow in 1640 to resume her position as a literary *Grande Dame* and when she died in 1649, Huygens compared her to the sun. Yet despite their obvious attributes and the frantic praises heaped upon them, the sisters never appear in any of the group portraits of the Muiden circle, and seem to have been regarded as prodigious ornaments. It took a 19th-century painter, J. C. Kruseman, to give the Visscher sisters pride of place among the male luminaries of the Muidenkring and today (if the painting's not in storage in the cellars) you can see the portrait hanging in the Rijksmuseum.

For 'castle' in Holland you can usually read 'stately home'. But Muiderslot is very much in the moated, turreted, impenetrable stone-wall mould. Most of the building dates back to the 13th and 14th centuries, though inside it has been restored in a style which rather effectively recreates an atmosphere that would have been more familiar to members of the Muiderkring. You can see the chamber where Floris met his fate, and the desk at which P. C. Hooft wrote his poems, standing up. The rooms are filled with such curiosities as a 'money table' (you detected counterfeit coins by clinking them on the limestone top), and a family box-bed (children in drawers underneath, parents shut into a wardrobe above, with a cord to pull that opened a vent when it all got a bit too pongy). Keep an eye open for a painting in which human figures have cabbages for heads—done a good 400 years before Magritte came up with the idea.

Loosdrechtse Plassen

The slow, wide river **Vecht**, that runs inland from Muiden, has long been the site of grand homes. Centuries ago rich Amsterdam merchants would build summer retreats along the banks. Many of these mansions are now given over to multimedia or advertising company offices, but many are still lived in. A cycle ride beside the river past the **Loosdrechtse Plassen** (a lake more than 5km long) is like a trip through the pages of *Homes and Gardens* (the smaller road along the eastern bank is the one to follow).

Naarden

Ten kilometres east of Muiden is **Naarden**, a town that, inconveniently, is perhaps best seen from the air. A ballooner's view would reveal the full pattern of its 17th-century fortifications—two concentric, star-shaped canals surrounding a circular town that juts six arrow-head shaped bastions out against the enemy. But most people will have to settle for a clamber about the walls and a walk through the tunnels of the **Vestingmuseum** (Fort Museum, Westwalstraat 6; *open March–Oct Tues–Fri 10.30–5; June–Aug, also Mon 10.30–5; Nov–Feb Tues–Sun noon–5; adm*). The **Raadhuis** (built 1601) is the oldest in 't Gooi, and the austere 14th-century **Grote Kerk** hosts a biennial performance of the Bach's *St Matthew Passion* that is to the Dutch at Easter what the King's College carol service is to Brits at Christmas. You can climb the tower for as near a bird's-eye view of the fortifications as most humans get.

Eating Out

Muiden ✆ (0294–)

Graf Floris V, Herengracht 72, ✆ 261 296 (*cheap*). Traditional café in the village, where you can get savoury and sweet pancakes, and simple meals.

Naarden ✆ (035–)

Het Arsenaal, Kooltjesburg 1, ✆ 694 9148 (*expensive*). Dine in a 17th-century arsenal, on dishes such as smoked monkfish with grilled tomato, prepared under the eagle eye of Paul Fagel, a member of a family that has produced some of the country's most renowned chefs.

Fishermen and Flevoland

Some 20km east of Naarden, on the banks of the Eemmeer, lies the quiet fishing village of **Spakenburg**, dating back to the 13th century. Even today, you can see women wearing the traditional local costume—a red, white and blue checked dress with flowery, American-football-style starched shoulder-pieces. You can still buy the checked and flower-patterned cotton-print fabrics in local shops, but the tradition is dying out. 'My grandmother wears *klederdracht* every day,' says a pancake waitress. 'But not me. Not ever.'

Once, Spakenburg was open to the sea, but the building of the Afsluitdijk (which made a freshwater lake of the Zuiderzee in 1932, *see* p.284) put an end to that. Then, in the 1960s, **Flevoland** appeared just off Spakenburg's coastline—an entire new province, 55 kilometres long and 22 kilometres wide, on land reclaimed from the southern Zuiderzee. So now Spakenburg lies on the narrow Eemmeer channel, and its fishing heyday is long past. But family boats still put out to sea, and Eemmeer eels are a delicacy. The village wafts with woodsmoke from backyard eel smokeries, and with the smell of freshly sawn wood from traditional boat builders.

Getting There

Spakenburg: Spakenburg is coupled with its neighbouring village, so most signs read 'Spakenburg-Bunschoten'. Take the train from Amsterdam Centraal Station to Amersfoort (twice an hour), there's a direct connection with bus 76 which will take you to the centre of Spakenburg. The journey takes 95mins. The VVV (*see* below) can arrange trips on traditional boats, with a skipper.

Batavia: A train goes directly to Lelystad from Amsterdam Centraal Station twice every hour. Bus 21 will then take you to Batavia Haven. The journey takes 50mins.

Oostvaardersplassen: Take the train to Lelystad from Amsterdam Centraal Station and bus 1 from Lelystad to Oostvaarderdijk/Houtritweg . The bird sanctuary begins a few minutes' walk from the bus stop.

Elburg: There's an hourly train to Harderwijk from Amsterdam Centraal Station; then, from outside the station, bus 100 will take you to Elburg. The whole journey takes nearly two hours. Alternatively, you can take bus 107 which leaves hourly from Lelystad to Harderwijk and then change to bus 100 to Elburg. The journey takes nearly 1½ hours.

Tourist Information

Spakenburg: VVV, Oude Schans 90, ✆ (033) 298 2156; open April–Oct Mon–Fri 10–5 and Sat 10–4; Oct–April Mon–Fri 1–5 and Sat 10–3.

Lelystad: VVV, Stationsplein 186, ✆ (0320) 243 444; open April–Oct Mon–Fri 9–5, Sat 9–3 and Thurs 7–9pm; Oct–April Mon–Fri 9–5 and Sat 9–1.

Elburg: VVV, Ledigestede 31, ✆ (0525) 681 520; open May–Sept Mon–Fri 9–5, Sat 10–4; Sept–April Mon noon–5, Tues–Fri 9–5 and Sat noon–4.

Festivals and When to Go

The **Spakenburg Days** (last two Wednesdays in July and first two in August) are festival days, with eel-smoking competitions, a street fair and lots of people wearing *klederdracht*. In mid-May traditional boats race on the Eemmeer during the **Zuidwal Botterwedstrijd**.

Spakenburg and Lelystad

Spakenburg is the home of the **Bruine Vloot** (the Brown Fleet), the largest traditional fishing fleet in the country. Around 17 of the elegant, shallow, slipper-shaped boats with their brown canvas sails, most dating from the 19th century, are moored in the harbour. The traditional shipyard on the wharf is kept busy repairing similar boats from all over the country, using time-tried techniques. The **Klederdracht en Visserijmuseum** (Costume and Fishing Museum, Kerkstraat 20; *open April–Sept Mon–Sat 10–5; adm*) gives you an idea of what life in Spakenburg was like, with reconstructed interiors and a herring smokery.

Southern Flevoland itself is flat, windswept and predominantly barren, dotted with dismal 1960s dormitory towns. But it contains two gems. Just outside **Lelystad** is the **Batavia-Werf** (Batavia Wharf; *open daily 10–5, July–Aug 10–8; adm exp*), where you can visit the *Batavia*, a far more authentic reconstruction of a Dutch East Indies sailing ship than the one at the Scheepvaartsmuseum in Amsterdam. The original *Batavia* was built in 1628, but foundered off the west coast of Australia a year later, while on a voyage to Java. The replica 45m-long three-master was built between 1985 and 1995 using traditional materials and techniques. You can walk below decks and marvel at how 341 people could squash in, with trading goods and all their supplies, for months on end; or stand on the bridge with the wind in your hair and the rigging clinking in your ears. The wharf is now busy with *De Zeven Provinciën*, a replica of the flagship of the famous Admiral de Ruyter (*see* pp.41 and 86). *During 2000 the Batavia will be in Sydney as part of the Olympics celebrations, and should arrive back home by April 2001.*

Beyond the Batavia-Werf lie the watery reaches of the **Oostvaardersplassen**, one of Europe's most important wetland reserves. Some 250 bird species (29 of which are on the endangered list) visit the reserve, including spoonbills, white-tailed eagles and rare varieties of goose. Yet until 1965 this marshland didn't even exist. It was one of the last parts of Flevoland to be reclaimed from the Zuiderzee, and work wasn't really even finished when nature moved in in full force. The mudflats and pools were invaded by larvae, bugs, flies and tiny crayfish, and hungry birds followed. The land, which had been set aside for industrial use, was declared a nature reserve amongst much controversy. Now herds of deer, long-horned cattle and tiny wild horses also roam the reserve. The nature reserve can only be visited with a forest guide (*info centre © (0320) 254 585*). Birdwatchers can also use the 5km signposted walking route called the 'Driehoek', which goes along the outskirts of the reserve.

Elburg

Back on the mainland, about 20km from Zwolle (*see* p.230) is the town of **Elburg**. Once Elburg lay on the coast and was heavily fortified against invaders. Parts of the fortification, such as the castle-keep-like **Vischpoort** (built 1592) remain, but nowadays these attract rather than repel invaders, and Elburg throngs with day-trippers. The Vischpoort now functions as a **museum** (Vischpoortstraat; *open mid-June–Aug Mon*

2–4.30, Tues–Fri 10am–noon and 1–4.30pm; adm ƒ3 in combination with Gemeente-museum and Kazematten) with a fairly missable collection of weaponry, though the ticket also allows you a look at the cramped **Kazematten** (artillery casemates)—the underground compartments where the guns were mounted, which form part of the fortifications—and the more interesting **Gemeentemuseum** (Municipal Museum, Jufferenstraat 6; *open Tues–Fri 10–5, but closed lunchtimes Sept–May; April–Sept also open Mon 2–5*), housed in a 15th-century former monastery just along the street. Here you'll find a mildly interesting collection of navigational instruments and other seafarer's bric-a-brac, as well as a few instruments of public shame, such as the red-painted wooden balls that 'sinful' women were made to wear around their necks in medieval times. Across the way is the 14th-century **St Nicolaaskerk**, whose 38m-high **tower** (*open daily July and Aug*), gives you a good view of what most people come to admire—the chessboard layout of the city, a great innovation when it was done back in 1392 by one Arent toe Boecop, who moved the entire town inland as a precaution against flooding. Ten minutes' walk northwest of the Vischpoort is Elburg's other main attraction, **De Vier Jaargetijden Tuinen** (Four Seasons' Gardens, Industriestraat 15; *open April–Oct Mon–Fri 9.30–4.30; June–Aug also Sat 10–4.30, guided tours only; adm free*), the vast homeopathic gardens established by Alfred Vogel. Homeopathic remedies have long been popular in Holland, and alternative treatments are covered by ordinary health insurance. Dr Vogel is a household name in this part of the world, and folk flock to the gardens where his herbs are grown—though for non-Dutch speakers it might all be a bit tedious.

Spakenburg ℰ (033–)   ***Eating Out***

Smulhuus, Havenstraat 12, ℰ 298 5274 (*cheap*). A cheery, child-friendly pancake house, with mum-and-dad-sized pancakes. Try the delicious *Boerenpannenkoek* (farmer's pancake), which comes with bacon, ham, mushrooms, cheese, raisins, pineapple and a curry sauce!

Marco's, Hoekstraat 10, ℰ 298 3249 (*moderate*). Upmarket but cosy fish restaurant, popular with local businessfolk at lunchtime. Smoked eel specialities, but also meat and game in season.

Hanseatic Towns

In the Middle Ages the river IJssel (*pronounced Ay-sill*), which connected the Zuiderzee to the Rhine (and hence the rich towns of the Baltic to western Europe's inland waterways) became a busy trade route. Towns along the river prospered, and many joined the Hanseatic League—a powerful cartel of cities that monopolized Baltic trade. But late in the 16th century the focus of Dutch trade moved westwards, as Amsterdam and other cities that hadn't bothered with the Hanseatic League's restrictive rules blossomed, and trade with the East Indies grew more important. Around the same time, the mouth of the IJssel began to silt up. Growth in the Hansa cities along the river came to a halt, and today many seem tiny by modern standards, yet they retain the architectural trappings of past grandeur.

Kampen: Take the train from Amsterdam Centraal Station to Zwolle then change for Kampen. The journey takes 90mins.

Zwolle: Trains go directly from Amsterdam Centraal Station to Zwolle once every hour. The journey takes 70mins.

Deventer: Take the train to Amersfoort and change for Deventer. Trains to Amersfoort leave hourly from Amsterdam Centraal Station, and trains to Deventer from Amesfoort go twice an hour. The journey takes 95mins including the transfer.

Zutphen: Take the train to Apeldoorn from Amsterdam Centraal Station and then change for Zutphen. The journey takes 80mins.

Tourist Information

Kampen: VVV, Botermarkt 5, ✆ (038) 331 3500; open Mon–Fri 9–5.30 and Sat 9–4.

Zwolle: VVV, Grote Kerkplein 14, ✆ (0900) 112 2375; open Mon 10–5.30, Tues–Fri 9–5.30 and Sat 9–4.

Deventer: VVV, Keiserstraat 22, ✆ (0570) 613 100; open Mon–Fri 9.30–6 and Sat 9.30–5; May–Nov also open Thurs evenings till 9.

Zutphen: VVV, Stationsplein 39, ✆ (0900) 2692 888; open Mon 10–4.30, Tues–Fri 9–4.30 and Sat 10–4.

Festivals and When to Go

The good folk of Kampen turn out every Thursday from mid-July to mid-August for street parties, fairs, feasting and evening concerts during the **Kamper Ui-t-dagen**. On the first Sunday in August, Deventer hosts the 'Biggest **Book Market** in Europe', stretching for three kilometres along the IJssel; and the city holds a **medieval fair** on Ascension Day.

Kampen

Kampen, at the mouth of the IJssel some 90km northeast of Amsterdam, joined the Hanseatic League late, in 1451, but was soon the foremost trading town in the northern Netherlands. By 1495 Kampen was so rich and powerful that Emperor Maximilian I granted it Free City status. The city went into decline along with other Hansa towns in the 16th and 17th centuries, but revived as a centre of cigar manufacture in the 1820s. Today, Kampen's main claim to fame is its Theological University, a source of sober Protestant ministers rather than partying students.

Oudestraat has been Kampen's main thoroughfare for centuries. Halfway along, the **Oude Raadhuis** (Oudestraat 133; *open Mon–Thurs 10–4; April–Sept also Sat 2–5; adm free*) with its spindly Gothic gable and onion-shaped tower looks the perfect palace for Rapunzel. Most of the building you see today dates from 1543, when the original 14th-century structure burned down and was rebuilt. You're allowed a peek into the council chamber, which is preserved almost in its original state, and can also see an exceedingly fussily carved 16th-century fireplace. Kampen can boast two city halls. The solid **Nieuwe Raadhuis** (Oudestraat 133; *open Mon–Thurs 10–4; April–Sept also Sat 2–5; adm free*), just behind its predecessor, grew up in fits and starts from the end of the 16th century until the 1950s. (Kampen is the sort of town where 'New' means anything after 1600.)

Capnisophiles should head down Botermarkt, behind the Nieuwe Raadhuis, to the **Kamper Tabakmuseum** (Kampen Tobacco Museum, Botermarkt 3; *open April–Dec Thurs–Sat 11–5; adm*) where they can gen up on the city's association with the wicked weed, and buy first-class cigars. Across the way from the Oude Raadhuis, you can climb the impressive **Nieuwe Toren** (Oudestraat 146; *open May–Sept Wed and Sat 2–5; July–Aug also Fri 2–5; adm*), built in the 17th century by renowned Amsterdam architect Philips Vingboons (*see* p.62), for a view across the whole town. A little farther along Oudestraat is the **Gotische Huis** (Gothic House), one of the finest merchant mansions from the Hanseatic heyday. Nowadays it houses the **Stedelijk Museum** (*open Tues–Sat 11–5; June–Sept also Sun 1–5; adm*), where you can view fine silver, old paintings, and even mint your own Kampen coins using the original mould.

Once, Kampen had 21 **city gates**. Today only three remain—one beside the river and two across town on Ebbingestraat. The most impressive is the **Koornmarktpoort** on the IJsselkade, described by English man of letters Sacheverell Sitwell as 'recalling the great gateway of the old Seraglio at Istanbul… It is the gateway, but without the janissaries, and with stalls of melons and cheeses instead of piles of heads.'

Zwolle

Just 10km from Kampen, Zwolle—larger and more industrialized than its neighbour—is a rail junction and capital of the surrounding province of Overijssel. Most famous past resident is the 15th-century monk and theologian **Thomas à Kempis**, who set down his *Imitation of Christ*—claimed to be the most influential devotional work ever written—while living at a local monastery. Though he worked mainly in nearby Deventer, the Golden Age painter **Gerard ter Borch** (1619–81; *see* p.53) is buried here, in the Grotekerk.

Zwolle, writes one Henri Havard, a Frenchman passing through in 1878, 'possesses large streets and pretty squares, which give it—pardon the expression—a very saucy look'. The pretty squares are still there, but the large streets are now lined with high-street stores, and the saucy look has matured into prim self-satisfaction. But the traces of old Zwolle that remain prevent it from subsiding into middle-sized-town mediocrity. Part of the old city fortifications are still intact, including stretches of moat and the **Sassenpoort**, a castle-like city gate south of the centre, built in 1409.

The town is worth a stopover to visit such sights as the Gothic **Grote- of St Michaëlskerk** (Great or St Michael's Church), with its 18th-century organ made by the renowned Schnitger brothers from Hamburg, and the old **patrician houses** around Grote Kerkplein. Clinging to the side of the church is the delicate Renaissance **Hoofdwacht** (Main Guardhouse)—appropriately enough still the offices of the Stadtswacht (City Watch—an auxiliary police force)—and across the square is a rugged *Adam* by the sculptor Rodin. The **Stedelijk Museum Zwolle** (Melkmarkt 41; *open Tues–Sat 10–5, Sun 1–5; adm*), just off Grote Kerkplein, has some beautiful period rooms, including a fully equipped 18th-century kitchen. Contemporary art goes on show in a flash modern wing. There are more fine period interiors just around the corner in **Het Vrouwenhuis** (Voorstraat 46, © (038) 422 4823; *open Mon–Sat by appointment; adm*), a 17th-century patrician mansion that was donated as a rest home for elderly women in 1742. It still has a peaceful atmosphere, and an interesting collection of paintings by woman artists. At the other end of the calm/disruption scale is the **Harley-Davidson and Indian Museum** (Oude Almeloseweg 2–4; bus 166; *open Mon–Sat 9–5; adm*), a bikers' paradise with around 100 classic machines, dating from 1912. On the southern outskirts of town, the **Ecodrome** (Willemsvaart 19; *open Wed, Sat, Sun 10–5; adm exp*), is an exciting nature theme park, complete with mammothgrave, tropical glasshouse, lots of fun and games, and swan-shaped water bicycles.

Deventer

Deventer, some 30km further south of Zwolle, is perhaps the least alluring of all the Hansa towns along the IJssel. It was founded some time in the 8th century by the Anglo Saxon missionary Liafwin, a.k.a. Lebuinus, (who named it after his home town of Daventry), and followed up its medieval glory days with a period of industrial expansion in the 19th century. Today many of the wide streets in the city centre have been pedestrianized, lined with high-street shops, and given over to headlong consumerism. But there are moments of respite. Head to the **Bergkwartier** around the Bergkerk ('mountain quarter/church'—though that's 'ever so slightly raised mound' in anyone else's language) on the eastern edge of the old centre, where the cobbled streets and crooked gables effectively evoke the middle ages. On the vast open square named **Brink**, long the commercial heart of town, is the solid, four-square **Waag** (Weighing House, built 1528). It once doubled as the City Watch guardhouse, but is now the **Historisch Museum** (Brink 56; *open Tues–Sat 10–5, Sun 1–5; adm f5; an additional guilder will give you access to the Toy and Tin Museum too*), with interesting displays on medieval and prehistoric Deventer, and an intriguing collection of antique bicycles (Holland's oldest among them).

Just behind the Waag, you'll find the **Speelgoed en Blikmuseum** (Toy and Tin Museum, Brink 47; *open Tues–Sat 10–5, Sun 1–5; adm f5, or in combination with a ticket from the Historisch Museum, f1*), full of doll's houses, kaleidoscopes, electric trains and other favourites. There's a pinball machine, and lots of buttons to push. The 'Tin' section displays a variety of containers, from 19th-century sweet tins to Coca-Cola cans. Just to the west of Brink, the Grote Kerkhof is taken up almost entirely by the **Grote Kerk**, parts of which date back to 1046, though the bare-brick interior is mainly of a later, Gothic style. The tower contains the oldest carillon in the Netherlands—47 bells made in 1647 by the Hemony brothers, who were renowned throughout the world.

Zutphen

The prettiest of the four towns, Zutphen, about 20km beyond Deventer, bustles with cheery burghers and preserves much of its medieval atmosphere. Attractive alleys lure you in to quiet squares and courtyards, or stop suddenly up against medieval walls or old city gates.

After a look at the attractive gables of the 15th-century **Stadhuis** on the main square, pop in to the neighbouring **Henriette Polak Museum** (Zaadmarkt 88; *open Tues–Fri 11–5, Sat–Sun 1.30–5; adm*). Housed in a former 16th-century inn, it shows choice works from its well-selected collection of post-war Dutch art. Up a narrow staircase, hidden in the attic, is a Roman Catholic *schuilkerk* (secret church, *see* p.89). In a former Dominican monastery around the corner, the **Stedelijk Museum** (Rozengracht 3; *open Tues–Fri 11–5, Sat–Sun 1.30–5; adm*) contains a mildly interesting stash of art, archaeological exhibits and other bits and pieces relating to Zutphen's history. But the gem of all Zutphen's attractions is the **St Walburgskerk** (St Walburgis Church) with its library. The church was begun in the 12th century, when Romanesque was still the vogue style, and was finished off in 16th-century Gothic. The church **Librije** (Kerkhof 3, *Ⓒ* (0575) 514178; *best to call beforehand as church sometimes closed for services; tours ƒ5*) was built in 1561. Until fairly recently, you could wander in and leaf through the tomes at will. But now that Zutphen's best-kept secret is out, and visitor numbers are rising, you need to wait for a guide to show you round. Only a handful of people are let in at a time, and the reading room (which is all you get to see) with its heavy volumes chained to the desks has hardly changed since it was built, and is dreamily evocative of monkish learning. You'll get to see some of the 750 ancient books, beautiful manuscripts and incunabula that are in the library's possession.

Where to Stay

Kampen *Ⓒ* (038–)

    De Stadsherberg, IJsselkade 48, 8261 AE, *Ⓒ* 331 2645, *✉* 332 7814 (*inexpensive*). Small hotel in historic building overlooking the IJssel. Rooms are large, though simply fitted out in a modern style.

Zwolle *Ⓒ* (038–)

    Hotel Wientjes, Stationsweg 7, 8011 CZ, *Ⓒ* 425 4254, *✉* 425 4260 (*moderate*). Old-style 'Grand Hotel', but on a petite scale. Neoclassical architecture fuses with smart modern décor, and every comfort is at hand. Just three minutes' walk from the station.

    Hotel Fidder, Koningin Wilhelminastraat 6, 8019 AM, *Ⓒ* 421 8395, *✉* 423 0298 (*moderate*). Three converted *Jugendstil* villas with gloriously camp

'Dutch castle meets 19th-century bordello' décor—canopied beds, lots of elaborate wood-carving, and heavily shaded lamps. The owners are charming and helpful, and there's an excellent breakfast buffet. About 15mins' walk from the centre.

City Hotel, Rode Torenplein 10, 8011 MJ, ✆ 421 8182, 📠 422 0829 (*inexpensive*). Only hotel within the city moat. Simple, but perfectly adequate establishment, with views over the IJssel and back on to the marketplace.

Deventer ✆ (0570–)

Gilde Hotel, Nieuwstraat 41, 7411 LG, ✆ 641 846, 📠 641 819 (*inexpensive*). Beautiful Gothic building in the heart of the Old Town. Inside there's an extraordinary carved staircase and many period features, though the rooms are modern and modestly done up.

Zutphen ✆ (0575–)

Best Western Zutphen Museum Hotel, De Stoven 37, 7206 AZ, ✆ 525 555, 📠 529 676 (*inexpensive*). Housed in a 17th-century mansion in the heart of the city. Inside, antiques, modern design and contemporary art live in happy harmony.

Berkhotel, Marspoortstraat 19, 7201 JA, ✆ 511 135, 📠 541 950 (*inexpensive*). Modest hotel beside a stream, yet just a few minutes' walk to the centre. Rooms in English country style add to the illusion of being far from town.

Eating Out

Kampen ✆ (038–)

Restaurant de IJssel, IJsselkade 59, ✆ 332 1001 (*moderate*). Large restaurant with 1930s grand-café air, looking out on a row of old sailing boats moored in the IJssel. Good for smoked eel and other Dutch cuisine.

Zwolle ✆ (038–)

De Librije, Broerenkerkplein 13, ✆ 421 2083 (*expensive*). Housed in the former library of a medieval monastery, and voted by influential Dutch foodie magazine *Lekker* to be the best restaurant in the country. The atmosphere is relaxed and friendly, as you savour such morsels as river bass with a 'foam' of smoked garlic, coriander pesto and sweet tomato compôte.

Poppe, Luttekestraat 66, ✆ 421 3050 (*moderate*). Busy restaurant with a lively bistro atmosphere, and good, tasty dishes such as pheasant served in two courses: thighs and leg roasted with jus, and then the breast with morels.

Grand Café Het Wijnhuis, Grote Kerkplein 7, ✆ 421 7495 (*moderate–cheap*). Spacious, softly lit café and restaurant that is good for the basics: soup, steaks, spare ribs, chips and salad.

Deventer ✆ (0570–)

Bussink's Koekwinkel, Brink 84, ✆ 614 246 (*cheap*). Home of the local speciality, Deventer Koek—a spicy gingerbread. You go in through the old-fashioned shop to a cosy tea room with a log fire...and plates of the home-bake.

't Arsenaal, Nieuwe Markt 33, ✆ 616 495 (*moderate*). Intimate, unpretentious little place where the food is good and wholesome, with a traditional Dutch leaning.

Zutphen ✆ (0575–)

De Pelikaan, Pelikaanstraat 6, ✆ 512 024 (*cheap*). Combined shop and tea room that has been providing tea and appropriate nibbles to genteel Zutpheners since the 1880s.

De Kloostertuin, Marspoortstraat 19, ✆ 511 135 (*moderate*). All the classic smart trappings—palm trees, candlelight, live piano music—and yet one of the few vegetarian restaurants around. Imaginative cuisine with an Asian touch.

Around the Green Heart

Hélène Müller loved art. Her husband, Anton Kröller, loved nature. She was heiress to a blast-furnace industry; he married the boss's daughter. Together they developed the family firm into a prosperous multinational and used their fortune to realize a dream. Between 1909 and 1914 Anton bought up tracts of wild land near Arnhem. Hélène built up a superb and inspired collection of late 19th- and early 20th-century art. They restocked the land with game, planted copses, built a lodge to live in and a museum for the paintings.

Today the **Kröller-Müller Museum**, set in the vast and varied landscape of **De Hoge Veluwe** national park, is one of the most delightful places to visit in the Netherlands. The estate now covers 5,500 hectares (13,000 acres) of land, the art collection is still growing and there really is something for everyone. You can picnic in forests or lie about on dunes, gallop through the fens on horseback or cycle sedately along leafy lanes. You can bird-watch, look for wild boar or nestle in animal hides waiting for red deer. The airy, intimate museum is a pleasure to walk around, and the collection is one of the best in the country. The sculpture park could detain you for hours and the lodge is unstuffy and well preserved. There are all the cafés, restaurants and children's playgrounds you could wish for, without the horrid ambience of a theme park or tourist trap.

On the outskirts of the park is Paleis Het Loo, a royal residence for three centuries, now open to public view. The villages around the park are good bases for longer stays and quick bites. **Bronkhorst**, just east of the park's borders, is especially worth a visit. It is known as the smallest town in the Netherlands, with just over 160 inhabitants—a pretty place with cobbled streets, an old inn, a church, a handful of farm houses and, curiously, the **Dickens Museum** (Onderstraat 2; *open April–Oct daily 10–5 and Nov–Easter Sat and Sun from 11–5; adm free*) which comprises a roomful of Charles Dickens curiosa.

Of the larger towns around the Green Heart, Apeldoorn and Arnhem are notable primarily as gateways to De Hoge Veluwe and surrounding attractions, though Amersfoort certainly merits a few hours' stopover.

Getting There and Around

The easiest way to get to and about **De Hoge Veluwe** and the surrounding villages is **by car**. You can drive about in the park, and abandon the car where you wish. Take the A1 to Apeldoorn or the A2 and A12 to Arnhem. There are gates to the park at the villages of Otterlo, Schaarsbergen and Hoenderloo. The journey takes about 1½ hours.

The nearest **railway stations** are at Arnhem and Apeldoorn. The journey from Amsterdam to **Arnhem** takes around 1½ hours and costs ƒ43 return. Trains leave twice an hour. Take bus 107 from Arnhem station for the park. There are about two trains an hour from Amsterdam to **Apeldoorn**. Journey time is one hour and tickets cost ƒ40 return. Bus 110 takes you in to the park, and bus 126 or 104 runs direct from Apeldoorn station to **Paleis Het Loo**.

Once in De Hoge Veluwe park you can get about on the (free) white **bicycles** (*see* next page).

Getting to surrounding villages by public transport is trickier. **Buses** 102 and 104 run from Appeldoorn to the stop 'De Echoput' near **Hoog Soeren** every half-hour, but then it's a half-hour's walk into the village. **Bronkhorst** is best reached by bus 52 from Zutphen, but again it's a 20min walk from the bus stop into the village.

Tourist Information

De Hoge Veluwe: Information is available from the Visitors' Centre (Hoenderloo Gate), ✆ (0318) 59162; open daily Nov–March 9–5.30; April 8–8, May–Aug 8–10, or VVV tourist offices in the area.

Apeldoorn: VVV, Stationstraat 72, ✆ (0900) 168 1636; open Mon–Fri 9–5.30 and Sat 9–4.

Arnhem: VVV, Stationsplein 45, ✆ (0900) 202 4075; open Mon–Fri 10–5.30 and Sat 10–4.

De Hoge Veluwe National Park

Open daily Nov–March 9–5.30, April 8–8, May–Aug 8am–10pm; adm ƒ14 per adult, ƒ7 per child, ƒ8 per car—includes admission to museum and sculpture park. From May to Sept no cars are allowed in parts of the park.

De Hoge Veluwe national park is a curious amalgam of drifting sand dunes, watery fens, thick cultivated forests and open heathland. Mrs Kröller-Müller loved autumn colours—so you'll find forests of oak, birch, beech and rowan trees as well as the older plantations of pine and junipers. In the summer there are gloriously coloured thickets of rhododendrons and purple heather covers the heath in August and September. Anton Kröller filled the park with magnificently antlered red deer, moufflons (a curly horned wild sheep from Sardinia), wild boar, roe deer and even kangaroos. All, except the poor roos, survive in multitudes and have such violent fun in the rutting season (*Sept–Oct*) that you're confined to your car in some parts of the park.

There are marked walks throughout the area, though you don't have to keep to the paths. The Visitors' Centre can put you in touch with a local stables if you'd like to hire a horse, or you can pick up a bicycle (*free, no deposit necessary*) from the shelter in the central square. The **Museonder** (*open daily 10–5; adm incl in park entrance*) is an intriguing underground museum, with exhibits on life below the earth's surface including the living roots of a giant tree.

Kröller-Müller Museum and Sculpture Park

Museum open April–Oct, Tues–Sun 10–5; Nov–Mar Tues–Sun 1–5; sculpture park open April–Nov Tues–Sun 10–4.30, Sun 11–4.30.

The Kröller-Müller Museum and Sculpture Park are now state-owned. A collection of exceptional quality is growing around the core of Hélène Kröller-Müller's bequest. It's a far more pleasant place to see **Van Goghs** than the crowded museum in Amsterdam— and Mrs Kröller-Müller had nearly 300 of the painter's works: a version of *The Potato Eaters*, fine self-portraits and landscapes, and some of his best drawings. You'll find good examples of Braque, Picasso and the rather neglected Cubist, Fernand Léger, colourful stippled Pointillist paintings by Seurat, and a touching study of an ageing clown by Renoir—in fact most major movements and artists of the last hundred years are represented. Before you leave have a look for Dutch artist Jan Toorop's eerie fairytale drawings and a dreamy pink and green screen by the French Symbolist painter, Odilon Redon.

Out in the **Sculpture Park** you'll find pieces not only by old familiars like Rodin, Henry Moore and Barbara Hepworth, but also exciting work by contemporary artists. The Park reflects Hélène Kröller-Müller's vision of the way art, nature and architecture can interrelate. The long, low, stone and glass museum blends perfectly into the surrounding landscape. In the pond outside, Marta Pan's enormous, curvaceous, abstract white *Swan* is gently blown about by the wind. In a little hollow, over a hill, rusty iron sheets seem to grow up from the soil. Boulders hang suspended in rope hammocks between the trees; giant, seed-shaped balls of clay, slate igloos and odd tent-like structures are scattered about open grass patches. A frail needle of aluminium pipes and steel wire towers 27m (92ft) into the sky, higher than most of the trees. Anyone under the age of 12 makes a beeline for Jean Dubuffet's *Jardin d'Email* (1972–3). From the outside it's a tall white wall, but once you climb the narrow stairs you're in a big, bumpy white landscape cut up by irregular black lines. Bemused adults sit around the edges, while children tear about, trip over the mounds and bang their heads. (*At present being restored; should be finished in the course of 2000*.)

Jachthuis St Hubertus

Open April–Oct, guided tours every half-hour 10.30–12.30 and 2–4.30; Dec–March 2–3; closed Jan.

Before leaving De Hoge Veluwe, pay a quick visit to the **Jachthuis St Hubertus** (St Hubert Hunting Lodge). The Kröller-Müller's family home and its artificial lake were built in 1914 by H. P. Berlage, the father of modern Dutch architecture (*see* p.63). It's a compact brick building with an ugly, incongruous tower. Inside, however, the house has a cosy 'lived-in' atmosphere—and some superb Art Deco furniture. Coloured bricks and brightly glazed tiles abound, and the motifs of hunting, of the story of St Hubertus (the patron saint of hunters), and of the sun, run throughout the interior design. Monstrous carp swim about in the lake and devour anything you drop in with a nightmarish 'plop'.

Paleis Het Loo

Open Tues–Sun 10–5; adm.

Adjoining the national park is the **Koninklijke Domeinen** (Royal Estate) and the magnificent Baroque **Paleis Het Loo** (Het Loo Palace). Built in 1685 as a hunting lodge for *stadhouder* William III (of 'William and Mary' fame), the palace was used as a royal residence until 1962. Nowadays it is open to the public. You wander through a succession of lavishly decorated state rooms and boudoirs. Each is done up using furniture that reflects the taste of one the of royal occupants, in sequence from the 17th century to the 1930s. But most splendid of all are the **gardens**, laid out again in the 1980s following the 17th-century plans by Daniël Marot, who also originally designed the palace interior. View the exquisite formal layout from the roof of the palace, then descend to stroll among rose bushes, brush against fragrant herbs and wander through the gazebo.

Apeldoorn and Arnhem

Apeldoorn, some 80km east of Amsterdam on the A1, grew from a nondescript farming village into a well-to-do town in 1684, when hangers-on arrived in the wake of William III, after he built the Paleis Het Loo. But nondescriptness soon crept up on it again. Today it serves mainly as a gateway to the surrounding attractions and, as with most gateways, the best thing to do is to pass through.

In addition to being the springboard for De Hoge Veluwe park and the palace, Apeldoorn is also the most convenient town for **Apenheul** (J. C. Wilslaan 31; *open April–Oct daily 9.30–5; June–Aug 9.30–6; adm exp*) an animal park where more than 30 varieties of ape and monkeys run free—and sometimes make free too, by sneaking up and nicking things from visitors' bags.

About 25km south of Apeldoorn along the A50, **Arnhem**, on the banks of the Lower Rhine, is best known for being the location of the 'bridge too far'. In September 1944, in a plan code-named **Operation Market Garden**, the Allies attempted to cut off

German forces entrenched in the eastern Netherlands by parachuting troops behind enemy lines, in order to seize bridges over the Rhine and surrounding rivers. It was the largest airborne operation of the Second World War. Two American landings near the towns of Veghel and Nijmegen proved relatively successful, but the 1st British Airborne Division, who parachuted into fields around the village of Oosterbeek, just outside Arnhem, ran into problems. Unbeknown to them, the entire 2nd SS Panzer Division was in the area. The British, together with Polish reinforcements, held out for an heroic eight days but were forced to withdraw, saving just over 2,100 of an original force of 10,000.

The **Airborne Cemetery** (*bus 1 from Arnhem Centraal Station to Oosterbeek leaves every 10mins and then it's a 10min walk*) is a secluded and sobering memorial to the event. The nearby **Airborne Museum** (Utrechtsweg 232; *open Mon–Sat 11–5, Sun 12–5; adm*) housed in the former British Airborne Division HQ, has an excellent audio-visual presentation about the battle, as well as poignant personal memorabilia.

Arnhem itself was devastated during the war, and though today it is quite a lively town, it isn't especially attractive. Old warehouses around the **Korenmarkt** in the city centre have been converted into restaurants and cafés giving the area some animation. The looming **Eusebiuskerk** (St Eusebius Church) to the south of the Korenmarkt, built in 1560 and almost entirely destroyed during the war, has now been massively restored. The **Museum voor Moderne Kunst** (Utrechtseweg 87; *open Tues–Fri 10–5, Sat and Sun 11–5; adm*) is walking distance from Arnhem Centraal Station, just west of the city centre. It stages mainly temporary exhibitions of contemporary Dutch art, but has a good permanent collection of Dutch **Magic Realists** (*see* p.60).

On the northern outskirts of town, on the edge of the Veluwe forest, is the **Nederlands Openluchtmuseum** (Schelmseweg 89; *open April–Nov 10–5; adm exp*) an enormous collection of rural buildings, including farmhouses, barns and more sorts of windmill than you would think possible. Inside some of them you'll encounter demonstrations of traditional baking, brewing and various crafts, as well as an extensive collection of national costume. Next door, the **Burger's Zoo** (Schelmseweg 85; *open summer daily 9–7, winter daily 9–sunset, but some sections close at 5pm; adm exp*) was the first 'zoo without bars' in the Netherlands and contains Europe's first safari park. It has developed into a 45ha zoological extravaganza, with thousands of animals and four completely different environments. You can watch big game animals from viewing platforms, clamber through the jungle in a 1.5ha tropical hall (complete with trilling birds, peeping frogs, bats and orchids), shudder at rattlesnakes and vultures in a recreated desert, and glimpse the underwater world of a coral reef. The effect is breathtaking—and at times utterly convincing.

Two **castles** near Arnhem are very much worth a visit. Solid and imposing, the medieval **Kasteel Doorwerth** (Fonteinallee 2; bus 88 leaves twice hourly from Arnhem Centraal Station; *open April–Nov, Tues–Fri 10–5, Sat and Sun 1–5; adm*) on the banks of the Rhine retains its moat, drawbridge, knights' hall and a few period rooms, and now also houses an ignorable nature museum. Main attraction for most is the restaurant (*see* below). **Kasteel Rosendael** (Rosendael 1; bus 31 leaves twice hourly from Arnhem Centraal Station; *open mid April–Nov, Tues–Sat 10–5; adm*) to the east of Arnhem has a 14th-century keep, 18th-century living quarters, and a splendid park—landscaped in the 19th century and including a **shell gallery**, complete with mini grottoes, mosaics and a small fountain. Highly popular with children are the **Bedriegertjes** ('Little Tricksters'), designed by Daniël Marot (architect of the Paleis Het Loo gardens)—hidden fountains that activate themselves as you pass by, resulting in shrieks, giggles and sometimes drenchings.

Where to Stay

Outside the Park

Herberg de Gouden Leeuw, Bovenstraat 2, 7226 LM Bronkhorst, ✆ (0575) 451 231, ✆ 452 566, *oechies@worldonline.nl* (*moderate–inexpensive*). Charming 17th-century country inn in the Netherlands' smallest village. The oak floors and open hearth of the public lounge are very much in period, though the rooms are simply furnished and more modern.

Hotel Hoog Soeren, Hoog Soeren 15, 7346 AB Hoog Soeren, ✆ (055) 519 1231, ✆ 519 1450 (*inexpensive*). Quiet family hotel set in the trees of a small village on the edge of the Hoge Veluwe, convenient for the park and surrounding sights. The rooms are clean and simple, and there's a good café/restaurant downstairs.

Het Roode Koper, Jonkheer Dr J. C. Sandbergweg 82, 3852 PV Ermelo, ✆ (0577) 407 393, ✆ 407 561 (*moderate*). Unpretentious, family-owned country-house hotel. A romantic 1910 villa, tastefully filled with antiques and equipped with pool, tennis court and a large garden. A gem—and good value for money.

Carnegie's Cottage, Onderlangs 35, 6731 BK Otterlo, ✆ (0318) 591 220, ✆ 592 093 (*cheap; breakfast extra*). A cosy white cottage with just 12 guest rooms, set all on its own up a dirt road in the woods. The management is friendly, the rooms have a comfortable, homey feel, and there's an excellent little restaurant.

Arnhem ✆ (026–)

Hotel Blanc, Coehoorn 4, 6811 LA, ✆ 442 8072, ✆ 443 4749 (*inexpensive*). Tastefully converted turn-of-the-century townhouse, just a few minutes' walk from the station, convenient for De Hoge Veluwe and all the surrounding attractions.

Hotel Molendal, Cronjéstraat 15, 6814 AG, ✆ 442 4858, ✆ 443 6614 (*inexpensive*). *Jugendstil* villa in a suburb of Arnhem, about 500m from the station. The rooms are spacious, and the management friendly.

Pension Parkzicht, Apeldoornsestraat 16, 6828 AB, ✆ 442 0698, 🖨 443 6202 (*cheap*). Small hotel in the centre of town. Rooms are done up in pastel colours and all have private facilities.

Eating Out

Paleis Het Loo and De Hoge Veluwe Park ✆ (0318–)

The Museum Café, Paleis Het Loo, ✆ 591 657 (*cheap*). Light snacks and cakes in the old orangerie, with a terrace that catches the sun.

Koperen Kop, Paleis Het Loo, ✆ 591 289 (*moderate*). Fuller meals in a grander setting.

The Kröller-Müller Museum Café, Kröller-Müller Museum, Hoge Veluwe, ✆ 591 041 (*cheap*). Good salads and a large terrace on the edges of the Sculpture Park.

De Hoge Veluwe is also the perfect place for a **picnic**. You can pick up supplies in Apeldoorn or Arnhem.

Outside the Park

Café-Restaurant Hoog Soeren, Hotel Hoog Soeren, Hoog Soeren 15, just off the N344 west of Apeldoorn, ✆ (055) 519 1231 (*cheap*). In a leafy village convenient for the park and Apenheul. Pleasant Old Dutch-style family restaurant complete with open hearth and hunting trophies, good for a game lunch.

Het Jachthuis, Hoog Soeren 55, ✆ (055) 519 1397 (*expensive*). Slightly stuffy atmosphere, but really excellent cuisine with game specialities in season.

De Gouden Leeuw, Bovenstraat 2, Bronkhorst, just off the N48 to the east of the park, ✆ (0575) 451 231 (*moderate*). Stylish restaurant in a 17th-century inn, where a young chef comes up with good Franco-Dutch cuisine and imaginative salads.

Arnhem ✆ (026–)

Mejuffrouw Janssen, Duizelsteeg 7, ✆ 351 4069 (*cheap*), is a popular *eetcafe* near the Kornmarkt, offering hearty chips-with-everything cooking.

Truffles, Rijnkade 54a, ✆ 443 3666 (*moderate*). Bustling brasserie with a terrace on the Rhine, and tasty dishes which, as the restaurant's name implies, often include the queen of the fungi.

Kasteel Doorwerth, Kasteel Doorwerth, Fonteinallee 4, ✆ 333 3420 (*expensive*). Situated in the former castle coach house, with a giant-sized open fire. Herbs and vegetables come from the castle gardens, game in season from the surrounding forest.

Nijmegen, just 20km south of Arnhem, is one of the oldest cities in the country. It was established as a Roman fort by Drusus in 12 BC, and named *Ulpia Noviomagus*. By AD 777 that name had transformed into *Numaga*, and in the next century the Holy Roman Emperor Charlemagne turned the fortress into a palace. The palace was trashed by Vikings, and rebuilt and named Valkhof by a subsequent emperor, Frederick Barbarossa, around 1155. Valkhof lasted up until the 18th-century French occupation of the Netherlands, when it was demolished as 'a symbol of feudalism' and the stones sold. During the Second World War, Nijmegen's bridges formed part of the objective of Operation Market Garden (*see* above), and the town was devastated by bombardment and shooting.

Getting There

Trains leave from Arnhem for Nijmegen four times an hour. The journey takes under 20 minutes.

The railway station is about a quarter of an hour's walk from the centre (follow Singel to the Keizer Karel roundabout, then head up Bisschop Hamerstraat and Molenstraat). Most buses at the station go to the centre.

Tourist Information

VVV, Keizer Karelplein 2, ✆ (0900) 112 2344; open May–mid-Sept Mon–Fri 9–5.30 and Sat 10–5; mid-Sept–April closes 5pm weekdays.

Much of today's town is new or reconstructed. In a park on the northeastern side of town, you can see scant ruins of the **Valkhof Palace**, plus the remains of a chapel built around 1030, and the still intact, octagonal **St Nicolaaskapel**, which survived because the French mistakenly thought it was part of the original Roman settlement. The edge of the park contains a **belvedere**, once part of the 15th-century city walls and now a restaurant (*see* below). Just south of the Valkhof ruins, on Kelfkensbos, is the brand new **Museum Het Valkhof** (*open Tues–Fri 10–5, Sat and Sun 12–5; adm*), which has garnered its impressive collection from a number of former museums around town. It displays a vast collection of Roman artefacts dug up in the Nijmegen area, as well as medieval and Renaissance pieces relating to city history, and a collection of paintings from the 17th century up to the modern day—with some quite good Pop Art. The Roman collection is so rich and varied that locals have nicknamed it 'the Roman Hema' (after the popular Dutch department-store chain).

On the Grote Markt, the main town square, you can see a much-restored Renaissance **Waag** (Weighhouse) built in the style of Hendrick de Keyser, and across the way the similarly much-renovated **St Stevenskerk**, built between 1250 and 1550 and varying in style from Romanesque to late Gothic. Inside is a richly carved pulpit from 1639 and a fine 18th-century organ.

Just out of town, you can visit the **Afrika Museum** (*open April–Oct Mon–Fri 10–5, Sat and Sun 11–5; Nov–March Tues–Fri 10–5, Sat and Sun 1–5; adm; bus 6 from Nijmegen station to stop Berg en Dal/Rust Wat, then a 20min walk*), which comprises an indoor section full of masks, musical instruments and other artefacts, and a large and interesting outdoor museum with reconstructed villages from various countries across the continent. An even more geographically disorientating experience is to be had at the **Bijbels Openluchtmuseum** (Open-air Bible Museum; bus 5 from Nijmegen station to stop Heilige Land Stichting; *open April–Oct Mon-Sun 9–5.30; adm*)—a 47ha park with reconstructions of villages and streets, wells and inns, Bedouin tents, and completely furnished houses, all to give a picture of life in Biblical times.

Nijmegen ✆ (024–)   **Where to Stay**

There are no really alluring hotels in Nijmegen, but if you need to spend the night try:

Hotel Belvoir Nijmegen, Grad van Roggenstraat 101, 6522 AX, ✆ 323 2344, ✆ 323 9960 (*moderate*). Situated near the Valkhof and other sights, with views over the Waal, and equipped with swimming pool, sauna and bowling alley.

Apollo, Bisschop Hamerstraat 14, 6511 NB, ✆ 322 3594, ✆ 323 3176 (*inexpensive*). Simple pension, convenient for station and sights.

Nijmegen ✆ (024–)   **Eating Out**

De Poortwachter, Belvedere, Voerweg, ✆ 360 0064 (*expensive*). Chic, yet cosy, restaurant in the historic belvedere, with dark wooden wainscoting, peach tablecloths and silver candlesticks. Service is friendly and attentive, and the food excellent—try the tender quail with a sweet raisin sauce, or succulent *coquilles St-Jacques.*

De Fusie, Waalkade 1, ✆ 360 6264 (*moderate*). Busy, lively restaurant with fusion-style cuisine, much influenced by the East.

Nijmegen ✆ (024–)   **Entertainment and Nightlife**

Curiously enough, among aficionados, Nijmegen is famed as the **tango** capital of Europe. Much of this is due to the presence of Eric Jorissen, ace dancer and teacher to the stars. On Friday nights at Eric's cavernous apartment-cum-dance hall you can join in a practice session, or if you're lucky you might tumble on one of the monthly salons. These attract dancers from all over Europe. The atmosphere is something between a private party and a speakeasy. Dancing goes on right through the night, and sometimes all weekend. Some people bring sleeping bags and crash out, then start dancing again when they wake up.

Tango El Corte, Graafseweg 108, ✆ 323 3063. Classes and workshops, salon every first Saturday from 10pm, practice nights every Friday from 11pm.

Forced unexpectedly to spend a night in Amersfoort on his way to St Petersburg in 1816, the Amsterdam merchant Willem de Clerq noted rather grumpily in his travel journal that he had nothing to report, except that the town was 'exceeding quiet, has one big tower without a church, and utterly dead streets'. He must have been in a particularly bad and unreceptive mood, because Amersfoort was—and remains—one of the most alluring towns in the district. The 'tower without a church' is a late-Gothic jewel, the 'dead streets' follow a maze-like pattern laid out in the 13th century, and the double wall of fortifications—Amersfoort was an important fortress town in the Middle Ages—is unique in the Netherlands. Today, Amersfoort has a busy, market-town charm, and its monuments and museums can divert you for at least a day.

Rock and Roll, Dutch-style

For centuries Amersfoort has been tagged with the epithet 'Keistad' (Boulder City). This has nothing to do with the terrain, but applies to an immense lump of rock that was transported from Scandinavia to the Netherlands by a glacier about 150,000 years ago. It ended up on the heaths outside the town. In 1661, local wag and rumbustious squire Everard Meyster bet his friends 3,000 guilders (a huge amount at the time) that he could persuade the gullible Amersfoorters to haul the rock into town. How he did this remains a mystery, but he won his bet. In 1672, overcome with shame at their stupidity (so the story goes), the good burghers buried the boulder, and it was redis-covered only in 1903. Today it stands on a plinth just south of the centre, on the corner of Arnhemseweg and the city ring road.

Getting There

Trains leave from Amsterdam to Amersfoort three times an hour. Journey time is just over half an hour. Trains from Utrecht to Amersfoort run every 12 minutes and take about a quarter of an hour to get there.

Tourist Information

Amersfoort: VVV, Stationsplein 9, ℰ (033) 463 5151 or (0900) 112 2364, open Oct–April Mon 1–5.30, Tues–Fri 9.30–5.30, Sat 10–2, May–Sept Sat 10–4.

Festivals and When to Go

Amersfoort hosts a modest, but generally good, **jazz festival** early in May and a three-day **summer festival** of spectacular street theatre, dance and music in the second week of July (details from the tourist office). Lovers of historical pageantry should try to make it for **De Keistad Feesten** (Boulder City Festivities) in mid-September, when there is a procession commemorating the Kei story, an outdoor market and fair.

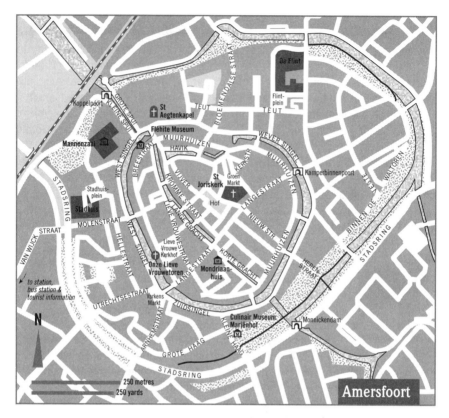

Along the Wall

Amersfoort is best seen working from the outside in, starting with a circuit along the moat of the second **city wall** (built 1380–1450), or its predecessor (built during the 13th and 14th centuries). The earlier ramparts were broken down when the second lot went up, and a solid wall of houses—***muurhuizen***—erected on the foundations. An amble along Muurhuizen (the houses gave their name to the street) takes you past a pleasing hotchpotch of styles—crumbly brick step-gables, poky cottages, haughty towers, solid bourgeois mansions—many dating from the 14th and 15th centuries.

The easiest landmark to head for is the delicate Gothic tower of **Onze Lieve Vrouwetoren** (Tower of Our Lady; *open July and Aug, Tues–Fri 10–5, Sat and Sun 12–5; adm free*), southwest of the centre, just inside the moat. Nearly 100m high and visible from miles around, the tower, with its faintly oriental top, was part of a church that was begun in 1444. But a gunpowder explosion in 1787 destroyed the nave and the tower was left standing alone (this is De Clerq's 'tower without a church'). In summer months you can climb up for a spectacular view over the town; there's a flower market in the space left by the blown-up church on Friday mornings, and a flea market on the first Saturday of the month. Coincidentally, the tower marks the exact geographical centre of the Netherlands.

Madonna in a Bucket

A tale is told of a humble serving maid who, though usually too taxed by her daily labours to do more than sleep the honest sleep of the truly exhausted, awoke one bright day in 1444 aware that she had dreamt clearly and vividly for the first time since she was a child. The dream instructed her to go and draw water from a particular spot in the Amersfoort canal, but beyond this it did not enlighten her. All day she tried to dismiss it from her mind—the canal was far and she was occupied—but her mind kept turning back and back to the dream and, instead of fading as dreams usually did, hourly the imperative grew clearer and stronger.

Eventually, realizing she would have no rest that night unless she obeyed, the serving maid took a bucket and went to the canal, drew the clearest, coldest water she could from its murky depths, and resentfully manhandled the full bucket home with her. She set it in a corner of her tiny room, not knowing what else to do, lay down on her narrow wooden bed and immediately fell fast asleep. No dreams came to her that night, and next morning she woke refreshed, rose, dressed—and behold! In the bucket floated a miniature Madonna.

At first she carried it with her everywhere tucked in a pocket of her apron, but, as time passed, the wooden statue proved to have miraculous properties of healing, causing the most hardened sinners to repent. Very soon this tiny holy symbol was bringing pilgrims flocking to Amersfoort from far and wide. The Madonna is now lost, but Amersfoort has not forgotten its miracle.

Walking clockwise along the moat, you soon come to the **Fléhite Museum** (Westsingel 50; *open Tues–Fri 11–5, Sat and Sun 1–5; adm includes adm to Mannenzaal*), a museum of city history occupying three restored *muurhuizen*. You can leaf through a book containing a saddening list of the 333 people deported from Amersfoort to concentration camps during the Second World War, examine a dangerous-looking 1915 motorbike, and admire a 17th-century cupboard-bed from which, without emerging from the blankets, a warmly ensconced mama would rock her baby to sleep in a cradle alongside by means of a long ribbon. Of the many old paintings on show is one that depicts the gullible Amersfoorters dragging the *kei* into town.

Far more worth a visit is the **Mannenzaal** (*same times as museum; adm inc. in museum ticket*) across the road. Founded in 1378 as a hospice, it soon became an old-age home for poor widows and widowers. Inmates had to hand over their worldly goods in exchange for a lifetime of care. (The inn Het Cromtje, a few doors down the road, was once handed over in payment.) Occasionally one of the old folk got the better of the deal—such as one Rijk van Bennekom in the 18th century who held in there until he was 102. Today, only the men's hall remains, but it is beautifully preserved, with rows of box beds each equipped with a chamber pot, chest, chair and bowl. In the hall outside you can see an example of a pipe and tobacco pouch that were also standard issue. In July and August, 'patients' pretending to be living in the year 1907 occupy the Mannenzaal and talk to you or answer questions.

The Gates

Three gates from the old city walls are still standing. Just around the corner from the Fléhite Museum is the most complete and sumptuous, the **Koppelpoort** (*open July and Aug, Tues–Fri 10–5; adm*), a combined land and water gate built over a canal in 1400. The original hoisting mechanism for the water gate still works, and visitors can walk the treadmills that lower the beam to block the canal. After viewing the Koppelpoort, pop in to micro-brewery **De Drie Ringen** (Kleine Spui 18, ✆ (033) 465 6575; *open Thurs–Sat 1–7; adm free*) for a taste of the spicy local beer.

Ten more minutes' walk along the moat brings you to the **Kamperbinnenpoort**, the only gate left from the first town wall. The **Monnickendam** on the south side of town is another water gate, also built around 1400, spanning a natural stream that was a popular means of access to the town. A few steps away from this is the **Culinair Museum Mariënhof** (Kleine Haag 2, ✆ (033) 463 1025; *open by appointment only, closed Sun and Mon*) a combined restaurant and museum housed in a 15th-century monastery. After viewing old cooking equipment, elegant silverware, ancient recipe books, an 18th-century teahouse and a Dutch East Indiaman galley, you can sit down to a meal in one of two restaurants (*see* below).

The Hof

The Hof (The Court) is the heart of town, and one of the most convivial market squares in the country. Other squares may cower in the shadow of a show-off Stadhuis or soaring church spire, but the Hof is ringed by modest two- and three-storey houses. As a result, the square seems cosy and human-sized, and when there's a market (on Saturdays) the mood is much the same as it must have been for hundreds of years.

On one side, the **St Joriskerk** (St Joris Church; *open end June–mid-Sept, Mon–Sat 2–4.30; adm free*) stands unobtrusively behind a classicist portico that was once a Weighhouse, and is now a public bicycle shed. The church dates back to 1340, though it has been much rebuilt since then. Inside, you can see traces of bright Gothic wall decoration, and a splendid organ raised on stilts above the central aisle. Don't be alarmed by the manic **carillon**: Amersfoort is home to one of two carillonists' schools in the world (the other is in Mechelen in Belgium), and students are sometimes let loose on the local bells.

The Mondriaanhuis

Kortegracht 11, open Tues–Fri 10–5, Sat and Sun 2–5; adm.

Piet Mondriaan (the painter who dropped the second 'a' in his name to make it sound more French, *see* p.59) was born in Amersfoort in 1872. The family home, together with the small primary school where his father was head teacher, has been converted into a museum in his honour. It is one of those rare instances where a museum with minimal resources manages to offer fascinating insights into its subject. In the first room, a display shows step by step how his style developed from naturalistic landscape to the bold, abstract blocks of primary colours for which he is famous (you can take it all in from a bright red sofa in the middle of the room). You also get let in on secrets, such as how the discovery of coloured tape in New York in the 1940s made his life so much easier, as it meant he could experiment with the positioning of his stripes without having to paint and repaint. Upstairs there is a full-scale recreation of Mondriaan's Paris studio—he was distressed by the irregular shape of the room, so with screens and geometric shapes of coloured paint turned it into a 3-D version of one of his paintings, astonishing his visitors. The museum also stages intriguing temporary exhibitions on aspects of Mondriaan's life—such as his love for dancing and jazz.

Amersfoort ✆ *(033–)*   ***Where to Stay***

Logies de Tabaksplant, Coninckstraat 15, 3811 WD, ✆ 472 9797, ✉ 470 0756 (*inexpensive*). Beautiful, early 17th-century town house, centrally situated and run as a largish B&B. Carefully decorated and well-run.

Kroonenburg, (also known as Terminus), Stationstraat 42, 3811 MK, ✆ 422 7050, ✉ 465 2144 (*inexpensive*). Clean, pleasant rooms above a café, near the station.

Huize den Treek, Treekerweg, 3832 RS Den Treek, ✆ 286 1426, ✉ 286 3007 (*inexpensive*). Rambling country house in 10,000 hectares of forest south of the city. The setting is romantic, and public rooms have a faded grandeur, though the bedrooms are fairly simply equipped and decorated.

Amersfoort ✆ *(033–)*   ***Eating Out***

In Den Kleinen Hap, Langestraat 95, ✆ 462 1365 (*cheap*). Warm, wooden-box of a café/restaurant near the Hof. Tuck into pancakes, apple pie, thick *erwetensoep* and other Dutch favourites.

't Madammeke, Lieve Vrouwstraat 6, ✆ 463 0155 (*moderate–cheap*). Lively Flemish eaterie serving up good helpings of hearty south-of-the-border cuisine, with (of course) excellent chips.

De Raadpensionaris, Krommestraat 52, ✆ 462 3006 (*expensive*). Intimate restaurant with a small terrace and excellent cuisine—think grilled red mullet with morels, nestling on fresh green noodles, or poached pear with pear ice cream, raspberry and strawberry coulis and fresh forest fruit. Excellent value for money.

Mariënhof, Kleine Haag 2, ✆ 463 2979 (*expensive*). The main restaurant attached to the Culinair Museum, in a 15th-century former monastery, ranks in the country's top twenty. Service is sparky, the wines superb and the cuisine inspired—Franco-Dutch, Michelin-star quality with lavish attention to detail. In the adjacent, somewhat less expensive **Rôtisserie** you can enjoy meat and fish cooked in the restaurant itself on a *grand feu* (vertical grill).

Utrecht

Anyone who arrives in Utrecht by train might be forgiven for thinking that half the city is a shopping mall. One of the Netherlands' most unfortunate 1960s architectural aberrations, a gigantic shoppers' warren (24ha in extent, with over 200 shops trailing along five kilometres of passageways, if you really want to know), sprawls around the station. It can take a determined ten-minute walk to reach the outside world.

But the ordeal is worth it. 'Amsterdam,' say the locals, 'was built by man, Utrecht by God himself.' The old centre of Utrecht is one of the most alluring in the land: spruce and stately, yet at the same time low-key and romantic—graced with two long canals and a network of side streets; rows of chic and quirky shops, a handful of top-rate museums, and an impressive Gothic spire to navigate by.

Getting There and Around

By train: Utrecht is about half an hour's drive from Amsterdam on the A2. If you arrive by car, bear in mind that the inner part of the city is a pedestrianized zone. There is ample parking beneath the aforementioned shopping mall (follow signs to Hoog Catharijne or Vredenburg).

By train: Trains leave Amsterdam for Utrecht four times an hour, and the journey takes just over 30mins. If you arrive at the railway station, follow the unobtrusive 'Centrum' signs to escape the shopping mall.

On foot: Utrecht's main sights are reachable on foot, though all but the bounciest will be in need of a little sit-down by the time they've made out to the Centraal Museum. For the Railway Museum and Rietveld-Schröder House you will need some sort of mechanization, but buses are prompt and plentiful, and your *strippenkaart* (*see* p.10) is valid here too.

By water: You can hire pedalos from **Canalbike**, on the Oudegracht opposite the Stadhuis.

Tourist Information

VVV, Vredenburg 90 (follow the signs through the shopping mall), ✆ (0900) 414 1414; open Mon–Fri 9–6, Sat 9–5.

When to Go

Utrecht's main festivals are cultural ones. There's a lively festival of **modern dance** and a **jazz festival** in April, and an experimental art festival in May. The city has a strong international reputation for Old Music—the **Festival Oude Muziek**, held in late August/early September, is world-renowned. The **Nederlands Filmfestival**, held in late September, is beginning to rival the Rotterdam Film Festival in reputation. The VVV can help with information on all of these.

History

The Romans were encamped at this strategic crossing over the river Rhine as long ago as AD 48, in a fort unimaginatively named *Trajectum ad Rhenum* (later shortened to 'de Trecht'). Next came the newly Christianized Franks, who set up a church in 620. The ever zealous British missionary monk Willibrordus lost little time in heading south from his usual stamping ground in Friesland to be installed as the first Bishop of Utrecht in 695—it was a position that, over the next few centuries, was to become one of the most powerful in the Low Countries. In the Middle Ages four churches were built at the points of an enormous cross, with the present Dom at the centre, in an attempt to make 'de Trecht' into a northern New Jerusalem. The city thronged with monks and canons, nuns and novices, curates and ecclesiastical hangers-on. Bald pates abounded, and barbers must have earned a pretty penny. But outside this holy city—'Uut-Trecht'—a thriving red-light quarter grew and, curiously, the name of this quarter has stuck.

Meanwhile, the river Rhine shifted naturally many kilometres south, and split to form the Lek and the Waal—leaving Utrecht with a trickle named the Leidse Rijn. As a religious metropolis the city grew ever more prosperous. It was granted its charter as early as 1122. The Bishops of Utrecht, together with their neighbours the Counts of Holland, were deeply involved in the wheeling, dealing and waging of war that led to the eventual unification of the Netherlands, and it was the Union of Utrecht, signed in the city in 1579, that first united the Seven Provinces against Spain (*see* p.40). Legend has it that two years earlier a Boadicean local woman, Katrijn van de Leemput, drove the Spaniards out of Utrecht almost single handed, then returned with a pick and her willing ad-hoc army to demolish their fort. She is commemorated by a fountain outside the Vredenburg Music Centre.

Ironically, it was the Union of Utrecht that marked the beginning of the city's slide from prominence, for the new Union was Protestant, and Utrecht's might had rested on the Roman Catholic church. In 1580 the monasteries were seized and Catholic worship forbidden. In the 17th century, while the rest of the country embarked on its Golden Age, Utrecht declined into genteel provincialism, though there was a brief flash of glory in 1810, when King Louis Bonaparte (*see* p.44) temporarily chose the city for his residence. The 20th century saw great expansion and industrialization, and Utrecht is still the seat of one of the most important bishops in the Netherlands—but it remains, essentially, a charming provincial town, somewhat enlivened by the presence of a university, founded in 1815.

Along the Oudegracht

The Oudegracht—a sunken canal, unique in the Netherlands—has run through the heart of Utrecht for more than 700 years. As the water level dropped over the centuries, the resourceful burghers responded by building a second sidewalk below street level, and digging cellars in the former canal walls. Today, many of these cellars are restaurants or cafés. Most of the tacky high-street stores have been sucked up by

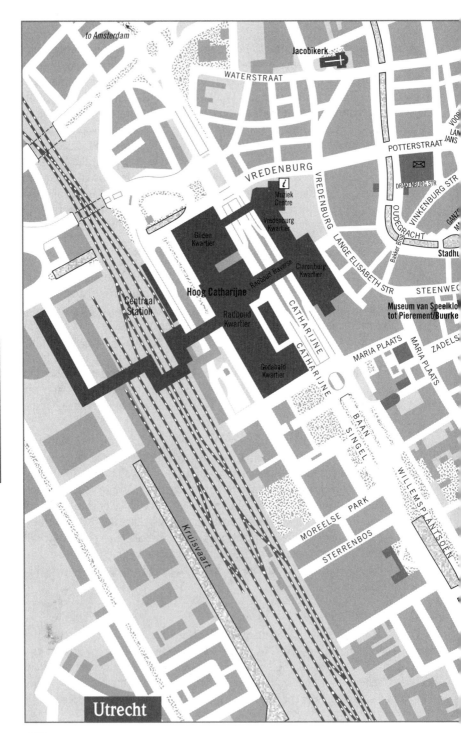

to Amsterdam

Jacobikerk

WATERSTRAAT

POTTERSTRAAT

VOOR
LAN
JANS

VREDENBURG

Muziek
Centre

Vredenburg
Kwartier

VREDENBURG

DRAKENBURG STR

VINKENBURG STR

OUDEGRACHT

GANZ
M

LANGE ELISABETH STR

Bakker Brug

Stadhu

Gilden
Kwartier

Radbout Traverse

Clarenburg
Kwartier

STEENWEC

Centraal
Station

Hoog Catharijne

Radbout
Kwartier

CATHARIJNE

Museum van Speelklo
tot Pierement/Buurke

MARIA PLAATS

MARIA PLAATS

ZADELS

Godabald
Kwartier

CATHARIJNE

BAAN

SINGEL

WILLEMSPLANTSOEN

Kruisvaart

MOREELSE PARK

STERRENBOS

Utrecht

250

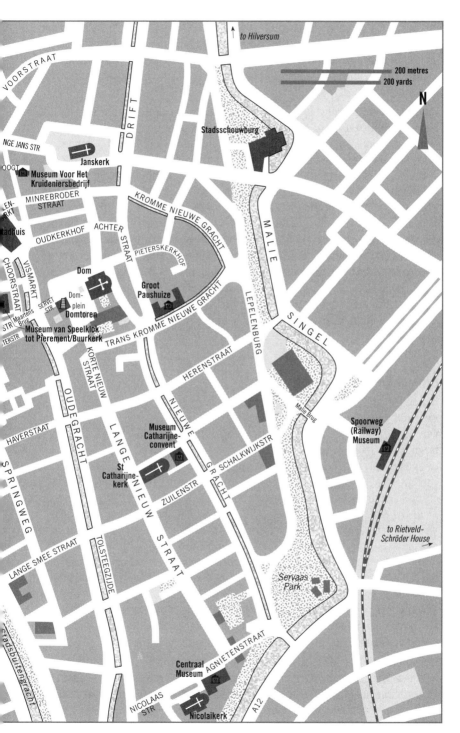

to Hilversum

200 metres
200 yards

N

VOORSTRAAT

DRIFT

Stadsschouwburg

NGE JANS STR

Janskerk

OOGT

Museum Voor Het
Kruideniersbedrijf

MINREBRODER
STRAAT

ELEN-
KT

KROMME NIEUWE GRACHT

tadhuis

OUDKERKHOF

ACHTER

STRAAT

PIETERSKERKHOF

MALIE

CHOORSTRAAT

VISMARKT

Dom

Servet
STR

Dom-
plein

Groot
Paushuize

LEPELENBURG

SINGEL

STR Maartens
Brug

Domtoren

TRANS KROMME NIEUWE GRACHT

Museum van Speelklok
tot Pierement/Buurkerk

TERSTR

KORTE NIEUW

STRAAT

HERENSTRAAT

Malie Brug

HAVERSTAAT

OUDEGRACHT

LANGE

NIEUWE

Museum
Catharijne-
convent

GRACHT

SCHALKWIJKSTR

Spoorweg
(Railway)
Museum

S
P
R
I
N
G
W
E
G

St
Catharijne-
kerk

NIEUW

ZUILENSTR

LANGE SMEE STRAAT

TOLSTEEGZIJDE

STRAAT

to Rietveld-
Schröder House

Servaas
Park

tadsbuitengracht

Centraal
Museum

AGNIETENSTRAAT

NICOLAAS
STR

A12

Nicolaikerk

Utrecht 251

the Hoog Catharijne complex; the shops here along the Oudegracht and in its surrounding squares and alleys sell designer clothes, antiques and knick-knacks, and curiosities from all over the world. Many of the streets are pedestrian-only, and—unlike so many other Dutch cities—care has been taken not to destroy old gables with hideous new shop fronts.

Just east of Oudegracht you can take a step in shopping nostalgia at the **Museum Voor Het Kruideniersbedrijf** (Grocer's Museum, Hoogt 6; *open Tues–Sat 12.30–4.30; adm free*), a reconstructed 1873 grocer's store complete with old-fashioned scales, open barrels of beans and rice, and rows of old tins and cartons. Following Oudegracht south, you pass the rather worse-for-wear neoclassical **Stadhuis**. Down an alley across the way, situated in a medieval church, is one of the delights of Utrecht, the **National Museum van Speelklok tot Pierement** (National Music Box and Barrel Organ Museum; *open Tues–Sat 10–5, Sun 12–5; adm*), a vast collection of automated musical instruments ranging from the 15th to the 20th centuries. You can wander about part of the museum alone, but would be strongly advised to wait for a tour (*also in English, duration 1hr, on the hour, but frequency according to demand at busy times, price incl in adm*), which not only shows you the full collection, but allows you to experience the twangs, tinkles and airy blasts of some of the machines in action— from a furry bunny that wiggles its ears in time to the music, through pianolas and a machine that plays three violins simultaneously, to the full-throated roar of a fairground organ.

Around the Dom

Bishop Hendrik van Vianden laid the first stone of Utrecht's **Dom** (cathedral) in 1254. An earlier cathedral had been razed to the ground, and its replacement was to be in the very latest French Gothic style—including a 112m-high tower that rises in three magnificent stages, and is topped by an octagonal filigreed cone. The tower was completed only in 1382, and building went on until 1517. But in 1674 a hurricane hit Utrecht, completely demolishing the nave. This was never rebuilt, so today only chancel and tower remain, separated by an open space. You can climb the **tower** (*open Mon–Sat 10–5, Sun 12–5, guided tours only, on the hour, last tour 4pm; adm*) for a view that reputedly includes Rotterdam and Amsterdam on a clear day, or pop in to the remaining building (*open May–Sept Mon–Fri 10–5, Sat 10–3.30, Sun 2–4; Oct–April, Mon–Fri 11–4, Sat 10–3.30, Sun 2–4; adm free*) for an idea of how vast and glorious the cathedral must once have been. Behind the chancel is a 15th-century cloister with a formal herb garden (divided into squares for medicinal, kitchen and dyeing plants), which was replanted in the 1960s. Have a look at one of the Gothic arches in the south-western corner of the cloister—a jokey stonemason has carved ropes around the Gothic tracery, apparently holding the delicate stonework together.

Domplein, the square beside the cathedral, has an appealing Parisian air, and just to the east (near the corner of Kromme Nieuwegracht) you can see the **Groot Paushuize**, an elegantly simple red-brick building put up as a residence for the only-ever Dutch pope,

Hadrian VI, in 1517. But Hadrian died less than a year after he had been elevated to the papacy, and never saw his Utrecht home. Today it is used for private functions and houses part of the university.

A short walk south of the Dom brings you to the **Museum Catharijneconvent** (Nieuwegracht 63; *open Tues–Fri 10–5, Sat and Sun 11–5; adm*), housed in a late-medieval convent. The museum offers an overview of Dutch religious art, with beautiful medieval manuscripts, richly embroidered vestments, carved altarpieces, and 16th- and 17th-century paintings by the likes of Rembrandt, Frans Hals and Saenredam. You can see the sobering influence of the Reformation on art (though there's also a painting of a pope that turns upside down to become a portrait of the devil), and the museum is known for excellent temporary exhibitions that draw on its substantial depot.

The Centraal Museum

Agnietenstraat 1; open Tues–Sun 11–5; adm.

Substantially renovated and extended in 1999, the Centraal Museum occupies a number of buildings around a large garden (to which visitors have access). You walk through underpasses and up spiral stairways, travel in glass-box lifts to Gothic chapels and large halls, explore cellars and suddenly discover attics. The collection is vast and varied, the presentation modern and imaginative, and the layout mind-boggling—though it's a pleasure to get lost. In the depths of one part of the building, accompanied by a whiff of creosote, is the skeleton of a wooden boat, dating from around AD 997. A long former stables building contains parallel exhibitions of fashion, interior design and contemporary art, arranged not chronologically, but along a spectrum from sober to extravagant. You begin with such exhibits as minimalist lampshades, geometric abstract paintings, a 1930s tennis frock and a white 1818 housecoat, and work your way to a neo-Gothic cabinet, a dramatic 3-D 'assemblage' on the wall, and an atomic-bomb silhouette overcoat by hot new Dutch designers Viktor and Rolf.

In the main building you can see part of the museum's extraordinary collection of **Golden Age** art—including Jan van Bronkhorst's beautifully pensive *Young Woman* (1655), and famed artists of the Utrecht School (*see* pp.51–2) such as Van Scorel, Bloemaert and Terbrugghen—as well as modern and contemporary Dutch painting. There are some particularly good pieces by Pyke Koch and Charley Toroop (*see* p.60), as well as by present-day artist Marlene Dumas. For a small fee, and after a short wait, you can order up anything from the museum's depot for a private view.

Across the way, an entire wing is devoted to *De Stijl* architect and designer Gerrit Rietveld (*see* pp.59–60), including a reconstruction of his studio and an apartment inte-rior, and lots of original Rietveld furniture.

On the Outskirts

Two more museums lure you further afield. To the east of the centre, just beyond the former city wall, is the **Nederland Spoorwegmuseum** (National Railway Museum, Maliebaan Station; bus 3 from Centraal Station; *open Tues–Fri 10–5, Sat and Sun*

11.30–5; adm). A converted 19th-century train station holds a buffed and shiny collection of over 60 old locomotives, trams and carriages, from the earliest days of steam and horse-drawn trams, to sleek electric trains.

A little farther east is the **Rietveld Schröder House** (Prins Hendriklaan 50, ℗ (030) 236 2310; bus 4 to De Hoogstraat; *open Wed–Sat 11–5, Sun 12–5, guided tours only, booking recommended, tours Wed–Sat 11, 11.30, 12.15, 1.45, 3.30, Sun 12.30, 1, 1.45, 2.45, 3.30; adm*), a highpoint of *De Stijl* architecture, designed by Gerrit Rietveld in 1924 for Mrs Truus Schröder, who lived there until her death in 1985. The house preserves original features, including bold yellow, red and blue colours, lamps and furniture designed by Rietveld, and an upper floor that is almost entirely subdivided by moving screens—a revolutionary concept at the time.

Utrecht ℗ (030–)   **Where to Stay**

Most of Utrecht's hotels are functional, unexciting places aimed at the trade-fair market. But there are a few exceptions.

Malie Hotel, Maliestraat 2, 3581 SL, ℗ 231 6424, ✆ 234 0661, *info@malie hotel.nl* (*moderate*). Converted from a smart 19th-century town house in a quiet residential area of town, reasonably convenient for the centre. The rooms are bright and modern, and the staff charming.

Ouwi, F. C. Donderstraat 12–14, 3572 JH, ℗ 271 6303, ✆ 271 4619 (*inexpensive*). Cared-for family hotel, with simple, clean rooms and a small terrace, a little way from the centre.

Smits Utrecht, Vredenburg 14, 3511 BA, ℗ 233 1232, ✆ 232 8451, *smits@ smits.nl* (*expensive–moderate*). Most pleasant of the standardized hotels, and certainly the best positioned, directly opposite the Vredenburg Music Centre.

There's a privately run B&B service that arranges rooms in family homes around town: Booking Office, Egelantierstraat 25, 3551 GB, ℗ (06) 504 34884, ✆ (030) 2448764, *amitie@xs4all.nl* (*double rooms cheap*).

Utrecht ℗ (030–)   **Eating Out**

Winkel van Sinkel, Oudegracht 158, ℗ 230 3030 (*cheap*). Busy, trendy, cavernous café built as a department store in the 1830s, and serving as a bank for most of the 20th century. The gigantic, cast-iron caryatids propping up the front portico were made in England, and were so heavy that they caused the canal wall beneath them to collapse. Pastas, salads and dishes of the day.

De Soepterrine, Zakkendragerssteeg 40, ℗ 231 7005 (*cheap*). Busy soup-kitchen down an alley near the Vredenburg Music Centre. Mouthwatering home-made soups include not only Dutch favourites, but exotica from Mexico or Japan. There's good bread, and a variety of salads too. An ideal stop for an inexpensive tummy-filler. Soups around *f*8.

Stadskasteel Oudaen, Oudegracht 99, ℗ 231 1864 (*moderate–cheap*). Grand old canalside mansion now converted into a large café with its own brewery. There are hearty meat-chips-and-salad meals downstairs to accompany your beer, and a smarter restaurant upstairs.

Het Grachtenhuys, Nieuwegracht 33, ℗ 231 7494 (*moderate*). Popular restaurant in a gracious old canal house. Good ingredients and careful, unfussy preparation make for an excellent meal. Good vegetarian options.

Sot-l'y-laisse, Zadelstraat 20, ℗ 232 1573 (*expensive*). Tiny, 'you're at a dinner party really' restaurant, with excellent cuisine. There's no menu, you choose your wine and set a limit to the number of courses you want, then just sit back and enjoy what comes—very much in a rich Franco-Dutch culinary tradition. Booking is advisable, as there are only 16 places.

Shopping

The area to head to for designer boutiques, quirky speciality shops, antiques and interiors stores is along the Oudegracht to Vismarkt, the alleys to the west of Vismarkt, and around the Dom.

There's a small **flower market** at the top end of the Oudegracht on Saturdays, and on Fridays the farmers come to town to sell **organic produce** in front of the Vredenburg.

Utrecht ℗ (030–)   ### Entertainment and Nightlife

Utrecht's students strike a lively note at cafés around the centre—during the week more than over weekends. Larger cafés such as **Winkel van Sinkel** and **Oudaen** (*see* above) are gathering spots for all ages. Hottest dance spot at the time of writing is Club Risk, late night at Winkel van Sinkel (latest info on *www.nachtwinkel.nl*).

The **Vredenburg Muziek Centre** (Vredenburgpassage 77, ℗ (030) 231 4544 for box office, ℗ 231 3144 for information) is the venue for most of the important classical music concerts in town.

Around Utrecht

Getting There

Oudewater: Bus 180 or 254 gets you from Utrecht bus station to Oudewater in about 35mins.

Schoonhoven: Bus 195 or 295 gets you from Utrecht to Schoonhoven in about ½hr.

Kasteel de Haar: Bus 126 from Utrecht Central Station plus short walk, or train to Vleuten then bus 127.

Slot Zuylens: Bus 36 from Utrecht Central Station, but doesn't run Sundays.

Oudewater: VVV, Kapellestraat 2, ✆ (0348) 564 636; open Tues–Fri 10–4, Sat 1–3.

Schoonhoven: Stadhuis, ✆ (0182) 385 009; open Tues–Fri 10–4, Sat 1–3.

Oudewater and the Witches' Weighing House

About 20km west of Utrecht, Oudewater is a prosperous little town criss-crossed by small canals and narrow brick-paved streets. Cutesy gabled buildings enclose fashion boutiques, pricey antiques shops and home interiors stores. The main attraction is the **Heksenwaag** (Witches' Weighing House, Leeuweringerstraat 2; *open April–Oct, Tues– Sat 10–5, Sun 12–5; adm*) on the main square. At the height of the witch-hunts that raged through Europe in the 16th century, there were three chief methods of identifying a witch: trial by fire (witches were supposed to burn less easily than innocents), trial by water (witches would float, innocents would sink) and trial by weight—in order to fly about on their broomsticks, witches, it was deduced, had to be extraordinarily light. Scales were set up all over the continent on which women were tested to see if they were suspiciously weightless. Weighmasters were notoriously corrupt and succumbed easily to bribes from jealous husbands, lovers, or anyone else who simply wanted to have a woman put to death. But the weighmasters at Oudewater were renowned for their honesty, and early in the 16th century were granted royal permission to issue certificates stating that 'The accused's weight is in accordance with the natural proportions of the body,' which were valid throughout the Burgundian empire. The certificates were valid in perpetuity, and women flocked to Oudewater for this valuable bit of life insurance. No one was ever condemned. Today, people of both genders can be weighed in the **Heksenwaag**, and are given a reassuring certificate to take home.

Schoonhoven and Silver

Some 10km farther south, **Schoonhoven** was long renowned as a centre for silversmiths, and today is worth a quick stopover for a wander along its old inland harbour and medieval **fortifications**. Don't miss the stumpy **Stadhuis** (built 1452) and only surviving town gate, the **Veepoort** (built 1601). The town is home to the national **Goud- Zilveran Klokkenmuseum** (Gold, Silver and Clock Museum, Kazerneplein 4; *open Tues–Sun 12–5; adm*). In addition to a clutter of gold and silver, and antique smiths' instruments, there is a large collection of timepieces, from the Meccano-like clock from the Jacobskerk in The Hague (dating from 1542) to delicate pocket watches. There are still a handful of silversmiths and jewellers working in Schoonhoven, and it's a good place to hunt for jewellery bargains. The most notable firm is **Rikkaert** (Haven 1–13, ✆ (0182) 383651), which has been bedecking fingers, necks and wrists for 120 years.

Two Castles

Two **castles** near Utrecht are worth a detour—even though one of them is a bit of a sham. **Kasteel de Haar** (near Haarzuilen; *open June–Aug Mon–Fri 11–4, Sat and Sun*

1–4; mid-March–May and Oct–mid-Nov Tues–Sun 1–4; Jan–mid-March and mid-Nov–end Nov Sun 1–4; adm exp), 10km northwest of the city centre, looks the classic fairytale medieval pile but was built in 1892 for the imposingly named Etienne, Baron van Zuylen van Nijevelt van de Haar, by the architect P .J. H. Cuypers, designer of Amsterdam's Centraal Station and Rijksmuseum (*see* p.63). Perhaps taking his cue from his patron's name, Cuypers came up with the biggest castle in the Netherlands. The family is still resident, but you can be taken on a tour of part of the building to view ancestral antiques, old paintings and rare 15th- and 16th-century Flemish tapestries. The magnificent park, which comprises both formal gardens and more wild landscapes, stretches for 100 hectares. The neighbouring village of Haarzuilens had to be moved a few kilometres eastwards to accommodate it.

The elegant **Slot Zuylen** (in Oud-Zuylen; *guided tour only, on the hour, mid-May–mid-Sept Tues–Thurs 11–4 except at noon, Sat 2–4, Sun 1–4; mid-March–mid-May and mid-Sept–mid-Nov Sat 2–4 and Sun 1–4; adm*) was built by a branch of the same family in the 12th century, though today's building dates from 1520 and underwent extensive renovations 200 years later. It was once home to the 18th-century writer and salon enchantress Belle van Zuylen. Inside, you'll find an interesting collection of 17th- and 18th-century furniture and tapestries, though the main attraction for many is the 'Snake Wall' in the grounds—a south-facing wall built with curves that catch every bit of the sun, warming up the bricks and enabling gardeners of yore to grow such exotica as peaches outdoors in dull northern climes.

Where to Stay

Oudewater ✆ (0348–)

> **Hotel Abrona**, Breckerstraat 20, 3421 BL, ✆ 567 466, ✉ 565 725, *www.abrona.nl* (*inexpensive*). Very pleasant small hotel in an historic building near the town centre. Rooms are simple, but tastefully furnished, and there's a garden courtyard out the back.

Schoonhoven ✆ (0182–)

> **Hotel Belvédère**, Lekdijk West 4, 2871 MK, ✆ 325 222, ✉ 325 229, *info@hotelbelvedere.demon.nl* (*inexpensive*). Romantic 1930s-style hotel atop the city fortifications, overlooking the river Lek.

> **Roos**, Voorhaven 21, 2871 CH, ✆ 383 461 (*cheap*). Homey B&B near the centre, with pretty backyard garden. Shared bathrooms only.

Eating Out

Oudewater ✆ (0348–)

> **'t Backertje**, Markt 14, ✆ 565 305 (*cheap*). Busy, friendly little café just next to the Heksenwaag, where you can get a good snack or light lunch.

Schoonhoven 𝄢 (0182–)

Eethuys de Waag, Dam, 𝄢 382 959 (*moderate–cheap*). Dinky 18th-century public weighing house, converted into a restaurant with just six tables, where you can get excellent pancakes and also more adventurous meals, such as a trio of turkey, rabbit and guinea fowl.

Gouda

Gouda (*pronounced with an aspirated guttural G, 'HGowda'*) is not all cheese and ersatz medieval markets. There's a thriving crafts industry, an imaginative historical museum and, in the longest church in the Netherlands, stained glass so beautiful that even the iconoclasts left it alone.

The first-known mention of Gouda was in a deed in 1139, though the area was settled long before that. The city got its charter from Count Floris V in 1272, and by 1400 was the fifth biggest in the land. During the 15th century Gouda prospered on the beer trade, then diversified into making pipes and ceramics—by 1750 about half the population was employed in the pottery trade. It wasn't until the mid-19th century that candlemaking took over as the dominant local industry.

Getting There

Gouda is 29km (18 miles) southwest of Amsterdam. The easiest way to get there is **by train** from Centraal Station. The journey takes about 50mins and it's a 15min walk from Gouda Station to the market square. Trains average two an hour and a day return costs ƒ29.25. The main tourist sights are clustered around the market square and are just a few minutes' walk apart.

Tourist Information

Gouda: VVV, Markt 24, 𝄢 (0182) 513 666; open Mon–Sat 9–5 (also open Sunday afternoons in summer).

Festivals and When to Go

In mid-December Gouda holds a candle festival. All electric lights in the market square are switched off. The Stadhuis windows and surrounding houses are decorated with candles, and an enormous Christmas tree is lit up. It's a breathtaking sight, and well worth a special trip.

Church and Market

An exuberantly Gothic **Stadhuis**, built in 1450 (*open Mon–Fri 9am–noon and 2–4pm, Sat 11–3, 11–4 in the summer*) is plonked right in the middle of the market square. With its pixie-capped spires, bright red shutters and cheerful carillon, it can't be missed. It's one of the most popular places in the country for weddings (in Holland you can plight your troth in any town you like) and couples are churned through every few minutes. Nip in between ceremonies for a look at the carved fireplaces and 17th-

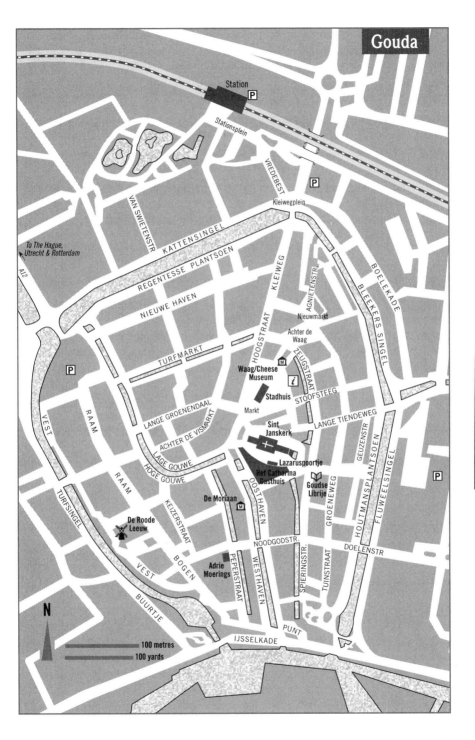

Gouda

Station
P
Stationsplein
Kleiwegplein
VREDEBEST
VAN SWIETENSTR
KATTENSINGEL
To The Hague,
Utrecht & Rotterdam
A12
REGENTESSE PLANTSOEN
NIEUWE HAVEN
KLEIWEG
HOOGSTRAAT
AGNIETENSTR.
BOELEKADE
BLEEKERS SINGEL
Nieuwmarkt
Achter de
Waag
TURFMARKT
ZEUGSTRAAT
Waag/Cheese
Museum
M
i
STOOFSTEEG
LANGE GROENENDAAL
Stadhuis
Markt
LANGE TIENDEWEG
P
VEST
RAAM
ACHTER DE VISMARKT
Sint
Janskerk
GEUZENSTR
HOUTMANSPLANTSOEN
FLUWEELSINGEL
P
LAGE GOUWE
Lazaruspoortje
Het Catharina
Gasthuis
HOGE GOUWE
RAAM
Goudse
Librije
GROENEWEG
KEIZERSTRAAT
De Moriaan
M
OOSTHAVEN
TURFSINGEL
BOGEN
De Roode
Leeuw
NOODGODSTR.
DOELENSTR
VEST
Adrie
Moerings
PEPERSTRAAT
WESTHAVEN
SPIERINGSTR.
TUINSTRAAT
BUURTJE
N
PUNT
IJSSELKADE
100 metres
100 yards

century tapestries. Remember to walk up the left-hand side of the double staircase at the entrance—criminals used to descend the one on the right on their way to the gallows, and it's considered bad luck to use it.

Behind the Stadhuis is the solid, square **Waag** (public weighing house), built in 1668. An enormous gable stone shows cheeses being weighed. Nowadays the Waag is a **Cheese Museum** (*open April–Oct Tues–Sun 1–5, Thurs 10–5; adm*), comprising mainly interactive computer installations that tell you all you ever wanted to know about cheese, and a lot more besides. Downstairs, on one of the original scales, an attendant weighs young visitors. Anyone weighing under 40 Dutch pounds gets in free.

Every Thursday morning during the summer, farmers and porters dress in traditional costume, and everyone goes through the rituals of an old market beside the Waag, mainly for the benefit of tourists. The *real* cheese-trading takes place a few hours earlier, at 9am, and has more of the appearance of a boot sale. A handful of farmers gather around the market square to sell their wares from the backs of cars, slapping hands with customers to seal the deal.

St Janskerk/Grotekerk (St John's Church/the Great Church; *open Mar–Oct Mon–Sat 9–5; Nov–Feb Mon–Sat 10–4; adm*), just off the market square, is the pride of the town. Earlier churches on the site seem to have been singled out by divine wrath; after three successive buildings had been destroyed by fire or lightning, the present cruciform basilica was begun in 1552. Soft soil precluded any towering Gothic spire, so the building spread horizontally and became the longest church in the Netherlands (123m/403ft). The church is famous for its 70 16th-century stained glass windows, the most detailed and richly coloured of which are by the brothers Dirck and Wouter Crabeth. Not only did the glass survive the scourges of the iconoclasts, but the Reformed Church added some of its own. Rather than scenes from lives of the saints, these depicted moments of historic glory—like the Relief of Leiden with its famous portrait of William of Orange. During the Second World War the windows were taken out and stored, and so survive beautifully intact.

Around Het Catharina Gasthuis

On the lane behind St Janskerk (helpfully called Achter de Kerk—'Behind the Church') is the tall red-brick **Lazaruspoortje** (Lazarus Gate) with a relief showing poor, pustule-ridden Lazarus and the rich man who will never make it to the bosom of Abraham (Luke 16:19–31). This 17th-century entrance to a Lepers' Hospice was transferred here in the 1960s to serve as the back entrance to **Het Catharina Gasthuis** (St Catherine's Hospital, now a municipal museum; *open Mon–Sat 10–5, Sun noon–5; adm; ticket also valid for De Moriaan Museum*), an intriguing collection of 14th–17th-century buildings. You can see a reconstructed 19th-century apothecary's shop (very much in demand as a period film set) and a medieval surgeon's room, a torture chamber and a lunatics' cell; there's a frightening similarity between the instruments used in each. The torture chamber sports an ingenious designer execution block. The victim was strapped down spreadeagled, there are holes for the blood to run through and a spike to display the head on afterwards. The museum also has a good collection of paintings from the French Barbizon school and from the Hague School (*see* p.58) and a fine collection of medieval silver (especially the ornate 15th-century *Chalice of Jacoba of Bavaria*). The director stages vigorous and adventurous exhibitions of contemporary art.

Five minutes' walk down the canal from the Catharina Gasthuis, you'll find **De Moriaan** ('The Blackamoor') at Westhaven 29, a 17th-century merchant's house and tobacco shop named after the carving over the door (*open Mon–Fri 10–5, Sat 10–12.30 and 1.30–5, Sun 12–5*). It has a vast collection of pipes, tiles and pottery. The **Goudse Librije**, Gouda Library, Spieringstraat 1, off the square behind the Catharina Gasthuis (*open Mon–Fri 2–4; adm free*) was used as an orphanage from the 17th century up to the 1940s. Now it houses a collection of 16th–19th-century books, some of which you can take down off the shelves and leaf through.

Arts and Crafts

Gouda bustles with craft industry. It's famous for its candles, and claims to produce 85 per cent of Holland's 'Delft' china. At **Het Tin en Keramiek Huis**, Lange Groenendaal 73 (*open Tues–Sat 10–5; adm free*) you can see award-winning designers paint the blue and white Delft patterns on to jugs and plates. Gouda also has its own ceramic style, which use richer colours, is far more beautiful and considerably more expensive. At Peperstraat 76, you can watch the luxuriously moustachioed Adrie Moerings make **clay pipes** in the traditional way (*open Mon–Fri 9–5, Sat 11–5; adm free*). Try to persuade him to make a *doorroker*. This pipe has a plain bowl, but as you use it, a pattern begins to emerge in the clay. At **De Roode Leeuw**, the windmill at Vest 65 (*open Thurs 9–2, Sat 9–4; adm*), you'll meet Marcel Koop, a real rosy-cheeked, flour-covered miller. In the early 1980s he gave up his job as an engineer to renovate the 17th-century windmill. Now it's the only working mill in the Netherlands also lived in by the miller. You can climb almost to the top, accompanied by the deep organic grumbling of the grindstones. And, of course, there's **cheese**. As well as the Thursday market, there are excursions and short bicycle rides to nearby dairy farms where you can follow the whole cheesemaking process from cow to bulging yellow cartwheel (*contact the VVV for details of which farms are open*).

Gouda ℭ (0182–)   ***Where to Stay***

Gouda is not overblessed with alluring hotels. You could consult the VVV for B&B possibilities, or try **De Utrechtsche Dom**, Geuzenstraat 6, 2801 XV, ℭ 528 833, ✆ 549 534 (*inexpensive*), a simple, but clean hotel, centrally situated, just a block or two behind St Jans.

Gouda ℭ (0182–)   ***Eating Out***

De Zalm Markt 34, ℭ 525 345 (*expensive*). Dutch royals drop by this 400-year-old inn when they're in town, to enjoy such dishes as Gelderland chicken fillets, stuffed with smoked ham, mushrooms and olives and served with tomato-and-sage sauce.

De Zes Sterren, Achter de Kerk 14, ✆ 516 095 (*expensive*). Authentic Old Dutch interior, complete with tiled stove and a clutter of antiques, in the basement of the Catharina Gasthuis. The menu comprises recipes researched from old Dutch cookbooks. Try *tailoor*—mushrooms with herbs and a poached egg—or *camallien*, grilled suckling pig with a bitter cinnamon-wine sauce.

Goudsche Salon, Wijdstraat 13, ✆ 512 330 (*cheap*). Friendly local café where you can sit and browse through magazines at the large central reading table, or order a filling lunch.

Het Goudse Winkeltje, Achter de Kerk 9a, ✆ 527 874 (*cheap*). Busy café just behind the Grotekerk that sells delicious pancakes and sandwiches.

Van den Berg, Lange Groenedaal 32, ✆ 529 975 (*cheap*). The place to go to savour the local speciality: sweet, sticky Gouda waffles.

The North

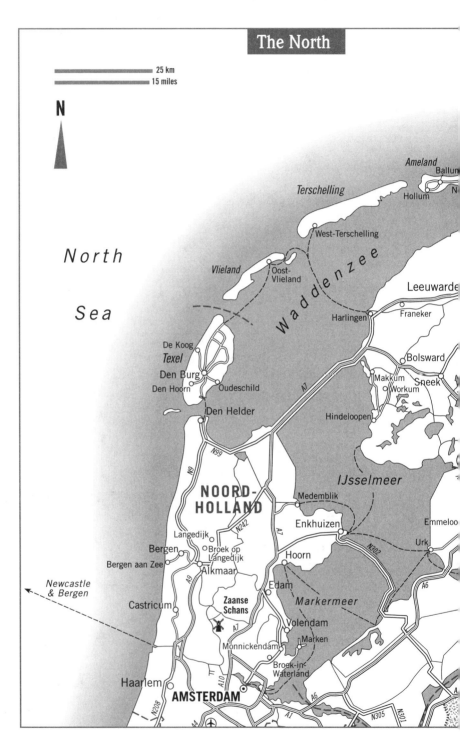

The northern part of the Netherlands is made up, working westwards, of a chunk of Noord-Holland (North Holland), a realm of touristy cheese-market towns and fishing villages; the province of Friesland, which retains a fierce sense of independence and its own language; Groningen in the northeast; and, running below that, Drenthe, which, as the writer Sacheverell Sitwell complained, is a 'sandy waste…a dreary and desolate part of Holland, though this aspect of it may not be apparent to those persons for whom this is their home'.

In between Noord-Holland and the other northern territories is the vast IJsselmeer, once known as the Zuiderzee, but now an inland freshwater sea cut off from the oceans by a 30km-long dyke, the Afsluitdijk. Flecked across the top of the map are the elongated shapes of the Wadden Islands, some of them close enough to shore to encourage intrepid mud-waders to slop across through the shallows of the Waddenzee on foot.

Being most accessible to the Randstad, the towns of Noord-Holland, such as Alkmaar, Edam and Volendam, tend to be the most tourist-drenched—some to the extent that they become twee, unrealistic and Disneyfied. But the area also offers charming spots unsullied by fake cheese markets and clog-wearers of dubious provenance.

Once, the Frisians occupied all of the territory east of the Zuiderzee, at a time when the land was prey to constant flooding. They habitually built houses or whole settlements on *terpelâns*, or 'terps': low hills created to raise a settlement out of the semi-tidal marshes. These 'living mounds' date back to 500 BC, and many towns remain on the sites of these ancient communities, including Harlingen and Franeker, although there is nothing to see of the old settlements. Before the Afsluitdijk was opened in 1932 (*see* p.284), much of this area, especially to the north-west, was relatively remote, cut off by the Zuiderzee and by distance from the Randstad towns. Once distinct in dress and dialect, the three provinces of Friesland, Groningen and Drenthe are now less individual-ized but still have a provincial feel to them, intensified by the occasional use of old languages, especially in Friesland.

Friesland is the most busy and immediately rewarding of these provinces. The West Fries towns of Workum, Makkum, Hindeloopen, Bolsward and Sneek were once all major harbour towns, and each bears the signs of past prosperity in huge churches, richly ornate town halls and streets of attractive gables. Franeker's university was once among the most renowned in Europe. Leeuwarden was the seat of the branch of the Nassau-Orange family that now sits on the throne.

Drenthe has the earliest signs of life discovered in the Netherlands, with traces of human existence around the Hondsrug range of hills dating from 2500 BC, but it remained a bleak and marshy place for most of its subsequent history: it did not drain its peat bogs until the 19th century. It's now a rich agricultural area but without much charm or historical interest.

Groningen province is similar in its expanses of rather bleak farmland. The city of Groningen is a buzzy, friendly place but over the centuries this mighty provincial capital has sucked much of the surrounding region dry. It's easy to be swamped by a picture of dull bogland, but there are numerous little jewels scattered, albeit sparsely, about the countryside.

Getting There

By car: The A7 and A9 are the main arterial roads from Amsterdam through North Holland. The A7 continues across the Afsluitdijk to connect Noord-Holland to Friesland, and this is genarally the quickest way to drive to the area around Leeuwarden (though note that the Afsluitdijk occasionally closes in bad weather). You can also get to Friesland via the A6 through Flevoland, whereas the A28 via Zwolle is handier for the eastern part of the territory.

By train: Trains to Leeuwarden and Groningen often leave Amsterdam as one unit, then split at Amersfoort—so make sure you're sitting in the right section. Travelling west to east (and vice versa) by train in the north can be difficult. Until recently there was no Groningen–Leeuwarden connection; now there is a privately run train, which leaves only once an hour. For most other journeys you'll have to travel all the way south to Zwolle, change trains, then head back north again.

Noord-Holland

Some of the most attractive parts of Noord-Holland are just a few minutes' journey out of Amsterdam—stretches of low-lying countryside where land and water seem divided fifty-fifty, and where wild swans, waterfowl and herons are as frequently sighted as cows and sheep. Amsterdammers and tourists invade in their thousands, on foot, in coaches, on bicycles—but there are still odd corners of calm.

Dunes and Waterland

The coasts and waterlands north of Amsterdam make ideal day-trip destinations—especially by bicycle—from the city. You can easily combine a cycling trip to Broek-in-Waterland with a visit to one of the Meer towns, such as Marken, in a day.

Getting There

Well-signposted cycle paths criss-cross the whole area.

Broek-in-Waterland: Bus 110/111 runs from Amsterdam Centraal Station.

Zaanse Schans: Take a train from Amsterdam to Koog Zaandijk, then an 8-minute walk; or bus 88 from Zaandam station. You can hire **bicycles** at the entrance to Zaanse Schans for *f*9 per half-day.

Bergen: Take the train to Alkmaar, then bus 160/162 to Bergen. Buses go every half-hour.

Broek op Langedijk: Take the train to Alkmaar then bus 155, every half-hour.

Museum Broeker Veiling: Take a train to Alkmaar, then bus 155 to Broek op Langedijk.

Tourist Information

Zaanse Schans: Visitors' Centre, Schansend 7, ℭ (075) 616 8218 (at the entrance); open daily 8.30–5 (8.30–6 in summer).

Bergen aan Zee: VVV, Van der Wijckplein 8, ℭ (072) 581 2400.

Broek-in-Waterland

Heading northeast out of Amsterdam, through a gentle landscape of fields and waterways, you come to the village of **Broek-in-Waterland**, a cluster of pretty wooden houses surrounded by canals and small lakes. Set in leafy gardens, some of these cottages date back 300 years and have become hot property amongst design-conscious moneyed Amsterdammers. At the heart of the hamlet is a 16th-century church that holds the grave of one Neeltje Pater, a whizz 18th-century businesswoman who built up a fleet of 16 merchant ships, and had a nest-egg of eight million guilders stashed away in the Bank of England.

Zaanse Schans

> *Free access and free entry, though individual sights have own opening times and fees; parking f15 for two hours.*

A few kilometres west, outside the town of Zaandam, you'll find the **Zaanse Schans**, resplendent with twelve working windmills. This cluster of green wooden houses dating from the 17th and 18th centuries was put up in the 1950s, to help convey the impression of what a village in the area was like at a time when more than 1,000 windmills ground away at various activities along the river Zaan. Though it throngs with tourists, the Zaanse Schans somehow manages to preserve some charm, and a visit to one or two of the mills is fascinating—one grinds mustard, another produces cooking oil, in a third a man makes paint from natural pigments (highly popular with Amsterdam artists). There's also a working dairy, a clog maker and a pewterer. You can see the first ever Albert Heijn grocery store (which grew into the nation's biggest chain of supermakets), and visit the Clock Museum, where a timepiece from 1520 thunks away in one corner, while in another a 31-bell carillon tinkles out folk tunes. At the entrance to the village, the **Zaans Museum** (*open Tues–Sat 10–5, Sun noon–5; adm*) offers an excellent multimedia presentation on the history of the district, which brands itself 'the oldest industrial area in Europe'.

The Western Coast

West of Zaandam, you come to the **Noord-Holland Duinreservaat** (*North Holland Dune reserve; free access*), one of the most beautiful stretches of coast in the country, and a far better destination on a hot summer's day than Zandvoort, 'Amsterdam's beach' farther south. In places the dunes are like rugged little mountains, at times they waft down into meadows. The north of the reserve is thick with forest, the beaches are long, sandy and often quite deserted. **Egmond aan Zee** gets very overrun—the towns to head for as a base are **Castricum aan Zee** and **Bergen aan Zee**.

At **Broek op Langedijk**, about 10km northeast of Bergen (just north of Alkmaar), is one of Holland's most curious museums. The **Museum Broeker Veiling** (Museumweg 2, Broek op Langedijk; *open April–Oct Mon–Fri 10–5, Sat and Sun 12–5; adm; with boat trip adm exp*) is a sail-in auction house dating back to the turn of the last (i.e. 19th–20th) century. Barges laden with fruit and vegetables would follow a canal into the middle of one of a number of auction halls, and moor there while the sale took place. Visitors can join in a Dutch auction in a *Jugendstil* hall, see a collection of old barges, and take a boat trip themselves out into the 'Realm of a Thousand Islands', a waterland nature reserve.

Where to Stay

Hotels along the coast tend, alas, to be pretty grotty, or soulless monstrosities. But if you want to spend an evening beside the seaside, and not head straight back to Amsterdam, one exception is **Villa de Horizon**, C. F. Zeilerboulevard 1, 1865 BB Bergen aan Zee, ✆ (072) 589 6868 (*inexpensive*), a friendly, family-run pension perched all alone on its own dune overlooking the beach. Rooms are furnished in a modern though not tacky style and most have balconies with sea views.

Eating Out

Broek-in-Waterland ✆ (020–)

De Witte Swaen, Dorpsstraat 11, ✆ 403 1525 (*cheap*). Old-fashioned pancake parlour in a traditional Broek-in-Waterland building, with a terrace that catches the sun.

Zaanse Schans ✆ (075–)

There's a busy pancake restaurant just near the entrance, or you could treat yourelf to **De Hoop Op d'Swarte Walvis**, Kalverringdijk 15 , ✆ 616 5629 (*expensive*). One of the region's top restaurants, housed in a complex of three historic buildings in the Zaanse Schans village. You can taste soup made with mustard ground at the windmill nearby, or lash out with veal served with creamy spinach, polenta, turnips and a laurel-leaf gravy.

The Dunes ✆ (072–)

Cheap 'n' cheerful eats are to be found in the beach pavilion restaurants at Egmond aan Zee (**de Uitkijk** is the most recommendable), but for something a little more special head to **De Kleine Prins**, Oude Prinsweg 29, Bergen, ✆ 589 6969 (*expensive–moderate*), where you can tuck into such delights as grilled rabbit with calvados sauce.

Fish and Cheese

Travelling along the shores of what was then the Zuiderzee in the 1920s, Aldous Huxley noted that: 'The people of Volendam are dressed as if for a musical comedy— *Miss Hook of Holland*—the men in baggy trousers and short jackets, the women in winged white caps, tight bodices and fifteen super-imposed petticoats. Five thousand tourists come daily to look at them...' Now that the Afsluitdijk has cut off revenues from trading and fishing, towns like Volendam, Marken and Monnickendam have set off in even hotter pursuit of the tourist dollar. Of the three, Monnickendam, which derives its living from watersports rather than nostalgia, is perhaps the least twee. The tiny cheese town of Edam is even more alluring.

Getting There

The most convenient way of getting around the area is by **bicycle** or **car**. Otherwise catch a **bus** from Amsterdam Central Station: Monnickendam, bus 111/116, one every 15 mins (journey time 25mins), 111 for Marken (30mins) or bus 116 for Volendam (35mins) and Edam (40mins).

The Marken Express **ferry** service connects Marken and Volendam, with boats running every 35mins (*f6.50 adults, f4.50 children*).

Tourist Information

Monnickendam: VVV, De Zaken 2, ✆ (0299) 651 998; open Mon–Fri 9–5, Sat 10–5

Volendam: VVV, Zeestraat 37, ✆ (0299) 363 747; open winter Mon–Fri 10–3; summer Mon–Sun 10–5.

Edam: VVV, Keizersgracht 1, ✆ (0299) 315 125; open winter Mon–Sat 10–5; summer Mon–Sat 10–5, Sun 1–5.

Monnickendam and Marken

Monnickendam, a few kilometres northeast of Broek-in-Waterland, was once one of the most important ports on the Zuiderzee. Nowadays yachts and windsurfers fill its harbour, but, as most day-trippers head for nearby Marken, the centre retains some of its old charm. Chief sights are the **Waag**, built on the harbour in 1600, then adorned with fancy pilasters 60 years later as city coffers got ever fuller, and the **Speeltoren**, which strongly resembles the tower of Amsterdam's Oude Kerk. The first written record of the

Speeltoren is in 1591, but it's been around a while longer than that. Certainly one of the bells in its carillon was cast as early as 1513.

A long causeway (built in 1957) connects Monnickendam to the former island of **Marken**, once a fishing and whaling port. The stripy shirts and embroidered waiscoats of the local traditional dress (now worn largely for the benefit of tourists) show a Scandinavian influence, perhaps a result of age-old whaling connections.

Despite the causeway and coachloads of tourists, Marken has managed to keep something of its atmosphere of island isolation. It's crammed with bottle-green wooden houses, and if you wander away from the harbour there are plenty of pretty side streets to explore. The **Marker Museum** (Kerkbuurt 44; *open Easter–Oct, Mon–Sat 10–5, Sun 12–4; adm*), housed in six former 'smokehouses' (cottages with an open fire in the middle for smoking fish) is well worth a visit for the impression it gives of the days when the people of Marken made their living from the sea.

Volendam and Edam

Edging farther along the coast, you come to the somewhat larger town of **Volendam**. People flock here from all over the world to ogle and photograph locals in traditional dress—men in fez-like black hats and wide lapels, women in pointy lace caps and long aprons. But there is real life in Volendam too—quaint, empty side streets lined with gabled houses, the occasional real fishing boat with a catch for sale, and even its own pop music style, '*palingbeat*' (eel beat), which emerged in the late 1980s. If you come in midwinter, you might find the harbour frozen over, the townsfolk turned out to skate, and barely a visitor in sight.

Now almost a suburb of Volendam, **Edam** is perhaps best known to outsiders because it gives its name to the round, rubbery cheese that the Dutch export in large quantities. Yet despite a tacky and utterly fake **cheese market** (*held on Wednesday mornings in summer*), Edam escapes the worst toy-town excesses, and is perhaps the most pleasant and atmospheric of all the towns on this stretch of coast. Founded in the 12th century, Edam enjoyed its high point in the 16th and 17th centuries, and still bears the architectural imprint of that time. The imperious Gothic **Grote Kerk** on the edge of the town centre was largely rebuilt in the 1620s, after it had been struck by lightning, and contains some beautiful stained glass—rare in the iconoclast-ravaged north. The slender, solitary **Speeltoren** (built 1561) was also once part of a church, demolished in the 19th century. In 1970, its original six-bell carillon was augmented by another 29 bells—so many that some had to hang outside, and the tower nearly fell over from the weight two years later.

The richly decorated **Kaaswaag** on the Kaasmarkt still weighs out Edamer cheese at the statutory 1000 or 1600 grams, though as far as décor goes it's upstaged by the ornate 18th-century **Stadhuis** on nearby Damplein. Next door to the Stadhuis, in a step-gabled house that dates back to 1550, is the **Edams Museum** (*open mid-April–Oct Tues–Sat 10–4.30, Sun 1.30–4.30; adm*), restored as a period merchant house but most famous for its floating cellar floor, supposedly built by a sea captain who just couldn't get to sleep on solid land.

All these little towns are mainly day-trip destinations from Amsterdam, but two hotels are worth special recommendation.

Volendam ✆ (0299–)

Hotel Spaander, Haven 15–19, 1131 EP, ✆ 363 595, ✉ 369 615, *spaander@ tref.nl* (*inexpensive*). Legendary hotel that is a testament to Volendam's long history of attracting tourist hordes—Renoir and Picasso were apparently once guests. Rooms range from standard to luxury and décor mixes traditional cosiness with Best Western modern, and the hotel can boast a fitness centre, large pool and Turkish bath.

Edam ✆ (0299–)

De Fortuna, Spuistraat 3–7, 1135 AV, ✆ 371 671, ✉ 371 469, *fortuna@ fortuna-edam.nl* (*inexpensive*). Family-run hotel occupying five 17th-century houses and two garden houses. Some rooms open directly on to the garden terrace. The décor has a traditional Dutch touch that manages to avoid kitsch.

Restaurants in this area cater almost exclusively to tourists, and are barely distinguishable from each other. Those overlooking the little harbour at **Markum** have the best views. All serve the usual range of pancakes, apple pie, mussels, fish dishes, and meat with salad and chips. One notable exception is in Edam, at the **De Fortuna** hotel (*see* above; *moderate*). Dinky step-gabled building belonging to a family-run hotel—heavy beams, soft lighting and superb food. Try the home-smoked lamb with mint and rocket couscous.

Along the Meer

The coming of the Afsluitdijk (*see* p.284) dealt a hard blow to the trading ports along the Zuiderzee coast. Denied access to the open sea, many have faded from prosperity into insignificance. But here and there are towns that might lure you out of Amsterdam for a day, or divert you for a while from your journey further north.

Note: Confusingly, you may see this little corner of Noord-Holland referred to as West Friesland, testament to the early occupation by the Frisians of the whole of the north of the Netherlands territory.

Hoorn is about 40mins from Amsterdam Centraal Station by train. Trains leave every half-hour. It's also on the tourist steam train route that runs through Medemblik and Enkhuizen in summer.

Enkhuizen is 23mins farther down the track.

Medemblik can be reached on bus 40/44 from Hoorn once every hour, and in summer you can take the steam train from Hoorn or the ferry from Enkhuizen.

Hoorn: VVV, Veemarkt 4, 1621 JC Hoorn, ✆ (0900) 403 1055, ✉ (0229) 215 023; open April Mon 1–5, Tues–Sat 9.30–5, Sun 1–5; June–Aug Mon 1–6, Tues–Fri 9.30–6, Thurs eve 7–9, Sat 9.30–5, Sun 1–5; Sept–Mar same as April but closed Sun.

Enkhuizen: VVV, Tussen Twee Havens 1 (opp. station), ✆ (0228) 313 164, ✉ 315 531; open Mon–Fri 9–5, Sat and Sun 9–2.

Medemblik: VVV, Stationsgebouw (next to the train station), ✆ (0227) 542 852; open April–Oct Mon–Sat 10–5, July–Aug also Sun 12–5.

Hoorn

Just half an hour up the A7 from Amsterdam, **Hoorn** is unimaginatively named after the bight (horn-shaped promontory) of the coastline on which it stands. It was one of the prosperous Golden Age harbour towns since blighted by the closing of the Afsluitdijk. A likeable place, with a compact centre friendly to the feet and plenty of relics of its glory days, it is best seen on a wander through the lovely old streets, and perhaps a stroll along the Westerdijk that curves around the western coast of the harbour.

The main sights centre on the square, Rode Steen, and the harbour area. Grote Noord, the otherwise bland shopping street connecting the station and Rode Steen, does boast a few interesting, tilting façades—look out for No.7 with an impressive door carved with lions. On the square itself is a statue of J. P. Coen, a major figure in the establishment of the Dutch East India Company empire, and the 1609 **Waag**, topped with a red and gilt unicorn and built by the renowned Amsterdam architect Hendrick de Keyser (*see* p.61). Nowadays it houses a restaurant.

Behind the ornate 1632 façade of a former *statencollege* (council hall of the States-General) is the **Westfries Museum** (Rode Steen 1; *open Mon–Fri 11–5, Sat and Sun 2–5; adm*). The museum's leaflet proudly quotes Aldous Huxley's summary: 'Hoorn with its absurd museum filled with rich mixed rubbish.' The observation is reasonably accurate but surely not in the right spirit: it's a charming treasure-trove inside a lovely old building, well worth exploration for the fine *stijlkamers* (period rooms), good silver, pottery and glass, and archaeology section with a second millennium BC corpse plus pots and stone sarcophagi. The attic contains the engagingly Heath-Robinson 17th-century clock machinery from the Hoofdtoren. Most fascinating, if gruesome, is Room 15, which recreates the study of a doctor and natural historian, with a model dodo, some rather unpleasant bottled and dried specimens (a goat foetus here, what looks suspiciously like half of somebody's head there), a selection of terrifying 17th-century surgical instruments, and a marvellous *rariteitenkabinet*—an inlaid bureau full of tiny drawers for specimens. The museum also holds good changing exhibitions.

The **Museum van de Twintigste Eeuw** (Museum of the Twentieth Century, Bierkade 4/4a, ✆ (0229) 214 001; *open Tues–Sun 10–5; adm*) is housed in two 1903 cheese warehouses. Huxley's denunciation would be rather more appropriate here: the exhibits are barely labelled even in Dutch and seem to bear little relation to one another except for their century of manufacture. There are *stijlkamers*—a turn-of-the-century school room, various sitting rooms, some shops (all using department-store-style mannequins); a display of old computers; some washing machines up to circa 1980; a few old motorbikes. It's hard to see the point.

Hoorn's **harbour** was once its heart, and it is still a good place to contemplate the IJsselmeer and the many pleasure boats that now fill the harbour. It's dominated by the astonishing 1532 Hoofdtoren. Its metre-thick walls that once guarded a mercantile empire's port now house a restaurant (*see* below). Also on the harbour are Johan Fabricius' famous statues of the Scheepsjongens (Ship's Boys) of Bontekoe, staring out to sea.

Willem Bontekoe, Master of Disaster

Willem Ysbrantzoon Bontekoe, master sailor, was the captain of the huge East Indiaman *Nieuw Hoorn*, a *Titanic* of its day at 1,100 tonnes, crewed by 206 men. In the severe Calvinist theology of the time, the sheer scale of this monster invited heavenly retribution for man's presumption and, according to Bontekoe, that, on his 1619 voyage, was what they got. When they reached the Sunda Straits in the East Indies fire broke out on board and the powder kegs caught light, blowing the *Nieuw Hoorn* and many of its crew into fragments.

As Bontekoe tells it, he is blasted high into the air before dropping back into the water within reach of a convenient spar. He and the other 72 survivors find one surviving lifeboat, put off the ship before the explosion, and drift on the ocean for days. They endure agonies of thirst and hunger, and eventually the crew decide 'first to eat the boys and when these were finished, they should draw lots who should be the next one'. By pious exhortation Bontekoe persuades his starving would-be cannibals to wait three more days before starting in on the boys and, amazingly, on the third day the ship strikes land. A series of violent encounters with wild beasts and murderous, spear-waving savages follow, further depleting their numbers, until the eventual rescue and return home.

How do we know? Bontekoe wrote up his journal as *The Memorable Account of the Voyage of the Nieuw Hoorn* and published it in 1646. It was a huge popular success, reprinted seventy times before 1800, and sparked off any number of other disaster epics, many of which seem even more cinematic and less likely. The unfortunate mariner and literary pioneer is thus a native son of whom Hoorn can be proud, even if one wonders whether the statues of his ships' boys are keeping watch for the return of the master or just a weather eye out for hungry mariners.

Hoorn offers a couple of attractions for smaller folk. The **Speelgoed Museum De Kijkdoos** (Italiaanse Zeedijk 106, ✆ (0229) 217 589; *open Tues–Sun 11–5; adm*) offers three floors of antique toys: train sets, doll's houses, cars, planes, carousels and more. The **Museumstoomtram** (Steam Tram Museum, Van Dedemstraat 8, ✆ (0229) 214 862, ✉ 216 653; *open 2 April–31 Oct; adm exp at between ƒ30 and ƒ50, children ƒ20–35 depending on trip*) is just on the other side of the railway tracks from the town. There's a little brick station with a cosy, old-fashioned interior and café. 'Museum' gives the wrong idea: what's on offer is a variety of trips on the old-fashioned little trains and trams. You can, for example, ride to Medemblik's Steam Train Museum, or to the ferry which takes you to the Zuiderzee Museum at Enkhuizen. There are trips through the countryside past tulip fields and windmills, and special candlelit dinner journeys in a real old-style dining car (*ƒ145, children ƒ85*). Call the museum or VVV for more details of trips and prices.

Enkhuizen

Enkhuizen (pronounced 'Enkhowzen', roughly), 15 kilometres farther along the 'hoorn', dates from 1000–1200. Its heyday came in the 16th and 17th centuries, when it was a base for herring fisheries and for the East and West India Companies. After the Zuiderzee was sealed off in 1932, the town withered away, its traditional way of life gone. With nothing left but its harbour and heritage, Enkhuizen is now making its money in those, with pleasure yachts and the nostalgic Zuiderzee museum to remind visitors of the old days.

In front of the station is Enkhuizen's **Buiten Haven**, a forest of yachts riding at anchor. Like everything in Enkhuizen these are old-style, with wooden sides and names like *Festina Lente* and *Nil Desperandum*—either of which could be the town's motto. Around to the left are the impressive gates of the **Snouck van Loosenpark**, an attractive spot with gardens beautifully laid out in the 19th century for Mrs Snouck van Loosen, a rich city benefactress. She also paid for the red-brick workers' cottages at the entrance to the park, with front gardens that might be posing for a still life: clogs on the windowsill, benches covered with pot of herbs, bowls of warty gourds and plates of mussel shells.

Near the harbour is the **Drommedaris** (Paktuinen 1, Postbus 50, 1600 AB Enkhuizen, ✆ (0228) 312 076/313 703), an old defence tower, built in 1540 during the VOC days to protect the harbour. Its gentle carillon was cast by the famous Hemony brothers. Note the elaborate gateway featuring a relief of Holland lions, cannons, fish and barrels—summing up the town's military and mercantile might. Now it's a cultural centre, café and dormitory, offering a cheap sleep for up to 25 people in its round tower. The park in front of the Drommedaris also offers, on one side of the path, a statue of painter of Holland's most famous painter of animals, Paulus Potter (*see* p.57) and, on the other, a statue of the goat he is sketching.

The **Flessenscheepjesmuseum** (Bottleship Museum, Zuiderspui 1, ✆ (0228) 318 583, ✉ 322 722; *open daily 10–5; adm; ticket gets you a free second beer or coffee in* *the Die Port van Cleve or Het Wapen van Enkhuizen restaurants*) is a marvellous little house crammed with bottled ships of all sizes, from a 2ft jug holding a small flotilla to a scent bottle so tiny that you look at it through a magnifying glass, to discover that it contains not one but two minuscule schooners. Most bottles contain scenery as well as their sailing vessels, from a simple seascape to an elaborate cliffside with people, trees, rearing horses and in one case a lighthouse with flashing lights. There are also other bottled scenes: a couple of plastic dolls next to a dresser with a picture hanging above it—not very attractive but how on earth did they get in through the narrow neck?—and several bottles containing a sailor at his desk putting a ship inside a bottle. To find out how it's done, go upstairs where there is a video and regular demonstrations during the summer months.

Inside the ornate **Stadhuis** on Breedstraat you can see the town collection of old skates, sledges and photos. To your left in a little square is the **Zuiderkerk**, an impressive onion-domed red brick building with a 65m spire, dating from 1445 to 1686. Nearby is the **Stadsgevangennis** (city prison), built in 1612 and tilted about 15 degrees off vertical, adding a new terror to the prospect of incarceration. The 15th-century Gothic **Westerkerk**, just off Breedstraat, is also worth a look.

Sprookjeswonderland (Fairytale Wonderland, Kooizandweg 9, ✆ (0228) 317 853, ✆ 322 226; *open April–Nov 10–5.30*), is to many a perfectly revolting theme park, but its fake turreted castle, plastic gingerbread cottages, dinky little train, home farm and big cutesy models of Mr Bunny, gnomes and the wolf from *Little Red Riding Hood* prove irresistible to smaller fry.

Zuiderzee Museum

Wierdijk 12–22, 1601 LA Enkhuizen, Postbus 42, 1600 AA Enkhuizen; ✆ (0228) 351 135, ✆ 351 111. Free parking, and in April–Oct you can take a ferry from the railway station.

Open April–Oct daily 10–5, Sun, hols 10–6; July and Aug daily 10–6; free guided tours at 12 and also 4 in July and Aug; adm exp (covers both parts of museum).

The region's biggest attraction comes in two parts. The **Buitenmuseum** (Open-air Museum) recreates the atmosphere of an old Zuiderzee town of the period 1880–1930, with houses, shops and workshops (an old laundry or bakery here, a chemist there, a row of cottages, a lime kiln) actually transported from different parts of the region. There are craft demonstrations, actors in period costume, activities for children and lots of space for simply wandering around soaking up the atmosphere. It's a little bit twee but done with great care and affection—it's impossible not to enjoy poking your nose into the interiors and petting the goats and sheep, especially if you have children. There's an information centre near the entrance by the Monnickendam cottages, and a restaurant (the bakery also sells pastries).

The **Binnenmuseum** (Indoor Museum; *open as above but also Nov–Mar 10–5; adm*) is less popular. It's based in a lovely old building, an enclosed square with a dizzying array of gables and angular rooftops and exposed beams in the walls. Unfortunately this has been extended to contain the museum with the use of acres of plate glass, concrete and steel, forming a distinctly unsuccessful hybrid. The labelling is in Dutch only and the exhibits not compellingly interesting: models of old towns, undistinguished paintings, applied art (including some wonderful old painted dressers). There's a mock-up of a 17th-century room where the 'Delft tiles' are actually vinyl wallpaper; and a display of old ships that gives very little sense of what it must have been like out at sea in these 10m tubs. The most interesting part is the room on whaling, featuring ship models, old prints and pictures (fervid images of disgruntled whales being harpooned in the Arctic), huge bones and an enormous pair of whaler's socks so sturdy you imagine that the idea was to kick the whale to death.

Medemblik

Another 15km around the coast, **Medemblik** is one of the oldest towns in the region, but it doesn't look it. The best old streets are Vooreiland and those along the harbour; otherwise the general impression is one of suburban neatness. Apart from the harbour, which flourishes with pleasure boats, the big attraction is **Radboud Castle** (Oudevaartsgat 8, ✆ (0227) 541 960; *open 15 May–15 Sept daily 10–5; 16 Sept–14 May Sun 2–5; adm*). 'Big' isn't really the word: it's a dinky four-square place, with conical-topped towers and all the other Gothic requirements: arched windows, a little moat, a cannon and pillory outside. It's quaint but not authentic: the round tower dates from its beginnings, built by Floris V, Count of Holland, in 1282, but most of the rest was built in the 19th century by P. J. H. Cuypers (architect of the Rijksmuseum in Amsterdam, *see* pp.63 and 110). The **Stadhuis** by the train station is another nostalgic reconstruction. Its gabled front may appear 17th century, but it was built in the 1940s.

More intriguing is the **Bakkerijmuseum** (Bakery Museum, Nieuwstraat 8, ✆ (0227) 545 014; *open April–Oct and school hols daily 12–5, Nov, Dec and Mar Sat and Sun 12–5; closed Jan–Feb; adm*) which offers an bakery (plus shop) dating from 1900, complete with kitchen implements, cookie moulds and frequent cookery demonstrations. Fans of steam trains can get excited about the **Nederlands Stoommachinemuseum** (Dutch Steam Engine Museum, Oosterdijk 4, ✆ (0227) 544 732; *open 1 April–31 Oct 10–5; closed Mon; adm*). Working machines show the development of the steam engine through the years; it's based in the old steam pumping station. You can also visit the windmill **Meelmolen de Herder** (Westerdijk 3, ✆ (0227) 543 198; *open Sat 10–5; adm f3, children f0.50*) to see how corn is ground.

Where to Stay

Hoorn ✆ (0229–)

Hoorn is quite expensive as a base, with nowhere offering outstanding value or particular character.

Petit Nord, Kleine Noord 53–55, 1621 JE Hoorn, ✆ 212 750, ✉ 215 745 (*moderate*) is a modern hotel, convenient for the station. Rooms are standard good hotel type, recently refurbished but still with somewhat 80s décor. There's a pleasant lounge, a lift, a number of non-smoking rooms, and pay-parking at the back.

De Keizerskroon, Breed 33, 1621 KA Hoorn, ✆ 212 717, ▨ 211 022 (*inexpensive*). Clean but rather bare rooms, with tiny bathrooms. But the popular, cosy restaurant is good, with full menus and cheaper snacks—note the elaborate china clock.

Enkhuizen ✆ (0228–)

De Port van Cleve, Dijk 74–8, 1601 GK, ✆ 312 510, ▨ 318 765 (*moderate-inexpensive*). Good, old-fashioned Dutch hospitality in a harbourside inn, part of which dates from the 16th century. Reasonably sized, comfortable modern rooms. Spacious and elegant restaurant with a French-style menu heavy on the fish. Cheaper snacks also available.

Het Wapen van Enkhuizen, Breedstraat 59, 1601 KB, ✆ 313 34, ▨ 320 020 (*moderate–inexpensive*). Friendly, modest hotel with modern, recently refurbished rooms, conveniently located next to the Stadhuis.

Hotel Villa Oud Enkhuizen, 217 Westerstraat, 1601 AH, ✆ 314 266, ▨ 318 171 (*inexpensive*). Slightly out of town, this is a lovely friendly little place with a charming lobby—black leather sofas, a green wrought-iron stove front, wooden floors and a quiet bar. There are rooms in the main building and a little extension out the back, all small, smart and modern.

Medemblik ✆ (0227–)

Medemblik only has one hotel, plus a few pensions.

Tulip Inn Medemblik, Oosterhaven 1, 1671 AA, ✆ 543 844, ▨ 542 397 (*inexpensive*). As with all the Tulip Inn chain, this is pleasant and comfortable. The bedrooms are large and decorated in quiet dark colours, well furnished with good sized bathrooms.

Pension Singelzicht, Hoogesteeg 11, 1671 HR, ✆ 544 380, ▨ 542 780 (*cheap*). This little white house offers three plainly decorated rooms and a large comfortable sitting room. The owner has an aviary with parrots and parakeets in his garden.

Eating Out

Hoorn ✆ (0229–)

Het Plafond, Kleine Noord 65, ✆ 216 923 (*cheap*). Café and grill bar reasonable for snacks, offering such goodies as satay baguette, mixed grill and steaks.

De Hoofdtoren, Hoofd 2, ✆ 215 487 (*moderate*). A cosy place for a drink or fuller meal in an extraordinary 16th-century building.

De Oude Rosmolen, Duinsteeg 1, ✆ 214 752 (*expensive*). Beautiful 17th-century building housing a restaurant that's been run by the same family for 50 years, and has long been one of the best restaurants in the country. Creations such as caramelized mini-pancakes with goose liver mousse have earned chef Constant Fonk two Michelin stars.

Enkhuizen ✆ (0228–)

Balkan Grill Restaurant, corner of Havenweg and Spoorstraat, ✆ 317 545 (*cheap*). Cosy, dark little place with plenty of plants, low lighting and a comfortable local clientele. Try a set menu of soup, then mussels or fish or schnitzel with chips and salad. The *à la carte* has a good selection of meats, fish and seafood.

De Admiral, Havenweg 4, ✆ 319 256, ✉ 318 928 (*moderate*). Lovely maritime-themed interior with wooden figureheads, an elaborate model ship in the entranceway and brass lamps and fittings. It's a thoroughly *gezellig* place with friendly staff. For lunch try a baguette with meat croquettes or with smoked eel and mackerel. Full main courses include several vegetarian options. You can eat on the pleasant terrace in summer and watch the ships go by. *Open from 12 noon.*

De Smederij, Breedstraat 158, ✆ 314 604 (*moderate*). Snug brasserie on the way to the Zuiderzee museum, and a good choice for a proper meal. Try the Smederij salad (with warm goat's cheese croutons and crispy bacon), or pie made of salmon with Chinese greens and banana. *Closed Wed, Thurs and in winter.*

Medemblik ✆ (0227–)

Eetcafe Royal, Nieuwstraat 38, ✆ 545 418 (*cheap*). A cosy, softly lit place with good-value food, featuring such comfort cooking as *stoofpotje* (traditional stew), or fillet of pork with spinach and potatoes.

De Tijd, Westerhaven 1, ✆ 541 386 (*moderate*) has an old-style wood interior fitted out with rustic elegance. It offers a modern Dutch menu with main courses such as guinea fowl in red wine sauce. Vegetarian options too. *Open from 12, closed Thurs.*

d'Artiest, Achtereiland 12a, ✆ 548 080 (*moderate*). Laid-back fish restaurant in an old warehouse—plain dishes and some imaginative concoctions too.

Alkmaar

Alkmaar is a cheesy place. It's a little medieval town whose main distinction over the years has been its long-running cheese market; and it retains a Disneyfied version of this as a tourist spectacle, attracting tens of thousands to the weekly markets all through summer.

Alkmaar is 35mins from Amsterdam Centraal Station by train; **trains** leave every half-hour. **Buses** go there from all the big towns in Noord-Holland.

Alkmaar is a small town with narrow lanes. Turn right out of the station and left down Scharlo at the lights; Scharlo becomes Geesterweg later on. It's a 5–10min walk into the centre of town.

Woltheus Cruises (✆ (072) 511 4840) offers a *Molenrondvaart* (trip past the mills) available on cheese-market Fridays, every 90mins from 10.30 till 3; or *Grachtenrondvaart* (canal trip), on cheese-market Fridays every 20mins from 9.30am; May–Aug daily on the hour from 11am; April, Sept and Oct Mon–Sat hourly from 11am.

Ask at the VVV about walking and cycling along the 126km Omringsdijk, which runs right across Noord-Holland to Medemblik.

VVV, Waagplein 2 (in the old Waag that also holds the cheese museum), 1811 JP Alkmaar, ✆ (072) 511 4284, ✉ 511 7513; open Tues 10–5.30, Wed 9–5.30, Thurs 9–9, Fri 9–6, Sat 9.30–5.

If you come to Alkmaar in season (April–Oct) it will probably be packed, especially on cheese-market days (mid-April–mid-Oct Fri mornings 10–12). If you visit out of season, even though the volume of visitors remains high, most of the major museums and sights will be closed.

History

Humans are thought to have inhabited this site since 4000 BC; the current town was established in 929 AD. Like so much of the area, it has been at constant risk of flooding; dykes around here date back as far as recorded habitation. In 1250 a number of West Friesland dyke systems were linked up to created the **Omringdijk**, running in a circle from Alkmaar to the Zuiderzee towns of Hoorn, Enkhuizen and Medemblik, back over to Schagen and closing the circle at Alkmaar to form the longest dyke in the Netherlands.

Alkmaar was awarded cheese-weighing rights in the 14th century and became a local administrative and industrial centre, with shipyards, breweries and potteries—but no cheese producers; Alkmaar has never actually made its own cheese. It was one of the rebel towns in the revolt against rule by Spain (*see* p.38). The Duke of Alva, governor general of the Netherlands under Philip II, decided to frighten the Dutch into obedience by sending soldiers to plunder some of the rebel towns. They laid siege to Alkmaar, but learned then what they would also find at Leiden a year later: that the ever-present menace of water could work for the Dutch as well as against them. The locals cut the dikes around the town and flooded the land, forcing the Spaniards to retreat on 8 October 1573, a date claimed (by Alkmaar) as the first true rebel victory and commemorated yearly with a display in the St Laurenskerk.

Around the Town

Alkmaar's medieval centre has survived the years more or less intact: it's a town of fanciful gables, narrow lanes, and a riot of carvings and gilding everywhere. This and the cheese market have made it a tourist magnet: the medieval streets are jammed with antique shops, boutiques, high-class souvenir shops, cheesemongers and any amount of places to eat—though with little sense of its being a living town. Certainly the youth seem disaffected. It must have taken ages for them to adorn one nameless alley off the Doelenstraat quite so thickly with chewing gum: from four feet to six like organic pebbledash. It makes you wonder what else there is to do here. What's more, the volume of the tourist trade seems to have made the locals almost contemptuous towards visitors in a way that is very unusual in the Netherlands, as if they resent the medieval charade on which so much revenue depends. People shove and jostle in the streets and the local VVV is surprisingly unhelpful, charging for the most basic information and offering little advice.

On Kerkplein, at the western edge of the Old Town, is the **St Laurenskerk** (*open Fri 9–5 in 'cheese time' (when the market is on), also June–Aug Tues–Sat 12–5*), a magnificent late-Gothic church dating from 1470–1520, its imposing grey stone bulk rearing above the town. It has a melodic carillon created by Melchior de Haze (1677–8) which plays at around 12.45, and a grand organ commissioned by Maria Tesselschade (*see* pp.223–4) with a case painted by Alkmaar artist Caesar Van Everdingen.

Across the way on Langestraat is the **Stadhuis** (*not open to the public*), which has a spectacular striped front: ornate gables, a gilded statue of Blind Justice, roaring Holland lions by the front stairs. Two doors up is the attractive **Moriaanshoofd**, an old patrician mansion dating from around 1730, built by then *burgemeester* Simon Schagen. Magdalenstraat, off Langestraat, is a winding alley of medieval houses, now occupied with quaint little shops. A right turn from here will bring you to the **Nederlands Bier Museum De Boom** (National Beer Museum, Houttil 1; *open April–Oct Tues–Fri 10–4, Sat and Sun 1.30–4; Nov–March Tues–Sun 1–4; adm*), named after the brewery that the building once housed. The large brick building dates from 1647 and contains a loving recreation of the brewing process in old times. There are displays of the processes of malting, brewing, cooping (making barrels) and bottling, plus lots of old equipment and bottles. The shop sells a good range of beers and assorted alcoholic merchandise and in the downstairs bar you can taste some of their 86 varieties of Dutch beer.

At the end of Houttil is Waagplein and Alkmaar's pride and joy, the **Waag** (Weighhouse). Its ornate tiered clocktower dates from the building's 14th-century origins as a chapel; the extravagant east gable, with gilt, lions and depictions of Holland personified, dates from 1582 and was put up to commemorate the town's victory in the 1573 siege. Inside the building is the VVV and, on the first floor, the **Hollands Kaasmuseum** (Dutch Cheese Museum; *open April–Oct Mon–Sat 10–4, on cheese-market Fridays 9–4; adm*). All you want to know about dairy production is here: implements for past and present production, scales for weighing, pictures, information about the current cheese industry and daily slideshows in several languages.

The Gouda, the Bad and the Ugly

Modern Alkmaar is a town built on cheese. Since the early Middle Ages the town has been the region's centre for cheese quality control as well as buying and selling. The Cheese Carrier's Guild is first recorded in the archives in 1619 but almost certainly existed for hundreds of years before: over the decades they have worked up the art of pulling cheese around on a big sledge into an arcane ritual, involving levels of skill, emblems to identify the more important officials, and a careful dress code. All of this is preserved in today's tourist spectacle-cum-market (little significant buying now goes on). Men in colour-coded straw hats lay out thirty thousand kilos of cheese in the town square, while women in the classic blue and red dresses and three-pointed white hats look decorative. They even wear clogs.

The market goes through the motions of what it did in medieval times. The *kaaszetters* (cheese arrangers) lay out the cheeses in long rows. Meanwhile the merchants assess what's on offer, sounding and smelling before taking a scoop of cheese from one of the wheels, crumbling it between the fingers to assess fat content and moisture, and tasting. Bargaining is conducted using a hand-clapping code. Sold cheese is then taken to the Waag for weighing on old wooden balances (the Guild motto is 'A false balance is an abomination to the Lord') and then returned to the Waagplein for packing and transport.

Those who only know Dutch cheese from the rubbery bland pre-packed Edam sold in supermarkets may now be wondering what all the fuss is about. But the kinds of cheese vary more than is often thought. Edam itself is not much eaten in the Netherlands. Try, for example, Beemste, Alkmaar's local speciality, or Leidse, creamy-textured with cumin seeds, or one of a variety of Goudas with holes in for extra sweetness. Cheeses are allowed to age, turning from the familiar soft sunny yellow into shades of deep amber and burnt sienna. As they age the taste changes completely, from mild *jong* (young) to tastier *belegen* (matured) and then *oud* (old—very tangy and rock-hard; an *oud* Edam is packed with fierce flavour). A 1.5kg Gouda will set you back perhaps ƒ18; a five-year-old version of the same cheese would be nearer ƒ30. The best cheeses are very good indeed, though few of them reach foreign markets in any great quantity. The Dutch like to keep them for themselves.

Taste the difference for yourself: you won't have any trouble finding cheese shops in this town. Two to try: **Kaan's Kaashandel** on Koorstraat just opposite the Laurenskerk is a friendly, old-fashioned place stocking only Dutch cheeses. Their oldest exhibit has been ageing for seven years and has a surface that looks like dried glue, but is extremely tasty.

Zelfkazer, Houttil 40, near the Waag, is a more wide-ranging deli, with plenty of French and other nationality cheeses, plus all you need for cheese consumption: biscuits, nuts, port and a cheese-scraper (*kaasschaaf*) of the kind the Dutch use to attack their mature morsels.

The **Stedelijk Museum** (Municipal Museum; *closed at the time of writing but should reopen in Canadaplein by October 2000*) has a wide collection of 16th- and 17th-century paintings, a modern assortment featuring a number of works by the Bergen School and a number of toys from the early 1900s, which children are allowed to touch.

Alkmaar ✆ (072–)   ***Where to Stay***

Alkmaar probably isn't somewhere you'd stay more than a day, which is lucky because there's only one convenient hotel: **Motel Stad en Land**, Stationsweg 92, near the station, ✆ 512 3911 (*inexpensive*). Clean, good-sized simple rooms. It's on a busy road but all rooms are double glazed and the buses stop running by 9pm. There's a basic restaurant, and a car park and a small garden out the back.

Alkmaar ✆ (072–)   ***Eating Out***

On the other hand there's a multitude of places to eat in Alkmaar, from the simplest snack to a sit-down blowout.

De Bonte Bengel, Kerkplein, ✆ 511 1713 (*cheap*). Pleasant café opposite the Laurenskerk. A cheerful young modern place with a startlingly multinational menu, featuring sweet or savoury pancakes, nachos, tagliatelle, Hindustani chicken, and Surinamese dishes.

De Vestibule, Ritsevoort 12, ✆ 512 5379 (*moderate–cheap*). Cheery, busy *eetcafe*, a long-time local favourite for croquettes, *uitsmijters* and other Dutch soul food. Also good vegetarian options, and a well-chosen wine list.

't Gulden Vlies, Koorstraat 30, ✆ 512 2442 (*moderate*). Comfortable, high-class restaurant near the water specializing in Dutch seasonal fare.

Friesland

The busiest of the northern provinces, Friesland can also be the most immediately rewarding, with its peaceful windswept coastline and the old university towns of Leeuwarden and Franeker. When the Frisians occupied the whole of the north, today's province of Friesland was only the central part of their territory, but it is still the heart of a land with its own language and its own separate identity.

Though now easily accessible over the Afsluitdijk, Friesland for centuries seemed isolated and difficult to reach, developing a strong identity of its own.

The Afsluitdijk today makes western Friesland visitable as part of a rather full day trip from Amsterdam, but there's enough in this western corner of the province to detain you for a longer stay.

The Afsluitdijk

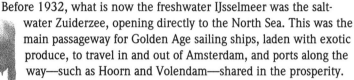

Before 1932, what is now the freshwater IJsselmeer was the salt-water Zuiderzee, opening directly to the North Sea. This was the main passageway for Golden Age sailing ships, laden with exotic produce, to travel in and out of Amsterdam, and ports along the way—such as Hoorn and Volendam—shared in the prosperity. But the low-lying land around the Zuiderzee was subject to terrible flooding. As early as the 17th century there had been proposals to close off the entrance to the Zuiderzee to prevent this, but the technology simply didn't exist. It wasn't until the late 19th century that such a scheme became feasible, and disastrous floods in 1916 catalyzed authorities into action. Objectors were vociferous: they feared that, as well as sounding a death knell for local fishing communities, the Afsluitdijk would cause a rise in the sea level around the Wadden Islands to the north.

But in 1920 work began on a small test dyke, and four years later construction on the Afsluitdijk began in earnest. On 28 May 1932 the last gap in the dyke was filled, and the Zuiderzee ceased to exist. The dyke stretches for 30km, and today some 30,000 vehicles drive along the A7 across it each week.

The Coastal Towns

The towns along the coast just south of the Afsluitdijk once enjoyed a prime strategic position at the entrance to the Zuiderzee, and traded with the world. Today, they're quiet backwaters, some noted for crafts such as ceramics and furniture painting—mainly reliant on tourism to survive, yet not as overrun as the towns nearer Amsterdam on the other side of the Meer.

Getting There and Around

Travelling around here **by bike** is much the easiest option, as public transport is relatively sparse and stations often inconveniently placed. If you aren't so energetic, next best is the **car**, although the roads tend to be narrow and the signposting sometimes disappears. The coast road from Makkum to Stavoren gives some lovely vistas of fields, canals and reed beds, although to see the sea you'll have to get out and clamber to the top of the dyke that runs along the coastline.

Trains run through Sneek and stop at Workum and outside Hindeloopen before the end of the line at Stavoren; **buses** also serve the area although with limited frequency, especially outside the season.

These towns get very busy with tourists in summer; between October and March many sights are closed or have reduced opening.

Tourist Information

Makkum: VVV in the Waag on Markt; open summer Mon–Sat 10–5 and Sun 1.30–5; winter Mon–Fri 10–12 and 1–4, ✆ (0515) 231 422.

Workum: VVV is at Noord 5, in a 1663 gabled house with plaster mouldings, ✆ (0515) 541 300; open winter Tues–Fri 1.30–5, Sat 9.30–4; summer Mon–Fri 9.30–5, Sat 9.30–4.

Makkum

The first stop after the Afsluitdijk is Makkum, whose main distinction is its status as a producer of ceramics that since the 17th century have rivalled Delft's in quality. The **Fries Aardwerk Museum** (in the 1698 Waag; *open same hours as VVV, adm*) has many examples of the local work, both blue and white and more colourful pieces. You can also visit the **Koninklijke Tichelaars Makkumer Aardewerk en Tegelfabriek** (Royal Tichelaar's Makkum Pottery and Tile Factory, Turfmarkt 65, ✆ (0515) 231 341; *open Mon–Fri 9–5.30, Sat 10–5*), the Tichelaar family workshops that have made Makkumware under royal licence for more than ten generations. Tiles, vases and more unusual objects, some plain, others with elaborate old-style patterns, are laid out in a large display area, and you can watch the craftspeople at work. There are plenty of other ceramics shops around the town but prices are high as this is the real, hand-painted thing.

Workum

A few miles farther south, Workum was already a prosperous town in the 14th century and did very well for itself in the Golden Age, cornering the market in shipping eels to London. It's based around one long street of little sloping-roofed houses, on which the few sights are clustered. This is **Noard**, which eventually (and reasonably) turns into **Sud**. At the north end of Noard is the neo-Gothic **St Werenfriduskerk** (1877) and its collection of religious artworks, the **Museum Kerkelijke Kunst** (Noard 175; *open June–15 Sept, Mon–Fri 1.30–5; adm*). At the other end of Noard is the **Jopie Huisman Museum** (Noard 6; *open Mar–Nov daily 1–5; April–Oct Mon–Sat from 10; adm*), featuring the works of an eccentric local eel-catcher, rag-and-bone man and self-taught artist who has achieved cult status in Holland for his finely detailed sketches and paintings of old dolls, shoes, and assorted flotsam and jetsam of anonymous lives. Noord terminates in Merk, a very attractive square, containing the mostly 18th-century Stadhuis and the oddly ornamented 1650 Waag. The latter has an ornate porch, and contains a small **local history museum** (*open Mar–Oct Tues–Fri 10–5, Sat–Mon 1–5; adm*). Merk also holds **St Gertrudskerk** (*open April–Sept Mon–Sat 11–5; Oct Tues, Thurs, Sat 1–5, Nov Sat only 1–5*), the biggest medieval church in Friesland and as such almost absurdly disproportionate to the little low town around it.

Hindeloopen

This amazingly neat and tidy coastal town of **Hindeloopen**, a few kilometres down the coast, is like others in this part of the country, a relic of past glories. Hindeloopen was once a wealthy Zuiderzee port and Hanseatic League town, trading with Norway and the Baltic. Its main claim to fame is its ornate **painted furniture**, with a background of red, green, white or dark blue covered with a complex pattern of tendrils and flowers, which originally emerged from a blend of Oriental and Scandinavian styles, thanks to the trading influences. You'll see examples all over Friesland. The women of Hindeloopen were once known for dressing in a related style, with vibrant colours and patterns, using different trinkets and materials to show their status.

Hindeloopen is very attractive on the surface, with its neat canals and footbridges, but it's somehow soulless: prettified, obsessively tidy, living off its past, its only industry tourism. As you walk past the pleasure-boat marina that was once a harbour or through the streets of quaint houses filled with souvenir furniture and cutesy art galleries, it's hard not to feel that stasis has spoiled Hindeloopen just as much as development could have. It isn't preserved, it's pickled.

The main relic of its greatness is the huge 17th-century **Grote Kerk**, just as in Workum dwarfing the little town. Note the gravestones lying almost flat around it, like fallen dominoes, so that the wind can't move them. By the church is the **Hidde Nijland Museum** (*open Mar–Oct Mon–Sat 10–5, Sun 1.30–5; adm*), which exhibits the town's history and characteristic clothes and furnishings in the 1683 Stadhuis. The **Schaats Museum** (Kleine Wiede 1, ✆ (0514) 521683; *open Mon–Sat 10–6, Sun 1–5; adm*) , offers a selection of old skates and pictures relating to the **Elfstedentocht**—the 'Eleven Towns Race', an ice-skating marathon that happens on the rare winters when the freeze is severe enough for participants to skate around a 200km route connecting 11 Frisian towns. When conditions are right, word goes out on the national news and thousands turn up to take part—though very few finish.

Where to Stay and Eating Out

Makkum ✆ (0515–)

> The good options here tend to be on the expensive side: there's nowhere outstanding for a reasonable quick lunch.
>
> **Hotel de Prins**, Kerkstraat 1, 8754 CN Makkum, ✆ 231 510 (*inexpensive*) is a small cosy place on the harbour whose traditional café/restaurant, offering Friese *koffietafel*, fish and pancakes as well as reasonable menus, is decorated by a marvellous wall of tiles with elaborate depictions of sailing ships. The friendly owner is currently renovating and it's not clear when the hotel will be completely open, but it's worth a try.
>
> **De Waag**, Markt 13, 8754 CM Makkum, ✆ 231 447, ✉ 232 737 (*inexpensive*), offers singles and doubles varying in size with price. The restaurant is on the pricey side, with dull starters but an interesting selection of game specialities including wild duck from the surrounding waterlands.

It Posthus, in the old Post- en Telegraaf Kantoor, Plein 15 (*moderate*), is a rather smart place with Frisian-style food: lamb shank cooked in beer, guinea-fowl fillets stuffed with chestnuts in juniper-berry sauce.

De Maitak, Markt 27, 232 850 (*moderate*) has a lighter and more varied menu to match its décor, with sole roulade with pesto in white wine. Try to sit in the room with the tiled wall.

Workum ✆ (0515–)

De Waegh, Merk 18, ✆ 541 900 (*moderate*), with elegant, bare-brick décor, offers French food with some Thai options and a good fish selection, including eels from the IJsselmeer, but no vegetarian options. There's a reasonable wine list.

Eetcafe de Witte, Sud 15 (*cheap*) has a good and reasonably priced selection of snacks. *Open from 4.30, closed Thurs.*

Herberg van oom Lammert en tante Klaasje, Merk 3, 8711 CL, Workum, ✆ 541 370, ✉ 543 815 (*inexpensive*). The first sign of something unusual here is probably the chicken-run on the landing. The 'rooms' are in fact a series of wooden cabins, each with front door looking on to a central brick-paved 'street'. Each cabin has an old-style Dutch cupboard-bed and relentlessly themed detail: the shower attachment appears to be a watering can, the modern toilet is fitted into a pine bench for that outhouse look. There are five double cabins and one with extra bunkbeds for the kids. The restaurant part is a spacious country pub, normally offering simple food at reasonable prices, occasionally hosting Frisian old-style theme banquets where you eat with your hands. Love it or avoid it.

Hindeloopen ✆ (0514–)

Cafe Restaurant De Drie Harinkjes (The Three Little Herrings), Buren 37–39, ✆ 522 222 (*moderate–cheap*), near the harbour, specialises in seafood.

Restaurant de Hinde, 't Oost 4, ✆ 521 478 (*moderate*) is a cosy and popular place with a bare wood floor, and nautical décor. It offers a short, simple, mainly fish-based menu with daily specials, smoked cod, and even eel as well as some vegetarian and meat options.

Hotel De Stads-Boerderij, Nieuwe Weide 7, 8713 JD, ✆ 521 278, ✉ 523 016 (*inexpensive*) is a large place. At the same address is the **Café Restaurant De Brabander**, offering a brown café and an old-style restaurant complete with florid local furniture.

Inland Towns

A network of inland waterways meant that not only coastal towns benefited from Golden Age trading prosperity. Sneek and Bolsward, in particular, still have something to show for their past riches.

Leeuwarden to Sneek: two trains an hour, and the journey takes about 20mins. Bus 98 or 99 goes from Sneek to Bolsward (links with train), but you can also go direct Leeuwarden–Bolsward on bus 92 (36mins).

Sneek: VVV, Marktstraat 18, ✆ (0515) 414 096, ✉ 423 703; open Mon–Fri 9–12 and 1–5.30, Sat 9–12.30 and 1–5.

Bolsward: VVV, Marktplein 1, ✆ (0515) 572 727, ✉ 577 718; open Mon 1.30–5, Tues–Fri 9.30–12.30 and 1.30–5, closed Sat and Sun.

The **Sneek Week** regatta in August is popular, but real *aficionados* come the month before for the *skûtjesilen*—races of old-fashioned sailing boats.

Sneek

Some 20km southwest of Leeuwarden, Sneek was once an important shipbuilding centre and Friesland's only walled town. It is still a lively place, now mainly known as a centre for boating activities and water sports. It holds a regatta, Sneek Week (regrettably, the town is pronounced 'snake'), in August each year, when the town is packed and all accommodation booked up. Sneek is a busy place and though there has been much new development it retains some old façades and has a sense of real life and fun.

Something of a city symbol, the twin-towered **Waterpoort** (Watergate, built 1613) is the only survivor of the city's fortifications, which were destroyed in the 18th century. But the commanding sight in town is the **Martinikerk** (*open mid-June–mid-Sept Mon–Sat 2.30–5; Aug also Sun–Fri 7.30pm–9pm*) on Martiniplein, founded in 1130. It is impressive in size if not stunningly attractive. Most of its exterior dates from the 16th century, the classical frontage from 1793, the ugly grey brick and wood Klokhuis to the side from 1681. On the other side of the Martinikerk, on Marktstraat, the rococo **Stadhuis** (*open mid-July–mid-Aug Mon–Fri 2–4*) is riotously ornate, with gargoyles, cherubs, gables and curlicues: be grateful its colour scheme is a subdued black, white, grey and dull red. It was built in 1475 but underwent major reworking in 1730–6. While on Marktplein don't miss No.22, whose yellow façade resembles an Art Nouveau castle but in fact conceals a nest of lawyers.

Marktplein and, off it to the east, Leeuwenburg contain most of Sneek's pubs and cafés. Leeuwenburg leads to pretty Kleinzand and the **Scheepvart Museum** and **Oudheidkamer** (Maritime Museum and Antiquity Room, Kleinzand 14, ✆ (0515) 414 057; *open Mon–Sat 10–5, Sun 12–5; adm*). The Maritime Museum offers model ships, naval machinery, displays on how sails and masts were made and more. The 'Oudheidkamer' features local silver, period rooms and displays on the history of the town, trade and skating. On Oosterdijk, a block north from Kleinzand, the **Hindelooper Kamer** is an Old Frisian coffeehouse with a Dutch menu and a Hindeloopen-style interior: a powerful riot of painted reds, blues and vivid flowers.

Bolsward

Bolsward, about 10km west from Sneek along the A7, was an old Hanseatic League town that became rich specializing in textiles. It hit the height of its prosperity in the 16th century and raised a couple of really impressive buildings. Today, it's an uneventful but attractive country town, with pleasant streets and canals to stroll along (Marktstraat and Dijlakker are worth a look), somewhat overwhelmed by tourism in summer. The undoubted highlight is the 1614 **Stadhuis** on Jongemastraat, a magnificent Renaissance confection exuberant with gables, swags, spires, curlicues, an elaborate outside staircase and an octagonal tiered pinnacle with a carillon. It holds a small local history museum, the **Stedelijk Oudheidkamer** (*open April–Oct Mon 2–4, Tues–Fri 9–12 and 2–4; adm*). Also worth visiting is the **Martinikerk** (*open Mon–Fri 10–12 and 2–4; July and Aug also Sat 2–4; adm*), a heavy hall church with a sonorous chime, built on a terp. It dates from the mid-15th century, with an older tower. The interior is special, with late 15th-century choir stalls adorned with misericords, a vault painting and a pulpit carved from a single tree decorated with such secular topics as the signs of the zodiac and the four seasons.

Where to Stay

Sneek ✆ (0515–)

De Wijnberg, Marktstraat 23, 8601 CS, ✆ 412 421, ✉ 413 369 (*inexpensive–cheap*). The best option in town: light, airy, fair-sized rooms with big bathrooms. The medieval pub/café part of the hotel is lovely, with bare brick, arches and pillars.

Hotel de Daaldersplaats, Stationstraat 66, 8601 GG Sneek, ✆ 413 175, ✉ 425 455 (*inexpensive*) is convenient for the station and has a small restaurant. It's a bit bleak and cheap-looking, and prices are high.

Hotel Ozinga, Lemmerweg 4–8, 8600 AD Sneek, ✆ 412 216 (*cheap*) is definitely the eccentric's option. Despite the name, this is a pension, B&B only, where they vet guests before deciding if any rooms are free (interest in history is an advantage, liking for luxury a no-no) and prefer to operate by word of mouth alone. You may not be able to book. The pub downstairs is dingy; the décor of the rooms escalates 'colour clash' to 'colour Armageddon'. However, rooms are clean and cheap.

Bolsward ✆ (0515–)

De Wijnberg, Marktplein 5, 8701 KG, ✆ 572 220, ✉ 572 665 (*inexpensive*). Unexciting rooms, all en suite, in a family-run hotel.

Pension Allemanshûs, Kleine Dijlakker 45, 8701 HX, ✆ 577 576, ✉ (0842) 129 088 (*inexpensive–cheap*). You're welcome to use the modern, comfortable sitting room in this family home. The rooms are homely, the décor arty and the owners friendly. Opposite the Martinikerk.

Sneek ✆ (0515–)

Haifa, Kleinzand 35–37, ✆ 423 261 (*cheap*) is an imaginative fish restaurant in a cool interior with plain walls and brick arches. Try salmon carpaccio for starters, then move on to fish *stoofpot* (stew) or succulent mussels. There are also non-fish options like chicken curry or a mixed Middle Eastern grill. Accepts credit cards, has terrace seating.

Lunchroom/Restaurant van der Wal, Leeuwenburg 3–11, ✆ 413 863 (*cheap*) is a no-frills option with lots of vegetarian and children's dishes and menus.

Onder de Linden, Marktstraat 30, ✆ 412 654 (*moderate*). Modern café set under lovely gables, looking out at the square through a row of linden trees. Choose from a modern fusion or a traditional Frysk (Frisian) menu.

't Stoofje, Oude Koemarkt 9–11, ✆ 417 438 (*moderate–cheap*). Cosy café-restaurant with a long list of pancakes, a variety of *stoofschotels* (stews/casseroles) and a few other main dishes.

Bolsward ✆ (0515–)

Dijkstraat is a good area to look for lunch.

Het Praethuys, Jongemastraat 19, ✆ 576 406 (*cheap*) offers lunch snacks from 12–3; evening meals 5–9. There's often live music.

It Ythuske, Rijkstraat 7, ✆ 547 936 (*expensive–moderate*). Classy Dutch food with a Frisian twist sits oddly with some more exotic ideas: hare stewed in honey and Frisian beer; or kingfish with papaya, mint and coriander. The interior is perhaps a little drab.

Northern Friesland

The northern part of Friesland has long formed a cultural and adminstrative focus for the Frisians. Country and coastal areas tend to be barren and windswept, but the regional capital, Leeuwarden, and its satellite towns have much to offer, from prize ceramics to tales of passion and intrigue.

Leeuwarden

Leeuwarden offers two excellent museums and a reasonably attractive Old Town, rather spoiled by thoughtless development: one of the visitor's first sights is an ugly modern fountain topped with a statue of Mercury, god of commerce, in front of an unappealing shopping mall. It's a university town with a provincial feel, prosperous though perhaps not as lively as it could be, with interesting public art that includes paving stones inscribed with poems.

History

Leeuwarden traces its origins back to a settlement of terps established at the confluence of the rivers Ee and Vlie with the now-drained Middelmeer. It avoided most of the ravages of war, and between 1584 and 1747 was the residence of the provincial *stadhouders*, the Nassau family, starting with Willem I ('The Silent') who eventually came to the throne of the Netherlands. His brother Willem Lodewijk was made *stadhouder* of Friesland, and his branch of the family held this position for over 150 years, acquiring *stadhoudership* of Groningen and Drenthe along the way, until Willem Carel Hendrik Friso was chosen as *stadhouder* of the United Provinces in 1747. Queen Beatrix is a direct descendant. Leeuwarden is proud of its most famous offspring: Mata Hari the exotic dancer and amateur spy (*see* pp.294–5).

Getting There

By car: The A31 connects Leeuwarden to the Afsluitdijk and Noord-Holland; the A32 heads down south towards Amsterdam. The quickest way to Groningen (and vice versa) is to head south on the A32, then back north again on the A7.

By train: There are two trains an hour to Leeuwarden from Amsterdam Centraal Station, one direct train and one with a transfer in Amersfoort. The journey takes 2½ hours. Trains leave every half-hour for Groningen.

Getting Around

Leeuwarden is small enough to be easily negotiable **on foot**; if you're travelling outside the city you can hire **bikes** from Stationsrijwielstalling, Stationsweg 1, ✆ (058) 213 9800; or Fietsenstalling Zaailand, ✆ (058) 212 8005.

The NS rail station and bus station are by the VVV on Stationsweg. Head up Sophialaan, averting your eyes from the unattractive Wilhelminaplein unless you wish to examine the neoclassical Gerichtshof (Palace of Justice, *c.* 1850), and carry straight on up trendy Doelensteeg to get to the interesting part of town.

Tourist Information

VVV, Stationsplein 1, (0900) 202 4060, ✆ (058) 215 3593; open Mon–Fri 9–5.30, Sat 10–2. There are no free town plans: it's ƒ2.50 for an advert-packed map. Ask here about the round trips by boat available in July and August.

The City Centre

Leeuwarden centres on Waagplein, on the southern part of the inner canal, which becomes Nieuwestad to the west. This stretch is broad and has some attractive gabled houses mostly converted to shops and restaurants. The **Waag** is a small foursquare building dating from 1595 in 'Friesland Renaissance' style, with comical moustachioed Holland lions holding up its shields. It's now a restaurant (✆ (058) 213 7250). As you pass, note the *gaper* ('yawner') above the shoe shop opposite.

To the northwest of the Waag, set in a large blank square at the end of Torenstraat, is **De Oldehove**, dubbed the Tower of Pisa of Leeuwarden, although the resemblance isn't striking—it's a Gothic red brick square tower dating from 1529–32. The point of similarity is the rather disturbing tilt of the building, although unlike the Italian edifice, which either tilted after completion or, some suspect, was meant to lean, De Oldehove started to go sideways even as it went up. The builders tried to correct the sagging by adjusting the placing of the windows and features of the façade as work continued to give an illusion of verticality, until they finally gave up. The church to which it belonged was demolished in 1595 because its foundations were even less reliable. You can, if you dare, climb the 40m tower for a wonderful view (*open Tues–Fri 2–4*).

North of the Oldehove is a pleasant park, looking over the river to the newer houses built as Leeuwarden expanded past its medieval bounds during this century. This is the **Prinsentuin**, the Nassau family's private pleasure garden from 1648 to 1750. From here you can see a bronze statue of a Frisian cow, locally known as 'Us Mem' ('Our Mother'; Willem Lodewijk, the first Frisian *stadhouder*, is 'Us Heit', 'Our Father'). The statue was presented to the town by the Frisian Cattle Syndicate and apparently has perfect proportions. The park often hosts concerts on summer Sundays. Off the park is one of Leeuwarden's major sights, the Princesshof.

Het Princesshof Ceramics Museum

Grote Kerkstraat 11, © (058) 212 7438; open Tues–Sun 11–5; adm.

Housed in a 17th-century palace, once the residence of Princess Marie-Louise, this is a must for those potty about pottery and surprisingly interesting even for non-fans, especially as there's labelling in English. Though the museum holds a wide variety of ceramic artefacts (check out the ceramic table in the period room on the ground floor), its bread and butter is tiles. There are acres of tiles, well laid out in the museum's cool white interior. The sets of Dutch tiles, shown mainly on the first floor, tend to be either groups of single tiles with similar designs (depictions of soldiers, flowers, children's games, mythological scenes) in which the variation and detail are fascinating; or the more expensive type in which a large number of tiles make up a single picture, so that a set of 16 might show a ship in full sail.

The second floor holds a seven-room collection of Oriental and especially Chinese ceramics through the ages. The earliest exhibits here are pots of red, grey or beige earthenware, dating from around 2500 BC. The collection runs through the centuries, with several lovely examples of Mongolian celadon (porcelain with a greenish glaze and decorations incised or in relief) and some marvellous Ming dynasty work, delicately painted in red and green with a light, spontaneous touch. There are examples too of the decline of Chinese ceramics in the 20th century with the production of less good work for export.

Those are the particular highlights but there's much more. Three rooms show the rise of European work: from crude Italian majolica to carefully sculpted French figurines and Art Nouveau objects and on to modern work. The cellars hold a selection of less good tiles from across Europe, plus some excellent examples from Iran, Syria and Turkey (the famous Iznik tiles). The **museum shop** has a selection of works on ceramics as well as books on the art of M. C. Escher (1902–72)—drawer of interlocking stairways, fish that turn into birds and other puzzles—who was born in the building.

Along Grote Kerkstraat

Grote Kerkstraat, a street with several good facades, holds the **Frisian Literary Museum** (FLMD, Grote Kerkstraat 212, ✆ (058) 212 0834; *open Mon–Fri 9–12.30 and 1.30–5; adm*), a collection of books, documents and portraits of Frisian literary figures of interest mainly to locals, though kept in a house where Mata Hari (*see* below) once lived. Farther up is the unexciting **Grote (Jacobijner) Kerk** (*open June–Aug, Tues–Fri 2–4*) dating mainly from the 13th and 15th centuries. It holds the tombs of various members of the House of Orange, a Müller organ and some good stained glass. The mid-17th-century Baroque southeast entrance is called the Oranjepoortje and topped with an orange tree.

West of the Grote Kerk, just one block north of Grote Kerkstraat, the **Fries Natuurmuseum** (Schoenmakersperk 2, ✆ (058) 212 9085; *open Tues–Sat 10–5, Sun and hols 1–5; adm*) is spacious, modern and well arranged but perhaps a little dull. There's an exhibition of whales with a rather unreal-looking 15m skeleton, but the main subject of the museum is Friesland wildlife: mussels, sticklebacks, snails, newts, small mammals. The underwater simulation is worth seeing for its ingenuity of presentation: you walk through displays as if you were at the bottom of a pond, with a thick translucent plastic ceiling above you mimicking the effect of the water's surface, broken by the occasional pair of duck's feet, a swimming rabbit or a cow's nose descending for a drink. Fish are suspended above the muddy banks and one display has a wrecked car, buried in mud, with a pike chasing its dinner in the interior. There's no sign of the driver though—maybe the pike ate him. A Walkman with English commentary is available. But Leeuwarden's main attraction is a short walk away, on Turfmarket.

The Frisian Museum

Turfmarkt 11; open Tues–Sun 11–5; adm.

The museum is housed in the 1566 spectacularly gabled late Gothic-early Renaissance Kanselarij (Chancellory) plus the 18th-century Eysinga house over the road, reached by an underground passageway. Entrance is through the post-modern iron-plated box structure, topped with a statue of a goat standing on a golden egg, to the left of the Kanselarij.

This excellent collection's highlight is perhaps the renowned display of **silver** in the vaults of the Kanselarij. This includes a drinking vessel made from a polished nautilus shell (1653) by Okke Jansen of Franeker, all kinds of decorative tableware, plates with carefully worked reliefs, a marvellously delicate filigree sugar spoon by Hendrik Dauw from the 18th century, and many other artefacts. On the top floor of the Kanselarij is the **Resistance Museum**, which offers a moving display on the period leading up to the Second World War and the Occupation. There are examples of the Resistance activities that went on, pictures of Resistance workers who were caught and killed, documents and artefacts from the Nazi occupation and examples of passive resistance in daily life. Interestingly, there's also a display on a fictional family of collaborators, taking a serious and humane look at how many Dutch people came to work with and even fight for the Nazis and the consequences they suffered after the war.

The Eysinga house contains a variety of period rooms. On the ground floor there's an accurate look at an 18th-century nobleman's house and lifestyle. The first floor holds several rooms furnished in the Hindeloopen style—blue- and red-painted furniture covered in elaborate floral designs in yellow and green, surrounded by walls of blue and white patterned Makkum tiles, all on a red and black tiled floor—to hallucinatory effect. There's also a wide collection of 16th-, 17th- and 19th-century paintings and some elaborately detailed 19th-century doll's houses. The second floor contains a small archaeological collection, with some lovely jewellery from Roman times to the Dark Ages (note the marvellously intricate inlaid fibula from *c.* 600 AD) and grave relics from the same era including a skeleton in the remains of a coffin adorned with a red, white and blue bead necklace. There's also a good collection of prints, with many works by **Hendrik Goltzius**, one of the most influential Dutch artists of the 16th century.

The modern part of the museum offers a permanent exhibition on the bizarre life of local heroine **Mata Hari**, with photos, documents (her scrapbook, the warrant for her execution) and skimpy dresses well displayed in salon-style surroundings.

Spy Stories

Margaretha Geertruida Zelle was born in Leeuwarden in 1876 to a well-off, successful middle-class family. It was a good start that didn't last: the family split up and she descended into poverty. At 19, broke and unhappy, Margaretha married Rudolph MacLeod, a Dutch East Indies army officer 20 years her senior, and went out to the East Indies. They had two children but the marriage was a disaster—she was flirtatious, he autocratic—and when their son died the couple returned to the Netherlands and separated. Margaretha left her daughter with MacLeod and went to Paris, determined, Scarlett O'Hara style, never to be hungry again.

She started her new career as a dancer under the name Lady MacLeod but soon decided that a more exotic approach would help. She called herself 'Mata Hari', Malaysian for 'eye of the day', announced that she was the daughter of a Scottish noble and a Javanese princess who had learned the art of dancing in the temples of India, and, most importantly, took all her clothes off. This novelty helped the press to disregard her less than exotic features and frequently varying stories. (She could not always maintain her mysterious Oriental sensuality: apparently she once announced to a lover that on the whole her greatest pleasure would be a cold beer and a piece of good cheese.)

As Mata Hari she was rich, famous, and desired by any number of wealthy men. She took numerous lovers, favouring men in uniform, both French and German, a habit that, along with her love of self-invention, led to disaster when war broke out. In 1916 she was recruited by the German intelligence services, presumably to exploit her close contacts with French officers; she returned to Paris and was promptly recruited by the French services as well. An egocentric fantasist, she had no idea what she was getting into, nor that playing the double agent in wartime is a dangerous game. Both sides rapidly came to distrust her and, less than a year from her original recruitment, she was arrested by the French and tried for pro-German activities. The trial was questionable—she seems to have passed little useful information in either direction—but she was sentenced to death and shot on 15 October 1917, leaving behind her the enduring myth of a mysterious, beautiful Eastern spy. Maybe Margaretha Zelle, storyteller extraordinaire, would have considered it worthwhile in the end.

Leeuwarden ✆ (058–)   **Where to Stay**

Hotel Palais Het Stadhouderlijk Hof, Hofplein 29, 8911 HJ Leeuwarden, ✆ 216 2180, ✉ 216 3890 (*luxury–moderate*). This imposing building used to be the palace inhabited by the family of Orange-Nassau from 1580 until 1795 (the suites have no numbers but are named after various members of the family). They keep *stadhouder* Prince William IV's chair in the lobby. The big double rooms have spacious sitting areas with comfortable well-chosen furniture, iron-framed four-poster beds, drapes everywhere, huge bathrooms and all the trimmings. Oddly the edges are a little shabby: walls and doors need a lick of paint, some rooms could do with jazzing up. The bridal suite, however, is amazing: an old-style four-poster, big sitting room area, in the corner marble steps up to a jacuzzi above which is a painted sky with little electric-light stars. It's worth getting married just to stay here. There's no restaurant, only breakfast. 'King's Suites' ƒ175–245, 'Imperial Suites' ƒ495, the bridal Willem Lodewijk Suite ƒ595.

Bilderberg Oranje Hotel, Stationsweg 4, 8911 AG Leeuwarden, ✆ 212 6241, ✉ 212 1441 (*moderate*). A pleasant upmarket hotel with 78 rooms combining modernity with quiet elegance. There's a luxury restaurant as well as an 'English-style pub'. The large rooms are well decorated, spacious and double-glazed; some have balconies.

Bastion Hotel Leeuwarden, Legedijk 6, 8935 DG Leeuwarden, ✆ 289 0112, ✉ 289 0512 (*inexpensive–cheap*) is a chain hotel outside the centre of town: large, modern, reasonably comfortable, unexciting.

't Anker, Eewal 73, ✆ 212 5216, ✉ 212 8293 (*inexpensive–cheap*) offers no-frills accommodation for all budgets. There are 23 rooms plus a big dormitory which can take up to 20 people at ƒ47.50 per person. The cheapest double room is ƒ87.50, rising to ƒ120 for en suite facilities. The hotel has a cheap bar and café.

De Pauw, Stationsweg 10 (*cheap*). The eating area is lovely, with carved settles, old oil lamps, paintings, caged birds, Turkish carpets and other evidence of *gezelligheid*. The rooms, however, are bare and plain, with campbeds. The restaurant offers a daily changing menu at ƒ25. *Closed Fri–Sun.*

Leeuwarden ✆ (058–)   **Eating Out**

Bilderberg Oranje Hotel, Stationsweg 4, ✆ 212 6241 (*expensive*) is classy with an interesting, mainly French menu. Starters (duck liver ravioli with sage, smoked ray with oyster mushrooms), main courses (lamb tenderloin with truffle sauce).

Het Haersma Huys, Tweebaksmarkt 49, ✆ 216 0120 (*moderate*) is a grand café that offers a good range of snacks and salads including vegetarian options such as goat's cheese salad and main courses like sweet and sour chicken casserole.

De Vliegende Hollander, Berlikumermarkt 15, ✆ 212 1717 (*moderate*) is a good, friendly place to bring children. The varied menu offers inexpensive salads and mains such as chicken schnitzel with Brie. There's a good vegetarian Indonesian selection and a tempting selection of desserts.

De Mulderij, Baljeestraat 19, ✆ 213 4802 (*moderate*). An elegant but pricey option, all smart linen and classy service with such starters as game ragout in puff pastry, then duck breast cooked with pineapple and Grand Marnier. *Open Tues–Fri 12–2.30, Mon–Sat 5.30–9.30.*

Eetcafe Spinoza, Eewal 50–52, ✆ 212 9393 (*cheap*). A stark, stripped-down place popular with students. *Open 4–11pm.*

Cafe Het Leven, Druifsteeg 57, ✆ 212 1233 (*cheap*) is a cosy place with an almost excessively international menu: gado-gado, saltimbocca, pepper steaks. It's popular and trendy, with walls covered in old posters.

For snacks **De Broodtrommel** on Nieuwestad 99, ✆ 212 2703 (*cheap*) offers *broodjes*, plate service and so on at around ƒ13–20. It's popular, light and airy with a young clientele. The *12-Uurtje* (soup, three small filled rolls, pickles and salad) is suitably filling and a bargain at ƒ13.75.

Leeuwarden ✆ (058–)   **Entertainment and Nightlife**

Coltrane's, 52 Eewel, is a café with a club downstairs after 10pm. **Roch It** and the **Fire Palace** on Doelesteeg both come recommended; the street is also the happening place to go for bars.

The Tivoli cinema, Nieuwestad 85, is open middays (except Thurs/Fri) and evenings, ✆ 212 5372.

Sauna Westenberg, Groet Kerkstraat 53, generally open for men and women 2pm–11pm, women only Tues 6–11pm and Thurs 9.30am–2pm, ✆ 213 7404.

Around Leeuwarden

The **Aqualutra Otterpark** (Kleine Wielen 4, Groene Ster, ✆ (0511) 431 214, a few kilometres out of town towards Dokkun; bus 10, 13, 50, 51, 62 from the train station run there; *open April–Oct Mon–Fri 9.30–5.30; Nov–Mar 10.30–4.30; adm*), to the east of town, exists solely for the conservation of otters, which are now extremely rare in the Netherlands.

Kinderboerderij (Children's Farm, Jeugdweg 3, ✆ (0511) 212 9256; *open April–Oct 10–6; winter Wed afternoons and Sat–Sun 10–6*) offers animals for petting, a playground and a *kabouterpad* ('gnome trail').

Franeker and Harlingen

Ten kilometres west of Leeuwarden along the A31, the charming town of **Franeker** was the seat of a major university from 1585 to 1811. After the university closed, the town subsided into gentle inaction and has kept much of its old centre intact. A few kilometres beyond Franeker, **Harlingen** is a passably pleasant harbour town, once prosperous as the main channel for foodstuffs coming in from the Baltic, and now the only Frisian harbour still connected to the open sea.

Getting There

Franeker is on the rail line from Harlingen to Groningen. Trains from Leeuwarden leave every half-hour, the journey takes about 75mins. The train station is to the southeast of town, about five minutes' walk. Follow Stationweg, cross the bridge and then follow Dijkstraat up to your left for Breedeplaats.

Harlingen is 7mins farther down the track. It has two stations: one for the town, the other, Harlingen Haven, for buses that connect with ferries to the islands. From the main station take Zuidoostersingel north; at the end take Eind to the left; this turns into Voorstraat. From Harlingen Haven walk straight down Havenplein and carry on to reach Voorstraat.

Harlingen is the port for **ferries** to Vlieland and Terschelling. From the train station to the harbour it's a 20min walk or take bus 79/99 to the ferry terminal.

Tourist Information

Harlingen: VVV, Voorstraat 34, ✆ (0900) 919 1999, ✆ (0517) 415 176; open Mon 1.30–4, Tues–Fri 10–12 and 1.30–4 (afternoons till 6 in summer), Sat 10–2 (till 5 in summer)

In shape **Franeker** is roughly rectangular, surrounded by a moat and with one canal inside the town confines. Most of the sights are on the main street, Voorstraat, or on the canal (called Eise Eisingastraat on the north side and Groenmarkt on the south). **Voorstraat** has a number of lovely houses with ornate façades and gables; notice the strange faces on the top of No.13, which resemble a blue-moustached Hitler. At Voorstraat 35 is the Martenastins, a fortified house dating from 1498 built by one Hessel van Martena.

Beyond is the **Museum 't Coopmanshuis** (Voorstraat 49–51, ✆ (0517) 392 192, also the VVV; *open Tues–Sat 10–5, April–Sept also Sun 1–5; adm*). This is made up of two 1746 university houses and the old weighing house, a 1662 building whose façade bears Baroque mouldings. The huge old oak balance still hangs above the desk. The museum has a variety of exhibits: the usual period rooms (including an interesting kitchen with huge wooden cookie moulds on the walls); collections of silver and porcelain; an old university senate room adorned with portraits of dead dons and a large astrolabe. There is a xylotheque—a collection of 158 boxes (shaped to resemble books), each made of a different kind of wood and containing specimens of the relevant tree's leaves, presented to the university by Louis Bonaparte in 1809.

There are also some of **Anna Maria van Schurman**'s artistic works. She was a famous intellectual, a friend of Descartes, fluent in Hebrew, Greek, Latin, Aramaic and Syriac, who published many logical disquisitions. One work, *The Learned Maid, or Whether a Maid may also be a Scholar*, was a powerful, crushingly intellectual and socially courageous tract asserting the rights of women to education and the use of their intelligence: 'whatsoever perfects and adorns the intellect of Man, that is fit and decent for a Christian woman.' She was also an artist, in the masculine worlds of portraiture and brass engraving as well as in embroidery, glass engraving and paper cut-outs. In the attic is a detailed model of Franeker in medieval times: it's best to see this after you have had a good look round the rest of the town so that you can see just how little has changed. The main difference is that the medieval castle no longer stands in the field at the end of Voorstraat, close to the site of De Bogt fen Guné.

From Voorstraat, close to the Martenastins, Raadhuisplein runs north up to the other cluster of sights. At its end is the 1591 **Stadhuis** (*open Mon–Fri 1.30–5.30; adm free*), an extravagant slice of very late Gothic cum Northern Dutch Renaissance, with twin gables and an octagonal tower.

Opposite, over the bridge, is the **Eise Eisinga Planetarium** (Eise Eisingastraat 3, (0517) 393 070; *open Tues–Sat 10–5, April–Sept also Sun and Mon 1–5; adm, no MJK; full explanatory booklet in English f5.50*). Eisinga was one of those mathematical geniuses who seem to come from nowhere and need no education. A wool-carder by profession, he published a work on mathematics at 17 and taught himself astronomy. In 1774 an unusual conjunction of planets was announced by certain astrologers and other charlatans as the imminent end of the world: the planets would bump into each other and throw the earth out of orbit so it would hit the sun. There was the usual result of mass panic; more productively, Eisinga's disgust at the ignorance around him prompted him to build this, now the oldest working planetarium in existence, in his own house.

The elaborate painted ceiling has small golden globes hanging from it to represent the planets, while various discs show the year, month, date, day of the week, moon cycle, time of sunrise and sunset, sign of the zodiac and so on. All these are accurate, as is the movement of the planets (as far as possible given the limitations of knowledge when he built it)—it still announces eclipses accurately, for example. Up the low winding stairs is the attic in which you can see the complex workings of the mechanism. The house-museum also contains a few exhibits on space and Eisinga's life, and a magnificent astronomical clock by Cornelius Jacobs van der Meulen.

East along Eisa Eisingastraat is the **Korendragers Huisje** (Wheat Transporter's Cottage) at the end of Noord, a tiny, sharply tilting house of 1634, hanging over the canal. There are plenty of other good houses to see: stroll around the Noordergracht (North Moat) to view the remains of the old city defences. Breedeplaats, a square to the east end of Voorstraat, holds the 1668 Botniastins, a charitable institution with painted figures over the door. This is a good example of the *stins*, a type of fortified house of which there are several here.

Off Breedeplaats is the heavy 1421 Gothic **Martinikerk**. Heading towards Voorstraat you pass the **Kaatsmuseum** (*open May–Sept Tues–Sat 1–5; adm*), also housed in a *stins*. Kaatsspel, the quintessential Fries sport, is similar to *pelota*, in that a hard ball is thrown at great speed using special leather gloves and identical to cricket in that unless you're an aficionado you'll be baffled. The museum tries to explain the basics of the game as well as displaying photos and trophies. Franeker holds a major yearly tournament up by De Bogt fen Guné pub on the fifth Wednesday of July (i.e. often in August). It's a very big event for the town and the place is packed for it. Seats sell out well in advance.

Harlingen is a good base for sailing activities: contact the VVV for details of the many firms who offer excursions. The town also used to be a ceramics centre (examples can be seen in the museum, *see* below). The last tile factories closed in the 1930s but a resurgence of interest led to the trade being restarted in the 1970s. The main street, Voorstraat, is now an unexciting shopping strip, but does hold the attractive 1730 Stadhuis (walk around it to see the projecting front and gilded statues) and **Het Hannemahuis Museum** (Voorstraat 56; *open April–June and 15 Sept–Nov Mon–Fri 1.30–5; July–14 Sept Tues–Sat 10–5; closed Dec–Easter; adm*). Based in a luxurious, high-ceilinged patrician's house dating from 1744, the museum manages to give a real sense of the life of the wealthy in the Golden Age. It offers a number of well-decorated period rooms—one on the ground floor has walls and doors completely covered in a diorama of ships at sea by Adrians Jan Oostendorp (1755–1827); another offers a magnificent fireplace with a multiple-tile depiction of a ship at sea. There's some good furniture, including a must-see clock whose face features moving waves, ships, whales and even sea monsters, all bobbing up and down in time with the tick. An impressive collection of Fries silver, including some excellent church pieces from St Michael's, and a modest selection of modern art at the back of the house complete a small but fascinating collection.

Franeker

Many of Franeker's hotels are in a transitional state at the time of writing, with two under renovation and the future of the third uncertain. It's a popular place so if you're keen to stay book in advance.

De Stadsherberg, Oud Kaatsveld 8, 8801 AB Franeker, ✆ 392 686, 🖷 398 095 (*inexpensive*). The hotel's recently renovated rooms are smart and modern with a few Frisian touches (some of the rooms are still to be completed). It's a very friendly, welcoming place with a classy restaurant. The décor is smart but traditional, with rustic touches like heavy beams and barrels, avoiding both cliché and clutter. It's on the canal; soon you should be able to moor your boat at their own jetty.

De Doelen, Breedeplaats 6, 8801 LZ Franeker, ✆ 392 261, 🖷 396 883 (*moderate*) is currently under renovation and should reopen in late 2000 with all rooms en suite.

Harlingen

Anna Caspari Hotel, Noorderhaven 67–71, 8861 AL Harlingen, ✆ 412 065, 🖷 414 540 (*inexpensive*), pleasantly located on the canal in the old town area, has 18 modern rooms with a few individual touches. The lounge area is cosy with lots of nautical décor and a magnificent clock; hundreds of ties hang above the bar. The restaurant (*cheap*) is European with a few Indonesian touches.

Hotel Zeezicht, Zuiderhaven 1, 8661 CJ Harlingen, ✆ 412 536, 🖷 419 001 (*moderate–inexpensive*). A friendly family-owned hotel with a lovely inviting lounge: comfy chairs, bookcases, smart décor and of course a British telephone box in the lobby. The rooms are cosy and well furnished with large bathrooms, and some have views over the water. The French-Dutch restaurant has an elegant evening part and a more casual terrace on the canal.

If you're broke **Wally's Pension**, 45 Voorstraat, ✆ 431 001, 🖷 431 003 (*cheap*), above a nice fast food place, has plain but clean rooms for ƒ65 per person including breakfast. No en suite, no frills, but friendly.

Pension Havenzicht, Noorderhaven 32a, ✆ 415 400 (closed for renovation at time of writing). The house is lovely, with ceiling mouldings and a fine staircase, lovely décor with bowls of flowers, a wood floor, old furniture and paintings, and a very modern kitchen.

Franeker

De Doelen, Breedeplaats 6, ✆ 392 261 (*cheap*), in a 1650 building with seating on the square in summer, is a light and comfortable eetcafe/restaurant with a Greek cook.

De Grillerije, Groenmarkt 14, ✆ 397 044 (*moderate*) is recommended by locals and has a pleasant interior, though the service isn't overwhelmingly friendly. The meat-based menu has a few unusual dishes (chicken and bacon rouleau as well as grills and casseroles).

Harlingen

De Gastronoom VOF, Voorstraat 38, ✆ 412 172 (*moderate*). Jolly, mildly chaotic family-run restaurant where helpings are generous and the cooking imaginative—try roast monkfish with spinach and a light curry sauce.

Graf Van Harlingen, corner of Vismarkt and Voorstraat, ✆ 430 003 (*moderate*). Loud and lively young bar in a 1647 gabled and shuttered building, with a steakhouse upstairs. Plain, meat-heavy fare.

De Tjotter, Rommelhaven 2, ✆ 414 691 (*expensive–moderate*) is a very comfortable and welcoming fish and seafood restaurant with much nautical paraphernalia scattered around for that fishy feel. *Open Wed–Sun 5–1.*

Noorderpoort Eetcafe, Noorderhaven 17–19, ✆ 415 043 (*moderate*) is a popular large 'brown café' in a classical building. Salads, stews, grills and fish dishes plus vegetarian and children's choices.

Galerie and Tearoom De Studio, 72 Noorderhaven (*cheap*) offers the usual range of snacks and light meals at reasonable prices, in a trendy French-style place, all wicker and plants, plus art out the back.

✆ (0517–)   *Entertainment and Nightlife*

Franeker

De Bogt fen Guné is the old university pub. It dates back to 1585 and has pictures, books and memorabilia of the glory days when the university was a significant centre of European study. There's a good tiled stove, old maps of the town and Kaatsspel trophies and relics (players' gloves and the like). The odd name is a corruption of 'The straits of Guinea' and refers to a long and complex story involving a discussion between Descartes and the landlord. It's often staffed by Leeuwarden university students, who are happy to tell the stories, and is a good place for a history-laden drink. The pub had a hotel, whose future is currently in doubt: it may be refurbished or closed by the time you get there. Call ✆ 392 416 to find out.

De Koornbeurs, the old Corn Exchange, Noord 1, ✆ 396 363, is now a cultural centre with concerts and theatrical performances.

Dokkum

Dokkum, Friesland's second oldest town after Stavoren, was once a significant port and the base for the Friesland and Groningen Admiralty. Its main claim to historical significance is that the Frisians murdered the missionary St Boniface here. Boniface had preached in Frisia and Germany for much of his life, setting up abbeys and bishoprics in Regensburg, Würzburg and Salzburg among other towns. The Frisians lost patience in AD 754 and martyred the monk (and over 50 of his friends), only to regret it later and dedicate many churches in his honour.

Dokkum's other claim to fame is its Beerenburg, a kind of gin made with 71 herbs, which is Friesland's national drink. The town retains some of its medieval fortifications, with restored bastions (two topped by windmills) and a moat. It's a pleasant place for an hour or so's exploration and has a few very fine hotels for a luxury break.

Getting There and Around

Dokkum is about 20km northeast of Leeuwarden, on the N361. It's half an hour by bus (bus 50), which goes once an hour. From the bus station it is a few minutes' walk to the north of the town: walk west along Stationsweg, then left down Aalsumerpoort and right down Koornmarkt and along Boterstraat to reach Markt.

Tourist Information

VVV, Grote Breedstraat 1, ✆ (0519) 293 800; open Mon 1–5, Tues–Fri 9–6 and 7–9, Sat 9–5.

The most notable church is the Martinuskerk on Kerkstraat, a double-naved 15th-century Gothic church with many tombstones set in the floor. The **Stadhuis** on De Zijk dates from around 1610 and has a carillon. The **Streeksmuseum** (Admiralitcitshuis, Diepswal 27, ✆ (0519) 293 134; *open Tues–Sat 10–5, Oct–Mar 2–5 only; adm f3.50*), based in the old HQ of the Fries and Groningen Admiralty, offers two millennia of culture in Northwest Friesland, including a display on the ubiquitous Boniface, period rooms, silver, textiles and folk art. There's also the **Natuurmuseum** (Keline Oosterstraat 12, ✆ (0519) 297 318; *open Mon–Fri 10–12 and 1–5; June–Sept also Sat and Sun 2–4.30; adm*), which resembles nothing so much as a primary school project on Friesland's natural history.

If all this has worn you down, the spring in **Boniface Park** down Bronlaan is said to have curative powers—try your luck.

Dokkum ✆ (0519–)   ### Where to Stay and Eating Out

De Abdij van Dockum, Markt 30–32, 9101 LS Dokkum, ✆ 220 422, ✉ 220 414, *www.abdijvandockum.nl* (*moderate–inexpensive*). This extremely smart hotel in a classical building, all chandeliers and silverware inside, offers some lovely rooms, many in the renovated and well-decorated 14th-century part of the building. The very elegant restaurant (*expensive–moderate*), run by a prize-winning chef, offers Franco-Dutch cuisine with three-course lunch and dinner menus. There's an excellent wine list.

Hotel Cafe Restaurant de Posthoorn, Diepswal 21, 9101 LA Dokkum, ✆ 293 500, ✉ 297 329 (*inexpensive*). Rooms are cosy but reasonably sized, with simple old-fashioned décor in dark colours, and large bathrooms. It's also a restaurant and *pannenkoekenhuis*.

Hotel Cafe Restaurant 't Raedhûs, Koningstraat 1, 9101 LP Dokkum, ✆ 294 082, ✆ 297 731 (*inexpensive*). This newly refurbished place is smart, friendly and warm. The pleasant modern rooms are all en suite, probably the best bargain in Dokkum. There's an inexpensive, light and airy café/restaurant.

De IJsherberg, Harddraversdijk 1, 9101 XA Dokkum, ✆ 229 500 (*cheap*), used to be a stopping-off point for skaters in the *Elfstedentocht*—hence the name, 'ice-auberge'. The restaurant (*cheap*), in the old library building, offers a 'culinary tour of Europe', where France is represented by steak with wild mushroom sauce, Norway by grilled salmon with red onions, Italy by lamb with tomato, garlic, basil and oregano. It has an outdoor terrace and also houses a theatre.

Eethuus De Waegh, Grote Breedstraat 1, ✆ 221 000 (*cheap*), is sited in the characteristic old 1752 weighing house. It has bare stone walls but enough rustic paraphernalia for cosiness. Hearty plain food.

The Province of Groningen

A treasured gem in a golden band
Is the town and surrounding land.

'Het Grönnens Laid', the Groningen Provincial anthem

The northeast corner of the Netherlands, the province of Groningen, is a divided place. The city of Groningen itself is a jewel, a lively, fun university town with a vibrant centre and some excellent museums and galleries. Yet it seems that the city has absorbed most of the region's prosperity. There are no other significant and interesting large towns and the northeast of the province in particular is not well off. It's sometimes referred to as the 'stepchild of Holland': poor, isolated, uncared for by its wealthy relatives. The inhabitants are seen by outsiders as being a closed community, unfriendly, with a peculiar dialect of their own. That pattern is changing slowly, with more investment going into the area to build up its industry and more tourism, but for now it remains the poor relation.

Groningen

Groningen, the capital of the province that bears its name, stands at the northern end of the Hondsrug (*see* p.317) alongside the Drentse Aa river. There has been a settlement here since the first millennium AD; the city is first recorded, under the name of the Villa Cruoninga, in a statute of the Holy Roman Emperor Henry III bestowing it upon the Bishop of Utrecht. The name probably comes from the Old Dutch '*grôn*', green place.

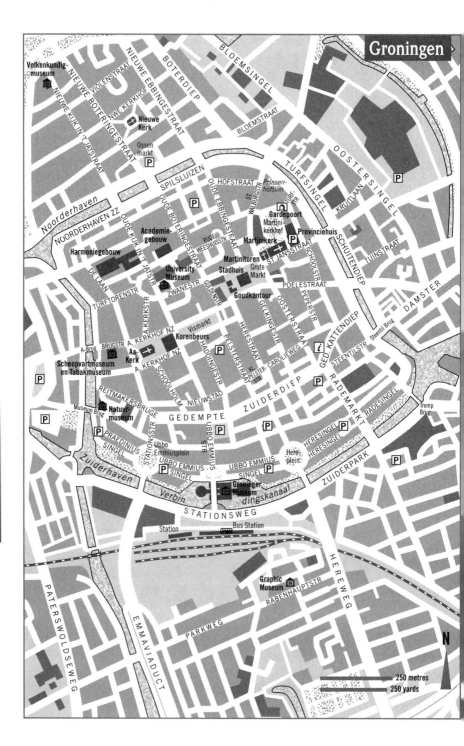

Groningen

Votkenkundig-
museum

NIEUWE VIOLENSTRAAT

NIEUWE BOTERINGESTRAAT

NIEUWE KIJK IN 'T JATSTRAAT

NWE KERKHOF

NWE KERKHOF

Nieuwe
Kerk

Ossen
markt

NIEUWE EBBINGESTRAAT

BOTERDIEP

BLOEMSINGEL

BLOEMSTRAAT

SPILSLUIZEN

HOFSTRAAT

Prinsen-
hoftuin

ST. WALBURGSTR

TURFSINGEL

OOSTERSINGEL

KRUTLAAN

Noorderhaven

NOORDERHAVEN ZZ

OUDE KIJK IN 'T JATSTRAAT

OUDE BOTERINGESTRAAT

OUDE EBBINGESTRAAT

RUDE WEESHUISSTR

Gardepoort

Martini-
kerkhof

Martinikerk

Provinciehuis

SCHUITENDIEP

TUINSTRAAT

DAMSTER

Academie-
gebouw

Harmoniegebouw

DE LAAN

University
Museum

ZWANESTR

GOLDKSTR

Martinitoren

Stadhuis

Grote
Markt

ST JANSSTRAAT

SCHOOLSTR

TURFTORENSTR

A. KERKSTR

Goudkantour

POELESTRAAT

OOSTERSTRAAT

PEPERSTR

PELSTERSTRAAT

GELKINGESTR

GED KATTENDIEP

STEENTILSTR

Steentil Brug

RADEMARKT

RADESINGEL

BRUGSTR

A. KERKHOF NZ

Vismarkt

Korenbeurs

A-Brug

Aa
Kerk

A. KERKHOF NZ

HADDINGESTR

HEERESTRAAT

KL. PELSTER-CAROLIEWEG STR

Scheepvartmuseum
en Tabakmuseum

SCHOOLHOLM

NIEUWSTAD

ZUIDERDIEP

REITMAKERSBRUGE

GEDEMPTE

Tromp
Brug

Museum Brug

Natuur-
museum

STATIONSSTR

UBBO EMMIUS STR

HEERESINGEL

HERESINGEL

ZUIDERPARK

PRAEDINIUS SINGEL

Ubbo
Emmiusplein

UBBO EMMIUS SINGEL

UBBO EMMIUS SINGEL

Here-
plein

Zuiderhaven

Verbin

dingskanaal

Groninger
Museum

STATIONSWEG

Station

Bus Station

PATERSWOLDSEWEG

EMMAVIADUCT

PARKWEG

Graphic
Museum

RABENHAUPTSTR

HEREWEG

N

250 metres
250 yards

Groningen's site gave it strategic and commercial importance: south of the fertile Frisian claylands and at the northernmost point of the province of Utrecht, it was perfectly sited as a marketplace. Its merchants traded with England and the Baltic lands, grew rich and, in the 13th century, decided to establish Groningen as an independent city-state, which they eventually achieved after much conflict with the Bishops of Utrecht. Groningen went on to become the most influential town of the region and made sure to exert its power: grain could only be sold at its market; only city breweries could produce beer for other than local consumption; those who traded outside Groningen's market could be arrested, fined and made to forfeit their goods. This did not endear Groningen to the surrounding areas and in the 16th century, when Groningen sided with the ruling Spanish, to whom the city had submitted the century before, the surrounding provinces broke out in rebellion and supported William of Orange. Nevertheless, when the town surrendered to the United Dutch Republic in 1594, it was confirmed in its authority over the surrounding area and its fortifications were expanded and strengthened. It was not until the 19th century that Groningen's political sway in the area was curtailed and its staple right over trading removed. Its disproportionate size and influence still cause resentment especially in the next-door Friesland region.

Groningen now has a population of some 170,000, with around 50,000 students: its status as a university town makes it one of the most fun and lively places to go in the area.

Getting There and Around

Trains leave Amsterdam for Groningen every half-hour (one train direct and one with a transfer in Amersfoort). The journey takes 2hrs 20mins. The train between Groningen and Leeuwarden takes about 50mins, leaves every half-hour and costs ƒ26.50. Groningen's **train and bus stations** are next to each other, to the south of the city.

If you arrive **by car**, note that the centre of Groningen is a car-free zone. There are a number of car parks in the city as well as Park and Ride facilities around its outskirts. There is no need to bring a car in: the pedestrianized area contains almost all the sights and the whole city centre, which forms a rough circle bounded by the canal, is no more than a kilometre across. The lack of traffic makes walking around the city a pleasant experience, though, as in Amsterdam, watch out for bikes.

Boat trips around the old moat can be taken in summer; book at the VVV.

Tourist Information

VVV, Gedempte Kattendiep 6, ✆ (0900) 202 3050 or ✆ (050) 313 9774, ✉ 313 6358; open Mon–Fri 9–5.30, Sat 10–5. Also a small booth in the station.

The first sight for most visitors is the 1896 **railway station**, a marvellous High Gothic-style building lavishly adorned with Art Nouveau tiles and spectacular ceilings. It was designed by prominent 19th-century Dutch architect I. Gosschalk (1838–1907) and recently renovated to its full glory. Just across from the station, nestling in the middle of a canal, is another startling sight, the 1994 Groninger Museum.

Groninger Museum

Museumeiland 1, © (0900) 821 2132, www.groninger-museum.nl; open Tues–Sun 10–5; adm.

The chief architect of this dramatic project was Alessandro Mendini, assisted by 'guest architects' Michele De Lucchi, Philippe Starck and Coop Himmelb(l)au (*sic*: without the 'l' his name means 'Heavenbuilding'), each of whom designed one of the four pavilions.

The complex is centred on a golden tower, which holds the entrance hall and expensive café. On one side is De Lucchi's square pavilion of typical Groningen bricks, sitting under Starck's contribution, a giant aluminium disc. On the other side Mendini's colourful mosaic-clad effort is topped with what appears to be an industrial accident but is in fact Coop Himmelb(l)au's deconstructivist pavilion. According to the blurb inside, this style releases the traditional elements of a building (walls, floor, windows, ceiling) from their usual context. The internal spaces thus created are 'the fallout from fields of tension'. This has been achieved by bolting together sheets of steel and glass, creating a chaotic effect which is certainly interesting, although perhaps not the best way to set off the art inside.

The pavilions were originally designed to reflect their purposes, so that De Lucchi's local brickwork was to hold the excellent local archaeology and history collection and Starck's construction the decorative arts (mainly ceramics and local silver), while the other buildings were for temporary collections and modern visual arts. However, following a flood that got into the lower pavilions, the permanent collections were taken off display and the entire museum used for a huge temporary exhibition of modern art and design which will last until June 2000. After that the Starck and De Lucchi Pavilions may return to their original uses, but this is not yet confirmed. Between this and the preference of the curators for fast rotation of the permanent collection, it is hard to predict what you'll see. It's worth visiting anyway, for the building's design, including the mosaic staircase inside the golden tower, and for the presentation of the exhibits— using gauze curtains inside the rooms to break up spaces, and displaying historical objects in settings reflecting those in which they were used, found or conceived. Thus a priceless collection of porcelain retrieved from a shipwrecked East Indiaman is partially displayed sunk in a fishtank set in the floor of the pavilion; a Jeff Koons mock-Baroque mirror is placed above a genuine Baroque table with appropriate silverware.

Grote Markt and Around

The old centre of Groningen suffered badly during the Second World War. Though much of the north and east side of the open space of the Grote Markt was destroyed, the south side retains some excellent gabled façades. At its west end is the **Goudkantour**, a tall twin-gabled tax collection house of 1635 (now a restaurant, built into a modern shopping mall). Heading across to the eastern end of Grote Markt you pass the neoclassical **Stadhuis** (1810) on the way to the **Martinitoren** (*open April–Sept daily 12–6.30;*

Oct–Mar Sat, Sun and school hols 12–6; adm). Known to Groningers as d'Olle Grieze (the Old Grey One), it was constructed in 1469–82, on the site where two previous towers had burned down. The tower, 127m high when first built, was set on a foundation of cow hides, but it collapsed in another fire and was reconstructed to a height of 97m in the 17th century; its foundations were replaced with cement only in the 1930s. The 49-bell carillon (by François Hemony) covers a four-octave range and is said to be one of the best in Europe. The Gothic **Martinikerk** itself (*open June–Sept Tues–Sat 12–4; adm*) contains paintings in the nave and the old choir from the 15th and 16th centuries, and has a renowned organ dating from 1470. If you find modern Groningen disappointing to look at, the church contains a detailed model of the town before it was all but destroyed by Allied bombing.

To the east of the Martinikerk in the attractive Martinikerkhof square is the neo-Renaissance **Provinciehuis** (seat of the province's government), in a former school, resplendent with gilt and with black and white shutters on the attic windows. The front façade is from 1916; the left side from 1559. On the north side of the square is the **Gardepoort**, a gate carved with impressive gaping monsters, that used to protect the entrance to the Prinsenhof (Princes' Court) but now adorns the local broadcasting service. To the right of this, a covered alley leads on to Turfsingel and the canal. North, up Turfsingel, are the **Prinsenhoftuin** (Princes' Gardens) (✆ (050) 318 3810; *open 1 April–15 Oct Mon–Fri 10–6, Sat and Sun 12–6*), elaborate rose and herb gardens laid out in 1625 by the Nassau-Orange *stadhouder* Ernst Casimir. The gate and gardens are adorned with the letters W and A, for later *stadhouder* Willem Frederik and his wife Albertine Agnes.

Vismarkt and Around

Southwest of Grote Markt is **Vismarkt**, which has some very attractive façades, especially on the south side, with flower-patterned tiles, decorative figures and elaborate gables—look above the Xenos kitchen shop for a fine example. To its west end is the neoclassical 1865 **Korenbeurs** (Corn Exchange), topped with a statue of Mercury, god of commerce, with Neptune, god of the sea, and Ceres, goddess of agriculture, at the front. It now houses a restaurant and cake shop. Behind the Korenbeurs is the **Aa-kerk** (Akerkhof 2, ✆ (050) 313 0902), named after the river Aa, which forms the town's moat. The bulky 15th-century nave has been frequently restored; the yellow and grey Baroque steeple dates from the 17th century. Its ornate white and gold interior, recently restored, is often the backdrop to concerts.

Off Akerkhof, along Brugstraat, is the **Noordelijk Scheepvartmuseum en Niemeyer Tabaksmuseum** (Maritime and Tobacco Museums, Brugstraat 24–26, ✆ (050) 312 2202; *open Tues–Sat 10–5, Sun 1–5; adm*), based in two houses. The Gothic house dates from the beginning of the 16th century and is a really excellent example of the style. The enjoyable and well laid out Maritime Museum, for which a welcome English leaflet is provided, offers displays on local styles of boat, the VOC and whaling; plus model ships, navigation instruments, old figureheads and a reconstructed victualling shop, with scales for weighing out goods and a sea serpent hanging over the desk. Don't miss the attic, a bewildering tangle of ropes and machinery. Nested in the middle of the Maritime Museum is the small Tobacco Museum, an engaging look at the history of the wicked weed, including Delft tiles of pipe-puffing angels and even sea monsters; plus models, pictures and smoking implements through history. There are some of 17th-century moralising engraver Jacob Cats' *Emblemata* here, in which (as usual) the one-man moral majority condemns all around him.

Other Museums

North of Vismarkt, the **Volkenkundigmuseum Gerardus van der Leew** (Ethnographic Museum, Nieuwe Kijk in 't Jatstraat 104, ✆ (050) 363 5791; *open Tues–Fri 10–4, Sat and Sun 1–5; adm free*) looks slightly old-fashioned but has some excellent exhibits in a clear and spacious layout. There are models of houses and waterwheels from Indonesia; jewellery from East Timor; Gujarati pottery animals; shadow puppets and masks; a complete Egyptian mummy with canopic jars, sarcophagi and a reconstruction of the face (looking unsurprisingly grumpy: call this eternal life?). Don't miss the marvellously evil Melanesian statues and masks on the top floor, near the gruesome display of decorated skulls.

Northeast of the town, outside the moat, is the **Museum of Anatomy** (Oostersingel 69, ✆ (050) 363 2460; *open Mon–Fri 9–5; adm free*), in the hospital medical science building. Outside the museum rooms are two old cabinets containing skulls, preserved human and animal foetuses, a square of skin bearing a tattoo in a jar, and much more. If you find this unpleasant, beware. This is a medical museum and there are some quite extraordinarily nasty exhibits, of professional interest to doctors, biologists and serial killers but which others, particularly children, may find disturbing (although look no further if you want to see where Damien Hirst gets his ideas).

South along the canal from Brugstraat is the **Natuurmuseum Groningen** (Natural History Museum, Praediniussingel 59, ✆ (050) 367 6170; *open Tues–Fri 10–5, Sat and Sun 1–5, closed hols; adm*). One of the most interesting things here is the layout. Stuck with a frankly old-fashioned collection of stuffed animals, the curators have used the exhibits in a variety of unusual ways to lift the museum out of a 19th-century rut. Sometimes this creates a bizarre impression—in the entrance hall dozens of posed stuffed seagulls dangle from the ceiling; the cloakroom pegs are, jaw-droppingly, antelope horns. In other cases it works brilliantly. One room on the first floor provides armchairs for the comfortable contemplation of curiosities; another lovely old room is enlivened by a huge tarantula on the wall and an owl perched on the roofbeams. Downstairs is a large, fun activity room for children.

Groningen offers yet more in the way of museums. There's the **Graphic Museum** (Rabenhauptstraat 65, southeast of the train station, ✆ (050) 525 6497; *open Tues–Sun 1–5; adm*) with displays of graphic design styles and equipment from typesetting to early DTP. There are also displays on local artists Hendrik Nico Werkman and Cornelis Jetses and regular special exhibitions. The **University Museum** (Zwanestraat 33, ✆ (050) 363 5562; *open Tues–Fri 12–4, Sat, Sun 1–4; closed Mon and hols; adm*) concentrates on Groningen as a university town, with a few displays of scientific instruments and so on. If you've become hooked on museums and need a final fix, the rather odd **Minimuseum** a little way north of the Groninger Museum (Ubbo Emmiusstraat 34a, ✆ (050) 314 6365; *open daily 11–6; adm*) offers a display of postcards of famous works of art.

Groningen ✆ (050–) **Where to Stay**

Auberge Corps de Garde, Oude Boteringestraat 72–4, 9712 GN Groningen, ✆ 314 5437, ✉ 313 6320, *www.corpsdegarde.nl* (*moderate*). This marvellous listed building has high-ceilinged rooms with lots of character, well decorated with funky lamps and lots of plants for a lived-in feel. The rooms possess good, large bathrooms. There's a small comfortable sitting area with leather chairs and a fire in winter, and an excellent restaurant (*set menus moderate, otherwise expensive*). The staff are terrifically friendly and charming. (Note: top floor holds five small twin-bedded rooms with two separate bathrooms. The rooms aren't normally used so they are plain, but perfectly serviceable and cosy, under the sloping roof. The staff can offer these rooms at a much cheaper rate, in the region of ƒ75 including breakfast. Ask about them if you're on a budget—you may get a relatively cheap stay at the nicest hotel in town.)

Schimmelpennick Huys, Oosterstraat 53, 9711 NR Groningen, ✆ 318 9502, ✉ 318 3164 (*moderate*) is a hotel, grand café and restaurant with a *pâtisserie/chocolatier* attached. Set in an 1723 patrician's house in Louis XVI style, the atmosphere is of faded grandeur—old brown oil paintings and leather chairs in the lounge, dark wood cellar bar-restaurant, Baroque dining room and 14th-century wine cellar. The rooms are large and old-fashioned in style and furnishings. There's a pleasant terrace restaurant.

Hotel De Ville, Oude Boteringestraat 43, 9712 GD Groningen, ✆ 318 1222, ✉ 318 1777 (*moderate*). The entrance hall is quite dauntingly posh, all mirrors and statues. The rooms are cool and spacious, with simple elegant design.

City Hotel, Gedempte Kattendiep 25, 9711 PM Groningen, ✆ 588 6565, ✉ 311 5100 (*moderate*). This ultramodern place boasts a very swish spacious lobby, with bare white walls and arty exposed brickwork. The rooms are simple, tasteful and modern, with Internet facilities. There's no restaurant but there is a free Turkish bath and sauna for the use of guests.

Hotel de Doelen, Grote Markt 36, 9711 LV Groningen, ✆ 312 7041, ✉ 314 6112 (*moderate*), surrounded by three-storey superpubs. The rooms are modern if on the small side, nicely decorated with reasonable bathrooms. The lounge areas are attractive, all dark wood and leather chairs; the hotel boasts a New York Steakhouse restaurant. A pity the staff aren't very friendly.

Weeva, Zuiderdiep 8, 9711 HG Groningen, ✆ 312 9919, ✉ 312 7904 (*inexpensive*) is big and bare and resembles à student hall of residence. Busy, impersonal, but reasonably priced. It has its own parking facilities.

Friesland, Kleine Pelserstraat 4, 9711 KN Groningen, ✆ 312 1307 (*cheap*), has reasonably sized rooms with haphazardly selected but adequate furnishings. It's clean, the shared bathrooms are perfectly acceptable and the price is good.

Tivoli, Gedempte Zuiderdiep 67, ✆ 312 5728, in case you can't find anywhere else (*cheap*). Little rooms with shabby furniture, threadbare carpets, and tiny, inconvenient facilities shared by many rooms.

Groningen ✆ *(050–)*   **Eating Out**

Bali, Rademarkt 15, ✆ 313 3355 (*moderate*). A fine Indonesian place with classy décor. The lengthy menu includes a wide range of dishes—*babi pangang*, lots of variations on *nasi goreng*, excellent satay, with *rijsttafels* at ƒ30 or ƒ40 per person. The food is well presented and comes in huge portions. *Open 12noon–10pm, closed Mon.*

Brussels Lof, A-kerkstraat 24, ✆ 312 7603 (*moderate*) has a rather bare, old-fashioned look, with pale green and wood effects. The traditional French/ Belgian menu (oysters, garlic mushrooms with Roquefort, *bouillabaisse*) includes several vegetarian dishes and is complemented by a good wine list.

Muller, Grote Kromme Elleburg 13, ✆ 318 3208 (*expensive*). Classy, pricey French restaurant, all crisp linen and silver in a very comfortable setting with statues on the walls. Voted best restaurant in the province by local foodie magazine *Lekker* for such mouthwatering creations as asparagus and *coquilles St-Jacques* with wild lettuce and raspberry dressing. *Open Tues–Sat 6–10.*

Soestdijk, Grote Kromme Elleboog 6, ✆ 314 5050 (*cheap*). An inviting little café-diner behind an old dark green front. Dishes such as ribeye steak or Zeeland mussels with chips and salad guaranteed to fill all empty corners.

De Pauw, Gelkingestraat 52, ✆ 318 1332 (*expensive*) is light, elegant and modern. Try salmon *mousseline* with crispy-fried herbed prawns, or pork in a pastry crust with a robust red wine and madeira sauce.

Koperen Kreeft, Gelkingestraat 50, ✆ 318 7082 (*moderate*) is a well-thought-of fish restaurant offering a variety of daily specials plus such dishes as poached cod with mussels or salmon with spinach and gorgonzola. The décor goes for the rough look, with whitewashed brick walls. *Open Tues–Sun 5–10.*

De Konings Vlinder, Ged. Kattendiep 15 (entrance on De Hornstraat), ✆ 314 3876 (*cheap*). Organic vegetarian food, with various soups, salads, pancakes (including a 'chilli-non-carne'), and a variety of fondues. *Open Wed–Sun from 5.30, kitchen closes at 9.30.*

Restaurant Dézart, Schuitendiep 44, ✆ 312 3730 (*moderate*). Brand-new Mediterranean-style eaterie, with arches in the walls and pale décor enhancing the bright contrasting upholstery of comfortable chairs. The menu is on a blackboard brought to your table. It offers French/international cuisine (salmon-trout terrine, shoulder of lamb in Belgian cherry beer), and also high tea from 3pm, when you can order sweet goodies or soups and starters from the dinner menu.

Goudkantour, in the 1675 gabled building at the centre of the Waagplein complex, ✆ 589 1888 (*moderate*). Stone floors in the entrance, velvet curtains and thick wax candles enhance the period feel, giving the place great atmosphere. It's on the pricey side, but then it used to be a tax office. A modern interesting menu includes sandwiches for lunch.

De Kleine Moghul, Nieuwe Boteringestraat 62, ✆ 318 8905 (*cheap*) is relatively far out of town but will be worth it for curryholics: this is one of the few Indian (rather than Indonesian) restaurants you'll encounter. Lots of *jalfrezi*, dopiaza and tandoori specialities.

Entertainment and Nightlife

Groningen has a thriving nightlife thanks to the number of students. Poelestraat and Peperstraat are generally the best places to go, Grote Markt is a little more brash. Gelkingestraat has **The Palace**, a huge and frankly evil-looking disco (*open Thurs–Sat after 11*) and a number of coffeeshops. Get a listings magazine from the VVV or newsagents to find out where the in-places are when you visit.

Cafe Kachel, Schuitendiep 62, is normally packed with a young crowd: noisy, smoky and fun. **Index Dansecafé**, above **'t Waegstuk Eetcafe**, Poelenstraat 55, offers club and trance tunes after 11pm. **Cafe Jansen**, Oude Kijk in 't Jatstraat, has a buzzing atmosphere and thumping tunes. **Blues Cafe-restaurant**, Oosterstraat 24, has a fun atmosphere and often live jazz. *Open Fri–Sat from 2pm, Sun–Mon from 4.* **Jazz-café De Spieghel**, Peperstraat 11, has live music nightly.

For those who like to sit down and hear conversation, **Cafe d'Opera**, Poelenstraat 15, also an *eetcafe*, is a rather more civilized place for a drink than most on this street. **Keyser** on Turftorenstraat is cosy, with candles on tables and a very friendly clientele; next door is **Cafe Wolthoorn**, which has a more stripped-down look but similar atmosphere. *Open Mon–Wed 4–1am, Thurs–Sat 4–2, Sun 8.30–2.*

Outside Groningen: Hortus Haren Botanical Gardens

Kerklaan 34, Haren, ✆ (050) 537 0053; bus 51/54 from Groningen station, get off at Botaniculaan stop before reaching the town. In summer cross the road and the garden entrance is up to the left; in winter this entrance is shut and you will have to walk towards town and follow the signs (about 15mins). Alternatively get a trein-taxi (see p.9) from Groningen station, or take the train to Haren (it's a 15min walk from there). There is parking by the main entrance.

Open summer daily 9–6; winter daily 9–5; adm exp, MJK free.

Hortus Haren is an extensive botanical garden featuring several different national styles, all worked out with care and love if not entirely convincing accuracy. The Hidden Ming Empire garden offers Chinese plants and trees in a setting of pagodas and statues (all authentic), little waterfalls and streams with stepping stones, a carp pond and so on.

The English garden is basically a large allotment, or rather 'cottage garden', with lots of vegetables (arranged by colour) as well as roses, offset by a red phone box and Dickens-themed tea room. The Ogham Garden, intensely green, has runic stones, mystical tree horoscopes and more. There's also a huge rockery, a Wild Plants Garden, a Bengal Garden, huge conservatories, and a really skin-crawling Insect House with tarantulas, scorpions, mantises, scarabs and giant snails. It's a charming place, perfect for a summer afternoon, with something new round every corner.

Groningen Province

Apart from the city of Groningen, there's not that much to see in the rest of the isolated, rather poor province around, but it's a good place for a cycling tour, with quiet roads near the coast and some trees to break the monotony. The province's image is of a flat, windswept, bleak, empty land—which doesn't seem so far from the truth if you travel in the winter. Yet it can be beautiful, with its vast, clear skies and empty, peaceful miles of country.

Getting Around

The most sensible way to explore is **by bike** (preferably) or **car**. If you're based in Groningen you can make forays from there by public transport: trains run from Groningen to Appingedam, to Uithuizen and to near Nieuweschans, and there are **bus services**. However, many of the places won't take more than a few hours to visit and you can spend just as long waiting for infrequent public transport and crossing the bleak scenery.

Lauwersoog: Bus 63 from Groningen leaves to co-ordinate with ferry departures to Schiermonnikoog and takes 55mins.

Uithuizen: There are hourly trains from Groningen (the station is 10–15mins' walk from the two big museums); bus 61 from Groningen takes you direct to the 1939–1945 Museum.

Appingedam: Trains run from Groningen every half-hour, take 30mins and cost *f*14.50. You can arrange waterbike or canoe hire or boat trips via Zaal De Klunder, located by Café Chez Bateau, Wijkstraat 26, on the Nieuwe Diep yacht harbour. ✆ (0596) 626 039.

Nieuweschans: You can reach the spa hotel by train, once an hour from Groningen, it takes 55mins and costs *f*23.

Bourtange: Reached by bus 7 from Groningen or more easily by car: follow the signs for Vesting.

Ter Apel: Bus 73 from Groningen; bus 270 from Bourtange.

Tourist Information

Lauwersoog: ExpoZee, ✆ (0519) 349 045; VVV, ✆ (0595) 401 957; both at Strandweg 1; open 10–5, both shut in winter when the winds are bitingly cold anyway.

Uithuizen: VVV, Mennonietenkerkstraat 13 (near the windmill), ✆ (0595) 434 051, ✆ 434 722; open April–Oct Mon–Fri 10–12 and 1–5, Sat 1–4; Nov–Mar Mon–Fri 10–12 and 1–4, Sat 2–4.

Appingedam: VVV, Wijkstraat 38 (to the left of the church), ✆ (0596) 620 300; open Mon–Fri 10–6, Sat 11–4.

Nieuweschans: VVV, Voorstraat 44; open Tues–Fri 2–4.

Bourtange: VVV/information centre offers an exhibition about the town's history (ƒ5, ƒ3 under 12); open April–Oct Mon–Fri 10–5, Sat/Sun 11–5; Nov–Mar Sat and Sun only 12.30–4.30.

Northern Groningen

At the northwest tip of Groningen province is the **Lauwersmeer**, which was closed off from the Waddenzee to become a freshwater lake by the Lauwersoog dam in the 1960s. It's a lovely, wild area, noted for its bird population, thanks to local conservationists' efforts to fend off development, and has now been declared a national park. It's a good place for outdoor activities; **Lauwersoog** holds the **ExpoZee** centre (also the VVV), which has lots of information on things to do, as well as background information on the Lauwersmeer, its flora and fauna, and ecological and land reclamation issues. They run boat trips for ƒ16.50, under 12 ƒ8. Lauwersoog is the port for ferries to Schiermonnikoog.

Some 20km east, off the N361 at **Leens** is the **Landgoed Verhildersum**, a *borg* (moated manor house) dating from the 14th century, inhabited by various owning families until 1953 (manor house ✆ (0595) 571 430, Welgelegen ✆ (0595) 572 400, restaurant ✆ (0595) 572 204; *open April–Nov 10.30–5; coachhouse and Welgelegen only 1.30–5; closed Mon; adm*). It's now been restored to display 19th-century local style and furnishings, and holds the Ommelander Museum of Agriculture and Crafts. In the grounds are the Schathuis (cattle barns, now a restaurant), the Welgelegen farmhouse museum, and the Koetshuis (coachhouse, holding temporary art exhibitions). The attractive gardens have an arbour and statuary by Eddy Roos.

Next along the N363 coastal road comes **Warffum**, which offers **Het Hoogeland** open-air museum (Schoolstraat 2, ✆ (0595) 422 233; *open April–Oct Tues–Sat 10–5, Sun 1–5; adm*), a collection of brick cottages and buildings that have been preserved and restored to show rural life in northeast Groningen in the 19th century: a school, shops, a kosher butcher's, a pub. There's not much of riveting interest but it gives a sense of the rather hard lives spent here.

The nearby town of **Uithuizen** isn't anything special but it has two interesting places to visit, close together on the east side of town. The prime reason to go is **Menkemaborg** (Menkemaweg 2, ✆ (0595) 431 970; *open April–Sept 10–12 and 1–5; Oct–Mar 10–12 and 1–4 and closed Mon; adm*), a fully furnished and restored *borg* (moated manor house) the ground floor and basement of which are open to the public. It was built in 1614 on the site of an older house that had been destroyed and remodelled by Allard Meyer, later city architect of Groningen, around 1705. The seven rooms give an idea of the life of a Dutch noble family, with rich furnishings, cabinets of valuable porcelain and elegant decoration: note particularly the five impressive carved oak mantelpieces, the work of Jan de Rijk. There is an angel-topped organ of 1777 in the state apartment (room 2) and an imposing four-poster bed, covered in yellow damask, in room 4. William III slept here in the 19th century; it's one of Menkemaborg's few pieces of original furniture (most of the rest is from other houses of the region.) In sharp contrast to this luxury is the ill-lit basement kitchen, the oldest part of the house, with its low ceiling and two tiny cupboard-beds for the servants. The formal gardens were laid out in the 18th century and have been reconstructed in this ornate and regular style, with walks, statues arbours, trellises, shaped yew trees and the odd peacock.

The **Internationaal Museum 1939–1945** (Dingeweg 1, ✆ (0595) 434 100; *open April–Oct 9–6; adm*) holds a huge amount of war memorabilia: photos, documents, battle plans, a working Sherman tank, weapons, uniforms and much more. Uithuizen also offers the **Kantmuseum** (Oude Dijk 7, ✆ (0595) 432 368; *open Mon and Wed– Fri 1–5; adm*), which features, not German philosophy, but lace. There are examples of both bobbin lace (Chantilly and Valenciennes style) and needlepoint (Point de Bruxelles) and many lacework items.

Along the N363 from Uithuizen or a train ride from Groningen, **Appingedam** is a charming town, well preserved, with some lovely buildings. It was a member of the Hanseatic League in the Middle Ages but excavations of terps date the original settlement to around 900. There isn't much to do beyond wandering the little streets of its centre, but it's a charming slice of old-style Holland that doesn't crawl with tourists in summer, and also a good example of how to integrate modern buildings without destroying the atmosphere of a town.

The main street, Wijkstraat, runs parallel with the canal; here you'll find the church complex that is Appingedam's main attraction. The earliest parts of the **Nikolaikerk** (*open 15 June–15 Sept Tues–Sat; or call ✆ (0596) 622 992*) date from 1225. It was originally built in a cruciform shape but later extended to become a hall church. Outside it's an imposing mostly Gothic structure in red brick; the lovely interior includes some wall-paintings, ornamented pews, a carved pulpit and a magnificent mid-18th-century organ. It has a tuneful carillon too. Next to it the arcaded Renaissance-style Raadhuis (1630), one of the smallest in the Netherlands, has a relief of the town's logo, an ornithologically inaccurate pelican feeding her chicks with blood from her own breast. The image is repeated on the walls of the Franse school attached to the church, as well as in the logo of the local football team, De Pelikanen. Solwerderstraat, which runs parallel to the canal on the other side from Wijkstraat, and the Damsterdiep canal are both especially worth a wander.

Uithuizen ✆ (0595–)

Cafe Restaurant 't Schathoes Menkemaborg, Menkemaweg 4, ✆ 431 858 (*cheap*) offers *koffietafels* (the local equivalent of a high tea) and pancakes in the old store-house building close to the manor house.

Appingedam ✆ (0596–)

Het Wapen van Leiden, Wijkstraat 44, 9901 AJ Appingedam, ✆ 622 963, ✆ 624 853 (*inexpensive*). Appingedam's solitary hotel has horrible carpeted walls but the rooms are pleasant enough, plain but light and spacious.

The other option for Appingedam is to stay in pensions. A marvellous choice, especially for lone travellers, is the **Fam. van den Ouden Lindenburg**, Heerd 35, 9932 CD Delfzijl, ✆ 626 907, mobile ✆ 06 20 41 84 55 (*cheap*), a little suburban house in the sprawl between Delfzijl and Appingedam, with just one twin-bedded guest room. The owners are welcoming, kind and friendly; Ineke is an expert on local history and delighted to tell you all the best places to go in the area; and breakfast is quite possibly the best spread in the Netherlands. A home from home for *f*35 per person. (*They mainly offer accommodation in April– Oct; no smoking in the house; small friendly dog.*)

The larger **Pension Kirsten**, 16 Stationsweg, ✆ 628 882 (*cheap*), has several rooms with shared bathrooms.

Grand Café de Oude Rechtbank, Wijkstraat 38, ✆ 628 234 (*cheap*) has a spacious, slightly old-fashioned interior. It offers a reasonable range of dishes— steaks and schnitzels, salmon in lime and coriander or fish in white wine—as well as vegetarian options and a children's menu.

Café Chez Bateau, Wijkstraat 26, ✆ 626 039 (*moderate*) offers 'steakhouse cooking': seafood starters, a variety of grilled meats for main course, vegetarian options on request. It's a cosy place on the harbour, full of plants and with a terrace out the back for summer dining.

Outside Appingedam is the **Landgoed Ekenstein**, Alberdaweg 70, 9901 TA Appingedam, ✆ 628 528, ✆ 620 621 (*moderate–inexpensive*). This old building, set in extensive grounds, offers a large pleasant park, children's playground, zoo, model boat harbour, canoe and kayak hire, as well as a very comfortable hotel.

Eastern Groningen

A novelty in the area, should you feel like a bit of pampering, is the spa town of **Nieuweschans** (just off the A7 near the German border), the site of one of the Netherlands' very few natural mineral springs. A large '**Kuurhotel**' has been created around the thermal spring, which is used to fill a smart outdoor pool. It's kept at body temperature, which along with the minerals has a detoxifying and relaxing effect. There are also all the other trappings—a normal pool, saunas (with piles of salt in urns by the side for body scrubbing), jacuzzi, gym, massage, beauticians, mud baths and seaweed wraps. You can come for the day at a price (*f17.50 for the thermal bath and relaxation room; f45 for a 30min massage and so on*). The village of Nieuweschans used to be surrounded by star-shaped fortifications until progress and the motorway removed all traces (they retain a fortress museum, the Vestingmuseum, by the VVV; *open Mon–Fri 1–5; also 9–12 in April–Oct*).

But 20km to the south you can see the best example of a star-shaped fortress village in the Netherlands. **Bourtange** (*pictured* p.263) was founded in 1580 to defend the approach to Groningen, but fell into disrepair until a remarkable restoration effort of the 1960s. The village is built inside a maze of moats forming concentric geometric patterns based around a five-pointed star shape, its astonishing regularity best shown by aerial photographs. Thread your way through the network of bridges and moats to reach the little gatehouse and the village itself. The perfectly restored 17th- and 18th-century houses and leafy main square give it more the atmosphere of period drama film set than a real place. The shops sell curiosities and antiques and tourist trinkets; any inhabitants trying to lead their own lives must feel like fish in an aquarium. A stab of reality comes with the plaque on the wall of the old synagogue, listing the names and ages of 46 Jews deported from this tiny place during the war; the oldest were over 80, the youngest just five years old.

Looming out of the woods southeast of Groningen is the **Museum-Klooster Ter Apel** (Boslaan 3, ☎ (0599) 581 370; *open Tues–Sat 10–5, Sun 1–5, April–Nov also Mon 10–5; adm*) a magnificent cruciform Gothic church, built in 1464 by the Order of the Crutched Friars, though the attached monastery wasn't completed until 1554. The expulsion of the occupying Catholic Spanish in 1594 and subsequent establishment of Calvinism as Groningen's official religion led to the closing of the monastic institutions of the province. Ter Apel, unlike many, was not destroyed, but new recruitment was banned and the last prior left to become a Calvinist priest in 1619. The monastery was used as a school, a house and a workshop before restoration in the 1930s. It's a fine place with attractive cloisters surrounding a traditional formal herb garden. The church retains some interesting features: the rood screen, 15th-century tripartite sedilia (where the priest and assistants sat during mass) and beautifully carved choir stalls with some fine misericords meant to represent vices and virtues. The east wing's chapter-room has a late Gothic ceiling of ornamented oak well worth seeing.

Where to Stay and Eating Out

Nieuweschans ☎ (0597–)

> **Golden Tulip Fontana Nieuweschans**, Weg naar de Bron 3–7, 9693 GA Nieuweschans, Postbus 44, 9693 ZG Nieuweschans, ☎ 527 777, ✉ 528 585 (*moderate–inexpensive*). The smart spa hotel has an expensive restaurant for dinner and lounges for lunch, but the rooms are surprisingly small and plain.

Bourtange ✆ (0599–)

Inside the fortified village everywhere to eat can be assumed to be old and quaint offering fairly standard fare. Try **Café-restaurant 's Lands Huys** (*moderate–cheap*), or **'t Oal Kroegle** (*cheap*), somewhat cosier, with plenty of lunch snacks. Both on the main square.

Hotel-restaurant de Staakenborgh, Vlagtwedderstraat 33, 9545 TA Bourtange, ✆ 354 216, ✉ 354 354 (*cheap*). A couple of kilometres down the road from the fortified village and through its modern extension. Rooms are bright and spacious if somewhat dormitory-style with twin campbeds in the rooms. There's a small farm attached, with tiny Shetland ponies, and a playground. The restaurant (*cheap*) is based in a lovely old barn, and offers plain country cooking. *Open 12–3 and 5–8.30, Sat and Sun 12–9.*

Ter Apel ✆ (0599–)

Boschhuis, Boslaan 6, 9561 LH Ter Apel, ✆ 581 208, ✉ 581 906 (*inexpensive*). An elegant old building opposite the monastery, with 10 large bedrooms, all in the same green-themed décor as the communal areas. It's the only place near to Ter Apel; this monopoly may account for the lack of effort that goes into making guests feel welcome. There's a smart restaurant (*moderate*)—halibut with chive sauce, lamb tournedos in honey, whisky and thyme. *Book at weekends.*

Drenthe and Northern Overijssel

> *...this province is one great peat bed, though without the mountains that give poetry to the Bog of Allen.*
>
> Sacheverell Sitwell

For most of its history Drenthe had the reputation of being the most thinly populated of provinces, a place of peat bogs and marshland, whose one ridge of low hills provided all its scenic excitement. In the 18th and 19th centuries many peat-cutting communities (*Veenkulunies*) were established here and drainage canals dug; after years of labour the land was dried out and cleared for agriculture, proving very fertile. It's now a prosperous area with several large towns.

Despite the unattractive qualities of the land before reclamation, Drenthe boasts a remarkable history of habitation. The 50km-long range of hills known as the Hondsrug (Dog's Back) that runs from Groningen to Emmen attracted prehistoric settlers in large numbers: the area was inhabited by 3000 BC. These settlers left a number of megalithic tombs (*hunebeds*), now among Drenthe's prime tourist attractions. After this burst of activity things seem to have slowed down until the 6th century AD, when it was invaded and subsequently ruled by Saxons. It then changed hands, going first to the Bishops of Utrecht (1024), then to the Habsburg empire (1538). Drenthe was not formally made a province until the 1796 establishment of the Batavian Republic, although it had had *stadhouders* of the House of Orange since 1722.

Assen and Emmen

Getting Around

The main towns are on rail lines, some served by inter-city trains, but local trains and buses are slow. The bus between Assen and Emmen, for example, takes an hour to creep 25km.

Assen: Trains travel four times an hour from Groningen, take 20mins and cost ƒ14.50.

Emmen: Bus 73 from Emmen runs to Ter Apel and bus 45 goes hourly to the Veenpark.

Tourist Information

Assen: VVV, Brink 42; open Mon 1–6, Tues–Thurs 9–6, Fri 9–9, Sat 9–5, ✆ (0592) 314 324. They have a good selection of walking and cycling maps for the area.

Emmen: VVV, Marktplein 9, ✆ (0591) 613 000, @ 644 106; open Mon 10–5, Tues–Fri 9–5, Sat 10–1.

Assen, the provincial capital of Drenthe, is not a town of any great interest with not much to visit apart from the **Drents Museum** (Brink 1 and 5, ✆ (0592) 312 741; *open Tues–Sat 11–5, also Mon on public holidays; adm*). The regional museum is housed in a complex of old buildings: the tiled 1885 Provinciehuis, two public officials' houses and the abbey church. The façades have not been altered, but the interiors are linked, giving the museum a pleasant rabbit-warren feel. The museum has a wide range of arts and crafts and many paintings of Drenthe landscapes (lots of sky and the occasional *hunebed* making it a popular subject with the Hague School). There's a particularly extensive Art Nouveau collection, with all kinds of artefacts and designs on display. The archaeological section offers some good finds, including an impressive treasure-trove of gold coins and jewellery from about AD 400 and, a less attractive discovery, the flaccid leathery corpse of a young woman who was strangled and thrown into a bog two thousand years ago. Other remarkable preserved artefacts include a plait of hair from 600 BC (red, as is all hair found in bogs), a ball of wool from 1500 BC, grave goods and brooches, and a Mesolithic canoe from around 7800 BC. All the museum's labelling is in Dutch and German.

South of Assen, near Hooghalen, is the **Herinneringscentrum Kamp Westerbork** (Oosthalen 8, 9414 TG Hooghalen, ✆ (0593) 592 600, @ 592 546; *open Mon–Fri 10–5, Sat and Sun 1–5 or 11–5 in July and Aug; adm*). Over 100,000 Dutch Jews were held here prior to transportation to the concentration camps. The camp itself has mostly been destroyed but there are moving artefacts and displays on the Holocaust.

Emmen, southeast of Assen, is an unexciting town centred on a very ugly shopping precinct. Fans of *hunebeds* might drop by, or you might also find it a convenient base to see the Veenpark (*see* below) or Ter Apel (*see* p.316).

There is a cluster of *hunebeds* around Emmen. The nearest is the **Emmerdennen Hunebed**, set in the woods a kilometre or so outside the town (signposted from the station). The *hunebed* is a low flat-topped structure of lichened stones set within a rough circle, not more than a metre high. It's incredibly old but not terribly impressive to a non-expert; any sense of age and brooding mystery tends to be dispelled by its popularity as a playground for small children. However, it's a good excuse for a walk in the woods among the pine and silver birch. The **National Hunebed Information Centre 't Flint'nhoes in Borger** can provide more information on these structures: ✆ (0599) 236 374. More impressive *hunebedden* can be seen just outside **Noordsleen**, 7km west of Emmen, which has two, and outside **Odoorn**, north of Emmen, which has three.

In nearby Barger Compascuum, the **Veenpark** (Berkenrode 4, Barger Compascuum, ✆ (0591) 324 444, @ 349 122; bus 45 from Emmenopen; *open April–Oct daily 10–5; July–Aug daily 10–6; adm exp*) is yet another outdoor theme park demonstrating local life in years gone by, with authentic buildings taken from around the region, costumes and demonstrations of crafts. You can see life in a peat colony *c*. 1870 and an exhibition of how to dig peat from a moor. There's a 1903 school, an 1870 windmill, a smithy, brown café, bakery, pancake house and more. (Naturally, food can be bought in all conceivable outlets.) A small old-style steam train runs through the park.

Where to Stay

Assen ✆ (0592–)

Hotel de Jonge, Brinkstraat 85, 9401 HZ Assen, ✆ 312 023, @ 313 114 (*inexpensive–cheap*). 54-room hotel across the alleyway from the restaurant. Unattractive smoke-smelling corridors and bare lobby but large comfortable rooms, well furnished, with good-sized bathrooms.

Christerus, Stationstraat 17, 9401 KV Assen, ✆ 313 517 (*cheap*) offers ten rooms, some with showers, in a family house run by an elderly couple. The rooms are clean but filled with some rather grotty furniture (this is where fluffy orange 1970s bedspreads come to die).

Emmen ✆ (0591–)

Hotel Boerland, Hoofdstraat 57, 7811 ED Emmen, ✆ 613 746, @ 616 525 (*inexpensive*). The rather kitsch building contains a pleasant hotel, light and cheerful, with comfortable pine furniture. The rooms are small but neat and modern.

Assen ✆ (0592–)

> **Cafe Restaurant de Passage**, Brinkstraat 2 (*cheap*) is a modern and reasonable place for filling up: *dagschotel f*17.50.
>
> **Centraal**, next to Hotel De Jonge, Brinkstraat (*moderate*) is a smoky, spacious Grand Café with wicker chairs and lots of light. Salads around *f*20, main courses around *f*30, with quite a young clientele for the modern food (steak with pineapple and rosemary chutney).
>
> The **Koffee- und Spijssalon**, 21 Brink (*cheap*) is an elegant stop for afternoon tea and pastries.

Emmen ✆ (0591–)

> **De Kamer**, Marktplein 7, ✆ 618 180 (*moderate–cheap*). This friendly café's dark bare wood interior combines café/restaurant with art gallery, showing regular exhibitions by local artists. The menu culinaire is arty too with lots of modern fusion food; more traditional food also available. There are also menus for children and vegetarians.

The Bible Belt

Hard-working farmers eking out a living in a harsh environment provide fertile ground for severe religions. The lands south and west of Drenthe are a stronghold of strict branches of the already super-Calvinist Dutch Reformed Church. There are still villages where mowing your lawn on the Sabbath is taboo, and where riding a bicycle on a Sunday—even to church—would be frowned upon.

Getting There and Around

Giethoorn: Bus 70 from Steenwijk station goes right through the village. The only way to truly appreciate Giethoorn is by **boat**, and craft ranging from canoes to motorboats are on hire all over the village, at prices ranging from *f*30 a day.

Urk: The only bus to Urk (bus 141) leaves from Kampen and Zwolle.

From May to mid-Sept there's a ferry connection to Enkhuizen two to three times daily (not Sun).

Tourist Information

Giethoorn: VVV, Beulakerweg 114a, ✆ (0521) 361 248.

Urk: VVV, Wijk 2, ✆ (0527) 684 040.

Staphorst, just south of Meppel beside the A28, is the heart of an especially strict community. This is one of the few towns in the country where people wear traditional dress—sober blue and black—for real. Photographs are not welcome, and there is little to see besides brightly painted farmhouses. Things are a bit more relaxed a few kilometres away at **Giethoorn**, just west of Meppel on the N334. A sort of miniature, rural Venice, Giethoorn is a patchwork of small farms and lush gardens interconnected by canals. Everything goes by boat—even cows being transported from one pasture to another. The greenery, pretty thatched cottages and romantic atmosphere make it a huge draw for tourists, but even that can't detract from its charm.

About 20 kilometres southwest, between the A6 and the N50, is **Schokland**. Until the surrounding land was reclaimed from the sea in the 19th century, Schokland was an island. Today it forms an odd 4.5km-long bump in a vast stretch of flat countryside. Lakenvelder cows (black and white cows bred so that they appear to be black ones with a white sheet thrown over their backs) graze around the edges. Today, it's a quiet and attractive museum village, where the **Museum Schokland** (*open April–Oct Tues–Sun 11–5; July and Aug also Mon; rest of year Sat and Sun 11–5; adm*) gives a brief history of the island and land-reclamation.

Urk, on the IJsselmeer coast a few kilometres west, was once also an island, and still holds on to its island sense of independence. Here, too, older people can still be seen wearing traditional dress, and even younger inhabitants speak an exclusive Urk dialect. When the Afsluitdijk was built, the people of Urk were the most active and violent in their opposition to the scheme, and extracted special concessions from the government. They still run their North Sea fishing fleet—though now it's based in Defzijl, north of Groningen—and operate heavily subsided fleets on the IJsselmeer. Apart from the attractive harbour and good fresh fish, there is little to detain you in Urk.

Where to Stay

Giethoorn ✆ (0521–)

> **Hotel De Jonge**, Beulakerweg 30, 8355 AH, ✆ 361 360, ✆ 362 549 (*inexpensive*). Quiet family hotel in the middle of the village, with a pleasant waterside terrace and restaurant filled with antiques. Rooms are more modern, but quite comfortable. From *f*104

> There are some good B&B's in Giethoorn. Try **Mol/Groenewegen**, Binnenpad 28, ✆ 361 359, ✆ 362 567 in the city centre, or the typical farmhouse belonging to **Mrs L. Mol Drost**, at Molenweg 21, ✆ 362 083 on the northern outskirts. (*Both cheap.*)

Urk ✆ (0527–)

> **Pension de Kroon**, Wijk 7 no.54, 8321 TA, ✆/✆ 681 216 (*cheap*). Small, simple pension outside the Old Town. Some rooms have a sea view.

Eating Out

Staphorst ✆ (0522–)

> **De Molenmeester**, Gemeenteweg 364, ✆ 463 116 (*moderate*). A sober village, maybe, but it offers some lavish cooking—try ostrich steaks with red

cabbage and blackberry sauce, or sardines toasted with paprika. Good vegetarian options and a pleasant terrace.

Giethoorn © (0521–)

De Lindenhof, Beulakerweg 77, © 361 444 (*expensive*). If you're not going to picnic on your punt, then opt for the best—a superb Michelin-starred restaurant in a typical Giethorn thatched farmhouse. Chef Martin Kruithof comes up with such delicacies as tender cod with oyster sauce. There's a large terrace under the trees and an imaginative range of vegetarian options.

Urk © (0527–)

De Kaap, Wijk 1 No.5, © 681 509 (*moderate*). A fine view over the harbour, and heaps of fresh fish—prepared with the minimum of fussy interference.

The Islands

The Wadden Islands (a.k.a the Frisian Islands) form a thin chain along the Netherlands' north coast. In between, the Wadden Sea is in places so shallow that it is possible simply to wade across. Most people—apart from the Dutch and the Germans—seem to forget that the islands are there, and they rarely form part of the ordinary visitor's itinerary. But from busy Texel to the rather quirky Schiermonnikoog, the islands are among the best seaside holiday destinations in the country—and not only in good weather. To be beside the seaside in a lonely spot on one of the Wadden Islands on a cloudy day, is like stepping into a minimalist painting. Just three stripes of colour. An undulating line of pale beige sand, paralleled by a strip of stone-grey sea, then a third band made by the soft, dove-coloured sky. Somewhere, a red speck—the coat of a solitary walker.

Getting There

Ferries for Texel leave from Den Helder in Noord-Holland. Ferries for Vlieland and Terschelling leave from Harlingen in Friesland. Ferries for Ameland leave from Holwerd, and those for Schiermonnikoog go from Lauwersoog in Groningen. Some involve a bus connection from a train station in another town (*details under individual islands*). The only inter-island conections are between Texel, Vlieland and Terschelling, though these are seasonal (*check with the VVV*).

If you're travelling from Amsterdam, ask at Centraal Station for a *waddenbiljet* ('vudin bill-yay'), which is a combined train/bus/ferry ticket all the way to one of the islands and back.

Waddenlopen (wading through the mudflats) is exhausting, exhilarating—and dangerous. You should not attempt it without a qualified guide. Local VVVs can help.

April and **May** are good months to come: the islands are carpeted with wild flowers and here and there beaches turn purple with samphire and sea lavender. Whitsun is a lively time to visit Schiermonnikoog—the islanders manage to stretch the festival out to last three days, and it ends with an enormous party and much daytime fun and games for children.

Thousands of holidaymakers invade in **July** and **August**. **June** and **September** are less busy and also warm and pleasant: Texel has more hours of sunshine than anywhere else in the Netherlands (the howling winds drive the clouds away) and in these months the sea is warm enough for swimming.

November is the least popular month with visitors: the wind comes from all directions at once, it rains horizontally and the wet that comes through the eyelets of your boots will make your socks squelch within minutes. No surprise that the Texel VVV brochure offers a winter holiday package consisting of a warm meal, a coffee laced with gin and a wind-cheater. Yet the raw emptiness of the dunes and the North Sea lend themselves to the bleak weather, and there is a real chance to feel alone with the elements.

December and **January** are more popular: the Waddensee coast freezes over some years, there is plenty of skating and the dunes may be covered with snow.

The Islands

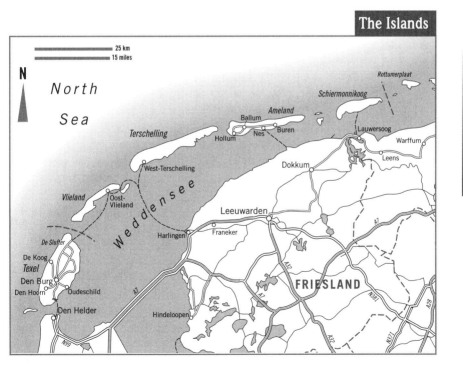

Texel (pronounced 'Tessel') is the largest and most touristy of the islands, and also makes its income from sheep-farming and bulb-growing. Den Hoorn is the centre for bulb culture, including narcissi, crocuses and (of course) tulips; and the lambs—which feed on island herbs—are sought after after by top restaurants around the country. The most important thing to remember about Texel is that in no circumstances should you visit in July and August. These are the peak months, when well over 30,000 visitors will be crammed into a few spots on an island just 15 miles long by 6 miles wide. Emergency camping grounds are opened on old football pitches as the island struggles to accommodate the massive influx of visitors, all searching for solitary, windswept charm.

Getting There

The only way to reach Texel is by ferry from Den Helder in Noord-Holland. The boat takes 20mins and goes hourly at 35mins past, though extra ferries may be put on in the peak season. Boats start running at 6am, later in slack periods or holidays. The return boat is at 5mins past the hour. You can't book a ticket on the ferry but shouldn't need to wait unless you're fool enough to go in high season—in which case you had better have booked your accommodation. The ticket is a return, costing *f*10 in summer (April–Oct), *f*8.25 in winter. It's possible to bring over a vehicle, from motorbike up to caravan, for a price, but it's a small place and you'd be better off on foot, bike or bus.

Getting Around

By bus: Texel has a good bus network that covers the seven villages regularly, usually a bus an hour in winter and more in summer. In summer you can buy a daily bus pass for *f*6. The buses stop at the ferry port and their arrivals coincide with the boat times.

By bike: You can bring your own over on the ferry for *f*6 summer, *f*5 winter, or hire one from one of the many hire shops ('Fiets Verhuur') on the island from *f*7.50 a day. Texel has 120km of cycle paths and four set routes to cover the main areas of beauty. The VVV has maps.

The *telekomtaxi* service, ✆ (0222) 322 211, runs all over the island, 6am–2am daily. It will take you from and to set pick-up points all over the island for just *f*7 per person, the snag being that you may have to wait for up to an hour.

Tourist Information

Emmalaan 66, 1791 AV Den Burg, ✆ (0222) 314 741, ✉ 310 054; open Oct–Mar Mon–Fri 9–6, Sat 9–5; April–Nov Mon–Thurs 9–6, Fri 9–9, Sat 9–5.30; July and Aug also Sun 10–1.30. The VVV is signed from the bus station. They have a special brochure with information for disabled travellers. They also offer a **Museum Ticket** for *f*20, *f*10 under 12s, giving admission to all five island museums (only worth it if you plan to visit more than the EcoMare and Beachcombers' Museum).

Den Burg

Nearly half of Texel's population lives in this pleasant little town. The streets follow their medieval pattern of concentric rings, although much of the centre was destroyed in 1945. It has a cinema and plenty of shops, most selling sheep-related ware (slippers, fleeces, cute toy lambs). It's not very exciting, with a couple of uninteresting churches and a few winding lanes for a quick wander, but makes a good base, less tacky than De Koog and with some nice places to eat. It also offers the **Oudheidkamer** (Antiquities Room; Kogerstraat 1; *open April–Oct only*), a small museum in 1900 style with a collection of prints, clothing, tools and folklore items and a very small herb garden.

De Koog

De Koog is a town with an identity crisis verging on psychosis. Its population is 825, rising to over 35,000 in summer. It should be a quiet little place of red-roofed houses, except that all along the main drag is a relentless series of hotels, restaurants, bars, bowling alleys and glitzy, uninspiring shops—a hairdresser adorned with pink neon scissors here, an Elvis-themed bar a few doors up, a bowling alley beyond. It's a kind of provincial Dutch Las Vegas without the excitement of gambling, and if that doesn't appeal to you, you're not alone. The locals put up with the invasion and afterwards count their money.

A Den Burg hotelier comments that De Koog was 'founded to keep the tourists off the rest of the island'. There's some truth in this: the old settlement was a fishing village whose coast silted up, making it hard for the fishing boats to reach the harbour. Many residents decamped for Den Hoorn and the old village was just about gone when mass tourism began at the beginning of the 20th century. The town was rebuilt for the purpose: it retains one old house plus a little white church, unfortunately located right in the middle of Dorpsstraat.

De Koog's big attraction is its beachside location, with long strands edged on one side by the magnificent dunes and the other by the North Sea. There are all kinds of watersports and activities on offer, and De Koog offers the most that the island has in the way of nightlife.

EcoMare

Ruyslaan 92, ℭ (0222) 317 741, reached from De Koog or Den Burg by bus 27 (summer), 28 (winter); the telekomtaxi stops here.

Open daily 9–5; seals fed at 11 and 3; adm.

Situated among the dunes by the coast, EcoMare is a nature centre concentrating on the wildlife of the Wadden and North Seas. It features a rehabilitation centre for wounded or sick seals and birds, many of which come in covered in oil. There are normally around 20 seals in its outdoor pools, fed at 11 and 3, and pups are born here every year. There are constantly changing exhibitions as well as core displays of the natural history of the region. These are small but well laid out with some English labelling. Several little aquaria hold various local fauna—a purple crab the size of a hand, ribbony butterfish, rays—as well as skeletons (a 5.5m whale jawbone) and plastic models. Exhibits have a strong ecological bias, naturally, and there's a lot of information on pollution—try to catch the jaw-dropping interactive display 'Whose Poo?' (roughly translated), where little lights flash as you match the picture of the bird, seal or child on potty to the appropriate plastic excrement.

The 70-hectare Dune Park itself is beautiful, in muted shades of burnt umber, dusty green and bright yellows and oranges, with three well-laid-out hiking paths of different lengths taking you through the hills and troughs to the glittering grey expanse of the North Sea. There's a free guided tour most days in summer, and excursions to the mud flats can also be arranged (*summer only, reserve in advance, call for details*). EcoMare can also give information on hiking and biking paths all over Texel.

Oudeschild

This is the island's seaport, with a marina and possibilities for shrimp- and sport-fishing. It's an unexciting place otherwise, with the usual little church and rows of neat new houses, except for its charming museum. The **Maritiem en Jutters Museum** (Maritime and Beachcombing Museum, Barentszstraat 21 (head for the windmill), © (0222) 314 956; *open Tues–Sat 10–5; adm*) is in the form of a little park of old sheds and houses with a windmill that you can go inside in summer. The barns contain various displays on the island's past: an old-style forge with blacksmith demonstrations in summer (you can also see fish-smoking and rope-making); a shipwright's workshop; an exhibition on Texel's history as a stopover point for East and West India Company ships, featuring tiles, paintings, prints, models of old ships and so on. The best display is the Beachcombery itself. The barn is packed with an extraordinary assortment of the stuff, ranging from intriguing to moving to pure junk, that has washed up on the shores over the years: huge bones, coconuts, a selection of ships' fire extinguishers, battered luggage, 400 kilos of cocaine (not actually on display). A large board is covered in shoes: some clean and paired as if simply left on the beach, others battered, mildewed and forlornly single. There are bits of machinery too: most alarming is a huge iron propeller with thick 5ft blades, twisted and bent almost double by the forces of the sea. It's an enchanting place.

Other Villages

To the north of the island, De Cocksdorp is the most isolated village, although a certain amount of hotel and apartment development is going on. It's bleak and windswept but attractive if isolation and nature are your thing.

Den Hoorn, De Waal and Oosterend are all protected villages, holding on to their heritage by banning further development. They're pretty places, with their white cottages with green-painted wooden fronts, and nice to wander around in for a while, but don't offer any further diversions (except for De Waal's Agrarian and Wagon Museum). Den Hoorn's pleasant little church is its biggest tourist attraction, possibly because its spire breaks the flatness of the scenery and provides a welcome relief to the eye. This is, after all, an island that noted that an area (between Den Burg and Oudeschild) was some 15 metres higher than most of the rest of the island, and consequently named it Hoge Berg—'High Mountain'.

There's a children's farm, **Funfarm de Mient**, in Den Hoorn (Rommelpot 11, ✆ (0222) 319 296; *open April–Oct daily 9.30–7; adm*), with lots of animals to see and pet (including a camel called Lizzie), play areas including minigolf and electrocars; pony rides available 2–5.30pm.

You can also see a working farm **De Noordkroon** (Nieuwlanderweg 10, ✆ (0222) 317 263; *open Mar–Oct Mon–Sat 2–6; adm*). Sheep are milked at 4, goats at 5.15. Visit in March and April when the lambs are born, for a real country experience.

When you're travelling round you'll notice the odd little thatched barns that look like normal barns cut in half. They are built like that with their backs to the prevailing winds to afford both farmers and animals a little shelter; in autumn and winter you'll see sheep huddled in front of them, locked in wet woolly misery.

Beaches on the West Coast

The long North Sea coast that runs down from De Cocksdorp at the top of the island past De Koog in the middle and Den Hoorn to the south offers a long stretch of beach, including some spectacular nature reserves edged with magnificent dunes. North of De Koog, the **De Slufter** tidal gully was created when the dyke broke in 1858. The dyke was never properly closed again, creating a unique area of saltwater flora and fauna deep inland.

South of De Slufter is the **De Muys** dune valley, whose little lake is a breeding ground for many birds, including blue herons and spoonbills. EcoMare and the Natuurmonumenten (nature reserve organization) organize bird-watching trips, *see* below.

Nudist beaches are south of marker 9 at Den Hoorn and south of De Cocksdorp between markers 26.7 and 27.7. Beaches are guarded June–Aug 9–6.

Texel ✆ (0222–)　　　　　　　　　　　　　　　**Sports and Activities**

Active types will not be short of things to do here, although some activities may only be offered or appropriate in season. Parachute-jumping, sea-fishing, minigolf, go-karting, bird-watching, sailing, riding, kayaking, tennis courts and saunas are all available. A few addresses are given here; contact the VVV in Den Burg for more information.

Walking: The VVV publishes a book of walks across the island: across forest, dunes or mud. There's even a special walk laid out for the blind and visually impaired, with tree stumps along the way as a guide and information in Braille. The marked 'Texel Walk' is an 80km ramble through the dunes, over mud flats and then inland.

Golf: Contact Golfbaan De Texelse, Roggeslootweg 3, 1795 JX De Cocksdorp, ✆ 316 539.

Riding school: Elzenhof, Oude Dijkje 16, De Koog, ✆ 317 469.

Pony riding: Manege Kikkert, Zijweg 16, Bosrandweg, De Koog, ✆ 317 516.

Tennis: Tennispark De Koog, Schumakersweg 1, De Koog, ✆ 317 888.

Catamaran sailing or windsurfing: Westerslag, beach marker 15, ✆ 312 013 or 314 847 (beach markers are clearly shown on the VVV's free map of the island); De Eilander, beach marker 33, ✆ 316 500; International Windsurf-centre, Dijkmanshuizen, ✆ 318 987 (windsurfing only); Canoe Centre, ✆/🖷 315 066; Kayak Centre, Seamount Tracks, ✆ 319 393.

Fishing: Angling is free along the dykes and on the beach. You can get bait, etc. from Watersportcentr. Duinker, Heemskerkstraat 11a, Oudeschild, ✆ 313 831; and Th. Eilander, Kikkertstraat 47, De Cocksdorp, ✆ 316 320.

Sport fishing and sailing on the Waddenzee can be arranged by De Zeester, ✆ 313 545; and M.S. Rival, ✆ 313 410, Het Sop, ✆ 310 533.

Texel ✆ (0222–)   ***Where to Stay***

Den Burg

't Koogerend, Kogerstraat 94, 1791 EV Den Burg-Texel, ✆ 313 301, 🖷 315 902 (*inexpensive*) is a wonderfully friendly and welcoming place to the north end of the town. The bedrooms are comfortable, recently renovated and warmly decorated, most are en suite and some have a whirlpool bath. The hotel has a good restaurant and bar plus garden.

De Smulpot, Binnenburg 5, 1791 CG Den Burg, ✆ 312 756 (*inexpensive*) is comfortable and central with 14 pleasant modern rooms. There's a good restaurant (*see* above) and the location is very convenient.

Hotel de Lindeboom, Groeneplaats 14, 1791 CC Den Burg-Texel, ✆ 312 041, 🖷 310 517 (*inexpensive*) offers reasonable if unexciting en suite rooms in the heart of Den Burg. There's a restaurant (*cheap*) offering lamb- and fish-based three-course menus, terraced seating and tables outside on the square in summer. The panelled doorway in the breakfast room is so ornately Baroque it could put you off your food.

Den Burg, Emmalaan 2–4, ✆ 312 106, 🖷 322 053 (*inexpensive*) was under renovation at the time of writing but should be reopened now. It has 30 en suite rooms. It prides itself on being homely and old style—the restaurant's menu is defiantly Dutch and it's a real family-run place, complete with huge boxer dog.

De Koog

Hotel Opduin, Ruyslaan 22, 1796 AD De Koog-Texel, ✆ 317 445, 🖷 317 777 (*moderate*). The only four star hotel on the island, it's located on the edge of De Koog by the dunes, about 15mins walk from EcoMare. Lots of extras—indoor pool, turkish bath, playroom, tennis courts, bike rental and beach huts. It's a large place (80 rooms) with an unattractive exterior and fairly typical expensive hotel interior. There's a good, pricey restaurant; rooms are well furnished with family suites available, there are two lifts and it generally offers the kind of service and detail you'd expect.

Greenside, Stappeland 6, 1796 BS De Koog, © 327 222, ✆ 327 333, *greenside BLAHtref.nl* (*moderate*). This large hotel complex on the edge of De Koog offers spacious en suite rooms, sauna, solarium and Turkish bath. It has both a restaurant and a Grand Café.

Hotel De Branding, Boodtlaan 6, © 317 233 (*inexpensive–cheap*) comes highly recommended by locals. The ground-floor rooms are well furnished and there's plenty of parking space. The restaurant specializes in fish. It also has a bowling alley attached with a giant skittle outside.

Boschrand, Bosrandweg 225, 1796 NA De Koog, © 317 281, ✆ 317 459 (*inexpensive*) is a modern hotel on the outskirts of town. All rooms en suite, there's a sauna and jacuzzi, also a lift. It offers bicycle hire and is close to a riding stables and heated pool. *Open Feb–Nov.*

Beatrix, Kamerstraat 45 (a slightly quieter road off Pontweg; *inexpensive*) has 13 en suite rooms. They are clean, sparse and pink, with friendly staff (it's a family place) and a comfortable breakfast room. It even has its own sauna.

Pension Boswinkel, Wintergroen 24, 1796 BL De Koog/Texel, De Koog, ©/✆ 317 596 (*cheap*), is a fine B&B to the north of De Koog, in a little suburb a few minutes from Dorpsstraat. Lex, the owner, is very friendly and helpful, running weekly barbecues in summer at which all the guests help out. The place is neatly decorated, comfortable and spotless, guests can use the nearby beach huts, all rooms have showers, breakfast is a wonderful array of pastries. *Book well in advance to be sure of a room.*

Den Burg

The best place to eat in Den Burg is at one of the restaurants on Gravestraat; locals say they're the best on the island.

De Gravenmolen, Gravenstr 4, © 312 204 (*cheap*) is a reasonably priced cosy *eetcafe* with a good *à la carte* selection.

Het Vierspan, Gravenstr 3, © 313 176 (*moderate–inexpensive*) is somewhat pricier and specializes in lamb dishes and game.

The hotel restaurants tend to be good. **De Smulpot**, Binnenburg 5, © 312 756 (*moderate*) has a cosy café/bar with green wicker chairs and a lighter, more spacious restaurant offering a good choice of fish and seafood dishes as well as the ubiquitous lamb and other meats.

De Koog

There is a non-stop stream of restaurants up Dorpsstraat.

Oranjerie, Dorpsstraat 204, ✆ 317 279 (*moderate–cheap*), a spacious, summery modern place with snacks (pancakes, mussels in mustard sauce) and main courses (spare ribs, chips and salad).

Het Binnenhof, across the road (next to the horrifying Cocky's hairdressers with pink neon scissors and plastic green-haired caryatids; *moderate*). Pleasant wood and tiled interior. It's a meat or fish with chips and salad sort of place, with grill-your-own on a volcanic stone a speciality.

Eethuis La Casserole, Dorpsstraat 100, ✆ 317 370 (*cheap*) is a good place for a large, comforting meal: fish and lamb casseroles. In summer cheap rooms are available above the restaurant.

De Taveerne, Dorpsstraat 119 (through the mall, opposite the Chinese restaurant, ✆ 317 585; *moderate*) is where the locals eat. It's somewhat Baroque, with pink swags and drapes everywhere, and the service is excellent. They specialize in lamb dishes (try the three different cuts in honey and thyme) but also offer good fish and seafood (though with disappointing bottled sauces).

Oudeschild

There are a couple of restaurants on the marina. **Havenzicht** has a warm wood and leather interior with marine décor, offering a range of snacks reasonably cheaply (*uitsmijters f9*).

Texel ✆ (0222–)	***Entertainment and Nightlife***

Piano Bar, Nikadel 9 (left up Badweg off north end of Dorpsstraat), De Koog, offers live 40s–70s music from 9.30pm to 2am, ✆ 327 376. You can't miss it: there's a giant illuminated piano outside.

Discos: The nightlife not really going to compete with Amsterdam but try **Metro en De Toekomst**, in De Koog, or **Question Plaza** or **Jelleboog** in Den Burg.

Vlieland, Terschelling and Ameland

Each island seems to attract its own brand of holidaymakers. Whilst Texel is undoubtedly the most commercial of the archipelago, Terschelling and Ameland come in a close second—though Terschelling attracts a slightly trendier crowd. Vlieland is more the realm of rich second-homers.

Getting There and Around

Ferries leave Harlingen for Terschelling and Vlieland about three times a day in summer, and twice daily in winter (phone ✆ (0900) 9292 for times and prices)

The crossing takes 1½ hours. In the summer months there is an additional ferry between the two islands, as well as a hydrofoil service from the mainland (about ƒ10 extra each way, but the journey is only about 45mins).

Ferries for Ameland leave from Holwerd (bus 66 from Leeuwarden, 35mins) once every two hours, and more frequently in summer (times and prices on ✆ (0900) 9292). Trips take 45mins.

No non-island cars are allowed on Vlieland, but you can hire taxis, and bicycle rental firms are abundant—a bicycle costs around ƒ8 a day.

Tourist Information

The island VVVs are a useful source of accommodation information, and can also supply information on walking and cycling routes and other activites. They also have material (though mainly in Dutch) on wildlife in the area.

Vlieland: VVV, Havenweg 10, ✆ (0562) 451 111; open Mon–Fri 9–5, Oct–April also Sat 11–12, May–Sept also Sat & Sun 11–12 and 4–5.

Terschelling: VVV, Willem Barentzkade 19a, near the ferry port, ✆ (0562) 443 000; open Mon–Fri 9–12 and 2–5.30, Sat 11–12 and 4–5.

Ameland: VVV, Rixt van Doniaweg 2, Nes, ✆ (0519) 542 020; open Mon–Fri 8.30–6.30 (closed lunch), Sat 8.30–4.

Vlieland

Vlieland is the narrowest (sometimes less than a kilometre) and quietest (no non-islanders' cars are allowed) of the Wadden Islands. Much of it is no-go military territory, and the rest occupied by drifting dunes. One town, West-Vlieland, got swallowed up by the sea in the 18th century, and was never rebuilt. The only other one, called Oost-Vlieland, is a pretty cluster of whitewashed holiday bungalows and old houses, some dating back to the 16th and 17th centuries.

Terschelling

The next island along the line, Terschelling, made its money from ship supply and repairs as well as whaling and fishing, before the tourists came along. The second biggest island after Texel, it is also the second busiest. The main town, West-Terschelling, is an unalluring sprawl, though the **Museum 't Behouden Huys** (Commandeurstraat 30–32; *open Jan–March Wed and Sat 1–5; April–Oct Mon–Fri 10–5; July also Sun 1–5; mid-June–Sept also Sat 1–5; adm*) near the ferry landing point is a marvellous clutter of treasures from various lands, boats in bottles, models of ships, and recreations of the Terschelling of yore, gathered together in two 17th-century commander's houses. West-Terschelling packs out with tourists, but as you move farther east throughout the island you'll find fields of wild orchids in the spring, marshland fluttering with waterbirds, pretty villages such as Hoorn and Oosterend, and even some deserted stretches of beach.

Ameland

Even a few decades ago, Ameland was still losing land (including a hotel and a few beach pavilions) to the sea. New dykes keep the ocean at bay, and Ameland has become a popular resort. The northern dunes are dry and desertlike; in the east there are wetlands teeming with birds—best viewed from a dune that reaches all of 24 metres high. Four villages dot the southern flatlands. **Hollum** is the most traditional and attractive, with a pretty church in an oval churchyard. **Nes** is the main town, with lively cafés and wavy-gabled 17th-century *commandeurswoningen* (captain's houses).

Sports and Activities

There are numerous opportunities for boating, windsurfing, cycling, walking and horse riding on the islands. The VVV has full information.

Where to Stay and Eating Out

Accommodation on the islands can fill quickly in summer months, and it is a good idea to book ahead. Often your best bet is a small privately run pension or B&B, and here the VVVs can be of help. They can also recommend chalets and bungalows for longer stays.

Terschelling ℭ (0562–)

Paal 8, Badweg 4, 8881 HB Terschelling-West, ℭ 449 090, ✉ 449 115 (*moderate–inexpensive*). One of the few hotels on the island with a good sea view (dykes and dunes tend to block out the vistas). Clean, 1950s modernist architecture allows in lots of light, and the breakfast room/dining room is gigantic. Rooms vary in quality, but many are spacious and some have sea views and balconies. Very acceptable restaurant (*cheap*) with three-course menus at under ƒ40. *Closed Dec–Mar.*

Pension de Wadvaarder, Westburen 30, 8891 GP, Midsland, Terschelling, ℭ 449 101, ✉ 449 308 (*cheap*). Homey, family-run pension on the edge of De Boschplaat nature reserve in the middle of the island. Ideal for walkers and birdwatchers.

De Grië, Hoofdstraat 43, Terschelling-West, ℭ 448 499 (*moderate*). A converted farmhouse (with open fire in colder months) that is one of the very few really good restaurants in the archipelago. Try the steak with a duck liver parfait and truffle sauce.

Vlieland ℭ (0562–)

Strandhotel Seeduyn, Badweg 3, 8899 BV Vlieland, ℭ 451 560, ✉ 451 115 (*moderate*). In the dunes on the North Sea coast, about a kilometre outside the village. A free buggy will cart your luggage from the ferry, so you can follow on hired bicycles. 'Family rooms' are small apartments, and there is a general ambience of quiet comfort. Guests have the use of indoor and outdoor pools, a sauna, tennis courts and bowling alley. There are two restaurants.

Badhotel Bruin, Dorpstraat 88, 8899 AL, Vlieland, ✆ 451 301, ✉ 451 227 (*inexpensive*). Comfortable hotel with individually decorated rooms and a good restaurant that specializes in fish dishes.

Ameland ✆ (0519–)

De Welvaart, Burenlaan 4, 9161 AK Hollum, Ameland, ✆ 554 634, ✉ 554 681 (*inexpensive*). Beside the church in the village of Hollum. Pleasant, modern rooms, a small garden terrace and reasonable restaurant. The friendly owner can help with advice on walking and cycling tours.

Schiermonnikoog

Schiermonnikoog is the most individual and alluring of the islands. You can't take a car, so it's just birds, beaches, bicycles and dunes. The island attracts its share of families on holiday, but it is also frequented by writers and artists—and occasionally members of the Dutch royal family hoping for a quiet time.

Getting There and Around

Ferries leave for Schiermonnikoog from the port of Lauwersoog. Bus 51 runs from Dokkum and Leeuwarden (1hr 30mins), and bus 63 from Groningen (1hr). There are about six a day (more in summer). Phone ✆ (0900) 9292 for times and prices.

Only residents' cars (and few of them at that) are allowed on the island, but you can hire **taxis**, there are **buses** from the ferry dock to the village, and numerous **bicycle** rental firms (about ƒ6 a day).

Tourist Information

VVV, Reeweg, ✆ (0519) 531 233; open Mon–Sat 9–1 and 2.30–6.30.

Most of Schiermonnikoog (pronounced 'Skee-er-monnik-oh-gh', with a guttural 'gh') is nature reserve, with no human habitation. The northern shore of the island is nearly 15km long, and for most of its length over 500m wide. Even at the busiest of times, half an hour's walk will leave you completely alone, a little like a desert explorer, with sand stretching in all directions, fading on one side into sea and bumping up on the other into scrubby dunes. Silence and solitude are delivered in full measure.

Nearer to the island's single village (also called Schiermonnikoog), dumpy thatched cottages appear between the dunes, and cycle paths take you through patches of pine forest and verdant corridors that smell of hawthorn, sweet grasses and wild roses. Families cycle past, toddlers perched in seats strapped to the carriers. Some come pulling wooden wagons—babies, buckets and spades, and provisions all piled in the back—heading for the beach, where they put up bright canvas windbreaks and settle in for the day.

The village comprises just a few streets of gabled houses, and centres on the church and two hotels—an upstart modern one, and Hotel Van der Werff, which is something of a legend. The entrance to the hotel is through its café—dim, wood-panelled and cosy, with a century's worth of accumulated bric-a-brac on the walls, the sort of café that has inhabitants rather than customers. Through an arch are the plush velvet armchairs, stopped grandfather clock and large fireplace of the Residents' Lounge. Prince Bernhard of the Netherlands, when he was younger, used to slip up to the Hotel Van der Werff for a little peace and quiet. His grandson Crown Prince Willem looks set to continue the tradition.

Schiermonnikoog © *(0519–)*　　　　　　　　　　　　　　　　　　**Where to Stay**

Hotel Van der Werff, Reeweg 2, © 531 203, ✉ 531 748 (*moderate–inexpensive*). You pile your luggage on top of a brightly painted 1950s bus that rattles you from the ferry to the oldest hotel on the island. Then Enid Blyton becomes Agatha Christie (*see* above). Rooms are generally spacious, but a little disapponting in décor given the rest of the hotel.

Pension Westerburen, Middenstreek 32, © 531 116, ✉ 531 985 (*cheap*). Pleasant pension in an old house in the village.

Schiermonnikoog © *(0519–)*　　　　　　　　　　　　　　　　　　**Eating Out**

Good food is not a Schiermonnikoog plus point. The restaurant at **Hotel Van der Werff** is massively overpriced, though the bar snacks offer better value. You can get reasonable meat-and-veg and big pancakes at **De Sapkûm** (Middenstreek 3, © 531 501) next door. The **Vis Bistro** (Badweg 91, © 531 287) has more adventurous fishy cuisine.

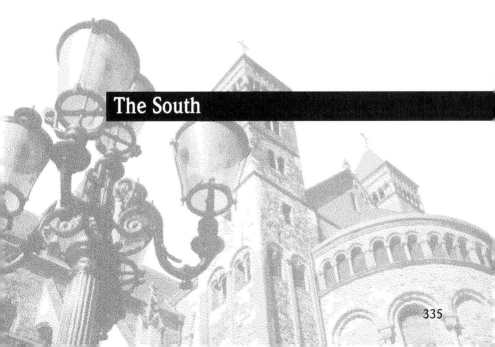

The South

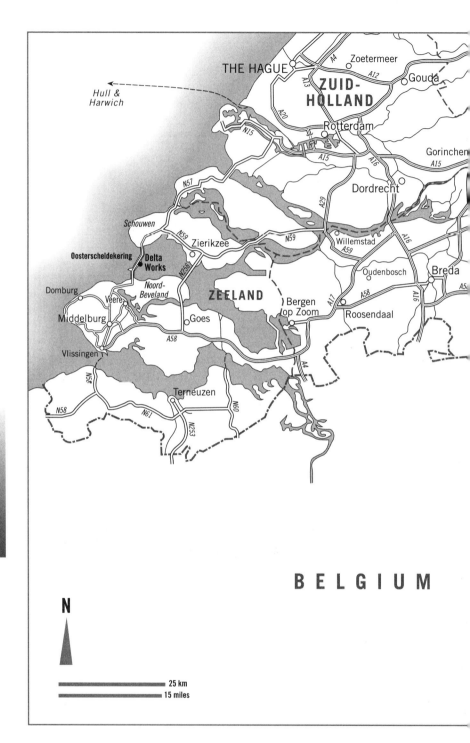

The South

Broad flows the Rhine—or at least it does until it hits the Dutch border, whereupon it splits into the Waal, the Lek, and a host of smaller rivers that tack 'Rijn' on to their names. This tangled band of waterways, together with the Maas that flows in from Belgium, cuts the country in two. The Dutch talk of 'south of the great rivers' as if it were another land—and, indeed, sometimes it feels as if it is. Accents are softer—the 'g' less guttural, and the 'r' sometimes rolled, as in French; towns, too, often have a Gallic flair, a different mood from the prim, neatly restored toytowns of the north.

Perhaps this is because much of the south is Roman Catholic. The sober northern Protestantism that underlay the Dutch Golden Age became such a permanent feature of the national image that it comes as a surprise to most people to learn that 35 per cent of the Netherlands' population is Roman Catholic. And most of this population is in the southeast. Here, once again, the churches have stained glass and there is a whiff of incense in the air. Maybe it's one's imagination playing tricks, but the streets seem to have a lighter, more festive air, more redolent of easygoing southern Europe, and the delights of good eating seem more central to life than in the north.

The southwestern corner of the country is the aptly named Zeeland—the province comprises almost more water than land, and is famed for its mussels, fishing and duney beaches. The province of Noord-Brabant, which stretches across the entire southern part of the country (Zuid Brabant is in Belgium), offers alluring towns like Breda and Den Bosch, welcome diversions in a fairly uneventful landscape. And as you move eastwards into Limburg, and down to Maastricht, the countryside raises itself into a series of gentle hills that in the context of the Low Countries seem positively mountainous.

Getting There

By car: The A2 is the main artery south from Amsterdam, with numerous other motorways connecting northern and southern cities. Lateral road travel across the region is relatively easy, too, with motorways running all the way from Middelburg in the furthest corner of Zeeland to Maastricht in the east.

By train: There are three main rail routes south, one running through Rotterdam and Dordrecht, another via Utrecht and Den Bosch, and a third through Arnhem and Nijmegen.

When to Go

In this Catholic patch, **Carnival**—that last wanton bash on the eve of Lent—is celebrated with fervour, fancy-dress street processions and partying in cafés being the dominant modes of merriment. Whilst revels seldom reach the giddy hedonistic heights that they do in Cologne across the German border, some towns put on a good show. Most notable are Maastricht, Den Bosch, and the otherwise unremarkable though whizzily named town of Bergen op Zoom in Zeeland. Note that many sights and museums, especially in Limburg, are closed for the Carnival weekend.

Zeeland

War and water have taken their toll on Zeeland. The patchwork of islands, semi-islands and meandering peninsulas that lie in the joint delta of the Waal, Maas and Schelde rivers saw some of the severest fighting of the Second World War, and in 1953 were ravaged by one of the most catastrophic floods in the Netherlands' history (*see* below). The construction of the Delta Works (*see* p.344), completed in 1986, has put paid to any possibility of another such disaster, and the now placid inland lakes behind the Delta Works dams are highly popular for diving and other water sports. And although many of Zeeland's buildings are post-1950s, it does boast some attractive historic towns.

Middelburg

Lucto et emergo.

'I struggle and emerge'—Middelburg's city motto; the coat of arms shows a lion rampant rising out of water.

Middelburg has surfaced from floods and the ruins of war admirably intact, if a little reconstructed. It was founded around 890, as a fort on a mound in the middle of the island of Walcheren, providing protection against the Vikings. ('Burg' means fort, and the centre of town still follows the circular shape of this early mound.) In the 12th century Middelburg was chosen as the site for what was to become an important abbey. The heyday of 'the pearl of Zeeland' lasted from the late Middle Ages through to 1574, when the city (which had long been faithful to Philip II, and had suffered a two-year siege in consequence) fell to forces loyal to the Prince of Orange. After a brief decline, Middelburg recovered during the Golden Age in the 17th century to become a power almost to rival Amsterdam. Today, attractive alleys lead into grand squares lined with patrician mansions, and the abbey tower still lords it over all.

Getting There

Take the train from Rotterdam Centraal Station, which goes once every hour, and takes 70mins.

Tourist Information

VVV, Nieuwe Burg 38–40, © (0118) 659 944; open Mon–Fri 9.30–5.30, Thurs 9.30–9, Sat 9.30–5, Sun 12–4.

Middelburg has a bustling Thursday market, popular with tourists and locals alike, and a good book and bric-a-brac market on Mondays (Easter–Oct), both on the Markt. The Vismarkt hosts a fleamarket on the first Saturday of the month (also on Thurs in summer).

The Abbey

Middelburg's abbey—**De Abdij**—covers nearly a quarter of the original 'burg'. It was founded in 1123 by an order of Norbertine monks, and grew in various stages as the order grew more prosperous, until they were ousted by William of Orange in 1574 (*see* above). The abbey's **three churches** (*open May–Sept Mon–Fri 10–5; adm free*) were then adapted for Protestant use, while the rest of the complex became the administrative seat of the Zeeland government, which it remains to this day. Both churches and abbey were badly damaged by German bombs in 1940, but have been so well rebuilt that you can hardly spot the seams—though the interiors remain rather bland and lack atmosphere. Perhaps the best part of the abbey today is the vast (and often eerily quiet) courtyard, from which you can admire the different architectural styles ranged around you.

The pride of the abbey complex, and indeed something of a totem for the whole of Zeeland, is **Lange Jan** ('Long John'), the 91m-high tower, its octagonal Gothic base topped with an 18th century Baroque flourish. The tower has four times been completely destroyed by fire—in 1476, 1512, 1568 and 1712—which is perhaps why, a couple of centuries ago, a group of late-night revellers, seeing the reflection of the moon on the roof, panicked and raised the fire alarm. The resultant efforts of the citizens to douse the 'flames' resulted in a nickname for Middelburgers that has stuck to this day—*maneblussers* ('moon-quenchers').

Housed in the former monks' quarters is the **Zeeuws Museum** (*open Mon–Sat 11–5, Sun 12–5; adm*), which tells the story of Zeeland from the time of fossilized bones to the present. Highlights include a Roman altar to the goddess Nehalennia, washed up on a nearby shore after a storm in 1647, interesting exhibitions on the time of the blossoming VOC trade, and a dim room lined with superb **tapestries**, commissioned at the end of the 16th century to commemorate the victory over the Spanish. In the abbey cloister the **Historama** (*open Mon–Sat 11–5, Sun 12–5; adm*) presents the history of the abbey in 3-D tableaux and a video. The abbey is also home to the **Roosevelt Study Centre** (*open Mon–Fri 10–12.30 and 1.30–4.30*), a well-stocked centre for the study of the historical links between America and Europe, particularly in the 20th century. There's an exhibition on Theodore, F. D. (both descendants of a Zeeland family) and Eleanor.

Before leaving the abbey, have a look at the decorative **Gistpoort** (literally 'Yeast Gate'), the abbey's southeast entrance.

Beyond the Abbey

Middleburg's other prime attraction is its 15th-century **Stadhuis**, a Gothic extravaganza complete with scores of red and white shutters, filigreed turrets, and its own tower with four minarets. Like many of the historical buildings in town, it was badly damaged by bombs in 1940, so most of what you see today is a clever reconstruction. Spread in front of the Stadhuis is a large market square, the scene of several busy general markets (see 'When to Go', left). For a flavour of old Middelburg, take a walk along the outskirts of the abbey, visit Damplein, and make a circuit of the old burg following the Lange Noordstraat (from behind the Stadhuis) around to Lange Delft. Children might enjoy **Miniatuur Walcheren** (*open April–Oct daily 10–6; July and Aug daily 10–7; adm*), just beyond Damplein, which has over 200 small-scale houses, farmyards, churches and other buildings from the island.

Middelburg ✆ (0118–)	*Where to Stay*

Le Beau Rivage, Loskade 19, 4331 HW, ✆ 638 060, ✆ 629 673 (*moderate–cheap*). Comfortable 19th-century villa hotel near the station. Rooms can vary quite a lot in size, but are all clean and decorated in a neutral modern style. Some have balconies, though the road out front can be noisy. There's a small garden at the back.

Hotel-Pension Roelant, Koepoortstraat 10, ✆ 627 659, ✆ 628 973 (*inexpensive*). Housed in a 16th-century town house just a few minutes' walk from the abbey. Supportive, comfortable beds and a tantalizing breakfast spread. Very good restaurant in the cellar downstairs, serving hearty Provençal food.

B&B Kaepstander, Koorkerkhof 10, ✆ 642 848 (*inexpensive–cheap*). Charming little B&B in a historic house just across from the abbey.

Middelburg ✆ (0118–)	*Eating Out*

Crêperie Pardoes, Reigerstraat 3, ✆ 635 759 (*cheap*). Attractive little café and crêperie with a garden out the back. Good home-made cakes and tasty French-style pancakes and savoury *galettes.*

Lunchroom de Gouden Bock, Damplein 17, ✆ 617 484 (*cheap*). Stylish venue for slap-up sandwiches, light lunches and genuine English high tea.

Nummer 7, Rotterdamsekaai 7, ✆ 627 077 (*cheap*). Bright and bonny poorer sister to Het Groot Paradijs (*see* below). Blue and yellow chunky cutlery, marble-topped tables and a *brasserie* atmosphere, with dishes such as rabbit stewed with beer and mustard.

Het Groot Paradijs, Damplein 13, ✆ 651 200 (*expensive*). Classically elegant restaurant run by the same team as Nummer 7 down the road. Fine *haute cuisine* with dishes such as beef *pot au feu* with truffle bouillon, or monkfish medallions with crayfish sauce. Keep an eye open especially for Zeeland seafood specialities.

'If it wasn't for the Germans, we might as well close Zeeland down.'

local hotelier

The Zeeland Delta offers long North Sea beaches, flat waterlands teeming with birds, and a flood barrier that displays engineering guaranteed to raise even the non-techie's eyebrow. A handful of towns are attractive enough to detain you for a while, but otherwise the area's attractions lie under the water (if the thousands of Belgium and German divers who flock here are to be believed), or skimming along its surface as a windsurfer.

Getting There

Domburg: Take bus 52 from Middelburg which goes once every hour; the journey takes 30mins.

Veere: Bus 53 from Middelburg goes once an hour; the journey will take around 20mins.

Delta Expo: Take bus 104 from Vlissingen or Middelburg stations, or from Spijkenisse metro station in Rotterdam.

Zierikzee: Take the train from Rotterdam to Goes, once every hour, then bus 132 to Zierikzee.

Tourist Information

Veere: VVV, Oude Straat 28, ✆ (0900) 202 0280; open Mon–Fri 11–5, Sat 1–4.

Zierikzee: VVV, Meelstraat 4, ✆ (0111) 412 450; open Mon 1–5, Tues–Fri 10–5, Sat 10–1.

When (not) to Go

In July and August the area is overrun with tourists (mainly from Germany) and the water teems with divers and windsurfers. Almost any other time of the year is a better bet.

Domburg

If the Dutch coast—its grey seas, usually grey skies, and windswept beige beaches—is an acquired taste, then the stretch of coast around **Domburg**, on the northwest edge of the island of Walcheren, is a good place to acquire it. Once this was the dipping place of artists (including Mondriaan and Charley Toroop) and members of the Dutch aristocracy, though nowadays the bathers are more mundane. From inland, all you can see is what appears to be a steep hill—the dyke that keeps the sea from flooding in. But from the top of the dyke you have on one side a vista of fields and old-fashioned farmsteads and, on the other, long beaches, wooden breakwaters and swooping seagulls. It's a fine setting for a bracing walk. Along the way are villages that retain some charm, even though they are now mainly tourist dormitories.

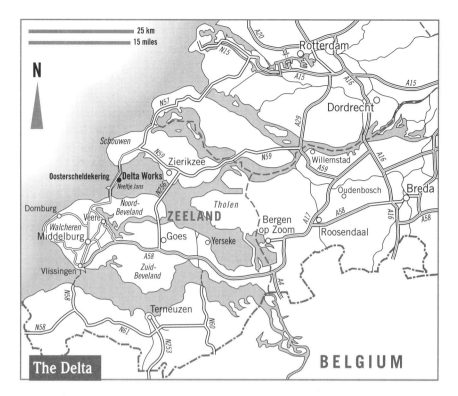

The Delta

Veere, Noord Beveland and the Delta Works

A little farther up the estuary, on the north side of the island, is the pretty little harbour town of **Veere**, which made its fortune from the unlikely combination of prawn-fishing and the wool trade. A testament to the latter are the **Schotse Huizen** (Scottish Houses), a row of dinky cottages built along the harbour in the 16th century as houses for Scottish wool merchants. In 1444 Mary, daughter of James I of Scotland, was espoused to a local lord, Wolfert van Borssele; a significant part of her dowry was a valuable monopoly for the Dutch on wool trading rights with her homeland. In addition, Scottish merchants were granted a range of special privileges, which they held for over three centuries, until the French arrived in 1795, and which attracted many of them to make their homes in this little Dutch port. One is open as a **museum** (Kaai 25; *open April–Oct Mon–Sat 12–5, Sun 1–5; adm*), with local traditional costumes, jewellery and domestic bits and bobs from Veere's prosperous trading era.

Nearby, the solid **Campveerse Toren** (built 1500), part of the original city fortifications, still stands guard over the harbour entrance—though nowadays it's used as a hotel and restaurant.

In the centre of town, look out for the diminutive Gothic **Stadhuis** (built 1474), with its oriental clock tower. The enormous **Grotekerk** (Great Church, built in the 15th and 16th centuries) is further evidence of Veere's former glories. After the decline of the wool trade, the church became a hospital and even suffered the ignominy of being a stables, before becoming the exhibition centre it is today.

The shoreline east of Veere, especially the part around the town of **Yerseke**, is famed for its oysters and mussels. You can see the shellfish farms on the water's edge.

From Veere, the road leads northwards across the island of Noord Beveland to the Oosterscheldekering storm barrier, the most impressive section of the **Delta Works** (*see* below). On the island of Neeltje Jans alongside the barrier is **Waterland Neeltje Jans** (*open April–Oct Mon–Sun 10–5.30; Nov–March Wed–Sun 10–5; adm f21.50, children f16.50; Nov–March excl. boat trip f14.50 and f9.50*). This comprises the Delta Expo, which tells the story of the building of the Delta Works and the storm barrier, and (*April–Oct only*) an interactive water museum, in the form of a beached whale. Here you're taken on a tour of the progress of water from rain via waterfalls to the sea, accompanied by lots of loud music. In the summer months the entrance tickets includes a short cruise around the delta area.

The Delta Works

At four in the morning on 1 February 1953, a combination of high spring tides and a violent storm broke the dykes around the estuary, and the North Sea crashed through and surged across Zeeland. There was no warning. People were swept away in their beds. Those who could clambered on to their roofs and used them as rafts. Around 47,000 homes were destroyed, the salt water ruined farmland, roads and railways were wrecked, and 1,835 people died.

To prevent such a catastrophe ever happening again, the Dutch set about an engineering project of awesome complexity, which has become known as the **Deltawerken** (Delta Works). The idea was to shorten and strengthen the coastline by damming the outermost openings of the estuary. The distances between some of the islands were small enough to make this feasible, if tricky. But the 10km stretch between Noord Beveland and Schouwen, across the mouth of the Oosterschelde, called for special measures. Work began on a dam in 1968, but opposition from local oyster farmers and environmentalists was furious. Damming the Oosterschelde would make it a freshwater sea, destroying the oyster and mussel farms and ruining breeding grounds for fish and water birds. Unlike their counterparts who opposed the Afsluitdijk in the 1930s (*see* p.284), these protesters were successful, and plans were drawn up instead for the **Oosterscheldekering**, a massive storm barrier. Enormous concrete pillars were made on the nearby island of Neeltje Jans, transported by special boats and sunk deep into a thick bed of boulders that had been laid on the estuary bottom between Noord Beveland and Schouwen. Massive hydraulic gates were hung between the pillars that closed only when the tide was adversely high—so the Oosterschelde kept its salt water and normal tidal flow.

The Delta Works project took some 30 years to complete. In addition to protecting Zeeland against floods, it dramatically improved communications, as roads were built across the tops of the dams, substantially cutting down journey times in this watery province of winding shorelines.

Zierikzee

Of all the towns around the estuary, nowhere is as well preserved as **Zierikzee**. Its narrow streets are lined by tiny, two-storey step- and spout-gabled houses, which contrast surprisingly with outsize remnants of the port's prosperous past. The most eye-catching of these is the aptly named **Dikke Toren** (Fat Tower), a gigantic sturdy base, begun in 1454, for what ought to have become an awe-inspiring steeple. But the tower was never finished, and the church to which it was attached burned down in 1832, leaving the stolid grey stump standing alone. Beside the tower is the equally imposing neoclassical **Nieuwe Kerk**, built after the 1832 fire.

To the east of the tower is a pleasant neighbourhood of pedestrian-only streets lined with small shops selling chic fashion, antiques and stylish designerware. In the heart of this quarter is the 16th-century former **Stadhuis** (Meelstraat 6; *open May–Oct Mon–Sat 10–5, Sun 12–5; adm*), now a museum with many of the old interiors intact, including a Louis XV wedding room, and a 1554 *schutterszaal* (civic guards' hall) with impressive wooden barrel-vaulting. Nearby, the **Maritiem Museum** (Mol 25; *open April–Oct Mon–Sat 10–5, Sun 12–5; adm*) has a mildly interesting collection on seafaring history, but the star attraction is the building itself—a 16th-century prison that was in use until 1923. On the upstairs floor, recent renovations uncovered the original walls (which had been whitewashed over in the 19th century)—revealing wooden-barred cells and screeds of graffiti, some of it dating from the 1570s. The Oude Haven (Old Harbour), farther down the road, is now the site of the **Museumhaven Zierikzee** (Oude Haven; *open July–mid-Sept; adm*), an intriguing collection of old ships from the area, most dating from the 19th century. At the entrance to the harbour stand two elegant **gatehouses**, which formed part of the original city fortifications.

Sports and Activities

Swimming

The best **beaches** are Domburg and Oostkapelle on Walcheren, and south of Renesse on Schouwen.

Diving

You can hire equipment and arrange lessons at: **Diving Centre Goes**, Nieuwstraat 72 (Goes), ✆ (0013) 251 951, ✉ 220 170; **Vakantiepark de Witte Boulevard**, Zeedistelweg 10 (Renesse), ✆ (0111) 461 238; **Diving Centre De Greveling**, Elkerszeeseweg 34 (Scharendijk), ✆ (0111) 671 500.

Sailing and Watersports

You can hire boats or windsurfing equipment and arrange classes through: **Surf Centre De Schotsman**, Canpensweg 1 (Kamperland) ✆ (0113) 376 039; **Sail Boat Hire Jan Hardenbol**, Baken 1 (Scharendijk), ✆ (0111) 671 513; **Sail and Surf School Het Veerse Gat**, Polredijk 21 (Veere), ✆ (0118) 501 398; **Sail Fleet De Zeeuwse Stromen**, Nieuwe Bogerdstraat 7 (Zierikzee), ✆ (0111) 415 830.

Fishing

Note, in some areas you may need a licence. Ask at a local fishing shop. Equipment is for sale or hire at **Sportvisserij Moermond**, 's-Heerlauwendorp 14 (Zierikzee), ✆ (0111) 414 309.

Where to Stay

Domburg ✆ (0118–)

Villa Duinvliet, Domburgseweg 44, 4357 NH, ✆ 583 921, ▨ 583 922 (*moderate*). Set in large meadow-like grounds (covered in daisies in season) just off the road between Domburg and Oostkapelle. One of the few old-style accommodations left in the area; a serene, white country house with moulded ceilings and oak wainscoting. Some rooms even have open fires, but sometimes bedroom décor doesn't quite measure up to the rest of the house. Only seven guest rooms.

Huis ter Duin, P. J. Eloufstraat 1, 4357 AH, ✆ 584 400, ▨ 584 614 (*moderate– inexpensive*). Roomy, unpretentious family hotel with garden, backing on to the dunes. Some rooms have a sea view.

Duinhotel Haga, Westkapelsweg 17, 4374 BA, Zoutlande, ✆/▨ 561 823 (*inexpensive*). Sun-catching 1930s hotel on the edge of the dunes. Simply decorated, but well-run.

Veere ✆ (0118–)

De Campveerse Toren, Kaai 2, 4351 AA, ✆ 501 291, ▨ 501 695 (*moderate*). Housed in a 16th-century tower that once formed part of the city wall, and which has long been an inn. William of Orange had his wedding banquet here in 1575. Nowadays it's tastefully done up with antiques. The rooms are stylishly decorated and many look out over the water, though they do vary a bit in size. There are two rooms in the tower itself.

Zierikzee ✆ (0111–)

Klaas Vaak, Nieuwe Bogerdstraat 24, 4301 CX, ✆ 414 204 (*cheap*). Amiable, attractive pension in a quiet street near the old harbour.

Domburg ✆ (0118–)

Most eateries along the North Sea coast cater to the passing tourist trade. You'll find no shortage of places for a quick fish and chips, grill, or coffee and *appel-gebak*. But, if you're looking for something special, try **In den Walcherschen Dolphyn**, Markt 9, ✆ 582 839 (*expensive–moderate*); an attractive restaurant on the small town square. Mussels are the thing here, and especially the 'mussel bouillabaisse', which includes oysters, crayfish, sole, salmon and tuna—and heaps of tasty garlic bread alongside.

Veere ✆ (0118–)

De Peperboom, Kapellestraat 11, ✆ 501 307 (*cheap*). Cheerful, relaxed atmosphere that offers great value for money, and good no-nonsense cuisine—plump oysters, baked sardines, artichoke and goat's cheese salad.

Yerseke ✆ (0113–)

Nolet's, Jachthaven 6, ✆ 572 101 (*expensive–moderate*). Busy restaurant beside the mussel farms, and—as you might expect—renowned for mussels and oysters, but also for super-fresh fish. Their fish soup is so popular that they now sell it to take away too.

Zierikzee ✆ (0111–)

Auberge Maritime, Nieuwe Haven 21, ✆ 417 156 (*expensive*). Cosy, inn-like hostelry on one of the old town harbours—though the menu is adventurous and modern. Try roast cod with pesto risotto and crispy fried vegetables.

Noord-Brabant

Noord-Brabant stretches almost the entire breadth of the country, from the North Sea to Germany. It contains some of the dullest towns in the land, places so bleak that your only reaction on passing through has to be a pang of sympathy for those who have to stay behind. But the province also offers some gems, most notably the towns of Breda and Den Bosch, and though the landscape begins uneventfully in the west, it later begins to display woods and gentle slopes that hint of what's to come in neighbouring Limburg.

Breda

Breda began life some time in the 12th century as a settlement in the marshy ground between the rivers Mark and Aa (the town's name is a compression of 'Brede Aa'—'Broad Aa'). A castle was built here in 1200, affording refuge to sailors and fishermen, and by 1500 Breda had become an important fortress and garrison town. It was occupied by the Spanish later the 16th century, but retaken by soldiers of Prince Maurits in 1590, using the Dutch equivalent of the Trojan Horse—the soldiers smuggled

themselves behind city defences hidden in a peat barge. The city's name may have resonance for British people who remember their history lessons, as it was the Peace of
Breda that ended the war between the Dutch Republic and England in 1667.

Breda's skyline is dominated by a gigantic, ash-white Gothic cathedral. Two- and three-
storey houses huddle closely around its walls like toddlers on the skirts of a Victorian
nanny. In the city centre, most of the stone-paved streets are for pedestrians only, and
this helps give Breda a cosy village-like atmosphere. But that doesn't mean it is dull.
Back in the 15th century, Breda had 15 breweries, and tax on beer accounted for 52
per cent of the city's income. Breda became known as 'Beer City'. The breweries have
disappeared, but the name has stuck, and nowadays the epithet has more to do with
consumption than production.

Getting There

Breda is about 100km south of Amsterdam along the A27.

Take a train from Rotterdam Centraal Station (twice an hour). The journey takes
35mins.

Tourist Information

VVV, Willemstraat 17–19, © (076) 522 2444; open Mon–Fri 9–6, Sat 9–5.

Around the Grote Kerk

Breda's **Grote Kerk of Onze Lieve Vrouwe Kerk** (Great Church or Church of Our
Lady; *open Mon–Sat 10–5, Sun 1–5, unless the church is in use; adm*) is in the delicate, rather restrained style known as Brabant Gothic. Though a fire in 1534 destroyed
the archives, it is known that a stone church existed on this site in 1269, and that the
choir of the present church was completed in 1410. Most of the building work took
place in the late 15th and early 16th centuries, and despite a tower that keeps threat-
ening to fall down (and has on occasions done so), this is pretty much the church you
see today. Inside, it has been very carefully restored—work in the 20th century uncovered some fine frescoes and returned exceptional ceiling paintings to their original
colours. There's a particularly beautiful 15th-century wall painting of the Annunciation
in the north transept, and an even earlier one of a rather wild-looking St Christopher in
the nave. The Prince's Chapel, to the left of the choir, is a burial place for the Counts of
Nassau, and contains a dramatic triptych, *The Discovery of the True Cross*, by Jan van
Scorel (*see* p.51). There are also some exceptional carved grave monuments.

A few minutes' walk northeast of the Grote Kerk is the **Begijnhof**, a quiet courtyard of
houses for *beguines* (*see* **Amsterdam** p.92), with a herb garden in the middle. The
tiny chapel is lined with Spanish-looking tiles, and chock-a-block with carved saints and
stained glass. Beyond the Begijnhof is the **Kasteel van Breda** (Breda Castle), begun in
the 16th century and much rebuilt, now a military academy. Next to it you can see an
old city watergate, the **Spanjaardsgat** (literally 'Spanish Hole', even though this is not
the gate that Prince Maurits' soldiers' peat barge slipped through).

Museums

Just east of the city centre, **De Beyerd** (Bochstraat 22; *open Tues–Fri 10–5, Sat and Sun 1–5; adm*) is a venue for temporary exhibitions of contemporary art and photography, while a block farther south is the **Breda's Museum** (Parade 12; *open Tues–Sun 10–5; adm*), which has an overview of the city's history—also with good, themed temporary exhibitions. The first hall, 'Tijdspiegels' (Mirrors of Time), juxtaposes exhibits across centuries (such as a modern photograph in a 17th-century frame), while in the others you'll find anything from paintings and liturgical embroidery to 1930s advertisements. Keep an eye open for the intricate silver reliquaries, J. C. Huysman's wistful *View of Breda* (1814), and the delightfully camp painting *Ghosts in the Attic*, done by a local artist in 1881.

Breda ✆ (076–)   ***Where to Stay***

Hotel van Ham, Van Coothplein 23, 4811 NC, ✆ 521 5229, ✉ 521 3157 (*inexpensive–cheap*). Pleasant hotel on the southern edge of the city centre, near the Breda's Museum. Rooms are comfortable, but facilities are not en suite. There's a popular café downstairs, and the owner's amiable attitude (plus a great terrace) has led to the nickname 'de Huyskamer van Breda' ('the sitting-room of Breda').

Hotel De Klok, Grote Markt 26, 4811 XR (*inexpensive*). Centrally located hotel, convenient for all the sights. Rooms are on the small side, but perfectly comfortable. There's a good café/brasserie downstairs.

Breda ✆ (076–)   ***Eating Out***

Café Beecker en Wetselaar, Grote Markt 45, ✆ 522 1100 (*cheap*). Spacious, popular grand café on the Grote Markt. Pop in for a drink or a simple but tasty full meal—salmon poached in wine; knuckles of ham and large salads.

De Beyerd, Pasbaan 1, ✆ 522 0222 (*moderate*). Lively family restaurant just east of the city centre, offering Dutch and Flemish cuisine. Dishes cooked in beer are a speciality—and there are over 100 brews to choose from to drink.

De Stadstuin, Ginnekenweg 138, ✆ 530 9636 (*expensive*). Bright, pale interior but a relaxed, friendly ambience. Fine, fairly traditional French cuisine such as salad with smoked goose breast, goose liver and truffles. There's a good-sized garden for al fresco dining.

's-Hertogenbosch (Den Bosch)

's-Hertogenbosch (the Duke's Forest) is a bit of a mouthful even for the Dutch, and you'll seldom hear the city referred to by any name other than the shortened form, Den Bosch (pronounced Den Boss). The duke in question was one Hendrik of Brabant, who in 1185 granted city rights to the fortress settlement at the confluence of the rivers Aa and Dommel, in the oak forests near his hunting lodge. Den Bosch flourished as a

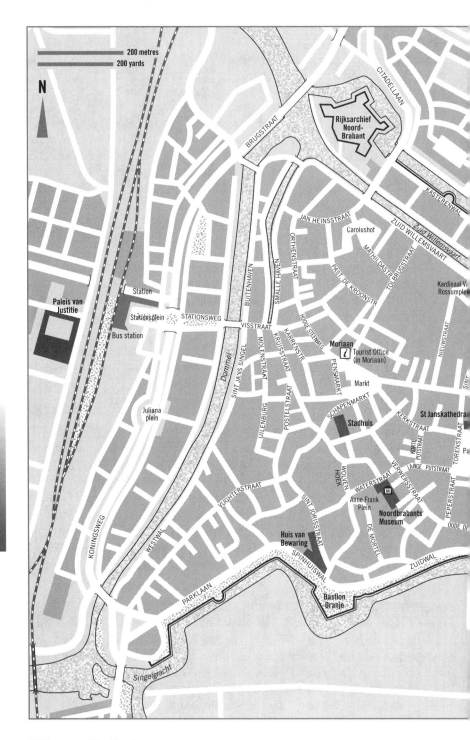

200 metres
200 yards

N

CITADELLAAN

BRUGSTRAAT

Rijksarchief
Noord-
Brabant

KASTERENWAL

JAN HEINSSTRAAT

Carolushof

ZUID WILLEMSVAART

Zuid Willemsvaart

ORTHENSTRAAT

MATHILDASTR

PAST. DE KROONSTR

TOLBRUGSTRAAT

Kardinaal Va
Rossumple

Paleis van
Justitie

Station

BUITENHAVEN

SMALLE HAVEN

HOOGE STEENWEG

NIEUWSTRAAT

Stationsplein

STATIONSWEG

VISSTRAAT

Moriaan

i Tourist Office
(in Moriaan)

Bus station

Dommel

SINT JANS SINGEL

MOLENSTRAAT

KRUISSTRAAT

KARRENSTR

PENSMARKT

Markt

SINT

Juliana
plein

UILENBURG

POSTELSTRAAT

SCHAPENMARKT

Stadhuis

KERKSTRAAT

St Janskathedraa

TORENSTRAAT

Pa

KORTE
PUTSTRAAT

VUGHTERSTRAAT

SINT JORISSTRAAT

WOLVEN
HOEK

WATERSTRAAT

VERWERSSTRAAT

LANGE PUTSTRAAT

PEPERSTRAAT

Anne Frank
Plein

M

OUDE DI

Noordbrabants
Museum

DE MORTEL

KONINGSWEG

WESTWAL

Huis van
Bewaring

SPINHUISWAL

ZUIDWAL

PARKLAAN

Bastion
Oranje

Singelgracht

's Hertogenbosch (Den Bosch)

trading city, in medieval times even rivalling nearby Brussels and Antwerp, and fending off invaders from north and south so successfully that it became known as the *Onoverwinnellijke Moerasdraak*, the 'Invincible Dragon of the Marshes'.

Den Bosch's most famous son is the painter **Hieronymus Bosch** (*c.* 1450–1516), who spent all his life in his home town. But there is not a single original painting of his to be seen anywhere in the city, although some murals in St Janskathedraal have been somewhat dubiously attributed to him.

Since 1815, Den Bosch has been capital of Noord-Brabant, and is one of the most exuberant and convivial cities in the country.

Getting There

Den Bosch is about 90km south of Amsterdam along the A2.

Trains from Breda go twice an hour. The journey takes 30mins.

Tourist Information

Markt 77, ℂ (0900) 112 2334; open Mon–Sat 9–5.

St Janskathedraal

By far Den Bosch's star attraction is the mighty, multi-buttressed **St Janskathedraal** (St John's Cathedral; *open daily 10–5 except when in use; adm free*), built between 1380 and 1520, and commonly regarded as the finest Gothic church in the country. The German painter and engraver Albrecht Dürer, who had taken in quite a few magnificent churches in his time, marvelled that St Jans was 'exuberantly beautiful'. Before going in, take a look at the wicked gargoyles—in this case devils, supposedly hindering the saints and other humans carved on the buttresses beneath in their ascent to heaven. Inside is a sumptuously carved **Altar of the Passion**, made in Antwerp around 1500. Near the west entrance, in her own chapel, is a brightly painted and richly bedecked 13th-century statue of the Virgin, dubbed **Zoete Lieve Vrouw** (Dear Sweet Lady) and said to have miraculous properties. A tall, throaty 17th-century **organ** was returned to prime working condition in the 1980s, and the freshly restored painting on the ceiling of the baldaquin stares down at you with an all-seeing Eye of God.

On the northeast side of the church, between the north transept and the ambulatory, is the chapel of the **Illustere Lieve Vrouwe Broederschap** (the Illustrious Brotherhood of Our Dear Lady, also known as the Zwanenbroeders), a society devoted to worship of the Virgin, and locally very popular because it regularly granted indulgences. Hieronymus Bosch was a member, which is perhaps why the murals in the chapel are sometimes attributed to him.

Around the Markt

Though it is a charming city, Den Bosch is not crammed with intriguing sights. In the middle of the triangular Markt (which shadows the shape of the original fort), you can see a restored medieval well and, across the way, the **Moriaan**, the city's oldest house. It's a quirky mix of step-gable, turret and half-timbering and nowadays is home to the tourist office. Just off the southern corner of the Markt is an elegant Classicist **Stadhuis** (built 1670), with four carved clockwork knights that charge out from below the pediment every half-hour.

Just west of the Markt, around Molenstraat, is the **Uilenberg** quarter, an old part of the city once packed back to back with cruddy medieval warehouses, but spruced up in the 1970s and now bursting at the seams with cafés and restaurants. A wander eastwards through the back streets brings you to the **Noordbrabants Museum** (Verwerstraat 41; *open Tues–Fri 10–5, Sat and Sun 12–5; adm*), located in the former residence of the Governors of Brabant, with a large modern extension. Much of the museum is devoted to art and artefacts concerning the history of Brabant, and there is also a sculpture garden, and good collection of contemporary art. Highlights include some really superb flower still lifes from the high point of the genre in the 17th and 18th centuries, and work by Peter Brueghel the Younger, including a desolate *Crucifixion*.

Den Bosch ✆ *(073–)*   **Where to Stay**

Curiously, although Den Bosch has many good restaurants (*see* below), it doesn't have any really special places to stay.

Golden Tulip Hotel Central, Burgemeester Loeffplein 98, 5211 RX, ✆ 692 6926, ✆ 614 5699, *info@hotel-central.nl* (*expensive–moderate*). Just what the name says—central, and offering all the unadventurous quality and comfort of the Golden Tulip chain, behind a 14th-century façade.

Best Western Eurohotel, Hinthamerstraat 63, 5211 MG, ✆ 613 7777, ✆ 612 8795 (*inexpensive*). Functional, family hotel near St Janskathedraal.

Van Beurden Versaevel B&B, Vughterstraat 163, 5211 GB, ✆ 614 4114 (*cheap*). Very comfortable family B&B, convenient for station and city centre.

Den Bosch ✆ *(073–)*   **Eating Out**

Den Bosch offers one of most varied and rewarding choices of restaurants outside of Amsterdam or Maastricht. Korte Putstraat, near St Janskathedraal, is lined with eateries—and, in contrast to similar streets around the country, most of them are excellent.

Corte, Korte Putstraat 10, ✆ 691 1430 (*moderate*). Cavernous, highly trendy grand café and brasserie. Stark décor with protruding metal and lots of geometry. The service is a bit of a disaster, but the food is excellent. Try the prawn and crab cannelloni with crayfish sauce, or monkfish with a tangy lemon sauce.

De Opera, Hinthamerstraat 115, ✆ 613 7457 (*expensive–moderate*). Long-standing favourite with locals and visitors alike. A tiny restaurant decorated with the abundance of a Peter Greenaway movie, and with really friendly staff. The cuisine is superb, with simple but knee-weakening dishes such as sauerkraut soup, or *waterzooi* (a delicate soupy stew made from sole and shellfish).

Café De Palm, Hinthamerstraat, ✆ 613 5727 (*cheap*). Neighbourhood café that from 6–8pm serves a set menu from De Opera across the road. There's no choice, but it's a great alternative to the pricier restaurant if you can't get a table, or don't want to fork out too much.

Eetcafe Javaanse Jongens, cnr Korte Putstraat and Lange Putstraat, ✆ 613 4107 (*moderate–cheap*). Bright and busy Indonesian restaurant decorated with colourful carvings, and serving inexpensive top-quality cuisine.

Entertainment and Nightlife

Den Bosch is a lively city with most nightlife activity centring on the area around Korte Putstraat and Hinthamerstraat, and along Karrenstraat. The local concert hall, **Het Muziekcentrum** (Prins Bernhardstraat, ✆ (073) 612 2123), offers a high standard of classical and contemporary music and jazz.

Around Noord-Brabant

Especially if you are travelling by car, which will make gadding about much easier, there are a number of small towns, one-off museums and wayside attractions around Noord-Brabant that merit a stopover.

Getting Around

Bergen op Zoom: Trains from Breda go twice an hour with a transfer in Roosendaal. The journey takes 35mins.

Willemstad: From Breda take bus 96 to Fernaard; change for bus 103 which will take you to Willemstad.

Oudenbosch: Take the train from Breda (twice an hour with a change in Roosendaal). The journey takes 25mins.

De Efteling: Take bus 137 from Breda once every hour. Journey time about 35mins. In the summer there are special buses laid on to De Efteling from all around the country; call ✆ (0900) 9292 or (0416) 288 111 for information.

Tilburg : Trains from Rotterdam Centraal Station go twice an hour to Tilburg. The journey takes 50mins.

Eindhoven: Take the train from Utrecht (four times an hour). The journey takes 50mins.

Tourist Information

Bergen op Zoom: Stationstraat 1, ✆ (0900) 202 0336; open Mon–Fri 10–5.30, Sat 10–4.

Willemstad: Hofstraat 1, ✆ (0168) 476 055; open Mon–Fri 9–4.30, Sat 11–4.30.

Eindhoven: Stationsplein 17, ✆ (0900) 112 2363; open Mon–Fri 9.30–5.30, Sat 10–5.

Bergen op Zoom, Carnival Town

Almost in Zeeland, on the edge of the Oosterschelde is the town of Bergen op Zoom, which has the 15th-century St Geertruidskerk, and an attractive city palace, **Het Markiezenhof** (Steenbergstraat 8; *open April–Sept Tues–Sun 11–5; Oct–March Tues–Sun 2–5; adm*), built between 1485 and 1511 and sporting a quaint oriental tower. Nowadays the Markiezenhof is a museum with grand period rooms, some interesting tapestries—and an exhibition of all you need for **Carnival**. For it is Carnival and Carnival alone that attracts most visitors to Bergen op Zoom, which reputedly holds one of the country's liveliest and most colourful processions.

Willemstad and Oudenbosch

Far more attractive as a town is Willemstad, just off the A29 some 25km north. Established by William of Orange as a fortress town in 1583, it preserves all seven of its original **bastions** (named after the Seven Provinces), has a charming main street and the grand Renaissance **Prinsenhof**, built as a hunting lodge for Prince Maurits in 1623. The octagonal **Koepelkerk** (Dome Church; *open Sat in summer 2–5; adm free*), especially commissioned by Prince Maurits, was one of the first churches purpose-built for Protestant services, and was finished in 1607.

Surely the most bizarre sight in all of Noord-Brabant is 10km down the way at Oudenbosch, just off the A59. In 1860 a band of swashbuckling Catholic soldiers left for Rome to defend the Pope against Garibaldi. They were not successful, but the Pope rewarded them amply and when they returned they commissioned Roman Catholic architect P. J. H. Cuypers (designer of Amsterdam's Rijksmuseum, *see* pp.63 and 110) to build a not-too downscaled replica of St Peter's (mixed in with a few other churches they had seen) in Oudenbosch. Named the **Basilica SS Agatha and Barbara**, it looms over the surrounding countryside. But there is little else to detain you in town.

De Efteling

> *Europalaan 1, © (0416) 288 111; opening times for 2000: 20 April–29 Oct daily 10–6; 8 July–27 Aug 10–9, on Sat in Aug open till midnight; adm exp and no discount for children, though children under 3 get in free.*

About halfway between Breda and Den Bosch, near the village of Kaatsheuvel just off the A59, is De Efteling, a truly magical theme park, completely devoid of the tackiness that often accompanies such ventures. The core of the park, designed in the 1950s by the illustrator of fairy-stories Anton Pieck, is an Enchanted Forest—a vast garden of real trees and flowers, where you might stumble upon Little Red Riding Hood, Snow White or Sleeping Beauty. They're models, but the attention to detail is exquisite. Sleeping Beauty's breasts rise and fall gently as she sleeps, Red Riding Hood knocks on the cottage door, while Wolf dressed as Granny peers out of the bedroom.

Though De Efteling gets very busy, you hardly notice—the crowds get lost in the forest. In addition to the Enchanted Wood, there are all manner of excellent rides, from the fast and deliciously scary to the utterly bewitching—such as a 'dream flight' in the dark through a castle, where you visit different elfin domains. You can smell the earth underground, feel the rain on your face as you're flying through the air. If you're bringing children to the Netherlands, this is the one absolute must. It's pretty high on the list of must-sees even if you're grown-up. It is expensive, but after your entrance ticket everything is free. Food and drink are for sale inside the park. Queues for rides can sometimes be long, but there are entertainers who help you keep your mind off the wait.

Tilburg and Eindhoven

By way of contrast, **Tilburg**, 10km south of De Efteling, is a front-runner for the title of the most horrid town in the Netherlands. Its one saving grace is perhaps the **Nederlands Textielmuseum** (National Textile Museum, Goirkestraat 96; *open Tues–Fri 10–5, Sat and Sun 12–5; adm*), which in addition to all sorts of antique weaving machines has an array of exotic and historical Dutch fabrics.

Close to Tilburg in the nastiness stakes and just 25km down the A58 is **Eindhoven**, sprawling home of the mighty Philips electronics multinational (though the administrative HQ has recently moved to Amsterdam). Apart from a good football team, Eindhoven's main claim to fame is the **Van Abbemuseum** (Bilderdijklaan 10, also temporarily at Vonderweg 1, © (040) 275 5275; *both open Tues–Sun 11–5; adm ƒ8 at each venue or ƒ12 combination ticket for both sites*). The Van Abbe has one of the best collections of modern and contemporary art in the country, but unfortunately rebuilding work at its official Bilderdijklaan building has dragged on for years, and both this building and the temporary premises across town at Vonderweg stage only temporary exhibitions drawn from part of the collection, so it's difficult to pin down what you might be able to see. But if 20th-century art appeals to you, then the museum is certainly worth a visit.

Where to Stay and Eating Out

Bergen op Zoom © (0164–)

> **Hotel Mercure De Draak**, Grote Markt 36, 4611 NT, © 252 050, @ 257 001 (*expensive*). Centrally situated and so lively lodgings during Carnival, though you'll have to book well in advance. The hotel claims to be the Netherlands' oldest inn, dating back to 1397. Now it spreads through three buildings, and has spacious, comfortable rooms, some of them air-conditioned. There's a restaurant downstairs.

Willemstad © (0168–)

> **Willemstad**, Voorstraat 42, © 472 250, @ 473 789, *info@wtours.nl* (*inexpensive–cheap*). Quiet, simple hotel, decorated in a modern style. On the main street, with back rooms overlooking a small church.

> **Het Wapen van Willemstad**, Benedenkade 12, 4797 AV, © 473 450, @ 473 705 (*inexpensive*). Relaxed, stylish hotel overlooking the small harbour. Rooms

are comfortable and decorated in soft pastel shades. There's a good restaurant downstairs, and an open hearth in the lounge.

De Rosmolen, Voorstraat 65, ✆ 472 466 (*cheap*). A shop in the 17th century, then for 200 years a flour mill, now a cosy café that serves salads, gigantic hamburgers and also fuller meals.

De Efteling/Kaatsheuvel ✆ (0416–)

Golden Tulip Efteling Hotel, Horst 31, 5171 RA, ✆ 282 000, ✉ 281 515, *informatie@efteling.nl* (*moderate*). Fun, fairytale-castle-shaped hotel very much in the same idiom as the theme park. There's a restaurant with good children's menus, and a playroom. The hotel is close to the park, and offers special combination prices.

De Joremeinshoeve, Lg Zandschel 1, 5971 TD, ✆ 274 527, ✉ 282 095 (*inexpensive*). Converted 18th-century farmhouse with a big garden (that includes a play area), in a quiet part of Kaatsheuvel village. Special combination prices with De Efteling available.

Limburg

Limburg, the tongue of land that prods its way between Germany and Belgium at the southernmost extremity of the country, joined the Netherlands late. Although Belgium declared itself an independent kingdom in 1830–31 (*see* p.44), bickering went on about borders and it wasn't until 1839 that the Dutch government, having negotiated the re-addition of Limburg to their territory, finally accepted the situation. But geologically Limburg is much older than the rest of the Netherlands. The coal from which Limburg once made its living formed 270 million years ago; the marl beneath Maastricht is over 60 million years old.

The mines are now closed, and today one of Limburg's prime attractions is its unspoiled landscape—in the north a patchwork of woods and farmland; around Roermond a watery wilderness of rivers and lakes; and to the south gentle hills, winding roads and swathes of green.

Getting There

The main **motorway** to Limburg from the north is the A2, which runs from Amsterdam through Utrecht and Den Bosch. If you're in Zeeland and don't wish to visit the rest of the south, it is quicker to drive to Maastricht via Antwerp in Belgium.

There are **trains** to Maastricht both via the Randstad and through the east of the country, via Arnhem and Nijmegen.

Maastricht

The capital of Limburg, Maastricht has a carefree, southern atmosphere, quite unlike any other Dutch town. For years it seemed to nestle in relative obscurity, known only to the Dutch and to the many Belgians and Germans who hopped across the border to do some shopping and have some fun. The signing of the 1992 Maastricht Treaty, a crucial stage in the cementing of European unity, shot Maastricht into the headlines but at the same time gave many people the false impression that the city was a bland realm of government bureaucrats. Nothing could be further from the truth. The oldest city in the country, it is also one of the most beautiful, and is European in the most attractive sense. People's conversation slips with ease between Dutch, German, French and English. Long before anyone thought of the euro, it was possible to pay for your purchases in Maastricht in any one of three currencies. There's something of the Belgian enjoyment of the good life, of French chic and café society, and of Dutch neatness and efficiency. And to top it all the restaurants are hard to beat.

History

The Romans settled beside the river Maas in 50 BC, building a crossing that they named *Mosae Trajectum*. Their wooden bridge, at the point where the St Servaasbrug is today, has long gone, but remains from the *castellum* they built beside the banks can still be seen in the Bonnefantenmuseum. The Maas (which connects with the inland waterways of the Netherlands) and its bridge laid the foundations for a prosperous trading city. But the strategic location of the bridge also made Maastricht an automatic focus for invaders, and the walled city was constantly besieged.

Around 350 AD Bishop Servatius (Servaas in Dutch), at a time when Christians in Northern Europe were a rare entity and were having a pretty hard time of things, made use of the protection of the Roman castle to establish a see at Maastricht, an initiative for which he was later canonized. Later, in 722, Bishop (also later Saint) Hubert transferred the see to Liège. From 1202, Maastricht was ruled jointly by the Duke of Brabant and the Prince-Bishop of Liège—an at times sticky arrangement that, in 1284, led to the signing of the 'Alde Caerte', which clearly defined temporal and ecclesiastical rights and privileges. The 'Alde Caerte' was in force until 1795, when the Low Countries were occupied by France. After Napoleon's defeat at Waterloo, Maastricht became part of the United Kingdom of Belgium and the Netherlands, and in 1839 was ceded to the Netherlands along with the rest of Limburg.

Getting There and Around

There's a direct **train** from Amsterdam Central Station to Maastricht every hour. Journey time is around 2½ hours.

The main sights are about 10mins' walk from the station, along Stationstraat and across the St Servaasbrug.

Maastricht, Kleine Staat 1, © (043) 325 2121; open Mon–Fri 9–6, Sat 9–5.

When to Go

Maastricht is one of the top **Carnival** cities, with the main parade happening the Sunday before Lent, a children's parade on the Monday and a brass band contest on the Tuesday. The **European Fine Art Fair** (usually late March) is one of the biggest arts and antiques fairs on the continent, and in the second week of May the **Feast of St Servaas** involves further processions and merry-making. Summer brings all manner of street events and cultural festivals and is a good time to visit this café-terrace-orientated city. From the second week of December through to the 23rd, there's a **Christmas market** on the Vrijthof.

Approaching the City

If you arrive in Maastricht by train, you get an immediate glimpse of one aspect of what the city has to offer, as the road into town is liberally dotted with restaurants and cafés.

You cross the river Maas over the **St Servaasbrug**, the oldest bridge in the Netherlands, built between 1280 and 1298. It's a solid stone structure with graceful rounded arches that has withstood attack by countless armies over the centuries; even explosives from both sides during the Second World War failed to make much of a dent.

To the left, just after you cross the bridge, is **Stokstraat**, a street of medieval and Golden Age houses that had fallen into rack and ruin, but which were considerably renovated in the 1980s, so now the quarter is one of the chicest shopping neighbourhoods in town. This quarter was the location of the original Roman fort. An alley off Stokstraat leads to the site of an erstwhile **Roman bathhouse**, though today it's just a quiet courtyard with the shadow of the old foundations marked out in the paving. At the end of Stokstraat, in a cellar beneath the Derlon hotel, you can see part of a 2nd- and 3rd-century **Roman square**, a 3rd-century well, and a 4th-century cobbled street and wall, at the **Museumlkelder Derlon** (Plankstraat 21; *open Sun 12–4; adm free*).

The Basilica and the City Walls

Just west of the Derlon Hotel is the shady **Onze Liewe Vrouweplein**, one of the most alluring squares in town. In good weather, the entire square is packed with café tables and chairs and echoes with conversation like a large dining hall.

Along the eastern end of the square is the **Onze Lieve Vrouwebasiliek** (Basilica of Our Dear Lady; *open daily 10–5, July and Aug 10–6; adm free*), a cruciform basilica begun around the year 1000, but built on the site of a number of much earlier churches, dating back to St Servaas's original place of worship (*see* 'History', above). The oldest parts are the west wing and the crypt; the nave and transept are a little later, and the choir dates from the 12th century. The capitals around the choir have some

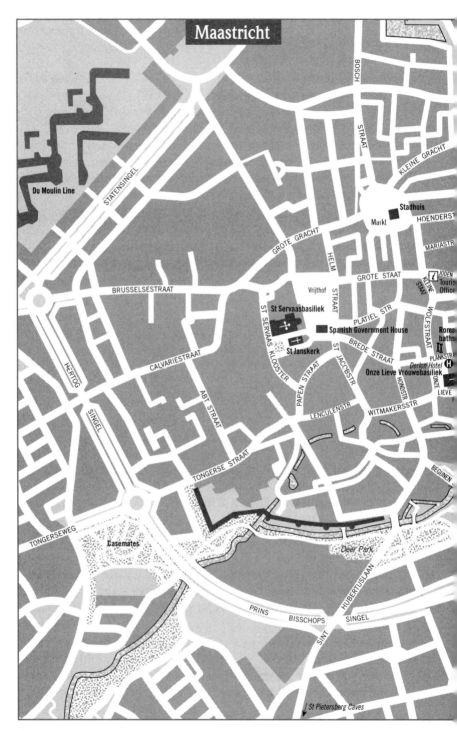

Maastricht

Du Moulin Line

BOSCH STRAAT

KLEINE GRACHT

STATENSINGEL

Stadhuis

Markt

HOENDERST

MARIASTR

GROTE GRACHT

BRUSSELSESTRAAT

HELM STRAAT

GROTE STAAT

JODEN Touris Office

KLEINE STAAT

Vrijthof

St Servaasbasiliek

PLATIEL STR

WOLFSTRAAT

Spanish Government House

Roma baths

PLANKSTR

ST SERVAAS KLOOSTER

ST JANSKERK

BREDE STRAAT

Derlon Hotel H

Onze Lieve Vrouwebasiliek

HERTOG

CALVARIESTRAAT

PAPEN STRAAT

ST JACOBSTR

LENCULENSTR

WITMAKERSSTR

LIEVE

HONDSTR

LIEVE

SINGEL

ABT STRAAT

TONGERSE STRAAT

BEGIJNEN

TONGERSEWEG

Casemates

Deer Park

PRINS BISSCHOPS SINGEL

HUBERTUSLAAN

SINT

St Pietersberg Caves

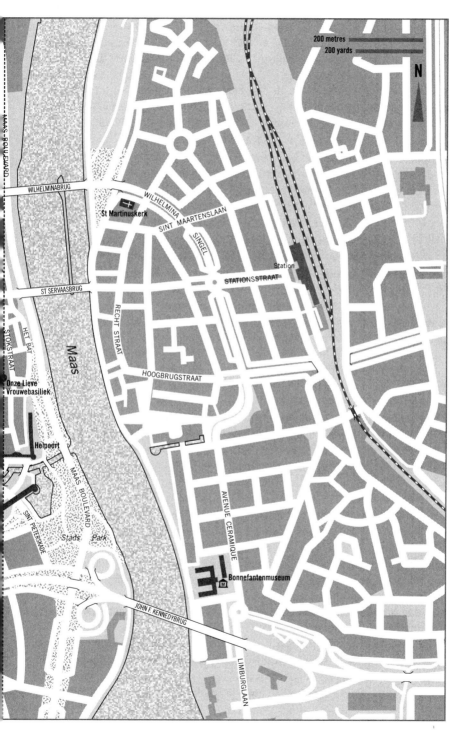

200 metres
200 yards

N

WILHELMINABRUG

St Martinuskerk

WILHELMINA
SINT MAARTENSLAAN
SINGEL

Station
STATIONSSTRAAT

ST SERVAASBRUG

RECHT STRAAT

HET BAT
STOKSTRAAT

Maas

Onze Lieve
Vrouwebasiliek

HOOGBRUGSTRAAT

Helpoort

MAAS BOULEVARD

SINT PIETERSKADE

Stads Park

AVENUE CERAMIQUE

Bonnefantenmuseum

JOHN F. KENNEDYBRUG

LIMBURGLAAN

MAAS BOULEVARD

particularly fine carvings of biblical scenes. There are hardly any windows in the church. The dim light, the residual aromas of centuries of incense and the soothing Romanesque architecture contribute to a feeling of indefinable holiness that could move even the most sceptical to prayer. And indeed a wave of heat hits you from all the candles placed before the image of Mare Stella in a side chapel near the entrance, an object of pilgrimage since the 15th century. In the **Treasury** (*open daily 10–5, July and Aug 10–6; adm*) there's a fine stash of silver, reliquaries and rich embroidery.

A block or two south of Onze Lieve Vrouwebasiliek, you come to the towering **Helpoort** (St Bernardusstraat; *open Easter to mid-Sept daily 2–5; adm donation*), part of the original 1229 city wall. It is the only city gate left standing in Maastricht and the oldest in the country. A second wall was built in 1350 as the city expanded, though the Helpoort was still an important gate. It formed a crucial part of the city defences until the 16th century, when an ever-growing population meant that a third wall had to be built beyond it. Inside, you can climb the tower and see a small exhibition on the development of Maastricht's defences. South of the Helpoort, in the park at the end of Begijnestraat, you can see part of the third city wall, and there's a long stretch of the second wall to the west, starting at Nieuwenhofstraat.

There are further fortifications just outside the ring road, in the Waldeckpark. The **Casemates** (*tours generally at 2pm, but check with VVV*) are based on mining tunnels built between 1575 and 1825, which were often used for refuge in times of siege and to sneak up behind enemy lines for surprise attacks. There are over ten kilometres of dark passageways, though the guided tour shows you only a small selection of the domed vaults, powder rooms and plunging steps. And if you're really enthusiastic about defence works, you should head off to the northwestern edge of town, where on Cabergerweg you can get in to see part of the **Du Moulin Line** (*guided tours leave from Meubelboulevard furniture store on Cabergerweg, Sun 3pm, except Carnival, duration 1hr; adm*), a complex system of dry trenches, bastions and bomb-proof shelters developed in the 18th century.

Around the Vrijthof

The **Vrijthof** is at the heart of Maastricht—a vast, open square with a line of cafés at one end and two imposing churches at the other. The name comes from an old word for graveyard. According to the chronicler Gregory of Tours (539–594), when St Servaas died in 384 he was buried, not in a church, but 'near a bridge by a public road'. Legend has it that the Vrijthof is the place, and the saint's relics are contained in the larger of the two churches on the square, the **St Servaasbasiliek** (*open daily 10–5, July and Aug 10–6; closed over Carnival; adm*). The basilica was built early in the 11th century, almost at the same time as the Onze Lieve Vrouwebasiliek.

It seems possible that the simultaneous sprouting of two great churches, almost next door and rivalling each other in size, was indicative of a growing tension between the powers ruling Maastricht—a tension that was later to lead to the 'Alde Caerte'. Unlike its rival church, St Servaas kept up with the latest trends in architectural fashion, and was the first Gothic church to be built in the area. Inside, it is all soaring arches and floods of light. Walls and ceiling have been restored to their original white-painted state, and decorated with bright designs. In the east crypt you can see the simple stone tomb of St Servaas, and in the St Servaas Chapel, beside the Sacristy, is an intricately carved 16th-century retable. Don't miss the sumptuous Bergportaal on the south side of the church—an elaborately carved, vividly coloured gateway built between 1225 and 1250, heavily influenced by sculptural trends that were just beginning to emerge in France. The collection in the **Treasury** is breathtaking. Look out especially for the exquisite 10th-century Cross of St Servaas, made of enamelled gold, ivory and jewels, and the saint's magnificent gold shrine.

To the south of the church is the much smaller, Gothic **St Janskerk**, sporting a pale red tower (*open Easter–mid-Oct, Mon–Sat 11–4; adm free to church, adm to tower*). Since 1633, Sint Jans has been Maastricht's main Protestant church, and the interior is appropriately sober. On the other side of St Servaas is an arcaded 18th-century **Watch House**, and on the south side of the square you'll find the **Spanish Government House** (Vrijthof 18; *open Wed–Sun 1–5; adm*), former seat of the Dukes of Brabant. Inside are a number of period rooms and good 17th- and 18th-century furniture.

Northeast of the Vrijfthof is the **Markt**, Maastricht's other main square and the scene of a busy general market on Wednesday and Friday mornings. Adorning the eastern end of the square is Maastricht's 17th-century **Stadhuis**. Legend has it that the grand double staircase was built so that the rival rulers from Brabant and Liège wouldn't have to argue about who should have precedence when going in and out.

Bonnefantenmuseum

> *Avenue Ceramique 250; on the banks of the Maas, about 10mins' walk from St Servaasbrug; buses 50, 54, 56, 57, 58 from the station; open Tues–Sun 11–5; closed over Carnival; adm.*

Limburg's provincial museum is housed in a spectacular new building—complete with a shiny metal bullet-shaped dome—by Italian architect Aldo Rossi. It is most renowned for its collection of medieval religious carvings unequalled anywhere else in the country. There is also some exceptionally fine Southern Netherlandish painting from the 16th and 17th centuries (including work by Brueghel the Younger), and beautiful early Italian painting from the period 1325 to 1525. A second part of the collection focuses on archaeological finds from the area, including Stone Age and Roman artefacts. And then there's an excellent (frequently changing) selection of contemporary art.

Outside the Centre

There is more troglodytic tramping to be done in the **St Pietersberg Caves** (*bus 4; generally one tour daily in English in summer, more frequent in Dutch; check with VVV for information; adm*), the result of centuries' worth of marl excavation in the all-of-112m-high 'Mount St Peter' on the southern outskirts of town. The mining passages provided useful protection in time of war, and were equipped as air-raid shelters during the Second World War—though hardly used. You can tour the cold, dark passages (take a jersey, the average temperature is 10°C) to view various provisions for emergencies, and old graffiti.

Shopping

Maastricht is renowned for its good shops: designer fashion boutiques, stylish home interiors shops, antiques stores and contemporary art galleries. The area around Stokstraat offers fruitful pickings, especially in **fashion** and **antiques**. There are more **antiques stores** to be found near the old city wall on St Pieterstraat. Contemporary **art galleries** are of a high standard; you'll find a few north of the centre along Brusselsestraat, and more around Tafelstraat (just south of Onze Lieve Vrouweplein). Across the Maas, you'll find a string of galleries and antiques stalls on the way to the Bonnefantenmuseum, along Rechtstraat and Hoogbrugstraat.

In addition to the Wednesday and Friday **general market** on the Markt, there is a **fleamarket** every Saturday along Stationstraat.

Maastricht © (043–) **Where to Stay**

Hotel Botticelli, Papenstraat 11, 6211, © 352 6300, ✆ 352 6336 (*expensive–moderate*). Converted 18th-century mansion, a stone's throw from St Servaas and retaining many original features, such as moulded ceilings, marble fireplaces and a beautiful staircase. Modern furniture has been stylishly integrated. Rooms vary in size.

Hotel Les Charmes, Lenculenstr 18, 6211 KR, © 321 7400, ✆ 325 8574 (*moderate*). A gem in central Maastricht. Six spacious rooms in an 18th-century town house. Each is individually decorated—one Art Deco, another stylishly modern. Downstairs is a very cosy, homey lounge.

D'Orangerie, Kleine Gracht 4, 6211 CB, © 326 1111, ✆ 326 1287 (*moderate–inexpensive*). Genteel, quiet hotel near the Markt in an elegant 18th-century building. Rooms are well-equipped and decorated in English country-house style.

Mabi, Kleine Gracht 24, 6211 CB, © 351 4444, ✆ 351 4455 (*moderate*). Straightforward, modern, comfortable central hotel in a converted cinema.

Dis Guesthouse, Tafelstraat 28, 6211 JD, © 321 5479, ✆ 325 7026 (*moderate*). Very stylish designer hotel above an art gallery in a Gothic townhouse near the old city wall.

Maison du Chêne, Boschstraat 104–106, 6211 AZ, © 321 3523, ✆ 325 8082 (*inexpensive*). Medium-sized, few-frills hotel in 19th-century inn, not far from the Markt.

Botel, Maasboulevard 95, 6211 JW, © 321 9023, ✆ 325 7988 (*cheap*). Bikes 'n' backpacker boat moored on the Maas, a short walk from the centre. Young, youth-hostelly atmosphere. Some rooms without private facilities.

De Bóbbel, Wolfstraat 32, ✆ 321 7413 (*cheap*). Traditional Maastricht café—sawdust on the floor, marble-topped bar and tables. There are eight beers on tap, a good range of wines, and wholesome dishes such as onion soup and chicken pasties. A good lunch venue.

Café In Den Oude Vogelstruys, Vrijthof 15, ✆ 321 4888 (*moderate–cheap*). One of the most popular cafés in town, with good soups, mussels, and asparagus dishes in season. Ideal for lunch and also good for an evening meal.

Reuben, Tongersestraat 23, ✆ 325 2843 (*moderate*). Warm brasserie atmosphere amidst wooden wainscoting and deep apricot walls. A mixed-aged crowd tuck into quails on a bed of tagliatelle and morels, or fat steak with a four-colour pepper sauce.

Au Coin Des Bons Enfants, Ezelmarkt 4, ✆ 321 2359 (*expensive–moderate*). Atmospheric restaurant in 16th-century building serving good, honest traditional French cuisine.

Alsacien Beaumont, Wycker Brugstraat 2, ✆ 325 4433 (*expensive*). Conventional hotel-restaurant décor, but top-rate Alsace wines and cuisine. Think goose breast with sauce of Pinot Noir, honey and raisins served with sauerkraut.

Toine Hermsen, Sint Bernardusstraat 2–4, ✆ 325 8400 (*expensive, but who cares?*). Toine Hermsen has been voted by his peers to be one of the top three chefs in the country; and his restaurant named the best in Limburg (and that's saying something!) by the foodie magazine *Lekker*. Yet the two-Michelin-starred restaurant just off Onze Lieve Vrouweplein retains an unpretentious homey ambience,and, year in, year out, the food remains heavenly.

Tongersestraat, in the university district, is lined with lively cafés. Pick your noise level. **D'Ouwe Klok** (Tongersestraat 13) is one of the more low-key bars on the strip, with a good range of Belgian beer and an array of clocks. There are a couple of late bars on Koestraat, and the cafés on Vrijthof and Onze Lieve Vrouweplein are popular night and day. **D'n Awwestiene** (a.k.a. Night Live Music) at Kesselkade 43 is a great live music and party venue, playing 'everything except house'.

The **Theater aan Het Vrijthof** (Vrijthof 47, ✆ 350 5555) is the main city venue for theatre, opera and concerts.

Traipsing around Limburg's gentle countryside is rewarding in itself. But there are added attractions along the way, from towering castles to thermal spas.

Getting There

Venlo: Take the train from Maastricht, which goes twice an hour, and transfer in Roermond. The journey will take around an hour.

Roermond: Take the train from Maastricht to Roermond (twice every hour). The journey takes 30mins.

Thorn: Take the train from Maastricht to Roermond and transfer to bus 73, which goes twice an hour. The journey takes 75mins in total.

Valkenburg: Take the train from Maastricht (twice an hour). The journey takes 15mins.

Heerlen: Take the train from Maastricht (twice an hour). The journey takes 30mins.

Tourist Information

Roermond: Kraanpoort 1, ✆ (0900) 202 5588; open Mon–Fri 9–5, Sat 10–2.
Thorn: Wijngaard 14, ✆ (0475) 562 761; open Tues–Sun 11–4.
Valkenburg: Th. Dorrenplein 5, ✆ (043) 609 8600; open Mon–Fri 9–5.30, Sat 9–1.
Heerlen: Honigmanstraat 100, ✆ (045) 571 6200; open Mon–Fri 9.30–6, Sat 9.30–4.

Venlo

Right up against the German border, the town of **Venlo** was on the front line during the Second World War, and suffered constant bombardment during 1944 and 1945. Most of the town was wrecked, but its grand twin-towered **Stadhuis** (built 1597–1600) still stands proud in the market place, and the 15th-century **St Martinuskerk** also survived reasonably intact. The **Limburgmuseum** (Goltziusstraat 21; *open Tues–Fri 10.30–4.30, Sat and Sun 2–5; adm*) has a large collection of historical exhibits. To the north of town, the 17th-century castle at **Arcen** (Lingsforternweg 26; bus 83 to stop Arcen Maasstraat, then 10min walk; *open April–Sept 10–6, Oct 11–5; adm exp*) has breathtaking gardens, including an abundant rosarium, as well as sub-tropical and oriental sections.

Roermond and Thorn

Some 20km farther south of Venlo, ostensibly Catholic **Roermond** is the birthplace of the architect P. J. H. Cuypers (*see* p. 63). The town's most beautiful building is the placid Romanesque **Onze Lieve Vrouwe Munster**, the last remains of a 13th-century Cistercian abbey to which Cuypers has added some rather unfortunate neo-Gothic towers. Inside the church is an extremely old carved stone retable, picturing Christ

Triumphant. Cuypers' neo-Gothic home and studio is now the **Stedelijk Museum Roermond** (Roermond Municipal Museum, Andersonweg 4; *open Tues–Fri 11–5, Sat and Sun 2–5; adm*), which features displays on the architect and his work, as well as on city history.

The main tourist attraction of the area is **Thorn**, a picturesque village 12km away to the east through rolling Limburg fields, where the streets are cobbled in patterns and all the houses are painted white, creating a somewhat Mediterranean air. For 800 years, up until 1794, Thorn was an independent state, ruled by a succession of aristocratic abbesses. The one non-white building in town (on the outside, anyway) is the 14th-century **Stiftskerk** (abbey church). Cuypers has plonked a neo-Gothic tower on this one too.

Valkenburg

Valkenburg, just a few minutes' journey east of Maastricht in the hilliest countryside in the land, sucks in hordes of tourists in all seasons. It has a pedestrianized old centre, around Grendelplein, though the modern focus is Theo Dorrenplein, a typical town centre piazza with outdoor cafés and the tourist information office. You can visit the ruins of the **Valkenburg Castle** (Daalhemerweg 27; *open daily 10–4, closed during Carnival; adm*) on a hill above the town, from which a secret underground passage, discovered in 1937, leads to the **Fluweelengrot Marl** caves nearby. In summer a cable car takes you to the top of the hill.

Oddly (given the rarity of hilly landscapes in the Netherlands) most of Valkenburg's attractions are underground. The **Roman Catacombs** (Plenkerstraat 55; *open April–Sept daily 10–5; adm*) are an imitation, built in 1909 by (guess who) P.J. H. Cuypers. In the **Steenkolenmijn** (Coal Mine, Daalhemerweg 31; *open April–Oct daily 10–5; Nov–Dec daily 1–3; Jan–March Sat and Sun 10–3; adm*), you're led about an equally artificial underground mine for an hour and a half by an ex-miner, who demonstrates the machines and tells you all about it. The **Gemeentegrot** (Municipal Cave, Cauberg 4; *open daily 10–6, closed Carnival; adm*) dates back to Roman times and has a little train that trundles you past portraits of local dignitaries and carvings cut into the rock face.

None of these attractions is especially riveting. A much better bet, for most adults anyway, is **Thermae 2000** (Cauberg 27, ✆ (043) 601 9419, ✉ 601 4815; *open daily 9–11; adm from ƒ30 for two hours, massage and beauty treatments extra, reservation for massage and beauty treatments advised*), a gigantic natural spa, complete with sauna and steam room, exercise room and a restaurant. You can also swim outdoors in the spa waters, with a great view over Limburg. There are facilities for mud baths and massage, and the spa complex includes luxurious accommodation. **Heerlen**, just a little closer to the German border, lies on the same net of mineral springs, and at the **Thermenmuseum** (Coriovallumnstraat 9; *open daily 10–5, closed Carnival; adm*) there are the well-preserved ruins of a Roman bath-house, complete with sound-and-light show to illustrate how it was used.

Roermond ✆ (0475–)

Willems, Godsweerdersingel 58, 6041 GM, ✆ 333 021, @ 337 951 (*inexpensive–cheap*). Very simple, but clean and perfectly adequate pension near the station. There's a traditional Limburg café downstairs.

Thorn ✆ (0475–)

Hostellerie la Ville Blanche, Hoogstraat 2, 6017 AR, ✆ 562 341, @ 562 828 (*moderate–inexpensive*). Pleasant hotel in the heart of 'White Town'. It has a pretty courtyard garden, and there's a brasserie downstairs.

Crasborn, Hoogstraat 6, 6017 AR, ✆ 561 281, @ 562 233 (*inexpensive*). Simple but comfortable family hotel across from the Stiftkerk. It has its own café and restaurant, with ample options for children, and a garden.

Valkenburg ✆ (043–)

Villa Martine, Broekhem 18, 6301 HH, ✆ 601 3804, @ 601 4720 (*inexpensive*). Beautiful, detached 19th-century villa in its own garden near the station. Comfortable, individually decorated rooms.

Parkhotel Rooding, Neerhem 68, 6301 CJ, ✆ 601 3241, @ 601 3240, *parkhotel@rooding.com* (*moderate*). Large and almost luxurious hotel in the hills, ten minutes' walk from the city centre. Big garden, swimming pool, and panoramic views. Offers special combination prices with Thermae 2000.

Prinses Juliana, Broekhem 11, ✆ 601 2244, @ 601 4405, *info@ juliana.nl* (*expensive*). A hotel-restaurant most renowned for its food. For the past 40 years it has ranked with the country's best, bouncing up and down between one and two Michelin stars. Exquisite French cuisine and a legendary wine list. Special dining/accommodation arrangements available. Spacious suite-style rooms.

The language spoken in the Netherlands is Nederlands. In the Middle Ages it was known as Dietse or Duutsc (hence the English 'Dutch'), an equivalent of the German Deutsch meaning 'the language of the people' (as opposed to Latin—the language of scholars and the Church). You can hear variations spoken in Belgium (Flemish or Vlaams) and South Africa (Afrikaans).

The standard form of the language goes by the rather grand title of Algemeen Beschaafd Nederlands (General Cultured Netherlandic or ABN), though there are a multitude of regional dialects. Most of the Dutch you'll hear in Amsterdam will be ABN. But relax in a neighbour-hood bar, or wander through one of the markets, and you'll hear the noisy rasping vowels of what detective story writer Nicolas Freeling called the rooks' caw of the Amsterdam dialect.

Historically, Dutch is the same language as German, a descendant of the language spoken by West Germanic tribes and the Salic Franks. Even today there are many similarities of sentence structure and vocabulary between the two languages. But Dutch doesn't have the gloss and edge of German. It's a softer, cosier, muddy language that seems to have grown out of the bogs and polders. Dutch is not an easy language to grapple with. However, to a short-term visitor to Amsterdam this need present no problem, as nearly everyone you meet will speak such good English that you could almost consider it to be the city's second language. The list of words and phrases below will help the polite and adventurous who wish to master everyday courtesies, interpret the menu, or disentangle themselves from sticky situations.

Pronunciation

Pronunciation is a question of tackling some rather difficult vowel sounds. Happily, spelling is phonetic, so once you've learned the sounds you'll be able to make a pretty accurate stab at pronouncing anything you read. The stress in Dutch, as in English, generally falls on the first syllable of a word.

Language

Consonants

Most consonants are pronounced the same as they would be in English. However, *p*s, *t*s and *k*s aren't aspirated (i.e. they're pronounced without the accompanying puff of air). Say *ch* and *g* as in the Scottish 'loch' (*g* is more strongly voiced in northern parts of the country). Good luck in getting your tongue around the combined *s* and *ch* sounds in words like *schip* (ship), *school* (school) or *schrijter* (writer). You have a choice for *r* — you can roll it at the back of your mouth or trill it behind your teeth, but you must *always* pronounce it. Say *w* halfway between the English 'w' and 'v', except before *r*, when you pronounce it 'v'. The Dutch *v* is closer to English 'f'. Say *j* as English 'y'; *sj* as English 'sh' and *tj* as English 'ch'.

Vowels

Pronounce the basic *a, e, i, o, u* sounds the same as you would in English, but *much shorter* (*a* as in 'hard', but shorter). Say *ie* as in 'neat', *oo* as in 'boat' and *oe* as in 'pool', but make all the sounds shorter. *aa* is like the 'a' in 'cat', but longer and *ee* is similar to the vowel sound in 'hail'. Say *eu* to rhyme with 'err', but round your lips tightly, and say *uu* as English *oo* in 'hoot'. The combination *ij* is a distinct letter in the Dutch alphabet, and is pronounced 'ay', whether it begins a word like *ijs* (ice/ice-cream), or comes in the middle, as in *wijn* (wine). The stretch of water north of Centraal Station is Het IJ, 'het ay'. The diphthong *ui* is a killer. In getting their tongues around the streetname Spui, Americans usually come up with 'Spew-ee' and the Brits manage 'Spow'. The Dutch sound is closer to the way a French person would say *œil*. If that leaves you none the wiser, try running together 'er-ee', but with no hint of an 'r' sound.

Here are some practice sentences:

Dag! Ik wil graag een fles wijn
darHg! ik vil HgrahHg ayn fles veyn
(Hello, I'd like a bottle of wine, please)

Waar is de wc?
Vahr iss de vay say?
(Where is the loo?)

Echt? Wat leuk!
EHgt? Vut lerk!
(Really? How nice!)

Useful Words and Phrases

do you speak English?	*spreekt u Engels?*	thank you/thanks	*dank u wel/bedankt*
I don't understand	*Ik begrijp het niet*	don't mention it	*niets te danken*
could you speak more slowly?	*kunt u wat lang- zamer spreken?*	there is/there are	*er is/er zijn*
		there isn't/aren't	*er is/zijn geen*
hello/goodbye	*dag*	I have	*ik heb*
hi	*hoi* (grating to some ears)	I don't have any	*ik heb geen*
		I'd like	*ik wil graag*
'bye	*doei* (grating)	we'd like	*wij willen graag*
goodbye	*tot ziens*	I like it	*ik vind het leuk*
see you later	*tot straks*	I don't like it	*ik vind het niet leuk*
good morning/ afternoon/night	*goede morgen/ middag/nacht*	where	*waar*
good evening	*goedenavond*	what	*wat*
yes/no/maybe	*ja/nee/misschien*	when	*waneer*
please	*alstublieft*	which	*welk*

who	wie	I'm hungry/thirsty	ik heb honger/dorst
why	waarom	I'm in a hurry	ik heb haast
where is the lavatory?	waar is het toilet?	I'm lost	ik ben verdwaald
may I	mag ik	call a doctor quickly	roep vlug een dokter
can you	kunt u		
how much is this/that?	hoeveel kost dit/dat?	call the police/ an ambulance	roep de politie/ een ambulance
expensive	duur	entrance/exit	ingang/uitgang
cheap	goedkoop	push/pull	duwen/trekken
can you help me?	kunt u mij helpen?	open/closed	open/gesloten (dicht)

Meeting People

how do you do?	(say your name and surname clearly)	may I get you a drink?	mag ik u iets te drinken aanbieden?
how are you?	hoe maakt u het?		
very well, thank you	uitstekend, dank u	do you have a light?	hebt u/je een vuurtje?
fine, thanks	heel goed, dank je		
and you?	en u/jij?	really?	echt?
my name is...	mijn naam is . . .	shall we go?	gaan we?
what are you having?	wat neem je?		

Hotel

single room	eenpersoonskamer
double room	tweepersoonskamer
with private bath/shower/toilet	met privé bad/douche/toilet
may I see the room?	mag ik de kamer zien?
did anyone telephone for me?	heeft er iemand voor mij gebeld?
may I see the manager, please?	mag ik de directeur spreken, alstublieft?

Transport

airport	luchthaven/vliegveld	how can I get to...?	hoe kom ik bij...?
customs	douane	where is...?	waar is...?
railway station	trein station	the ticket office	het loket
platform	perron	I'd like a ticket to...	ik wil graag een kaartje naar...
platform five	spoor vijf		
car	auto	single/return	enkeltje/retourtje
bicycle	fiets/rijwiel	change (trains)	overstappen
ticket	kaartje	when does the next/ first/last train leave?	wanner vertrek de volgende/eerste/ laatste trein?
occupied/reserved	bezet/gereserveerd		
where can I get a taxi?	waar kan ik een taxi krijgen?		
		how long does it take?	hoe lang duurt het?
what's the fare to...?	wat kost het naar...?	near/far	dichtbij/ver weg
take me to this address	breng me naar dit adres	left/right/ straight ahead	links/rechts/ vooruit
I want to go to...	ik wil naar...		

Driving

car hire	*auto verhuur*	parking place	*parkeerplaats*
petrol/diesel	*benzine/diesel*	parking garage	*parkeer garage*
leaded/unleaded	*lood/loodvrij*	no parking	*verboden te park*
filling station	*benzinestation*		*eren/niet parkeren*
garage (for repairs)	*garage*	speed limit	*snelheidslimiet*

Numbers

nought	*nul*	seventy	*zeventig*
one/two/three	*een/twee/drie*	eighty	*tachtig*
four/five/six	*vier/vijf/zes*	ninety	*negentig*
seven/eight/nine	*zeven/acht/negen*	hundred	*honderd*
ten/eleven/twelve	*tien/elf/twaalf*	two hundred and	*tweehonderd-*
thirteen, fourteen etc.	*dertien/veertien* etc.	twenty	*twintig*
twenty	*twintig*	thousand	*duizend*
twenty-one	*eenentwintig*	million	*een miljoen*
twenty-two	*tweeëntwintig* (etc.)	first/1st	*eerste/1e*
thirty	*dertig*	second/2nd	*tweede/2e*
forty	*veertig*	third/3rd	*derde/3e*
fifty	*vijftig*	fourth/4th	*vierde/4e*
sixty	*zestig*	eighth/8th	*achtste/8e*

Time

what time is it?	*hoe laat is het?*	tomorrow	*morgen*
one o'clock	*een uur*	morning/afternoon	*morgen/middag*
a quarter past one	*kwart over een*	evening/night	*avond/nacht*
half past one	*half twee* [sic]	Monday	*maandag*
a quarter to two	*kwart voor twee*	Tuesday	*dinsdag*
ten to/past three	*tien voor/over drie*	Wednesday	*woensdag*
twenty past five	*tien voor half zes*	Thursday	*donderdag*
twenty-five to eight	*vijf over half acht*	Friday	*vrijdag*
I'll come at 2 o'clock	*ik kom om twee uur*	Saturday/Sunday	*zaterdag/zondag*
today	*vandaag*	day/week/month	*dag/week/maand*
yesterday	*gisteren*	year	*jaar*

Menu Guide

may I see the menu/wine list?	*mag ik de spijskaart/wijnkaart zien?*
bon appétit	*eet smakelijk*
it tastes good/bad	*het smaakt lekker/niet lekker*
may I have the bill, please?	*mag ik de rekening, alstublieft?*
waiter/waitress	*ober/serveerster*
service	*bediening*
starter	*voorgerecht*
soup	*soep*
main course	*hoofdgerecht*
dish of the day	*dagschotel*
dessert	*nagerecht*

Drinks

a beer, please	*een pils, alstublieft*	fizzy mineral water	*spa rood* (brand)
a bottle of wine	*een fles wijn*	still mineral water	*spa blauw*
red/white	*rode/witte*	coffee (with milk)	*koffie (verkeerd)*
sweet/dry	*zoete/droge*	tea	*thee*
fresh orange juice	*jus d'orange*	(with milk/lemon)	*(met melk/citroen)*
tomato juice	*tomatensap*		

Fish

cod	*kabeljauw*	herring	*haring*
bass	*zeebaars*	trout	*forel*
eel	*paling*	salmon	*zalm*
halibut	*heilbot*	sole	*tong*

Meat, Poultry and Game

veal	*kalfsvlees*	duck	*eend*
lamb	*lamsvlees*	turkey	*kalkoen*
beef	*rundvlees*	rabbit	*konijn*
pork	*varkensvlees*	venison	*wild*
chicken	*kip*		

Vegetables

garlic	*knoflook*	spinach	*spinazie*
mushrooms	*champignons*	potatoes	*aardappelen*
carrots	*worteltjes*	potato chips	*patat frites*
asparagus	*asperge*	salad	*sla*

Dessert

whipped cream	*slagroom*	ice-cream and	
fruit	*vrucht*	chocolate sauce	*dame blanche*
ice-cream	*ijs*		

Preparation

poached	*gepocheerd*	grilled	*geroosterd*
fried	*gebakken*	stuffed	*gevuld*
roast	*gebraden*	rare	*rood*
boiled	*gekookt*	medium	*half doorbakken*
braised	*gestoofd*	well-done	*gaar*

Dutch Specialities

amandelbroodje	sweet roll with almond-paste filling
appelgebak	world-famous apple pie
appelmoes	apple sauce (with everything)
belegd broodje	bread roll with variety of fillings

bitterbal	ball of meat purée covered in breadcrumbs and deep fried
blinde vink	slice of veal rolled around stuffing
boerenomelet	omelette with vegetables and bacon
drie-in-de-pan	fluffy pancake with currants
erwtensoep	thick pea soup with sausages in it
frikandel	meatballs
hete bliksem	potatoes, bacon and apples cooked in butter, salt and sugar
Hollandse nieuwe	freshly caught filleted herring
hutspot	hotchpotch, i.e. hotpot (beef and vegetable stew)
kroket	croquette (with any filling imaginable)
pannekoek	pancake
poffertjes	mini doughnut-like pancakes
rolpens	fried slices of beef and tripe with apple
speculaas	spiced almond biscuit
uitsmijter	bread, ham and fried eggs (and variations)
vla	custard, served with everything that doesn't have *appelmoes* (q.v.)
Vlaamse karbonade	braised beef and onions—usually with beer
wentelteefje	bread fried in egg batter, then sprinkled with cinnamon and sugar

Indonesian Dishes and Terms

ayam	chicken
babi pangang	roast suckling pig with sweet and sour sauce
bami goreng	casserole of noodles, vegetables, pork and shrimps
daging	beef
gado gado	vegetables with peanut sauce
goreng	fried
ikan	fish
kroepoek	fluffy deep-fried prawn crackers
loempia	enormous spring roll
nasi	rice
nasi goreng	fried rice (with meat and vegetables)
nasi rames	mini *rijsttafel* on a single plate
pedis	spicy (tongue-searing)
pisang	banana
rendang	beef stewed in a dry, fiery sauce
rijsttafel	plain rice, and up to 30 side dishes of spicy meats, vegetables, sauces and fruit
sambal	hot chilli paste
saté	skewered meat with peanut sauce
seroendeng	spicy, fried coconut
tauge	bean sprouts

History/General

Bolt, Rodney, *Xenophobe's Guide to the Dutch* (Oval Press, 2000). Affectionate, irreverent cure for xenophobia.

Cotterell, Geoffrey, *Amsterdam* (Saxon House, 1972). Readable romp through the history of the city right up to the 1960s.

Geyl, Pieter, *The Revolt of the Netherlands 1555–1609* and *The Netherlands in the 17th Century 1600–1648* (Cassell, 1988). Definitive histories of the uprising against Spain, the unification of the Netherlands and the Golden Age.

Hibbert, Christopher, *Cities and Civilizations* (Weidenfeld & Nicolson, 1987). Interesting chapter on everyday life in the 17th century.

Farber, Jules, *But give me Amsterdam* (Kosmos, 1995/6). Full of interesting titbits.

Kistemaker, Renée and Van Gelder, Roeloef, *Amsterdam: The Golden Age* (Abbeville Press, 1975). Wittily written illustrated account of 17th-century Amsterdam.

Kruizinga, Jaap, *Het XYZ van Amsterdam* (2 vols., Amsterdam Publishers, 1995/6). Detailed encyclopaedia of the city; a lifetime's work. At present only in Dutch, but keep an eye open for the translation.

Rietenbergen, P.J.A.N., *A Short History of the Netherlands* (Bekking 1998). Text-booky but accessible general history of the Ice Age up to today.

Schama, Simon, *The Embarrassment of Riches: An interpretation of Dutch culture in the Golden Age* (Abbeville Press, 1975). An erudite book that wears its immense research very lightly. A wonderful read.

van der Horst, H, *The Low Sky*. Excellent, scholarly though not dry look at the Dutch nation and its beliefs.

Art and Architecture

Clark, Kenneth, *Civilisation* (BBC Publications, 1969). Accessible and perceptive chapter on the Golden Age.

Derwig, Jan and Mattie, Erik, *Functionalism in the Netherlands* (Architectura & Natura, 1995). An informed, sympathetic view of concrete-and-glass architecture.

Fromentin, Eugène, *The Masters of Past Time: Dutch and Flemish painting from Van Eyck to Rembrandt* (Phaidon, 1981). Impressions of an articulate art critic wandering about the towns and galleries of 19th-century Netherlands. A gem.

Fuchs, R. H., *Dutch Painting* (Thames & Hudson, 1978). By the current director of the Stedelijk Museum. A good general introduction, if at times a little disjointed.

Jaffe, H. L. C., *De Stijl 1917–1931* (Alec Tiranti, 1956). Comprehensive history of the Netherlands' most influential modern art movement.

Further Reading

Janse, Herman, *Building Amsterdam* (De Brink, 1994). Helpfully illustrated beginner's guide to Amsterdam architecture.

Kloos, Maarten (ed.), *Amsterdam: An architectural lesson* (THOTH, 1988). Lectures by renowned architects on modern Amsterdam architecture.

McQuillan, Melissa, *Van Gogh* (Thames & Hudson, 1989). Life, letters and works.

Meischke, R. et al., *Huizen in Nederland: Amsterdam* (Waanders, 1995). Photos and floor plans of most of the historical buildings in town. Text in Dutch.

Rosenberg, Jakob et al., *Dutch Art and Architecture 1600–1800* (Penguin, 1978). Comprehensive, clearly written account of the Golden Age and beyond.

Stone, Irving, *Lust for Life* (Methuen, 1980). Interesting semi-fictional (though at times cringingly awful) biography of Van Gogh.

White, Christopher, *Rembrandt* (Thames & Hudson, 1988). Easy and wide-ranging account of Rembrandt's chaotic life and his work.

Guides

Kemme, Guus, *Amsterdam Architecture: A guide* (THOTH, 1989, revised 1996). Photographs and brief accounts of important buildings in the city—from the oldest standing, up to the 1990s.

Stoutenbeek, Jan, and Vigeveno, Paul, *A Guide to Jewish Amsterdam* (De Haan, 1985). Every nook and cranny of the city with a significance to Jewish people listed and discussed. Now sadly out of print, but still available second-hand.

Amsterdam in Cameracolour (Ian Allen, 1980). Good photos and witty snippets of text.

Fiction

Dutch fiction is unjustifiably neglected by the English-speaking world. Authors mentioned below are very much worth exploring. Penguin Books has a good Dutch list.

Carmiggelt, Simon, *I'm Just Kidding* (publ. in English 1972). Wry observations on life in Amsterdam—an anthology of pieces he wrote weekly for the newspaper *Het Parool* under the penname 'Kronkel'.

Frank, Anne, *The Diary of Anne Frank* (Pan). No matter how many times you read it, you'll be moved by its honesty and awed by its perception.

Freeling, Nicolas, *Because of the Cats, Love in Amsterdam* etc. (Penguin, 1963). The creator of Van der Valk of the BBC TV series writes good classic detective stories—many set in Amsterdam.

Hillesum, Etty, *Etty* (Triad Grafton, 1985). War diary of a young Jewish woman who died in Auschwitz. More knowing than Anne Frank's diary, and not as compelling.

Mulisch, Harry, *Last Call* (Penguin, 1985). From one of Holland's foremost authors. The story of an old actor unearthed to play Prospero in *The Tempest*—it examines the national guilt about the lack of intervention to save the Jews in the Second World War. (Mulisch also wrote *The Assault*, which was made into an Oscar-winning film.)

Multatuli, *Max Havelaar: or the coffee auctions of the Dutch Trading Company* (Penguin, 1987). Neglected Dutch classic, a satirical indictment of Dutch colonialism which shocked 19th-century Holland.

Nooteboom, Cees, *A Song of Truth and Semblance* (Penguin, 1990). Two different fictions, separated by centuries, interweaved. A witty novel that seems to reveal the essence of Dutch writing. (Try also *Rituals* and *In the Dutch Mountains*.)

Stockum, Hilda van, *The Winged Watchman* (Farrar Strauss, 1962; Bethlehem Press, 1999). Moving story of Dutch family during the German occupation—a great book for children to read before coming.

Wolkers, Jan, *Turkish Delight* (Marion Boyars). Deliberately offensive misogynistic work by one of Holland's most provocative writers and artists.

AD **50**	Roman occupation.
AD **600ff**	Gradual Christianization. Eventual unification under Charlemagne.
AD **814**	Charlemagne dies. Kingdom divided into areas roughly corresponding to France, Germany and the Low Countries.
AD **922**	King of France creates first Count of Holland.
1100ff	Fisherman's huts and Gijsbrecht van Amstel's castle appear at mouth of Amstel.
1275	First recorded reference to city. Floris V grants toll tax exemption to Aemstelledamme.
1296	Gijsbrecht IV rebels against Floris.
1300	Amsterdam granted first charter.
1419	Philip the Good of Burgundy begins to unite the provinces.
1421	First Great Fire of Amsterdam.
1425	Singel, the first girdle canal, begun in Amsterdam.
1452	Second Great Fire of Amsterdam.
1467	Philip the Good dies, his son Charles the Bold assumes power.
1477	Charles's daughter Mary in power, marries Maximilian of Austria.
1482	Mary dies and Maximilian rules alone.
1494	Maximilian becomes Holy Roman Emperor, transfers power to his son Philip the Handsome, and later to grandson Charles V.
1516	Charles becomes King of Spain.
1555	Charles abdicates. Spain, Italy and Low Countries go to his fanatical son Philip II.
1559	Reaction to Philip II's campaigns of persecution of Protestants force Philip into tactical withdrawal, leaving sister Margaret to rule.
1565	Winter famine. Wave of iconoclasm.
1566	City regents protest to Margaret. They persuade her to sign the 'Moderation' offering greater religious tolerance.
1567	Duke of Alva takes over. Establishes the Council of Blood and begins reign of terror.
1568	William of Orange attempts invasion, but receives little support from terrified Protestants. This marks the beginning of the Eighty Years' War with Spain.

Chronology

1573	Alva and his son Frederic massacre Calvinists at Haarlem. Dykes cut and Netherlanders use superior naval power to force a withdrawal. Philip replaces Alva with De Resquesens. Siege of Alkmaar.

1574	Siege of Leiden
1575–6	Siege of Amsterdam
1576	De Resquesens dies. Unpaid troops mutiny. Outrage at this gives William support.
1579	The Union of Utrecht unites the seven northern provinces as the United Provinces with William as *stadhouder*. The southern provinces declare allegiance to Spain in the Union of Arras. Duke of Parma takes control of cities in the south.
1584	William assassinated. Aggression continues from south.
1585	Fall of Antwerp. Refugees flood Amsterdam.
1588	Maurits (William's son) becomes *stadhouder* of the United Provinces.
1597	Compagnie van Verre (Far Away Company) formed. The Dutch begin to look East.
1602	East India Company formed.
1622	Northern provinces renew war with Spain (part of the Thirty Years' War).
1624	West India Company formed.
1648	Final defeat of Spain. Peace of Westphalia formally recognizes Dutch independence.
1652	First Anglo-Dutch War (for sea supremacy).
1664	Second Anglo-Dutch War.
1667	Dutch Fleet reaches the Medway. Peace of Breda ends war. Louis XIV of France invades Spanish Netherlands. Holland, England and Sweden form Triple Alliance.
1688	William of Orange crowned King of England after secret negotiations to replace James II.
1701	War of the Spanish Succession .
1702	William dies heirless.
1713	Treaty of Utrecht ends war—both sides exhausted. France renounces all claim to Spanish Netherlands, passes control to Charles VI of Austria.
1734	Dutch Republic unwillingly enters the war of Austrian Succession.
1778	Trade treaty in support of rebellious American colonies.
1780	England discovers this. War.
1791	West India Company ends and East India Co goes into liquidation.
1792	France defeats Austria.
1793	France declares war on England and the Dutch Republic.
1795	French enter Amsterdam and set up Batavian Republic—end of the Dutch Republic.
1806	Napoleon's brother, Louis Bonaparte, installed as King.
1810	Louis forced to abdicate. Holland is incorporated into France.

1813	Prince of Orange returns after riots and Napoleon's retreat from Moscow.
1814	Unification of Netherlands under Prince of Orange by Congress of Vienna.
1815	Belgium is joined to Netherlands.
1824	North Holland Canal built to bypass the Zuider Zee. Bigger ships reach Amsterdam.
1831	Belgium forms independent kingdom
1839	First railway line—Amsterdam to Haarlem. Netherlands officially recognizes Belgium.
1848	William panics at European revolts and rushes through liberal constitution.
1876	North Sea Canal opens to supplement ineffectual North Holland Canal.
1880	Amsterdam University founded. Bicycles and trams begin to appear in the city.
1889	Amsterdam Centraal Station built.
1890	Queen Wilhelmina ascends the throne.
1914	Netherlands neutral in First World War.
1921	The world's first air travel booking office open at Schiphol.
1928	Olympic Games held in Amsterdam.
1939	Attempt to remain neutral in Second World War.
1940	German invasion.
1941	Round-up of Jews begins. General strike in protest.
1945	Canadians liberate Amsterdam.
1948	Queen Wilhelmina abdicates and is succeeded by Queen Juliana.
1980	Queen Juliana abdicates in favour of her eldest daugher Beatrix.
1983	Ed van Thijn assumes office as *burgemeester* in Amsterdam.
1992	After a Euro summit, the Maastricht Treaty moves the former European Economic Community towards today's European Union.
1994	Schelto Patijn assumes office as Burgomaster.
1995/6	Patijn attempts to give Amsterdam sleeker image by tightening up on drugs and prostitution.
1997	Another summit leads to the Treaty of Amsterdam, which further cements European Unity.
1999	Gay marriage legalized on an equal footing with heterosexual marriage.

Main page references are in **bold**. Page references to maps are in *italics*.

Also Available from Cadogan Guides...

Country Guides

Antarctica
Belize
Central Asia
China: The Silk Routes
Egypt
France: Southwest France;
    Dordogne, Lot & Bordeaux
France: Southwest France;
    Gascony & the Pyrenees
France: Brittany
France: The Loire
France: The South of France
France: Provence
France: Côte d'Azur
Germany: Bavaria
Greece: The Peloponnese
Holland
India
India: South India
India: Goa
Ireland
Ireland: Southwest Ireland
Ireland: Northern Ireland
Italy
Italy: The Bay of Naples and Southern Italy
Italy: Lombardy, Milan and the Italian Lakes
Italy: Venetia and the Dolomites
Italy: Tuscany and Umbria
Italy: Tuscany
Italy: Umbria
Italy: Italian Riviera
Italy: Rome and the Heart of Italy
Japan
Morocco
Portugal
Portugal: The Algarve
Scotland
Scotland's Highlands and Islands
South Africa, Swaziland and Lesotho
Spain
Spain: Southern Spain
Spain: Northern Spain
Syria & Lebanon
Tunisia
Turkey
Yucatán and Southern Mexico
Zimbabwe, Botswana and Namibia

City Guides

Amsterdam
Brussels, Bruges, Ghent & Antwerp
Bruges
Edinburgh
Florence, Siena, Pisa & Lucca
Italy: Three Cities—Rome, Florence, Venice
Italy: Three Cities—Venice, Padua, Verona
Italy: Three Cities—Rome, Naples, Sorrento
Italy: Three Cities—Rome, Padua, Assisi
Japan: Three Cities—Tokyo, Kyoto and
    Ancient Nara
Spain: Three Cities—Granada, Seville,
    Cordoba
London
London–Paris
London–Brussels
Madrid
Manhattan
Moscow & St Petersburg
Paris
Prague
Rome
St Petersburg
Venice

Island Guides

Caribbean and Bahamas
Jamaica & the Caymans

Greek Islands
Crete
Mykonos, Santorini & the Cyclades
Rhodes & the Dodecanese
Corfu & the Ionian Islands

Madeira & Porto Santo
Malta
Sardinia
Sicily

Plus...

Southern Africa on the Wild Side
Bugs, Bites & Bowels
London Markets
Take the Kids Travelling
Take the Kids London
Take the Kids Paris and Disneyland

Available from good bookshops or via, in the UK, **Grantham Book Services**, Isaac Newton Way, Alma Park Industrial Estate, Grantham NG31 9SD, ✆ (01476) 541 080, ✉ (01476) 541 061; and in North America from **The Globe Pequot Press**, 246 Goose Lane, PO Box 480, Guilford, Connecticut 06437–0480, ✆ (800) 243 0495, ✉ (800) 820 2329.